Properties and Dynamics of Neutron Stars and Proto-Neutron Stars

Properties and Dynamics of Neutron Stars and Proto-Neutron Stars

Editors

Veronica Dexheimer
Rodrigo Negreiros

MDPI • Basel • Beijing • Wuhan • Barcelona • Belgrade • Manchester • Tokyo • Cluj • Tianjin

Editors
Veronica Dexheimer
Kent State University
USA

Rodrigo Negreiros
Universidade Federal Fluminense
Brazil

Editorial Office
MDPI
St. Alban-Anlage 66
4052 Basel, Switzerland

This is a reprint of articles from the Special Issue published online in the open access journal *Universe* (ISSN 2218-1997) (available at: https://www.mdpi.com/journal/universe/special_issues/Neutron_ProtoNeutron_Stars).

For citation purposes, cite each article independently as indicated on the article page online and as indicated below:

LastName, A.A.; LastName, B.B.; LastName, C.C. Article Title. *Journal Name* **Year**, *Volume Number*, Page Range.

ISBN 978-3-0365-5399-3 (Hbk)
ISBN 978-3-0365-5400-6 (PDF)

© 2022 by the authors. Articles in this book are Open Access and distributed under the Creative Commons Attribution (CC BY) license, which allows users to download, copy and build upon published articles, as long as the author and publisher are properly credited, which ensures maximum dissemination and a wider impact of our publications.

The book as a whole is distributed by MDPI under the terms and conditions of the Creative Commons license CC BY-NC-ND.

Contents

About the Editors vii

Preface to "Properties and Dynamics of Neutron Stars and Proto-Neutron Stars" ix

Veronica Dexheimer
Properties and Dynamics of Neutron Stars and Proto-Neutron Stars
Reprinted from: *Universe* **2022**, *8*, 434, doi:10.3390/universe8080434 1

Débora Peres Menezes
A Neutron Star Is Born
Reprinted from: *Universe* **2021**, *7*, 267, doi:10.3390/universe7080267 5

Parit Mehta, Rana Nandi, Rosana de Oliveira Gomes, Veronica Dexheimer and Jan Steinheimer
Low Density Neutron Star Matter with Quantum Molecular Dynamics: The Role of Isovector Interactions
Reprinted from: *Universe* **2022**, *8*, 380, doi:10.3390/universe8070380 47

Hoa Dinh Thi, Chiranjib Mondal and Francesca Gulminelli
The Nuclear Matter Density Functional under the Nucleonic Hypothesis
Reprinted from: *Universe* **2021**, *7*, 373, doi:10.3390/universe7100373 65

Armen Sedrakian and Arus Harutyunyan
Equation of State and Composition ofProto-Neutron Stars and Merger Remnants with Hyperons
Reprinted from: *Universe* **2021**, *7*, 382, doi:10.3390/universe7100382 87

Daniela Curin, Ignacio Francisco Ranea-Sandoval, Mauro Mariani, Milva Gabriela Orsaria and Fridolin Weber
Hybrid Stars with Color Superconducting Cores in an Extended FCM Model
Reprinted from: *Universe* **2021**, *7*, 370, doi:10.3390/universe7100370 103

Efrain J. Ferrer and Vivian de la Incera
Magnetic Dual Chiral Density Wave: A Candidate Quark Matter Phase for the Interior of Neutron Stars
Reprinted from: *Universe* **2021**, *7*, 458, doi:10.3390/universe7120458 123

José C. Jiménez and Eduardo S. Fraga
Radial Oscillations of Quark Stars Admixed with Dark Matter
Reprinted from: *Universe* **2022**, *8*, 34, doi:10.3390/universe8010034 149

Rachid Ouyed
The Macro-Physics of the Quark-Nova: Astrophysical Implications
Reprinted from: *Universe* **2022**, *8*, 322, doi:10.3390/universe8060322 173

Mark G. Alford, Alexander Haber, Steven P. Harris and Ziyuan Zhang
Beta Equilibrium under Neutron Star Merger Conditions
Reprinted from: *Universe* **2021**, *7*, 399, doi:10.3390/universe7110399 197

Daniel A. Godzieba and David Radice
High-Order Multipole and Binary Love Number Universal Relations
Reprinted from: *Universe* **2021**, *7*, 368, doi:10.3390/universe7100368 225

Daniel A. Godzieba and David Radice
Correction: Godzieba, D.A.; Radice, D. High-Order Multipole and Binary Love Number Universal Relations. *Universe* 2021, 7, 368
Reprinted from: *Universe* **2021**, *7*, 456, doi:10.3390/universe7120456 . . . . **239**

About the Editors

Veronica Dexheimer

Dr. Dexheimer is a theoretical nuclear/particle astrophysicist who specializes in the study of dense and hot matter in compact stars. After completing her Bachelor and Master degrees in Universidade Federal do Rio Grande do Sul in Porto Alegre, Brazil, she received her PhD from the Frankfurt Institute for Advanced Studies in Frankfurt, Germany, in 2009. Currently, Dr. Dexheimer is an Associate Professor at Kent State University in Kent, OH, where she has been since 2013. Her research group focuses on finding evidence for exotic matter in neutron stars and their mergers while connecting high-energy astrophysical data with high-energy laboratory data here on Earth.

Rodrigo Negreiros

Prof. Negreiros obtained his Ph.D. at San Diego State University in 2010 followed by a research appointment at the Frankfurt Institute for Advanced Studies in Frankfurt, Germany. His research is dedicated to the study of neutron stars—seeking a better understanding of the multifaceted aspects of such astonishing objects. Dr. Negreiros has published over 40 papers in diverse journals concerning several aspects of compact stars: from their microscopic composition to their macroscopic and global properties. Currently, he is a professor at the physics department of Universidade Federal Fluminense in Niteroi, Brazil.

Preface to "Properties and Dynamics of Neutron Stars and Proto-Neutron Stars"

Following new developments in the measurement of gravitational waves from neutron–star mergers and the modification or construction of particle colliders to reach larger densities, we are entering a new era, during which we can begin to understand dense and hot matter for the first time. This, together with future supernova explosion data, will provide us with the opportunity to have truly multimessenger data on hot and dense matter, which is, to some extent, similar to the matter present in the core of proto-neutron stars.

This Special Issue focuses on the theory necessary to understand present and future data. It includes state-of-the-art theoretical models that describe dense and hot matter and the dynamic stellar simulations that make use of them, with the ultimate goal of determining which degrees of freedom are relevant under these conditions and how they affect the matter equation of state and stellar evolution.

Veronica Dexheimer and Rodrigo Negreiros
Editors

Editorial

Properties and Dynamics of Neutron Stars and Proto-Neutron Stars

Veronica Dexheimer

Department of Physics, Kent State University, Kent, OH 44242, USA; vdexheim@kent.edu

Citation: Dexheimer, V. Properties and Dynamics of Neutron Stars and Proto-Neutron Stars. *Universe* **2022**, *8*, 434. https://doi.org/10.3390/universe8080434

Received: 1 August 2022
Accepted: 9 August 2022
Published: 21 August 2022

Publisher's Note: MDPI stays neutral with regard to jurisdictional claims in published maps and institutional affiliations.

Copyright: © 2022 by the author. Licensee MDPI, Basel, Switzerland. This article is an open access article distributed under the terms and conditions of the Creative Commons Attribution (CC BY) license (https://creativecommons.org/licenses/by/4.0/).

This Special Issue provides a comprehensive collection of papers that present modern theories to describe neutron star interiors and dynamics. It includes state-of-the-art theoretical models that describe dense and hot matter and simulations that test how different models affect the birth, evolution, and coalescence of neutron stars. While following diverse approaches, the different papers that constitute the Special Issue are motivated by the same recent developments in nuclear physics and astrophysics, concerning new data provided by the measurement of electromagnetic and gravitational waves from neutron-stars and their mergers and new laboratory constraints for nuclear matter from heavy-ion collisions.

Since the observation of the first neutron star 55 years ago, we have learned a great amount about them: how they are formed, typical masses, radii, surface magnetic fields, etc., culminating in the detection of the merger of two neutron stars in 2017, from a galaxy 140 million light years away. Nevertheless, properties of their most inner layers, such as composition, density, and magnetic fields remain a mystery, which we are only starting to understand systematically. To do so, one starts with a theory or model, which provides a thermodynamic description (the equation of state, or EoS) that can be used to reproduce observable stellar properties, ultimately confronted with experimental data. See Ref. [1] from Débora Peres Menezes for a review.

The different regions inside neutron stars are defined based on the presence (or absence) of nuclei. While in the core all nuclei have been dissolved into bulk nuclear matter, in the crust they are still present. More specifically, in the inner crust, larger structures can appear when nuclei combine into shapes, referred to as nuclear pasta. To study pasta phases, one can either assume particular configurations or make use of Quantum Molecular Dynamics (QMD) simulations to determine which configurations appear at different densities inside the star. However, unlike atomic nuclei, neutron stars are very asymmetric with respect to isospin. The effect of isospin-dependent nuclear forces on nuclear clusters in the inner crust of neutron stars is the topic of Ref. [2] by Parit Mehta, Rana Nandi, Rosana de Oliveira Gomes, Veronica Dexheimer and Jan Steinheimer. There, the authors study the relation between the poorly known vector–isovector couplings and the density dependence of the symmetry energy, a quantity that can be measured in the laboratory at low densities.

Concerning the core of neutron stars, the uncertainty in the particle composition and how they interact grows with density (towards the center). The most basic hypothesis assumes that the constituents of the core are the same ones that make up the nuclei in the crust, protons and neutrons (and electrons). In this case, direct connections can be made, using Bayesian analysis, between dense matter equation of state, nuclear equation of state parameters, and recent observational data collected by LIGO-Virgo and NASA NICER. In particular, Ref. [3] by Hoa Dinh Thi, Chiranjib Mondal, and Francesca Gulminelli extracts the behavior of the energy per particle of symmetric matter and the density dependence of the symmetry energy.

Alternatively, exotic particles (not present in normal nuclei) can be produced in the inner core of neutron stars. These are hyperons, more massive than neutrons and protons, that also contain strange quarks. Hyperons become particularly important when the temperature is comparable (roughly >10%) to the Fermi energy of the particles present in the star. This is the case in proto-neutron stars, immediately after being formed in supernova explosions, and when neutron stars merge. Ref. [4] by Armen Sedrakian and Arus Harutyunyan makes use of a covariant density functional (CDF) theory to describe neutrons, protons, and hyperons with interactions that are density-dependent. The role of leptons, electrons, muons, and neutrinos are also investigated by fixing the lepton fraction. See Figure 1 below for examples of particle content for different snapshots of proto-neutron star evolution.

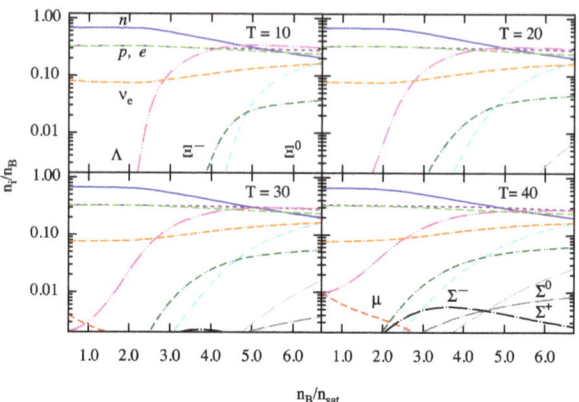

Figure 1. Normalized particle content as a function of density (in nuclear saturation units). Several temperatures are shown for a fixed lepton fraction $Y_{L,e} = 0.4$.

If the density is such that neutrons, protons, and hyperons start to overlap, the description of matter needs to explicitly account for the quark degrees of freedom. Descriptions that include different types of degrees of freedom (including deconfined quarks) are called hybrid models. Ref. [5] by Daniela Curin, Ignacio Francisco Ranea-Sandoval, Mauro Mariani, Milva Gabriela Orsaria and Fridolin Weber studies the possibility of a sharp phase transition to quark matter in the inner core of neutron stars, modeled by an extended version of the field correlator method (FCM) with repulsive vector interactions and color superconductivity. The latter is important because the attraction between quarks can lead to quark–matter pair condensation, a phenomenon similar to the Bardeen–Cooper–Schrieffer (BCS) theory in condensed matter. The parameters of the model are constrained by observational data on massive pulsars and, again, LIGO-Virgo and NASA NICER data, pointing towards a slow deconfinement of the quarks, which gives rise to stable neutron stars with extended quark-matter inner cores.

The picture of neutron-star interiors becomes even more interesting when strong magnetic fields are considered. In particular, they can affect color superconductivity. Furthermore, phases in dense quark matter can be spatially nonuniform, in which case the ground state spatial structure of the theory takes the form of a standing wave. Ref. [6] by Efrain J. Ferrer and Vivian de la Incera discusses the characteristics of the magnetic dual chiral density wave (MDCDW) phase, possibly formed inside neutron stars. This could give rise to topological properties and anomalous electric transport, leading to γ-ray photons being converted into gapped axion-polaritons (quasiparticles resulting from strong coupling of electromagnetic waves, equivalent to phonons) and causing stars to collapse. This mechanism could provide an explanation for the a long-standing puzzle in astrophysics concerning observing electromagnetically fewer pulsars than expected close to the galactic center.

Another ingredient for the description of neutron stars being currently discussed in the literature is dark matter, which comprehends 85% of the matter content of the universe. As it is expected to interact weakly with normal matter, dark matter is described inside stars as a separate fluid. Within this framework, Ref. [7] by José C. Jiménez and Eduardo S. Fraga investigate cold quark matter (described by the MIT bag model) and (weakly and strongly self-interacting) fermionic dark matter. By studying their fundamental-mode radial oscillations, they find that dark strange planets and very small dark strangelets can be stable.

Although there is strong indications for quark matter being present in neutron stars (especially when they merge), the dynamics of deconfinement in neutron stars is far from being completely understood. This is because stars cannot be exactly probed in the laboratory, where it is impossible to achieve extreme densities with comparative very low temperature, not to mention the important influence of gravity. For example, a conversion to quark matter could trigger another stellar explosion (after the supernova that created the neutron star), referred to as a quark-nova. Ref. [8] by Rachid Ouyed comprehensively discusses the theory behind such explosions and how to simulate them numerically using the Burn-UD computer code. The authors also discuss neutrino signatures for such events and the possibility of measuring those here on Earth.

Another astrophysical scenario in which temperature is relevant, in addition to supernovae and proto-neutron stars, is the merger of neutron stars. A question worth asking is whether the low-temperature beta-equilibrium condition (or relation among chemical potentials), $\mu_n = \mu_p + \mu_e$, still holds at the higher temperatures reached in mergers. Ref. [9] by Mark G. Alford, Alexander Haber, Steven P. Harris and Ziyuan Zhang shows the need for corrections to this condition when the temperature is in the range $1~\text{MeV} \lesssim T \lesssim 5~\text{MeV}$. They make use of IUF and SFHo relativistic mean field models with relativistic dispersion relations of protons and neutrons and find that such corrections are very important when calculating Urca process rates, which are essential in modeling the thermal evolution of neutron stars.

Finally, in order to better understand neutron star mergers, we need to understand the relation between important quantities, such as the stars' masses, radii, and tidal deformability, which is a measurement of how much neutron stars are deformed while they merge. Universal relations, that do not depend on the equation of state, provide such correlations in a reliable way. To obtain these, Ref. [10] by Daniel A. Godzieba and David Radice used approximately 2 million phenomenological equations of state, all causal and consistent with observational constraints, to find new and improved universal relations.

With all these tools in hand, we are ready for the next generation of astrophysical observations and terrestrial particle collision data to be analyzed and interpreted, with the ultimate goal of reaching a comprehensive understanding of dense matter and neutron stars.

Funding: The Guest Editor's activity received no external funding.

Conflicts of Interest: The author declares no conflict of interest.

References

1. Menezes, D.P. A Neutron Star Is Born. *Universe* **2021**, *7*, 267. [CrossRef]
2. Mehta, P.; Nandi, R.; Gomes, R.d.O.; Dexheimer, V.; Steinheimer, J. Low Density Neutron Star Matter with Quantum Molecular Dynamics: The Role of Isovector Interactions. *Universe* **2022**, *8*, 380. [CrossRef]
3. Dinh Thi, H.; Mondal, C.; Gulminelli, F. The Nuclear Matter Density Functional under the Nucleonic Hypothesis. *Universe* **2021**, *7*, 373. [CrossRef]
4. Sedrakian, A.; Harutyunyan, A. Equation of State and Composition of Proto-Neutron Stars and Merger Remnants with Hyperons. *Universe* **2021**, *7*, 382. [CrossRef]
5. Curin, D.; Ranea-Sandoval, I.F.; Mariani, M.; Orsaria, M.G.; Weber, F. Hybrid Stars with Color Superconducting Cores in an Extended FCM Model. *Universe* **2021**, *7*, 370. [CrossRef]
6. Ferrer, E.J.; de la Incera, V. Magnetic Dual Chiral Density Wave: A Candidate Quark Matter Phase for the Interior of Neutron Stars. *Universe* **2021**, *7*, 458. [CrossRef]
7. Jiménez, J.C.; Fraga, E.S. Radial Oscillations of Quark Stars Admixed with Dark Matter. *Universe* **2022**, *8*, 34. [CrossRef]
8. Ouyed, R. The Macro-Physics of the Quark-Nova: Astrophysical Implications. *Universe* **2022**, *8*, 322. [CrossRef]

9. Alford, M.G.; Haber, A.; Harris, S.P.; Zhang, Z. Beta Equilibrium under Neutron Star Merger Conditions. *Universe* **2021**, *7*, 399 [CrossRef]
10. Godzieba, D.A.; Radice, D. Correction: Godzieba, D.A.; Radice, D. High-Order Multipole and Binary Love Number Universal Relations. Universe 2021, 7, 368. *Universe* **2021**, *7*, 456. [CrossRef]

Article

A Neutron Star Is Born

Débora Peres Menezes

Departamento de Física, Universidade Federal de Santa Catarina, Florianópolis 88040-900, Brazil; debora.p.m@ufsc.br

Abstract: A neutron star was first detected as a pulsar in 1967. It is one of the most mysterious compact objects in the universe, with a radius of the order of 10 km and masses that can reach two solar masses. In fact, neutron stars are star remnants, a kind of stellar zombie (they die, but do not disappear). In the last decades, astronomical observations yielded various contraints for neutron star masses, and finally, in 2017, a gravitational wave was detected (GW170817). Its source was identified as the merger of two neutron stars coming from NGC 4993, a galaxy 140 million light years away from us. The very same event was detected in γ-ray, X-ray, UV, IR, radio frequency and even in the optical region of the electromagnetic spectrum, starting the new era of multi-messenger astronomy. To understand and describe neutron stars, an appropriate equation of state that satisfies bulk nuclear matter properties is necessary. GW170817 detection contributed with extra constraints to determine it. On the other hand, magnetars are the same sort of compact object, but bearing much stronger magnetic fields that can reach up to 10^{15} G on the surface as compared with the usual 10^{12} G present in ordinary pulsars. While the description of ordinary pulsars is not completely established, describing magnetars poses extra challenges. In this paper, I give an overview on the history of neutron stars and on the development of nuclear models and show how the description of the tiny world of the nuclear physics can help the understanding of the cosmos, especially of the neutron stars.

Keywords: neutron stars; equations of state; relativistic models; gravitational waves

Citation: Menezes, D.P. A Neutron Star Is Born. *Universe* **2021**, *7*, 267. https://doi.org/10.3390/universe7080267

Received: 16 June 2021
Accepted: 17 July 2021
Published: 26 July 2021

Publisher's Note: MDPI stays neutral with regard to jurisdictional claims in published maps and institutional affiliations.

Copyright: © 2021 by the author. Licensee MDPI, Basel, Switzerland. This article is an open access article distributed under the terms and conditions of the Creative Commons Attribution (CC BY) license (https://creativecommons.org/licenses/by/4.0/).

1. Introduction

Two of the known existing interactions that determine all the conditions of our Universe are of nuclear origin: the strong and the weak nuclear forces. It is not possible to talk about neutron stars without understanding them, and especially the strong nuclear interaction, which is well described by the Quantum Chromodynamics (QCD). However, note that a good description through a Lagrangian density does not mean that the solutions are known for all possible systems subject to the strong nuclear force.

Based on the discovery of asymptotic freedom [1], which predicts that strongly interacting matter undergoes a phase transition from hadrons to the quark–gluon plasma (QGP) and on the possibility that a QGP could be formed in heavy-ion collisions, the QCD phase diagram has been slowly revealed. While asymptotic freedom is expected to take place at both high temperatures, as in the early universe and high densities, as in neutron star interiors, heavy-ion collisions can be experimentally tested with different energies at still relatively low densities but generally quite high temperatures. If one examines the QCD phase diagram shown in Figure 1, it is possible to see that the nuclei occupy a small part of the diagram at low densities and low temperatures for different asymmetries. One should notice the temperature log scale, chosen to emphasize the region where nuclei exist. Neutron stars, on the other hand, are compact objects with a density that can reach 10 times the nuclear saturation density, which discussed later on along this paper. While heavy ion collisions probe experimentally some regions of the diagram, lattice QCD (LQCD) calculations explain only the low density region close to zero baryonic chemical potential.

Hence, we rely on effective models to advance our understanding, and they are the main subject of this paper.

Since the beginning of the last century, many nuclear models have been proposed. In Section 2.1, the first models are mentioned and the notion of nuclear matter discussed. The formalisms that followed, either non-relativistic Skyrme-type models [2] or relativistic ones that gave rise to the quantum hadrodynamics model, were based on some basic features described by the early models, the liquid drop model [3] and the semi-empirical mass formula [4]. Once the nuclear physics is established, the very idea of a neutron star can be tackled. However, it is very important to have in mind the model extrapolations that may be necessary when one moves from the nuclei region shown in Figure 1 to the neutron star (NS) region. A simple treatment of the relation between these two regions and the construction of the QCD phase transition line can be seen in [5].

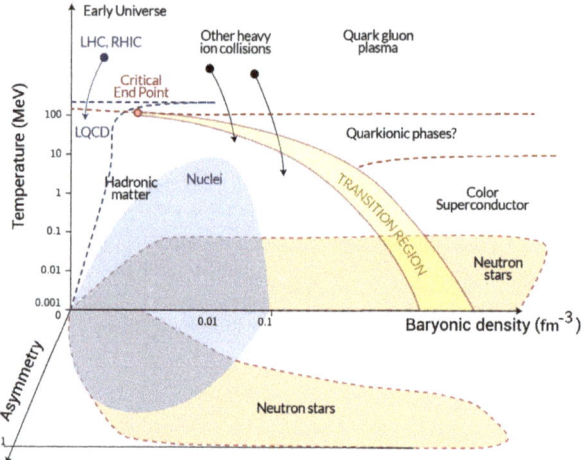

Figure 1. QCD phase diagram. On the left of the transition region stands hadronic matter and on the right side, the quark gluon plasma. Quarkyonic phases represent a region where chiral symmetry has been restored but matter is still confined. Figure taken and adapted from [6].

The exact constitution of these compact objects, also commonly named pulsars due to their precise rotation period, is still unknown, and all the information we have depends on the confrontation of theory with astrophysical observations. As the density increases towards their center, it is believed that there is an outer crust, an inner crust, an outer core and an inner core. The inner core constitution is the most controversial: it can be matter composed of deconfined quarks or perhaps a mixed phase of hadrons and quarks. I will try to comment and describe every one of the possible layers inside a NS along this text.

NASA's Neutron Star Interior Composition Explorer (NICER), an X-ray telescope [7] launched in 2017, has already sent some news [8]: by monitoring the X-ray emission of gas surrounding the heaviest known pulsar, PSR J0740 + 6620 with a mass of 2.08 ± 0.07, it has measured its size, and it is larger than previously expected, a diameter of around 25 to 27 km, with consequences on the possible composition of the NS core.

In this paper, I present a comprehensive review of the main nuclear physics properties that should be satisfied by equations of states aimed to describe nuclear matter, the consequences arising from the extrapolation necessary to describe objects with such high densities as neutron stars, and how they can be tuned according to observational constraints. At the end, a short discussion on quark and hybrid stars is presented and the existence of magnetars is rapidly outlined. Not all important aspects related to neutron stars are treated in the present work, rotation being the most important one that is disregarded, but the interested reader can certainly use it as an initiation to the physics of these compact objects.

2. Historical Perspectives

I divide this section, which concentrates all necessary information for the development of the physics of neutron stars, into two parts. In the first one, I discuss the development of the nuclear physics models based on known experimental properties and introduce the very simple Fermi gas model, whose calculation is later used in more realistic relativistic models. The second part is devoted to the history of compact objects from the astrophysical point of view.

2.1. From the Nuclear Physics Point of View

The history of nuclear physics modeling started with two very simple models: the liquid drop model, introduced in 1929 [3], and the semi-empirical mass formula, proposed in 1935 by Bethe and Weizsäcker [4].

The liquid drop model idea came from the observation that the nucleus has behavior and properties that resemble the ones of an incompressible fluid, such as the following: (a) the nucleus has low compressibility due to its almost constant internal density; (b) it presents a well-defined surface; (c) the nucleus radius varies with the number of nucleons as $R = R_0 A^{1/3}$, where $R_0 \simeq 1.2 \times 10^{-15}$ m; and (d) the nuclear force is isospin-independent and saturates.

Typical nuclear density profiles are shown in Figure 2, in which one can observe some of the features mentioned above; e.g., the density is almost constant up to a certain point and then it drops rapidly close to the surface, determining the nucleus radius. The mean square radius is usually defined as

$$R_i^2 = \frac{\int d^3r \, r^2 \rho_i(\mathbf{r})}{\int d^3r \, \rho_i(\mathbf{r})}, \quad i = p, n \tag{1}$$

where ρ_p is the number density of protons and ρ_n the number density of neutrons.

A nucleus with an equal number of protons and neutrons has a slightly larger proton radius because they repel each other due to the Coulomb interaction. A nucleus with more neutrons than protons (as most of the stable ones) has a larger neutron radius than its proton counterpart and the small difference between both radii is known as neutron skin thickness, given by [9–12]:

$$\theta = R_n - R_p. \tag{2}$$

For the last two decades, a precise measurement of both charge and neutron radii of the ^{208}Pb nucleus has been tried at the parity radius experiment (PREX) at the Jefferson National Accelerator Facility [13] using polarized electron scattering. The latest experimental results [12] point to $\theta = 0.283 \pm 0.071$ fm and to the interior baryon density $\rho_0 = 0.1480 \pm 0.0036(\exp) \pm 0.0013(\text{theo})$ fm^{-3}. These quantities have been shown to be important for the understanding of some of the properties of the neutron star. I will go back to this discussion later on.

The binding energy B of a nucleus $^A_Z X_N$ is given by the difference between its mass and the mass of its constituents (Z protons and N neutrons):

$$B = (Zm_p + Nm_n - (m(^A_Z X) - Zm_e))c^2 = (Zm(^1 H) + Nm_n - m(^A_Z X))c^2, \tag{3}$$

where $m(^A_Z X)$ is the mass of the chemical element $^A_Z X$ and is given in atomic mass units. The binding energy per nucleon $\frac{B}{A}$ is shown in Figure 3, from where it is seen that the curve is relatively constant and of the order of 8.5 MeV except for light nuclei. The semi-empirical mass formula, which is a parameter-dependent expression was used to fit the experimental results successfully and it reads:

$$B(Z, A) = a_v A - a_s A^{\frac{2}{3}} - a_c e^2 \frac{Z(Z-1)}{A^{\frac{1}{3}}} - a_i \frac{(N-Z)^2}{A} + \delta(A). \tag{4}$$

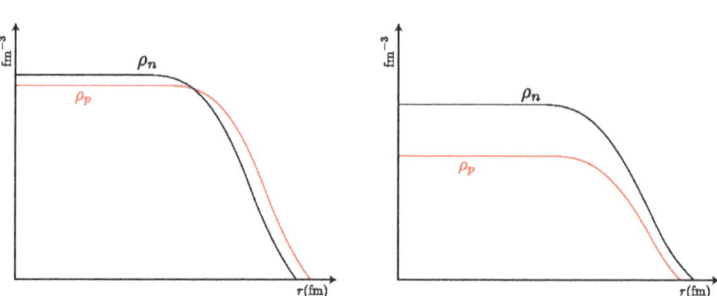

Figure 2. Schematic representation of the nuclear densities with equal number of protons and neutrons (**left**) and a larger number of neutrons than protons (**right**). The proton and neutron densities depend on the number of nucleons such that heavier elements present larger densities. Typical theoretical densities for ^{208}Pb are of the order of 0.09 fm^{-3} for neutrons and 0.06–0.07 fm^{-3} for protons [10].

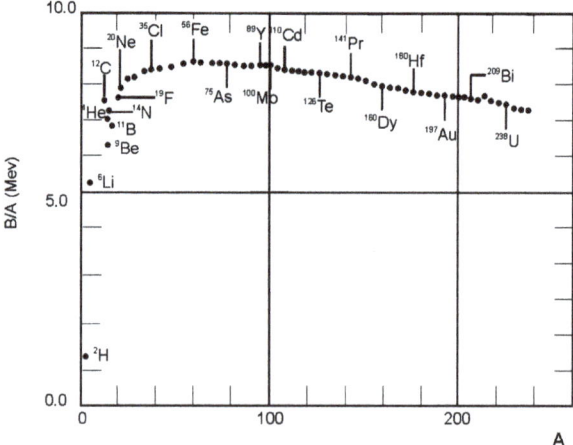

Figure 3. Binding energy per nucleon as a function of the number of nucleons.

In this equation, from left to right, the quantities refer to a volume term, a surface term, a Coulomb term, an energy symmetry term and a pairing interaction term [14,15]. Of course, with so many parameters, other parameterisations can be obtained from the fitting of the data. One possible set is $a_v = 15.68$ MeV, $a_s = 18.56$ MeV, $a_c \times e^2 = 0.72$ MeV, $a_i = 18.1$ MeV and

$$\delta = \begin{cases} 34\ A^{-3/4} \text{MeV}, & \text{even-even nuclei}, \\ 0, & \text{even-odd nuclei}, \\ -34\ A^{-3/4} \text{MeV}, & \text{odd-odd nuclei}. \end{cases} \tag{5}$$

Although quite naive, these two models combined can explain many important nuclear physics properties, such as nuclear fission [15].

Parameter-dependent nuclear models can also explain the fusion of the elements in the stars and the primordial nucleosynthesis with the abundance of chemical elements in the observable universe, which is roughly the following: 71% is hydrogen, 27% is helium,

1.8% is carbon to neon elements, 0.2% is neon to titanium, 0.02% is lead and only 0.0001% is elements with atomic number larger than 60. By observing Figure 3, one easily identifies the element with the largest binding energy, ^{56}Fe. Hence, it is possible to explain why elements with atomic numbers $A \leq 56$ are synthesised in the stars by nuclear fusion that are exothermic reactions, and heavier elements are expected to be synthesized in other astrophysical processes, such as supernova explosions and more recently also simulated in the mergers of compact objects. For a simplistic and naive but didactic idea of the stellar fusion chains, I show the possible synthesized chemical elements in Figure 4.

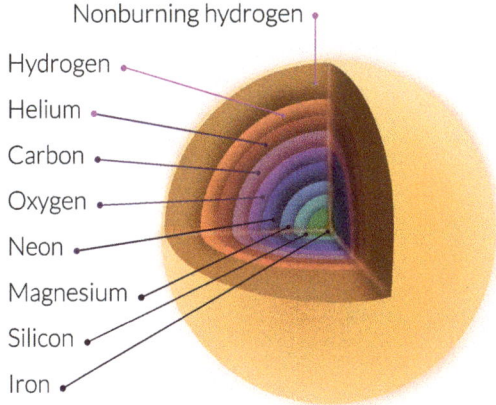

Figure 4. Naive schematic representation of the possible chemical elements synthesized in stellar fusion. Heavier elements are produced in dense stellar matter. Notice that these elements are produced in normal stars, not neutron stars.

After a star is born, it takes some time to fuse all the chemical elements in its interior, until its death, which is more or less spectacular depending on its mass. One of the most useful diagrams in the study of stellar evolution is the Hertzsprung and Russel (HR) diagram [16], developed by Ejnar Hertzsprung and Norris Russel independently in the early 1900s. According to the HR diagram, displayed in Figure 5, the star spends most of its life time in the central line of the diagram, the main sequence. Our Sun will become a white dwarf after its death, the kind of objectt shown at lower luminosities and higher temperatures, towards the left corner of the diagram. More massive stars, with masses higher than eight solar masses ($M_\odot$) become either a neutron star or a black hole, and these compact objects are not shown in the HR Diagram since they do not emit visible light waves. Moreover, neutron stars were only detected much later, as discussed in Section 2.2. For a better comprehension of the HR diagram, please refer to [17].

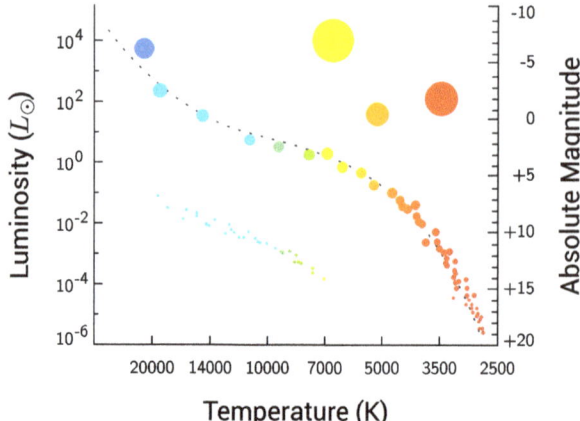

Figure 5. Hertzspring and Russel diagram: luminosity (in terms of the Sun luminosity) as a function of the star temperature. Notice that the temperature increases from right to left. The yellow, orange, and red big dots on the right top represent red giants, the blueish sequence on the bottom left represents white dwarfs, and the central line is the main sequence, where the red stars are red dwarfs and the blue ones are blue giants.

The main idea underlying nuclear models is to satisfy experimental values and nuclear properties, and to achieve this purpose, in almost one century of research, they became more and more sophisticated. The most important of these properties are the binding energy, the saturation density, the symmetry energy, its derivatives, and the incompressibility, all of them already explored in the semi-empirical mass formula given in Equation (4). An important question to be answered is what happens when one moves to higher densities or to finite temperature in the QCD phase diagram shown in Figure 1.

To better understand this point, let us discuss the concept of nuclear matter. This is a common denomination for an infinite matter characterized by properties of a symmetric nucleus in its ground state and without the effects of the Coulomb interaction. If one divides Equation (4) by the number of nucleons A, one can see that under the conditions just mentioned, the third and forth term disappear. If one assumes an infinite radius, $A \to \infty$ and no surface effects exist. The pairing interaction would be an unnecessary correction. Hence, the binding energy per nucleon becomes approximately

$$\frac{B(Z, A)}{A} = a_v \simeq 16 \text{ MeV}, \qquad (6)$$

which is what one gets for a two-nucleon system if compared with the average value shown in Figure 3. However, the deuteron binding energy is much smaller, around only 2 MeV. This means that nuclear matter is not an appropriate concept if one wants to describe the properties of a specific nucleus, but it is rather useful to study, for instance, the interior of a neutron star. Normally, it is described by an equation of state, which consists of a set of correlated equations, such as pressure, energy, and density. The equation of state that describes the ground state of nuclear matter is calculated at zero temperature and is a function of the proton and the neutron densities, which are the same in symmetric matter. Useful definitions are the proton fraction $y_p = \frac{\rho_p}{\rho}$ and the asymmetry $\delta = \frac{\rho_n - \rho_p}{\rho}$, which are respectively 0.5 and 0 in the case of symmetric nuclear matter. In these equations, $\rho = \rho_p + \rho_n$ is the total nuclear (or baryonic) density. The macroscopic nuclear energy can be obtained from the microscopic equation of state if one assumes that

$$E_N = \int \mathcal{E}(\rho, \delta) d^3\mathbf{r}, \qquad (7)$$

where $\mathcal{E}(\rho, \delta)$ is the energy density. Thus,

$$\frac{B(Z,A)}{A} = \frac{E_N}{A} - m_n = \frac{\mathcal{E}}{\rho} - m_n, \tag{8}$$

where $m_n = 939$ MeV is the neutron mass ($c = 1$). The binding energy as a function of the density is shown in Figure 6. We will see how it can be obtained later in the text. The minimum corresponds to what is generally called saturation density, and the value inferred from experiments ranges between $\rho_0 = 0.148 - 0.17$ fm^{-3}, as mentioned earlier when the PREX results were given.

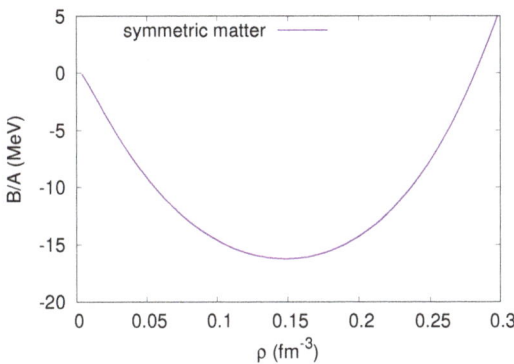

Figure 6. Nuclear matter binding energy per nucleon.

The pressure can be easily obtained from thermodynamics

$$-PV = E_N - TS - \mu A, \tag{9}$$

or, dividing by the volume,

$$-P = \mathcal{E} - TS - \mu\rho = \Omega, \tag{10}$$

where T is the temperature, S is the entropy density, μ is the chemical potential, and Ω the thermodynamical potential. When we take $T = 0$, the expression becomes even simpler because the term TS vanishes.

To demonstrate how a simple equation of state (EOS) can be obtained from a relativistic model, we use the free Fermi gas and assume that $\hbar = c = 1$, known as natural units. Within this model, the fermions can be either neutrons or nucleons, but I would like to emphasize that it is not adequate to describe nuclear matter properties, as will be obvious later. Its Lagrangian density reads:

$$\mathcal{L}_0 = \bar{\psi}(i\gamma^\mu \partial_\mu - m)\psi. \tag{11}$$

From the Euler–Lagrange equations

$$\partial_\mu \left(\frac{\partial \mathcal{L}}{\partial(\partial_\mu \psi)} \right) - \frac{\partial \mathcal{L}}{\partial \psi} = 0, \tag{12}$$

the Dirac equation is obtained:

$$(i\gamma^\mu \partial_\mu - m)\psi = 0. \tag{13}$$

Its well known solution has the form $\psi = \Psi(\mathbf{k}, \lambda)e^{i(\mathbf{k}\cdot\vec{r}-E(\mathbf{k})t)}$, where $\Psi(\mathbf{k}, \lambda)$ is a four-component spinor and λ labels the spin. The energy can be calculated from

$$(\vec{\alpha} \cdot \mathbf{k} + \beta M)^2 \Psi(\mathbf{k}, \lambda) = E(\mathbf{k})^2 \Psi(\mathbf{k}, \lambda), \tag{14}$$

where $\alpha = \gamma_0 \vec{\gamma}$ or

$$(\mathbf{k})^2 + M^2 = E(\mathbf{k})^2, \quad E(\mathbf{k}) = \pm\sqrt{\mathbf{k}^2 + M^2}. \tag{15}$$

Moreover, one gets

$$<\Psi|\Psi> = \gamma \int \frac{d^3k}{(2\pi)^3}(f_+ - f_-) = \rho, \tag{16}$$

where $f_\pm$ represents the Fermi–Dirac distribution for particles and antiparticles [18]. For $T = 0$, f_+ is simply the step function, and there are no antiparticles in the system. In this case,

$$<\Psi|\Psi> = \gamma \int \frac{d^3k}{(2\pi)^3}\theta(k_F^2 - k^2) = \frac{\gamma}{2\pi^2} \int_0^{k_F} k^2 dk = \frac{\gamma k_F^3}{6\pi^2} = \rho, \tag{17}$$

with k_F being the Fermi momentum and γ the degeneracy of the particle. If one considers only a gas of neutrons, the degeneracy is 2 due to the spin degeneracy. However, if one considers a gas of nucleons, i.e., symmetric matter with the same amount of protons and neutrons, it is 4 because it accounts for the isospin degeneracy as well.

One can then write

$$<\Psi|\vec{\alpha} \cdot \mathbf{k} + \beta M|\Psi> = \int \frac{d^3k}{(2\pi)^3}\sqrt{\mathbf{k}^2 + M^2}(f_+ + f_-) \tag{18}$$

or

$$\mathcal{E} = \frac{\gamma}{2\pi^2}\int k^2 dk \sqrt{\mathbf{k}^2 + M^2}(f_+ + f_-). \tag{19}$$

For $T = 0$, it becomes

$$\mathcal{E} = \frac{\gamma}{2\pi^2}\int_0^{k_F} k^2 dk \sqrt{\mathbf{k}^2 + M^2}. \tag{20}$$

As we still do not know the value of the chemical potential in Equation (10), the pressure can be obtained from the energy momentum tensor:

$$T_{\mu\nu} = -g_{\mu\nu}\mathcal{L} + \partial_\nu \psi \left(\frac{\partial \mathcal{L}}{\partial(\partial^\mu \psi)}\right), \tag{21}$$

having in mind that

$$\mathcal{E} = <T_{00}>, \quad P = \frac{1}{3}<T_{ii}> \tag{22}$$

and is given by

$$P = \frac{1}{3}\psi^\dagger(-i\vec{\alpha} \cdot \nabla)\psi. \tag{23}$$

From Equation (18), one can write

$$<\Psi|\vec{\alpha} \cdot \mathbf{k}|\Psi> = k\frac{\partial}{\partial k}<\Psi|\vec{\alpha} \cdot \mathbf{k} + \beta M|\Psi> = k\frac{\partial}{\partial k}<\Psi|E(\mathbf{k})|\Psi> \tag{24}$$

and finally

$$\psi^\dagger(-i\vec{\alpha} \cdot \nabla)\psi = \frac{\gamma}{(2\pi)^3}\int d^3k k \frac{\partial E}{\partial k} = \frac{\gamma}{2\pi^2}\int k^2 dk \cdot \frac{k^2}{\sqrt{\mathbf{k}^2 + M^2}},$$

$$P = \frac{\gamma}{6\pi^2} \int dk \frac{k^4}{\sqrt{k^2 + M^2}} (f_+ + f_-), \tag{25}$$

and for $T = 0$,

$$P = \frac{\gamma}{6\pi^2} \int_0^{k_F} dk \frac{k^4}{\sqrt{k^2 + M^2}}. \tag{26}$$

The entropy density of a free Fermi gas is given by

$$S = -\gamma \int \frac{d^3 p}{(2\pi)^3} \left(f_+ \ln\left(\frac{f_+}{1 - f_+}\right) + \ln(1 - f_+) \right. \tag{27}$$

$$\left. + f_- \ln\left(\frac{f_-}{1 - f_-}\right) + \ln(1 - f_-) \right), \tag{28}$$

By minimizing Equation (10), the distribution functions are obtained:

$$\frac{\partial \Omega}{\partial f_+} = 0 \rightarrow f_+ = \frac{1}{1 + e^{(\mathcal{E} - \mu)/T}} \tag{29}$$

and

$$\frac{\partial \Omega}{\partial f_-} = 0 \rightarrow f_- = \frac{1}{1 + e^{(\mathcal{E} + \mu)/T}}. \tag{30}$$

On the other hand, the minimization of the thermodynamical potential with respect to the density yields the chemical potential, i.e.,

$$\frac{\partial \Omega}{\partial \rho} = 0 \rightarrow \mu. \tag{31}$$

For $T = 0$,

$$\frac{\partial \Omega}{\partial k_F} = 0 \rightarrow \mu = \sqrt{k_F^2 + M^2}. \tag{32}$$

In order to go back to the discussion of nuclear matter, we are lacking exactly the nuclear interaction and its introduction will be seen in Section 3.

2.2. From the Compact Objects Point of View

I have already discussed the evolution process of a star while it remains in the main sequence of Figure 5. When the fusion ends, it is believed that one of the possible remnants is a neutron star. We see next how it was first predicted and then observed.

In fact, the history of neutron stars started with the observation of a white dwarf and its description with a degenerate free Fermi gas equation of state, as the one just introduced, but with the fermions being electrons instead of neutrons. In 1844, Frederich Bessel observed a very bright star that described an elliptical orbit [19], known as Sirius. He proposed that Sirius was part of a binary system, whose companion was not possible to see. In 1862, it was observed by Alvan Clark Jr. This companion, named Sirius B, had a luminosity many orders of magnitude lower than Sirius, but approximately the same mass, of the order of the solar mass (1 $M_\odot$). In 1914 Walter Adams concluded, through spectroscopy studies, that the temperature at the surface of both stars should be similar, but the density of one of them should be much higher than the density of the companion. This high-density star was called a white dwarf, and its properties were explained only in 1926 by Ralph Fowler [20] with the help of quantum mechanics. He claimed that the internal constituents of the white dwarf should be responsible for a degeneracy pressure that would compensate the gravitational force. This hypothesis was possible since the electrons are fermions and hence obey the Pauli Principle. In 1930, Subrahmanyan Chandrasekhar calculated the maximum densities of a white dwarf [21] and subsequently its maximum mass [22] that he thought should be 0.91 $M_\odot$ due to an incorrect value of the atomic mass to charge number ratio. It is interesting to note that the correct Chandrasekhar limit, 1.44 $M_\odot$ was actually obtained by Landau [23].

Concomitantly, Lev Landau reached the same conclusion as Chandrasekhar and went further: he proposed that even denser objects could exist, and in this case, the atomic nuclei would overlap and the star would become a gigantic nucleus [24]. Landau's hypothesis is considered the first forecast of a neutron star, although the neutrons had not been detected yet. Landau's paper was written in the beginning of 1931 but published one year later, just when the neutron was discovered by James Chadwick [25]. The first explicit proposition of the existence of neutron stars was made by Baade and Zwick [26], soon after Chadwick's discovery.

In 1939, Toman and, independently, Oppenheimer and Volkoff (TOV) [27,28] used special and general relativity to correct Newton's equations that described the properties of a perfect isotropic fluid, which they considered could be the interior of compact objects (white dwarfs and neutron stars). While Tolman proposed eight different solutions for the system of equations, Oppenheimer and Volkoff used the equation of state of a free neutron gas (exactly the one introduced in the previous section) and obtained a maximum mass of 0.7 $M_\odot$ for the neutron star, which was very disappointing because it was lower than the Chandrasekhar limit. However, soon, the limitations of this EOS were noticed: the inclusion of the nuclear interaction could make it harder and then generate higher masses. These calculations will be shown in the next section.

In 1940, Mario Shenberg and George Gamow proposed the Urca process [29], responsible for cooling down the stars by emitting neutrinos, which can carry a large amount of energy with very little interaction.

In 1967, the first neutron star (NS) was detected by Jocelyn Bell and Anthony Hewish [30]. At first, they believed they were capturing signals from an extraterrestrial civilization and the booklet *The Little Green Men* really existed. However, they soon realised that the radio signals were coming from a compact object with a very stable frequency (pulse) and the object was called a pulsar.

It is worth pointing out that white dwarfs and neutron stars bear very different internal constituents and densities. Neutron stars are much denser. This means that general relativity is a very important component in the study of NS, but this is not true for white dwarfs. Hence, it would be expected that only relativistic models, as the ones introduced in the present text, could be used to describe neutron star macroscopic properties. However, there are non-relativistic models, known as Skyrme models, which can be used to describe NS, as far as they do not violate causality. Moreover, some non-relativistic models lead to symmetry energies that decrease too much after three times saturation density, which is a very serious problem if we want to apply them to the study of neutron stars, which are highly asymmetric systems. These problems can be solved with the inclusion of three-body forces, which makes the calculations much more complicated. For a review of Skyrme models, please see Reference [2]. On the other hand, relativistic models are generally causal and always Lorentz invariant and when extended to finite temperature, anti-particles appear naturally. Thus, only relativistic models are discussed in the present work.

Let us go back to history because it continues. In 1974, Russel Hulse and Joseph Taylor identified the first binary pulsar PSR1913+16 [31] with a radio-telescope in Arecibo and proposed that the system was losing energy in the form of gravitational waves (GW), the same kind of waves foreseen by relativistic theories. Note that they did not detect gravitational waves directly but instead proved their existence via pulsar timing and were laureated with the Nobel prize for this discovery. In 2015, the first GW produced by two colliding black holes was finally detected directly by LIGO [32], and in 2017, GW170817, produced by the merger of two NS [33], initiated the era of multi-messenger astronomy [34]. These gravitational waves have become an excellent source of constraints to the EOS used to describe neutron stars, as will be discussed in a future section.

3. Relativistic Models for Astrophysical Studies

In Section 2.1, the EOS of a free Fermi gas was introducedl and in Section 2.2, I mentioned that the EOS can satisfactorily describe a white dwarf, as shown by Chandrasekhar, if the free Fermi gas is a gas of electrons. However, if the fermions are neutrons, it cannot describe neutron stars. One important ingredient, besides the already mentioned relativistic effects, is still missing in the recipe: the nuclear interaction. Therefore, let us go back to nuclear matter.

3.1. The $\sigma - \omega$ Model

This model, also known as the Walecka model [35] or quantum hadrodynamics (QHD-1), is based on the fact that the interaction inside the nucleus has two contributions: an attractive contribution at *large* distances and a repulsive one at short distances, and both can be reasonably well described by Yukawa-type potentials and represented by fields generated, respectively, by scalar and vector mesons. This idea was first proposed by Hans Peter Durr in his Ph.D. thesis in 1956, supervised by Edward Teller, who, in 1955, also proposed a version of the model based on classical field theory [36]. However, the quantum version proposed by Walecka was the one that gained the most popularity, and until now, it is largely applied with different versions and extensions. This simplified model does not take pions into account because, as will be seen next, it is usually solved in a mean field approximation and in this case, the pion contribution disappears. As the $\sigma - \omega$ model is a relativistic model, this simpler and more common approximation is always known as relativistic Mean Field Theory (RMF) or relativistic Hartree approximation.

As the name suggests, the $\sigma - \omega$ model considers that the central effective potential for the nucleon–nucleon interaction is given by

$$V(r) = \frac{g_\omega^2}{4\pi}\frac{e^{-m_\omega r}}{r} - \frac{g_\sigma^2}{4\pi}\frac{e^{-m_\sigma r}}{r},$$

where r is the modulus of the vector that defines the relative distance between two nucleons, the two constants g_σ and g_ω are adjusted to reproduce the nucleon–nucleon interaction and the meson masses are, respectively, $m_\sigma = 550$ MeV and $m_\omega = 783$ MeV. The interested reader can look at the potential $V(r)$ obtained with the coupling constants and masses used in this section in [15]. To obtain the binding energy that corresponds to this potential in RMF, a Lorentz invariant Lagrangian density is necessary, and it reads:

$$\mathcal{L} = \bar{\psi}[\gamma_\mu(i\partial^\mu - g_\omega \omega^\mu) - (M - g_\sigma \sigma)]\psi$$
$$+ \frac{1}{2}(\partial_\mu \sigma \partial^\mu \sigma - m_\sigma^2 \sigma^2) + \frac{1}{2}m_\omega^2 \omega_\mu \omega^\mu - \frac{1}{4}F_{\mu\nu}F^{\mu\nu}, \quad (33)$$

where

$$F_{\mu\nu} = \partial_\mu \omega_\nu - \partial_\nu \omega_\mu, \quad (34)$$

ψ represents the baryonic field (nucleons), σ and ω^μ represent the fields associated with the scalar and vector mesons and M is the nucleon mass, generally taken as 939 MeV. By comparing Equations (11) and (33), one can see that besides the Fermi gas representing the nucleons, the latter contains two interaction terms and kinetic and mass terms for both mesons. The usual prescription is to use the Euler–Lagrange Equation (12) for each field to obtain the equations of motion. They read:

$$\left(\partial_\mu \partial^\mu + m_\sigma^2\right)\sigma = g_\sigma \bar{\psi}\psi, \quad (35)$$

$$\partial_\mu F^{\mu\nu} + m_\omega^2 \omega^\nu = g_\omega \bar{\psi}\gamma^\nu \psi \quad (36)$$

and

$$[\gamma_\mu(i\partial^\mu - g_\omega \omega^\mu) - (M - g_\sigma \sigma)]\psi = 0. \quad (37)$$

Note that Equation (35) is a Klein–Gordon equation with a scalar source, Equation (36) is analogous to quantum electrodynamics with a conserved baryonic current ($\bar{\psi}\gamma^\nu\psi$), instead of the electromagnetic current, and Equation (37) is a Dirac equation for an interacting (not free) gas.

In an RMF approximation, the meson fields are replaced by their expectation values that behave as classical fields:

$$\sigma \to \langle\sigma\rangle \equiv \sigma_0 \tag{38}$$

and

$$\omega_\mu \to \langle\omega_0\rangle \equiv \omega_0, \quad \langle\omega_k\rangle = 0. \tag{39}$$

The equations of motion can then be easily solved and they read:

$$\sigma_0 = \frac{g_\sigma}{m_\sigma^2} <\bar{\psi}\psi> = \frac{g_\sigma}{m_\sigma^2}\rho_s \tag{40}$$

and

$$\omega_0 = \frac{g_\omega}{m_\omega^2} <\psi^\dagger\psi> = \frac{g_\omega}{m_\omega^2}\rho, \tag{41}$$

where ρ_s is a scalar density and ρ is a baryonic number density. The Dirac equation becomes simply

$$\left[(i\gamma_\mu\partial^\mu - g_\omega\gamma_0\omega^0) - (M - g_\sigma\sigma_0)\right]\psi = 0, \tag{42}$$

and

$$M^* = M - g_\sigma\sigma_0, \tag{43}$$

is the effective mass. To obtain the EOS, the recipe is the same as already shown for the free Fermi gas, which leads to expressions for the energy density and pressure. Assuming $C_s^2 = g_\sigma^2(M^2/m_\sigma^2) = 267.1$ and $C_v^2 = g_\omega^2(M^2/m_\omega^2) = 195.9$, the binding energy $E/N - M = -15.75$ MeV at the saturation density $\rho = 0.19$ fm^{-3}, a little bit too high.

Other important quantities directly related with nuclear matter EOS are the symmetry energy, its derivatives and the incompressibility. The symmetry energy is roughly the necessary energy to transform symmetric matter into a pure neutron matter, as shown in Figure 7, i.e.,

$$\mathcal{E}(\rho,\delta) \simeq \mathcal{E}(\rho,\delta=0) + E_{sym}(\rho)\delta^2. \tag{44}$$

Its value can be inferred from experiments and it is of the order of 30–35 MeV and it can be written as

$$E_{sym} = \frac{1}{8}\left(\frac{\partial^2(\mathcal{E}/\rho)}{\partial y_p^2}\right)_{y_p=0.5} = \frac{1}{2}\left(\frac{\partial^2(\mathcal{E}/\rho)}{\partial\delta^2}\right)_{\delta=0}. \tag{45}$$

It is common to expand the symmetry energy around the saturation density in a Taylor series as

$$E_{sym} = J + L_0(\frac{\rho-\rho_0}{3\rho_0}) + \frac{K_{sym}}{2}(\frac{\rho-\rho_0}{3\rho_0})^2 + \mathcal{O}(3), \tag{46}$$

where J is the symmetry energy at the saturation point and L_0 and K_{sym} represent, respectively, its slope and curvature:

$$L_0 = 3\rho_0\left(\frac{\partial E_{sym}(\rho)}{\partial\rho}\right)_{\rho=\rho_0}, \tag{47}$$

and
$$K_{sym} = 9\rho_0^2 \left(\frac{\partial^2 E_{sym}(\rho)}{\partial \rho^2}\right)_{\rho=\rho_0}. \tag{48}$$

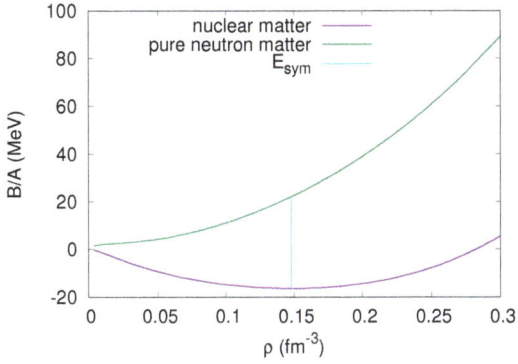

Figure 7. Schematic representation of the nuclear matter symmetry energy.

Experimental data for the symmetry energy can be inferred from heavy-ion collisions, giant monopole (GMR) and giant dipole (GDR) resonances, pygmy dipole resonances and isobaric analog states. Accepted values for the slope until very recently lay in between 30.6 and 86.8 MeV [37,38] and for the curvature, in between -400 and 100 MeV [39,40]. These two quantities are correlated with macroscopic properties of neutron stars, as will be seen later on in this manuscript. Based on 28 experimental and observational data, restricted bands for the values of J ($25 < J < 35$ MeV) and L_0 ($25 < L_0 < 115$ MeV) were given in [41]. More recently, results obtained by the PREX2 experiment [12] point to a different band, given by $L_0 = 106 \pm 37$ MeV [42]. If confirmed, this result rehabilitates many of the EOS already ruled out and points to a neutron star radius much larger than previously expected, as also discussed later on in the present paper.

Another important quantity is the incompressibility, already mentioned when the liquid drop model idea was introduced. It is a measure of the stiffness of the EOS; i.e., it defines how much pressure a system can support and it is calculated from the relation

$$K_0 = 9\left(\frac{\partial P}{\partial \rho}\right)_{\rho=\rho_0,\, y_p=0.5} \tag{49}$$

and ranges between 190 and 270 MeV [37,38]. These values can be inferred from both theory and experiments.

I will go back to the importance of these nuclear matter bulk properties and their connection with neutron star properties later on.

3.2. Extended Relativistic Hadronic Models

I next present one example of a complete Lagrangian density that describes baryons interacting among each other by exchanging scalar-isoscalar (σ), vector-isoscalar (ω), vector-isovector (ρ), and scalar-isovector (δ) mesons:

$$\mathcal{L} = \mathcal{L}_{nm} + \mathcal{L}_\sigma + \mathcal{L}_\omega + \mathcal{L}_\rho + \mathcal{L}_\delta + \mathcal{L}_{\sigma\omega\rho}, \tag{50}$$

where [43]

$$\mathcal{L}_{nm} = \bar{\psi}(i\gamma^\mu\partial_\mu - M)\psi + g_\sigma\sigma\bar{\psi}\psi - g_\omega\bar{\psi}\gamma^\mu\omega_\mu\psi - \frac{g_\rho}{2}\bar{\psi}\gamma^\mu\vec{\rho}_\mu\cdot\vec{\tau}\psi + g_\delta\bar{\psi}\vec{\delta}\cdot\vec{\tau}\psi, \quad (51)$$

$$\mathcal{L}_\sigma = \frac{1}{2}(\partial^\mu\sigma\partial_\mu\sigma - m_\sigma^2\sigma^2) - \frac{A}{3}\sigma^3 - \frac{B}{4}\sigma^4, \quad (52)$$

$$\mathcal{L}_\omega = -\frac{1}{4}F^{\mu\nu}F_{\mu\nu} + \frac{1}{2}m_\omega^2\omega_\mu\omega^\mu + \frac{C}{4}(g_\omega^2\omega_\mu\omega^\mu)^2, \quad (53)$$

$$\mathcal{L}_\rho = -\frac{1}{4}\vec{B}^{\mu\nu}\vec{B}_{\mu\nu} + \frac{1}{2}m_\rho^2\vec{\rho}_\mu\cdot\vec{\rho}^\mu, \quad (54)$$

$$\mathcal{L}_\delta = \frac{1}{2}(\partial^\mu\vec{\delta}\partial_\mu\vec{\delta} - m_\delta^2\vec{\delta}^2), \quad (55)$$

and

$$\mathcal{L}_{\sigma\omega\rho} = g_\sigma g_\omega^2 \sigma\omega_\mu\omega^\mu\left(\alpha_1 + \frac{1}{2}\alpha_1' g_\sigma\sigma\right) + g_\sigma g_\rho^2\sigma\vec{\rho}_\mu\cdot\vec{\rho}^\mu\left(\alpha_2 + \frac{1}{2}\alpha_2' g_\sigma\sigma\right) + \frac{1}{2}\alpha_3' g_\omega^2 g_\rho^2\omega_\mu\omega^\mu\vec{\rho}_\mu\cdot\vec{\rho}^\mu. \quad (56)$$

In this Lagrangian density, $\mathcal{L}_{nm}$ represents the kinetic part of the nucleons plus the terms standing for the interaction between them and mesons σ, δ, ω, and ρ. The term $\mathcal{L}_j$ represents the free and self-interacting terms of the meson j, where $j = \sigma, \delta, \omega$, and ρ. The σ self-interaction terms were the first ones to be introduced [44] to correct some of the values of the nuclear bulk properties. The last term, $\mathcal{L}_{\sigma\omega\rho}$, accounts for crossing interactions between the meson fields. The antisymmetric field tensors $F_{\mu\nu}$ and $\vec{B}_{\mu\nu}$ are given by $F_{\mu\nu} = \partial_\nu\omega_\mu - \partial_\mu\omega_\nu$ and $\vec{B}_{\mu\nu} = \partial_\nu\vec{\rho}_\mu - \partial_\mu\vec{\rho}_\nu - g_\rho(\vec{\rho}_\mu\times\vec{\rho}_\nu)$. The nucleon mass is M and the meson masses are m_j.

In a mean field approximation, the meson fields are treated as classical fields and the equations of motion are obtained via Euler–Lagrange equations. Translational and rotational invariance are assumed. The equations of motion are then solved self-consistently and the energy momentum tensor, Equation (21), is used in the calculation of the EOS. The calculations follow the steps shown in Sections 2.1 and 3.1. The interested reader can also check them, for instance, in [35,37]. Nevertheless, some of the important steps are mentioned in what follows. Within a RMF approximation, the common substitution mentioned below is again performed:

$$\sigma \to \langle\sigma\rangle \equiv \sigma_0, \quad \omega_\mu \to \langle\omega_0\rangle \equiv \omega_0, \quad \vec{\rho}_\mu \to \langle\vec{\rho}_0\rangle \equiv \bar{\rho}_{0(3)}, \quad \vec{\delta} \to <\vec{\delta}> \equiv \delta_{(3)}, \quad (57)$$

and the equations of motion read:

$$m_\sigma^2\sigma_0 = g_\sigma\rho_s - A\sigma_0^2 - B\sigma_0^3 + g_\sigma g_\omega^2\omega_0^2(\alpha_1 + \alpha_1' g_\sigma\sigma) + g_\sigma g_\rho^2\bar{\rho}_{0(3)}^2(\alpha_2 + \alpha_2' g_\sigma\sigma), \quad (58)$$

$$m_\omega^2\omega_0 = g_\omega\rho - Cg_\omega(g_\omega\omega_0)^3 - g_\sigma g_\omega^2\sigma_0\omega_0(2\alpha_1 + \alpha_1' g_\sigma\sigma_0) - \alpha_3' g_\omega^2 g_\rho^2\bar{\rho}_{0(3)}^2\omega_0, \quad (59)$$

$$m_\rho^2\bar{\rho}_{0(3)} = \frac{g_\rho}{2}\rho_3 - g_\sigma g_\rho^2\sigma_0\bar{\rho}_{0(3)}(2\alpha_2 + \alpha_2' g_\sigma\sigma_0) - \alpha_3' g_\omega^2 g_\rho^2\bar{\rho}_{0(3)}\omega_0^2, \quad (60)$$

$$m_\delta^2\delta_{(3)} = g_\delta\rho_{s3}, \quad (61)$$

and

$$[i\gamma^\mu\partial_\mu - \gamma^0 V_\tau - (M + S_\tau)]\psi = 0, \quad (62)$$

where

$$\rho_s = \langle\bar{\psi}\psi\rangle = \rho_{sp} + \rho_{sn}, \quad \rho_{s3} = \langle\bar{\psi}\tau_3\psi\rangle = \rho_{sp} - \rho_{sn}, \quad (63)$$

$$\rho = \langle\bar{\psi}\gamma^0\psi\rangle = \rho_p + \rho_n, \quad \rho_3 = \langle\bar{\psi}\gamma^0\tau_3\psi\rangle = \rho_p - \rho_n = (2y_p - 1)\rho, \quad (64)$$

with

$$\rho_{sp,n} = \frac{\gamma M^*_{p,n}}{2\pi^2}\int_0^{k_{Fp,n}}\frac{k^2 dk}{\sqrt{k^2 + M^{*2}_{p,n}}}, \quad (65)$$

$$\rho_{p,n} = \frac{\gamma}{2\pi^2} \int_0^{k_{F_{p,n}}} k^2 dk = \frac{\gamma}{6\pi^2} k_{F_{p,n}}^3, \qquad (66)$$

$$V_\tau = g_\omega \omega_0 + \frac{g_\rho}{2} \bar{\rho}_{0(3)} \tau_3, \qquad S_\tau = -g_\sigma \sigma_0 - g_\delta \delta_{(3)} \tau_3, \qquad (67)$$

with $\tau_3 = 1$ and -1 for protons and neutrons respectively and $\gamma = 2$ to account for the spin degeneracy. The proton and neutron effective masses read:

$$M_p^* = M - g_\sigma \sigma_0 - g_\delta \delta_{(3)} \quad \text{and} \quad M_n^* = M - g_\sigma \sigma_0 + g_\delta \delta_{(3)}. \qquad (68)$$

Due to translational and rotational invariance, only the zero components of quadrivectors remain. From the energy-momentum tensor, the following expressions are obtained:

$$\begin{aligned}
\mathcal{E} =\ & \frac{1}{2} m_\sigma^2 \sigma_0^2 + \frac{A}{3} \sigma_0^3 + \frac{B}{4} \sigma_0^4 - \frac{1}{2} m_\omega^2 \omega_0^2 - \frac{C}{4}(g_\omega^2 \omega_0^2)^2 - \frac{1}{2} m_\rho^2 \bar{\rho}_{0(3)}^2 + g_\omega \omega_0 \rho + \frac{g_\rho}{2} \bar{\rho}_{0(3)} \rho_3 \\
& + \frac{1}{2} m_\delta^2 \delta_{(3)}^2 - g_\sigma g_\omega^2 \sigma \omega_0^2 \left(\alpha_1 + \frac{1}{2}\alpha_1' g_\sigma \sigma_0\right) - g_\sigma g_\rho^2 \sigma \bar{\rho}_{0(3)}^2 \left(\alpha_2 + \frac{1}{2}\alpha_2' g_\sigma \sigma_0\right) \\
& - \frac{1}{2} \alpha_3' g_\omega^2 g_\rho^2 \omega_0^2 \bar{\rho}_{0(3)}^2 + \mathcal{E}_{kin}^p + \mathcal{E}_{kin}^n,
\end{aligned} \qquad (69)$$

with

$$\mathcal{E}_{kin}^{p,n} = \frac{\gamma}{2\pi^2} \int_0^{k_{F_{p,n}}} k^2 (k^2 + M_{p,n}^{*2})^{1/2} dk \qquad (70)$$

and

$$\begin{aligned}
P =\ & -\frac{1}{2} m_\sigma^2 \sigma_0^2 - \frac{A}{3} \sigma_0^3 - \frac{B}{4} \sigma_0^4 + \frac{1}{2} m_\omega^2 \omega_0^2 + \frac{C}{4}(g_\omega^2 \omega_0^2)^2 + \frac{1}{2} m_\rho^2 \bar{\rho}_{0(3)}^2 + \frac{1}{2} \alpha_3' g_\omega^2 g_\rho^2 \omega_0^2 \bar{\rho}_{0(3)}^2 \\
& - \frac{1}{2} m_\delta^2 \delta_{(3)}^2 + g_\sigma g_\omega^2 \sigma_0 \omega_0^2 \left(\alpha_1 + \frac{1}{2}\alpha_1' g_\sigma \sigma_0\right) + g_\sigma g_\rho^2 \sigma \bar{\rho}_{0(3)}^2 \left(\alpha_2 + \frac{1}{2}\alpha_2' g_\sigma \sigma\right) \\
& + P_{kin}^p + P_{kin}^n,
\end{aligned} \qquad (71)$$

with

$$P_{kin}^{p,n} = \frac{\gamma}{6\pi^2} \int_0^{k_{F_{p,n}}} \frac{k^4 dk}{(k^2 + M_{p,n}^{*2})^{1/2}}. \qquad (72)$$

3.3. Too Many Relativistic Models

In [37], a large number of relativistic models were confronted with two sets of nuclear bulk properties, one more and one less restrictive. The interested reader should check the chosen ranges of properties in both sets and the respective values of 363 models. In what follows, I will restrict myself to three parameter sets: NL3 [45], NL3$\omega\rho$ [46], which is an extension of the NL3 parameter set with the introduction of a vector–isovector interaction, and IUFSU [47]. These models are chosen because they are frequently used in various applications in the literature. Moreover, NL3$\omega\rho$ and IUFSU satisfy all nuclear matter bulk properties, but it will be seen throughout the text that recent astrophysical observations are not completely satisfied by them. The inclusion of NL3 and its comparison with NL3$\omega\rho$ help the understanding of the importance of the $\omega - \rho$ interaction. Other parameter sets shown along the next sections are GM1 [48], GM3 [49], TM1 [50], and FSUGZ03 [51]. All of them are contemplated in [37], and the interested reader can check their successes and failures in satisfying the main nuclear bulk properties. Notice that none of the parameter sets explicitly mentioned in the present work includes the δ meson, which distinguishes protons and neutrons, and consequently, the effective masses given in Equation (68) are identical. The mesonic crossing terms weighted by the parameters $\alpha_1, \alpha_1', \alpha_2, \alpha_2'$ are not included either. In Table 1, the parameter values for the three parametrizations mostly used are presented and in Table 2, their main nuclear properties are shown.

Table 1. Parameter sets used in this section-all meson masses and A are given in MeV, $\Lambda_v = \alpha_3'/2$ and $M = 939$ MeV.

Model	m_σ	m_ω	m_ρ	g_σ	g_ω	g_ρ	A	B	C	Λ_v
NL3	508.194	782.501	763	10.217	12.868	8.948	2.055×10^{-3}	-2.65×10^{-3}	0	0
NL3$\omega\rho$	508.194	782.501	763	2.192	12.868	11.276	2.055×10^{-3}	-2.65×10^{-3}	0	0.03
IUFSU	491.5	782.5	763	9.971	13.032	13.590	1.80×10^{-3}	4.9×10^{-5}	0.18	0.046

In Figure 8 left, I plot the binding energy per nucleon for the three parameter sets, and one can clearly see the slightly different saturation densities and binding energy values. Notice that the $\omega - \rho$ channel does not influence the binding energy of symmetric nuclear matter but plays an important role in asymmetric matter. In Figure 8 right, the symmetry energy is depicted, and it is easy to see that they are very similar at sub-saturation densities but completely different at larger densities. As a consequence of what is seen in Figure 8, the incompressibility, the slope, and the curvature of the three models are different, as shown in Table 2.

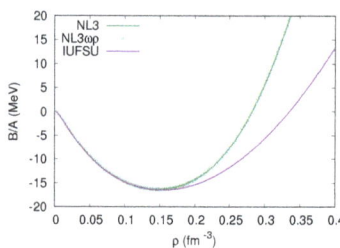
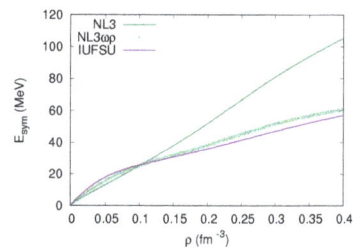

Figure 8. (Left) Binding energy and (right) symmetry energy as a function of the baryonic density for the three parameter sets used in this section.

Table 2. Saturation and stellar properties. These values are commented along the text.

Model	ρ_0 fm^{-3}	B/A MeV	K_0 MeV	M^*/M	J MeV	L MeV	$M_{max}/M_\odot$	$R_{1.4M_\odot}$ km
NL3	0.148	−16.24	271.53	0.60	37.40	118.53	2.78	14.7
NL3$\omega\rho$	0.148	−16.24	271.60	0.60	31.70	55.50	2.76	13.7
IUFSU	0.155	−16.40	231.33	0.61	31.30	47.21	1.94	12.5

4. Stellar Matter

The idea of this section is to show how the relativistic models presented so far can be applied to describe stellar matter, and, in this case, we refer specifically to neutron stars. Looking back at the QCD phase diagram presented in the Introduction, one can see that neutron stars have internal densities that are 6 to 10 times higher than the nuclear saturation density and that their temperature is low. Actually, if we compare their thermal energy with the Fermi energy of the system, the assumption of zero temperature is indeed reasonable. At these very high densities, the onset of hyperons is expected because their appearance is energetically favorable as compared with the inclusion of more nucleons in the system. To deal with this fact, the first term in the Lagrangian density of Equation (51) has to be modified to take into account, at least, the eight lightest baryons, and it becomes:

$$\mathcal{L}_{Bm} = \sum_B \overline{\psi_B}(i\gamma^\mu \partial_\mu - M_B)\psi_B + g_{\sigma B}\sigma\overline{\psi_B}\psi_B - g_{\omega B}\overline{\psi_B}\gamma^\mu \omega_\mu \psi_B - \frac{g_{\rho B}}{2}\overline{\psi_B}\gamma^\mu \vec{\rho}_\mu \vec{\tau}\psi_B. \quad (73)$$

The meson-baryon coupling constants are given by

$$g_{jB} = \chi_{Bj} g_j, \tag{74}$$

where g_j is the coupling of the meson with the nucleon and χ_{jB} is a value obtained according to symmetry groups or by satisfying hyperon potential values. These are important quantities when hyperons are included in the system [49,52]. We come back to the discussion of these quantities below. If we perform once again an RMF approximation and use the Euler–Lagrange equations to obtain the equations of motion, we find:

$$\sigma_0 = \sum_B \frac{g_{\sigma B}}{m_\sigma^2} \rho_{sB} - \frac{1}{m_\sigma^2}\left(A\sigma_0^2 - B\sigma_0^3\right), \tag{75}$$

$$\omega_0 = \sum_B \frac{g_{\omega B}}{m_\omega^2} \rho_B - \frac{1}{m_\omega^2}\left(2\Lambda_v g_\omega^2 g_\rho^2 \bar{\rho}_{0(3)}^2 \omega_0\right), \tag{76}$$

$$\bar{\rho}_{0(3)} = \sum_B \frac{g_{\rho B}}{m_\rho^2} \frac{\tau_3}{2} \rho_B - \frac{1}{m_\rho^2}\left(2\Lambda_v g_\omega^2 g_\rho^2 \omega_0^2 \bar{\rho}_{0(3)}\right), \tag{77}$$

where ρ_{sB} is the scalar density and ρ_B is the baryon B density, given by:

$$\rho_{sB} = \frac{\gamma}{2\pi^2} \int_0^{k_{fB}} \frac{M_B^*}{\sqrt{k^2 + M_B^{*2}}} k^2 dk, \tag{78}$$

$$\rho_B = \frac{\gamma}{6\pi^2} k_{fB}^3, \quad \text{and} \quad \rho = \sum_B \rho_B, \tag{79}$$

where k_{fB} is the Fermi momentum of baryon B. The terms $\mathcal{E}_{kin}^p$ and $\mathcal{E}_{kin}^n$ that appear in Equation (69), must now be substituted by

$$\mathcal{E}_B = \frac{\gamma}{2\pi^2} \sum_B \int_0^{k_{fB}} \sqrt{k^2 + M_B^{*2}} k^2 dk \tag{80}$$

and

$$M_B^* = M_B - g_\sigma \sigma_0. \tag{81}$$

Whenever stellar matter is considered, β-equilibrium and charge neutrality-conditions have to be imposed, and hence, the inclusion of leptons (generally electrons and muons) is necessary. These conditions read:

$$\mu_B = \mu_n - q_B \mu_e, \quad \mu_e = \mu_\mu, \quad \sum_B q_B \rho_B + \sum_l q_l \rho_l = 0, \tag{82}$$

where μ_B and q_B are the chemical potential and the electrical charge of the baryons, q_l is the electrical charge of the leptons, ρ_B, and ρ_l are the number densities of the baryons and leptons.

After the supernova explosion, the remnant is, at first, a protoneutron star. Before deleptonisation takes place, neutrinos are also present in the system and in this case, the chemical stability condition becomes

$$\mu_B = \mu_n - q_B(\mu_e - \mu_{\nu_e}), \quad \mu_e = \mu_\mu. \tag{83}$$

In this process, entropy is usually fixed at values compatible with simulations of neutron star cooling, and the lepton fractions reach values of the order of 0.3–0.4. This scenario is not considered in the present paper, but examples of this calculation can be seen in [53].

To satisfy the above conditions of chemical equilibrium and charge neutrality, leptons must be incorporated in the system, and this is done with the introduction of a free Fermi gas, i.e.,

$$\mathcal{L}_{lep} = \sum_{l} \bar{\psi}_l [i\gamma^\mu \partial_\mu - m_l] \psi_l, \tag{84}$$

where the sum runs over the electron and the muon and their eigenenergies are

$$E_l = \sqrt{k^2 + m_l^2}, \tag{85}$$

so that their energy density becomes

$$\mathcal{E}_l = \frac{\gamma}{2\pi^2} \sum_l \int_0^{k_{fl}} \sqrt{k^2 + m_l^2} k^2 dk. \tag{86}$$

The total pression of the system can be either obtained separately for its baryonic and leptonic parts as in the previous section or by thermodynamics:

$$P = \sum_f \mu_f \rho_f - \mathcal{E}_f, \tag{87}$$

where f stands for all fermions in the system and it is common to define the particle fraction (including leptons) as $Y_f = \frac{\rho_f}{\rho}$.

As already mentioned, an important point is how to fix the meson–hyperon coupling constants $g_{iB}, i = \sigma, \omega, \rho$. There are two methods generally used in the literature. The first one is phenomenological and is based on the fitting of the hyperon potentials [49]:

$$U_Y = g_{\omega B} \omega_0 - g_{\sigma B} \sigma_0, \tag{88}$$

which, unfortunately, are not completely established. The only well-known potential is the Λ potential depth $U_\Lambda = -28$ MeV [48]. Common values for the Σ and Ξ potentials are $U_\Sigma = +30$ MeV and $U_\Xi = -18$ MeV [54,55], but their real values remain uncertain. According to [48], appropriate values for the meson–hyperon coupling constants defined in Equation (74) are obtained if $\chi_{B\sigma} = 0.7$ and $\chi_{B\omega} = \chi_{B\rho}$ is given by 0.772 for NL3 and 0.783 if another common parametrization, the GM1, is used. However, in these cases, the value of $\chi_{B\rho}$ remains completely arbitrary. We have mentioned GM1 here because it is very often used in the description of neutron star matter since it was one of the first parameter sets with a high effective mass at the saturation density ($M^*/M = 0.7$) as compared with 0.6 given by NL3, for instance (see Table 2). This high effective mass helps the convergence of the codes when the hyperons are introduced because Equation (81) accounts for a large contribution of the σ_0 field, which in turn, carries the information of the scalar densities of eight baryons. The situation is very different from the one in nuclear matter, where the effective mass only carries the σ_0 field coming from the nucleonic scalar density. This means that whenever the eight lightest baryons are included, the negative contribution in Equation (81) can make the nucleon mass reach zero very rapidly if the effective mass is too low.

Other examples of how to fit these couplings based on phenomenological potentials can be seen in [56,57]. The second possibility to choose the meson–hyperon couplings is based on the relations established among them by different group symmetries, the most common being SU(3) [52,58] and SU(6) [59].

In the present work, we have used the following sets of couplings, for which $U_\Lambda = -28$ MeV, $U_\Sigma = +30$ MeV and $U_\Xi = -18$ MeV:

- for NL3 and NL3$\omega\rho$: $\chi_{\Lambda\sigma} = 0.613$, $\chi_{\Sigma\sigma} = 0.460$, $\chi_{\Xi\sigma} = 0.317$,
- for IUFSU: $\chi_{\Lambda\sigma} = 0.611$, $\chi_{\Sigma\sigma} = 0.454$, $\chi_{\Xi\sigma} = 0.316$,

and $\chi_{\Lambda\omega} = \chi_{\Sigma\omega} = 0.667$, $\chi_{\Xi\omega} = 0.333$ in all cases due to the SU(6) symmetry and $\chi_{B\rho} = 1$ for all hyperons in all cases.

In Figure 9, six different EOSs are shown, for the three parameter sets identified above, with and without the inclusion of the hyperons. The EOSs for the IUFSU with and without hyperons are reproduced with different units (fm^{-4}) instead of the more intuitive (MeV/fm^3) because those are common units used in stellar matter studies. Notice that $\hbar c = 197.326$ MeV.fm and Natural units are used in these calculations.

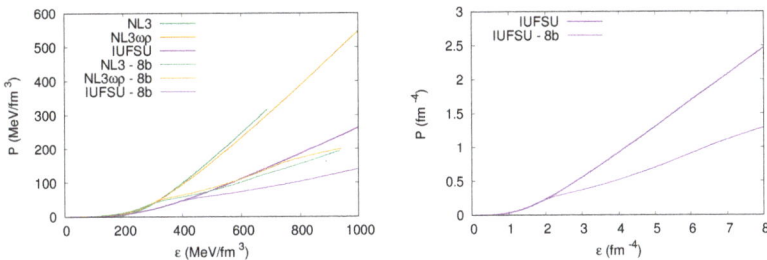

Figure 9. (**Left**) Stellar matter EOS obtained with different parametrizations. Thick solid lines show EOS with nucleons only and thin lines represent EOS with the eight lightest baryons and (**right**) the same EOS for IUFSU with and without hyperons but with different units for pressure and energy density.

In Figure 10, the particle fractions obtained with IUFSU are displayed for the two cases shown in Figure 9 right. Notice that when the hyperons are included, these particle fractions depend on the meson–hyperon couplings discussed above. A different choice for these couplings would generate different particle fractions for the same nuclear parametrisation. One can see that the constituents of the neutron stars change with the increase in the density, making their core richer in terms of particles than the region near the crust. From these plots, the conditions of charge neutrality and chemical equilibrium become clear.

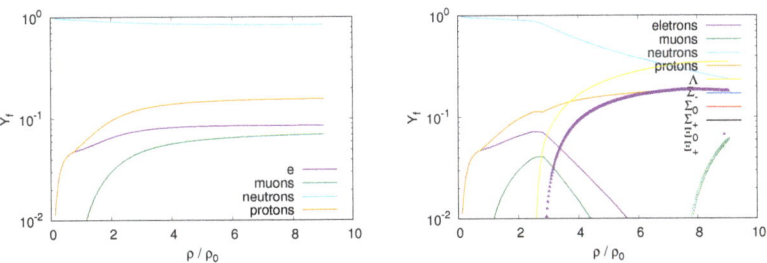

Figure 10. Particle fractions obtained with IUFSU for an EOS with (**left**) nucleons only and (**right**) lightest eight baryons.

4.1. The Tolman–Oppenheimer–Volkoff Equations

As it was just seen, essential nuclear physics ingredients for astrophysical calculations are appropriate equations of state (EOS). After the EOSs are chosen, they enter as input to the Tolman–Oppenheimer–Volkoff equations (TOV) [27,28], which in turn give as output some macroscopic stellar properties: radii, masses, and central energy densities. Static properties, as the moment of inertia and rotation rate can be obtained as well. The EOSs are also necessary in calculations involving the dynamical evolution of supernova, protoneutron star evolution and cooling, conditions for nucleosynthesis and stellar chemical composition, and transport properties, for instance.

The TOV equations were obtained by Tolman [27] and independently by Oppenheimer and Volkoff [28], as already mentioned, and they read:

$$\frac{dP}{dr} = -G\frac{(\mathcal{E}+P)(M(r)+4\pi Pr^3)}{r^2-2M(r)r},$$

$$= -\frac{G\mathcal{E}M(r)}{r^2}\left[1+\frac{P}{\mathcal{E}}\right]\left[1+\frac{4\pi r^3 P}{M(r)}\right]\left[1-\frac{2GM(r)}{r}\right]^{-1} \quad (89)$$

$$\frac{dM}{dr} = 4\pi\mathcal{E}r^2,$$

$$\frac{dM_{Baryonic}}{dr} = 4\pi m_n r^2 \rho(r)\left[1-\frac{2M(r)}{r}\right]^{-1/2},$$

where M is the gravitational mass, $M_{Baryonic}$ is the baryonic mass, m_n is the nucleon mass, and r is the radial coordinate and also the circumferential radius. Be aware that $M_{Baryonic}$ refers to the baryonic mass of the star, and it is not the same as the M_B, the individual baryonic masses used to compute the EOS.

The first differential equation is also shown in such a way that the corrections obtained from special and general relativity are clearly separated.

The EOSs shown on the r.h.s. of Figure 9 are then used as input to the above TOV equations and the corresponding mass-radius diagram is shown in Figure 11. Each curve represents a family of stars, being the maximum point of the curves related to the maximum stellar mass of the family. By comparing the curves shown in Figures 9 and 11, one can clearly see that the harder EOS yields higher maximum mass. Hence, the inclusion of hyperons makes the EOS softer, as expected, but results in lower maximum masses. As there is no reason to believe that the hyperons are not present, this connection of softer EOS with lower neutron star mass gave rise to what is known as the *hyperon puzzle*. I will go back to this debate in the next section.

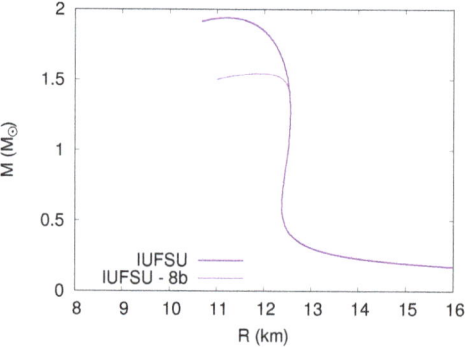

Figure 11. Mass–radius diagram obtained with the IUFSU parametrization for hadronic matter with (8b) and without hyperons.

I would like to call the attention of the reader for the values of the symmetry energy slope (L_0), which has been extensively discussed in the last years. Although its true value is still a matter of debate, most studies indicate that it has non-negligible implications on the neutron star macroscopic properties [38,60–66]. The slope can be controlled by the inclusion of the $\omega - \rho$ interaction, as can be seen in Table 2. In general, the larger the value of the interaction, the lower the values of the symmetry energy and its slope [60]. As a general trend, it is also true that the lower the value of the slope, the lower the radius of the canonical star, the one with 1.4 $M_\odot$. In Table 2, the values of the maximum stellar masses obtained without the inclusion of hyperons and the radii of the canonical stars are displayed. Notice, however, that the value of the radius of the canonical stars depends on the EOS of the crust. To obtain the values shown in Table 2, I used the BPS EOS [67] for the outer crust and interpolated the inner crust. As far as the maximum mass is concerned, the crust barely affects it, since the involved densities are too low. I will discuss this subject further when discussing the pasta phase in Section 4.3. Another interesting correlation noticed in [68] is that the onset of the charged (neutral) hyperons takes place at lower (larger) densities for smaller values of the slope.

4.2. Structure of Neutron Stars and Observational Constraints

Although the internal constitution of a neutron star cannot be directly tested, it is reasonably well understood. A famous picture of the NS internal structure was drawn by Dany Page and can be seen in [69]. Close to the surface of the star, there is an outer and an inner crust, and towards the center, an outer and an inner core are believed to exist. The solid crust is expected to be formed by nonuniform neutron-rich matter in β-equilibrium. This inhomogeneous phase is known as pasta phase, and calculations predict that it exists at densities lower than 0.1 fm^{-3}, where nuclei can coexist with a gas of electrons and neutrons that have dripped out. The center of the star is composed of hadronic matter, and the true constituents are still a matter of debate, as one can conclude from the results presented in the last section. The fact that the core should contain hyperons is widely accepted, although this possibility excludes many EOS that become too soft to explain the existing massive stars, namely, MSP J0740+6620, whose mass range lies at 2.07 ± 0.08 $M_\odot$ [8,70], PSR J0348+0432 with mass of 2.01 ± 0.04 $M_\odot$ [71] and PSR J1614-2230, which is also a massive neutron star [72]. Until around 2005, these massive NS had not been detected and practically all EOS could satisfy a maximum 1.4 $M_\odot$ star.

Since the appearance of hyperons is energetically favorable, different possibilities were considered in the literature such that the EOS would be stiffer, such as the tuning of the unknown meson–hyperon coupling constants. Another mechanism that increases the maximum mass of neutron stars with hyperons in their core is the inclusion of an additional vector meson that mediates the hyperon–hyperon interaction [52,58]. In Figure 12, mass–radius curves are shown for different hyperon–meson coupling constants of the GM1 parametrization [52]. One can see that all choices produce results with high maximum masses, satisfying the new massive star constraints. I refer the reader to [52] and references therein for explanations of the introduction of the strange meson channel on the Lagrangian density and the corresponding strange meson–hyperon couplings.

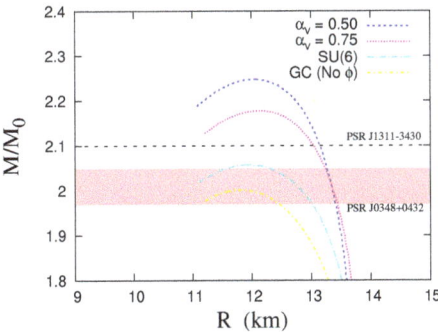

Figure 12. Mass–radius curve for the GM1 parametrisation based on [52].

As already mentioned in Section 2.2, the observation of the binary neutron star system GW170817 [33] by the LIGO-Virgo scientific collaboration and also in the X-ray, ultraviolet, optical, infrared, and radio bands gave rise to the new era of multi-messenger astronomy [34]. The detection of the corresponding gravitational wave helped the establishment of additional constraints to the physics of neutron stars. This subject is discussed in more detail below, but at this point, I would like to mention that a series of papers based on the these constraints imposed restricted values for the neutron star radius [73–77], not always compatible among themselves.

The dimensionless tidal deformability, also called tidal polarisability and its associated Love number, are related to the induced deformation that a neutron star undergoes by the influence of the tidal field of its neutron star companion in the binary system. The idea is analogous to the tidal response of our seas on Earth as a result of the Moon's gravitational field. The theory of Love numbers emerges naturally from the theory of tidal deformation, and the first model was proposed in 1909 by Augustus Love [78] based on Newtonian theory. The relativistic theory of tidal effects was deduced in 2009 [79,80], and since then the computing of Love numbers of neutron stars has become a field of intense investigation.

As different neutron star EOS and related composition have different responses to the tidal field, the tidal polarizability can be used to discriminate between different equations of state. A complete overview on the theory of Love numbers in both Newtonian and General Relativity theories can be found in [81]. Here, I show next only the main equations for the understanding of the constraints on NS.

The second order Love number k_2 is given by

$$k_2 = \frac{8C^5}{5}(1-2C)^2[2+C(y_R-1)-y_R]$$
$$\times \left\{2C[6-3y_R+3C(5y_R-8)]\right.$$
$$+4C^3[13-11y_R+C(3y_R-2)+2C^2(1+y_R)]$$
$$\left.+3(1-2C^2)[2-y_R+2C(y_R-1)]\ln(1-2C)\right\}^{-1}. \tag{90}$$

where $C = M/R$ is the star compactness, M and R are the total mass and total circumferential radius of the star, respectively, and $y_R = y(r = R)$, which is obtained from

$$r\frac{dy}{dr} + y^2 + yF(r) + r^2 Q(r) = 0. \tag{91}$$

Here, the coefficients are given by

$$F(r) = [1 - 4\pi r^2(\mathcal{E} - P)]/E \tag{92}$$

and

$$Q(r) = 4\pi\left[5\mathcal{E} + 9P + (\mathcal{E}+P)\left(\frac{\partial P}{\partial \mathcal{E}}\right) - \frac{6}{4\pi r^2}\right]/E$$
$$-4\left[\frac{m+4\pi r^3 P}{r^2 E}\right]^2, \tag{93}$$

where $E = 1 - 2m/r$, $\mathcal{E}$, and P are the energy density and pressure profiles inside the star. Notice that Equation (91) has to be solved coupled to the TOV equations.

Finally, one can obtain the dimensionless tidal deformability Λ, which is connected to the compactness parameter C through

$$\Lambda = \frac{2k_2}{3C^5}. \tag{94}$$

In Figure 13, the second-order Love number as a function of the compactness is shown for the three equations of state discussed in Section 3.2, as well as the corresponding tidal deformabilities (Λ_1, Λ_2) for the binary system (M_1, M_2), with $M_1 > M_2$. The plots are calculated from the equation for the chirp mass

$$M_{chirp} = (M_1 M_2)^{3/5}(M_1 + M_2)^{-1/5}, \tag{95}$$

and the diagonal dotted line corresponds to the case $M_1 = M_2$. The lower and upper dashed lines correspond to LIGO/Virgo collaboration 50% and 90% confidence limits, respectively, which are obtained from the GW170817 event. The EOS used to obtain these curves do not include hyperons to avoid the uncertainties related to the meson–hyperon couplings. It is important to mention the matching procedure used to compute the Love number and the tidal polarizabilities. The outer crust is a BPS EOS, the inner crust is a polytropic function, which interpolates between the outer crust and the core. A detailed explanation is given in [82], Section 2.2. More advanced crustal EOSs are available [83,84], and I discuss the sensitivity of some results on the crust model later on. One can see from these figures that the Love numbers are very different for the three models and so are the tidal polarisabilities, the NL3 and NL3$\omega\rho$ not being able to reproduce the GW170817 data satisfactorily. Actually, this behavior of the NL3 and NL3$\omega\rho$ had already been observed in [85], but one should notice that in [85], the confidence lines were taken from a preliminary version of the LIGO/Virgo data [33], while in the present paper, they are taken from [86], where the consideration of massive stars was neglected.

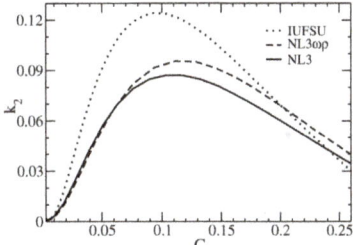 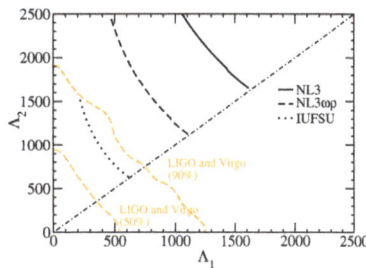

Figure 13. (**Left**) Love number as a function of the compactness and (**Right**) tidal deformabilities of both NS in the binary system before the merger.

Another important constraint concerns the radii of the canonical stars, the ones with $M = 1.4\ M_\odot$. According to the LIGO/Virgo collaboration, the tidal polarizability of canonical stars should lie in the range $70 \leq \Lambda_{1.4} \leq 580$ [86], a restriction that imposed a constraint to the radii of the corresponding stars, which should lie in the range 10.5 km $\leq R_{1.4M_\odot} \leq 13.4$ km. This constraint, which does not take into account a maximum stellar mass of 1.97 $M_\odot$, only excludes the NL3 parameter set from the ones we are analyzing (see Table 2), exactly the one that was shown not to describe nuclear bulk properties well enough. However, the history has become more complicated: a recently published paper concludes that the canonical neutron star radius cannot be larger than 11.9 km [77]. If this small radius is confirmed, it could imply a revision of the EOSs or of the gravity theory itself, as done in [87]. Notice, however, that this small radius is in line with older works that predicted that the maximum mass of a canonical star should be 13.6 km [73,74], whose authors claimed that any NS, independently of its mass, should bear a radius smaller than 13 km. Moreover, the new information sent by NICER [8] supports the evidence that the detected massive PSR J0740+6620 has a radius of the order of 12.35 ± 0.75 km and that a star with a mass compatible with a canonical star, J0030+0451, has a radius of the order of 12.45 ± 0.65 km [88], or $12.71^{+1.14}_{-1.19}$ km [75] or even $13.02^{+1.24}_{-1.06}$ km [76], depending on the analysis performed. These recent detections point to the fact that the radii of canonical and massive stars are of the same order, and this feature is not easily reproduced by most EOSs. On the other hand, one of the analyses of the results from the PREX experiment implies that 13.25 km $\leq R_{1.4M_\odot} \leq 14.26$ km corresponding to a tidal polarizability in the range $642 \leq \Lambda_{1.4M_\odot} \leq 955$ [42], also much higher than the above mentioned value obtained from GW170817 data. Notice, however, that the recent PREX results seem to contradict previous understandings on the softness of the symmetry energy [89]. Hence, the sizes of these objects are still a source of debate. One of the conclusions in [42] is that a precise knowledge of the crust of these compact objects may help to minimize the systematic uncertainties of these results.

A detailed analysis of the relativistic mean field models shown to be consistent with all nuclear bulk properties in [37] according to the masses and radii they yield when applied to describe NS can be found in [90]. Thirty four models were analyzed, and only twelve were shown to describe massive stars with maximum masses in the range $1.93 \leq M/M_\odot \leq 2.05$ without the inclusion of hyperons. In another paper [91], the very same models were confronted with the constraints imposed by the LIGO/Virgo collaboration. In this case, 24 models were shown to satisfy them. However, only five models could, at the same time, describe massive stars and constraints from GW170817. These studies did not use EOSs with hyperons, what poses an extra degree of complication due to the uncertainties on the meson–hyperon coupling constants. Looking at the three sets used in the present work, one can clearly see the difficulty. The two models that can describe massive stars are outside the range of validity of the GW170817 tidal deformabilities. On the other hand, IUFSU gives a mass a bit lower than desired, a deficiency that can be made correct with some tuning.

Another aspect that deserves to be mentioned refers to the inclusion of Δ baryons in the EOS. If they are considered as a possible constituent of neutron stars, at least with the parametrisations studied (GM1 and GM1$\omega\rho$), no "Δ puzzle" is observed [92].

4.3. The Importance of the Inner and Outer Crusts

When examining neutron star merger, the coalescence time is determined by the tidal polarizability, which as already explained, is a direct response of the tidal field of the companion that induces a mass quadrupole. This scenario suggests that the neutron star crust should play a role in this picture. If one looks at the famous figure drawn by Dany Page [69], one can see that the crust is divided into two pieces, the outer and the inner crust, the latter being the motive for the present section. It may include a *pasta phase*, the result of a frustrated system in which there is a unique competition between the Coulomb and the nuclear interactions, possible at very low baryonic densities. In the simplest interpretation of the geometries present in the pasta phase, they are known as droplets (3D), rods (2D), and slabs (1D) and their counterparts (bubbles, tubes, and slabs) are also possible. Much more sophisticated geometries such as waffles, parking garages and triple periodic minimal surface have been proposed [93–95], but I next describe only the more traditional picture.

The pasta phase is the dominant matter configuration if its free energy (binding energy at $T = 0$) is lower than its corresponding homogeneous phase. Depending on the model, the used parametrization and the temperature [96], typical pasta densities lie between 0.01 and 0.1 fm^{-3}. Different approaches are used to compute the pasta phase structures: the coexisting phases (CP) method, the Thomas–Fermi approximation, numerical simulations, etc. For detailed calculations, one can look at [96–98], for instance. In what follows, I only show the main equations used to build the pasta phase with the CP method.

According to the Gibbs conditions, both pasta phases have the same pressure and chemical potentials for proton and neutron and, at a fixed temperature, the following equations must be solved simultaneously:

$$P^I = P^{II}, \tag{96}$$

$$\mu_p^I = \mu_p^{II}, \tag{97}$$

$$\mu_n^I = \mu_n^{II}, \tag{98}$$

$$f(\rho_p^I - \rho_e) + (1-f)(\rho_p^{II} - \rho_e) = 0. \tag{99}$$

where I (II) represents the high (low) density region, ρ_p is the global proton density, ρ_e is the electron density taken as constant in both phases and f is the volume fraction of the phase I, which reads

$$f = \frac{\rho - \rho^{II}}{\rho^I - \rho^{II}}. \tag{100}$$

The total hadronic matter energy reads:

$$\mathcal{E}_{matter} = f\mathcal{E}^I + (1-f)\mathcal{E}^{II} + \mathcal{E}_e, \tag{101}$$

where $\mathcal{E}^I$ and $\mathcal{E}^{II}$ are the energy densities of phases I and II, respectively, and $\mathcal{E}_e$ is the energy density of the electrons, included to account for charge neutrality. The total energy can be obtained by adding the surface and Coulomb terms to the matter energy in Equation (101),

$$\mathcal{E} = \mathcal{E}_{matter} + \mathcal{E}_{surf} + \mathcal{E}_{Coul}. \tag{102}$$

Minimizing $\mathcal{E}_{surf} + \mathcal{E}_{Coul}$ with respect to the size of the droplet/bubble, cylinder/tube or slabs, we obtain [97] $\mathcal{E}_{surf} = 2\mathcal{E}_{Coul}$ where

$$\mathcal{E}_{Coul} = \frac{2\alpha}{4^{2/3}}(e^2\pi\Phi)^{1/3}\left[\sigma^{surf}D(\rho_p^I - \rho_p^{II})\right]^{2/3}, \tag{103}$$

with $\alpha = f$ for droplets, rods and slabs, and $\alpha = 1-f$ for tubes and bubbles. The quantity Φ is given by

$$\Phi = \begin{cases} \left(\frac{2-D\alpha^{1-2/D}}{D-2} + \alpha\right)\frac{1}{D+2}, & D = 1,3 \\ \frac{\alpha-1-\ln\alpha}{D+2}, & D = 2 \end{cases} \tag{104}$$

where σ^{surf} is the surface tension, which measures the energy per area necessary to create a planar interface between the two regions. The surface tension is a crucial quantity in the pasta calculation, and it is normally parametrized with the help of more sophisticated formalisms. Another important aspect is that the pasta phase is only present at the low-density regions of the neutron stars, and in this region, muons are not present, although they are present in the EOS that describes the homogeneous region.

In Figure 14, I plot the binding energy of the homogeneous matter (dashed line) as compared with the pasta phase binding energy (solid line with different colours representing the different structures). One can see that the pasta-phase binding energy is lower up to a certain density, when the homogeneous phase becomes the preferential state. In Figure 15, I show various phase diagrams obtained with the CP and TF methods for fixed proton fractions at different temperatures. As the temperature increases, the pasta phase shrinks. Here I have mentioned the TM1 parameter set [50], not used before in the present work but also quite common in the literature. The purpose is only to show that different approximations and different parametrizations result in different internal structures with different transition densities from one phase to another.

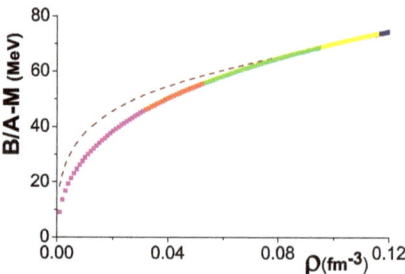

Figure 14. *npe* matter binding energy obtained with the CP method and NL3 parametrisation [45]. Figure taken from [96].

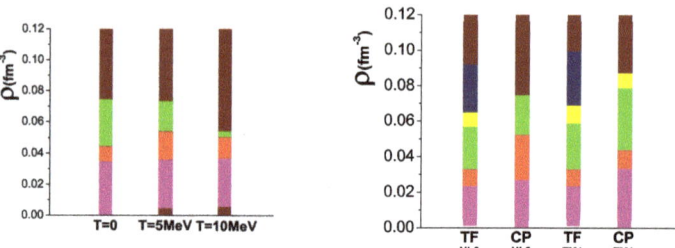

Figure 15. Phase diagrams obtained with (**Left**) NL3 parametrisation and CP method for $Y_p = 0.5$. From bottom to top, the colors represent homogeneous phase ($T = 5$ and 10 MeV only), droplets, rods, and homogeneous phase. (**Right**) NL3 and TM1 parametrizations with CP and TF methods for $Y_p = 0.3$ and $T = 0$. Figures taken from [96].

However, what is the influence of the pasta phase on the calculation of the tidal polarizability, and if this structure is not well determined, how much does its uncertainty contribute to the final calculations? This problem was tackled in [99], and, as the model used in that paper is quite different from the RMF models we use in the present work, we do not include any figures, but it is fair to say that the contribution is indeed minor. In [99], the BPS EOS was used for the outer crust. For the inner crust, two possibilities were considered: the existence of the pasta phase and a simple interpolation between the outer crust and the core. It was observed that, although the explicit inclusion of the pasta phase affected the Love number in a visible way, it almost did not change the tidal polarizabilities, a result that corroborated the findings in [100]. These results can be explained by the fact that, for a fixed compactness, even if the Love number is sensitive to the inner crust structure, the tidal polarizability scales with the fifth power of C, and hence, the influence is small.

Furthermore, what about the outer crust? Indeed, in this case, the tidal effects should be even more sensitive. In what follows, I test how much the use of a modern EOS for the outer crust, which we call *reliable* [84], changes the results as compared with the BPS generally used and mentioned below. A modified version of the IUFSU model known as FSUGZ03 [51] was used to plot Figure 16, and we trust that the qualitative results would be the same for any other parametrisation. In this Figure, the outer crust is linked directly to the core EOS, as seen on the top figure. Log-scale is used because the differences cannot be seen in linear scale. Then, the different prescriptions are used to compute the tidal polarisabilities shown on the bottom. Once again, one can see that the influence is very small.

Although we have seen that neither the outer nor the inner crust significantly alter the tidal polarizabilities, they do have an impact, which was quantified in [101,102]. The authors of these works concluded that the impact of the crust EOS is not larger than 2%, but the matching procedure (crust-core) can account for a 5% difference in the determination of the low mass NS radii and up to 8% on the tidal deformability. In another recent work [103], the inner crust was parametrised in terms of a polytropic-like EOS and the sound velocity and canonical star radii were computed. EOS for the inner crust with different sound velocities produced radii with up to 8% difference when the same EOS was used for the core.

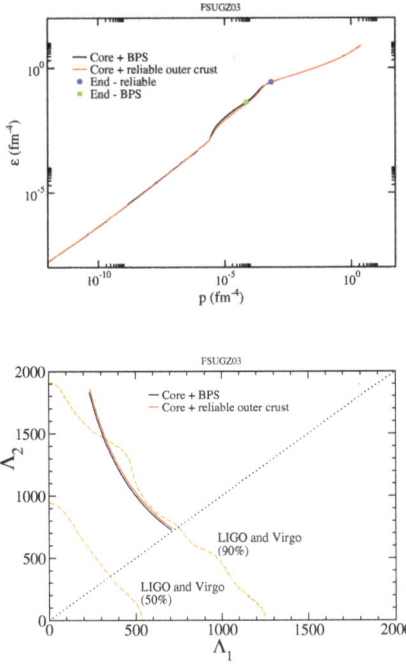

Figure 16. (**Top**) EOSs obtained with the outer crust described by BPS and by a reliable model [84]; (**Bottom**) tidal polarizabilities for both NSs with the EOSs shown on the right.

Despite the fact that present results show that the inclusion of the pasta phase is not essential when the above discussed macroscopic properties of NSs are computed, it may indeed be important for the thermal [104], magnetic evolution [105,106], and neutrino diffusion of NS [107,108], processes that take place at different epochs. This means it is able to handle properly the pasta phase structure is still a matter or concern. The first issue worth discussing is the possible existence of baryons that are more massive than nucleons and carry strangeness in the pasta phase. In [109], it was verified that the Λ hyperons can indeed be present, although in small amounts, as seen in Figure 17, where the Λ fraction is shown as a function of temperature in phases I (clusters) and II (gas). For the parametrization used, NL3$\omega\rho$, the pasta phase disappears at $T = 14.45$ MeV, the Λs being present for electron fractions ranging from 0.1 to 0.5 and in quantities larger than 10^{-11} for $T > 7$ MeV. The Ξ^- can also be found, but in much smaller amounts, on the order of 10^{-12}.

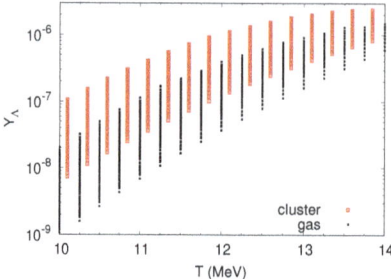

Figure 17. Λ fraction as a function of temperature in the cluster and gas phases with the NL3ωρ parametrization [46]. Figure taken from [109].

The second important point refers to the fact that the CP method just presented and also another commonly used method, the Thomas–Fermi approximation [110], can only provide one specific geometry for each density, temperature, and proton (or electron) fraction, but it is well known that this picture is very naive. In fact, different geometries can coexist at thermal equilibrium [98,111,112]. The problem with these more sophisticated approaches is that the computational cost is tremendous, making them inadequate to be joined to other expensive computational methods that may be necessary to calculate neutrino opacities and transport properties, for instance. In a recent paper, a prescription with a very low computational cost was presented [113]. In that paper, fluctuations are taken into account in a reasonably simple way by the introduction of a rearrangement term in the free energy density of the cluster. A simple result can be seen in Figure 18, where one can see that different geometries can coexist at a certain temperature for a fixed density. If different proton fractions are considered, the dominant geometry changes as in the CP or TF method, but the other geometries can still be present. The complete formalism has been revised and extended to asymmetric matter and can be found in [114].

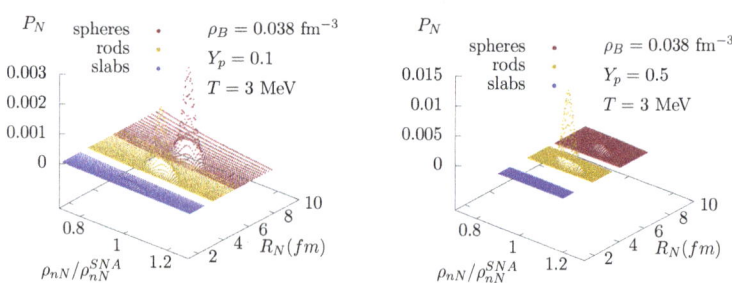

Figure 18. 3D probability distribution as a function of the pasta linear dimension and the normalized cluster density with different geometries obtained with the IUFSU parametrization for different proton fractions. Notice the vertical scale differences.

5. Hybrid Stars

So far, I have discussed the possibility that hadronic matter exist in the core of a neutron star and that nuclear physics underlies the models that describe it. The idea of a hybrid star containing a hadronic outer core that has a different composition than the inner core, which could be composed of deconfined quarks, was first proposed by Ivanenko and Kurdgelaidze [115] in the late 1960s. In their papers, they have even foreseen that a transition to a superconducting phase would be possible. This idea has gained credibility lately. A model-independent analysis based on the sound velocity in hadronic and quark matter points to the fact that the existence of quark cores inside massive stars should be considered the standard picture [116]. In this case, one would be dealing with what is known as hybrid star, and, from the theoretical point of view, its description requires a sophisticated recipe: a reliable model for the outer hadronic core and another model for the inner quark core. The ideal picture would be a chiral model that could describe both matters as density increases, but those models are still rarely used [117–120]. Generally, what we find in the literature are Walecka-type models such as the ones presented in Section 3.2 or density-dependent models, whose density dependence is introduced on the meson–baryon couplings as in [121,122] for the hadronic matter and the MIT bag model [123] or the Nambu–Jona–Lasinio (NJL) model [124] for the quark matter. While the MIT bag model is very simplistic, the NJL model is more robust and accounts for the expected chiral symmetry but cannot satisfy the condition of absolutely stable strange matter that will be discussed next. The MIT bag model EOS is simply the EOS calculated for a free Fermi gas in Section 2.1, where the masses are the ones of the u, d, s quarks, generally taken as $m_u = m_d = 5$ MeV and m_s varying from around 80 to 150 MeV and the inclusion of a bag constant B of arbitrary value, which is responsible for confining the quarks inside a certain surface. B enters with a negative sign in the pressure equation and consequently a positive one in the energy density equation. The NJL EOS is more complicated and, besides accounting for chiral symmetry breaking/restoration, also depends on a cut-off parameter. The derivation of the EOS can be obtained in the original papers [124] in an excellent review article [125] or in one of the papers I have co-authored, [126], for instance, and I will refrain from copying the equations here. Contrary to the MIT bag model, the NJL model does not offer the possibility of free parameters. All of them are adjusted to fit the pion mass, its decay constant, the kaon mass, and the quark condensates in the vacuum. There are different sets of parameters for describing the SU(2) (only considers u and d quarks) and the SU(3) versions of the model.

When building the EOS to describe hybrid stars, two constructions are commonly made: one with a mixed phase (MP) and another without it, where the hadron and quark phases are in direct contact. In the first case, neutron and electron chemical potentials are continuous throughout the stellar matter, based on the standard thermodynamical rules for phase coexistence known as Gibbs conditions. In the second case, the electron chemical potential suffers a discontinuity, and only the neutron chemical potential is continuous. This condition is known as Maxwell construction. The differences between stellar structures obtained with both constructions were discussed in many papers [127–129], and I just reproduce the main ideas next.

In the mixed phase, constituted of hadrons and quarks, charge neutrality is not imposed locally but only globally, meaning that quark and hadron phases are not neutral separately. Instead, the system rearranges itself so that

$$\chi \rho_c^{QP} + (1-\chi)\rho_c^{HP} + \rho_c^l = 0,$$

where ρ_c^{iP} is the charge density of the phase $i = H, Q$; χ is the volume fraction occupied by the quark phase; and ρ_c^l is the electric charge density of leptons. The Gibbs conditions for phase coexistence impose that [49]:

$$\mu_n^{HP} = \mu_n^{QP}, \quad \mu_e^{HP} = \mu_e^{QP} \quad \text{and} \quad P^{HP} = P^{QP},$$

and consequently,

$$\langle \mathcal{E} \rangle = \chi \mathcal{E}^{QP} + (1-\chi)\mathcal{E}^{HP} + \mathcal{E}^l \tag{105}$$

and

$$\langle \rho \rangle = \chi \rho^{QP} + (1-\chi)\rho^{HP}. \tag{106}$$

The Maxwell construction is much simpler than the case above and it is only necessary to find the transition point where

$$\mu_n^{HP} = \mu_n^{QP} \quad \text{and} \quad P^{HP} = P^{QP},$$

and then construct the EoS.

In Figure 19, different EOS are built with both constructions, and the respective mass radius curves are also shown. In all cases, the hadronic matter was described with either GM1 [48] or GM3 parametrizations [49] and the quark phase with the two most common parametrizations for the NJL model (HK [130] and RKH [131]). On the left, one can see that under the Maxwell construction, the EOS presents a step at fixed pressure, and under the Gibbs construction, the EOS is continuous. It is then easy to see that for both constructions, the mass radius curves are indeed very similar and yield almost indistinguishable results for gravitational masses and radii. In these cases, the differences in the hadronic EOSs dominate over the differences in quark EOSs. Hence, the maximum mass is mostly determined by the hadronic part. It is also important to stress that the quark core is not always present in the star even if the quark matter EOS is included in the EOS. This fact is noticed when one compares the density where the onset of quarks takes place with the star central density. If the star-central density is lower than the quark onset, no quark core exists.

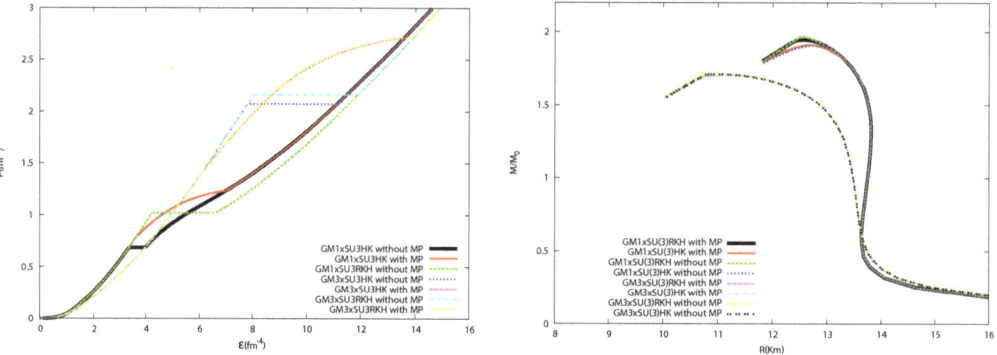

Figure 19. (**Left**) EOS built with Maxwell (without MP) and Gibbs (with MP) constructions; (**Right**) corresponding mass–radius diagram. Figure based on the results presented in [129].

A more recent analysis of the dependence of the macroscopic properties of hybrid stars on meson–hyperon coupling constants and on the vector channel added to the NJL model can be seen in [59].

In 2019, the LIGO/Virgo collaboration detected yet another gravitational wave, the GW190814 [132], resulting from the merger of a 23 $M_\odot$ black hole and another object with $2.59^{+0.08}_{-0.09} M_\odot$, which falls in the mass-gap category, i.e., too light to be a black hole and too massive to be a NS. In [118], a chirally invariant model was used to describe hybrid stars with a variety of different vector interactions, and this compact object could be explained as a massive, rapidly rotating NS. A comprehensive discussion on ultra-heavy NS (masses larger than 2.5 $M_\odot$) and the possibility that they are hybrid objects can be found in [133].

If the reader is interested in understanding the effects of different quark cores that also include trapped neutrinos at fixed entropies, reference [53] can be consulted.

6. Quark Stars

All experiments that can be realized in laboratories show that hadrons are the ground state of the strong interaction. Around 50 years ago, Itoh [134] and Bodmer [135], in separate studies, proposed that under specific circumstances, such as the ones existing in the cores of neutron stars, strange quark matter (SQM) may be the real ground state. This hypothesis, later on also investigated by Witten, became known as the Bodmer–Witten conjecture, and it is theoretically tested with the search of a stability window, defined for different models in such a way that a two- flavor quark matter (2QM) must be unstable (i.e., its energy per baryon must be larger than 930 MeV, which is the iron-binding energy) and SQM (three-flavour quark matter) must be stable, i.e., its energy per baryon must be lower than 930 MeV [135,136]. As shown in the previous section, although the Nambu–Jona–Lasinio (NJL) model [124] can be used to describe the core of a hybrid star [120,126], it cannot be used in the description of absolutely stable SQM as shown in [137–140]. The most common model, the MIT bag model [123] satisfies the Bodmer–Witten conjecture, but cannot explain massive stars J0348+0432 [71], J1614-2230 [72] and J0740+6620) [8,70], as can be seen in Figure 20, from where one can observe that the maximum attained mass is 1.94 $M_\odot$ obtained for a non-massive strange quark.

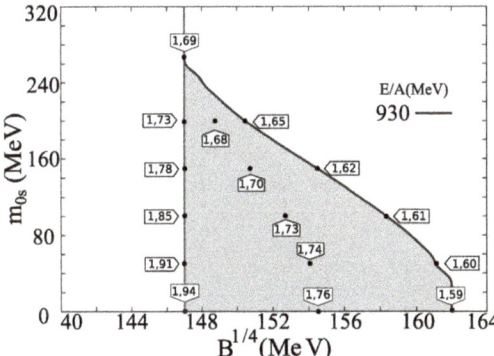

Figure 20. Stability window shown in the shaded area. The flags indicate the maximum stellar masses obtained with various B and strange quark mass values. Figure taken from [141].

Hence, we next mention another quark matter model that satisfies de Bodmer–Witten conjecture at the same time that can describe massive stars and canonical stars with small radii, the density-dependent quark mass (DDQM) proposed in [142,143] and investigated in [144]. In the DDQM model, the quark masses depend on two arbitrary parameters and are given by

$$m_i = m_{i0} + m_I \equiv m_{i0} + \frac{D}{\rho_b^{1/3}} + C\rho_b^{1/3}, \tag{107}$$

where the index I stands for the medium corrections and the baryonic density is written in terms of the quark densities as

$$\rho_b = \frac{1}{3}\sum_i \rho_i, \quad \rho_i = \frac{g_i \nu_i^3}{6\pi^2}, \tag{108}$$

and ν_i is the Fermi momentum of quark i, which reads:

$$\nu_i = \sqrt{\mu_i^{*2} - m_i^2} \tag{109}$$

and μ_i^* is the i quark effective chemical potential. The energy density and pressure are respectively given by

$$\mathcal{E} = \Omega_0 - \sum_i \mu_i^* \frac{\partial \Omega_0}{\partial \mu_i^*}, \tag{110}$$

and

$$P = -\Omega_0 + \sum_{i,j} \frac{\partial \Omega_0}{\partial m_j} n_i \frac{\partial m_j}{\partial \rho_i}, \tag{111}$$

where Ω_0 stands for the thermodynamical potential of a free system with particle masses m_i and effective chemical potentials μ_i^* [142]:

$$\Omega_0 = -\sum_i \frac{g_i}{24\pi^2}\left[\mu_i^* \nu_i\left(\nu_i^2 - \frac{3}{2}m_i^2\right) + \frac{3}{2}m_i^4 \ln\frac{\mu_i^* + \nu_i}{m_i}\right], \tag{112}$$

with g_i being the degeneracy factor 6 (3 (color) x 2 (spin)) and the relation between the chemical potentials and their effective counterparts is simply

$$\mu_i = \mu_i^* + \frac{1}{3}\frac{\partial m_I}{\partial n_b}\frac{\partial \Omega_0}{\partial m_I} \equiv \mu_i^* - \mu_I, \tag{113}$$

On the left of Figure 21 the stability window is plotted for a fixed value of C, so that it displays a shape that can be compared with Figure 20. For other values of the constants, more stability windows are shown in [144]. On the right of Figure 21, different mass–radius curves are shown, and one can see that very massive stars can indeed be obtained. At this point, it is worth mentioning that quark stars are believed to be bare (no crust is supported), and for this reason, the shape of the curves shown in Figure 21 are very different from the ones obtained for hadronic stars and shown in Figures 11 and 12 and for hybrid stars, as seen in Figure 19.

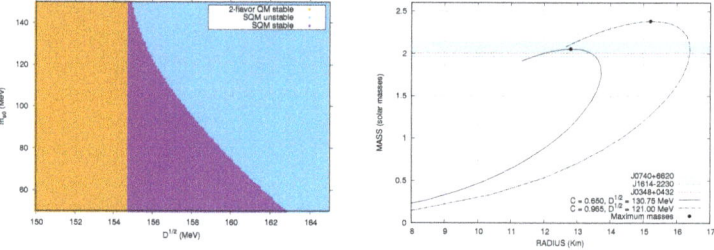

Figure 21. (**Left**) Stability window for fixed $C = 0$, (**Right**) mass–radius diagram for different values of C and $\sqrt{D}$. Figures based on the results shown in [144].

There is still another very promising model: an extension of the MIT bag model based on the ideas of the QHD model. In this extended version, the Lagrangian density accounts for the free Fermi gas part plus a vector interaction and a self-interaction mesonic field and reads [145]:

$$\mathcal{L} = \sum_{u,d,s}\{\bar{\psi}_q[\gamma^\mu(i\partial_\mu - g_{qq}V V_\mu) - m_q]\psi_q - B\}\Theta(\bar{\psi}_q\psi_q) + \frac{1}{2}m_\omega^2 V_\mu V^\mu + b_4\frac{(g_{uuV}^2 V_\mu V^\mu)^2}{4}, \tag{114}$$

where the quark interaction is mediated by the vector channel V_μ representing the ω meson, in the same way as in QHD models [35]. The relative quark–vector field interaction is fixed by symmetry group and results in

$$g_{ssV} = \frac{2}{5}g_{uuV} = \frac{2}{5}g_{ddV}, \tag{115}$$

with adequate redefinitions given by

$$(g_{uuV}/m_V)^2 = G_V, \quad X_V = \frac{g_{ssV}}{g_{uuV}} \tag{116}$$

and b_4 taken as a free parameter. Using a mean field approximation and solving the Euler–Lagrange equations of motion, the following eigenvalues for the quarks and V_0 field can be obtained:

$$E_q = \mu = \sqrt{m_q^2 + k^2} + g_{qqV} V_0, \quad (117)$$

$$g_{uuV} V_0 + \left(\frac{g_{uuV}}{m_\omega}\right)^2 \left(b_4 (g_{uuV} V_0)^3\right) = \left(\frac{g_{uuV}}{m_\omega}\right) \sum_{u,d,s} \left(\frac{g_{qqV}}{m_\omega}\right) n_q.$$

With this new approach, when the self-interaction vector channel is turned off, the stability window increases, and a 2.41 $M_\odot$ quark star that satisfies all astrophysical constraints is obtained. The self-interaction vector channel does not change the stability window, but it allows even more flexibility in the calculation of the tidal polarizability and the canonical star radius due to the inclusion of the free parameter b_4. In this case, a 2.65 $M_\odot$ quark star corresponding to a 12.13 km canonical star radius and a tidal polarizability within the expected observed range is obtained along many other results that satisfy all presently known astrophysical constraints. Some of the results are displayed in Figure 22. After all the discussion on the radii of NS constrained with the help of gravitational wave observation and neutron skin thickness experimental results presented in Section 4.2 and on the uncertainty of these values, I just would like to add one comment: contrary to what is obtained for a family of hadronic stars (maximum mass stars are generally associated with a smaller radii than their canonical star counterparts), a family of quark stars may produce canonical stars with radii that can be approximately the same as the maximum mass star radii, depending on the model used [145], and this feature could accommodate the recent NICER detections for J0030+0451 and J0740+6620.

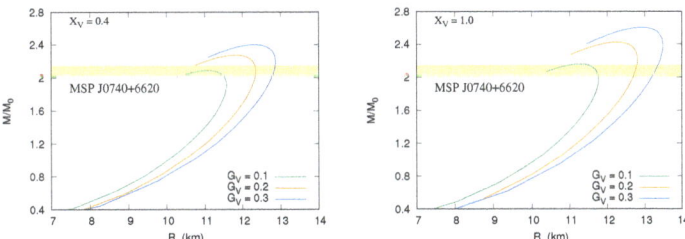

Figure 22. Mass–radius diagram obtained with the minimum value of the bag pressure that produces stable quark stars with different values of G_v and left) $X_v = 0.4$, right) $X_v = 1.0$. Figure based on the results presented in [145].

This modified MIT bag model has also been used to investigate the finite temperature systems and to obtain the QCD phase diagram in [5] with the help of a temperature dependent bag $B(T)$, as discussed in the Introduction of the paper. Some of the possible phase diagrams are shown in Figure 23.

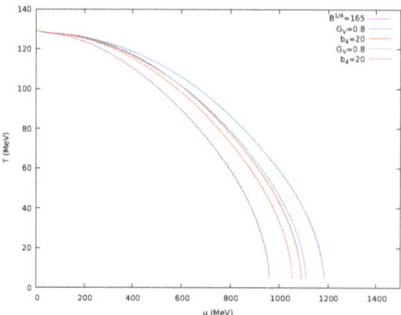

Figure 23. Phase diagram for neutral matter in β-equilibrium with a temperature dependent bag pressure $B(T)$. Dashed lines stand for $X_v = 0.4$ and solid lines for $X_v = 1.0$. Figure based on the results presented in [5].

I have outlined the main aspects concerning the internal structure of quark stars, but the discussion about their bare surface [146,147] is not completely settled [148] and important problems as its high plasma frequency and neutrinosphere are out of the scope of the present work but should not be disregarded.

7. Magnetars: Crust–Core Transitions and Oscillations

I cannot end this review without mentioning magnetars [149,150], a special class of neutron stars with surface magnetic fields three orders of magnitude (reaching up to 10^{15} G at the surface) stronger than the ones present in standard neutron stars (10^{12} G at the surface). Most of the known magnetars detected so far are isolated objects; i.e., they are not part of a binary system and manifest themselves as either transient X-ray sources, known as soft-γ repeaters or persistent anomalous X-ray pulsars. They are also promising candidates for the recent discovery of fast radio bursts [151]. So far, only about 30 of them have been clearly identified [152] but more information is expected from NICER [7] and ATHENA [153], launching foreseen to take place in 2030. So far, NICER has already pointed to the fact that the beams of radiation emitted by rapidly rotating pulsars may not be as simple as is often supposed: the detection of two hot spots in the same hemisphere suggests a magnetic field configuration more complex than perfectly symmetric dipoles [8].

From the theoretical point of view, there is no reason to believe that the structure of the magnetars differs from the ones I have mentioned in this article. Thus, they can also be described as hadronic objects [81,154–158], as quark stars [138,139,157–160] or as hybrid stars [155,157].

At this point, it is fair to claim that the best approach to calculate macroscopic properties of magnetars is the use of the LORENE code [161], which takes into account Einstein–Maxwell equations and equilibrium solutions self consistently with a density dependent magnetic field. LORENE avoids discussions on anisotropic effects and violation of Maxwell equations as pointed out in [160], for instance. However, at least two important points involving matter subject to strong magnetic fields can be dealt with even without the LORENE code. The first one is the crust core transition density discussed in [156,162]. Although the magnetic fields at the surface of magnetars are not stronger than 10^{15} G, if the crust is as large as expected (about 10% of the size of the star), at the transition region the magnetic field can reach 10^{17} G. The transition density can then be estimated by computing the spinodal sections, both dynamically and thermodynamically. The point where the EOS crosses the spinodal defines the transition density [163]. An interesting aspect is that the spinodals of magnetized matter are no longer smooth curves. Due to the filling of the Landau levels, more than one crossing point is possible [156,162], which introduces an extra uncertainty into the calculation.

The second aspect refers to possible oscillations in magnetars caused by the violent dynamics of a merging binary system. One has to bear in mind that so far, all observed magnetars are isolated compact objects, but there is no reason to believe that binary systems do not exist. In this case, the perturbations on the metric can couple to the fluid through the field equations [164,165]. For a comprehensive discussion of the equations involved, please refer to [81]. The gravitational wave frequency of the fundamental mode is expected to be detected in the near future by detectors such as the Einstein Telescope. In [81], the effect of strong magnetic fields on the fundamental mode was investigated. From the results presented in that paper, one can clearly see that magnetars with masses below 1.8 $M_\odot$ present practically the same frequencies. Nevertheless, more massive stars present different frequencies depending on their constitution: nucleonic stars present frequencies lower than their hyperonic counterparts, a feature that may define the internal constitution of magnetars.

The DDQM described in Section 6 was also investigated under the effects of strong magnetic fields, and the main expressions can be found in [166]. This may be an interesting model for future calculations of the fundamental models.

8. Final Remarks

From the existence of a massive ordinary star that is alive due to nuclear fusion, to its explosive ending and its aftermath, I have tried to tell the history of the neutron star. All these stages can be explained thanks to nuclear physics, and I have revisited the main aspects and models underlying each one.

I have also tried to emphasize that nuclear models are generally parameter-dependent, and a plethora of models have been proposed in recent decades, but it is unlikely that the very same models can be used to describe different aspects of nuclear matter and, at the same time, all macroscopic properties of neutron stars. I do not advocate that the models I have chosen to use are the best ones, but the main idea is to show that different models should be used at the discretion of the people who employ them. I have not used density-dependent hadronic models such as the ones proposed, for instance, in [122,167], to avoid extra theoretical complications, but they are indeed very good options, since they can describe nuclear matter, finite nuclei, and NS properties well, as seen in [37,90,91].

As far as detections of gravitational waves are concerned, a window was opened in 2015, and many observations will certainly be disclosed even before I finish writing this paper. Besides the ones already mentioned, I would like to comment on the GW190425 [168], GW200105, and GW200115 [169]. The first one was used in conjunction with a chiral effective field theory to constrain the NS equation of state [170]. The authors obtained a radius equal to $11.75^{+0.86}_{-0.81}$ for a canonical star, which was also quite small as compared with the ones obtained from the PREX experiment. The other two probably refer to neutron star–black hole mergers, systems that have been conjectured for a long time and will probably contribute to the understanding of NS EOS.

Before concluding, I would like to mention that many aspects regarding either isolated NS or binary systems have not been tackled in this manuscript and, in my opinion, rotation is the most important one. A better understanding of these compact objects depends on many rich features, including thermal and magnetic evolution. Different observation manifestations such as pulsars, accreting X-ray binaries, soft γ-repeaters, and anomalous X-ray pulsars also deserve an attentive investigation. Hence, this review is just one step towards the incredible exotic world of neutron stars.

As far as the QCD phase diagram is concerned, many aspects have been extensively studied and are well understood: matter at zero temperature; symmetric nuclear and pure neutron matter; low density matter; including clusterisation and the pasta phase; high density matter; and matter in β-equilibrium. Nevertheless, an EOS that covers the complete QCD phase diagram parameter space in (T, μ_B) in a single model is not available yet. Some of the EOS can be found on the CompOSE (CompStar Online Supernovae Equations of State) website [171].

Funding: This work is a part of the project INCT-FNA Proc. No. 464898/2014-5. D.P.M. is partially supported by Conselho Nacional de Desenvolvimento Científico e Tecnológico (CNPq/Brazil) under grant 301155.2017-8.

Institutional Review Board Statement: Not applicable.

Informed Consent Statement: Not applicable.

Acknowledgments: Figures 1–5 were drawn by Kevin Schroeder, the data used to draw Figure 16 with the reliable crust was obtained by Thomas Carreau and Francesca Gulminelli. Figure 13 were drawn by Odilon Lourenço, Figure 18 by Mateus Renke Pelicer, Figure 21 by Betânia C.T. Backes, Figure 22 by Luiz L. Lopes and Figure 23 by Carline Biesdorf. I thank them all and also Constança Providência for useful comments and suggestions.

Conflicts of Interest: The author declares no conflict of interest.

References

1. Gross, D.J.; Wilczek, F. Ultraviolet Behavior of Non-Abelian Gauge Theory. *Phys. Rev. Lett.* **1973**, *30*, 1343. [CrossRef]
2. Dutra, M.; Lourenço, O.; Sá Martins, J.S. Delfino; A. Stone, J.R.; Stevenson, P.D. Skyrme interaction and nuclear matter constraints. *Phys. Rev. C* **2012**, *85*, 035201. [CrossRef]
3. Mackie, F.D.; Baym, G. Compressible liquid drop nuclear model and mass formula. *Nucl. Phys. A* **1977**, *285*, 332. [CrossRef]
4. von Weizsäcker C.F. Zur Theorie der Kernmassen. *Z. Phys.* **1935**, *96*, 431.
5. Lopes, L.L.; Biesdorf, C.; Marquez, K.D.; Menezes, D.P. Modified MIT Bag Models—Part II: QCD phase diagram and hot quark stars. *Phys. Scr.* **2021**. [CrossRef]
6. Watts, A.; Xu, R.; Espinoza, C.; Andersson, N.; Antoniadis, J.; Antonopoulou, D.; Buchner, S.; Dai, S.; Demorest, P.; Freire, P.; et al. Advancing Astrophysics with the Square Kilometre Array. *arXiv* **2014**, arXiv:1501.00042.
7. Neutron Star Interior Composition Explorer Mission–NICER. 2016. Available online: https://heasarc.gsfc.nasa.gov/docs/nicer/ (accessed on 20 July 2021).
8. Miller, M.C.; Lamb, F.K.; Dittmann, A.J.; Bogdanov, S.; Arzoumanian, Z.; Gendreau, K.C.; Guillot, S.; Ho, W.C.G.; Lattimer, J.M.; Loewenstein, M.; et al. The Radius of PSR J0740+6620 from NICER and XMM-Newton Data. *arXiv* **2021**, arXiv:2105.06979.
9. Avancini, S.S.; Marinelli, J.R.; Menezes, D.P.; Moraes, M.M.W.; Schneider, A.S. Reexamining the neutron skin thickness within a density dependent hadronic model. *Phys. Rev. C* **2007**, *76*, 064318. [CrossRef]
10. Avancini, S.S.; Marinelli, J.R.; Menezes, D.P.; Moraes, M.M.W.; Providência, C. Density dependent hadronic models and the relation between neutron stars and neutron skin thickness. *Phys. Rev. C* **2007**, *75*, 055805. [CrossRef]
11. Abrahamyan, S.; Ahmed, Z.; Albataineh, H.; Aniol, K.; Armstrong, D.S.; Armstrong, W.; Averett, T.; Babineau, B.; Barbieri, A.; Bellini, V.; et al. Measurement of the Neutron Radius of ^{208}Pb through Parity Violation in Electron Scattering. *Phys. Rev. Lett.* **2012**, *108*, 112502. [CrossRef]
12. Adhikari, D.; Albataineh, H.; Androic, D.; Aniol, K.; Armstrong, D.S.; Averett, T.; Ayerbe Gayoso, C.; Barcus, S.; Bellini, V.; Beminiwattha, R.S.; et al Accurate Determination of the Neutron Skin Thickness of ^{208}Pb through Parity-Violation in Electron Scattering. *Phys. Rev. Lett.* **2021**, *126*, 172502. [CrossRef]
13. Aniol, K.A.; Armstrong, D.S.; Averett, T.; Benaoum, H.; Bertin, P.Y.; Burtin, E.; Cahoon, J.; Cates, G.D.; Chang, C.; Chao, Y.; et al. Parity-Violating Electron Scattering from ^{4}He and the Strange Electric Form Factor of the Nucleon. *Phys. Rev. Lett.* **2006**, *96*, 022003. [CrossRef]
14. Krane, K.S. *Introductory Nuclear Physics*; John Wiley and Sons, Inc.: New York, NY, USA, 1988.
15. Menezes, D.P. *Introdução à Física Nuclear e de Partículas Elementares*; Editora da UFSC: Florianópolis, Brazil, 2002.
16. Britannica. "Hertzsprung–Russell Diagram". Encyclopedia Britannica. Available online: https://www.britannica.com/science/Hertzsprung-Russell-diagram (accessed on 30 March 2021).
17. Chaisson, E.; McMillan, S. *Astronomy Today*; Pearson Prentice Hall, Pearson Education, Inc.: Upper Saddl River, NJ, USA, 2005.
18. Greiner, W.; Neise, L.; Stocker, H. *Thermodynamics and Statistical Mechanic*; Springer: New York, NY, USA, 1995.
19. Srinivasan, G. *Life and Death of the Stars*; Springer: Berlin/Heidelberg, Germany, 2014
20. Fowler, R.H. On Dense Matter. *Month. Not. R. Astron. Soc.* **1926**, *87*, 114–122. [CrossRef]
21. Chandrasekhar, S. The density of white dwarf stars. *Philos. Mag.* **1930**, *11*, 592–596. [CrossRef]
22. Chandrasekhar, S. The Maximum Mass of Ideal White Dwarfs. *Astrophys. J.* **1931**, *74*, 81. [CrossRef]
23. Landau, L. On the Theory of Stars. *Phys. Z. Sowjetunion* **1932**, *1*, 285.
24. Yakovlev, D.G.; Haensel, P.; Baym, G.; Pethick, C. Landau and the Concept of Neutron Stars. *Phys. Uspekhi* **2013**, *56*, 289–295. [CrossRef]
25. Webster, H.C. Possible existence of a neutron. *Nature* **1932**, *129*, 312. [CrossRef]
26. Baade, W.; Zwicky, F. On Super-Novae. *Proc. Natl. Acad. Sci. USA* **1934**, *20*, 254–259. [CrossRef]
27. Tolman, R.C. Static Solutions of Einstein's Field Equations for Spheres of Fluid. *Phys. Rev.* **1939**, *55*, 364. [CrossRef]
28. Oppenheimer, J.R.; Volkoff, G.M.; On Massive Neutron Cores. *Phys. Rev.* **1939**, *55*, 374. [CrossRef]
29. Gamow, G.; Schenberg, M. The Possible Role of Neutrinos in Stellar Evolution. *Phys. Rev.* **1940**, *58*, 1117. [CrossRef]

30. Hewish, A.; Bell, S.J.; Pilkington, J.D.H.; Scott, P.F.; Collins, R.A. Observation of a Rapidly Pulsating Radio Source. *Nature* **1968**, *217*, 709. [CrossRef]
31. Hulse, R.A.; Taylor, J.H. Discovery of a pulsar in a binary system. *Astrophys. J.* **1975**, *195*, L51–L55. [CrossRef]
32. Abbott, B.P.; Abbott, R.; Abbott, T.D.; Abernathy, M.R.; Acernese, F.; Ackley, K.; Adams, C.; Adams, T.; Addesso, P.; Adhikari, R.X.; et al. Observation of Gravitational Waves from a Binary Black Hole Merger. *Phys. Rev. Lett.* **2016**, *116*, 061102. [CrossRef] [PubMed]
33. Abbott, B.P.; Abbott, R.; Abbott, T.D.; Acernese, F.; Ackley, K.; Adams, C.; Adams, T.; Addesso, P.; Adhikari, R.X.; Adya, V. B.; et al. GW170817: Observation of Gravitational Waves from a Binary Neutron Star Inspiral. *Phys. Rev. Lett.* **2017**, *119*, 161101. [CrossRef] [PubMed]
34. Cowperthwaite, P.S.; Berger, E.; Villar, V.A.; Metzger, B.D.; Nicholl, M.; Chornock, R.; Blanchard, P.K.; Fong, W.; Margutti, R.; Soares-Santos, M.; et al. Multi-messenger Observations of a Binary Neutron Star Merger. *Astrophys. J. Lett.* **2017**, *848*, L17. [CrossRef]
35. Walecka, J.D. A theory of highly condensed matter. *Ann. Phys.* **1974**, *83*, 491. [CrossRef]
36. Johnson, M.H.; Teller, E. Classical Field Theory of Nuclear Forces. *Phys. Rev.* **1955**, *98*, 783. [CrossRef]
37. Dutra, M.; Lourenço, O.; Avancini, S.S.; Carlson, B.V.; Delfino, A.; Menezes, D.P.; Providencia, C.; Typel, S.; Stone, J.R. Relativistic mean-field hadronic models under nuclear matter constraints. *Phys. Rev. C* **2014**, *90*, 055203. [CrossRef]
38. Oertel, M.; Hempel, M.; Klähn, T.; Typel, S. Equations of state for supernovae and compact stars. *Rev. Mod. Phys.* **2017**, *89*, 015007. [CrossRef]
39. Tews, I.; Lattimer, J.M.; Ohnishi, A.; Kolomeitsev, E.E. Symmetry Parameter Constraints from a Lower Bound on Neutron-matter Energy. *Astrophys. J.* **2017**, *848*, 105. [CrossRef]
40. Zhang, N.B.; Cai, B.J.; Li, B.A.; Newton, W.G.; Xu, J. How tightly is the nuclear symmetry energy constrained by a unitary Fermi gas? *Nucl. Sci. Tech.* **2017**, *28*, 181. [CrossRef]
41. Li, B.-A.; Han, X. Constraining the neutron-proton effective mass splitting using empirical constraints on the density dependence of nuclear symmetry energy around normal density. *Phys. Lett. B* **2013**, *727*, 276. [CrossRef]
42. Reed, B.T.; Fattoyev, F.J.; Horowitz, C.J.; Piekarewicz, J. Implications of PREX-2 on the Equation of State of Neutron-Rich Matter. *Phys. Rev. Lett.* **2021**, *126*, 172503. [CrossRef] [PubMed]
43. Agrawal, B.K. Asymmetric nuclear matter and neutron skin in an extended relativistic mean-field model. *Phys. Rev. C* **2010**, *81*, 034323. [CrossRef]
44. Boguta, J.; Bodmer, A.R. Relativistic calculation of nuclear matter and the nuclear surface. *Nucl. Phys.* **1977**, *A292*, 413. [CrossRef]
45. Lalazissis, G.A.; König, J.; Ring, P. New parametrization for the Lagrangian density of relativistic mean field theory. *Phys. Rev. C* **1997**, *55*, 540. [CrossRef]
46. Horowitz, C.J.; Piekarewicz, J. Neutron Star Structure and the Neutron Radius of ^{208}Pb. *Phys. Rev. Lett.* **2001**, *86*, 5647. [CrossRef]
47. Fattoyev, F.J.; Horowitz, C.J.; Piekarewicz, J.; Shen, G. Relativistic effective interaction for nuclei, giant resonances, and neutron stars. *Phys. Rev. C* **2010**, *82*, 055803. [CrossRef]
48. Glendenning, N.K.; Moszkowski, S.A. Reconciliation of neutron-star masses and binding of the Λ in hypernuclei. *Phys. Rev. Lett.* **1991**, *67*, 2414. [CrossRef]
49. Glendenning, N.K. *Compact Stars*; Springer: New York, NY, USA, 2000.
50. Sumiyoshi, K.; Kuwabara, H.; Toki, H. Relativistic mean-field theory with non-linear σ and ω terms for neutron stars and supernovae. *Nucl. Phys. A* **1995**, *581*, 725. [CrossRef]
51. Kumar, R.; Agrawal, B.K.; Dhiman, S.K. Effects of ω meson self-coupling on the properties of finite nuclei and neutron stars. *Phys. Rev. C* **2006**, *74*, 034323. [CrossRef]
52. Lopes, L.L.; Menezes, D.P. Hypernuclear matter in a complete SU(3) symmetry group. *Phys. Rev. C* **2014**, *89*, 025805. [CrossRef]
53. Menezes, D.P.; Providência, C. Warm stellar matter with neutrino trapping. *Phys. Rev. C* **2004**, *69*, 045801. [CrossRef]
54. Pile, P.H.; Bart, S.; Chrien, R.E.; Millener, D.J.; Sutter, R.J.; Tsoupas, N.; Peng, J.-C.; Mishra, C.S.; Hungerford, E.V.; Kishimoto, T.; et al. Study of hypernuclei by associated production. *Phys. Rev. Lett.* **1991**, *66*, 2585. [CrossRef] [PubMed]
55. Schaffner-Bielich, J.; Gal, A. Properties of strange hadronic matter in bulk and in finite systems. *Phys. Rev. C* **2000**, *62*, 034311. [CrossRef]
56. Torres, J.R.; Gulminelli, F.; Menezes, D.P. Liquid-gas phase transition in strange hadronic matter with relativistic models. *Phys. Rev. C* **2016**, *93*, 024306. [CrossRef]
57. Torres, J.R.; Gulminelli, F.; Menezes, D.P. Examination of strangeness instabilities and effects of strange meson couplings in dense strange hadronic matter and compact stars. *Phys. Rev. C* **2017**, *95*, 025201. [CrossRef]
58. Weissenborn, S.; Chatterjee, D.; Schaffner-Bielich, J. Hyperons and massive neutron stars: The role of hyperon potentials. *Nucl. Phys. A* **2012**, *881*, 62. [CrossRef]
59. Lopes, L.L.; Menezes, D.P. Broken SU(6) symmetry and massive hybrid stars. *Nucl. Phys. A* **2021**, *1009*, 122171. [CrossRef]
60. Cavagnoli, R.; Menezes, D.P.; Providencia, C. Neutron star properties and the symmetry energy. *Phys. Rev. C* **2011**, *84*, 065810. [CrossRef]
61. Lopes, L.L.; Menezes, D.P. Effects of the Symmetry Energy and its Slope on Neutron Star Properties. *Braz. J. Phys.* **2014**, *44*, 744. [CrossRef]

62. Tsang, M.B.; Stone, J.R.; Camera, F.; Danielewicz, P.; Gandolfi, S.; Hebeler, K.; Horowitz, C.J.; Lee, J.; Lynch, W.G.; Kohley, Z.; et al. Constraints on the symmetry energy and neutron skins from experiments and theory. *Phys. Rev. C* **2012**, *86*, 015803. [CrossRef]
63. Lattimer, J.M.; Steiner, A. Constraints on the symmetry energy using the mass-radius relation of neutron stars. *Eur. Phys. J. A* **2014**, *50*, 40. [CrossRef]
64. Pais, H.; Providencia, C. Vlasov formalism for extended relativistic mean field models: The crust-core transition and the stellar matter equation of state. *Phys. Rev. C* **2016**, *94*, 015808. [CrossRef]
65. Dexheimer, V.; Gomes, R.O.; Schramm, S.; Pais, H. What do we learn about vector interactions from GW170817? *J.Phys. G* **2019**, *46*, 034002. [CrossRef]
66. Providencia, C.; Fortin, M.; Pais, H.; Rabhi, A. Hyperonic Stars and the Nuclear Symmetry Energy. *Front. Astron. Space Sci.* **2019**, *26*. doi:10.3389/fspas.2019.00013 [CrossRef]
67. Baym, G.; Pethick, C.; Sutherland, P. The Ground State of Matter at High Densities: Equation of State and Stellar Models. *Astrophys. J.* **1971**, *170*, 299. [CrossRef]
68. Providência, C.; Avancini, S.S.; Cavagnoli, R.; Chiacchiera, S.; Ducoin, C.; Grill, F.; Margueron, J.; Menezes, D.P.; Rabhi, A.; Vidaña, I. Imprint of the symmetry energy on the inner crust and strangeness content of neutron stars. *Eur. Phys. J. A* **2014**, *50*, 44. [CrossRef]
69. Lattimer, J. Researchgate. 2004. Available online: https://www.researchgate.net/publication/253849889_Neutron_Stars_as_a_Probe_of_the_Equation_of_State (accessed on 1 June 2021)
70. Cromartie, H.T.; Fonseca, E.; Ransom, S.M.; Demorest, P.B.; Arzoumanian, Z.; Blumer, H.; Brook, P.R.; De Cesar, M.E.; Dolch, T.; Ellis, J.A.; et al. Relativistic Shapiro delay measurements of an extremely massive millisecond pulsar. *Nat. Astr.* **2020**, *4*, 72. [CrossRef]
71. Antoniadis, J.; Freire, P.C.C.; Wex, N.; Tauris, T.M.; Lynch, R.S.; van Kerkwijk, M.H.; Kramer, M.; Bassa, C.; Dhillon, V.S.; Driebe, T.; et al. A Massive Pulsar in a Compact Relativistic Binary. *Science* **2013**, *340*, 1233232. [CrossRef] [PubMed]
72. Demorest, P. B.; Pennucci, T.; Ransom, S.M.; Roberts, M.S.; Hessels, J.W.T. A two-solar-mass neutron star measured using Shapiro delay. *Nature* **2010**, *467*, 1081. [CrossRef]
73. Annala, E.; Gorda, T.; Kurkela, A.; Vuorinen, A. Gravitational-Wave Constraints on the Neutron-Star-Matter Equation of State. *Phys. Rev. Lett.* **2018**, *120*, 172703. [CrossRef]
74. Raithel, C.; Ozel, F.; Psaltis, D. Tidal Deformability from GW170817 as a Direct Probe of the Neutron Star Radius. *Astrophys. J. Lett.* **2018**, *857*, L23. [CrossRef]
75. Riley, T.E.; Watts, A.L.; Bogdanov, S.; Ray, P.S.; Ludlam, R.M.; Guillot, S.; Arzoumanian, Z.; Baker, C.L.; Bilous, A.V.; Chakrabarty, D.; et al. A NICER View of PSR J0030+0451: Millisecond Pulsar Parameter Estimation. *Astrophys. J. Lett.* **2019**, *887*, L21. [CrossRef]
76. Miller, M.C.; Lamb, F.K.; Dittmann, A.J.; Bogdanov, S.; Arzoumanian, Z.; Gendreau, K.C.; Guillot, S.; Harding, A.K.; Ho, W.C.G.; Lattimer, J.M.; et al. PSR J0030+0451 Mass and Radius from NICER Data and Implications for the Properties of Neutron Star Matter. *Astrophys. J. Lett.* **2019**, *887*, L24. [CrossRef]
77. Capano, C.D.; Tews, I.; Brown, S.M.; Margalit, B.; De, S.; Kumar, S.; Brown, D.A.; Krishnan, B.; Reddy, S. Stringent constraints on neutron-star radii from multimessenger observations and nuclear theory. *Nat. Astron.* **2020**. [CrossRef]
78. Love, A.E.H. The yielding of the earth to disturbing forces. *Proc. R. Soc. Lond. A* **1909**, *82*, 551. [CrossRef]
79. Damour, T. Alessandro Nagar. Relativistic tidal properties of neutron stars. *Phys. Rev. D* **2009**, *80*,084035. [CrossRef]
80. Binnington, T. ;Poisson E. Relativistic theory of tidal Love numbers. *Phys. Rev. D* **2009**, *80*, 084018. [CrossRef]
81. Flores, C.V.; Lopes, L.L.; Castro, L.B.; Menezes, D.P. Gravitational wave signatures of highly magnetized neutron stars. *Eur. Phys. J. C* **2020**, *80*, 1142. [CrossRef]
82. Lourenço, O.; Dutra, M.; Lenzi, C.; Biswal, S.K.; Bhuyan, M.; Menezes, D.P. Consistent Skyrme parametrizations constrained by GW170817. *Eur. Phys. J. A* **2020**, *56*, 32. [CrossRef]
83. Pearson, J.M.; Chamel, N.; Potekhin, A.Y. Unified equations of state for cold nonaccreting neutron stars with Brussels-Montreal functionals. II. Pasta phases in semiclassical approximation. *Phys. Rev. C* **2020**, *101*, 015802. [CrossRef]
84. Fantina, A.F.; Ridder, S.D.; Chamel, N.; Gulminelli, F. Crystallization of the outer crust of a non-accreting neutron star. *Astron. Astrophys.* **2020**, *633*, A149. [CrossRef]
85. Malik, T.; Alam, N.; Fortin, M.; Providência, C.; Agrawal, B.K.; Jha, T.K.; Kumar, B.; Patra, S.K. GW170817: Constraining the nuclear matter equation of state from the neutron star tidal deformability. *Phys. Rev. C* **2018**, *98*, 035804. [CrossRef]
86. Abbott, B.P.; Abbott, R.; Abbott, T.D.; Acernese, F.; Ackley, K.; Adams, C.; Adams, T.; Addesso, P.; Adhikari, R.X.; Adya, V.B.; et al. GW170817: Measurements of Neutron Star Radii and Equation of State. *Phys. Rev. Lett.* **2018**, *121*, 161101. [CrossRef]
87. Mota, C.E.; Santos, L.C.N.; Grams, G.; Silva, F.M.; Menezes, D.P. Combined Rastall and rainbow theories of gravity with applications to neutron stars. *Phys. Rev. D* **2019**, *100*, 024043. [CrossRef]
88. Bogdanov, S.; Dittmann, A.J.; Ho, W.C.G.; Lamb, F.K.; Mahmoodifar, S.; Miller, M.C.; Morsink, S.M.; Riley, T.E.; Strohmayer, T.E.; Watts, A.L.; et al. Constraining the Neutron Star Mass–Radius Relation and Dense Matter Equation of State with NICER. III. Model Description and Verification of Parameter Estimation Codes. *arXiv* **2021**, arXiv:2104.06928.
89. Piekarewicz, J. Implications of PREX-2 on the electric dipole polarizability of neutron rich nuclei. *arXiv* **2021**, arXiv: 2105.13452.
90. Dutra, M.; Lourenço, O.; Menezes, D.P. Stellar properties and nuclear matter constraints. *Phys. Rev. C* **2016**, *93*, 025806. [CrossRef]

91. Lourenço, O.; Dutra, M.; Lenzi, C.H.; Flores, C.V.; Menezes, D.P. Consistent relativistic mean-field models constrained by GW170817. *Phys. Rev. C* **2019**, *99*, 045202. [CrossRef]
92. Dexheimer, V.; Marquez, K.D.; Menezes, D.P. Delta baryons in neutron-star matter under strong magnetic fields. *Eur. Phys. J. A* **2021**, *57*, 216. [CrossRef]
93. Schneider, A.S.; Caplan, M.E.; Berry, D.K.; Horowitz, C.J. Domains and defects in nuclear pasta. *Phys. Rev. C* **2018**, *98*, 055801. [CrossRef]
94. Newton, W.G.; Stone, J.R. Modeling nuclear "pasta" and the transition to uniform nuclear matter with the 3D Skyrme-Hartree-Fock method at finite temperature: Core-collapse supernovae. *Phys. Rev. C* **2009**, *79*, 055801. [CrossRef]
95. Schuetrumpf, B.; Martínez-Pinedo, G.; Afibuzzaman, M.; Aktulga, H.M. Survey of nuclear pasta in the intermediate-density regime: Shapes and energies. *Phys. Rev. C* **2019**, *100*, 045806. [CrossRef]
96. Avancini, S.S.; Menezes, D.P.; Alloy, M.D.; Marinelli, J.R.; Moraes, M.M.W.; Providência, C. Warm and cold pasta phase in relativistic mean field theory. *Phys. Rev. C* **2008**, *78*, 015802. [CrossRef]
97. Maruyama, T.; Tatsumi, T.; Voskresensky, D.N.; Tanigawa, T.; Chiba, S. Nuclear "pasta" structures and the charge screening effect. *Phys. Rev. C* **2005**, *72*, 015802. [CrossRef]
98. Schneider, A.S.; Berry, D.K.; Caplan, M.E.; Horowitz, C.J.; Lin, Z. Effect of topological defects on "nuclear pasta" observables. *Phys. Rev. C* **2016**, *93*, 065806. [CrossRef]
99. Lourenço, O.; Lenzi, C.; Dutra, M.; Frederico, T.; Bhuyan, M.; Negreiros, R.P.; Flores, C.V.; Grams, G.; Menezes, D.P. Neutron star cooling and GW170817 constraint within quark-meson coupling models. *Chin. Phys. C* **2021**, *45*, 025101. [CrossRef]
100. Piekarewicz, J.; Fattoyev, F.J. Impact of the neutron star crust on the tidal polarizability. *Phys. Rev. C* **2019**, *99*, 045802. [CrossRef]
101. Ferreira, M.; Providência, C. Effect of the crust on neutron star empirical relations. *arXiv* **2010**, arXiv:2010.05588.
102. Ferreira, M.; Providência, C. Neutron Star Properties: Quantifying the Effect of the Crust–Core Matching Procedure. *Universe* **2020**, *6*, 220; doi:10.3390/universe6110220. [CrossRef]
103. Lopes, L.L. The neutron star inner crust: an empirical essay. *arXiv* **2020**, arXiv:2012.05277.
104. Deibel, A.; Cumming, A.; Brown, E.F.; Reddy, S. Late-time Cooling of Neutron Star Transients and the Physics of the Inner Crust. *Astrophys. J.* **2017**, *839*, 95. [CrossRef]
105. Pons, J.A.; Viganó D.; Rea, N. A highly resistive layer within the crust of X-ray pulsars limits their spin periods. *Nat. Phys.* **2013**, *9*, 431. [CrossRef]
106. Horowitz, C.J.; Berry, D.K.; Briggs, C.M.; Caplan, M.E.; Cumming, A.; Schneider, A.S. Disordered Nuclear Pasta, Magnetic Field Decay, and Crust Cooling in Neutron Stars. *Phys. Rev. Lett.* **2015**, *114*, 031102. [CrossRef] [PubMed]
107. Alloy, M.D.; Menezes, D.P. Nuclear "pasta phase" and its consequences on neutrino opacities. *Phys. Rev. C* **2011**, *83*, 035803. [CrossRef]
108. Horowitz, C.J.; Berry, D.K.; Caplan, M.E.; Fischer, T.; Lin, Z.; Newton, W.G.; O'Connor, E.; Roberts, L.F. Nuclear pasta and supernova neutrinos at late times. *arXiv* **2016**, arXiv:1611.10226.
109. Providencia, C.; Menezes, D.P. Hyperons in the nuclear pasta phase. *Phys. Rev. C* **2017**, *96*, 045803.
110. Avancini, S.S.; Chiacchiera, S.; Menezes, D.P.; Providência, C. Warm "pasta" phase in the Thomas-Fermi approximation. *Phys. Rev. C* **2010**, *82*, 055807. [CrossRef]
111. Okamoto, M.; Maruyama, T.; Yabana, K.; Tatsumi, T. Nuclear "pasta" structures in low-density nuclear matter and properties of the neutron star crust. *Phys. Rev. C* **2013**, *88*, 025801. [CrossRef]
112. Fattoyev, F.J.; Horowitz, C.J.; Schuetrumpf, B. Quantum nuclear pasta and nuclear symmetry energy. *Phys. Rev. C* **2017**, *95*, 055804. [CrossRef]
113. Barros, C.C., Jr.; Menezes, D.P.; Gulminelli, F. Fluctuations in the composition of nuclear pasta in symmetric nuclear matter at finite temperature. *Phys. Rev. C* **2020**, *101*, 035211. [CrossRef]
114. Pelicer, M.R.; Menezes, D.P.; Barros, C.C., Jr.; Gulminelli, F. Fluctuations in the pasta phase. *arXiv* **2021**, arXiv:2105.03318.
115. Ivanenko, D.; Kurdgelaidze, D.F. Hypothesis concerning quark stars. *Astrophysics* **1965**, *1*, 251–252. [CrossRef]
116. Annala, E.; Gorda, T.; Kurkela, A.; Nättilä, J.; Vuorinen A. Evidence for quark-matter cores in massive neutron stars. *Nat. Phys.* **2020**, *16*, 907–910. [CrossRef]
117. Dexheimer, V.A.; Schramm, S. Novel approach to modeling hybrid stars. *Phys. Rev. C* **2010**, *81*, 045201. [CrossRef]
118. Dexheimer, V.; Gomes, R.O.; Klahn, T.; Han, S.; Salinas, M. GW190814 as a massive rapidly rotating neutron star with exotic degrees of freedom. *Phys. Rev. C* **2021**, *103*, 025808. [CrossRef]
119. Pais, H.; Menezes, D.P.; Providência, C. Neutron stars: From the inner crust to the core with the (extended) Nambu–Jona-Lasinio model. *Phys. Rev. C* **2016**, *93*, 065805. [CrossRef]
120. Graeff, C.A.; Alloy, M.D.; Marquez, K.D.; Providencia, C.; Menezes, D.P. Hadron-quark phase transition: The QCD phase diagram and stellar conversion. *J. Cosm. Astrop. Phys.* **2019**, *1*, 024. [CrossRef]
121. Fuchs, C.; Lenske, H.; Wolter, H.H. Density dependent hadron field theory. *Phys. Rev. C* **1995**, *52*, 3043. [CrossRef] [PubMed]
122. Typel S.; Wolter, H.H. Relativistic mean field calculations with density-dependent meson-nucleon coupling. *Nucl. Phys. A* **1999**, *656*, 331. [CrossRef]
123. Chodos, A.; Jaffe, R.L.; Johnson, K.; Thorne, C.B.; Weisskopf, V.F. New extended model of hadrons. *Phys. Rev. D* **1974**, *9*, 3471. [CrossRef]

124. Nambu, Y.; Jona-Lasinio, G. Dynamical Model of Elementary Particles Based on an Analogy with Superconductivity. I. *Phys. Rev.* **1961**, *122*, 345. [CrossRef]
125. Buballa, M. NJL-model analysis of dense quark matter. *Phys. Rep.* **2005**, *407*, 205. [CrossRef]
126. Menezes, D.P.; Providência, C. Warm stellar matter with deconfinement: Application to compact stars. *Phys. Rev. C* **2003**, *68*, 035804. [CrossRef]
127. Maruyama, T.; Chiba S.; Schulze H.J, Tatsumi T. Hadron-quark mixed phase in hyperon stars. *Phys. Rev. D* **2007**, *76*, 123015 [CrossRef]
128. Voskresensky, D.N.; Yasuhira, M.; Tatsumi, T. Charge screening in hadron–quark mixed phase. *Phys. Lett. B* **2002**, *541*, 93. [CrossRef]
129. de Paoli, M.G.; Menezes, D.P. Effects of the existence of a mixed phase in hybrid neutron stars. *Int. J. Mod. Phys. D* **2010**, *19*, 1525–1529. [CrossRef]
130. Hatsuda, T.; Kunihiro, T. QCD Phenomenology based on a Chiral Effective Lagrangian. *Phys. Rep.* **1994**, *247*, 221. [CrossRef]
131. Rehberg, P.; Klevansky, S.P.; Hüfner, J. Hadronization in the SU (3) Nambu–Jona-Lasinio model. *Phys. Rev. C* **1996**, *53*, 410. [CrossRef]
132. Abbott, R.; Abbott T.D.; Abraham S.; Acernese F.; Ackley K.; Adams C.; Adhikari R.X.; Adya V.D.; Affeldt C.;Agathos M.; et al. GW190814: Gravitational Waves from the Coalescence of a 23 Solar Mass Black Holewith a 2.6 Solar Mass Compact Object. *Astrophys. J. Lett.* **2020**, *896*, L44. [CrossRef]
133. Tan, H.; Dore, T.; Dexheimer, V.; Noronha-Hostler, J.; Yunes, N. Extreme Matter meets Extreme Gravity: Ultra-heavy neutron stars with crossovers and first-order phase transitions. *arXiv* **2021**, arXiv: 2106.03890.
134. Itoh, N. Hydrostatic Equilibrium of Hypothetical Quark Stars. *Prog. Theor. Phys.* **1970**, *44*, 291. [CrossRef]
135. Bodmer, A.R. Collapsed Nuclei. *Phys. Rev. D* **1971**, *4*, 1601. [CrossRef]
136. Witten, E. Cosmic separation of phases. *Phys. Rev. D* **1984**, *30*, 272. [CrossRef]
137. Buballa, M. The problem of matter stability in the Nambu-Jona-Lasinio model. *Nucl. Phys. A* **1996**, *611*, 393. [CrossRef]
138. Menezes D.P.; Pinto M.B.; Avancini S.S.; Pérez Martinez A.; Providência C. Quark matter under strong magnetic fields in the Nambu–Jona-Lasinio model. *Phys. Rev. C* **2009**, *79*, 035807. [CrossRef]
139. Menezes, D.P.; Pinto, M.B.; Avancini, S.S.; Providência, C. Quark matter under strong magnetic fields in the su(3) Nambu–Jona-Lasinio Model. *Phys. Rev. C* **2009**, *80*, 065805. [CrossRef]
140. Dexheimer, V.; Torres, J.R.; Menezes, D.P. Stability windows for proto-quark stars. *Eur. Phys. J. C* **2013**, *73*, 2569. [CrossRef]
141. Torres, J.R.; Menezes, D.P. Quark matter equation of state and stellar properties. *Europhys. Lett.* **2013**, *101*, 42003. [CrossRef]
142. Peng, G.X.; Chiang, H.C.; Zou, B.S.; Ning, P.Z.; Luo, S.J. Thermodynamics, strange quark matter, and strange stars. *Phys. Rev. C* **2000**, *62*, 025801. [CrossRef]
143. Xia, C.J.; Peng, G.X.; Chen, S.W.; Lu, Z.Y.; Xu, J.F. Thermodynamic consistency, quark mass scaling, and properties of strange matter. *Phys. Rev. D* **2014**, *89*, 105027. [CrossRef]
144. Backes, B.C.; Hafemann, E.; Marzola, I.; Menezes, D.P. Density-dependent quark mass model revisited: Thermodynamic consistency, stability windows and stellar properties. *J. Phys. G* **2021**. [CrossRef]
145. Lopes, L.L.; Biesdorf, C.; Menezes, D.P. Modified MIT Bag Models—Part I: Thermodynamic Consistency, Stability windows and symmetry group. *Phys. Scr.* **2021**. Available online: https://iopscience.iop.org/article/10.1088/1402-4896/abef34 (accessed on 20 July 2021). [CrossRef]
146. Melrose, D.B.; Fok, R.; Menezes, D.P. Pair emission from bare magnetized strange stars. *Mon. Not. R. Astron. Soc.* **2006**, *371*, 204–210. [CrossRef]
147. Menezes, D.P.; Providência, C.; Melrose, D.B. Quark stars within relativistic models. *J. Phys. G* **2006**, *32*, 1081–1096. [CrossRef]
148. Haensel, D.G.Y.P.; Potekhin, A.Y. *Neutron Stars 1: Equation of State and Structure*; Springer: New York, NY, USA, 2007.
149. Thompson, C.; Duncan, R.C. The soft gamma repeaters as very strongly magnetized neutron stars—I. Radiative mechanism for outbursts. *Mon. Not. R. Astron. Soc.* **1995**, *275*, 255. [CrossRef]
150. Mereghetti, S.; Pons, J.A.; Melatos, A. Magnetars: Properties, Origin and Evolution. *Space Sci. Rev.* **2015**, *191*, 315. [CrossRef]
151. Bochenek, C.D.; Ravi. V.; Belov, K.V.; Hallinan, G.; Kocz, J.; Kulkarni, S.R.; McKenna, D.L. A fast radio burst associated with a Galactic magnetar. *Nature* **2020**, *587*, 59–62. [CrossRef]
152. Olausen, S.A.; Kaspi, V.M. The McGill Magnetar Catalog. *Astrophys. J.* **2014**, *212*, 6. [CrossRef]
153. Athena X-ray Observatory. 2016. Available online: http://www.the-athena-x-ray-observatory.eu/ (accessed on 20 July 2021).
154. Lopes, L.L.; Menezes, D.P. The Influence of Hyperons and Strong Magnetic Field in Neutron Star Properties. *Braz. J. Phys.* **2012**, *42*. [CrossRef]
155. Casali, R.; Castro, L.B.; Menezes, D.P. Hadronic and hybrid stars subject to density dependent magnetic fields. *Phys. Rev. C* **2014**, *89*, 015805. [CrossRef]
156. Chatterjee, D.; Gulminelli, F.; Menezes, D.P. Estimating magnetar radii with an empirical meta-model. *J. Cosmol. Astropart. Phys.* **2019**, *3*, 035. [CrossRef]
157. Lopes, L.L.; Menezes, D.P. Role of vector channel in different classes of (non)magnetized neutron stars. *Eur. Phys. J. A* **2020**, *56*, 122. [CrossRef]
158. Lopes, L.L.; Menezes, D.P. On magnetized neutron stars. *J. Cosmol. Astropart. Phys.* **2015**, *8*, 002. [CrossRef]

59. Dexheimer, V.; Menezes, D.P.; Strickland, M. The influence of strong magnetic fields on protoquark stars. *J. Phys. G Nucl. Part. Phys.* **2014**, *41*, 015203. [CrossRef]
60. Menezes, D.P.; Lopes, L.L. Quark matter under strong magnetic fields. *Eur. Phys. J. A* **2016**, *52*, 17. [CrossRef]
61. LORENE. Available online: https://lorene.obspm.fr/ (accessed on 20 July 2021).
62. Fang, J.; Pais, H.; Pratapsi, S.; Avancini, S.; Li, J.; Providência, C. Effect of strong magnetic fields on the crust-core transition and inner crust of neutron stars. *Phys. Rev. C* **2017**, *95*, 045802. [CrossRef]
63. Brito, L.; Providência, C.; Santos, A.M.; Avancini S.S.; Menezes, D.P.; Chomaz, P. Unstable modes in relativistic neutron-proton-electron (npe) matter at finite temperature. *Phys. Rev. C* **2006**, *74*, 045801. [CrossRef]
64. Thorne, K.; Campolattaro, A. Non-Radial Pulsation of General-Relativistic Stellar Models. I. Analytic Analysis for L >= 2. *Astrophys. J.* **1967**, *149*, 591. [CrossRef]
65. Hinderer, T. Tidal Love Numbers of Neutron Stars. *Astrophys. J.* **2008**, *677*, 1216. [CrossRef]
66. Backes, B.C.T.; Marquez, K.D.; Menezes, D.P. Effects of strong magnetic fields on the hadron-quark deconfinement transition. *Eur. Phys. J. A* **2021**, *57*, 229. [CrossRef]
67. Gogelein, P.; van Dalen, E.N.E.; Fuchs, C.; Muther, H. Nuclear matter in the crust of neutron stars derived from realistic NN interactions. *Phys. Rev. C* **2008**, *77*, 025802. [CrossRef]
68. Abbott, B.P.; Abbott, R.; Abbott, T.D.; Abraham, S.; Acernese, F.; Ackley, K.; Adams, C.; Adhikari, R.X.; Adya, V.B.; Affeldt, C.; et al. GW190425: Observation of a Compact Binary Coalescence with Total Mass 3.4 M$\odot$. *Astrophys. J. Lett.* **2020**, *892*, L3. [CrossRef]
69. Abbott, R.; Abbott, T.D.; Abraham, S.; Acernese, F.; Ackley, K.; Adams, A.; Adams, C.; Adhikari, R.X.; Adya, V.B.; Affeldt, C.; et al. Observation of Gravitational Waves from Two Neutron Star–Black Hole Coalescences. *Astrophys. J. Lett.* **2021**, *915*, L5. [CrossRef]
70. Dietrich, T.; Coughlin, M.W.; Pang, P.T.H.; Bulla, M.; Heinzel, J.; Issa, L.; Tews, I.; Antier, S. Multimessenger constraints on the neutron-star equation of state and the Hubble constant. *Science* **2020**, *370*, 1450. [CrossRef]
71. Available online: http://compose.obspm.fr (accessed on 20 July 2021).

Article

Low Density Neutron Star Matter with Quantum Molecular Dynamics: The Role of Isovector Interactions

Parit Mehta [1,*], Rana Nandi [2], Rosana de Oliveira Gomes [3], Veronica Dexheimer [4] and Jan Steinheimer [5]

1. I. Physikalisches Institut, Universität zu Köln, Zülpicher Str. 77, 50937 Köln, Germany
2. Polba Mahavidyalaya, Hooghly 712148, India; nandi@fias.uni-frankfurt.de
3. Hakom Time Series GmbH, Lemböckgasse 61, 1230 Vienna, Austria; rosana.gomes@hakom.at
4. Department of Physics, Kent State University, Kent, OH 44242, USA; vdexheim@kent.edu
5. Frankfurt Institute for Advanced Studies, Ruth-Moufang-Str. 1, 60438 Frankfurt am Main, Germany; steinheimer@fias.uni-frankfurt.de
* Correspondence: mehta@ph1.uni-koeln.de

Abstract: The effect of isospin-dependent nuclear forces on the inner crust of neutron stars is modeled within the framework of Quantum Molecular Dynamics (QMD). To successfully control the density dependence of the symmetry energy of neutron-star matter below nuclear saturation density, a mixed vector-isovector potential is introduced. This approach is inspired by the baryon density and isospin density-dependent repulsive Skyrme force of asymmetric nuclear matter. In isospin-asymmetric nuclear matter, the system shows nucleation, as nucleons are arranged into shapes resembling nuclear pasta. The dependence of clusterization in the system on the isospin properties is also explored by calculating two-point correlation functions. We show that, as compared to previous results that did not involve such mixed interaction terms, the energy symmetry slope L is successfully controlled by varying the corresponding coupling strength. Nevertheless, the effect of changing the slope of the nuclear symmetry energy L on the crust-core transition density does not seem significant. To the knowledge of the authors, this is the first implementation of such a coupling in a QMD model for isospin asymmetric matter, which is relevant to the inner crust of neutron and proto-neutron stars.

Keywords: neutron star crust; nuclear matter; meson interactions; quantum molecular dynamics

1. Introduction

Matter in neutron stars presents the largest densities achieved in the Universe, making their equation of state (EOS) hard to determine. Seeking the EOS of neutron-star matter (NSM) is a flourishing field of interest due to the presence of neutron rich matter with magnetic fields that can be larger than 10^{12} G with the possibility of exotic particles, and a phase transition to deconfined quark matter. The crust of a neutron star contains nuclei embedded in a sea of electrons. As the density increases from the surface of the neutron star towards its core, these nuclei undergo a neutronization process, eventually reaching a state of high neutron to proton asymmetry, which is followed by a transition to uniform nuclear matter at the core. Since matter above nuclear saturation density is unattainable in terrestrial conditions (except in heavy ion collisions with larger temperatures), neutron stars are considered to hold the key to the mysteries of dense nuclear matter.

Several approaches have been employed to study the properties of nuclear matter in the context of neutron stars. One of the prominent methods is Quantum Molecular Dynamics (QMD), which allows for the incorporation of competing nuclear forces of attraction and repulsion in dynamical simulations. QMD as a framework for simulating heavy-ion collisions was proposed by J. Aichelin and H. Stöcker [1]. Until then, nuclear matter simulations were only possible microscopically through one-body models, such as the Vlaslov–Uehling–Uhlenbeck (VUU) theory, and macroscopically by fluid dynamical models [2,3]. QMD combines classical molecular dynamics with quantum corrections, the most important of which is the Pauli principle. Peilert et al. [4] used QMD for the first time to simulate clustering in nuclear matter at sub-saturation densities. They performed uniform nuclear matter simulations with nucleons, which were sampled only in momentum space, for the density range $0 < \rho < 2\rho_0$ (where ρ_0 is the nuclear saturation density). These were then compared with simulations where nucleons were free to move in position space, showing a decrease in binding energy per nucleon (E/A), for the latter case, of about 8 MeV towards a more bound system for sub-saturation densities at a near-zero temperature. In the same work, the authors also took snapshots of simulated nuclear matter for different mean densities below ρ_0, which was useful to visualize clustered matter at $\rho = 0.1\rho_0$, but did not help deduce the properties of single clusters (unless a computationally expensive time average of many simulations could be done).

Later, results for sub-saturation density nuclear matter at zero temperature were published by Maruyama et al. [5], where the the number of nucleons was significantly expanded (by ≈4 times) in the simulated infinite nuclear matter system. In addition to partially observing transient shapes like holes, slabs, and cylinders in clustered nuclear matter, they also extended the calculations to asymmetric nuclear matter, and obtained similar clusterization effects. This is necessary to evaluate the properties of NSM, which is highly asymmetric at saturation and sub-saturation densities. Further improvements to NSM simulations were made by Watanabe et al. [6] by implementing larger relaxation time scales and analyses of spatial distribution of nucleons. In a similar analysis, utilizing the Indiana University Molecular Dynamics framework, Sagert et al. [7] have shown nuclear pasta through similar 3D Skyrme Hartree–Fock (SHF) simulations. Recently, Schramm and Nandi [8] studied the asymmetry dependence of the transition density from asymmetric to homogeneous nuclear matter in the inner crust using QMD.

In this article, the asymmetry dependence shown by R. Nandi and S. Schramm [8] is modified to have better control on the symmetry energy slope (L). The inspiration is taken from the coupling of omega (ω) and rho (ρ) meson fields in the Relativistic Mean-Field (RMF) theory. The model is first applied to isospin chains of finite nuclei, and then to nuclear matter at ρ_0. Symmetry energy at saturation density is re-evaluated along with its slope L. The primary aim of this work is to successfully control the density dependence of symmetry energy, and of pure neutron matter, by calibrating the $\omega - \rho$ type coupling according to established constraints. The expected clustering of nuclear matter at densities ≈$0.1\rho_0$ is also addressed.

The structure of the article is as follows: the general formalism is outlined in Section 2. Then a study of parameters of different strengths of the $\omega - \rho$ coupling in elucidated in Section 3. The conclusions are presented in Section 4, along with an outlook for the model under study.

2. Formalism
2.1. The Canonical Formalism: Hamiltonian and Equations of Motion

Quantum Molecular Dynamics (QMD) is a model used to accomplish dynamical simulations of nuclear matter by incorporating correlation effects between the constituents of the simulated N-body system. Peilert et al. [4] studied non-uniformities that give rise to clustering in nuclear matter. A model based on QMD for heavy-ion collisions through an N-body approach was proposed as early as the late 1980s (Aichelin and Stöcker [1]). The reader can refer to Ref. [9] for a thorough review of the method and its theoretical background. A brief insight into the working of QMD and the relevance to this project is provided in this section based on a review by Maruyama et al. [10].

In a Classical Molecular Dynamics (CMD) simulation of nucleons, particles are simulated as solid elastic spheres, and their motion is governed by Newton's equations of motion. Inter-particle potentials quantify the force experienced by a particle, given the positions of other particles. QMD introduces quantum behavior to the system of nucleons by including the following modifications:

(a) In QMD for nuclear matter, a nucleon is represented by a fixed-width Gaussian wavepacket in the form of a single particle wave function

$$\psi(\mathbf{r_i}) = \frac{1}{(2\pi C_W)^{3/4}} exp\left(-\frac{(\mathbf{r}-\mathbf{R_i})^2}{4 C_W} + i\mathbf{r}\cdot\mathbf{P_i}\right), \quad (1)$$

with $\mathbf{R_i}$ and $\mathbf{P_i}$ as the centers of position and momentum of the wave packet, respectively. C_W denotes the width of the wave packet. The motion of the wave packet or 'nucleon' is determined by forces derived from inter-particle potentials in the QMD Hamiltonian. The total wave function of the N-nucleon system is obtained through a direct product given by

$$\Psi(\mathbf{r}) = \prod_i^N \psi(\mathbf{r_i}), \quad (2)$$

(b) The nucleon wavefunctions are not anti-symmetrized to explicitly manifest fermionic characteristics. As a result, the energy states violate the Pauli principle, as they all attain minimum energy. This problem was addressed phenomenologically (see the review in Ref. [10] for further references) by mimicking the Pauli principle through a repulsive 2-body potential called the Pauli potential (V_{Pauli}). The potential effectively repels nucleons with the same spin and isospin from coming close in phase space, since it is a function of both distance in coordinate and momentum space. In the ground state, nucleons have non-zero momentum values and do not all exist in the lowest energy state.

The Hamiltonian of the nucleon-nucleon interaction is given by Ref. [11]

$$\mathcal{H} = K + V_{Pauli} + V_{Skyrme} + V_{sym} + V_{MD} + V_{Coul}, \quad (3)$$

where K is the kinetic energy, V_{Pauli} is the Pauli potential, V_{Skyrme} is the potential similar to Skyrme like interactions, V_{sym} is the isospin dependent potential, V_{MD} is the momentum dependent potential, and V_{Coul} is the Coulomb potential. The expressions for the potential and kinetic terms are

$$K = \sum_i \frac{\mathbf{P_i}^2}{2m_i}, \quad (4)$$

$$V_{Pauli} = \frac{C_P}{2}\left(\frac{1}{q_0 p_0}\right)^3 \sum_{i,j(\neq i)} exp\left[-\frac{(\mathbf{R_i}-\mathbf{R_j})^2}{2q_0^2} - \frac{(\mathbf{P_i}-\mathbf{P_j})^2}{2p_0^2}\right] \delta_{\tau_i \tau_j} \delta_{\sigma_i \sigma_j}, \quad (5)$$

$$V_{Skyrme} = \frac{\alpha}{2\rho_0}\sum_{i,j(\neq i)}\rho_{ij} + \frac{\beta}{(1+\theta)\rho_0^\theta}\sum_i\left[\sum_{j(\neq i)}\tilde{\rho}_{ij}\right]^\theta, \quad (6)$$

$$V_{Sym} = \frac{C_s}{2\rho_0}\sum_{i,j(\neq i)}(1-2|\tau_i-\tau_j|)\rho_{ij}, \quad (7)$$

$$V_{MD} = \frac{C_{ex}^{(1)}}{2\rho_0}\sum_{i,j(\neq i)}\frac{1}{1+\left[\frac{\mathbf{P_i}-\mathbf{P_j}}{\mu_1}\right]^2}\rho_{ij} + \frac{C_{ex}^{(2)}}{2\rho_0}\sum_{i,j(\neq i)}\frac{1}{1+\left[\frac{\mathbf{P_i}-\mathbf{P_j}}{\mu_2}\right]^2}\rho_{ij}, \quad (8)$$

$$V_{Coul} = C_{coul}\frac{e^2}{2}\sum_{i,j(\neq i)}\left(\tau_i+\frac{1}{2}\right)\left(\tau_j+\frac{1}{2}\right)\iint d^3r\, d^3r'\,\frac{1}{|\mathbf{r}-\mathbf{r}'|}\rho_i(\mathbf{r})\rho_j(\mathbf{r}'), \quad (9)$$

where the nucleon mass, spin, and isospin are represented by m_i, σ_i and τ_i, respectively. The values of the parameters are listed in Table 1.

Table 1. Parameter set for nucleon-nucleon interaction (values from Ref. [5] parameterized to reproduce properties of the ground states of the finite nuclei and saturation properties of the nuclear matter). The parameters are optimized to give $E/A \approx -16$ MeV for symmetric nuclear matter at saturation ρ_0.

Parameter	Value
C_P (MeV)	207
p_0 (MeV/c)	120
q_0 (MeV)	1.644
α (MeV)	-92.86
β (MeV)	169.28
θ	1.33333
$C_{ex}^{(1)}$ (MeV)	-258.54
$C_{ex}^{(2)}$ (MeV)	375.6
μ_1 (fm^{-1})	2.35
μ_2 (fm^{-1})	0.4
ρ_0 (fm^{-3})	0.165
C_S (MeV)	25
C_W (fm^2)	2.1
C_{coul}	0 or 1

The overlap between single nucleon densities ρ_{ij} and $\tilde{\rho}_{ij}$, which depends on positions $\mathbf{R}_i$ and $\mathbf{R}_j$, is calculated as

$$\rho_{ij} \equiv \int d^3 r \rho_i(\mathbf{r})\rho_j(\mathbf{r}), \quad \tilde{\rho}_{ij} \equiv \int d^3 r \tilde{\rho}_i(\mathbf{r})\tilde{\rho}_j(\mathbf{r}), \tag{10}$$

where the single nucleon densities are given by

$$\rho_i(\mathbf{r}) = |\psi_i(\mathbf{r})|^2 = \frac{1}{(2\pi C_W)^{3/2}} \exp\left[-\frac{(\mathbf{r}-\mathbf{R}_i)^2}{2C_W}\right],$$

$$\tilde{\rho}_i(\mathbf{r}) = \frac{1}{(2\pi \tilde{C}_W)^{3/2}} \exp\left[-\frac{(\mathbf{r}-\mathbf{R}_i)^2}{2\tilde{C}_W}\right], \tag{11}$$

along with the modified width

$$\tilde{C}_W = \frac{1}{2}(1+\theta)^{1/\theta} C_W, \tag{12}$$

which is calculated in this form to incorporate the effect of density-dependent term in Equation (6) (see Section II.B. of Ref. [5] for details).

2.2. Vector-Isovector Interaction Formalism

As the numerical model to simulate nuclear matter in conditions pertaining to neutron star crusts has been outlined above, we now move on to the introduction of a nucleon-nucleon interaction potential based on the RMF $\omega - \rho$ vector interaction.

C. J. Horowitz and J. Piekarewicz [12,13] added isoscalar-isovector coupling terms to the non-linear Lagrangian for nuclear matter, and achieved softening of symmetry energy to control the neutron skin thickness in ^{208}Pb. They introduced a RMF Lagrangian density, where the interaction part has the following terms:

$$\begin{aligned}\mathcal{L}_{int} = & \bar{\psi}\left[g_s\phi - \left(g_v V_\mu + \frac{g_\rho}{2}\boldsymbol{\tau}\cdot\mathbf{b}_\mu + \frac{e}{2}(1+\tau_3)A_\mu\right)\gamma^\mu\right]\psi \\ & -\frac{\kappa}{3!}(g_s\phi)^3 - \frac{\lambda}{4!}(g_s\phi)^4 + \frac{\zeta}{4!}g_v^4(V_\mu V^\mu)^2 + \frac{\tilde{\zeta}}{4!}g_\rho^4(\mathbf{b}_\mu\cdot\mathbf{b}^\mu)^2 \\ & + g_\rho^2 \mathbf{b}_\mu\cdot\mathbf{b}^\mu\left[\Lambda_4 g_s^2\phi^2 + \Lambda_v g_v^2 V_\mu V^\mu\right],\end{aligned} \tag{13}$$

where ψ and $\bar{\psi}$ are the baryon and conjugate baryon fields, respectively. V represents the isoscalar ω meson field, ϕ represents the isoscalar-scalar σ meson field, isovector **b** is the ρ-meson field, and the photon is denoted by A. g_v, g_s, and g_ρ are the respective coupling constants. A similar Lagrangian with a non-linear $\omega - \rho$ interaction term is employed by F. Grill, H. Pais et al. [14] to study the effect of the symmetry energy slope parameter, L, on the profile of the neutron star crust within a Thomas–Fermi formalism.

Note that a softening of the symmetry energy around saturation can also be achieved through the use of density dependent couplings (See Figure 4 and the right panel of Figure 2 of Ref. [15]).

According to the RMF framework, the equation of motion for the ω-meson field takes the form,

$$m_\omega^2 \langle V_0 \rangle - \sum_{B=n,p} g_v \rho_B + \frac{\zeta}{3!} g_v^4 \langle V_0 \rangle^3 + 2 g_\rho^2 \Lambda_v g_v^2 \langle b_0 \rangle^2 \langle V_0 \rangle = 0 , \quad (14)$$

and similarly for the the ρ-meson field:

$$m_\rho^2 \langle b_0 \rangle - \sum_{B=n,p} g_\rho(\rho_p - \rho_n) + \frac{\tilde{\zeta}}{3!} g_\rho^4 \langle b_0 \rangle^3 + 2 g_\rho^2 \Lambda_4 g_s^2 \langle b_0 \rangle \langle \phi_0 \rangle^2 + 2 g_\rho^2 \Lambda_v g_v^2 \langle b_0 \rangle \langle V_0 \rangle^2 = 0 . \quad (15)$$

From Equations (14) and (15), it is clear that the mean ω and ρ meson fields depend on the baryon density ρ_B and isospin density $\rho_I = \rho_p - \rho_n$, respectively (linearly, if we ignore higher-order contributions). Equation (13) shows how the mixed coupling $\omega - \rho$ potential part of the Lagrangian density depends quadratically on the ω and ρ meson fields, from which we can conclude its dependency to be $\sim \rho_B^2 \rho_I^2$. Let us approximate it for our QMD model, motivated by the density-dependent repulsive Skyrme potential as in Equation (6) with a term quadratic in both the ρ_B, and in ρ_I as

$$V_{\omega\rho} = \frac{C_{\omega\rho}}{5\rho_0^4} \sum_{i,k} <\rho_i>^2 <\tilde{\rho}_k>^2 , \quad (16)$$

where $<\rho_i>$ and $<\tilde{\rho}_k>$ are the averaged ρ_B and ρ_I respectively, with the following expressions:

$$<\rho_i> = \sum_{j(\neq i)} \rho_{ij} = \sum_{j(\neq i)} \frac{e^{-(R_i - R_j)^2 / 4 C_W}}{(4\pi C_W)^{3/2}} \quad (17)$$

$$<\tilde{\rho}_k> = \sum_{l(\neq k)} c_{kl} \rho_{kl} = \sum_{l(\neq k)} (1 - 2|\tau_k - \tau_l|) \frac{e^{-(R_k - R_l)^2 / 4 C_W}}{(4\pi C_W)^{3/2}} . \quad (18)$$

The summation needs to be calculated before squaring in Equation (16). A similar calculation has already been made for the repulsive part of the Skyrme potential.

The components of force for the $\omega - \rho$ term can be derived from the potential

$$\begin{aligned}
-f_m^x &= \frac{\partial V_{\omega\rho}}{\partial X_m} \\
&= \frac{2 C_{\omega\rho}}{5 \rho_0^4} \Sigma_{j,k} \left[(<\rho_m> + <\rho_j>) \frac{X_m - X_j}{2L} \rho_{mj} <\tilde{\rho}_k>^2 \right. \\
&\quad \left. + (<\tilde{\rho}_m> + <\tilde{\rho}_j>) <\rho_k>^2 \frac{X_m - X_j}{2L} c_{mj} \rho_{mj} \right] \\
&= \frac{2 C_{\omega\rho}}{5 \rho_0^4} \left[\Sigma_k <\tilde{\rho}_k>^2 \left\{ \Sigma_j \rho_{mj} \frac{dX_{mj}}{2L} (<\rho_m> + <\rho_j>) \right\} \right. \\
&\quad \left. + \Sigma_k <\rho_k>^2 \left\{ \Sigma_j C_{mj} \rho_{mj} \frac{dX_{mj}}{2L} (<\tilde{\rho}_m> + <\tilde{\rho}_j>) \right\} \right]
\end{aligned} \quad (19)$$

51

where X_m and X_j are the x-coordinates of the centers of the positions of m-th and j-the particles, respectively.

2.3. Modeling of Infinite Systems: Achieving the Ground State Configuration

Different methods can be employed to achieve the ground state configuration of nuclear matter for a given density or temperature. Peilert et al. [4] calculated E/A values for finite nuclei, and subsequently studied infinite nuclear matter using a version of the QMD model. They found that nuclear matter simulated at temperatures near $T = 0$ MeV showed clustering among nucleons at sub-saturation densities. Later, Maruyama et al. [5] employed QMD to study the dynamical evolution of nuclear matter into pasta phases. In this work, we follow the method employed by Maruyama et al., obtaining the energy-minimum configuration of nuclear matter by distributing nucleons randomly in phase space, and then cooling down the system to achieve the minimum energy state of the system. This allows for arbitrary nuclear shapes and incorporates thermal fluctuations, giving an insight into the formation process of such structures.

To achieve equilibrium in the nuclear matter system, we use the following equations of motion along with damping factors ξ_R and ξ_P:

$$\dot{\mathbf{R}}_i = \frac{\partial \mathcal{H}}{\partial \mathbf{P}_i} - \xi_R \frac{\partial \mathcal{H}}{\partial \mathbf{R}_i},$$
$$\dot{\mathbf{P}}_i = -\frac{\partial \mathcal{H}}{\partial \mathbf{R}_i} - \xi_P \frac{\partial \mathcal{H}}{\partial \mathbf{P}_i}, \tag{20}$$

where $\mathcal{H}$ is given by Equation (3) and the factors ξ_R and ξ_P are adjusted according to the relaxation time scale, with a fixed value of either 0 or -0.1.

The system is cooled from an initial temperature maintained by the Nosé–Hoover thermostat. The thermostat introduces additional coordinates and velocities in the Hamiltonian of the system in order to mimic a thermal bath in contact with the system. The extended Hamiltonian $\mathcal{H}_{Nose}$ appears as

$$\mathcal{H}_{Nose} = \sum_{i=1}^{N} \frac{\mathbf{P}_i^2}{2m_i} + \mathcal{U}(\{\mathbf{R}_i\}, \{\mathbf{P}_{ij}\}) + \frac{sp_s^2}{2Q} + g\frac{\ln s}{\beta}$$
$$= \mathcal{H} + \frac{sp_s^2}{2Q} + g\frac{\ln s}{\beta}, \tag{21}$$

where s is the additional dynamical variable for time scaling, p_s is the momentum conjugate to s, $\mathcal{U}(\{\mathbf{R}_i\}, \{\mathbf{P}_i\}) = \mathcal{H} - K$ is the potential which depends on both positions and momenta, Q is the thermal inertial parameter corresponding to a coupling constant between the system and thermostat, g is a parameter to be determined as $3N$ by a condition for generating the canonical ensemble in the classical molecular dynamics simulations, and β is defined as $\beta \equiv 1/(k_B T_{set})$ [16,17]. The energy of the nuclear matter system is not conserved, but $\mathcal{H}_{Nose}$ is. The most important variables here are $\beta = 1/k_B T_{set}$, where T_{set} is the desired input temperature, and $Q \approx 10^8$ MeV (fm/c)^2. More details can be found in Refs. [17,18] and sources therein.

At sub-saturation densities, local minima may take place around the actual global energy-minimum value of the ground state that the damping coefficients lead to if not chosen carefully. The simulation results should be checked to avoid local energy minima by repeating the cooling procedure.

3. Results

3.1. Simulation Procedure

Using the theoretical framework established in the previous chapters, the QMD simulation of a system of neutrons and protons is carried out. The final temperature after cooling down from a finite temperature was set to 0, so as to imitate the conditions in a neutron star's inner crust.

A cubic box confines the nucleons. The size of the box is determined by the number of nucleons N and average density ρ_{av}. Periodic boundary conditions are imposed and the motion of nucleons is imitated across 26 cells surrounding the central primitive cell. The value of N is set to 1024, such that for homogeneous symmetric nuclear matter the number for protons/neutrons with spin up and protons/neutrons with spin down is equal (proton fraction Y_p = 0.5 with 512 particles each of protons and neutrons). Hence, there is no magnetic polarization. Electrons are treated as a uniform background gas that makes the system charge neutral.

The nucleons are initially distributed randomly in phase space. The system is brought to thermal equilibrium at T = 20 MeV for about 1000 fm/c. The system, initially kept at a constant temperature by the Nosé–Hoover thermostat, is slowly cooled down in accordance with the equations of motion (Equation (20)), until the temperature is 0. To attain the ground state configuration, the simulation requires about 1–2 days of computation time to reach 10^4 fm/c when carried out on the Goethe-HLR CPU cluster at Goethe-University Frankfurt. The computer code for the simulations in this project was first used for QMD calculations in Ref. [8].

The set of values for the parameters used in interaction potentials constituting the Hamiltonian Equation (3) is given in Table 1. Additionally, the set of values for the coefficient $C_{\omega\rho}$ of $V_{\omega\rho}$ in Equation (16) are listed in Table 2.

Table 2. Optimized values for coefficient of $V_{\omega\rho}$.

Set	$C_{\omega\rho}$ (MeV)
I	0.02
II	0.01
III	0.005
IV	−0.01
V	−0.02

3.2. Finite Nuclei

We first calculate the binding energies of ground states of a number of finite nuclei and their isotopes. Five different values of the coefficient $C_{\omega\rho}$ are tested. All five reproduce the trend of binding energies per nucleon of various nuclear isotopes, as can be seen in Figure 1. Individual simulated energy values (E_{calc}) deviate from the experimental (E_{exp}) counterparts [19] by less than 10% in all cases. Considering a reasonable expectation of accuracy within the QMD model employed in this paper, there is a minor spread in the calculated values. It is clear that varying $C_{\omega\rho}$ does not have a significant impact on the binding energies per nucleon of finite nuclei, which can be explained by the non-dependence of symmetry energy in a finite nucleus to its slope L, and the fact that it rather depends on other parameters: the symmetry energy coefficient at saturation density, ratio of the surface symmetry coefficient to the volume symmetry coefficient, surface stiffness and obviously the mass number of the nucleus (see Refs. [20,21] and sources therein.) The nuclei chosen are heavy with Z larger than 40. Good results for lighter nuclei are not expected, based on the results in Figure 4 of Ref. [5]. For each isotope family, three nuclei are selected with Y_P ranging from 0.3 to 0.5 to analyze the effect of isospin dependent interactions.

There is an anomaly in the form of binding energies per nucleon being about 0.65 MeV too deep compared with experimental values for all nuclei. Given the realistically achievable accuracy within a molecular dynamics approach, this deviation is acceptable. Nevertheless, the model reproduces the overall trends of the binding energies of various nuclei reasonably well, for all values of $C_{\omega\rho}$.

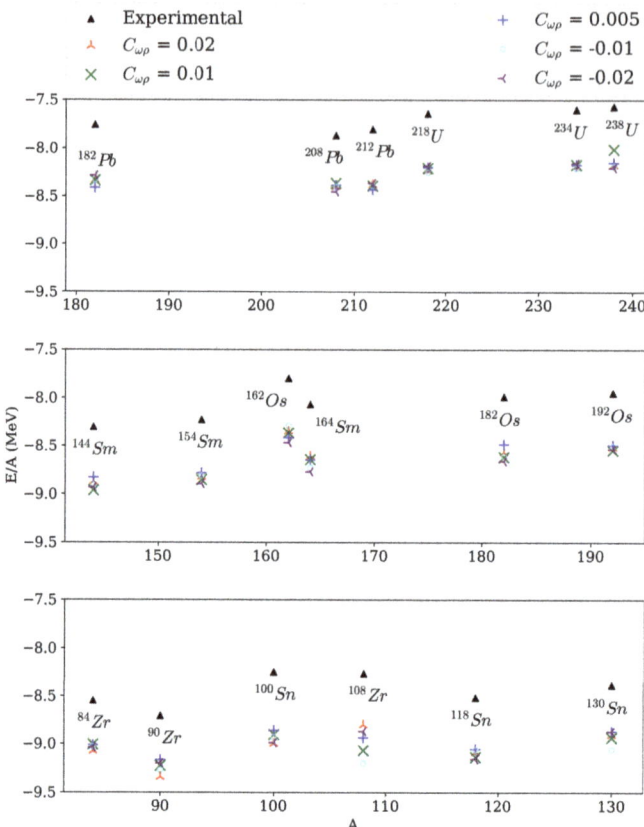

Figure 1. Binding energies per nucleon for three nuclear isotopes each of Zr, Sn, Sm, Os, Pb, and U obtained from simulation for five different parameter sets listed above the image. The experimental values are taken from AME2016 [19].

3.3. Pure Neutron Matter

An important final test of the model is the examination of the behavior of a pure neutron gas at nuclear and sub-nuclear densities. The energy per nucleon $(E/N)_n$ of pure neutron matter affects the densities at which NSM becomes uniform.

For this case, the same system is adapted to simulate nuclear matter with $Y_P = 0.0$, i.e., 1024 neutrons in the primitive cell without protons. The results for pure neutron matter simulations for nuclear and sub-nuclear densities are shown in Figure 2. The density dependence of neutron matter (or the neutron matter EoS) is crucial, as E/N is an input in the calculation of the symmetry energy.

In Figure 2, the neutron matter EoSs for different $C_{\omega\rho}$ from the QMD model can be compared with two other non-linear RMF models (IUFSU [23] and FSUgold [24]), which also include the $\omega - \rho$ coupling. The shaded area shows the results from Chiral EFT [22], providing robust theoretical constraints for neutron-matter equations of state. For $C_{\omega\rho} = 0.02$, the EoS indicates a bit too much repulsion around the nuclear saturation density. For all values of $C_{\omega\rho}$ at low densities, binding is weaker than expected. In spite of these issues, all parameter sets with different strengths of the coefficient $C_{\omega\rho}$ appear to be in good qualitative agreement with the constraints.

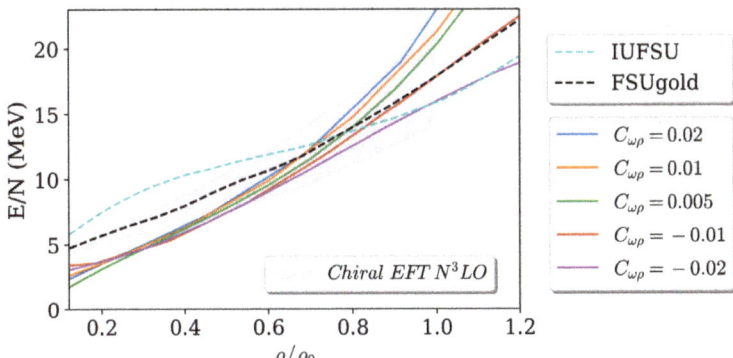

Figure 2. Energy per nucleon of pure neutron matter as a function of density for 5 different parameter sets. The shaded area corresponds to Chiral EFT constraints as provided in Ref. [22]. The RMF models FSUgold and IUFSU, which also include the $\omega - \rho$ interaction, are shown for comparison. Note that here the saturation density $\rho_0 = 0.165\, fm^{-3}$.

The slope of the symmetry energy L and the pure neutron matter EoS are related, shown by Equation (19) in Ref. [11]:

$$L = 3\rho_0 \frac{\partial}{\partial \rho_n}\left(\frac{\varepsilon_n}{\rho_n}\right)_{\rho_0}, \tag{22}$$

where the energy density of pure neutron matter is given by ε_n. The slope of the neutron-matter EoS decreases as $C_{\omega\rho}$ is lowered, which is consistent with the trend of the L values in Table 3. Therefore, varying the slope (and by extension the strength of the $\omega - \rho$ interaction) has a direct impact on the densities at which neutrons drip out of nuclei, and consequently on the nuclear pasta phases in NSM.

Table 3. Symmetry energies and corresponding slope values (parabolic approximation).

Set	$C_{\omega\rho}$ (MeV)	$S(\rho)$	L
I	0.02	37.40	135.26
II	0.01	35.63	102.71
III	0.005	34.72	100.41
IV	−0.01	32.23	66.38
III	−0.02	30.52	48.32

3.4. Determination of Symmetry Energy and Slope Parameter

In a free fermion gas of nucleons, the expression for energy per particle is

$$\frac{E}{A} \approx \frac{E}{A}(\beta_{asy} = 0) + E_{sym}\beta_{asy}^2 + \cdots, \tag{23}$$

where β_{asy} defined as

$$\beta_{asy} = \frac{n_n - n_p}{n_n + n_p} = \frac{N - Z}{A}, \tag{24}$$

or in terms of proton and neutron densities ρ_p and ρ_n,

$$\beta_{asy} = \frac{\rho_n - \rho_p}{\rho}. \tag{25}$$

For an initial determination of E_{sym} and L at saturation density, a parabolic approximation is applied, such that only the lowest-order non-vanishing term in β_{asy} is retained. Rewriting the equation with the approximation gives

$$\frac{E}{A} = \frac{E}{A}(\beta_{asy} = 0) + S(\rho)\beta_{asy}^2 , \qquad (26)$$

where $\frac{E}{A}(\beta_{asy} = 0) = (E/A)_0$ is the energy per nucleon of symmetric matter, and $S(\rho)$ is the nuclear symmetry energy. Keeping the Coulomb interaction switched off, the simulation is run for many values of Y_P at ρ_0 for all $C_{\omega\rho}$ in Table 2. The values for E/A are fitted in Equation (26), and $S(\rho_0)$ is obtained as a fit parameter from the plot of energies per nucleon shown in Figure 3.

The slope parameter L quantifies the density dependence of the symmetry energy, which can be used to practically calculate the possible L values as [25]

$$L = 3\rho_0 \frac{S(1.1\rho_0) - S(0.9\rho_0)}{1.1\rho_0 - 0.9\rho_0} . \qquad (27)$$

Here, $S(1.1\rho_0)$ and $S(0.9\rho_0)$ are determined with the same procedure as for $S(\rho_0)$ described above. The obtained values for $S(\rho)$ and L are listed in Table 3.

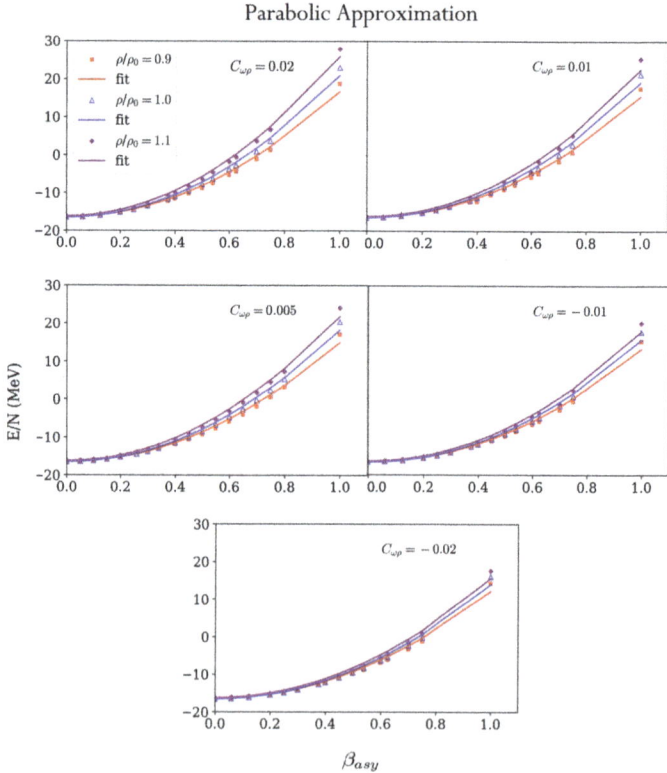

Figure 3. Fit of energy per nucleon vs. neutron excess using Equation (26) for different parameter sets (parabolic approximation). β_{asym} is the neutron excess with 1.0 being pure neutron matter, and 0.0 being symmetric nuclear matter. A list of the corresponding slope values is given in Table 3.

The calculations discussed above can be improved. Chen et al. [26] suggested that the description of the nuclear matter EoS can be made better by improving on the parabolic approximation. Through a systematic study of isospin dependence of saturation properties of asymmetric nuclear matter, it was concluded that the parabolic approximation produces good results for $\beta_{asy}^2 \leq 0.1$, but for higher asymmetries the quartic term should also be included. In this work, where higher isospin asymmetries are simulated, the fit using the function in Equation (26), as can be seen in Figure 3, is not satisfactory. The slope values for $\beta_{asy}^2 > 0.1$ can therefore be modified by adding a quartic term to Equation (26), which now expands to

$$\frac{E}{A} = \frac{E}{A}(\beta_{asy} = 0) + S_{(2)}(\rho)\beta_{asy}^2 + S_{(4)}(\rho)\beta_{asy}^4, \quad (28)$$

where $S_{(2)}(\rho) = S(\rho)$ and $S_{(4)}(\rho)$ is the fourth order term of nuclear symmetry energy. The binding energies for different β_{asy} values are fitted to the Equation (28) and $S_{(2)}(\rho) = S(\rho)$ and $S_{(4)}(\rho)$ are obtained as fitting parameters. A better fit for energy per nucleon is achieved, as shown in Figure 4. The updated values for symmetry energy and slope are listed in Table 4. Figure 5 shows the density dependence of symmetry energy for 5 different parameter sets. The difference between results obtained using different parameter sets increases with density due to the quadratic dependence of $V_{\omega-\rho}$ on baryon and isospin densities, being very small for densities below $0.5\rho_0$.

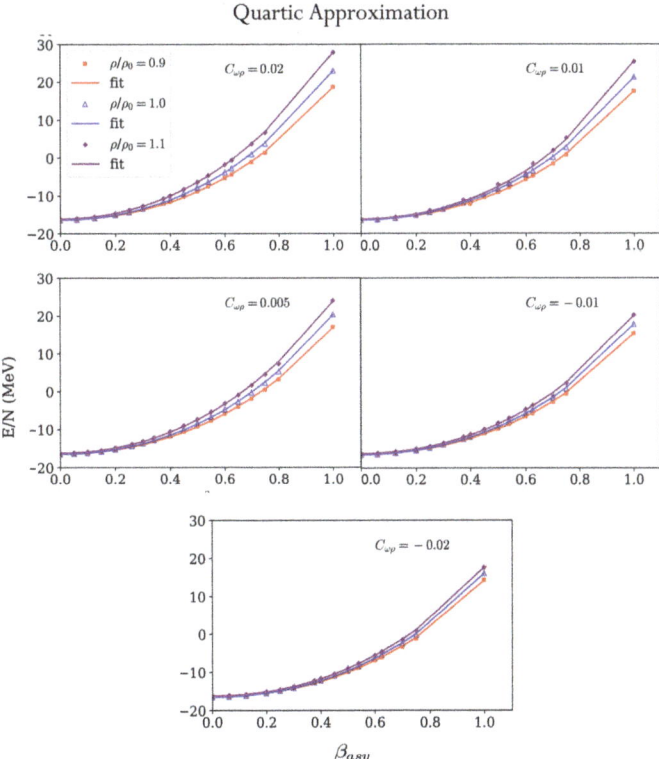

Figure 4. Fit of energy per nucleon vs. neutron excess using Equation (28) (quartic approximation) for different parameter sets. β_{asym} is the neutron excess with 1 being pure neutron matter and 0 being symmetric nuclear matter. A list of the corresponding slope values is given in Table 4. This approximation results in better fitting compared to the parabolic approximation in Figure 3.

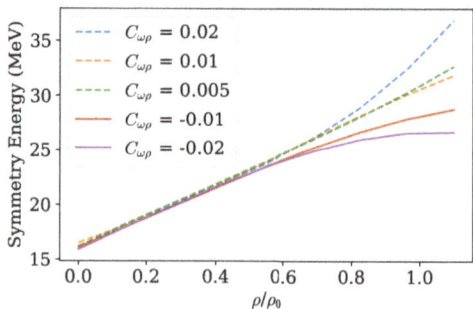

Figure 5. Density dependence of symmetry energy for 5 different parameter sets is shown. The $\omega - \rho$ term determines the coupling of two vector fields, which are sub-leading at low densities, where the attraction represented by the scalar fields dominates. As the density increases beyond $\rho_B = 0.5$ fm^{-3}, the $\omega - \rho$ effects can clearly be seen in this figure.

Comparing Tables 3 and 4, the effect of adding a fourth order term is a decrease in the symmetry energy in all cases. However, the decrease in L is not straightforward and is only seen for Sets II, III, and IV in the quartic case (as compared to the parabolically approximated case). It is clear in Table 4 that, with a decrease in $C_{\omega\rho}$, L can be lowered to optimal values for Sets II, III, VI, and V. However, the L for Set III was expected to be lower than that for Set II, in agreement with the trend of decreasing values going from Sets I to V. It appears that this value is indeed much closer to previous results in Ref. [8], where a symmetry energy of $\approx$29 MeV is associated with an $L \approx 92$ MeV. This can be interpreted in terms of the strength of the $\omega - \rho$ interaction energy being too low for Set III, which causes the prediction to agree closely with previous results that excluded it. Note that the values of symmetry energy and slope for set I are high when compared with experimental values [27–29].

Table 4. Symmetry energies and corresponding slope values (quartic approximation).

Set	$C_{\omega\rho}$ (MeV)	$S_{(2)}(\rho)$	$S_{(4)}(\rho)$	$L_{(2)}$	$L_{(4)}$
I	0.02	32.81	6.56	135.52	−0.38
II	0.01	30.93	6.72	71.88	44.11
III	0.005	30.18	6.59	99.52	1.30
IV	−0.01	27.56	6.68	61.32	7.24
V	−0.02	25.88	6.63	49.32	−1.43

3.5. Nucleon Distributions

Nuclear clustering cannot only occur in NSM, but also for more isospin symmetric matter as it undergoes the liquid-gas transition. Such matter can be studied, for example, in high energy nuclear collisions. In order to bridge the gap between such studies and NSM, the proper isospin dependence of the existence and occurrence of the liquid-gas phase separation needs to be understood. In the following we will show how our model can be used to study the occurrence of clustering of nuclear matter for nuclear matter with proton fractions between $0.3 < Y_e < 0.5$.

The nucleon distribution of nuclear matter at $T = 0$ can be visualized in the simulation box. At every grid point, the density contribution of each nucleon is added to produce a density map. Since the Coulomb interaction is included, clusterization of nucleons in a lattice-like structure is clearly seen in the system.

In Figures 6–8, clusterization is seen in the system at $T = 0$. At every grid point in the simulation box, the density contribution of each nucleon gaussian wave packet is added to calculate the density map. In Figure 7, an increased $C_{\omega\rho}$ decreases the density of clusters, so they seem to break up into smaller clusters of lower densities. This implies that neutrons will drip out at lower densities for $C_{\omega\rho} = 0.02$ than for 0.01. As the density is increased 3-folds (shown in Figure 8), the density map morphs into a more interesting structure.

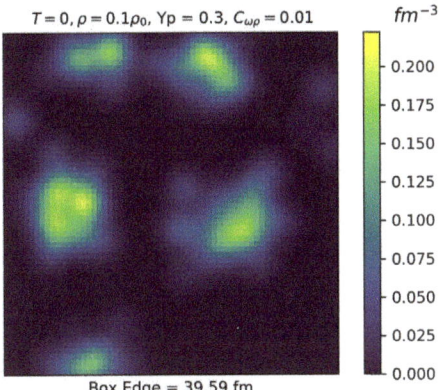

Figure 6. Density map of simulation box with $C_{\omega\rho} = 0.01$.

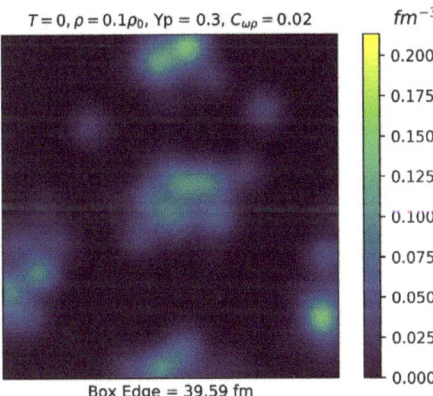

Figure 7. Density map of simulation box with $C_{\omega\rho} = 0.02$.

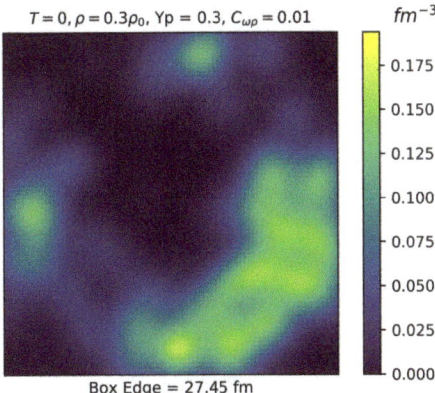

Figure 8. Density map of simulation box with $C_{\omega\rho} = 0.01$, but at three times the density of Figure 6.

3.6. Transition from Clustered to Uniform Nuclear Matter

Long-range correlations between nucleons can determine the density at which a liquid-gas phase transition occurs. To this end, a useful tool to analyse the spatial distribution of nucleons is the two-point density fluctuation correlation function $\tilde{\zeta}_{NN}$ for nucleon density fluctuations defined as [8]:

$$\tilde{\zeta}_{NN} = \langle \Delta_N(\mathbf{x})\Delta_N(\mathbf{x}+\mathbf{r}) \rangle. \qquad (29)$$

Here, the average denoted by $\langle \ldots \rangle$ is taken over the position x and in the direction of r. The fluctuation $\Delta_N(\mathbf{x})$ of the nucleon density field $\rho_N(\mathbf{x})$ is defined as

$$\Delta_N = \frac{\rho_N(\mathbf{x}) - \rho_{av}}{\rho_{av}}, \qquad (30)$$

where ρ_{av} is the average density of the simulation box. Two-point correlation functions for $Y_P = 0.3$ and 0.5 (for $C_{\omega\rho} = 0.01$, 0.005, and -0.01) are plotted in Figure 9. In all cases, an increase in density decreases the amplitude of $\tilde{\zeta}_{NN}$, indicating a smoother nucleon density distribution. Correlations are highest near the origin as the nucleons have the strongest influence on their nearest neighbors. This also indicates clusterization at low densities. A negative value of $\tilde{\zeta}_{NN}$ at a given r implies anti-clustering or regularity, which means the point at that r has a density lower than the average density of the simulation box.

All curves at densities higher than $0.8\rho_0$ are almost flat-lined at $\tilde{\zeta}_{NN} = 0$, indicating uniform matter above $0.8\rho_0$. Clear trends in the variation of cluster size and densities with $C_{\omega\rho}$ and L could not be deduced.

When nuclear matter is uniform, the two-point correlation vanishes. At a certain average density, the long-range correlations suddenly disappear (instead of gradually), indicating the density turning to uniform matter through a first-order phase transition, which corresponds to the liquid-gas transition. Similar conclusions were obtained in previous studies [6,8]. For all cases of $C_{\omega\rho}$ in Figure 9, more data is needed to find out the point of transition although the transition from asymmetric to uniform matter seems to occur between ρ/ρ_0=0.6 and 0.8.

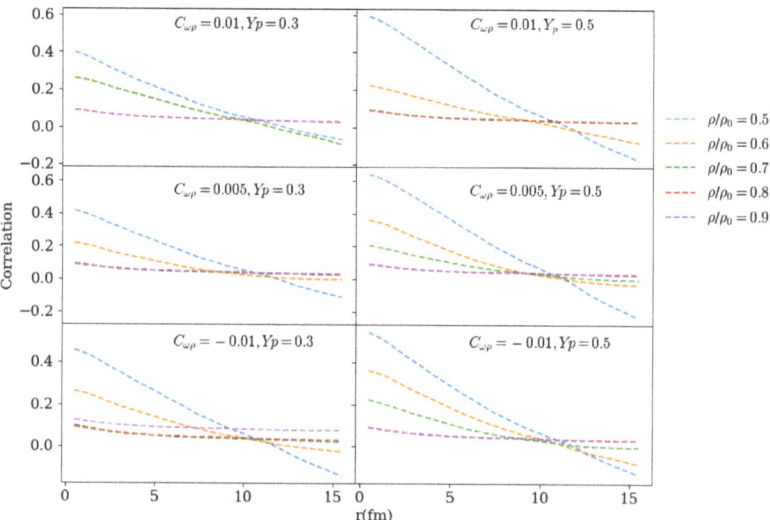

Figure 9. Two-point correlation function $\tilde{\zeta}_{NN}$ of nucleon density fluctuations for $C_{\omega\rho} = 0.01$, $C_{\omega\rho} = 0.005$ and $C_{\omega\rho} = -0.01$ and proton fractions $Y_P = 0.3$ (**left**) and 0.5 (**right**).

Note that it has been shown using relativistic mean field models that effects on the slope of the symmetry energy induced by an additional $\omega - \rho$ interaction affect the crust-core transition: a smaller slope reproduces a larger onset [30–32]. Similar results were found within the Brueckner–Hartree–Fock approach [33] and in a detailed study involving different approaches [34].

4. Conclusions

The conditions in the inner crust of neutron stars have been simulated within a Quantum Molecular Dynamics (QMD) approach with periodic boundary conditions to imitate infinite uniform nuclear matter. The nucleon-nucleon interaction Hamiltonian for QMD was successively developed in earlier works by Aichelin and Stöcker [1], Peilert et al. [4], and Watanabe et al. [6] and consists of effective interaction potentials that take into account the Pauli principle, the Yukawa interaction, Coulomb interaction, and density dependent terms. In the current project, an isospin-dependent potential term to take into account the repulsion from interaction of omega and rho mesons has been implemented in the QMD Hamiltonian. The idea to include a mesonic self-interaction in nuclear matter calculations is not new. It was first introduced in an attempt to reduce the neutron-skin thickness of ^{208}Pb [12]. In a work proposing the IUFSU effective interaction [23], it was shown that increasing the $\omega - \rho$ coupling constant softens the EoS of nuclear matter at around saturation density and that the density dependence of symmetry energy is highly sensitive to it. This was done within a model based on a relativistic effective field theory. Later, it was shown to improve the radius and tidal deformability of neutron stars, leading RMF models to be in better agreement with observations [35].

The new $\omega - \rho$-inspired term in the QMD model Hamiltonian in this work is inspired from the density dependent repulsive Skyrme force and depends on the baryon density and isospin density of asymmetric nuclear matter. A few values for the coefficient of the $\omega - \rho$ potential were tested, which resulted in very different behavior of the symmetry energy and its slope L. First, the values and trends of binding energies per nucleon of ground states of several nuclear isotopes were reasonably reproduced compared with experimental values. Simulations for pure neutron matter resulted in a density dependent behavior that is largely similar for all $C_{\omega\rho}$ (coefficient of $\omega - \rho$ meson field interaction) below nuclear saturation density and is in good qualitative agreement within constraints from Chiral EFT. Around ρ_0, we can see a large divergence in the trend of E/N and a decrease in maximum energies as $C_{\omega\rho}$ is lowered. The numerical data obtained by simulating asymmetric nuclear matter was fitted to the energy per nucleon expanded as Taylor series, keeping both the lowest and the second highest order term. The approximation in the second-order term, also called the parabolic approximation, gave a trend of symmetry energies that decreases as the coefficient of the $\omega - \rho$ potential also decreases. The corresponding slopes L exhibit a similar trend, although four of five tested parameter sets produced L values within established constraints [27–29]. The higher-order approximation, which is necessary to obtain a better fitting of the data to energy per nucleon, further reduced the symmetry energies for the same coefficient values whereas there are more variations in the corresponding L values amidst a general decrease. This behavior requires the inclusion of data for higher and in-between values of proton fractions to further improve fitting and obtain better symmetry energy and slope values.

The dependence of clusterization in the system, due to the nuclear liquid-gas transition, on the isospin properties was also explored by calculating two-point correlation functions. Although a detailed study of the structure of inhomogenous phases could not be accomplished due to inaccurate Coulomb energies, a visualization of the simulated system shows interesting pasta-like shapes. The transition from inhomogeneous to uniform matter is evaluated using a two-point density fluctuation correlation function and points to a first-order phase transition. Only a small change was observed in the effect of varying L on the transition density, which cannot be deemed as significant. The properties of the mixed phase with the newly integrated $\omega - \rho$-inspired interaction can be studied in a similar fashion to a work conducted earlier in Ref. [36] with the aim of giving a better range for the critical end-point of the liquid-gas phase transition in dense nuclear matter.

The analysis of two-point density fluctuation correlations also reveals the size of clumps of nucleons in the system. If the evolution of clump sizes is tracked with respect to time, one can deduce where density fluctuations are amplified enough to have matter separate into domains of high and low densities forming a coexisting phase. The growth of instabilities or fluctuations point to a region of negative compressibility in the phase diagram of nuclear matter, where at a constant temperature an increase of density results in a decrease in pressure [37]. This region is called the spinodal region. Therefore, further study is needed to shed more light on the nuclear phase diagram. Steinheimer et al. [38,39] have conducted detailed analyses on experimental signals of the expected phase transition at large baryon densities and identifying spinodal clumping in high energy nuclear collisions. Studies of temperature, pressure, and time evolution of density fluctuations in nuclear matter are outside the scope of this project but is an interesting prospect for the future.

QMD has an advantage over other types of models in the possibility to track the trajectory of nucleons and study the non-averaged properties of clusters in nuclear matter at inner crust densities, unlike mean-field approaches. Implementing the $\omega - \rho$ interaction in a QMD model is an important step in efforts to constrain the density dependence of symmetry energy and at the same time observe effects of this interaction on the structure of nuclear matter within a dynamical framework. Pressure can be calculated using the simulated data to obtain the full equation of state, and subsequently a M-R curve for the model used in this work. We also aim to find a way to reconcile the model with the causality of sound speed, which is ensured in Relativistic Mean Field models but can be problematic in microscopic simulations. An exciting prospect is finite temperature calculations to check for phases of hot nuclear matter at sub-saturation densities, which is relevant for proto-neutron stars.

Author Contributions: Formal analysis, P.M., R.N. and J.S.; Investigation, R.N.; Supervision, R.N., R.d.O.G. and J.S.; Validation, V.D.; Visualization, P.M.; Writing—original draft, P.M.; Writing—review & editing, R.N., R.d.O.G. and V.D. All authors have read and agreed to the published version of the manuscript.

Funding: V. Dexheimer acknowledges support from the National Science Foundation under grant PHY-1748621 and PHAROS (COST Action CA16214). Centre for Scientific Computing (CSC) at the J. W. Goethe-University provided computational support for this project. P. Mehta acknowledges support from the Rolf and Edith Sandvoss-Scholarship awarded by the Walter Greiner Gesellschaft, Frankfurt a.M.

Institutional Review Board Statement: Not applicable.

Informed Consent Statement: Not applicable.

Data Availability Statement: Not applicable.

Acknowledgments: P. Mehta would like to thank Horst Stoecker for guidance and enriching discussions. This manuscript is dedicated to the memory of late Stefan Schramm.

Conflicts of Interest: The authors declare no conflict of interest.

References

1. Aichelin, J.; Stöcker, H. Quantum molecular dynamics—A novel approach to N-body correlations in heavy ion collisions. *Phys. Lett. B* **1986**, *176*, 14–19. [CrossRef]
2. Peilert, G.; Stocker, H.; Greiner, W. Physics of high-energy heavy-ion collisions. *Rep. Prog. Phys.* **1994**, *57*, 533–602. [CrossRef]
3. Bohnet, A.; Aichelin, J.; Pochodzalla, J.; Trautmann, W.; Peilert, G.; Stöcker, H.; Greiner, W. Multifragmentation near the threshold. *Phys. Rev. C* **1991**, *44*, 2111–2129. [CrossRef] [PubMed]
4. Peilert, G.; Randrup, J.; Stöcker, H.; Greiner, W. Clustering in nuclear matter at subsaturation densities. *Phys. Lett. B* **1991**, *260*, 271–277. [CrossRef]
5. Maruyama, T.; Niita, K.; Oyamatsu, K.; Maruyama, T.; Chiba, S.; Iwamoto, A. Quantum molecular dynamics approach to the nuclear matter below the saturation density. *Phys. Rev. C* **1998**, *57*, 655–665. [CrossRef]
6. Watanabe, G.; Sato, K.; Yasuoka, K.; Ebisuzaki, T. Structure of cold nuclear matter at subnuclear densities by quantum molecular dynamics. *Phys. Rev. C* **2003**, *68*, 035806. [CrossRef]

7. Sagert, I.; Fann, G.I.; Fattoyev, F.J.; Postnikov, S.; Horowitz, C.J. Quantum simulations of nuclei and nuclear pasta with the multiresolution adaptive numerical environment for scientific simulations. *Phys. Rev. C* **2016**, *93*, 055801. [CrossRef]
8. Nandi, R.; Schramm, S. Low density nuclear matter with quantum molecular dynamics: The role of the symmetry energy. *Phys. Rev. C* **2016**, *94*, 025806. [CrossRef]
9. Aichelin, J. "Quantum" molecular dynamics—A dynamical microscopic n-body approach to investigate fragment formation and the nuclear equation of state in heavy ion collisions. *Phys. Rep.* **1991**, *202*, 233–360. [CrossRef]
10. Maruyama, T.; Watanabe, G.; Chiba, S. Molecular dynamics for dense matter. *Prog. Theor. Exp. Phys.* **2012**, *2012*, 01A201. [CrossRef]
11. Sonoda, H.; Watanabe, G.; Sato, K.; Yasuoka, K.; Ebisuzaki, T. Phase diagram of nuclear "pasta" and its uncertainties in supernova cores. *Phys. Rev. C* **2008**, *77*, 035806. [CrossRef]
12. Horowitz, C.J.; Piekarewicz, J. Neutron star structure and the neutron radius of 208Pb. *Phys. Rev. Lett.* **2001**, *86*, 5647–5650. [CrossRef]
13. Carriere, J.; Horowitz, C.J.; Piekarewicz, J. Low mass neutron stars and the equation of state of dense matter. *Astrophys. J.* **2003**, *593*, 463–471. [CrossRef]
14. Grill, F.; Pais, H.; Providência, C.; Vidaña, I.; Avancini, S.S. Equation of state and thickness of the inner crust of neutron stars. *Phys. Rev. C* **2014**, *90*, 045803. [CrossRef]
15. Typel, S. Relativistic Mean-Field Models with Different Parametrizations of Density Dependent Couplings. *Particles* **2018**, *1*, 3–22. [CrossRef]
16. García, M.Á.P. The Nosé-Hoover thermostat in molecular dynamics for nuclear matter. *J. Math. Chem.* **2006**, *40*, 63–69. [CrossRef]
17. Watanabe, G.; Sato, K.; Yasuoka, K.; Ebisuzaki, T. Phases of hot nuclear matter at subnuclear densities. *Phys. Rev. C* **2004**, *69*, 055805. [CrossRef]
18. Nandi, R.; Schramm, S. Transport Properties of the Nuclear Pasta Phase with Quantum Molecular Dynamics. *Astrophys. J.* **2018**, *852*, 135. [CrossRef]
19. Wang, M.; Audi, G.; Kondev, F.G.; Huang, W.J.; Naimi, S.; Xu, X. The AME2016 atomic mass evaluation (II). Tables, graphs and references. *Chin. Phys. C* **2017**, *41*, 030003. [CrossRef]
20. Centelles, M.; Roca-Maza, X.; Viñas, X.; Warda, M. Nuclear Symmetry Energy Probed by Neutron Skin Thickness of Nuclei. *Phys. Rev. Lett.* **2009**, *102*, 122502. [CrossRef]
21. Brown, B.A. Constraints on the Skyrme Equations of State from Properties of Doubly Magic Nuclei. *Phys. Rev. Lett.* **2013**, *111*, 232502. [CrossRef]
22. Krüger, T.; Tews, I.; Hebeler, K.; Schwenk, A. Neutron matter from chiral effective field theory interactions. *Phys. Rev. C* **2013**, *88*, 025802. [CrossRef]
23. Fattoyev, F.J.; Horowitz, C.J.; Piekarewicz, J.; Shen, G. Relativistic effective interaction for nuclei, giant resonances, and neutron stars. *Phys. Rev. C* **2010**, *82*, 055803. [CrossRef]
24. Todd-Rutel, B.G.; Piekarewicz, J. Neutron-rich nuclei and neutron stars: A new accurately calibrated interaction for the study of neutron-rich matter. *Phys. Rev. Lett.* **2005**, *95*, 122501. [CrossRef]
25. Baldo, M.; Burgio, G.F. The nuclear symmetry energy. *Prog. Part. Nucl. Phys.* **2016**, *91*, 203–258. [CrossRef]
26. Chen, L.W.; Cai, B.J.; Ko, C.M.; Li, B.A.; Shen, C.; Xu, J. Higher-order effects on the incompressibility of isospin asymmetric nuclear matter. *Phys. Rev. C* **2009**, *80*, 014322. [CrossRef]
27. Li, B.A.; Krastev, P.G.; Wen, D.H.; Zhang, N.B. Towards Understanding Astrophysical Effects of Nuclear Symmetry Energy. *Eur. Phys. J. A* **2019**, *55*, 117. [CrossRef]
28. Reed, B.T.; Fattoyev, F.J.; Horowitz, C.J.; Piekarewicz, J. Implications of PREX-2 on the Equation of State of Neutron-Rich Matter. *Phys. Rev. Lett.* **2021**, *126*, 172503. [CrossRef]
29. Reinhard, P.G.; Roca-Maza, X.; Nazarewicz, W. Information Content of the Parity-Violating Asymmetry in ^{208}Pb. *Phys. Rev. Lett.* **2021**, *127*, 232501. [CrossRef]
30. Xia, C.J.; Maruyama, T.; Yasutake, N.; Tatsumi, T.; Zhang, Y.X. Nuclear pasta structures and symmetry energy. *Phys. Rev. C* **2021**, *103*, 055812. [CrossRef]
31. Ducoin, C.; Margueron, J.; Providencia, C.; Vidana, I. Core-crust transition in neutron stars: Predictivity of density developments. *Phys. Rev. C* **2011**, *83*, 045810. [CrossRef]
32. Pais, H.; Providência, C. Vlasov formalism for extended relativistic mean field models: The crust-core transition and the stellar matter equation of state. *Phys. Rev. C* **2016**, *94*, 015808. [CrossRef]
33. Vidana, I.; Providencia, C.; Polls, A.; Rios, A. Density dependence of the nuclear symmetry energy: A Microscopic perspective. *Phys. Rev. C* **2009**, *80*, 045806. [CrossRef]
34. Pais, H.; Sulaksono, A.; Agrawal, B.K.; Providência, C. Correlation of the neutron star crust-core properties with the slope of the symmetry energy and the lead skin thickness. *Phys. Rev. C* **2016**, *93*, 045802. [CrossRef]
35. Dexheimer, V.; Gomes, R.d.O.; Schramm, S.; Pais, H. What do we learn about vector interactions from GW170817? *J. Phys. G Nucl. Part. Phys.* **2018**, *46*, 034002. [CrossRef]
36. Nandi, R.; Schramm, S. Effect of the Coulomb interaction on the liquid-gas phase transition of nuclear matter. *Phys. Rev. C* **2017**, *95*, 065801. [CrossRef]

37. Borderie, B.; Frankland, J. Liquid–Gas phase transition in nuclei. *Prog. Part. Nucl. Phys.* **2019**, *105*, 82–138. [CrossRef]
38. Steinheimer, J.; Pang, L.; Zhou, K.; Koch, V.; Randrup, J.; Stoecker, H. A machine learning study to identify spinodal clumping in high energy nuclear collisions. *J. High Energy Phys.* **2019**, *2019*, 122. [CrossRef]
39. Steinheimer, J.; Randrup, J.; Koch, V. Non-equilibrium phase transition in relativistic nuclear collisions: Importance of the equation of state. *Phys. Rev. C* **2014**, *89*, 034901. [CrossRef]

Article

The Nuclear Matter Density Functional under the Nucleonic Hypothesis

Hoa Dinh Thi, Chiranjib Mondal and Francesca Gulminelli *

Laboratoire de Physique Corpusculaire, CNRS, ENSICAEN, UMR6534, Université de Caen Normandie, CEDEX, 14050 Caen, France; dinh@lpccaen.in2p3.fr (H.D.T.); mondal@lpccaen.in2p3.fr (C.M.)
* Correspondence: gulminelli@lpccaen.in2p3.fr

Abstract: A Bayesian analysis of the possible behaviors of the dense matter equation of state informed by recent LIGO-Virgo as well as NICER measurements reveals that all the present observations are compatible with a fully nucleonic hypothesis for the composition of dense matter, even in the core of the most massive pulsar PSR J0740+6620. Under the hypothesis of a nucleonic composition, we extract the most general behavior of the energy per particle of symmetric matter and density dependence of the symmetry energy, compatible with the astrophysical observations as well as our present knowledge of low-energy nuclear physics from effective field theory predictions and experimental nuclear mass data. These results can be used as a null hypothesis to be confronted with future constraints on dense matter to search for possible exotic degrees of freedom.

Keywords: neutron stars; gravitational waves; equation of state; dense matter

1. Introduction

The exceptional progress of multi-messenger astronomy on different astrophysical sources of dense matter has very recently led to quantitative measurements of various properties of neutron stars (NS), such as the correlation between mass and radius (M-R) from X-ray timing with NICER [1–4] and the tidal polarizability from gravitational wave (GW) LIGO/Virgo data [5–9]. These observations, together with the plethora of upcoming data [10], are expected to unveil in the near future exciting open questions such as the structure and degrees of freedom of baryonic matter in extreme conditions, particularly the presence of phase transitions and the existence of deconfined matter in the core of neutron stars [11].

This direct connection between astrophysical measurements and the microphysics of dense matter is due to the well-known fact that, under the realm of general relativity, there is a one-to-one correspondence between any static observable and the dense matter equation of state (EoS) [12]. However, this task is complicated by the fact that there is no ab initio calculation of ultra-dense matter in the hadronic or partonic sectors; therefore, effective models are used. Information about the composition of high-density matter is blurred by the uncertainty on the effective energy functional, and similar equations of state can be obtained under different hypotheses on the underlying microphysics [13,14].

Tension was reported between the GW observational data that tend to favor stiffer EoS, and ab initio nuclear physics calculations, which point towards a slightly softer density dependence [15]. This tension could, in principle, suggest the emergence of new degrees of freedom at high density. However, the statistical significance of the dispersion is not sufficient to lead to strong conclusions, and could even be reduced if the new measurement of the neutron-skin thickness of ^{208}Pb by the PREX-II collaboration [16] will confirm a higher value for the skin than previously estimated [17,18]. In addition to this, the most recent M-R estimations from the two objects PSR J0740+6620 and PSR J0030+0451 do not report any significant reduction in the NS radius with increasing mass [3,4], in qualitative agreement with the expectations for purely hadronic models for the EoS [19].

For these reasons, the hypothesis of a purely nucleonic composition of the NS cores cannot be ruled out. To identify the observables pointing towards more exotic constituents, it is important to quantitatively evaluate the space of parameters and observables that are compatible with the nucleonic hypothesis. To this end, meta-modelling techniques were proposed [19–25], which allow for exploring the complete parameter space of hadronic equations of state, and predicting the astrophysical observables with uncertainties controlled by our present theoretical and experimental knowledge of nuclear physics. This approach can be viewed as a way of transforming experimental and observational constraints into empirical parameters of nuclear physics to guide the elaboration of phenomenological and microscopic nuclear models, and it can also be used as a null hypothesis to search for exotic degrees of freedom.

In this paper, we address this timely issue by performing a Bayesian statistical analysis of the semi-agnostic meta-modelling technique of Refs. [21,24], including both nuclear physics and astrophysical constraints. With respect to previous works by different groups [19–25], we include the most recent NICER results [4] which provide constraints in the density region where many-body perturbation theory (MBPT) cannot be applied, and use a fully unified EoS approach [26] allowing for the constraints from nuclear mass measurements [27] to be included in the posterior distributions. We have not included the recent skin measurement by PREX II [16] in the considered constraints because our model is not presently able to calculate nuclear radii. An extension in this direction would be of interest, and is left for future work. In the present work, the information from the PREX II experiment can only be incorporated as an interval of the empirical parameter L_{sym} in the prior distribution. The prior that we have chosen already overlaps with the lower end of the constraint given on L_{sym} by PREX-II. Increasing the range of L_{sym} to include the higher values compatible with the PREX experiment would not modify our results, as the corresponding equations of state are filtered out by the chiral EFT constraint.

The paper is organized as follows. In Section 2, we summarize the basic ideas of nucleonic metamodelling developed in References [19,21]. We explain the different filters from low-energy nuclear physics and astrophysical observations used for the Bayesian analysis in Section 3. The results obtained in the present work are described in Section 4. We make our concluding remarks in Section 5.

2. Meta-Modelling of the EoS

Within the assumption that the core of neutron stars is composed of neutrons, protons, electrons, and muons in weak equilibrium, a prior distribution of the viable unified EoS model is generated by Monte-Carlo sampling of a large parameter set of 10 independent, uniformly distributed empirical parameters corresponding to the successive density derivatives at saturation up to order 4 of the uniform matter binding energy in the isoscalar and isovector channels. These parameters characterize the density dependence of the energy in symmetric matter, as well as of the symmetry energy, and their prior distribution is consistent with the present empirical knowledge for a large set of nuclear data [21]. They are complemented by five additional surface and curvature parameters [28] that are optimized, for each set of uniform matter parameters, to the experimental Atomic Mass Evaluation 2016 (AME2016) nuclear mass table [27]. The expression of the surface and curvature energy we employ [29] was optimized on Thomas–Fermi calculations at extreme isospin asymmetries, and also subsequently employed in different works on neutron star crust and supernova modelling within the compressible liquid drop approximation [26,28,30–33]. Two additional parameters rule the density dependence of the effective mass and the effective mass splitting, and an extra parameter enforces the correct behavior at zero density; see Reference [21] for details. The use of the same functional to describe the inhomogeneous crust [26,28] guarantees a consistent estimation of the crust–core transition and is known to be important for a correct estimation of the NS radius [34].

3. Bayesian Analysis

The posterior distributions of the set $\mathbf{X}$ of EoS parameters are conditioned by likelihood models of the different observations and constraints $\mathbf{c}$ according to the standard definition:

$$P(\mathbf{X}|\mathbf{c}) = \mathcal{N} P(\mathbf{X}) \prod_k P(c_k|\mathbf{X}), \tag{1}$$

where $P(\mathbf{X})$ is the prior, and $\mathcal{N}$ is a normalization factor. The different constraints c_k used in the present study are as follows: (a) nuclear mass measurements in the AME2016 mass table [27]; (b) the bands of allowed region in symmetric and pure neutron matter produced by many-body perturbation theory (MBPT) calculations from Reference [35] based on two- and three-nucleon chiral effective field-theory (EFT) interactions at next-to-next-to-next-to leading order (N3LO), which are interpreted as a 90% confidence interval; (c) mass measurement from radio-timing observations of pulsar PSR J0348+0432 [36], $M_{J03} = 2.01 \pm 0.04 M_\odot$, where $M_\odot$ is the solar mass; (d) constraints on the tidal deformability of the binary NS system associated to the gravitational wave event GW170817, detected by the LIGO/Virgo Collaboration (LVC) [7]; (e) X-ray pulse-profile measurements of PSR J0030+0451's mass, $M_{J00} = 1.44^{+0.15}_{-0.14} M_\odot$, and radius, $R_{J00} = 13.02^{+1.24}_{-1.06}$ km from Reference [2]; (f) the radius measurement with NICER and XMM-Newton data [4] of the PSR J0740+6620 pulsar of mass $M_{J07} = 2.08 \pm 0.07 M_\odot$ [37], $R_{J07} = 13.7^{+2.6}_{-1.5}$ km [4].

Posterior distributions of different observables Y are calculated by marginalizing over the EoS parameters as:

$$P(Y|\mathbf{c}) = \prod_{k=1}^{N} \int_{X_k^{min}}^{X_k^{max}} dX_k \, P(\mathbf{X}|\mathbf{c}) \delta(Y - Y(\mathbf{X})), \tag{2}$$

where $N = 13$ is the number of parameters in the metamodel. $Y(\mathbf{X})$ is the value of any observable Y obtained with the $\mathbf{X}$ parameter set, with $X_k^{min(max)}$ being the minimum (maximum) value in the prior distribution taken as in Reference [26]. To see the impact of different constraints on the nuclear physics informed prior, we consider four distributions, with each containing around $\sim$18,000 models. They are labeled as follows:

1. *Prior*: models in this set are required to result in meaningful solutions for the crust, that is, the minimization of the canonical thermodynamic potential at a given baryon density leads to positive gas and cluster densities. In addition, the fit of the surface and curvature parameters $\{\sigma_0, b_s, \sigma_{0c}, \beta\}$ to the nuclear masses in the AME2016 table must be convergent. These criteria are characterized by the pass-band filter ω_0. Given that the mentioned conditions are satisfied, i.e., $\omega_0 = 1$, the probability of each model, associated to a parameter set $\mathbf{X}$, is then quantified by the goodness of the optimal fit,

$$P_1(\mathbf{X}) \propto \omega_0 e^{-\chi^2(\mathbf{X})/2} P(\mathbf{X}), \tag{3}$$

in which the original prior $P(\mathbf{X})$ contains uniformly distributed EoS parameters, and the cost function $\chi^2(\mathbf{X})$ has the following form:

$$\chi^2(\mathbf{X}) = \frac{1}{N_{dof}} \sum_n \frac{\left(M_{cl}^{(n)}(\mathbf{X}) - M_{AME}^{(n)}\right)^2}{\sigma_n^2}. \tag{4}$$

The sum in Equation (4) runs over all the nuclei in the AME2016 [27] mass table, with M_{AME} and $M_{cl}(\mathbf{X})$ being the experimental and theoretical nuclear masses, respectively, in which the latter is calculated within a compressible liquid drop model (CLDM) approximation using the best-fit surface and curvature parameters for each EOS model; σ_n represents the systematic theoretical error; $N_{dof} (= n - 4)$ is the number of degrees of freedom. The distributions obtained with this prior represent the most general predictions, within a purely nucleonic composition hypothesis, which are compatible with low-energy nuclear physics experiments.

2. LD: in this sample, the models are selected by the strict filter from the chiral EFT calculation, where the energy per nucleon of symmetric nuclear matter (SNM) and pure neutron matter (PNM) of the model are compared with the corresponding energy bands of Reference [35], enlarged by 5%. This constraint is applied in the low-density region, from 0.02 fm^{-3} to 0.2 fm^{-3}. The posterior probability can be written as:

$$P_2(\mathbf{X}) \propto \omega_{LD}(\mathbf{X})P_1(\mathbf{X}), \quad (5)$$

in which $\omega_{LD}(\mathbf{X}) = 1$ if the model $\mathbf{X}$ is consistent with the EFT bands, and $\omega_{LD}(\mathbf{X}) = 0$ otherwise. Implementing this low-density (LD) filter amounts to including in the nucleonic hypothesis the information from ab initio nuclear theory.

3. HD + LVC: the posterior probability of this distribution is written as:

$$P_3(\mathbf{X}) \propto \omega_{HD} P(J03|\mathbf{X}) P(LVC|\mathbf{X}) P_1(\mathbf{X}). \quad (6)$$

Here, ω_{HD} is also a pass-band type filter similar to ω_{LD} in Equation (5). It only accepts models satisfying all the following conditions: causality, thermodynamic stability, and non-negative symmetry energy at all densities. The second term in Equation (6), $P(J03|\mathbf{X})$, is the likelihood probability from the mass measurement of PSR J0348+0432 [36], which is $M_{J03} = 2.01 \pm 0.04 M_\odot$. This likelihood is defined as the cumulative Gaussian distribution function with a mean value of 2.01 and a standard deviation of 0.04:

$$P(J03|\mathbf{X}) = \frac{1}{0.04\sqrt{2\pi}} \int_0^{M_{max}(\mathbf{X})/M_\odot} e^{-\frac{(x-2.01)^2}{2\times 0.04^2}} dx, \quad (7)$$

where $M_{max}(\mathbf{X})$ is the maximum NS mass at equilibrium, determined from the solution of the Tolmann–Oppenheimer–Volkoff (TOV) equations [38,39].

We expect these different conditions not to be selective on the low-order EOS parameters, but to constitute stringent constraints on the high-density (HD) behavior of the EOS that is essentially governed, within the nucleonic hypothesis, by the third- and fourth-order effective parameters Q_{sat}, Z_{sat}, Q_{sym} and Z_{sym} [21].

The constraint from the GW170817 event, measured by the LVC, evaluates the weight of a model based on its prediction for the tidal deformability $\tilde{\Lambda}$. The likelihood is written as:

$$P(LVC|\mathbf{X}) = \sum_i P_{LVC}(\tilde{\Lambda}(q^{(i)}), q^{(i)}), \quad (8)$$

in which q is the ratio of the lighter component mass m_2 to the heavier component mass m_1, $q = m_2/m_1 \leq 1$, and $P_{LVC}(\tilde{\Lambda}(q), q)$ is the joint posterior distribution of $\tilde{\Lambda}$ and q taken from References [7,40]. In References [7,40], the authors performed a Bayesian inference with four different waveform models. The distribution for $\tilde{\Lambda}$ and q, which we are using for this work, is the one obtained with the PhenomPNRT waveform, which is mentioned as their "reference model". The tidal deformability $\tilde{\Lambda}$ is expressed in the form of the component masses, m_1 and m_2, and the two corresponding dimensionless tidal deformabilities, Λ_1 and Λ_2, as:

$$\tilde{\Lambda} = \frac{16}{13} \frac{(m_1 + 12m_2)m_1^4 \Lambda_1 + (m_2 + 12m_1)m_2^4 \Lambda_2}{(m_1 + m_2)^5}. \quad (9)$$

The dimensionless tidal deformability Λ is related to the mass M through the expression:

$$\Lambda = \frac{2}{3} k_2 \left[\frac{c^2}{G} \frac{R(M)}{M} \right]^5, \quad (10)$$

where c, G, $R(M)$, and k_2 are the speed of light, gravitational constant, NS radius at mass M, and Love number, respectively [41–43]. In our analysis, q is chosen to be in the one-sided 90% confidence interval obtained in Reference [7], $q \in [0.73, 1.00]$. In Reference [7], it was shown that the chirp mass $\mathcal{M}_c$ of the binary NS system associated to the GW170817 event was accurately determined, $\mathcal{M}_c = 1.186 \pm 0.001 M_\odot$ at the median value with 90% confidence limits. The chirp mass $\mathcal{M}_c$ can be expressed as a function of m_1 and q as:

$$\mathcal{M}_c = \frac{(m_1 m_2)^{3/5}}{(m_1 + m_2)^{1/5}} = \frac{q^{3/5} m_1}{(1+q)^{1/5}}. \tag{11}$$

Since the uncertainty in the chirp mass $\mathcal{M}_c$ is negligible, for each value of the mass ratio q, we calculate m_1 directly from the median value of $\mathcal{M}$ through Equation (11).

4. *All*: Including the three constraints mentioned above, together with the likelihood from the joint mass-radius distributions of the two NICER measurements from References [2,4], the posterior probability for the final distribution is written as:

$$P_4(\mathbf{X}) \propto \omega_{LD} \omega_{HD} P(J03|\mathbf{X}) P(LVC|\mathbf{X}) P(NICER|\mathbf{X}) P_1(\mathbf{X}). \tag{12}$$

The NICER likelihood probability is given by:

$$P(NICER|\mathbf{X}) = \sum_i p_{NICER1}(M_1^{(i)}, R(M_1^{(i)})) \sum_j p_{NICER2}(M_2^{(j)}, R(M_2^{(j)})), \tag{13}$$

where $p_{NICER1}(M, R)$ is the two-dimensional probability distribution of mass and radius for the pulsar PSR J0030+0451 obtained using the waveform model with three uniform oval spots by Miller et al. in [2]; and $p_{NICER2}(M, R)$ is the probability distribution for PSR J0740+6620 using NICER and XMM–Newton data by Miller et al. [4]. The intervals of M_1 and M_2 are chosen to be sufficiently large so that they cover most of the associated joint mass-radius distributions, $M_1 \in [1.21, 1.70] M_\odot$ and $M_2 \in [1.90, 2.25] M_\odot$.

To ensure that the differences in the posterior distributions are induced by the impact of the different constraints, care is taken to obtain comparable statistics from the four distributions for each plot shown in this paper. Moreover, for all the shown observables, we have checked that an increase in statistics does not affect the results within the chosen precision for the numerical values given in this paper.

4. Results and Discussions
4.1. Empirical Parameters

In Figures 1 and 2 we show the probability density distributions (PDFs) of isoscalar and isovector empirical parameters of order $N < 4$, respectively. As we have described previously, the distributions labeled as "Prior" in these figures are not flat, but carry the information from the experimental nuclear mass measurement. For example, E_{sat}, the energy per particle in SNM at saturation, already has a peaked shape (see Figure 1a) because of this reason. From the HD+LVC distribution in these figures, we can see that the astrophysical constraints on NS mass and tidal deformability have almost no effect on low-order parameters. The impact of the chiral EFT filter on the isoscalar parameters of order $N < 3$, i.e., E_{sat}, K_{sat}, along with n_{sat} is not prominent. This knowledge can be further reinforced by looking at Table 1, where the LD filter hardly improves the constraints on the aforementioned isoscalar parameters. This can be explained by the fact that the prior intervals of the empirical parameters are chosen based on the current knowledge provided by nuclear physics, in which the deviations of E_{sat}, n_{sat}, and K_{sat} are already relatively small.

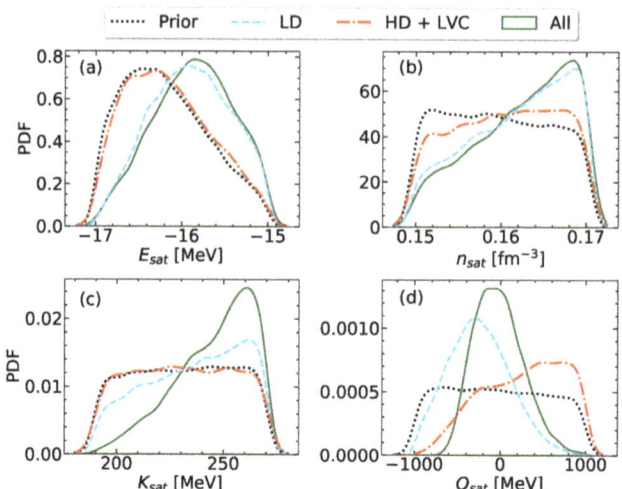

Figure 1. Probability density distributions of isoscalar empirical parameters E_{sat} (panel (**a**)), n_{sat} (panel (**b**)), K_{sat} (panel (**c**)), and Q_{sat} (panel (**d**)), for the prior distribution informed by experimental nuclear masses (black dotted line) and for posteriors of models passing through the low-density (chiral EFT) constraint (blue dashed line), high-density constraints (causality, stability, $e_{sym} \geq 0$, maximum NS mass, and tidal deformability) (red dash-dotted line), and all constraints combined (green shaded region). See texts for details.

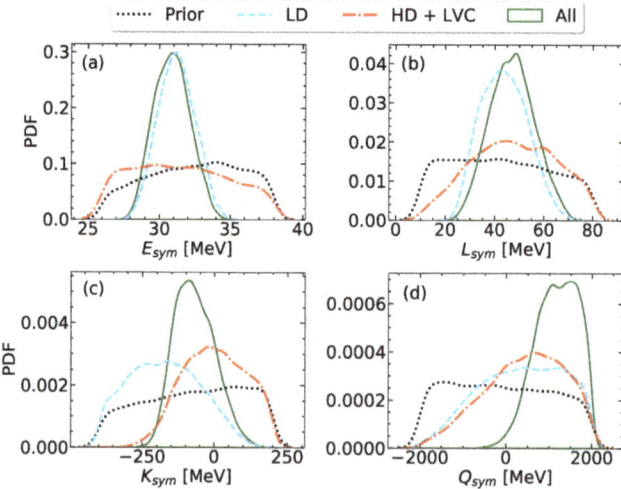

Figure 2. Same as Figure 1 but for isovector empirical parameters E_{sym} (panel (**a**)), L_{sym} (panel (**b**)), K_{sym} (panel (**c**)), and Q_{sym} (panel (**d**)).

Table 1. Medians and 68% confidence limits of EoS empirical parameters of order $N < 4$ in the four distributions.

	E_{sat} [MeV]	n_{sat} [fm^{-3}]	K_{sat} [MeV]	Q_{sat} [MeV]	E_{sym} [MeV]	L_{sym} [MeV]	K_{sym} [MeV]	Q_{sym} [MeV]
Prior	$-16.25^{+0.61}_{-0.46}$	$0.159^{+0.008}_{-0.006}$	231^{+27}_{-28}	-44^{+693}_{-650}	$32.6^{+3.5}_{-3.9}$	42^{+24}_{-22}	-62^{+181}_{-210}	-132^{+1394}_{-1290}
LD	$-15.90^{+0.51}_{-0.50}$	$0.163^{+0.005}_{-0.008}$	239^{+22}_{-30}	-264^{+383}_{-356}	$31.2^{+1.3}_{-1.3}$	43^{+11}_{-9}	-175^{+136}_{-131}	406^{+1026}_{-1116}
HD+LVC	$-16.20^{+0.60}_{-0.47}$	$0.161^{+0.006}_{-0.008}$	231^{+27}_{-27}	321^{+467}_{-596}	$31.4^{+4.0}_{-3.6}$	48^{+18}_{-19}	-2^{+121}_{-113}	502^{+891}_{-1054}
All	$-15.86^{+0.49}_{-0.50}$	$0.163^{+0.006}_{-0.007}$	249^{+15}_{-23}	-41^{+310}_{-267}	$30.9^{+1.3}_{-1.3}$	47^{+9}_{-9}	-74^{+78}_{-65}	1207^{+491}_{-539}

Unlike the lower-order parameters in the isoscalar sector, the isovector counterparts are quite poorly determined by nuclear physics experiments. As a result, once the constraint from the chiral EFT calculation is included, E_{sym}, L_{sym} and K_{sym} are strongly affected (see Figure 2 and Table 1). Interestingly, the LD filter also has a non-negligible impact on the high-order parameters Q_{sat} and Q_{sym}. This is because the chiral EFT calculation gives very precise predictions at very low densities, far from nuclear saturation. In this region, the high-order parameters have a non-negligible contribution to the nuclear matter energy. It was shown by References [28,44] that constraining the EoS at very low densities $n \sim 0.02$–0.1 fm^{-3} is crucial when studying the crust–core transition.

As one may expect, the constraints from NS observables (HD+LVC) play an important role in high-order parameters, such as Q_{sat} and Q_{sym}, as well as on the poorly constrained isovector compressibility K_{sym}. One can observe that, for these parameters, higher values of the chosen intervals are preferred in the nucleonic hypothesis, with a low preference for the softer EoSs. However, note that this is the net effect of both the radio mass and GW180817 measurements. We have checked that without the constraint on the tidal deformability, the resulting nuclear matter energies are even higher, which means that the constraint from GW170817 softens the EoS.

As discussed in detail in Reference [21], the density behavior of realistic functionals can be accurately reproduced up to the central density of massive neutron stars by a Taylor expansion truncated at the fourth order; however, because of the truncation, the parameters of order $N \geq 3$ have to be considered as effective parameters that govern the high-density behavior of the EOS, and do not need to be equal to the corresponding density derivatives at saturation. On the other hand, in the sub-saturation regime, the deviations from the Taylor expansion are accounted for by the low-density corrective term that imposes the correct zero-density limit [21]. With these two effects being completely independent, the meaning of the third- and fourth-order parameters as explored by the EFT calculation and the astrophysical observations is not the same, and we can expect that low- and high-density constraints might point to different values for those parameters. Comparing the dashed and dashed-dotted lines in Figure 1, we can see that low-density constraints impose lower values of Q_{sat} with respect to high-density ones. This means that low-energy experiments aimed towards a better measurement of Q_{sat} will not improve our empirical knowledge of the high-density EOS. Interestingly, the same is not true for Q_{sym}, for which the dotted and dash–dotted distributions closely overlap. Even if the present constraints are quite loose, it appears that the skewness of the symmetry energy at saturation Q_{sym} gives a fair description of the behavior of the EOS at high density, while a deviation is observed at the level of compressibility K_{sym}. We do not include results for the fourth-order parameters Z_{sat}, Z_{sym}, because they have very large uncertainties and very little impact from the different constraints. Furthermore, we will see that they have almost no correlations to other parameters, as well as observables.

In Figure 3, we plot the bands for SNM energy per nucleon and symmetry energy at 50% and 90% confidence intervals for the four posterior distributions, as explained in the previous section. The impact of LD and HD+LVC filters can be observed by looking at panels (b) and (c) of Figure 3, respectively. Their effects are appreciated at different density regimes, as is also evident from the analysis carried out in Figures 1 and 2 and Table 1.

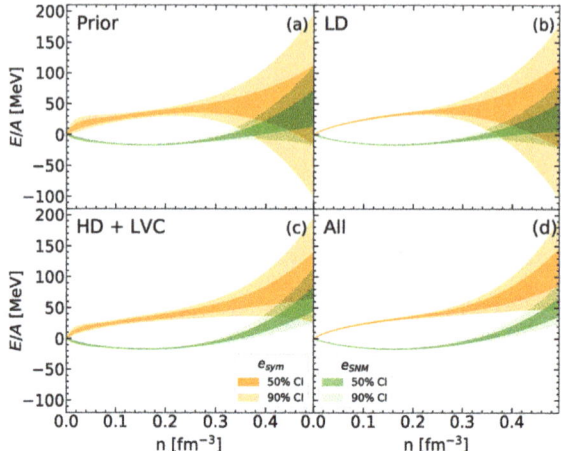

Figure 3. 50% (darker color) and 90% (lighter color) confidence intervals of energy per nucleon of symmetric nuclear matter (e_{SNM}, color green) and symmetry energy (e_{sym}, color orange) as a function of density n in the four distributions: Prior (panel (**a**)), LD (panel (**b**)), HD+LVC (panel (**c**)), and All (panel (**d**)).

4.2. Properties of NS Crust

In our calculation, the transition from the solid crust to the liquid outer core is determined by comparing the corresponding energy density of clusterized matter to that of homogeneous matter at β-equilibrium with the metamodel. For the crust part, the metamodel is extended by introducing surface parameters within the compressible liquid drop model (CLDM) approach [26]. The precision in the prediction of the crust–core transition point is crucial in estimating crustal observables, such as crustal mass, thickness, and moment of inertia. These quantities are in particular thought to have an influence on the origin of the pulsar glitches [45]. In the literature, there are various works devoting to determining the crust–core transition density n_{CC} with different many-body methods and nuclear functionals, spanning a large range of values, such as $n_{CC} = 0.0548$ fm^{-3} in [46] obtained using Thomas–Fermi calculations for the NL3 functional, or $n_{CC} = 0.081$ fm^{-3} in [47] within the full fourth-order extended Thomas–Fermi approach for the BSk24 functional. For this reason, an estimation for the uncertainties of the crustal properties with Bayesian tools using both the current nuclear physics and astrophysical data, provided by LVC and NICER, are of great importance.

In Figure 4, we display the joint distributions of the crust–core transition density n_{CC} and pressure P_{CC}. The chiral EFT calculation plays an important role in the determination of the crust–core transition point, which is evident from the LD distribution in Figure 4b. One can observe that the chiral EFT filter puts stringent limits on both the crust–core transition density n_{CC} and pressure P_{CC}; very high and very low values of n_{CC} and P_{CC} get eliminated. In Figure 4c for the HD+LVC distribution, the most noticeable fact is the suppression of models with high transition pressures. However, the probability densities of these models are tiny, and they are outside of the 95% contour in the prior distribution (see Figure 4a). Moreover, they are associated to models violating at least one of the following conditions required in the HD+LVC posterior: causality, thermodynamics stability, or non-negative symmetry energy. In other words, the astrophysical constraints on NS maximum mass and tidal deformability have very little effect on the crust–core transition. This is consistent with our observations for the nuclear matter energy in Figure 3c: the nuclear matter energy in the HD+LVC distribution is not notably constrained at densities around $n \sim n_{sat}/2$.

The crust–core transition point determines astrophysical observables, such as crust thickness, or moment of inertia [24]. In this study, we have chosen the crust thickness to be the demonstrative quantity. Figure 5 presents the PDFs of NS crust thicknesses for $1.4 M_\odot$ and $2.0 M_\odot$ NSs. In both cases, the uncertainties in the LD distributions are narrowed down compared to the prior, while the effect in the HD+LVC distribution is only marginal. This agrees with our conclusions for the crust–core transition point, that is, the role of the chiral EFT filter is more dominant in the determination of crustal properties. When all constraints are taken into account, the crust thicknesses of both $1.4 M_\odot$ and $2.0 M_\odot$ NSs are known with relative uncertainties of up to 10%. For a quantitative estimation of the effects of different filters, in Table 2 we present crust–core transition density n_{CC} and pressure P_{CC}, along with a crustal thickness of $1.4 M_\odot$ and $2.0 M_\odot$ NSs accompanied by errors on them at 68% confidence interval. One can quite conclusively comment that the primary effect comes from the LD chiral EFT filter, which also puts stringent constraints when all the filters are combined together, denoted as "All".

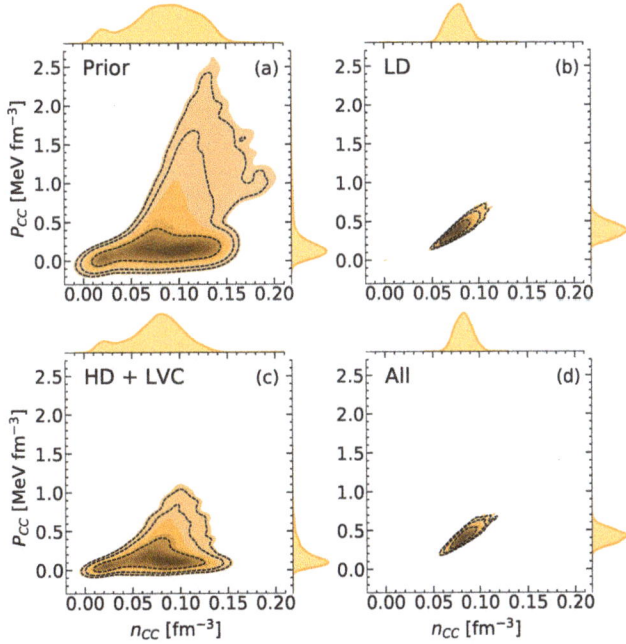

Figure 4. Joint probability density plots of crust–core transition density n_{CC} and pressure P_{CC} in the four distributions: Prior (panel (**a**)), LD (panel (**b**)), HD+LVC (panel (**c**)), and All (panel (**d**)). The dashed black contours in each panel indicate the 68%, 95%, and 99% confidence regions.

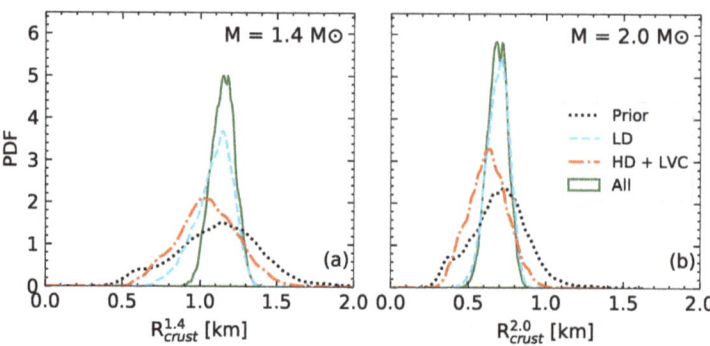

Figure 5. Probability density distributions of crust thickness at $M = 1.4 M_\odot$ (panel (**a**)) and $M = 2.0 M_\odot$ (panel (**b**)).

Table 2. Estimations of NS crustal properties in four distributions. The results are presented with medians and 68% confidence limits.

	n_{CC} [fm^{-3}]	P_{CC} [MeV fm^{-3}]	$R_{crust}^{1.4}$ [km]	$R_{crust}^{2.0}$ [km]
Prior	$0.087^{+0.033}_{-0.037}$	$0.163^{+0.281}_{-0.095}$	$1.13^{+0.25}_{-0.29}$	$0.706^{+0.165}_{-0.191}$
LD	$0.078^{+0.011}_{-0.011}$	$0.385^{+0.104}_{-0.097}$	$1.11^{+0.10}_{-0.14}$	$0.693^{+0.070}_{-0.079}$
HD+LVC	$0.079^{+0.023}_{-0.033}$	$0.141^{+0.202}_{-0.076}$	$1.05^{+0.20}_{-0.20}$	$0.627^{+0.126}_{-0.128}$
All	$0.084^{+0.009}_{-0.010}$	$0.423^{+0.093}_{-0.090}$	$1.15^{+0.10}_{-0.08}$	$0.687^{+0.067}_{-0.067}$

4.3. NS Equation of State

Unlike the crustal properties, HD+LVC filter is expected to put tighter bounds on global NS properties, which is governed chiefly by the high-density part of the EoS. The effects of different filters on the EoS are shown in Figure 6. The light (dark) orange band indicates 90% (50%) confidence interval. For comparison, we also display the result inferred from the gravitational wave data GW170817 by LVC at the 90% level in dashed blue lines [6]. We have also used the same units for mass-density g cm^{-3} as in Reference [6] for the same reason. In this unit the saturation density n_{sat} is denoted as ρ_{sat} ($\simeq 2.8 \times 10^{14}$ g cm^{-3}). In Reference [6], Abbott et al. have sampled their EoSs at high density using the spectral parametrization [48]. These EoSs are then matched with SLy EoS [49] at around $\sim \rho_{sat}/2$. Incidentally, the authors also utilized some prior criteria similar to our analysis, which are causality, thermodynamic stability, and consistency of NS maximum mass with the observation. For the last condition, they put a sharp limit ($M_{max} \geq 1.97 M_\odot$) instead of using a likelihood probability as in our analysis (see Equation (7)). However, we have verified that the difference in the maximum NS treatment does not lead to sizable deviation in the final results. In Figure 6a, we can see that our prior distribution perfectly covers the whole posterior band given by GW170817 event [6] with good agreement. In our case, the prior distribution carries information from nuclear physics experiments and theoretical calculations via the chosen prior intervals of empirical parameters as well as the mass fit. This is why the EoS in our prior distribution at low densities is relatively narrow compared to other analyses. Note that the uncertainty below ρ_{sat}, appears to be large due to the visual effect of the logarithmic scale in the pressure. Once the chiral EFT filter is applied, this uncertainty is vastly reduced (see Figure 6b), resulting in a very well-constrained band and excellently compatible with the posterior constrained by GW170817 data [6]. Contrarily, the behavior of the EoS at supra-saturation densities is not constrained by the chiral EFT filter. As a result, a larger dispersion is observed at high densities. This dispersion is not as important as in fully agnostic studies [50] because of the nucleonic hypothesis that imposes an analytic behavior of the EoS at all densities. This strong hypothesis can be challenged by the astrophysical measurements, and any inconsistency with the observations will reveal the presence of exotic degrees of freedom.

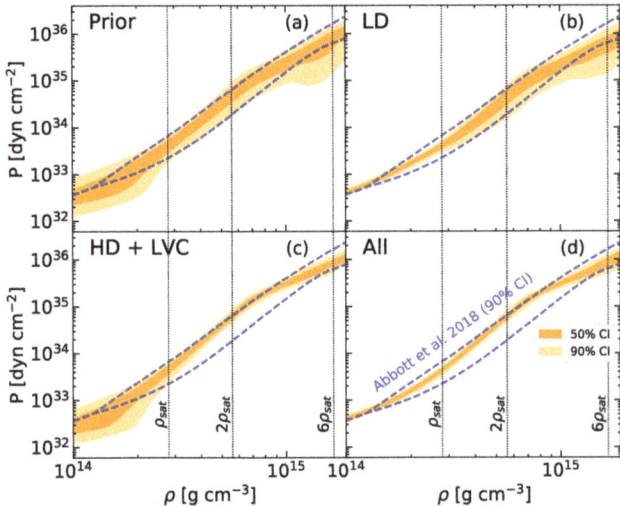

Figure 6. 50% (dark orange) and 90% (light orange) confidence intervals of pressure P as a function of mass density ρ in comparison with the 90% confidence interval of the posterior obtained in Abbott et al. 2018 [6] (blue dashed lines) in the four distributions: Prior (panel (**a**)), LD (panel (**b**)), HD+LVC (panel (**c**)), and All (panel (**d**)). See text for details.

By incorporating the pass band filter ω_{HD} as well as the condition on the NS maximum mass in Figure 6c, the deviation in the lower limit of the pressure at density $\rho \gtrsim 10^{15}$ g cm^{-3} observed in the prior, is eliminated. In particular, the constraint on the NS maximum mass sets a stringent limit on the lower bound of the pressure, and posterior EoS is shifted significantly towards higher values of pressure. Conversely, the constraint from LVC prefers softer EoS, hence setting the limit on the upper bound of the pressure band. In Figure 6d, when all constraints are combined, as expected, we obtain a narrower band for the EoS than the one obtained exclusively from GW170817 data [6]. In addition, we observe that our EoS is lightly stiffer than the one of Reference [6] at around $2 - 3\rho_{sat}$. The small width of the EoS and its stiffness are assigned to the semi-agnostic hadronic prior, which represents current nuclear physics knowledge. Nevertheless, the overall agreement is excellent. Thus, it indicates the compatibility of the nucleonic EoS with the gravitational wave GW170817 data.

Comparing the "HD+LVC" and "All" distributions in Figure 6c,d, it can be observed that the inclusion of the new NICER measurement does not show any significant impact on the EoS. Similar conclusions have been drawn in other studies in the literature. Pang et al. [51] carried out a Bayesian analysis using the data from Riley et al. [3] and Miller et al. [4]. In both cases, they found that the effect of the constraint from the radius measurement of PSR J0740+6620 only marginally impact the EoS. In Reference [52], Raaijmakers et al. performed the Bayesian inference with two EoS parametrizations: a piece-wise polytropic (PP) model and a speed-of-sound (CS) model drawing similar conclusions. For the constraint on PSR J0740+6620, they employed the data from Riley et al. [3], in which the error bar of the radius is smaller than that obtained in Miller et al. [4]. They concluded that, for the PP models, the impact on the EoS mainly comes from the high mass value of PSR J0740+6620 because their prior distribution in that mass range is within the 68% level of the radius measurement (see Figure 4 in [52]).

4.4. Speed of Sound in Medium

In Figure 7, we plot the velocity of sound in medium as a function of mass density ρ obtained with four different filters at the 50% and 90% confidence intervals, together with the behavior of some selected models [53–56]. One can observe that, for all the filters, the most probable equations of state remain causal up to very high densities ($\sim 6\rho_{sat}$), even though we do not explicitly put this requirement in our "Prior" and the "LD" filters in Figure 7a,b, respectively. As expected, the behavior of the sound speed is globally structureless. However, we can surprisingly see a trend for a peaked structure, which is typically presented in the literature as a signature of a transition to exotic matter. This peak may arise from the shoulder observed in Figure 6 above, which is due to the combined constraints of a relatively soft EoS at low density, and the necessity of reaching the maximal mass. These conditions lead to a peak in the global distribution; note, however, that this is not true for all models individually (see lines in Figure 7d). A very small fraction of non-causal models are present due to the fact that we plot the EoS only up to densities where the nucleon sound velocity is in the interval between 0 and 1. Residual non-causalities (not visible within 90% confidence interval of Figure 7) originate from the additional lepton contribution in beta-equilibrated matter.

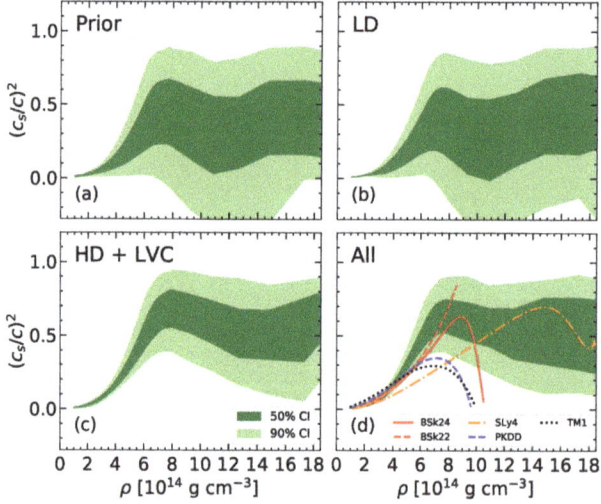

Figure 7. 50% (dark green) and 90% (light green) confidence intervals of sound speed $\left(\frac{c_s}{c}\right)^2$ as a function of mass density ρ in the four distributions: Prior (panel (**a**)), LD (panel (**b**)), HD+LVC (panel (**c**)), and All (panel (**d**)). Curves in panel (**d**) show the sound speed of some selected models [53–56] up to the central density corresponding to the maximum mass. See text for details.

4.5. NS Observables

4.5.1. Masses and Radii

In Figure 8 we plot, for different filters, three shaded regions (from light to dark) sequentially containing 99%, 95%, and 68% confidence intervals for two-dimensional distribution for the mass and radius of NSs. The two black contour lines, at low mass and high mass, respectively, indicate 68% of the mass-radius distributions for PSR J0030+0451 [2] and PSR J0740+6620 [4]. One can observe in Figure 8a that our prior is already quite compatible with both the recent NICER observations [2,4]. This explains why the effect of the constraints from NICER is globally small in all our distributions. Moreover, since in Figure 8c we already included the constraint from the radio mass measurement of the high-mass pulsar PSR J0348+0432, the impact from the mass of PSR J0740+6620 is obscured in Figure 8d. Additionally, the large uncertainty in the new radius measurement does not help to further constrain the EoS. The compatibility of NICER measurement and our distributions implies that a nucleonic EoS is flexible enough to reproduce those dense-matter observations. In Reference [51], Pang et al. computed the Bayes factor to study the possibility of a strong first-order phase transition from nuclear to quark matter in NS. If the data from Miller et al. [4] is used, the Bayes factor changes from 0.265 to 0.205. Even though the effect from PSR J0740+6620 is not significant, a decrease in the Bayes factor points to the fact that a first-order phase transition to quark matter is disfavored. Similarly, Legred et al. [57] found that the Bayes factor for EoSs with one stable branch against those with at least one disconnected hybrid star branch is 0.156 (0.220) with (without) the PSR J0740+6620 measurement. Both these studies censure the possibility of a strong phase transition and support the suitability of the hadronic EoS with respect to NS observables, which is in line with our present analysis.

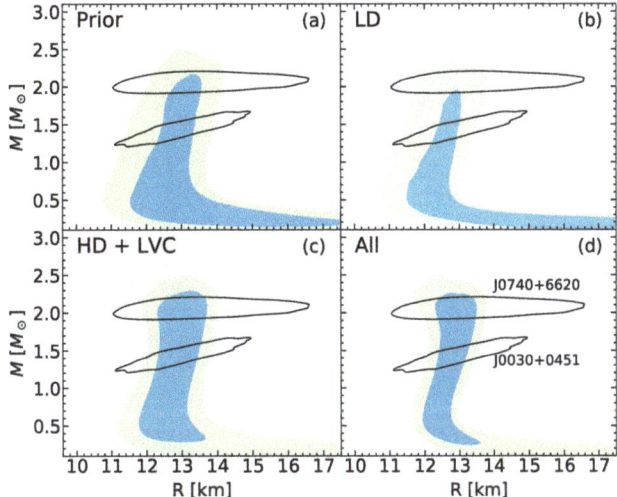

Figure 8. Probability density plots of NS mass M as a function of radius R in comparison with two NICER measurements at 68% (black contours) in the four distributions: Prior (panel (**a**)), LD (panel (**b**)), HD+LVC (panel (**c**)), and All (panel (**d**)). The three shaded regions in each panel contain 68%, 95%, and 99% of the distribution. See text for details.

Figure 9 displays the marginalized distributions of NS radii, $R_{1.4}$ and $R_{2.0}$, of the canonical mass $1.4 M_\odot$ (panel (a)) and the typical high mass $2.0 M_\odot$ (panel (b)), respectively. The dashed blue lines represent the PDFs obtained when a chiral EFT (LD) filter is applied. We can see from the figure that this filter puts a constraint on the upper bound of the distributions. It rejects models with $R_{1.4} \gtrsim 13.6$ km and $R_{2.0} \gtrsim 14.0$ km. In the HD+LVC distribution for $1.4 M_\odot$ NS, the constraint from GW170817 softens the EoS, hence constraining the upper bound of $R_{1.4}$, while the requirement on the NS maximum mass filters out very soft EoSs, which places a limit on the the lower bound of $R_{1.4}$. As a result, these two competing effects provide us with a relatively narrow range on the radius. In particular, $R_{1.4} \in [11.8, 14.0]$ km (see red dashed-dotted line in panel (a)). In the case of $R_{2.0}$, the constraint from radio mass measurement of PSR J0348+0432 becomes redundant because all distributions must support $2.0 M_\odot$ NS, resulting in no effect being shown in the lower value of $R_{2.0}$. Therefore, in the HD+LVC distribution of $R_{2.0}$, the constraint only comes from the LVC measurement. Furthermore, this figure also tells us that the impacts on $R_{2.0}$ from the gravitational signal GW170817 and chiral EFT calculation are very similar, even though they affect two different regions of the EoS. Specifically, the former controls the EoS in the NS core, hence the core radius, while the latter dominates the crust EoS, hence the crust thickness. The prediction in the form of median and 68% credible limits for $R_{1.4}$ ($R_{2.0}$) when all constraints are applied together is $12.78^{+0.30}_{-0.29}$ ($12.96^{+0.38}_{-0.37}$) km. In Miller et al. [4], the authors employed three EoS models, namely Gaussian, spectral, and PP. The values of $R_{1.4}$ for these three models are, respectively, $12.63^{+0.48}_{-0.46}$ km, $12.30^{+0.54}_{-0.51}$ km, and $12.56^{+0.45}_{-0.40}$ km at 68% confidence limit. Despite the difference in EoS sampling methods, these results are in excellent agreement with the results obtained in the present work. Using also the likelihood from PREX-II measurement of R^{208}_{skin} [16], Reference [58] obtains $R_{1.4} = 12.61^{+0.36}_{-0.41}$ km, which is also consistent with our prediction.

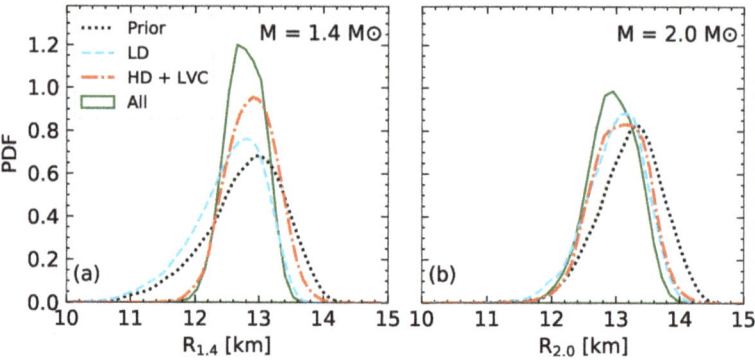

Figure 9. Probability density distributions of NS radii at $M = 1.4 M_\odot$ (panel (**a**)) and $M = 2.0 M_\odot$ (panel (**b**)).

The dimensionless tidal deformability Λ in Equation (10) suggests a relation between Λ and R for a NS of given mass M. However, this relationship is not straightforward due to the complex radius dependence of the tidal Love number k_2 [41–43]. The relation between R and Λ, particularly for the mass $M = 1.4 M_\odot$ has been investigated in several works [59–62]. Interestingly, Figure 10 shows that the distributions of $\Lambda_{1.4}$ and $\Lambda_{2.0}$ behave in accordance with the corresponding radius distributions in Figure 9. This may indicate a strong positive correlation between these two quantities, which will be discussed later. In addition, we estimate the 90% confidence boundaries of $\Lambda_{1.4}$ ($\Lambda_{2.0}$) to be $\Lambda_{1.4} \in [463, 757]$ ($\Lambda_{2.0} \in [43, 94]$). This prediction of $\Lambda_{1.4}$ agrees excellently with the upper bound extracted from GW170817 signal in Reference [5] using TaylorF2 model, that is, $\Lambda_{1.4} \leq 800$. The limit in $\Lambda_{1.4}$ has been improved in Reference [6], in which the more realistic waveform PhenomPNRT was employed, and they obtained $\Lambda_{1.4} \in [70, 580]$ at 90% confidence level for the EoS-insensitive analysis [5,6]. Our distribution is still compatible with this result, but it suggests a slightly too stiff EoS in the nucleonic hypothesis.

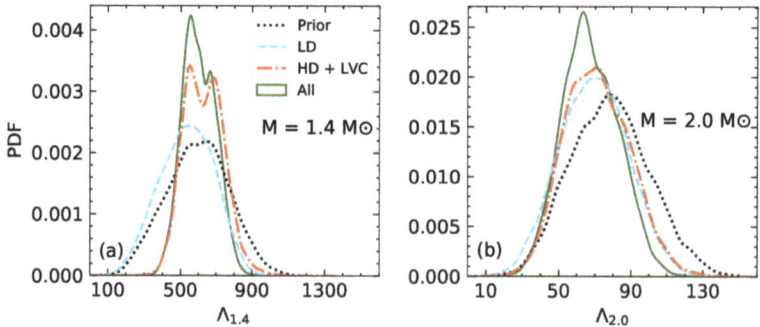

Figure 10. Probability density distributions of NS dimensionless tidal deformabilities at $M = 1.4 M_\odot$ (panel (**a**)) and $M = 2.0 M_\odot$ (panel (**b**)).

4.5.2. Composition

The determination of the proton fraction is crucial for studying NS cooling. The most efficient cooling mechanism of NS is through the direct Urca (dUrca) neutrino emission process. This process is described by the following successive reactions:

$$n \to p + l + \bar{\nu}_l \tag{14}$$

$$p + l \to n + \nu_l, \tag{15}$$

where $l = \{e^-, \mu^-\}$. From the momentum and charge conservations, one can derive the expression for the threshold, below which the dUrca process is forbidden:

$$x_{DU} = \frac{1}{1 + (1 + x_{ep}^{1/3})^3}, \tag{16}$$

where $x_{ep}(= x_e/x_p)$ is the ratio between electron and proton fraction. Values of x_{DU} can vary in the range from $x_{DU} \simeq 1/9$ in the case of no muons ($x_{ep} = 1$) to $x_{DU} \simeq 0.148$ at the limit of massless muons ($x_{ep} = 0.5$) [30,63].

Figure 11 shows the PDFs of proton fractions calculated at the center of NS with $M = 1.4 M_\odot$ and $M = 2.0 M_\odot$. The black arrow in each panel indicates the most probable value of x_{DU}, calculated for the central density, denoted as x_{DU}^{mp}. We find that this quantity is independent of the constraint used. Furthermore, x_{DU}^{mp} only depends weakly on NS mass, $x_{DU}^{mp} \simeq 0.134$ (0.138) for $M = 1.4$ (2.0) $M_\odot$. For both masses, the distributions of x_p extend to higher values than the corresponding threshold x_{DU}^{mp}. Therefore, it is possible for the dUrca process to operate even in NS of mass $1.4 M_\odot$. Nevertheless, this fast cooling channel is more likely to occur in heavier NSs due to the higher median and deviation of the x_p distribution. By integrating the PDF to find the area under the curve for $x_p \geq x_{DU}^{mp}$, we estimate the possibility for the dUrca process in NS of mass $1.4 M_\odot$ ($2.0 M_\odot$) to be approximately 26% (72%). For a more definitive evaluation, the predictions of NS central proton fractions, along with the radius and tidal deformability for NSs of mass $1.4 M_\odot$ and $2.0 M_\odot$ at 68% confidence limit, are listed in Table 3.

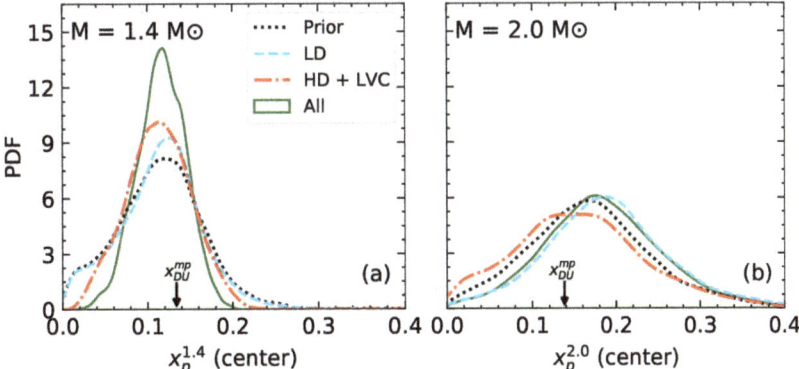

Figure 11. Probability density distributions of central proton fractions of NS at $M = 1.4\ M_\odot$ and $M = 2.0\ M_\odot$. The arrow in each panel indicates the most probable value of x_{DU}. Panel (a): $x_{DU}^{mp} \simeq 0.134$. Panel (b): $x_{DU}^{mp} \simeq 0.138$. At each value of mass, value of x_{DU}^{mp} are very similar in four distributions. See text for details.

Table 3. Medians and 68% confidence intervals of NS radii, dimensionless tidal deformabilities, and central proton fractions at $M = 1.4 M_\odot$ and $M = 2.0 M_\odot$.

	$R_{1.4}$ [km]	$R_{2.0}$ [km]	$\Lambda_{1.4}$	$\Lambda_{2.0}$	$x_p^{1.4}$	$x_p^{2.0}$
Prior	$12.85^{+0.52}_{-0.69}$	$13.26^{+0.45}_{-0.52}$	601^{+171}_{-182}	78^{+23}_{-22}	$0.115^{+0.047}_{-0.052}$	$0.166^{+0.073}_{-0.070}$
LD	$12.61^{+0.45}_{-0.64}$	$13.03^{+0.39}_{-0.49}$	541^{+151}_{-162}	70^{+19}_{-19}	$0.117^{+0.041}_{-0.052}$	$0.187^{+0.072}_{-0.067}$
HD+LVC	$12.89^{+0.38}_{-0.40}$	$13.07^{+0.42}_{-0.44}$	626^{+114}_{-107}	71^{+20}_{-17}	$0.113^{+0.038}_{-0.039}$	$0.154^{+0.079}_{-0.074}$
All	$12.78^{+0.30}_{-0.29}$	$12.96^{+0.38}_{-0.37}$	598^{+105}_{-85}	66^{+18}_{-14}	$0.117^{+0.027}_{-0.030}$	$0.181^{+0.070}_{-0.065}$

4.6. Pearson Correlations

Studying correlations among parameters and observables reveals a great deal about the many facets of multi-parametric model calculations [64]. The most frequently employed tool for this purpose is the linear Pearson correlation, which is defined for two quantities, x and y (x, y can be parameters of the model or any observable calculated from it) as,

$$corr(x, y) = \frac{cov(x, y)}{\sigma_x \sigma_y}, \qquad (17)$$

where $cov(x, y)$ is the covariance between x and y, and σ_x (σ_y) is the standard deviation on x (y).

Figure 12 displays the Pearson correlation coefficients among all bulk, surface, and curvature parameters in the case where all constraints are applied. Since the bulk parameters are initially by construction uncorrelated in the flat prior distribution, we can easily assign the induced correlations to the different filters employed. It is shown in the figure that there is a perfect negative correlation between the surface tension of symmetric matter σ_0 and the saturation energy E_{sat}, with $corr(\sigma_0, E_{sat}) = -1$. A similar result was found in Reference [26]. The parameters associated to the curvature (σ_{0c} and β), on the other hand, exhibit strong positive correlations with E_{sat}. These correlations appear due to the fit of the surface and curvature parameters to the experimental nuclear mass table. In addition, if the prior is only constrained by the experimental masses of nuclei, we also find a strong correlation between b_s and E_{sym}, which are the two main parameters governing the energy of asymmetric nuclear matter. However, once the filter from chiral EFT calculation is applied, E_{sym} is tightly constrained, and hence the correlation becomes blurred. Similar to References [19,26], no significant correlations are found to be induced by the astrophysical constraints. The correlations among the bulk parameters shown in Figure 12 are resulted from the chiral EFT constraint. In particular, the symmetry energy E_{sym} has a moderate (anti)correlation with (E_{sat}) n_{sat}. Stronger correlations are found among the isovector parameters, which are $corr(E_{sym}, L_{sym}) = 0.67$ and $corr(L_{sym}, K_{sym}) = 0.67$. The former is found in several works (see References [23,26,65] and references therein for a review), and the latter is also studied in References [66–72]. Slight correlations between high-order parameters, $K_{sat} - Q_{sat}$ and $K_{sym} - Q_{sym}$, are also induced due to the narrow EFT energy bands at very low densities.

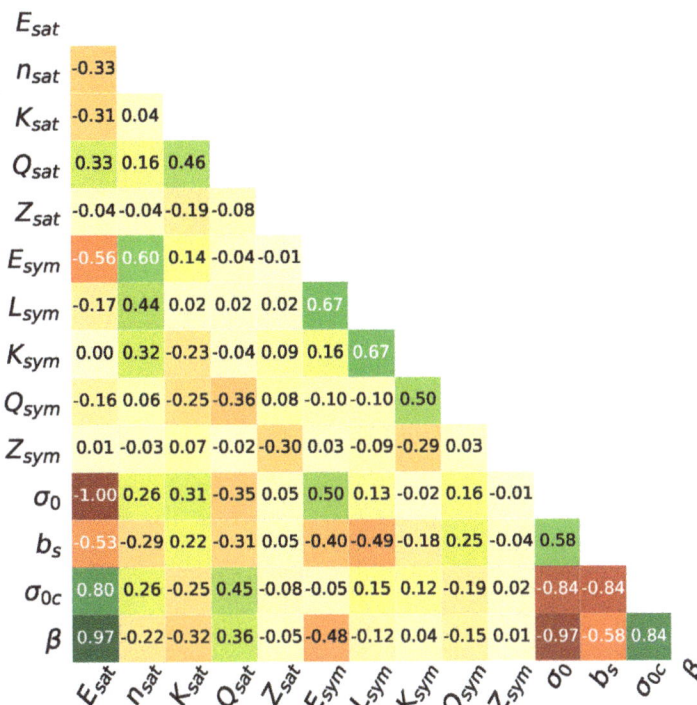

Figure 12. Pearson correlation coefficients matrix among bulk and surface empirical parameters in the case all filters are applied.

Correlations among different observables found in our study are plotted in Figure 13. The strongest correlations in this matrix are the well-known ones between radius and dimensionless tidal deformability, $corr(R_{1.4}, \Lambda_{1.4}) = 0.97$ and $corr(R_{2.0}, \Lambda_{2.0}) = 0.98$. This explains the similarity in the distributions of R and Λ seen in Figures 9 and 10. There is also a strong positive correlation between n_{CC} and P_{CC}. This correlation is also visible in the joint distribution plot in Figure 4. We have mentioned before that the determination of the transition point from crust to core is important in predicting crustal observables; this is again confirmed by the correlation coefficients between the crust thickness with the transition density and pressure. Finally, the correlations between the observables and parameters are also computed. The correlation matrix is shown in Figure 14. For most of the cases, the most influential parameters are from the isovector channel, which are L_{sym}, K_{sym}, and Q_{sym}. The only exception is for the proton fraction, where high-order isoscalar parameters have negative correlations. This correlation study clearly demonstrates that astrophysical observables have a marginal influence on the higher order nuclear matter properties, which points towards two conclusions: (a) the low-density nuclear physics data have a large influence on constraining the lower-order parameters; (b) we need more precise astrophysical data to tighten the constraints on higher order parameters. Conversely, to obtain a more accurate prediction of astrophysical properties, we need to reduce the uncertainties in these higher-order parameters from other sources, e.g., heavy ion collisions [73].

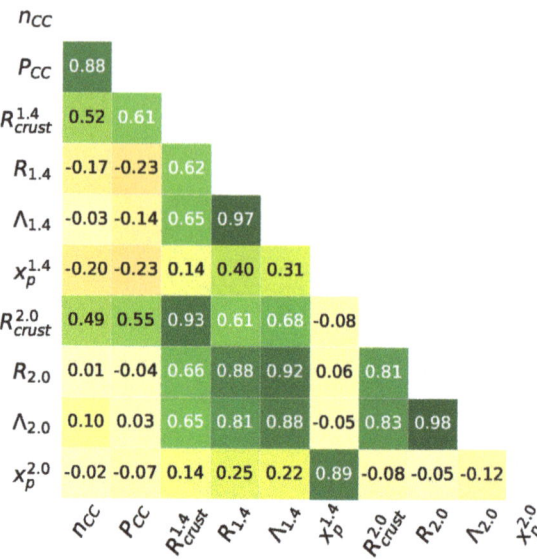

Figure 13. Pearson correlation coefficients matrix among some observables in the case all filters are applied.

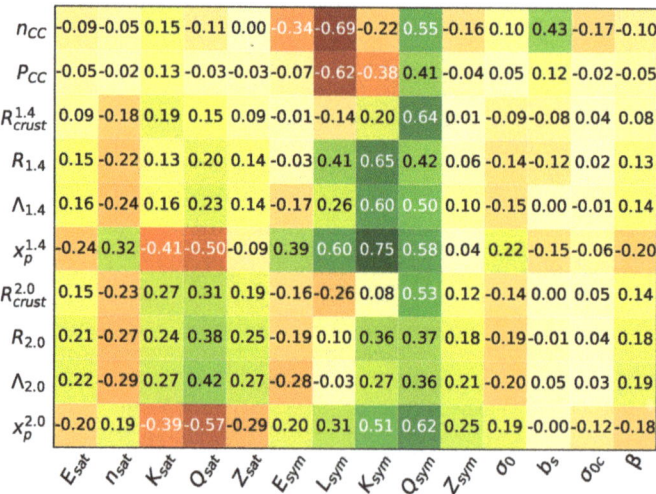

Figure 14. Pearson correlation coefficients between some observables with the empirical and surface parameters in the case all filters are applied.

5. Conclusions

To conclude, we have jointly analyzed different constraints on the nuclear matter EoS coming from nuclear experiments, ab initio nuclear theory, and several new astrophysical observational data, including the very recent simultaneous observation of mass-radius of PSR J0348+0432 and PSR J0740+6620 from NICER collaboration as well as LIGO-Virgo observations of tidal deformability in GW170817 event. Imposing all these different constraints in a Bayesian framework, we have challenged the hypothesis of a fully analytical (continuous and derivable at all orders) EoS, as obtained in the case where dense baryonic matter is purely constituted of neutrons and protons without any phase transition or exotic degrees of freedom.

Notably, we have observed that if we have a nuclear physics informed prior including the binding energy data of the whole nuclear chart and chiral EFT constraints on low-density SNM and PNM, the posterior for mass-radius of NSs are already in line with NICER observations. Contrarily, bounds on high-density matter from a radio astronomy observation of NS of 2 solar mass and GW170817 data on tidal deformability are reasonably appreciated. With the present knowledge of astrophysical observations, we predict that the direct Urca cooling is possible with non-negligible probability (27%), even in an NS with a mass as low as $1.4 M_\odot$, which increases much further $\sim 72\%$ for a NS of $2.0 M_\odot$. This might also be very crucial when (in)validating the nucleonic hypothesis of high-density matter. As all current data on astrophysical observations comply with the nucleonic hypothesis within our metamodel approach, we need much more stringent constraints from the observations to conclusively establish (reject) the presence of exotic degrees of freedom in high-density matter.

Author Contributions: All the authors contributed equally to the writing with H.D.T. performing the calculations and preparing the first draft of the manuscript. All authors have read and agreed to the published version of the manuscript.

Funding: The authors acknowledge partial support from the IN2P3 Master Project "NewMAC".

Institutional Review Board Statement: This manuscript has gone through VIRGO document review system as C.M. and F.G. are obliged to make sure any infringement of the VIRGO data has not taken place, being part of the VIRGO collaboration through Caen-Meudon group.

Informed Consent Statement: Not applicable.

Data Availability Statement: Not applicable.

Conflicts of Interest: The authors declare no conflict of interest.

References

1. Riley, T.E.; Watts, A.L.; Bogdanov, S.; Ray, P.S.; Ludlam, R.M.; Guillot, S.; Arzoumanian, Z.; Baker, C.L.; Bilous, A.V.; Chakrabarty, D.; et al. A NICER View of PSR J0030+0451: Millisecond Pulsar Parameter Estimation. *Astrophys. J. Lett.* **2019**, *887*, L21. [CrossRef]
2. Miller, M.C.; Lamb, F.K.; Dittmann, A.J.; Bogdanov, S.; Arzoumanian, Z.; Gendreau, K.C.; Guillot, S.; Harding, A.K.; Ho, W.C.G.; Lattimer, J.M.; et al. PSR J0030+0451 Mass and Radius from NICER Data and Implications for the Properties of Neutron Star Matter. *Astrophys. J. Lett.* **2019**, *887*, L24. [CrossRef]
3. Riley, T.E.; Watts, A.L.; Ray, P.S.; Bogdanov, S.; Guillot, S.; Morsink, S.M.; Bilous, A.V.; Arzoumanian, Z.; Choudhury, D.; Deneva, J.S.; et al. A NICER View of the Massive Pulsar PSR J0740+6620 Informed by Radio Timing and XMM-Newton Spectroscopy. *arXiv* **2021**, arXiv:2105.06980.
4. Miller, M.C.; Lamb, F.K.; Dittmann, A.J.; Bogdanov, S.; Arzoumanian, Z.; Gendreau, K.C.; Guillot, S.; Ho, W.C.G.; Lattimer, J.M.; Loewenstein, M.; et al. The Radius of PSR J0740+6620 from NICER and XMM-Newton Data. *arXiv* **2021**, arXiv:2105.06979.
5. Abbott, B.P.; Abbott, R.; Abbott, T.D.; Acernese, F.; Ackley, K.; Adams, C.; Adams, T.; Addesso, P.; Adhikari, R.X.; Adya, V.B.; et al. GW170817: Observation of Gravitational Waves from a Binary Neutron Star Inspiral. *Phys. Rev. Lett.* **2017**, *119*, 161101. [CrossRef]
6. Abbott, B.P.; Abbott, R.; Abbott, T.D.; Acernese, F.; Ackley, K.; Adams, C.; Adams, T.; Addesso, P.; Adhikari, R.X.; Adya, V.B.; et al. GW170817: Measurements of Neutron Star Radii and Equation of State. *Phys. Rev. Lett.* **2018**, *121*, 161101. [CrossRef] [PubMed]
7. Abbott, B.P.; Abbott, R.; Abbott, T.D.; Acernese, F.; Ackley, K.; Adams, C.; Adams, T.; Addesso, P.; Adhikari, R.X.; Adya, V.B.; et al. Properties of the Binary Neutron Star Merger GW170817. *Phys. Rev. X* **2019**, *9*, 011001. [CrossRef]
8. The LIGO Scientific Collaboration; Aasi, J.; Abbott, B.P.; Abbott, R.; Abbott, T.; Abernathy, M.R.; Ackley, K.; Adams, C.; Adams, T.; Addesso, P.; et al. Advanced LIGO. *Class. Quantum Grav.* **2015**, *32*, 074001. [CrossRef]
9. Acernese, F.; Agathos, M.; Agatsuma, K.; Aisa, D.; Allemandou, N.; Allocca, A.; Amarni, J.; Astone, P.; Balestri, G.; Ballardin, G.; et al. Advanced Virgo: a second-generation interferometric gravitational wave detector. *Class. Quantum Grav.* **2015**, *32*, 024001. [CrossRef]
10. Abbott, B.P.; Abbott, R.; Abbott, T.D.; Acernese, F.; Ackley, K.; Adams, C.; Adams, T.; Addesso, P.; Adhikari, R.X.; Adya, V.B.; et al. Prospects for observing and localizing gravitational-wave transients with Advanced LIGO, Advanced Virgo and KAGRA. *Living Rev. Relativ.* **2020**, *23*, 1–69. [CrossRef]

11. Oertel, M.; Hempel, M.; Klähn, T.; Typel, S. Equations of State for Supernovae and Compact Stars. *Rev. Mod. Phys.* **2017**, *89*, 015007. [CrossRef]
12. Hartle, J.B. Slowly Rotating Relativistic Stars. 1. Equations of Structure. *Astrophys. J.* **1967**, *150*, 1005–1029. [CrossRef]
13. Horowitz, C.J. Neutron Rich Matter in the Laboratory and in the Heavens after GW170817. *Ann. Phys.* **2019**, *411*, 167992. [CrossRef]
14. Fiorella Burgio, G.; Vidaña, I. The Equation of State of Nuclear Matter: From Finite Nuclei to Neutron Stars. *Universe* **2020**, *6*, 119. [CrossRef]
15. Güven, H.; Bozkurt, K.; Khan, E.; Margueron, J. Multimessenger and Multiphysics Bayesian Inference for the GW170817 Binary Neutron Star Merger. *Phys. Rev. C* **2020**, *102*, 015805. [CrossRef]
16. Adhikari, D.; Albataineh, H.; Androic, D.; Aniol, K.; Armstrong, D.S.; Averett, T.; Ayerbe Gayoso, C.; Barcus, S.; Bellini, V.; Beminiwattha, R.S.; et al. Accurate Determination of the Neutron Skin Thickness of ^{208}Pb through Parity-Violation in Electron Scattering. *Phys. Rev. Lett.* **2021**, *126*, 172502. [CrossRef]
17. Reed, B.T.; Fattoyev, F.J.; Horowitz, C.J.; Piekarewicz, J. Implications of PREX-2 on the Equation of State of Neutron-Rich Matter. *Phys. Rev. Lett.* **2021**, *126*, 172503. [CrossRef]
18. Essick, R.; Tews, I.; Landry, P.; Schwenk, A. Astrophysical Constraints on the Symmetry Energy and the Neutron Skin of ^{208}Pb with Minimal Modeling Assumptions. *arXiv* **2021**, arXiv:2102.10074. [CrossRef]
19. Margueron, J.; Hoffmann Casali, R.; Gulminelli, F. Equation of State for Dense Nucleonic Matter from Metamodeling. II. Predictions for Neutron Star Properties. *Phys. Rev. C* **2018**, *97*, 025806.
20. Steiner, A.W.; Lattimer, J.M.; Brown, E.F. The Neutron Star Mass-Radius Relation and the Equation of State of Dense Matter. *Astrophys. J. Lett.* **2013**, *765*, L5. [CrossRef]
21. Margueron, J.; Hoffmann Casali, R.; Gulminelli, F. Equation of State for Dense Nucleonic Matter from Metamodeling. I. Foundational Aspects. *Phys. Rev. C* **2018**, *97*, 025805. [CrossRef]
22. Zhang, N.-B.; Li, B.-A.; Xu, J. Combined Constraints on the Equation of State of Dense Neutron-Rich Matter from Terrestrial Nuclear Experiments and Observations of Neutron Stars. *Astrophys. J.* **2018**, *859*, 90. [CrossRef]
23. Lim, Y.; Holt, J.W. Bayesian Modeling of the Nuclear Equation of State for Neutron Star Tidal Deformabilities and GW170817. *Eur. Phys. J. A* **2019**, *55*, 209. [CrossRef]
24. Carreau, T.; Gulminelli, F.; Margueron, J. General Predictions for the Neutron Star Crustal Moment of Inertia. *Phys. Rev. C* **2019**, *100*, 055803. [CrossRef]
25. Tsang, C.Y.; Tsang, M.B.; Danielewicz, P.; Lynch, W.G.; Fattoyev, F.J. Impact of the Neutron-Star Deformability on Equation of State Parameters. *Phys. Rev. C* **2020**, *102*, 045808. [CrossRef]
26. Carreau, T.; Gulminelli, F.; Margueron, J. Bayesian Analysis of the Crust-Core Transition with a Compressible Liquid-Drop Model. *Eur. Phys. J. A* **2019**, *55*, 188. [CrossRef]
27. Huang, W.J.; Audi, G.; Wang, M.; Kondev, F.G.; Naimi, S.; Xu, X. The AME2016 Atomic Mass Evaluation (I). Evaluation of Input Data; and Adjustment Procedures. *Chin. Phys. C* **2017**, *41*, 030002. [CrossRef]
28. Dinh Thi, H.; Carreau, T.; Fantina, A.F.; Gulminelli, F. Uncertainties in the Pasta-Phase Properties in Catalysed Neutron Stars. *Astron. Astrophys.* **2021**. [CrossRef]
29. Ravenhall, D.G.; Pethick, C.J.; Wilson, J.R. Structure of Matter below Nuclear Saturation Density. *Phys. Rev. Lett.* **1983**, *50*, 2066. [CrossRef]
30. Lattimer, J.M.; Douglas Swesty, F. A Generalized Equation of State for Hot, Dense Matter. *Nucl. Phys. A* **1991**, *535*, 331–376. [CrossRef]
31. Lorenz, C.P.; Ravenhall, D.G.; Pethick, C.J. Neutron Star Crusts. *Phys. Rev. Lett.* **1993**, *70*, 379–382. [CrossRef]
32. Newton, W.G.; Gearheart, M.; Li, B.A. A Survey of the Parameter Space of the Compressible Liquid Drop Model as Applied to the Neutron Star Inner Crust. *Astrophys. J. Suppl. Ser.* **2013**, *204*, 9. [CrossRef]
33. Balliet, L.E.; Newton, W.G.; Cantu, S.; Budimir, S. Prior Probability Distributions of Neutron Star Crust Models. *Astrophys. J.* **2021**, *918*, 79. [CrossRef]
34. Fortin, M.; Providência, C.; Raduta, A.R.; Gulminelli, F.; Zdunik, J.L.; Haensel, P.; Bejger, M. Neutron Star Radii and Crusts: Uncertainties and Unified Equations of State. *Phys. Rev. C* **2016**, *94*, 035804. [CrossRef]
35. Drischler, C.; Hebeler, K.; Schwenk, A. Asymmetric Nuclear Matter Based on Chiral Two- and Three-Nucleon Interactions. *Phys. Rev. C* **2016**, *93*, 054314. [CrossRef]
36. Antoniadis, J.; Freire, P.C.C.; Wex, N.; Tauris, T.M.; Lynch, R.S.; van Kerkwijk, M.H.; Kramer, M.; Bassa, C.; Dhillon, V.S.; Driebe, T.; et al. A Massive Pulsar in a Compact Relativistic Binary. *Science* **2013**, *340*. [CrossRef]
37. Fonseca, E.; Cromartie, H.T.; Pennucci, T.T.; Ray, P.S.; Kirichenko, A.Y.; Ransom, S.M.; Demorest, P.B.; Stairs, I.H.; Arzoumanian, Z.; Guillemot, L.; et al. Refined Mass and Geometric Measurements of the High-Mass PSR J0740+6620. *Astrophys. J. Lett.* **2021**, *915*, L12. [CrossRef]
38. Oppenheimer, J.R.; Volkoff, G.M. On Massive Neutron Cores. *Phys. Rev.* **1939**, *55*, 374–381. [CrossRef]
39. Tolman, R.C. Static Solutions of Einstein's Field Equations for Spheres of Fluid. *Phys. Rev.* **1939**, *55*, 364–373. [CrossRef] [PubMed]
40. LIGO Document P1800370-v5: Parameter Estimation Sample Release for GWTC-1. Available online: doi:10.7935/KSX7-QQ51 (accessed on 22 July 2021). [CrossRef]
41. Hinderer, T. Tidal Love Numbers of Neutron Stars. *Astrophys. J.* **2008**, *677*, 1216–1220. [CrossRef]

42. Binnington, T.; Poisson, E. Relativistic Theory of Tidal Love Numbers. *Phys. Rev. D* **2009**, *80*, 084018. [CrossRef]
43. Damour, T.; Nagar, A. Relativistic Tidal Properties of Neutron Stars. *Phys. Rev. D* **2009**, *80*, 084035. [CrossRef]
44. Dinh Thi, H.; Fantina, A.F.; Gulminelli, F. The Effect of the Energy Functional on the Pasta-Phase Properties of Catalysed Neutron Stars. *Eur. Phys. J. A* **2021**, submitted. [CrossRef]
45. Espinoza, C.M.; Lyne, A.G.; Stappers, B.W.; Kramer, M. A Study of 315 Glitches in the Rotation of 102 Pulsars. *Mon. Not. R. Astron. Soc.* **2011**, *414*, 1679–1704. [CrossRef]
46. Grill, F.; Providência, C.; Avancini, S.S. Neutron Star Inner Crust and Symmetry Energy. *Phys. Rev. C* **2012**, *85*, 055808. [CrossRef]
47. Pearson, J.M.; Chamel, N.; Potekhin, A.Y. Unified Equations of State for Cold Nonaccreting Neutron Stars with Brussels-Montreal Functionals. II. Pasta Phases in Semiclassical Approximation. *Phys. Rev. C* **2020**, *101*, 15802.
48. Lindblom, L. Spectral Representations of Neutron-Star Equations of State. *Phys. Rev. D* **2010**, *82*, 103011. [CrossRef]
49. Lattimer, J.M.; Prakash, M. Neutron Star Structure and the Equation of State. *Astrophys. J.* **2001**, *550*, 426–442. [CrossRef]
50. Landry, P.; Essick, R.; Chatziioannou, K. Nonparametric constraints on neutron star matter with existing and upcoming gravitational wave and pulsar observations. *Phys. Rev. D* **2020**, *101*, 123007. [CrossRef]
51. Pang, P.T. H.; Tews, I.; Coughlin, M.W.; Bulla, M.; Van Den Broeck, C.; Dietrich, T. Nuclear-Physics Multi-Messenger Astrophysics Constraints on the Neutron-Star Equation of State: Adding NICER's PSR J0740+6620 Measurement. *arXiv* **2021**, arXiv:2105.08688. [CrossRef]
52. Raaijmakers, G.; Greif, S.K.; Hebeler, K.; Hinderer, T.; Nissanke, S.; Schwenk, A.; Riley, T.E.; Watts, A.L.; Lattimer, J.M.; Ho, W.C.G. Constraints on the Dense Matter Equation of State and Neutron Star Properties from NICER's Mass-Radius Estimate of PSR J0740+6620 and Multimessenger Observations. *arXiv* **2021**, arXiv:2105.06981. [CrossRef]
53. Goriely, S.; Chamel, N.; Pearson, J.M. Further Explorations of Skyrme-Hartree-Fock-Bogoliubov Mass Formulas. XIII. the 2012 Atomic Mass Evaluation and the Symmetry Coefficient. *Phys. Rev. C* **2013**, *88*, 024308. [CrossRef]
54. Chabanat, E.; Bonche, P.; Haensel, P.; Meyer, J.; Schaeffer, R. A Skyrme Parametrization from Subnuclear to Neutron Star Densities Part II. Nuclei Far from Stabilities. *Nucl. Phys. A* **1998**, *635*, 231–256.
55. Sumiyoshi, K.; Kuwabara, H.; Toki, H. Relativistic mean-field theory with non-linear σ and ω terms for neutron stars and supernovae. *Nucl. Phys. A* **1995**, *581*, 725–746.
56. Long, W.; Meng, J.; Van Giai, N.; Zhou, S.G. New Effective Interactions in Relativistic Mean Field Theory with Nonlinear Terms and Density-Dependent Meson-Nucleon Coupling. *Phys. Rev. C* **2004**, *69*, 034319. [CrossRef]
57. Legred, I.; Chatziioannou, K.; Essick, R.; Han, S.; Landry, P. Impact of the PSR J0740+6620 Radius Constraint on the Properties of High-Density Matter. *arXiv* **2021**, arXiv:2106.05313. [CrossRef]
58. Biswas, B. Impact of PREX-II and Combined Radio/NICER/XMM-Newton's Mass-Radius Measurement of PSRJ0740+6620 on the Dense Matter Equation of State. *arXiv* **2021**, arXiv:2105.02886. [CrossRef]
59. Malik, T.; Alam, N.; Fortin, M.; Providência, C.; Agrawal, B.K.; Jha, T.K.; Kumar, B.; Patra, S.K. GW170817: Constraining the Nuclear Matter Equation of State from the Neutron Star Tidal Deformability. *Phys. Rev. C* **2018**, *98*, 035804. [CrossRef]
60. Fattoyev, F.J.; Piekarewicz, J.; Horowitz, C.J. Neutron Skins and Neutron Stars in the Multimessenger Era. *Phys. Rev. Lett.* **2018**, *120*, 172702.
61. Annala, E.; Gorda, T.; Kurkela, A.; Vuorinen, A. Gravitational-Wave Constraints on the Neutron-Star-Matter Equation of State. *Phys. Rev. Lett.* **2018**, *120*, 172703.
62. Lourenço, O.; Dutra, M.; Lenzi, C.H.; Flores, C.V.; Menezes, D.P. Consistent Relativistic Mean-Field Models Constrained by GW170817. *Phys. Rev. C* **2019**, *99*, 045202. [CrossRef]
63. Klähn, T.; Blaschke, D.; Typel, S.; van Dalen, E.N.E.; Faessler, A.; Fuchs, C.; Gaitanos, T.; Grigorian, H.; Ho, A.; Kolomeitsev, E.E.; et al. Constraints on the High-Density Nuclear Equation of State from the Phenomenology of Compact Stars and Heavy-Ion Collisions. *Phys. Rev. C* **2006**, *74*, 035802. [CrossRef]
64. Dobaczewski, J.; Nazarewicz, W.; Reinhard, P.-G. Error estimates of theoretical models: A guide. *J. Phys. G* **2014**, *41*, 074001. [CrossRef]
65. Margueron, J.; Gulminelli, F. Effect of High-Order Empirical Parameters on the Nuclear Equation of State. *Phys. Rev. C* **2019**, *99*, 025806. [CrossRef]
66. Danielewicz, P.; Lee, J. Symmetry Energy I: Semi-Infinite Matter. *Nucl. Phys. A* **2009**, *818*, 36–96. [CrossRef]
67. Chen, L.-W.; Cai, B.-J.; Ko, C.M.; Li, B.-A.; Shen, C.; Xu, J. Higher-Order Effects on the Incompressibility of Isospin Asymmetric Nuclear Matter. *Phys. Rev. C* **2009**, *80*, 014322. [CrossRef]
68. Vidaña, I.; Providência, C.; Polls, A.; Rios, A. Density Dependence of the Nuclear Symmetry Energy: A Microscopic Perspective. *Phys. Rev. C* **2009**, *80*, 045806. [CrossRef]
69. Ducoin, C.; Margueron, J.; Providência, C. Nuclear Symmetry Energy and Core-Crust Transition in Neutron Stars: A Critical Study. *Europhys. Lett.* **2010**, *91*, 32001. [CrossRef]
70. Santos, B.M.; Dutra, M.; Lourenço, O.; Delfino, A. Correlations between the Nuclear Matter Symmetry Energy, Its Slope, and Curvature from a Nonrelativistic Solvable Approach and Beyond. *Phys. Rev. C* **2014**, *90*, 035203. [CrossRef]
71. Mondal, C.; Agrawal, B.K.; De, J.N.; Samaddar, S.K.; Centelles, M.; Viñas, X. Interdependence of different symmetry energy elements. *Phys. Rev. C* **2017**, *96*, 021302. [CrossRef]

72. Mondal, C.; Agrawal, B.K.; De, J.N.; Samaddar, S.K. Correlations among symmetry energy elements in Skyrme models. *Int. J. Mod. Phys. E* **2018**, *27*, 1850078. [CrossRef]
73. Adamczewski-Musch, J.; Arnold, O.; Behnke, C.; Belounnas, A.; Belyaev, A.; Berger-Chen, J.C.; Blanco, A.; Blume, C.; Böhmer, M.; Bordalo, P.; et al. Directed, Elliptic, and Higher Order Flow Harmonics of Protons, Deuterons, and Tritons in Au + Au Collisions at $\sqrt{s_{NN}}$ = 2.4 GeV. *Phys. Rev. Lett.* **2020**, *125*, 262301. [CrossRef]

Article

Equation of State and Composition of Proto-Neutron Stars and Merger Remnants with Hyperons

Armen Sedrakian [1,2,*] and Arus Harutyunyan [3,4]

[1] Frankfurt Institute for Advanced Studies, Ruth-Moufang-Straße, 1, 60438 Frankfurt am Main, Germany
[2] Institute of Theoretical Physics, University of Wrocław, 50-204 Wrocław, Poland
[3] Byurakan Astrophysical Observatory, Byurakan 0213, Armenia; arus@bao.sci.am
[4] Department of Physics, Yerevan State University, Yerevan 0025, Armenia
* Correspondence: sedrakian@fias.uni-frankfurt.de

Abstract: Finite-temperature equation of state (EoS) and the composition of dense nuclear and hypernuclear matter under conditions characteristic of neutron star binary merger remnants and supernovas are discussed. We consider both neutrino free-streaming and trapped regimes which are separated by a temperature of a few MeV. The formalism is based on covariant density functional (CDF) theory for the full baryon octet with density-dependent couplings, suitably adjusted in the hypernuclear sector. The softening of the EoS with the introduction of the hyperons is quantified under various conditions of lepton fractions and temperatures. We find that Λ, Ξ^-, and Ξ^0 hyperons appear in the given order with a sharp density increase at zero temperature at the threshold being replaced by an extended increment over a wide density range at high temperatures. The Λ hyperon survives in the deep subnuclear regime. The triplet of Σs is suppressed in cold hypernuclear matter up to around seven times the nuclear saturation density, but appears in significant fractions at higher temperatures, $T \geq 20$ MeV, in both supernova and merger remnant matter. We point out that a special isospin degeneracy point exists where the baryon abundances within each of the three isospin multiplets are equal to each other as a result of (approximate) isospin symmetry. At that point, the charge chemical potential of the system vanishes. We find that under the merger remnant conditions, the fractions of electron and μ-on neutrinos are close and are about 1%, whereas in the supernova case, we only find a significant fraction ($\sim$10%) of electron neutrinos, given that in this case, the μ-on lepton number is zero.

Keywords: equation of state; neutron stars; neutrinos; hyperons

Citation: Sedrakian, A.; Harutyunyan, A. Equation of State and Composition of Proto-Neutron Stars and Merger Remnants with Hyperons. *Universe* **2021**, *7*, 382. https://doi.org/10.3390/universe7100382

Academic Editor: Nicolas Chamel

Received: 4 September 2021
Accepted: 8 October 2021
Published: 15 October 2021

Publisher's Note: MDPI stays neutral with regard to jurisdictional claims in published maps and institutional affiliations.

Copyright: © 2021 by the authors. Licensee MDPI, Basel, Switzerland. This article is an open access article distributed under the terms and conditions of the Creative Commons Attribution (CC BY) license (https://creativecommons.org/licenses/by/4.0/).

1. Introduction

Several astrophysical scenarios lead to the formation of hot, neutrino-rich compact objects which contain nuclear and hypernuclear matter at finite temperature. One such scenario arises in the core-collapse supernova and proto-neutron star context, where a hot proto-neutron star is formed during the contraction of the supernova progenitor and subsequent gravitational detachment of the remnant from the expanding ejecta [1–7]. A related scenario arises in the case of stellar black-hole formation when the progenitor mass is so large (typically tens of solar masses) that the formation of a stable compact object is not possible and a black hole is inevitably formed [8–11]. Finally, the binary neutron star mergers offer yet another scenario where finite temperature nuclear and hypernuclear matter play an important role [12–15]. In the "hot" stage of evolution of these objects the thermodynamics of the matter is characterized by several parameters, for example, density, temperature and lepton fraction. This is in contrast to the case of cold (essentially zero-temperature) compact stars whose thermodynamics is fully determined by a one-parameter EoS relating pressure to energy density under approximate β-equilibrium. An important feature of the hot stages of evolution of compact stars is the trapped neutrino component above the trapping temperature $T_{tr} \simeq 5$ MeV—a regime where the neutrino mean-free-path is shorter than the size of the star [16]. As is well known, neutrinos affect significantly the composition of matter and are important for the energy transport and dynamics of supernova and binary neutron star mergers.

After the first observation of a massive compact star in 2010 [17] which was followed by further observations of such objects [18,19] the interest in the covariant density functional (CDF) theories of superdense matter resurged because its parameters became subject to astrophysical constraints in addition to the (low-density) constraints coming from laboratory nuclear physics (for reviews see [20–22]). CDF based models tuned to the astrophysical constraints that account for the finite temperature, neutrino component, and strangeness in the form of hyperons appeared in recent years [23–34].

In this work, we study the EoS and composition of nuclear and hypernuclear matter both in the neutrino free and neutrino-trapped regimes within the CDF formalism. Our numerical implementation is based on that of Ref. [24] but also includes the hidden strangeness σ^* and ϕ mesons which account for the interactions amongst hyperons. In addition, instead of using SU(3) symmetry arguments of Ref. [24] in the scalar sector, we adjust the parameters to the depths of hyperon potentials, as already done in Refs. [35–37] in the case of zero-temperature EoS. In this work, we use, for the sake of conciseness, a single nucleonic CDF with parameters chosen according DDME2 parameterization [38]. A similar nucleonic DDME2-model-based finite temperature EoS has been presented in Ref. [32], where the couplings in the hyperonic sector were taken from Ref. [39] which differ from the ones adopted here. In this work, we do not address microscopic models of hypernuclear matter which predict too low masses associated for hyperonic stars, see Refs. [22,40] for reviews.

This work is organized as follows. Section 2 is devoted to the formal aspects of EoS and the composition of matter at finite temperatures. The CDF formalism is discussed in Section 2.1 and the choice of the baryon–meson coupling constants is addressed in Section 2.2. The thermodynamic conditions of baryonic matter relevant to neutron star mergers and supernovas are discussed in Section 2.3. Our numerical results are given in Section 3. Section 4 provides a short summary. We use the natural (Gaussian) units with $\hbar = c = k_B = 1$, and the metric signature $g^{\mu\nu} = \mathrm{diag}(1, -1, -1, -1)$.

2. Relativistic Density Functional with Density-Dependent Couplings

2.1. Equation of State

We start with a description of the formalism of CDF as applied to hyperonic matter. In this work, we adopt the DDME2 parameterization [38] which is based on the version of the theory that uses density-dependent coupling constants for the meson-baryon interactions [41].

The Lagrangian of the stellar matter is given by

$$\mathcal{L} = \mathcal{L}_b + \mathcal{L}_m + \mathcal{L}_\lambda + \mathcal{L}_{em}, \qquad (1)$$

where the baryon Lagrangian is given by

$$\mathcal{L}_b = \sum_b \bar{\psi}_b \left[\gamma^\mu \left(i \partial_\mu - g_{\omega b} \omega_\mu - g_{\phi b} \phi_\mu - \frac{1}{2} g_{\rho B} \boldsymbol{\tau} \cdot \boldsymbol{\rho}_\mu \right) - (m_b - g_{\sigma b} \sigma - g_{\sigma^* b} \sigma^*) \right] \psi_b, \qquad (2)$$

where the b-sum is over the $J_B^P = \frac{1}{2}^+$ baryon octet; ψ_b are the Dirac fields of baryons with masses m_b; $\sigma, \sigma^*, \omega_\mu, \phi_\mu$, and $\boldsymbol{\rho}_\mu$ are the mesonic fields and g_{mb} are the coupling constants that are density-dependent. The σ^*- and ϕ-meson fields only couple to hyperons. The mesonic part of the Lagrangian is given by

$$\begin{aligned}\mathcal{L}_m &= \frac{1}{2}\partial^\mu\sigma\partial_\mu\sigma - \frac{m_\sigma^2}{2}\sigma^2 - \frac{1}{4}\omega^{\mu\nu}\omega_{\mu\nu} + \frac{m_\omega^2}{2}\omega^\mu\omega_\mu - \frac{1}{4}\rho^{\mu\nu}\cdot\rho_{\mu\nu} + \frac{m_\rho^2}{2}\rho^\mu\cdot\rho_\mu \\ &+ \frac{1}{2}\partial^\mu\sigma^*\partial_\mu\sigma^* - \frac{m_\sigma^{*2}}{2}\sigma^{*2} - \frac{1}{4}\phi^{\mu\nu}\phi_{\mu\nu} + \frac{m_\phi^2}{2}\phi^\mu\phi_\mu,\end{aligned} \quad (3)$$

where m_σ, m_{σ^*}, m_ω, m_ϕ and m_ρ are the meson masses and $\omega_{\mu\nu}$, $\phi_{\mu\nu}$ and $\rho_{\mu\nu}$ stand for the field-strength tensors of vector mesons

$$\omega_{\mu\nu} = \partial_\mu\omega_\nu - \partial_\mu\omega_\nu, \quad \phi_{\mu\nu} = \partial_\mu\phi_\nu - \partial_\mu\phi_\nu, \quad \rho_{\mu\nu} = \partial_\nu\rho_\mu - \partial_\mu\rho_\nu. \quad (4)$$

The leptonic Lagrangian is given by

$$\mathcal{L}_\lambda = \sum_\lambda \bar{\psi}_\lambda(i\gamma^\mu\partial_\mu - m_\lambda)\psi_\lambda, \quad (5)$$

where ψ_λ are leptonic fields and m_λ are their masses. The lepton index λ includes electrons and μ-ons. In hot stellar matter, one needs to include also the three flavors of neutrinos whenever they are trapped. An approximate estimate of the temperature above which neutrinos are trapped is $T_{tr} = 5$ MeV. We will neglect henceforth the strong magnetic fields present in certain classes of compact stars and drop the gauge part $\mathcal{L}_{em}$ of the Lagrangian. For the inclusion of these effects see Refs. [42–44]. We do not consider in this work the non-strange $J = \frac{3}{2}$ members of the baryons decuplet—the Δ-resonances [35,45–50]; for a review, see [21].

The partition function $\mathcal{Z}$ of the matter can be evaluated in the mean-field and infinite system approximations from which one finds the pressure and energy density

$$P = P_m + P_b + P_\lambda, \quad \mathcal{E} = \mathcal{E}_m + \mathcal{E}_b + \mathcal{E}_\lambda, \quad (6)$$

with the contributions due to mesons and baryons given by

$$P_m = -\frac{m_\sigma^2}{2}\sigma^2 - \frac{m_\sigma^{*2}}{2}\sigma^{*2} + \frac{m_\omega^2}{2}\omega_0^2 + \frac{m_\phi^2}{2}\phi_0^2 + \frac{m_\rho^2}{2}\rho_{03}^2, \quad (7)$$

$$\mathcal{E}_m = \frac{m_\sigma^2}{2}\sigma^2 + \frac{m_\sigma^{*2}}{2}\sigma^{*2} + \frac{m_\omega^2}{2}\omega_0^2 + \frac{m_\phi^2}{2}\phi_0^2 + \frac{m_\rho^2}{2}\rho_{03}^2, \quad (8)$$

$$P_b = \frac{1}{3}\sum_b \frac{2J_b+1}{2\pi^2}\int_0^\infty \frac{dk\,k^4}{E_k^b}\left[f(E_k^b - \mu_b^*) + f(E_k^b + \mu_b^*)\right], \quad (9)$$

$$\mathcal{E}_b = \sum_b \frac{2J_b+1}{2\pi^2}\int_0^\infty dk\,k^2 E_k^b\left[f(E_k^b - \mu_b^*) + f(E_k^b + \mu_b^*)\right], \quad (10)$$

where $2J_b + 1$ is the spin degeneracy factor of the baryon octet. The lepton contribution is given by

$$P_\lambda = \frac{1}{3}\sum_\lambda \frac{2J_\lambda+1}{2\pi^2}\int_0^\infty \frac{dk\,k^4}{E_k^\lambda}\left[f(E_k^\lambda - \mu_\lambda) + f(E_k^\lambda + \mu_\lambda)\right], \quad (11)$$

$$\mathcal{E}_\lambda = \sum_\lambda \frac{2J_\lambda+1}{2\pi^2}\int_0^\infty dk\,k^2 E_k^\lambda\left[f(E_k^\lambda - \mu_\lambda) + f(E_k^\lambda + \mu_\lambda)\right], \quad (12)$$

where $2J_\lambda + 1 = 2$ for electrons and μ-ons and 1 for neutrinos of all flavors. The single particle energies of baryons and leptons are given by $E_k^b = \sqrt{k^2 + m_b^{*2}}$ and $E_k^\lambda = \sqrt{k^2 + m_\lambda^2}$, respectively, where the effective (Dirac) baryon masses in the mean-field approximation are given by

$$m_b^* = m_b - g_{\sigma b}\sigma - g_{\sigma^* b}\sigma^*. \quad (13)$$

Next, $f(E) = [1 + \exp(E/T)]^{-1}$ is the Fermi distribution function at temperature T. The effective baryon chemical potentials are given by

$$\mu_b^* = \mu_b - g_{\omega b}\omega_0 - g_{\phi b}\phi_0 - g_{\rho b}\rho_{03}I_{3b} - \Sigma^r, \qquad (14)$$

where μ_b is the chemical potential, I_{3b} is the third component of baryon isospin and the rearrangement self-energy Σ^r, which arises from density-dependence of the coupling constants, is given by

$$\Sigma^r = \sum_b \left(\frac{\partial g_{\omega b}}{\partial n_b}\omega_0 n_b + \frac{\partial g_{\rho b}}{\partial n_b}I_{3b}\rho_{03}n_b + \frac{\partial g_{\phi b}}{\partial n_b}\phi_0 n_b - \frac{\partial g_{\sigma b}}{\partial n_b}\sigma n_b^s - \frac{\partial g_{\sigma^* b}}{\partial n_b}\sigma^* n_b^s \right). \qquad (15)$$

In the mean-field approximation the meson expectation values are given by

$$m_\sigma^2 \sigma = \sum_b g_{\sigma b} n_b^s, \quad m_{\sigma^*}^2 \sigma^* = \sum_b g_{\sigma^* b} n_b^s, \qquad (16)$$

$$m_\omega^2 \omega_0 = \sum_b g_{\omega b} n_b, \quad m_\phi^2 \phi_0 = \sum_b g_{\phi b} n_b, \qquad (17)$$

$$m_\rho^2 \rho_{03} = \sum_b I_{3b} g_{\rho b} n_b, \qquad (18)$$

where the meson fields now stand for their mean-field values; the scalar number density is given by $n_b^s = \langle \bar\psi_b \psi_b \rangle$, whereas the baryon number density is given by $n_b = \langle \bar\psi_b \gamma^0 \psi_b \rangle$. Explicitly, they are given by

$$n_b = \frac{2J_b + 1}{2\pi^2} \int_0^\infty k^2 dk \left[f(E_k^b - \mu_b^*) - f(E_k^b + \mu_b^*) \right], \qquad (19)$$

$$n_b^s = \frac{2J_b + 1}{2\pi^2} \int_0^\infty k^2 dk \, \frac{m_b^*}{E_k^b} \left[f(E_k^b - \mu_b^*) + f(E_k^b + \mu_b^*) \right]. \qquad (20)$$

2.2. Choice of Coupling Constants

The coupling constants are functions of baryon density, n_B. This accounts for modifications of interactions by the medium at zero temperature; the extrapolation to finite temperature neglects the influence of temperature on the self-energies of baryons at beyond-mean-field level. The nucleon–meson couplings are given by

$$g_{iN}(n_B) = g_{iN}(n_{sat}) h_i(x), \qquad (21)$$

where n_{sat} is the saturation density, $x = n_B/n_{sat}$ and

$$h_i(x) = \frac{a_i + b_i(x + d_i)^2}{a_i + c_i(x + d_i)^2}, \quad i = \sigma, \omega, \quad h_\rho(x) = e^{-a_\rho(x-1)}. \qquad (22)$$

For completeness, we list the values of parameters in Table 1.

Table 1. The values of parameters of the DDME2 CDF.

Meson (i)	m_i (MeV)	a_i	b_i	c_i	d_i	g_{iN}
σ	550.1238	1.3881	1.0943	1.7057	0.4421	10.5396
ω	783	1.3892	0.9240	1.4620	0.4775	13.0189
ρ	763	0.5647	—	—	—	7.3672

The density-dependent functions $h_i(x)$ are subject to constraints $h_i(1) = 1$, $h_i''(0) = 0$ and $h_\sigma''(1) = h_\omega''(1)$.

Fixing the hyperonic coupling constants involves two sources of information: (a) the couplings of hyperons to the vector mesons are chosen according to the SU(6) spin-flavor symmetric model [51]; (b) their couplings to the scalar mesons are chosen such as to reproduce their phenomenological potential depths at the saturation density, which are determined from experiments.

We express the hyperonic couplings in terms of their ratios to the corresponding couplings of nucleons: $R_{iY} = g_{iY}/g_{iN}$ for $i = \{\sigma, \omega, \rho\}$ and $R_{\sigma^*Y} = g_{\sigma^*Y}/g_{\sigma N}$, $R_{\phi Y} = g_{\phi Y}/g_{\omega N}$. For Λ-hyperons, we adopt $R_{\sigma\Lambda} = 0.6106$ [35], which is close to the value determined in Ref. [52] through fits to the Λ-hypernuclei. The likely range of the potentials for Σ and Ξ hyperons are

$$-10 \leq U_\Sigma(n_{\text{sat}}) \leq 30 \text{ MeV}, \quad (23)$$

$$-24 \leq U_\Xi(n_{\text{sat}}) \leq 0 \text{ MeV}, \quad (24)$$

where the value $U_\Xi(n_{\text{sat}}) = -24$ MeV has been given in [53] and is much deeper than the one expected from Lattice 2019 results [54,55]. The adopted values of the coupling constants are taken from Ref. [35] and are listed in Table 2. Note that it is implicitly assumed that the couplings of mesons to hyperons have the same density dependence as for nucleons. The hidden strangeness mesons have masses $m_{\sigma^*} = 980$ and $m_\phi = 1019.45$ MeV, with the density dependence of their couplings coinciding with those of the couplings of the σ- and ω-mesons, respectively.

Table 2. The ratios of the couplings of hyperons to mesons. See text for explanations.

$Y\backslash R$	$R_{\omega Y}$	$R_{\phi Y}$	$R_{\rho Y}$	$R_{\sigma Y}$	$R_{\sigma^* Y}$
Λ	2/3	$-\sqrt{2}/3$	0	0.6106	0.4777
Σ	2/3	$-\sqrt{2}/3$	2	0.4426	0.4777
Ξ	1/3	$-2\sqrt{2}/3$	1	0.3024	0.9554

2.3. Thermodynamic Conditions in Supernovas and Merger Remnants

Next, we adopt our hypernuclear CDF to the stellar conditions, specifically to the cases of supernovas and binary neutron star mergers. As already mentioned, two regimes arise depending on the ratio of the neutrino mean-free-path to the size of the system: the neutrino free regime in the case of this ratio being much larger than unity, and the trapped neutrino regime in the opposite case. Trapped neutrinos are in thermal equilibrium and are characterized by appropriate Fermi distribution functions at the matter temperature. Numerical simulations provide the lepton fractions that we adopt in our static (time-independent) description. We assume that the lepton number is conserved in each family, which implies that the neutrino oscillations are neglected. The τ-leptons are neglected because of their large mass. For supernova matter, the predicted electron and muon lepton numbers are typically $Y_{L,e} \equiv Y_e + Y_{\nu_e} = 0.4$ and $Y_{L,\mu} \equiv Y_\mu + Y_{\nu_\mu} = 0$ [1,6,29], where we introduced partial lepton densities normalized by the baryon density $Y_{e,\mu} = (n_{e,\mu} - n_{e^+,\mu^+})/n_B$, where e^+ refers to the positron and μ^+—to the anti-muon. Note, however, that Y_e may vary significantly along with a supernova profile in a time-dependent manner. Furthermore, muonization in the matter can lead to a small (of the order 10^{-3}) fraction of μ-ons [56,57] which we neglect here. In the case of neutron star mergers, the hot remnant emerges from the material of initial cold neutron stars, and the lepton fractions $Y_{L,e} = Y_{L,\mu} = 0.1$ are assumed for the remnant of a merger. The adopted values reflect (approximately) those of the pre-merger cold neutron stars.

The stellar matter is in weak equilibrium and is charge neutral. The equilibrium with respect to the weak processes requires

$$\mu_\Lambda = \mu_{\Sigma^0} = \mu_{\Xi^0} = \mu_n = \mu_B, \tag{25}$$

$$\mu_{\Sigma^-} = \mu_{\Xi^-} = \mu_B - \mu_Q, \tag{26}$$

$$\mu_{\Sigma^+} = \mu_B + \mu_Q, \tag{27}$$

where μ_B and $\mu_Q = \mu_p - \mu_n$ are the baryon and charge chemical potentials, μ_b with $b \in \{n, p, \Lambda, \Sigma^{0,\pm}, \Xi^{0,-}\}$ are the thermodynamic chemical potentials of the baryons. The charge neutrality condition is given in terms of the partial densities of charged baryons as

$$n_p + n_{\Sigma^+} - (n_{\Sigma^-} + n_{\Xi^-}) = n_Q. \tag{28}$$

Introducing the partial charge density normalized by the baryonic density $Y_Q = n_Q/n_B$, the charge neutrality condition can be written

$$Y_Q = Y_e + Y_\mu. \tag{29}$$

The free streaming and trapped neutrino regimes are characterized by

$$\mu_e = \mu_\mu = -\mu_Q = \mu_n - \mu_p, \quad \text{(free streaming)} \tag{30}$$

$$\mu_e = \mu_{L,e} - \mu_Q, \quad \mu_\mu = \mu_{L,\mu} - \mu_Q, \quad \text{(trapped)} \tag{31}$$

where $\mu_{L,e/\mu}$ are the lepton chemical potentials which are associated with the lepton number $Y_{L,e} = Y_e + Y_{\nu_e}$ and $Y_{L,\mu} = Y_\mu + Y_{\nu_\mu}$, which are conserved separately. Combining the weak-equilibrium and charge neutrality conditions we are now in a position to compute the EoS of stellar matter both in the trapped and free streaming neutrino regimes. Note that it is implicitly assumed that the matter is under detailed balance with respect to Urca processes; if this condition is violated, then an additional "isospin chemical potential" arises [58,59]. Additionally, note that we do not constrain particles to their Fermi surfaces and any corrections associated with the finite temperature features of the Fermi distribution function are included in our β-equilibratium condition.

3. Numerical Results

Our numerical procedure involves a solution of self-consistent equations for the meson fields and the scalar and baryon densities for fixed values of temperature, density, and lepton numbers $Y_{L,e}$ and $Y_{L,\mu}$, which are chosen according to the physical conditions characteristic for supernovas and merger remnants, as specified in Section 2.3. In this work, we concentrate on the features of EoS and particle fractions (or abundances) in the matter under various thermodynamic conditions.

Figure 1 shows the EoS for nucleonic and hyperonic matter at temperature $T = 0.1$ MeV in the β-equilibrium and neutrino-free case, as well as at $T = 5$ and 50 MeV with trapped neutrinos and several values of $Y_{L,e}$. The μ-on fractions are chosen as $Y_{L,\mu} = 0$ for $Y_{L,e} = 0.2, 0.4$ and $Y_{L,\mu} = Y_{L,e} = 0.1$. The non-zero $Y_{L,\mu}$ is characteristic of merger remnants whereas zero $Y_{L,\mu}$ is characteristic for supernovas. The key well-known feature of the onset of hyperons seen in Figure 1 is the softening of the EoS, i.e., the shift of pressure to lower values above the energy-density for the onset of hyperons. It is further seen that for a higher temperature, the pressure is larger at low densities and is lower at high densities independent of the presence of hyperons.

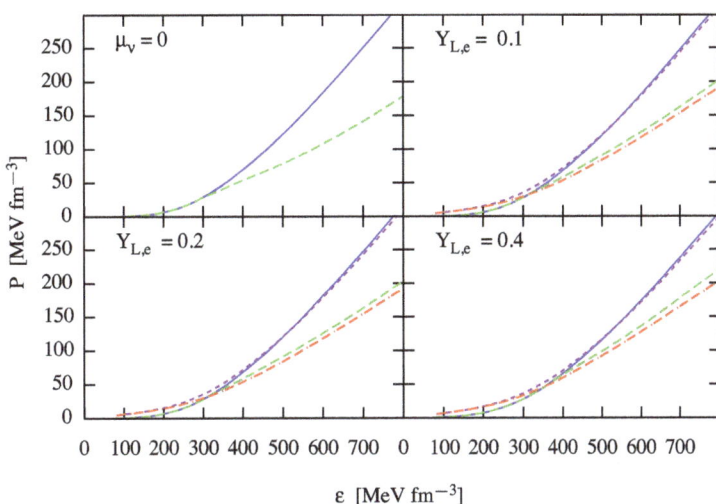

Figure 1. Dependence of the pressure on the energy density. The panel labeled $\mu_\nu = 0$ corresponds to neutrino-free β-equilibrium case without (solid) and with (dashed) hyperons at $T = 0.1$ MeV. (Varying the temperature up to T_{tr} does not produce visible changes.) The remaning panels show results for the neutrino trapped matter at $T = 5$ MeV (solid—without hyperons and long-dashed—with hyperons) and 50 MeV (short-dashed—without hyperons and double-dash-dotted—with hyperons) for $Y_{L,e} = 0.1, 0.2, 0.4$. The μ-on fractions are $Y_{L,\mu} = Y_{L,e} = 0.1$ (upper right panel) and $Y_{L,\mu} = 0$ for $Y_{L,e} = 0.2$ and 0.4 (lower row). The case $Y_{L,e} = 0.1$ is characteristic of a merger remnant, whereas $Y_{L,e} = 0.2, 0.4$—to supernova.

Figure 2 shows the particle number densities n_i/n_B in $npe\mu$-matter normalized by baryon density as a function of baryon density normalized by $n_{sat} = 0.152$ fm^{-3}. The case $\mu_\nu = 0$ corresponds to the β-equilibrium neutrino-free case at $T = 1$ MeV, whereas the cases $Y_{L,e} = 0.1, 0.2, 0.4$ correspond to the trapped neutrino regime at $T = 50$ MeV. The choices of $Y_{L,\mu}$ match those of Figure 1. In contrast to the neutrino-transparent case, where the muons appear above a threshold density around n_{sat} where $\mu_e \geq m_\mu$, in the neutrino-trapped regime, the electron and muon contributions are almost equal under merger conditions ($Y_{L,e} = 0.1$), and there is a visible fraction of μ-on neutrinos. Thus, the charge neutrality is maintained through the balance of negative charges of both types of leptons with protons. From the upper right panel of Figure 2, we see that the net neutrino numbers become negative at low densities for both lepton families, indicating that there are more antineutrinos than neutrinos in the low-density and high-temperature regime of neutron star merger matter.

Note that the proton fraction remains below the threshold for the Urca processes to operate in the low-temperature neutrino-free regime. In the high-temperature regime, the phase-space for Urca processes opens due to the thermal smearing of Fermi surfaces of baryons. This has important ramifications on the oscillations of post-merger remnants through the damping effect of the bulk viscosity driven by Urca processes [34,58,60–62].

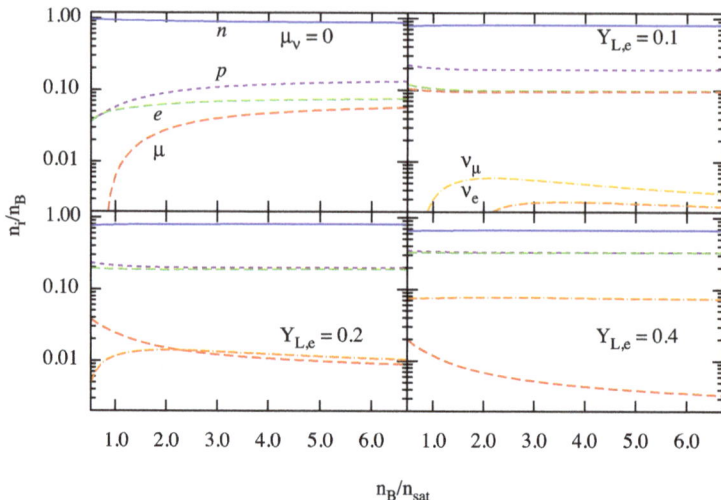

Figure 2. Dependence of the particle fractions n_i/n_B on the baryon density n_B normalized by the saturation density. The panels show the composition of $npe\mu$ matter in β-equilibrium at $T = 1$ MeV in the neutrino-free case ($\mu_\nu = 0$) and for neutrino-trapped matter at $T = 50$ MeV for several values of the electron lepton faction $Y_{Le} = 0.1, 0.2, 0.4$., with the μ-on component satisfying $Y_{L\mu} = Y_{Le} = 0.1$ and $Y_{L\mu} = 0$ for $Y_{Le} = 0.2, 0.4$, where $Y_{L\mu}$ is the μ-on lepton fraction.

Under the supernova conditions, μ-ons are greatly suppressed and the corresponding neutrinos are extinct. Then, the near equality of proton and electron abundances is required by charge neutrality. Note that the μ-on abundances need not vanish, as $Y_{L,\mu}$ also includes the contributions from muonic neutrinos and antineutrinos. The small μ-on fraction seen in the lower panels of Figure 2 is compensated by an equal fraction of muonic antineutrinos $\bar{\nu}_\mu$ required by the condition $Y_{L,\mu} = 0$. The isospin asymmetry in supernova matter is reduced with increasing $Y_{L,e}$ and, consequently, the difference between the neutron and proton abundances gradually vanishes. The electron-neutrino population increases as well. In the cases $Y_{L,e} = 0.1$, the μ-on neutrino fraction is comparable to that of electron-neutrinos, as their lepton numbers are set equal. In the lower panels of Figure 2, they are absent because we enforced the condition $Y_{L,\mu} = 0$.

Figure 3 shows the same as Figure 2, but it includes the full baryon octet. Hyperons appear at densities above the saturation, in the following sequence: Λ, Ξ^- and Ξ^0. The onset of Σ^- hyperon in the low-temperature matter occurs at densities outside the range shown. The reason for the shift of Σ^- hyperons to high densities is the adopted highly repulsive potential value in nuclear matter [63–68]. This ordering is at variance to the case of free hyperonic gas, where Σ^- was predicted to be the first hyperon to nucleate [69], and more elaborate models which assign weakly repulsive potential, see, e.g., [24]. However, the triplet of $\Sigma^{\pm,0}$ is present for $T = 50$ MeV independent of the values of lepton numbers. It is interesting that Σ^- and Σ^+ fractions interchange their roles from being most abundant to least abundant Σ-hyperon with increasing density at a special intersection point where the abundances of all the Σs coincide. Note that the location of this special point depends on the choice of $Y_{L,e}$. Furthermore, it is seen that the intersection point of n and p fractions, as well as that of Ξ^- and Ξ^0 fractions, are located close to the intersection point of Σs.

This feature can be understood by examining the β-equilibrium conditions (25)–(27). If there is a point within the density range considered where the proton fraction reaches the neutron fraction (which means $\mu_n^* = \mu_p^*$ due to Equation (19)), then the charge chemical potential $\mu_Q = \mu_p - \mu_n$ vanishes at that point (due to the density scaling (22), the contribution of the ρ-meson mean-field to the effective baryon chemical potentials (14) is negligible at high densities, resulting in $\mu_n^* - \mu_p^* \simeq \mu_n - \mu_p$). This results in a single chemical potential $\mu_b = \mu_B$ for the full baryon octet at that special *isospin degeneracy* point. This implies, in turn, almost equal values of effective chemical potentials and, therefore, equal baryon fractions within a given isospin-multiplet.

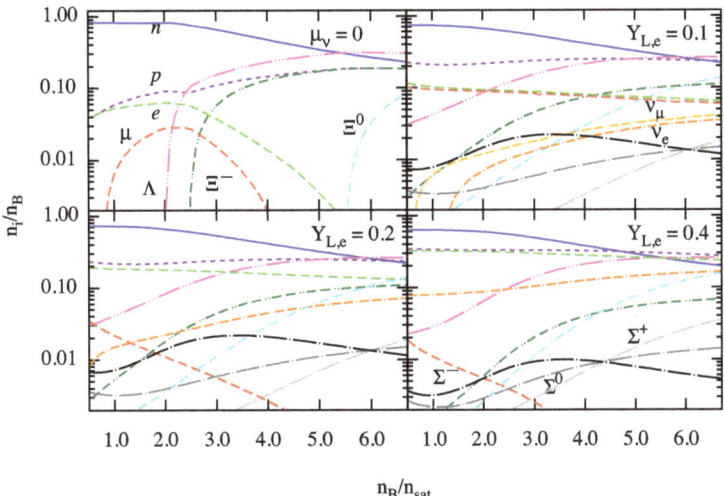

Figure 3. Same as in Figure 2, but for the full baryon octet with the μ-on component satisfying the conditions $Y_{L,\mu} = Y_{L,e} = 0.1$ (**upper right**) and $Y_{L,\mu} = 0$ for $Y_{L,e} = 0.2, 0.4$ (**lower row**). In the low-temperature, β-equilibrium case, the Λ, Ξ^- and Ξ^0 appear in the given order with a sharp increase in their fractions at the corresponding density thresholds. At high temperature $T = 50$ MeV the density thresholds are located at lower densities (some are outside figure's scale) and the triplet $\Sigma^{0,\pm}$ appears. The fractions of Λ hyperons are shown by dash-triple-dot lines, that of $\Xi^{0,-}$ by double-dash-double-dot lines and that of $\Sigma^{0,\pm}$ by dash-single-dot lines. The electron and μ-ons neutrinos are shown by double-dash-dot lines; the electrons and μ-ons by long-dashed lines, protons by short-dashed lines and, finally, neutrons by solid lines.

Figure 4 shows the effective masses of baryons as a function of density at $T = 0.1$ MeV and in β-equilibrium. The effective masses of isospin multiplets (n, p), $\Sigma^{0,\pm}$ and $\Xi^{0,-}$ are degenerate. The temperature dependence of the effective masses of baryons is very weak and, for the sake of clarity, is not shown.

Figure 5 shows the effective baryon chemical potentials minus their effective masses, which clearly show the special intersection points within each multiplet at all values of the lepton fractions in the neutrino-trapped matter. Note that the effective masses within each multiplet are equal in our model, see Figure 4 above. On the left side of the intersection point we have $\mu_Q \leq 0$, which according to the conditions (25)–(27) puts the baryon abundances within each multiplet in the charge-decreasing order (i.e., baryons with smaller charges are more abundant). Above the intersection point $\mu_Q \geq 0$, the ordering of baryon fractions within each multiplet is reversed. Similar behaviour of baryon abundances was found also in Refs. [6,32], where the composition of hot stellar matter was shown at constant entropy-per-baryon and the composition of matter also included the quartet of Δ-resonances. Note that in the ideal case of exact isospin symmetry, the intersection points of the three isospin-multiplets $n - p$, $\Sigma^{0,\pm}$ and $\Xi^{0,-}$ would be located exactly at the same density. The small deviations of these three points from each other (which increase gradually with increasing $Y_{L,e}$) reflect the fact that the isospin symmetry is approximate.

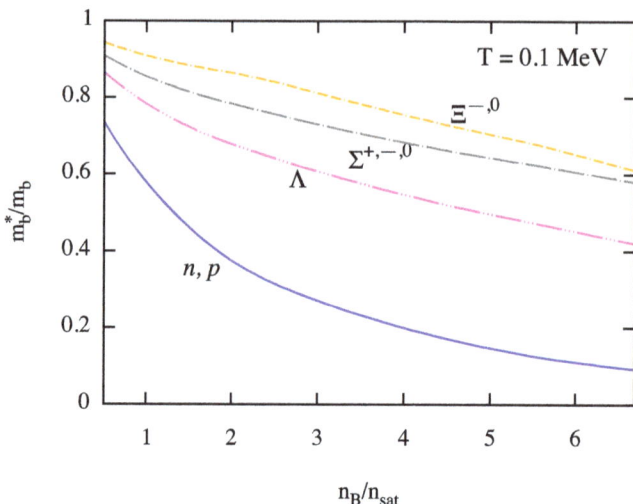

Figure 4. Dependence of effective masses of baryons on the density at $T = 0.1$ MeV and in β-equilibrium. Each isospin multiplet is shown by a single line due to the degeneracy in their masses.

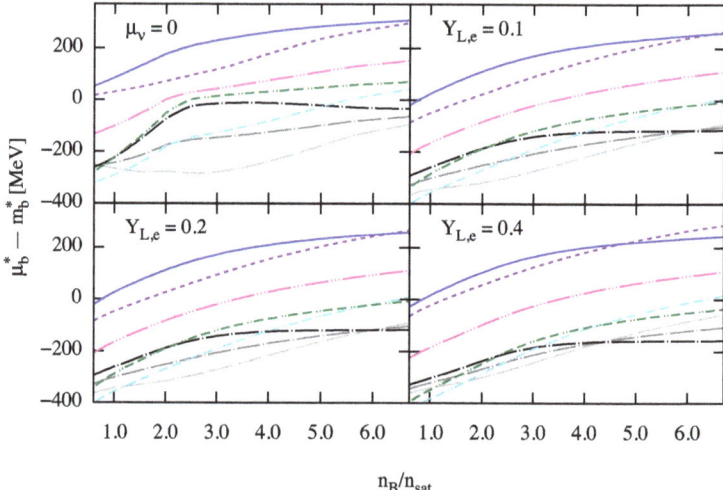

Figure 5. Dependence of baryon effective chemical potentials (computed from their effective masses) on the normalized baryon density n_B/n_{sat}. The line styles for each baryon and the values of the temperature and lepton fractions for each panel match those in Figure 3. The intersection (isospin degeneracy) points of chemical potentials of the same isospin-multiples is clearly visible at all values of lepton fractions in the neutrino-trapped matter.

The difference between almost equal abundances of leptons for $Y_{L,e} = 0.1$ and the remaining cases $Y_{L,e} = 0.2, 0.4$ is related to our choice of $Y_{L,\mu}$ to reflect merger remnant conditions (first case) and supernova conditions (second case). This difference also propagates to the abundances of electron and μ-on neutrinos, which are present in almost equal quantities in the first case, whereas in the second case, the μ-on neutrinos are replaced by a much smaller amount of μ-on antineutrinos. Hyperons affect the way the charge neutrality is maintained at high density. In low-temperature and β-equilibrated matter it is enforced by equal abundances of protons and Ξ^- hyperons with electrons and μ-ons being extinct at high densities. At finite temperature, the electrons are abundant and the presence of Ξ^- hyperon only induces some splitting between the electron and proton fractions, which becomes less pronounced with increasing $Y_{L,e}$. The fractions of μ-ons and their neutrinos in the merger remnant case ($Y_{L,e} = Y_{L,\mu} = 0.1$) are as significant as those of electrons and electron-neutrinos, respectively, but they do not play any significant role in the supernova case where $Y_{L,\mu} = 0$. In contrast to the pure nucleonic matter where the neutrino abundances remain constant or decrease slowly with baryon density, the hypernuclear matter features increasing neutrino abundances with density because of decreasing lepton fractions at fixed $Y_{L,e}$ and $Y_{L,\mu}$.

It is further seen that finite temperatures induce a significant shift of the hyperon thresholds to lower densities (which lie outside of the density range considered). This is in accordance with the recent observation that low-density hot nuclear matter may feature a significant fraction of strangeness (Λ-particles) as well as Δ-resonances in addition to light clusters and free nucleons [70]. Note also that the Λ-hyperon abundances become larger than those of neutrons at high density, i.e., these species are the dominant baryonic component in the matter for $n_B/n_{sat} \gtrsim 5.5$. This results mainly from the weaker repulsive coupling of Λs to ω-meson which enhances their abundances compared to neutrons. The weaker renormalization of Λ's mass due to coupling to σ and σ^* mesons than that of neutron is less important.

Figure 6 shows the particle fractions in the hypernuclear matter in the temperature range $10 \leq T \leq 40$ MeV and electron and μ-on fraction fixed by the condition $Y_{L,e} = Y_{L,\mu} = 0.1$ characteristic of neutron star binary mergers. It is seen that the abundances of neutrons, protons, electrons and μ-ons are weakly dependent on the temperature. Due to equal lepton numbers, the electron and μ-on abundances are close to each other with the small electron excess reflected in the dominance of μ-on neutrinos over the electron-neutrinos. At high densities, the neutrino abundances are almost independent of the temperature as well, but they decrease with increasing temperature and, eventually, become negative at temperatures between 40 and 50 MeV in the low-density domain (see also the upper right panel of Figure 3).

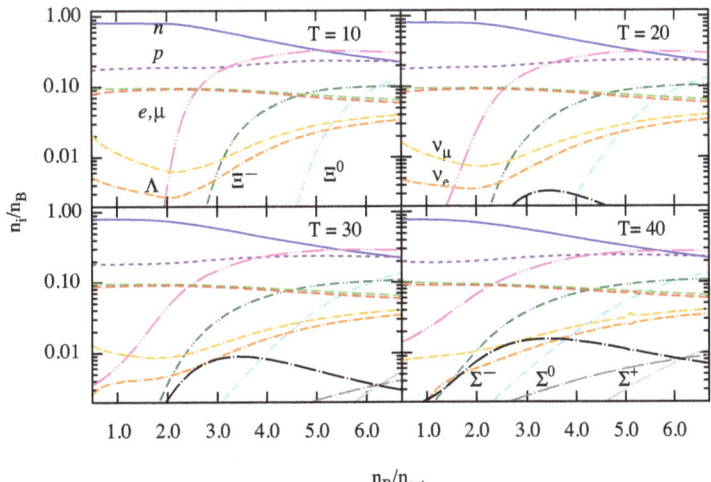

Figure 6. Same as in Figure 3, but for the fixed electron and μ-on lepton fractions $Y_{L,e} = Y_{L,\mu} = 0.1$ and temperatures $T = 10, 20, 30$ and 40 MeV. The lepton number fractions are characteristic for binary neutron star mergers.

Hyperons have sharply increasing fractions at the thresholds at $T = 10$ MeV, which replicates those at low temperatures and in neutrino-free regimes. With increasing temperature, the thresholds of the appearance of the hyperons move to the lower densities, with the Λ threshold moving to a density below $n_{\rm sat}/2$. The high-density limit shows the following new features: (a) the Λ becomes the most abundant baryon by exceeding the neutron fraction; the Ξ^0 hyperon overtakes Ξ^- and becomes the second-most abundant hyperon. Note that the upper right panel of Figure 3 differs from the panels shown here only by the temperature ($T = 50$ MeV); therefore, our comments here parallel the statements made earlier in the context of Figure 3. Turning to the Σs, we note that their abundances are noticeable for $T \geq 20$ MeV and the occurrence of the special interchange point of isospin degeneracy is seen again for $T = 30$ MeV and $T = 40$ MeV.

In Figure 7, we show the same as in Figure 6 but for $Y_{L,e} = 0.4$ and $Y_{L,\mu} = 0$, which physically corresponds to the case of supernova matter. Many general trends seen for baryon abundances remain the same under these new conditions. An interesting new feature is the near equipartition between neutrons, Λ, and protons at high density $n_B/n_{\rm sat} \geq 5$, with Ξ^0 fraction approaching this group above $6n_{\rm sat}$. As for leptons, the main effect arises from the drop of μ-on fraction to below 1% and less for $T \leq 40$ MeV. For $T = 50$, this number climbs to a few percent (see Figure 3, lower panels). Because of this, the charge neutrality is mainly maintained by the equality of the abundances of protons and electrons, with slight disparity introduced by Ξ^- at high density. The most striking difference is the strong enhancement of electron-neutrino abundances for all temperatures, with a very weak dependence on the temperature of the environment.

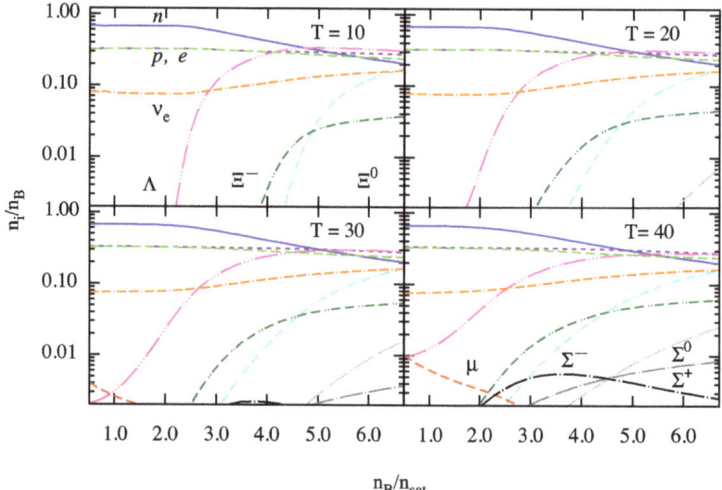

Figure 7. Same as in Figure 6, but for the fixed $Y_{L,e} = 0.4$ and $Y_{L,\mu} = 0$, i.e., the lepton number fractions are characteristic for supernova.

4. Conclusions

In this work, we explored the finite-temperature EoS of nuclear and hypernuclear matter within the CDF formalism. Formally, our study uses essentially the same approach as that of Ref. [24], but it includes additional hidden-strangeness mesons and employs a different strategy to fix the hyperonic couplings in the scalar sector by adjusting these to the depths of hyperon potential in nuclear matter. We performed parameter studies varying the temperature, density and lepton fraction within two scenarios: the binary merger remnant scenario with equal numbers of electron and μ-on lepton numbers and the supernova scenario with non-zero electron and zero μ-on lepton numbers. In all cases, the well-known feature of softening of the EoS with the inclusion of hyperons is reproduced. Even though the temperature dependence of the EoS is not strong (see Figure 1), it has significant impact on the radii and masses of compact stars (see for example, refs. [32,71]). The abundances of particles in a baryon–lepton mixture in a merger remnant and a supernova were explored within the CDF formalism. The main features are: (a) at finite temperatures, the sharp increase in hyperon fractions at the thresholds is replaced by a gradual increase over a density range allowing for a significant fraction of hyperons, especially Λs, at sub-saturation densities, as shown in Figures 3, 6, and 7. (b) At large densities $n_B/n_{sat} \geq 5$, the most abundant baryon is Λ, as in the strongly relativistic regime, the difference between the (bare) masses of the neutron and Λ is not important. The weaker coupling of σ meson to Λ than to nucleon results in a a weaker renormalization of Λ mass (see Figure 4) which disfavors Λ hyperons. However, the weaker repulsive coupling of Λs to ω-meson promotes their abundances compared to neutrons, which eventually leads to their dominance at high densities. Note that the ρ-meson coupling is exponentially suppressed at high densities and it does not play any considerable role. Note also that the roles played by σ^*- and ϕ-mesons are similar to that of σ- and ω-mesons, but are quantitatively less important. (c) The triplet of Σ hyperons, which is completely suppressed in the cold regime of hypernuclear matter, emerges at temperatures above 20 MeV, with significant fractions of Σ^- compatible to that of Ξ^- at low densities $n_B \leq 2n_{sat}$ and high temperatures $T \geq 40$ MeV. (d) In the neutrino-trapped regime, there is always a special isospin degeneracy point where the charge chemical potential of the system vanishes. At that point, the baryon abundances within each of the three isospin-multiplets are equal to each other as a result of (approximate) isospin symmetry. (e) We find a significant difference between the neutrino abundances in the merger remnant and supernova cases. In the first case, there are comparable numbers $\sim 1\%$ of electron and μ-on neutrinos (the electron and μ-on lepton numbers being equal). In the second case, electron neutrino abundance is much larger $\sim 10\%$ and μ-on neutrinos are absent (there is only a small fraction of μ-on anti-neutrinos in this case, typically less than a percent). This, of course, reflects the choices of $Y_{L,e}$ and $Y_{L,\mu}$ for these cases, but the abundances are not trivially related to lepton numbers.

Author Contributions: A.S. and A.H. equally contributed to all stages of this project. All authors have read and agreed to the published version of the manuscript.

Funding: This research was funded by the Volkswagen Foundation (Hannover, Germany) grant No. 96 839. A. S. was funded by Deutsche Forschungsgemeinschaft (DFG) Grant No. SE1836/5-1.

Institutional Review Board Statement: Not applicable.

Informed Consent Statement: Not applicable.

Data Availability Statement: The data underlying this article will be shared on reasonable request to the corresponding author.

Acknowledgments: The author acknowledge the networking opportunities offered by the European COST Action "PHAROS" (CA16214).

Conflicts of Interest: The authors declare no conflict of interest.

References

1. Prakash, M.; Bombaci, I.; Prakash, M.; Ellis, P.J.; Lattimer, J.M.; Knorren, R. Composition and structure of protoneutron stars. *Phys. Rep.* **1997**, *280*, 1–77. [CrossRef]
2. Pons, J.A.; Reddy, S.; Prakash, M.; Lattimer, J.M.; Miralles, J.A. Evolution of Proto–Neutron Stars. *Astrophys. J.* **1999**, *513*, 780–804. doi:10.1086/306889 [CrossRef]
3. Janka, H.T.; Langanke, K.; Marek, A.; Martinez-Pinedo, G.; Mueller, B. Theory of core-collapse supernovae. *Phys. Rep.* **2007**, *442*, 38—74. [CrossRef]
4. Mezzacappa, A.; Lentz, E.J.; Bruenn, S.W.; Hix, W.R.; Messer, O.E.B.; Endeve, E.; Blondin, J.M.; Harris, J.A.; Marronetti, P.; Yakunin, K.N.; et al. A Neutrino-Driven Core Collapse Supernova Explosion of a 15 M Star. *arXiv* **2015**, arXiv:1507.05680.
5. O'Connor, E.P.; Couch, S.M. Exploring Fundamentally Three-dimensional Phenomena in High-fidelity Simulations of Core-collapse Supernovae. *Astrophys. J.* **2018**, *865*, 81. [CrossRef]

6. Malfatti, G.; Orsaria, M.G.; Contrera, G.A.; Weber, F.; Ranea-Sandoval, I.F. Hot quark matter and (proto-) neutron stars. *Phys. Rev. C* **2019**, *100*, 015803. [CrossRef]
7. Burrows, A.; Radice, D.; Vartanyan, D.; Nagakura, H.; Skinner, M.A.; Dolence, J.C. The overarching framework of core-collapse supernova explosions as revealed by 3D FORNAX simulations. *Mon. Not. R. Astron. Soc.* **2020**, *491*, 2715–2735. [CrossRef]
8. Sumiyoshi, K.; Yamada, S.; Suzuki, H. Dynamics and Neutrino Signal of Black Hole Formation in Nonrotating Failed Supernovae. I. Equation of State Dependence. *Astrophys. J.* **2007**, *667*, 382–394. [CrossRef]
9. Fischer, T.; Whitehouse, S.C.; Mezzacappa, A.; Thielemann, F.K.; Liebendörfer, M. The neutrino signal from protoneutron star accretion and black hole formation. *Astron. Astrophys.* **2009**, *499*, 1–15. [CrossRef]
10. O'Connor, E.; Ott, C.D. Black Hole Formation in Failing Core-Collapse Supernovae. *Astrophys. J.* **2011**, *730*, 70. [CrossRef]
11. da Silva Schneider, A.; O'Connor, E.; Granqvist, E.; Betranhandy, A.; Couch, S.M. Equation of State and Progenitor Dependence of Stellar-mass Black Hole Formation. *Astrophys. J.* **2020**, *894*, 4. [CrossRef]
12. Shibata, M.; Taniguchi, K. Coalescence of Black Hole-Neutron Star Binaries. *Living Rev. Relativ.* **2011**, *14*, 6. [CrossRef]
13. Faber, J.A.; Rasio, F.A. Binary Neutron Star Mergers. *Living Rev. Relativ.* **2012**, *15*. [CrossRef]
14. Rosswog, S. The multi-messenger picture of compact binary mergers. *Int. J. Mod. Phys. D* **2015**, *24*, 1530012–1530052. [CrossRef]
15. Baiotti, L. Gravitational waves from neutron star mergers and their relation to the nuclear equation of state. *Prog. Part. Nucl. Phys.* **2019**, *109*, 103714. [CrossRef]
16. Alford, M.G.; Harris, S.P. β equilibrium in neutron-star mergers. *Phys. Rev. C* **2018**, *98*, 065806. [CrossRef]
17. Demorest, P.B.; Pennucci, T.; Ransom, S.M.; Roberts, M.S.E.; Hessels, J.W.T. A two-solar-mass neutron star measured using Shapiro delay. *Nature* **2010**, *467*, 1081–1083. [CrossRef]
18. Cromartie, H.T.; Fonseca, E.; Ransom, S.M.; Demorest, P.B.; Arzoumanian, Z.; Blumer, H.; Brook, P.R.; DeCesar, M.E.; Dolch, T.; Ellis, J.A.; et al. Relativistic Shapiro delay measurements of an extremely massive millisecond pulsar. *Nat. Astron.* **2020**, *4*, 72–76. [CrossRef]
19. Fonseca, E.; Pennucci, T.T.; Ellis, J.A.; Stairs, I.H.; Nice, D.J.; Ransom, S.M.; Demorest, P.B.; Arzoumanian, Z.; Crowter, K.; Dolch, T.; et al. The NANOGrav Nine-year Data Set: Mass and Geometric Measurements of Binary Millisecond Pulsars. *Astrophys. J.* **2016**, *832*, 167. [CrossRef]
20. Oertel, M.; Hempel, M.; Klähn, T.; Typel, S. Equations of state for supernovae and compact stars. *Rev. Mod. Phys.* **2017**, *89*, 015007. [CrossRef]
21. Sedrakian, A.; Li, J.J.; Weber, F. Hyperonization in Compact Stars. *arXiv* **2021**, arXiv:2105.14050.
22. Burgio, G.F.; Schulze, H.J.; Vidaña, I.; Wei, J.B. Neutron stars and the nuclear equation of state. *Prog. Part. Nucl. Phys.* **2021**, *120*, 103879. [CrossRef]
23. Oertel, M.; Fantina, A.F.; Novak, J. Extended equation of state for core-collapse simulations. *Phys. Rev. C* **2012**, *85*, 055806. [CrossRef]
24. Colucci, G.; Sedrakian, A. Equation of state of hypernuclear matter: Impact of hyperon-scalar-meson couplings. *Phys. Rev. C* **2013**, *87*, 055806. [CrossRef]
25. Oertel, M.; Gulminelli, F.; Providência, C.; Raduta, A.R. Hyperons in neutron stars and supernova cores. *Eur. Phys. J.* **2016**, *A52*, 50. [CrossRef]
26. Marques, M.; Oertel, M.; Hempel, M.; Novak, J. New temperature dependent hyperonic equation of state: Application to rotating neutron star models and $I-Q$ relations. *Phys. Rev. C* **2017**, *96*, 045806. [CrossRef]
27. Dexheimer, V.; de Oliveira Gomes, R.; Schramm, S.; Pais, H. What do we learn about vector interactions from GW170817? *J. Phys. G* **2019**, *46*, 034002. [CrossRef]
28. Fortin, M.; Oertel, M.; Providencia, C. Hyperons in hot dense matter: What do the constraints tell us for equation of state? *Publ. Astron. Soc. Aust.* **2018**, *35*, 44. [CrossRef]
29. Weber, F.; Farrell, D.; Spinella, W.M.; Malfatti, G.; Orsaria, M.G.; Contrera, G.A.; Maloney, I. Phases of Hadron-Quark Matter in (Proto) Neutron Stars. *Universe* **2019**, *5*, 169. [CrossRef]
30. Stone, J.R.; Dexheimer, V.; Guichon, P.A.M.; Thomas, A.W. Hot Dense Matter in The Quark-Meson-Coupling Model (QMC): Equation of State and Composition of Proto-Neutron Stars. *arXiv* **2019**, arXiv:1906.11100.
31. Roark, J.; Du, X.; Constantinou, C.; Dexheimer, V.; Steiner, A.W.; Stone, J.R. Hyperons and quarks in proto-neutron stars. *Mon. Not. R. Astron. Soc.* **2019**, *486*, 5441–5447. [CrossRef]
32. Raduta, A.R.; Oertel, M.; Sedrakian, A. Proto-neutron stars with heavy baryons and universal relations. *Mon. Not. R. Astron. Soc.* **2020**, *499*, 914–931. [CrossRef]
33. Stone, J.R.; Dexheimer, V.; Guichon, P.A.M.; Thomas, A.W.; Typel, S. Equation of state of hot dense hyperonic matter in the Quark-Meson-Coupling (QMC-A) model. *Mon. Not. R. Astron. Soc.* **2021**, *502*, 3476–3490. [CrossRef]
34. Alford, M.G.; Haber, A. Strangeness-changing rates and hyperonic bulk viscosity in neutron star mergers. *Phys. Rev. C* **2021**, *103*, 045810. [CrossRef]
35. Li, J.J.; Sedrakian, A.; Weber, F. Competition between delta isobars and hyperons and properties of compact stars. *Phys. Lett. B* **2018**, *783*, 234–240. [CrossRef]
36. Li, J.J.; Sedrakian, A. Implications from GW170817 for Δ-isobar Admixed Hypernuclear Compact Stars. *Astrophys. J. Lett.* **2019**, *874*, L22. [CrossRef]

37. Li, J.J.; Sedrakian, A.; Alford, M. Relativistic hybrid stars with sequential first-order phase transitions and heavy-baryon envelopes. *Phys. Rev. D* **2020**, *101*, 063022. [CrossRef]
38. Lalazissis, G.A.; Nikšić, T.; Vretenar, D.; Ring, Ring. New relativistic mean-field interaction with density-dependent meson-nucleon couplings. *Phys. Rev. C* **2005**, *71*, 024312. [CrossRef]
39. Fortin, M.; Providência, C.; Raduta, A.R.; Gulminelli, F.; Zdunik, J.L.; Haensel, P.; Bejger, M. Neutron star radii and crusts: Uncertainties and unified equations of state. *Phys. Rev. C* **2016**, *94*, 035804. [CrossRef]
40. Sedrakian, A. The physics of dense hadronic matter and compact stars. *Prog. Part. Nucl.Phys.* **2007**, *58*, 168–246. [CrossRef]
41. Typel, S. Relativistic Mean-Field Models with Different Parametrizations of Density Dependent Couplings. *Particles* **2018**, *1*, 3–22. [CrossRef]
42. Sinha, M.; Mukhopadhyay, B.; Sedrakian, A. Hypernuclear matter in strong magnetic field. *Nucl. Phys. A* **2013**, *898*, 43–58. [CrossRef]
43. Thapa, V.B.; Sinha, M.; Li, J.J.; Sedrakian, A. Equation of State of Strongly Magnetized Matter with Hyperons and Δ-Resonances. *Particles* **2020**, *3*, 660–675. [CrossRef]
44. Dexheimer, V.; Marquez, K.D.; Menezes, D.P. Delta Baryons in Neutron-Star Matter under Strong Magnetic Fields. *arXiv* **2021**, arXiv:2103.09855.
45. Drago, A.; Lavagno, A.; Pagliara, G.; Pigato, D. Early appearance of Δ isobars in neutron stars. *Phys. Rev. C* **2014**, *90*, 065809. [CrossRef]
46. Cai, B.J.; Fattoyev, F.J.; Li, B.A.; Newton, W.G. Critical density and impact of $\Delta(1232)$ resonance formation in neutron stars. *Phys. Rev. C* **2015**, *92*, 015802. [CrossRef]
47. Zhu, Z.Y.; Li, A.; Hu, J.N.; Sagawa, H. $\Delta(1232)$ effects in density-dependent relativistic Hartree-Fock theory and neutron stars. *Phys. Rev. C* **2016**, *94*, 045803. [CrossRef]
48. Kolomeitsev, E.E.; Maslov, K.A.; Voskresensky, D.N. Delta isobars in relativistic mean-field models with σ-scaled hadron masses and couplings. *Nucl. Phys. A* **2017**, *961*, 106–141. [CrossRef]
49. Sahoo, H.S.; Mitra, G.; Mishra, R.; Panda, P.K.; Li, B.A. Neutron star matter with Δ isobars in a relativistic quark model. *Phys. Rev. C* **2018**, *98*, 045801. [CrossRef]
50. Ribes, P.; Ramos, A.; Tolos, L.; Gonzalez-Boquera, C.; Centelles, M. Interplay between Δ Particles and Hyperons in Neutron Stars. *Astrophys. J.* **2019**, *883*, 168. [CrossRef]
51. de Swart, J.J. The Octet Model and its Clebsch-Gordan Coefficients. *Rev. Mod. Phys.* **1963**, *35*, 916–939. [CrossRef]
52. van Dalen, E.N.E.; Colucci, G.; Sedrakian, A. Constraining hypernuclear density functional with Λ-hypernuclei and compact stars. *Phys. Lett. B* **2014**, *734*, 383–387. [CrossRef]
53. Friedman, E.; Gal, A. Constraints on Ξ^- nuclear interactions from capture events in emulsion *arXiv* **2021**, arXiv:2104.00421.
54. Inoue, T.; HAL QCD Collaboration. Strange nuclear physics from QCD on lattice. In Proceedings of the 13th International Conference on HyperNuclear and Strange Particle Physics: HYP2018, Portsmouth, VR, USA, 24–29 June 2018, American Institute of Physics Conference Series; 2019; Volume 2130, p. 020002.
55. Sasaki, K. $\Lambda\Lambda$ and $N\Xi$ interactions from Lattice QCD near the physical point. *Nucl. Phys. A* **2020**, *998*, 121737.
56. Bollig, R.; Janka, H.T.; Lohs, A.; Martinez-Pinedo, G.; Horowitz, C.; Melson, T. Muon Creation in Supernova Matter Facilitates Neutrino-driven Explosions. *Phys. Rev. Lett.* **2017**, *119*, 242702. [CrossRef]
57. Guo, G.; Martínez-Pinedo, G.; Lohs, A.; Fischer, T. Charged-Current Muonic Reactions in Core-Collapse Supernovae. *Phys. Rev. D* **2020**, *102*, 023037. [CrossRef]
58. Alford, M.G.; Harris, S.P. Damping of density oscillations in neutrino-transparent nuclear matter. *Phys. Rev. C* **2019**, *100*, 035803. [CrossRef]
59. Alford, M.G.; Haber, A.; Harris, S.P.; Zhang, Z. Beta equilibrium under neutron star merger conditions. *arXiv* **2021**, arXiv:2108.03324.
60. Alford, M.; Harutyunyan, A.; Sedrakian, A. Bulk viscosity of baryonic matter with trapped neutrinos. *Phys. Rev. D* **2019**, *100*, 103021. [CrossRef]
61. Alford, M.; Harutyunyan, A.; Sedrakian, A. Bulk Viscous Damping of Density Oscillations in Neutron Star Mergers. *arXiv* **2020**, arXiv:2006.07975.
62. Alford, M.; Harutyunyan, A.; Sedrakian, A. Bulk viscosity from Urca processes: $npe\mu$-neutrino-trapped matter. *arXiv* **2021**, arXiv:2108.07523.
63. Bart, S.; Chrien, R.E.; Franklin, W.A.; Fukuda, T.; Hayano, R.S.; Hicks, K.; Hungerford, E.V.; Michael, R.; Miyachi, T.; Nagae, T.; et al. Σ Hyperons in the Nucleus. *Phys. Rev. Lett.* **1999**, *83*, 5238–5241. [CrossRef]
64. Dover, C.; Gal, A. Hyperon-nucleus potentials. *Prog. Part. Nucl. Phys.* **1984**, *12*, 171–239. [CrossRef]
65. Maslov, K.A.; Kolomeitsev, E.E.; Voskresensky, D.N. Relativistic Mean-Field Models with Scaled Hadron Masses and Couplings: Hyperons and Maximum Neutron Star Mass. *Nucl. Phys. A* **2016**, *950*, 64–109. [CrossRef]
66. Lopes, L.L.; Menezes, D.P. Hypernuclear matter in a complete SU(3) symmetry group. *Phys. Rev. C* **2014**, *89*, 025805. [CrossRef]
67. Gomes, R.O.; Dexheimer, V.; Schramm, S.; Vasconcellos, C.A.Z. Many-body forces in the equation of state of hyperonic matter. *Astrophys. J.* **2015**, *808*, 8. [CrossRef]
68. Miyatsu, T.; Cheoun, M.K.; Saito, K. Equation of State for Neutron Stars With Hyperons and Quarks in the Relativistic Hartree-Fock Approximation. *Astrophys. J.* **2015**, *813*, 135. [CrossRef]

69. Ambartsumyan, V.A.; Saakyan, G.S. The Degenerate Superdense Gas of Elementary Particles. *Sov. Astron.* **1960**, *4*, 187.
70. Sedrakian, A. Light clusters in dilute heavy-baryon admixed nuclear matter. *Eur. Phys. J. A* **2020**, *56*, 258. [CrossRef]
71. Khadkikar, S.; Raduta, A.R.; Oertel, M.; Sedrakian, A. Maximum mass of compact stars from gravitational wave events with finite-temperature equations of state. *Phys. Rev. C* **2021**, *103*, 055 811. [CrossRef]

Article

Hybrid Stars with Color Superconducting Cores in an Extended FCM Model

Daniela Curin [1,†], Ignacio Francisco Ranea-Sandoval [1,2,†], Mauro Mariani [1,2,†], Milva Gabriela Orsaria [1,2,†] and Fridolin Weber [3,4,*,†]

[1] Grupo de Gravitación, Astrofísica y Cosmología, Facultad de Ciencias Astronómicas y Geofísicas, Universidad Nacional de La Plata, Paseo del Bosque S/N, La Plata 1900, Argentina; danielacurin@fcaglp.unlp.edu.ar (D.C.); iranea@fcaglp.unlp.edu.ar (I.F.R.-S.); mmariani@fcaglp.unlp.edu.ar (M.M.); morsaria@fcaglp.unlp.edu.ar (M.G.O.)
[2] CONICET, Godoy Cruz 2290, CABA 1425, Argentina
[3] Department of Physics, San Diego State University, 5500 Campanile Drive, San Diego, CA 92182, USA
[4] Center for Astrophysics and Space Sciences, University of California at San Diego, La Jolla, CA 92093, USA
* Correspondence: fweber@sdsu.edu or fweber@ucsd.edu
† These authors contributed equally to this work.

Abstract: We investigate the influence of repulsive vector interactions and color superconductivity on the structure of neutron stars using an extended version of the field correlator method (FCM) for the description of quark matter. The hybrid equation of state is constructed using the Maxwell description, which assumes a sharp hadron-quark phase transition. The equation of state of hadronic matter is computed for a density-dependent relativistic lagrangian treated in the mean-field approximation, with parameters given by the SW4L nuclear model. This model described the interactions among baryons in terms of σ, ω, ρ, σ^*, and ϕ mesons. Quark matter is assumed to be in either the CFL or the 2SC+s color superconducting phase. The possibility of sequential (hadron-quark, quark-quark) transitions in ultra-dense matter is investigated. Observed data related to massive pulsars, gravitational-wave events, and NICER are used to constrain the parameters of the extended FCM model. The successful equations of state are used to explore the mass-radius relationship, radii, and tidal deformabilities of hybrid stars. A special focus lies on investigating consequences that slow or fast conversions of quark-hadron matter have on the stability and the mass-radius relationship of hybrid stars. We find that if slow conversion should occur, a new branch of stable massive stars would exist whose members have radii that are up to 1.5 km smaller than those of conventional neutron stars of the same mass. Such objects could be possible candidates for the stellar high-mass object of the GW190425 binary system.

Keywords: neutron stars; hybrid star; equation of state; color superconductivity; diquark

1. Introduction

Neutron stars (NSs) are compact stellar remnants which are born in type-II supernova explosions [1]. Within just a few minutes after birth, they turn into cold (on the nuclear scale) stellar objects with temperature of just a few MeV [2]. Their masses can be as high as $\sim 2\,M_\odot$, and their radii range from $\sim$10 to $\sim$13 km, depending on mass. The mean density of a NS with a canonical mass of 1.5 $M_\odot$ is higher than the nuclear saturation density of $n_0 = 2.5 \times 10^{14}$ g cm^{-3} and the density reached in the central core is expected to be several times higher than n_0 [3]. Paired with the unprecedented current progress in observational astronomy [4–8] these characteristic features make NSs superb astrophysical laboratories for a wide range of physical studies, which help us to understand the nature of matter subjected to most extreme conditions of pressure and density [9,10].

Traditionally, NSs are though as three-layer compact objects composed by an inner core, an outer core and a crust. Densities in the crust are lower than n_0. Experimental nuclear physics data from terrestrial laboratories have been extremely useful to reduce the uncertainties in the low-density regime of such NS matter and its associate equation of state (EoS). The situation is different for matter with densities above n_0, for which there is no general agreement about the structure and composition. This lack of knowledge increases with increasing central density [11,12]. Over the years, several different theoretical possibilities regarding the unknown nuclear composition have been explored, including those that take into account a possible hadron-quark phase transition (see, e.g., Refs. [10,12], and references therein). Neutron stars containing hadrons and deconfined quarks in their center are referred to as hybrid stars (HS). The situation is different for matter at densities above n_0, for which no general agreement on the structure and composition exists. This lack of knowledge deepens with increasing density. Several different theoretical possibilities of the central composition of NSs are being explored, including some which account for a possible hadron-quark phase transition (see, for example, Refs. [10,12], and references therein). NSs containing hadrons and deconfined quarks in their centers, are known as hybrid stars (HSs).

Observations of the 2 $M_\odot$ pulsars PSR J1614-2230 [13,14], PSR J0348+0432 [15] and PSR J0740+6620 [16] have imposed strong constraints to the EoS of matter inside NSs. In addition, the merger of two binary NSs (BNSs) known as GW170817, together with the detection of the electromagnetic radiation associated with this event, has been used to put constraints on the radius and dimensionless tidal deformability of the merging compact objects and, therefore, indirectly on their nuclear EoSs [4]. The analysis of the data from this event has been used to set new limits on the radius of a 1.4 $M_\odot$ NS which is estimated to be between 9.2 and 13.76 km [17]. Moreover, the upper bound to the maximum-mass of cold and slowly rotating NS has been estimated to be $\sim$ 2.3 $M_\odot$ [18]. A second BNS merger, named GW190425, has been detected by the LIGO Livingston interferometer. In this case, the inferred total mass of the NSs that merged has been estimated to be $M_{tot} = 3.4^{+0.4}_{-0.1}$ $M_\odot$ [6]. This is higher than the expected Galactic mean mass for this kind of binary systems [19]. To date, no electromagnetic counterpart associated with GW190425 has been detected (see, for example, Ref. [20], and references therein).

In 2019 the NICER collaborations have determined the mass and radius of the isolated NS PSR J0030+0451 with values of $1.34^{+0.15}_{-0.16}$ $M_\odot$ and $12.71^{+1.14}_{-1.19}$ km [21] and $M = 1.44^{+0.15}_{-0.14}$ $M_\odot$ and $13.02^{+1.24}_{-1.06}$ km [22]. Very recently, data from NICER and XMM-Newton were used to determine the radius of PSR J0740+6620 with a value of $13.7^{+2.6}_{-1.5}$ km [8] and $12.39^{+1.30}_{-0.98}$ km [7]. These values show that the radius of PSR J0030+0451 is similar to the radius of the much more massive NS PSR J0740+6620, whose mass is $2.072^{+0.067}_{-0.066}$ $M_\odot$ [7]. This constrains the nuclear EoS to a greater degree than previously possible.

For a comprehensive study of the properties of matter in the cores of neutron stars and the EOS associated with such matter, it is necessary to resort to Quantum Chromodynamics (QCD), the theory of strong interactions. Besides quark confinement, asymptotic freedom is one of the main features of QCD, which states that matter at high density and/or temperatures exhibits a phase transition in which hadrons merge leading to the formation of a plasma of quarks and gluons. QCD has inherent computational problems that make it extremely difficult to perform analytic calculations at finite densities to be performed. For this reason, several phenomenological and/or effective models have been proposed that reproduce (some of) the key features and symmetries of the QCD Lagrangian density (see Ref. [10] and references therein).

If the hadron-quark phase transition occurs in the cores of NSs, it has been shown that the liberated quarks should form a color superconductor (CSC) [23–25]. This phase is characterized by the formation of quark Cooper pairs, similarly to the formation of electron Cooper pairs in ordinary condensed matter superconductivity, which is energetically favored since it lowers the energy of the Fermi sea of fermions [26]. A Cooper pair of quarks can not be a in a color singlet state as the corresponding condensate breaks the QCD local color symmetry, $SU(3)_{color}$. Hence the notion color superconductivity. Since the pairing among the quarks is quite robust, quark matter, if existing in the cores of

NSs, ought to be a CSC. In contrast to ordinary condensed matter superconductivity, however, the condensation patterns of CSC quark matter are much more complex as up to three different quark flavors and three different color states are involved in the diquark formation [24,25].

Two of the most studied color superconducting phases are the two flavor color superconducting (2SC) phase and the color-flavor-locked (CFL) phase. In the 2SC phase, only up, u, and down, d, quarks pair. The strange quark, s, has a mass that is by two orders of magnitude higher than the masses of u and d quarks. This favors the formation of the 2SC phase at intermediate densities, while at high densities, where the mass of the strange quark plays a less dominant role, the CFL phase may replace the 2SC phase. CFL is a more symmetric phase of matter in which all three quark flavors are involved in the pairing process. There is also the possibility that a phase known as 2SC+s is formed at intermediate densities, where the strange quarks are treated as a gas of free massive fermions [27]. The formation of diquarks lower the energy of the system by an amount related to the size of the CSC gap, Δ. This quantity is a function of the chemical potential, but can be treated as a free parameter of the model [28]. This phenomenological approach is useful as it gives theoretical insight into CSC. The occurrence of each of these phases is directly related to the mass of the strange quark mass, the energy gap, and the electron chemical potential [25].

In addition to the possibility of diquarks formation in HSs, it is known that the inclusion of the repulsive vector interaction in quark models allows HSs to satisfy the 2 $M_\odot$ constraint [29–31].

In this work, we study the influence of color superconductivity and of vector interactions among quarks on the composition and structure of HSs. Using an extended version of the Field Correlator Method (FCM) for the description of quark matter [32–34], the effects of 2SC+s and CFL superconductivity is included in the quark model in a phenomenological way. To model the hadronic phase of the hybrid EoS, we use the SW4L parametrization of the density dependent relativistic mean-field theory which includes all particles of the baryon octet as well as the Δ resonance [35].

We assume that the surface tension at the hadron-quark interface is high so that a sharp hadron-quark phase transition occurs, which is modeled as a Maxwell transition (see Ref. [10], and references therein). In this context we analyze the possibilities of rapid versus slow conversions of matter at the hadronic and quark matter interface [36]. This phenomenon requires a modification of the traditional stability criteria of compact objects.

The paper is organized as follows. In Section 2 we provide some details of the treatment of phase transitions in HSs. Chemical and mechanical equilibrium conditions for the construction of the hybrid EoS are also given. Section 3 is devoted to the description of the hadronic model used to describe the outer cores of HSs. The model used to describe quark matter in the inner core of HSs is introduced in Section 4. The model accounts for vector interactions among quarks and the effects of color superconductivity. The results of our comprehensive analysis of quark matter parameters, phase transitions and hybrid configurations will be discussed in Section 5. Finally, a summary and discussion of our key findings are presented in Section 6.

2. Quark-Hadron Phase Transition in Neutron Stars

Properties such as the surface tension at the hadron-quark interface, σ_{HQ}, and nucleation timescale are only poorly known. These two quantities define the nature of the hadron-quark phase transition. For example, whether the hadron-quark phase transition separating both types of matter is sharp or smooth is determined by the value of the surface tension between the two phases. If the value of the surface tension is larger than a critical value of $\sigma_{HQ} \sim 70$ MeV fm^{-2}, a (sharp) Maxwell phase transition is favored [37–39]. Otherwise, a (smooth) Gibbs phase transition would be expected. It is important to note that for the Gibbs formalism, the global electric charge neutrality condition leads to the appearance of geometrical structures in the mixed hadron-quark phase. This so-called pasta phase is highly dependent on the EoS used to construct the phase transition as well as on the value of σ_{HQ} (see, for example Refs. [40,41], and references therein).

Although the analysis of data from GW170817 and its electromagnetic counterpart led to the conclusion that high-mass NSs may be expected to have quark matter in their inner cores [42], there is no direct observational evidence of the occurrence of a hadron-quark phase transition in the interior of such objects. In this work, we assume that the favored transition scenario is that of a sharp hadron-quark phase transition.

Within this theoretical framework, we study two different regimes related to the nucleation timescales of the sharp phase transition: the slow and the rapid conversion. The importance of considering these different theoretical scenarios has been introduced in Ref. [36]. In that work, the authors showed the huge impact these two types of conversions have on the structure and stability of HSs against radial oscillations. The main result was that when a slow conversion rate is considered to occur inside of a HS, the star continues to remain stable against radial oscillations (i.e., the fundamental radial mode remains real valued) even beyond the gravitational mass peak, where the mass is decreasing with increasing central energy density (for details, see Ref. [43]). This finding differs drastically from the standard stability criterion established for compact stars whereupon stability of stars against radial oscillations is only possible if the mass is monotonically increasing with density.

The concept of slow and rapid conversion is linked to the relationship between two very different timescales. These are the nucleation timescale, i.e., the characteristic time during which a hadron (quark) fluid element is converted into quark (hadronic) matter, and the characteristic timescale of the oscillation of the fluid elements. As to the latter, the fluid elements located near the transition interface oscillate to regions of larger (smaller) pressures as the oscillation stretches and compresses the matter in the star. The hadron-quark conversion is slow (rapid) if the nucleation timescale is much larger (smaller) that the one associated with the oscillations at the interface separating the two phases.

The strong and weak interactions have times scales that differ from each other by many orders of magnitude ($\tau_{strong} \sim 10^{-23}$ s, $\tau_{weak} \sim 10^{-8}$ s). For this reason it has been proposed that the hadron-quark deconfinement process ought to consist of two separate steps: the formation of a virtual drop of out-of-β-equilibrium quark matter that will subsequently reach chemical equilibrium. The characteristic time scale of this process is related to the difference between the Gibbs free energies of equilibrium and out-of-β-equilibrium quark matter (for a more detailed discussion, see, for example, Ref. [44]). Present results for this energy difference are strongly model dependent and inconclusive (for details, see, for example, Refs. [45–49]). Therefore, in this work we shall account for both theoretical possibilities and analyze the astrophysical consequences and observational differences that might help understand in detail the microphysics of the hadron-quark phase transition.

The composition of the matter in the interior of a HS is determined by the condition of β-equilibrium and electric charge neutrality [50,51]. These condition imposes a relationship between the chemical potentials of the different particle species in the hadronic phase,

$$\mu_B = \mu_n + q_B \mu_e, \tag{1}$$

and in the quark phase with flavors $f = u, d, s$,

$$\mu_f = \mu_n/3 + q_f \mu_e, \tag{2}$$

where q_B and q_f are the baryon and quark electric charges, μ_n is the neutron chemical potential, and μ_e the electron chemical potential.

To calculate the hybrid EoS within the Maxwell construction at zero temperature, $T = 0$, we impose the mechanical equilibrium condition that reads

$$P_h(\mu_n, \mu_e) = P_q(\mu_n, \mu_e). \tag{3}$$

Charge neutrality is imposed locally in the Maxwell formalism, i.e., each phase has to be independently electrically neutral. This condition is satisfied if $\partial P_{h(q)}/\partial \mu_e = 0$, where $P_{h(q)}$ is the pressure of the hadronic (quark) phase, which will be defined later.

3. The Hadronic Phase

To describe hadronic matter in the outer core of HSs we use the SW4L parametrization of the density dependent non-linear relativistic mean-field model [52–54]. This family of models have gained popularity since the density-dependent couplings allows one to account for the latest slope values of the symmetry energy consistent with experimental data [55,56]. This quantity plays a significant role for the determination of the radii of NSs [57].

For the SW4L parametrization, the interactions between baryons are described by the exchange of scalar (σ, σ^*), vector (ω, ϕ) and isovector (ρ) mesons. The pressure and the energy density of the model are given by

$$\begin{aligned} P_h &= \frac{1}{\pi^2}\sum_B \int_0^{p_{F_B}} dp \, \frac{p^4}{\sqrt{p^2+m_B^{*2}}} - \frac{1}{2}m_\sigma^2 \bar{\sigma}^2 \\ &- \frac{1}{2}m_{\sigma^*}^2 \bar{\sigma}^{*2} + \frac{1}{2}m_\omega^2 \bar{\omega}^2 + \frac{1}{2}m_\rho^2 \bar{\rho}^2 + \frac{1}{2}m_\phi^2 \bar{\phi}^2 \\ &- \frac{1}{3}\tilde{b}_\sigma m_N (g_{\sigma N}\bar{\sigma})^3 - \frac{1}{4}\tilde{c}_\sigma (g_{\sigma N}\bar{\sigma})^4 + n\tilde{R}, \end{aligned} \quad (4)$$

$$\begin{aligned} \varepsilon_h &= \frac{1}{\pi^2}\sum_B \int_0^{p_{F_B}} dp \, \sqrt{p^2+m_B^{*2}} + \frac{1}{2}m_\sigma^2 \bar{\sigma}^2 \\ &+ \frac{1}{2}m_{\sigma^*}^2 \bar{\sigma}^{*2} + \frac{1}{2}m_\omega^2 \bar{\omega}^2 + \frac{1}{2}m_\rho^2 \bar{\rho}^2 + \frac{1}{2}m_\phi^2 \bar{\phi}^2 \\ &+ \frac{1}{3}\tilde{b}_\sigma m_N (g_{\sigma N}\bar{\sigma})^3 + \frac{1}{4}\tilde{c}_\sigma (g_{\sigma N}\bar{\sigma})^4, \end{aligned} \quad (5)$$

where the sum over B sums all members of the baryon octet, $p, n, \Lambda, \Sigma, \Xi$, as well as the Δ resonance. The quantities $g_{\rho B}(n)$ denote density dependent meson–baryon coupling constants that have a functional form given by

$$g_{\rho B}(n) = g_{\rho B}(n_0)\exp\left[-a_\rho\left(\frac{n}{n_0}-1\right)\right], \quad (6)$$

where n is the total baryon number density. The last term in Equation (4) is the rearrangement term which guarantees the thermodynamic consistency of the model [58],

$$\tilde{R} = [\partial g_{\rho B}(n)/\partial n]I_{3B}n_B\bar{\rho}. \quad (7)$$

The quantity I_{3B} is the 3-component of isospin, and $n_B = p_{F_B}^3/3\pi^2$ are the particle number densities of each baryon B with Fermi momentum p_{F_B}. The effective baryon mass in Equations (4) and (5) is given by

$$m_B^* = m_B - g_{\sigma B}\bar{\sigma} - g_{\sigma^* B}\bar{\sigma}^*. \quad (8)$$

The parameters of SW4L are presented in Table 1. These values are adjusted to the properties of nuclear matter at saturation density shown in Table 2 (for details, see Ref. [54], and references therein).

Table 1. Parameters of the SW4L parametrization that lead to the properties of symmetric nuclear matter at saturation density shown in Table 2.

Quantity	Numerical Value
m_σ (GeV)	0.5500
m_ω (GeV)	0.7826
m_ρ (GeV)	0.7753
m_{σ^*} (GeV)	0.9900
m_ϕ (GeV)	1.0195
$g_{\sigma N}$	9.8100
$g_{\omega N}$	10.3906
$g_{\rho N}$	7.8184
$g_{\sigma^* N}$	1.0000
$g_{\phi N}$	1.0000
$\tilde{b}_\sigma$	0.0041
$\tilde{c}_\sigma$	-0.0038
a_ρ	0.4703

Table 2. Energy per nucleon E_0, nuclear compressibility K_0, effective nucleon mass m^*, symmetry energy J_0, and slope of the symmetry energy L_0 of nuclear matter at saturation density, n_0, obtained for the SW4L parametrization.

Saturation Properties	Numerical Values
n_0 (fm^{-3})	0.15
E_0 (MeV)	-16.0
K_0 (MeV)	250.0
m_N^*/m_N	0.7
J_0 (MeV)	30.3
L_0 (MeV)	46.5

4. The Quark Phase

To describe quark matter in the inner core of cold HSs we use an extended version of the FCM model, including the effects of repulsive vector interactions among quarks and of color superconductivity.

The FCM model is based on the calculation of the amplitudes of the color electric $D^E(x)$, $D_1^E(x)$ and color magnetic $D^H(x)$, $D_1^H(x)$ Gaussian correlators. $D^E(x)$ and $D^H(x)$ are directly related with the confinement of quarks, and $D_1^E(x)$, $D_1^H(x)$ contain perturbative terms related to the perturbation expansion over the strong coupling constant at a given order [32,59]. The method has been generalized to finite temperature and baryonic density using the single line approximation (SLA) which neglects, to first order, all perturbative and non-perturbative interactions of the system. In this way, it is possible to factorize the partition function into the products of one gluon and one quark (anti-quark) contributions and thus calculate the corresponding thermodynamic potential [33].

For zero-temperature HS matter, $D^E(x) = D^H(x)$ and $D_1^E(x) = D_1^H(x)$, leaving two field correlators which can be parametrized through the large distance $q\bar{q}$ potential, V_1, and the gluon condensate, G_2. In addition, the main consequence of repulsive vector interactions for HSs is to stiffen the EoS of quark matter to obtain 2 $M_\odot$ stellar configurations, in agreement with recent observations of massive pulsars. We also mention that the onset of quark matter in the interior of HSs is affected by this interaction.

Both vector interactions among quarks and color superconductivity are taken into account by FCM model.

4.1. Inclusion of Vector Interactions in the FCM Model

The inclusion of vector interactions among quarks modifies the SLA of the quark pressure in the following way

$$P_f = \frac{T^4}{\pi^2}\left[\phi_v^+\left(\frac{\mu_f^* - V_1/2}{T}\right) + \phi_v^-\left(\frac{\mu_f^* + V_1/2}{T}\right)\right]$$
$$+ P_{VI}(T, \mu_f^*),\tag{9}$$

where

$$\phi_v^\pm(a) = \int_0^\infty dz \frac{z^4}{\sqrt{z^2+v^2}} \frac{1}{e^{\sqrt{z^2+v^2}\pm a}+1},\tag{10}$$

and $v = m_f/T$, m_q is the bare quark mass of a quark flavor f and T is the temperature. The effective chemical potential is given by

$$\mu_f^* = \mu_f - K_V w(T, \mu_f^*),\tag{11}$$

where μ_f is the chemical potential of a quark of flavor f, K_V is the coupling constant of the vector interactions, and $w(T, \mu_f^*)$ is the associated condensate.

An expression similar to the first term in Equation (9) can be deduced for the pressure of the gluons, which vanished at zero temperature. The second term is the pressure due the vector condensates given by

$$P_{VI}(T, \mu_f^*) = \frac{K_V}{2} w^2(T, \mu_f^*).\tag{12}$$

Taking the limit $T \to 0$ in Equation (9), we obtain a simplified expression for the total pressure of the system that reads

$$P_q = \sum_{f=u,d,s} P_f = \sum_{f=u,d,s}\left[\frac{3}{\pi^2}\int_0^{p_F^*} z^2(\tilde{\mu}_f^* - z)\, dz\right.$$
$$\left.+ \frac{K_V}{2} w_f^2\right] + \Delta\epsilon_{vac},\tag{13}$$

where $\tilde{\mu}_f^* = \mu_f^* - V_1/2$, $p_F^* = \sqrt{\tilde{\mu}_f^{*2} - m_f^2}$, $w_f = w(\tilde{\mu}_f^*)$, and

$$\Delta\epsilon_{vac} = -\frac{11 - \frac{2}{3}N_f}{32} \frac{G_2}{2}\tag{14}$$

is the vacuum energy density for N_f flavors [32].

The EoS of the system can be computed using the Euler thermodynamic relation given by

$$\varepsilon = -P_q + \sum_{f=u,d,s} \mu_f \frac{\partial P_f}{\partial \mu_f}.\tag{15}$$

The effective chemical potential of Equation (11) is determined in a self-consistent way by minimizing Equation (13) with respect to the vector condensate, from which it follows that $w_f = n(\mu_f^*)$, where $n(\mu_f^*)$ is the number density quark flavor f.

4.2. Effects of Color Superconductivity on the Quark EoS

The working hypothesis of our study is that in the inner cores of HSs deconfined up, down and strange quarks are paired in the CFL phase. However, since the mass of the strange quark is around two orders of magnitude greater than that of up and down quarks, paired up and down quark condensates should appear first, in a phase known as 2SC+s. The quark masses in the 2SC+s and CFL color superconducting phases are taken as $m_u = m_d = 0$ and $m_s \neq 0$.

To include the effect of color superconductivity, we work to order Δ^2 in the diquark energy gap Δ, which simplifies the calculation considerably [51]. In this way, it is possible to consider Equation (13) as a fictional state made of unpaired quark matter that transforms to a superconducting state once the quarks involved in the pairing reach a common Fermi momentum. Thus, analogously to what happens in BSC theory, the diquarks formed in the 2SC+s and CFL phases are conventional zero-momentum Cooper pairs.

For each quark forming a diquark, we have a contribution $(\Delta \bar{\mu}/2\pi)^2$ to the binding energy of the diquark pairing [51], where

$$\bar{\mu} = \frac{1}{N} \sum_i \tilde{\mu}_i^* \tag{16}$$

is the mean chemical potential related to N quarks participating in the pairing. In the 2SC+s phase, four of the nine quarks (three flavors times three colors) form pairs while in the CFL phase all quarks form diquarks. The condensation terms that contribute to the pressure are given by

$$P_{\Delta_{2SC+s}} = 4 \left(\frac{\Delta \bar{\mu}}{2\pi} \right)^2 \tag{17}$$

for the 2SC+s phase and by

$$P_{\Delta_{CFL}} = \left(\frac{\Delta_1 \bar{\mu}}{2\pi} \right)^2 + 8 \left(\frac{\Delta_2 \bar{\mu}}{2\pi} \right)^2 \simeq 3 \left(\frac{\Delta \bar{\mu}}{\pi} \right)^2 \tag{18}$$

in for the CFL phase.

In the case of the CFL phase, the nine quarks forming pairs give rise to a singlet and an octet state of quasi-particles (see Equation (18)) that satisfy the approximate relation $\Delta_1 = 2\Delta_2 = 2\Delta$ [60].

Due to the breaking of the SU(3)$_{color}$ symmetry in the subgroup $U(1)_3 \times U(1)_8$, Equation (11) becomes

$$\mu_i^* = \mu_f + T_3 \mu_3 + T_8 \mu_8 - K_v w_i, \tag{19}$$

where the matrices are defined in color space as $T_3 = \text{diag}(1/2, 1/2, 0)$ and $T_8 = \text{diag}(1/3, 1/3, -2/3)$. The subscript i in Equation (19) accounts for the nine possible combinations of flavor and color, as given in Table 3. The quantities μ_3 and μ_8 are the chemical potentials associated with the color charges. For the 2SC+s phase, we consider $\mu_3 = 0$ because the symmetry that is broken in this phase is $U(1)_8$, leaving the $U(1)_3$ intact. Only u and d quarks carrying green and red colors are paired in the 2SC+s phase, while blue colored quarks do not participate in the formation of Cooper pairs. The vector condensate in that phase is $w_f = \sum_i w_i$.

Table 3. Flavor and color combinations associated with Equations (21) and (22).

i	r	g	b
u	1	2	5
d	3	4	6
s	7	8	9

Considering the possibility of diquark formation, Equation (13) is modified as

$$P_q = P' + P_\Delta + \sum_{f=u,d,s} \frac{K_v}{2} w_f^2 + \Delta \epsilon_{vac}, \tag{20}$$

where P_Δ is either given by Equation (17) or Equation (18), depending on which superconducting phase is being considered. The quantity P' is given by

$$P'_{2SC} = \frac{1}{\pi^2} \sum_{i=1}^{4} \int_0^{p_{FC}} z^2 (\tilde{\mu}_i^* - z) dz$$
$$+ \frac{1}{\pi^2} \sum_{i=5}^{9} \int_0^{p_{FC}} z^2 \left(\tilde{\mu}_i^* - \sqrt{z^2 + m_i}\right) dz, \quad (21)$$

or

$$P'_{CFL} = \frac{1}{\pi^2} \sum_{i=1}^{9} \int_0^{p_{FC}} z^2 \left(\tilde{\mu}_i^* - \sqrt{z^2 + m_i}\right) dz, \quad (22)$$

where $\tilde{\mu}_i^* = \mu_i^* - V_1/2$ and p_{FC} are determined by minimizing Equation (20). Color charge neutrality is imposed by the conditions $\partial P_q / \partial \mu_3 = \partial P_q / \partial \mu_8 = 0$. The breaking of color symmetry increases the number of coupled equations that are to be solved in order to compute the quark matter EoS. The system of equations consists of nine coupled equations for the 2SC+s phase and twelve coupled equations for the CFL phase.

5. Results

The hybrid configurations studied in this work consist of an inner core, an outer core, and a crust. The latter has been modeled in out study by the Baym-Pethick-Sutherland (BPS) and Baym-Bethe-Pethick (BBP) EoSs [61,62].

The FCM model has already been used in several works to model the inner cores of HSs [34,43,63–66]. In these studies, the parameter space (V_1, G_2) of the model has been analyzed by accounting for constraints from Lattice QCD simulations, the existence of 2 $M_\odot$ pulsars, as well as the limits set by the gravitational-wave event GW170817. In our work, we expand the (V_1, G_2) space by accounting for vector interactions and color superconductivity, which introduces the additional parameters K_V and Δ, respectively. To investigate this new parameter space spanned by V_1, G_2, K_V, Δ, we have chosen $V_1 = 20$ MeV and $G_2 = 0.009$ GeV^4, following the results presented in Ref. [34]; these values for V_1 and G_2 are qualitatively representative of the parameters space. In this way, we focus our attention on the values of K_V and Δ.

In this context, it should be mentioned that one of the methods used to combine and analyze different sets of data is Bayesian analysis, which analyzes the ranges of parameters using probability techniques. The application of Bayesian methods is frequently used in astrophysics (e.g., neutron star physics [67,68]), particularly when dealing with large data sets. A Bayesian analysis of the parameters of our model, however, is out of the scope of this paper.

To calculate the properties of HSs, such as gravitational mass, radius, tidal deformability and study their stability under slow and rapid conversion of hadronic matter to quark matter, we solve the relativistic hydrostatic equilibrium equation of Tolman, Oppenheimer, and Volkoff (TOV) [69,70].

5.1. Analysis of the FCM Parameter Space Spanned by V_1, G_2, K_V, Δ

We start by analyzing the effects of varying K_V and Δ values on the EoS and the mass-radius relationship (M–R) of HSs shown in Figures 1–4. All the hybrid EoSs shown in these figures satisfy the constraints presented in [42]; besides, these EoSs have one common characteristic feature, namely that the hadron-quark transition pressure must be larger than about 200 MeV fm^{-3} so that the 2 $M_\odot$-mass constraint condition can be satisfied.

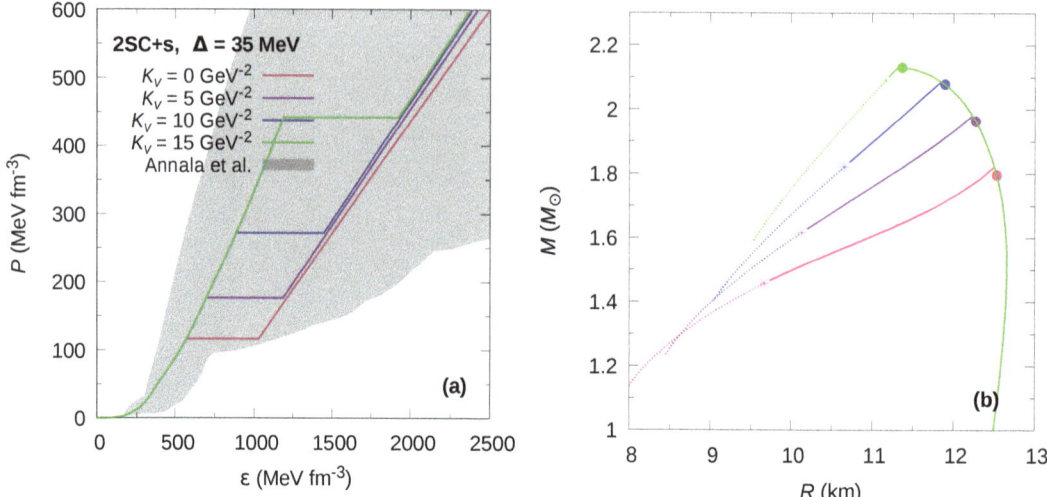

Figure 1. (Color online) Hybrid EoS (panel (**a**)) and mass-radius relationship (panel (**b**)) for the 2SC+s phase at fixed gap value of $\Delta = 35$ MeV, for different values of the K_v parameter. In panel (**a**), the grey region shows the constraints presented in [42]. The solid dots in panel (**b**) indicate the appearance of the color superconducting phase, just before the maximum mass peak. For rapid conversions, the stellar configurations to the left of each maximum mass are unstable and the existence of HSs is only marginal. For slow conversions, an extended stability branch exists. The stable configurations are shown by continuous lines. The terminal configurations are marked with asterisks.

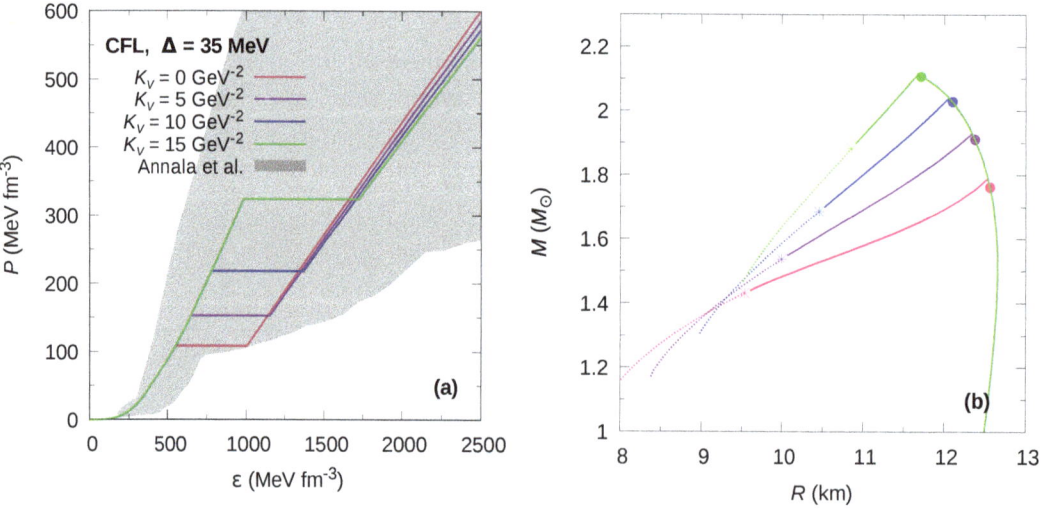

Figure 2. Hybrid EoS (panel (**a**)) and mass-radius relationship (panel (**b**)) for the CFL phase at fixed gap value of $\Delta = 35$ MeV, for different values of the K_v parameter. In panel (**a**), the grey region shows the constraints presented in [42]. The solid dots in panel (**b**) indicate the appearance of the color superconducting phase, just before the maximum mass peak. For rapid conversions, the stellar configurations to the left of each maximum mass are unstable and the existence of HSs is only marginal. For slow conversions, an extended stability branch exists. The stable configurations are shown by continuous lines. The terminal configurations are marked with asterisks.

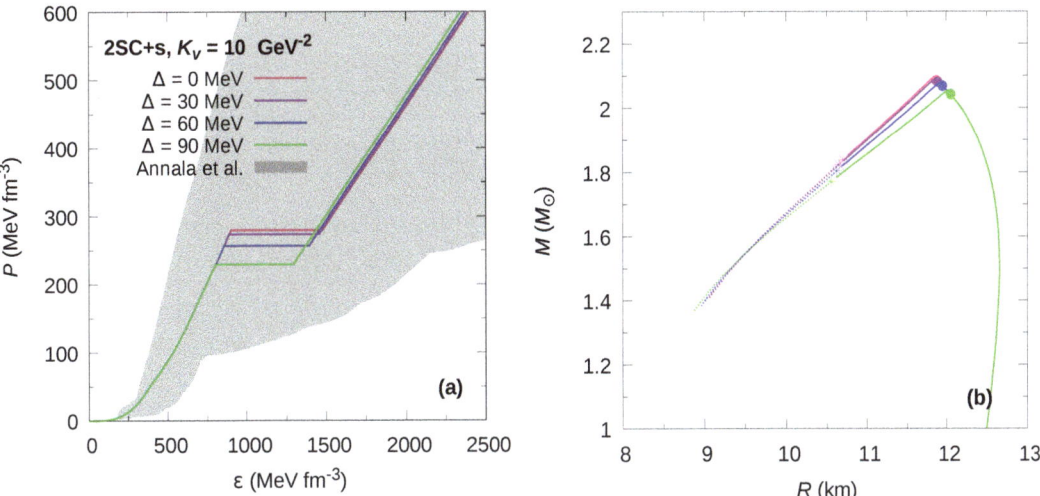

Figure 3. Hybrid EoS (panel (**a**)) and mass-radius relationship (panel (**b**)) for the 2SC+s phase at fixed gap value of $K_v = 10\,\text{GeV}^{-2}$, for different values of the Δ parameter. In panel (**a**), the grey region shows the constraints presented in [42]. The solid dots in panel (**b**) indicate the appearance of the color superconducting phase, just before the maximum mass peak. For rapid conversions, the stellar configurations to the left of each maximum mass are unstable and the existence of HSs is only marginal. For slow conversions, an extended stability branch exists. The stable configurations are shown by continuous lines. The terminal configurations are marked with asterisks.

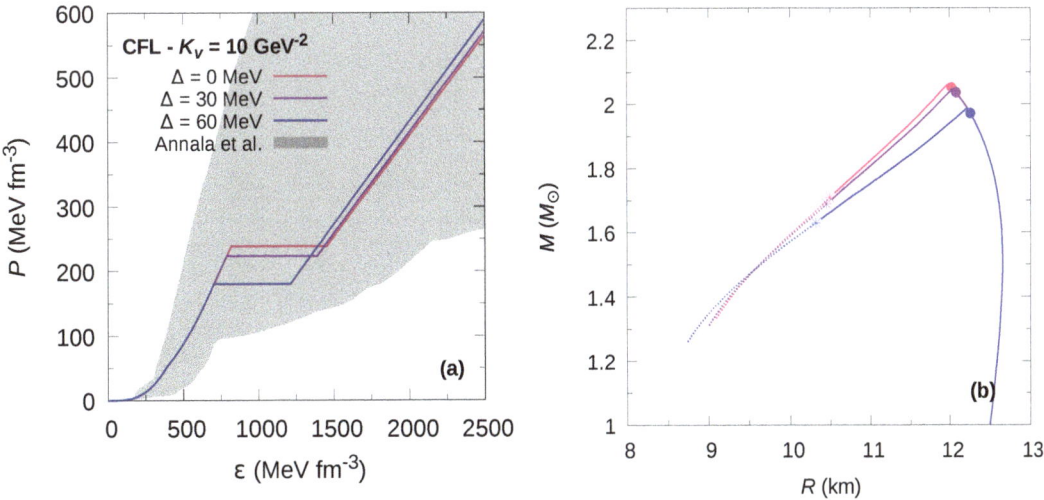

Figure 4. (Hybrid EoS) (panel (**a**)) and mass-radius relationship (panel (**b**)) for the CFL phase at fixed gap value of $K_v = 10\,\text{GeV}^{-2}$, for different values of the Δ parameter. In panel (**a**), the grey region shows the constraints presented in [42]. The solid dots in panel (**b**) indicate the appearance of the color superconducting phase, just before the maximum mass peak. For rapid conversions, the stellar configurations to the left of each maximum mass are unstable and the existence of HSs is only marginal. For slow conversions, an extended stability branch exists. The stable configurations are shown by continuous lines. The terminal configurations are marked with asterisks.

This has direct implications for the appearance of quark Matter in the cores of HSs. A comprehensive study of the range of values of K_v and Δ (including the values of V_1 and G_2) shows that only a rapid conversion of hadronic matter to quark matter destabilized HSs. This finding is independent of the type of the color superconducting phase and is in agreement with the results obtained in a previous study of HSs, where quark matter was modeled with NJL-type models [71].

In Figures 1 and 2 we show the hybrid EoSs and the corresponding M–R relationships of HSs computed for the 2SC+s and CFL phases. The value for the superconducting gap is $\Delta = 35$ MeV, and the K_v values range from zero to 15 GeV^{-2}. In panels (a), we see how the pressure at which the phase transition occurs increases and the energy density gap widens as K_v increases. For the 2SC+s EoS (Figure 1) the increase in K_v stiffens the EoS of the color superconducting phase, which in turn increases the speed of sound ($c_s^2/c^2 = \partial P/\partial \epsilon$) in that phase. On the contrary, for the CFL EoS (Figure 2) we find that increasing values of K_v lead to decreasing speeds of sound.

The solid dots shown in the M–R relationships shown in panels (b) of Figures 1 and 2 mark the appearance of color superconducting quark matter cores of these stars. Most interestingly, the appearance of such matter does not destabilize the stars if the conversions from hadronic matter to quark matter proceed slowly. Instead, such stars remain stable over an extended regime in the M–R diagram. Their final termination points are marked with asterisks in Figures 1 and 2).

In Figures 3 and 4, we present the EoSs and M–R relationships of HSs with 2SC+s and CFL matter in their cores, but for which the value of K_v is kept constant while the diquark energy gap taken on several different values. We can see that varying the value of Δ in the 2SC+s phase has little impact on the hybrid EoS. For the CFL phase, however, the impact is more pronounced. In both cases, the speed of sound in the quark superconducting phase does not change significantly with changes in Δ. An increase in Δ leads to a somewhat smaller changes in energy density in the transition region. This effect is more noticeable in the CFL phase than in the the 2SC+s phase. The main differences appear in the transition pressure where a higher value of Δ leads to a lower transition pressure. This, of course, has consequences for the appearance of superconducting quark cores in HSs and, in particular, reverberates on the extended stable branch of HSs, panels (b) of Figures 3 and 4. One common feature is that the increase of the value of K_v leads to a shortening of the extended branch of stable compact objects.

5.2. Astrophysical Constraints

In Figure 5, we explore the maximum-mass values of HSs in the K_v-Δ plane. Panel (a) shows the results for 2SC+s stars while panel (b) is for CFL stars. The 2.01 $M_\odot$ gravitational mass constraint imposed by PSR J1614-2230, PSR J0348+0432, and PSR J0740+6620 is shown by the white curve. It can be seen that our models satisfy this mass constraint for a wide range of K_v and Δ values. A combination of such values is compiled in Table 4, which will be used for subsequent investigations below. It is worth noting that HSs with $V_1 = 20$ MeV and $G_2 = 0.009$ GeV^4 do not satisfy the $M_{max} = 2.01\ M_\odot$ constraint unless vector interactions and color superconductivity are included in the model. Furthermore, the possibility of obtaining sufficiently massive HSs with color superconducting quark matter in their cores increases if Δ increases, for a wide range of K_v values. This is most noticeable in panel (b) for stars with a CFL core. Comparing panels (a) and (b) with each other shows that the parameter space that leads to sufficiently massive HSs with 2SC+s cores is narrower. For the 2SC+s phase, shown in panel (a), stars with M_{max} (along the white curve) correspond to K_v values that scatter around 7 GeV^{-2}. This situation is quite different when the CFL phase is considered (see panel (b) in Figure 5) where it is shown that the maximum masses depend on both K_v and Δ rather strongly.

Table 4. Selected sets of parameters for the quark matter EoS.

Set	Quark Phase	K_V (GeV^{-2})	Δ (MeV)
1	2SC+s	15	90
2	2SC+s	10	30
3	CFL	10	30
4	CFL	15	30

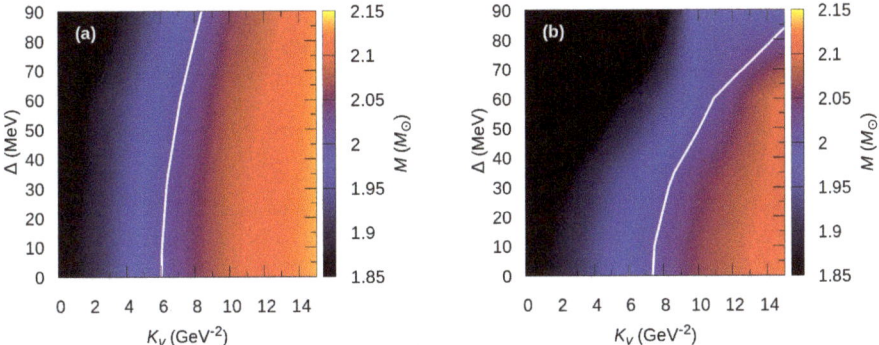

Figure 5. (Text) Maximum mass of stars as a function of Δ and K_V, for the 2SC+s quark matter (panel (**a**)) and CFL quark matter (panel (**b**)). The white curve marks the maximum mass constraint $M_{max} = 2.01 M_\odot$.

In Figure 6, we show the M-R curves that correspond to hybrid star configurations constructed with EoSs whose parameters are listed in Table 4. These curves are consistent with the 2 $M_\odot$ mass constraint set by massive pulsars, NICER observations, as well as the NS data extracted from the gravitational-wave event GW170817 and GW190425. We see that, when assuming slow hadron-quark conversion, each model predicts the existence of high-mass twin stars. And because of this possibility, the observed 2 $M_\odot$ pulsars could be either NSs or HSs. The radii of the latter could be up to 1.5 km smaller than those of the NSs. Furthermore, for parameter set 3 of Table 4 we find that the corresponding extended hybrid-star branch could even explain the stellar high-mass component of the GW190425 binary system [6].

We have also explored the possibility of sequential phase transitions between the two different quark matter EoSs, i.e., the occurrence of a transition of quark matter from the 2SC+s to the CFL phase. We find that such a sequential transition is possible, but the M–R relationships do not fulfill 2 $M_\odot$ mass constraint. The main reasons for this is a low speed of sound of $c_s^2/c^2 \sim 0.33$ in the extended FCM EoS and a high phase transition pressure.

In Figure 7, we present the dimensionless tidal deformability, Λ, as a function of gravitational mass for the stellar hybrid configurations of Figure 6. All models present pure hadronic stars for masses $M \leq 1.4 \, M_\odot$, and are consistent with the $\Lambda_{1.4} \sim 500$ constraint deduced from GW170817. One also sees that the HSs along the twin stellar branch have tidal deformabilities that lie on an almost straight horizontal line. This opens up the possibility that future observations of NS mergers may help to shed light on the actual existence of twin stars and hence on the behavior of matter in the inner cores of compact objects.

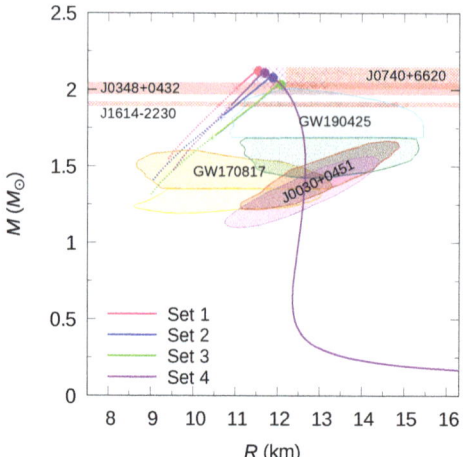

Figure 6. (Color online) M–R relationship of the selected EoSs (Table 4) of this work. The solid dots indicate the appearance of color superconducting quark matter in HSs, which happens just before the maximum-mass peaks are reached. For a rapid conversion of matter, the stellar configurations to the left of each maximum-mass star are unstable. For slow conversions there exist extended branches of stable stars which end at the locations marked with asterisks. The shaded regions (clouds) correspond to constraints imposed by GW170817, GW190425, and NICER observations of PSR J0030+0451. The horizontal pink stripped bands, indicate constraints imposed by pulsars J0740+6620, J0348+0432, and J1614-2230.

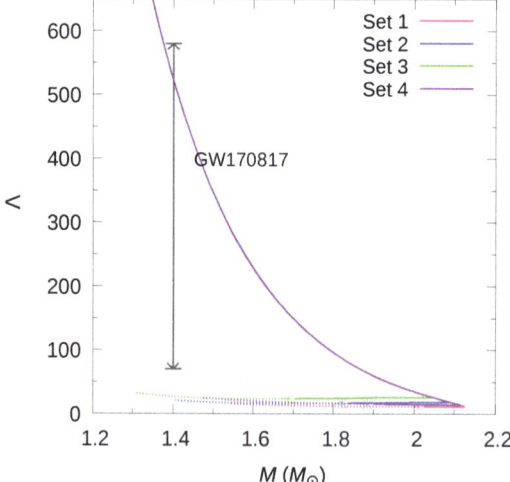

Figure 7. (Color online) Dimensionless tidal deformability as a function of gravitational mass, with the constraint obtained from GW170817 [5]. Stable stellar configurations beyond the maximum mass have very small values of Λ, which are almost independent of mass. The positions of the terminal stars of the twin HSs branch (obtained for slow hadron-quark conversion) are marked with asterisks.

In Figure 8, we show the individual dimensionless tidal deformabilities of the hybrid configurations consistent with the observational constraints obtained after GW170817 and its electromagnetic counterpart. The black line represents the situation in which the two merging objects are purely hadronic NSs.

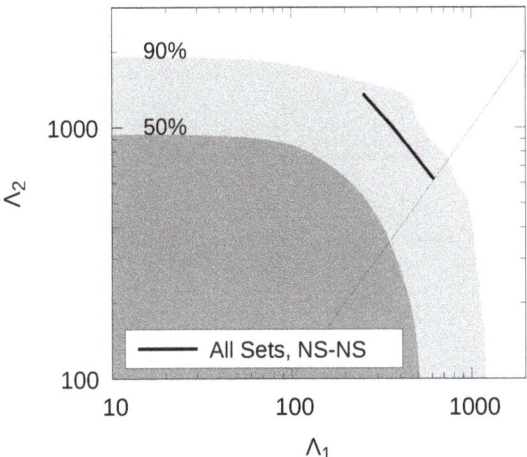

Figure 8. Text Dimensionless tidal deformabilities Λ_1 and Λ_2 for the selected EoSs. The solid black line represents the results obtained for a purely hadronic NS-NS merger with masses consistent with data from GW170817. The dark (light) gray areas represent the 50% (90%) confidence limit of the probability contour of GW170817 and the dotted line corresponds to $\Lambda_1 = \Lambda_2$.

6. Summary and Conclusions

In this work, we have studied hybrid EoSs and the structure of HSs considering the effects of color superconductivity (2SC+s and CFL phases) and vector interactions in quark matter in the framework of the FCM model. Both color superconductivity and vector interactions were included in the model in a phenomenological way, taking advantage of the similarity of the FCM with the MIT bag model at the zero temperature limit. For the description of the hadronic phase, we used the SW4L parametrization of the RMF model. We have assumed a sharp hadron-quark phase transition and considered the the implications of slow versus rapid conversions of matter at the hadron-quark interface. This assumption dramatically modifies the traditional picture of stability in the M–R diagram of HSs. For instance, if we consider a soft Gibbs phase transition, instead of a Maxwell sharp transition, the extended stable branch does not exist. Since in the Gibbs case the EoS has no discontinuity or jump, the stability criterion for hybrid stars is the traditional one, in which case $\partial M / \partial \epsilon_c < 0$ indicates unstable configurations and the maximum mass configuration is the last stable star in the mass-radius diagrams.

After extending the parameter space of the FCM model, we performed a systematic analysis of the parameters of this new space. The goal was to find out whether the parameters lead to equations of state that are consistent with present astrophysical observations. For this purpose we investigated the dependencies of the EoS and the M–R relationship of compact stars on the K_V and Δ parameters, which are related to vector interactions and color superconductivity of the extended FCM model. Fixed values were assumed for the other two parameters, V_1 and G_2, of the model. As our investigations show, the hybrid EoSs we determined successfully satisfy the constraints set by Annala et al. [42] and by PSR J1614-2230, PSR J0348+0432, PSR J0740+6620, GW170817, GW190425, and NICER observations.

In addition, using a specific FCM model parameter set, we have shown that the inclusion of vector interactions and color superconductivity plays a central role in satisfying the mass constraint set by massive pulsars. Specifically, we found that increasing K_V leads to a stiffer hybrid EoS, which increases the maximum stellar mass. However, this increase leads to shorter stability branches for the twin stars. In contrast, an increase in the Δ parameter leads to softer EoSs, both for the 2SC+s and CFL phase, which lowers the maximum mass but leads to extended branches of stellar stability. In general, changes in the value of K_V have a more pronounced effect on the system properties than changes in Δ. An exception is the CFL phase, where changes in Δ dominate the mass-radius relationship.

We have also explored the possibility of a sequential phase transition in HSs. We have found that although that possibility exists, the hybrid configurations obtained from these EoSs do not satisfy the restrictions imposed by massive pulsars. This is due to a low speed of sound in the quark phase and a high value of the hadron-quark transition pressure. It is worth a short discussion of this point since the authors of Refs. [72,73] obtained HSs with sequential phase transitions in the constant speed of sound framework, which fulfill the $2\,M_\odot$ mass constraint. This was possible by using a parametric EoS for the quark phase and by fixing the hadron-quark phase transition pressure (at $p_t \sim 100$ MeV fm^{-3}) as well as the quark-quark phase transition pressure (at $p_t \sim 250$ MeV fm^{-3}). Furthermore, a high value of the speed of sound in quark matter phases ($c_s^2/c^2 \gtrsim 0.7$) was assumed in that paper.

Massive HSs with sequential phase transitions were also obtained with Nambu-Jona-Lasinio type models of quark matter [74,75]. However, extra ingredients are needed in these models to achieve a hadron-quark followed by a quark-quark phase transition, because in these models $c_s^2/c^2 \sim 0.33$. Besides that, an effective bag can be added to the model to lower the transition pressure, considering a large diquark coupling [74]. In these works, the transition pressures (i.e., $p_t \sim 40$ to 60 MeV fm^{-3} for the hadron-quark transition and $p_t \sim 100$ to 130 MeV fm^{-3} for the quark-quark transition) are lower than in Ref. [72]. In a recent study [31] it was shown that in NJL models a higher speed of sound can be achieved through the incorporation of higher-order repulsive interactions. This affects the size of the quark core in HSs, leading to massive hybrid configurations with extended cores of quark matter in the rapid conversion scenario.

Regarding the tidal deformability results, our models satisfy the GW170817 constraint of a $1.4\,M_\odot$ star. Also the restrictions coming from the constraints in the Λ_1–Λ_2 plane are fulfilled. In this case, the purely hadronic branch already lies, for all four parameters sets of Table 4, inside the confidence region. Remarkably, the slow hadron-quark conversion scenario, which leads to new stable hybrid-star branches, helps to satisfy astrophysical constraints (similar conclusions have already been presented in Refs. [43,54,73]).

Author Contributions: Conceptualization, D.C., A.F.R.-S., M.M., M.G.O.; methodology, A.F.R.-S., M.M., M.G.O.; investigation, D.C., A.F.R.-S., M.M., M.G.O., F.W.; writing—original draft preparation, D.C., A.F.R.-S., M.M., M.G.O.; writing—review and editing, F.W.; supervision, F.W. All authors have read and agreed to the published version of the manuscript.

Funding: D.C. is a fellow of UNLP. D.C., I.F.R.-S., M.M. and M.G.O. thank CONICET and UNLP (Argentina) for financial support under grants PIP-0714 and G157, G007. I.F.R.-S. is also partially supported by PICT 2019-0366 from ANPCyT (Argentina). I.F.R.-S., M.G.O. and F.W. are supported by the National Science Foundation (USA) under Grants PHY-2012152.

Institutional Review Board Statement: Not applicable.

Informed Consent Statement: Not applicable.

Acknowledgments: The authors would like to thank V. Dexheimer and R. Negreiros for inviting us to submit a contribution to the Special Issue of Universe entitled "Properties and Dynamics of Neutron Stars and Proto-Neutron Stars".

Conflicts of Interest: The authors declare no conflict of interest.

References

1. Lattimer, J.M.; Prakash, M. The Physics of Neutron Stars. *Science* **2004**, *304*, 536–542. [CrossRef] [PubMed]
2. Pons, J.A.; Reddy, S.; Prakash, M.; Lattimer, J.M.; Miralles, J.A. Evolution of Proto-Neutron Stars. *Astrophys. J.* **1999**, *513*, 780–804. [CrossRef]
3. Potekhin, A.Y. The physics of neutron stars. *Phys.-Uspekhi* **2010**, *53*, 1235–1256. [CrossRef]
4. Abbott, B.P.; Abbott, R.; Abbott, T.D.; Acernese, F.; Ackley, K.; Adams, C.; Adams, T.; Addesso, P.; Adhikari, R.X.; Adya, V.B.; et al. [The LIGO Scientific Collaboration and the Virgo Collaboration]. GW170817: Measurements of Neutron Star Radii and Equation of State. *Phys. Rev. Lett.* **2018**, *121*, 161101. [CrossRef] [PubMed]
5. Abbott, B.P.; Abbott, R.; Abbott, T.D.; Acernese, F.; Ackley, K.; Adams, C.; Adams, T.; Addesso, P.; Adhikari, R.X.; Adya, V.B.; et al. [The LIGO Scientific Collaboration and the Virgo Collaboration]. Properties of the binary neutron star merger GW170817. *Phys. Rev. X* **2019**, *9*, 011001. [CrossRef]
6. Abbott, B.P.; Abbott, R.; Abbott, T.D.; Abraham, S.; Acernese, F.; Ackley, K.; Adams, C.; Adhikari, R.X.; Adya, V.B.; Affeldt, C.; et al. GW190425: Observation of a Compact Binary Coalescence with Total Mass $\sim$ 3.4 $M_\odot$. *Astrophys. J. Lett.* **2020**, *892*, L3. [CrossRef]
7. Riley, T.E.; Watts, A.L.; Ray, P.S.; Bogdanov, S.; Guillot, S.; Morsink, S.M.; Bilous, A.V.; Arzoumanian, Z.; Choudhury, D.; Deneva, J.S.; et al. A NICER View of the Massive Pulsar PSR J0740+6620 Informed by Radio Timing and XMM-Newton Spectroscopy. *Astrophys. J. Lett.* **2021**, *918*, L27. [CrossRef]
8. Miller, M.C.; Lamb, F.K.; Dittmann, A.J.; Bogdanov, S.; Arzoumanian, Z.; Gendreau, K.C.; Guillot, S.; Ho, W.C.G.; Lattimer, J.M.; Loewenstein, M.; et al. The Radius of PSR J0740+6620 from NICER and XMM-Newton Data. *Astrophys. J. Lett.* **2021**, *918*, L28. [CrossRef]
9. Baym, G.; Hatsuda, T.; Kojo, T.; Powell, P.D.; Song, Y.; Takatsuka, T. From hadrons to quarks in neutron stars: A review. *Rept. Prog. Phys.* **2018**, *81*, 056902. [CrossRef]
10. Orsaria, M.G.; Malfatti, G.; Mariani, M.; Ranea-Sandoval, I.F.; García, F.; Spinella, W.M.; Contrera, G.A.; Lugones, G.; Weber, F. Phase transitions in neutron stars and their links to gravitational waves. *J. Phys. G* **2019**, *46*, 073002. [CrossRef]
11. Weber, F. *Pulsars as Astrophysical Laboratories for Nuclear and Particle Physics*; Series in High Energy Physics, Cosmology and Gravitation; CRC Press: Boca Raton, FL, USA, 1999. [CrossRef]
12. Weber, F. Strange quark matter and compact stars. *Prog. Part. Nucl. Phys.* **2005**, *54*, 193–288. [CrossRef]
13. Demorest, P.; Pennucci, T.; Ransom, S.; Roberts, M.; Hessels, J. Shapiro Delay Measurement of A Two Solar Mass Neutron Star. *Nature* **2010**, *467*, 1081–1083. [CrossRef]
14. Arzoumanian, Z.; Brazier, A.; Burke-Spolaor, S.; Chamberlin, S.; Chatterjee, S.; Christy, B.; Cordes, J.M.; Cornish, N.J.; Crawford, F.; Cromartie, H.T.; et al. The NANOGrav 11-year Data Set: High-precision Timing of 45 Millisecond Pulsars. *Astrophys. J. Suppl. Ser.* **2018**, *235*, 37. [CrossRef]
15. Antoniadis, J.; Freire, P.C.; Wex, N.; Tauris, T.M.; Lynch, R.S.; Van Kerkwijk, M.H.; Kramer, M.; Bassa, C.; Dhillon, V.S.; Driebe, T.; et al. A Massive Pulsar in a Compact Relativistic Binary. *Science* **2013**, *340*, 6131. [CrossRef] [PubMed]
16. Cromartie, H.T.; Fonseca, E.; Ransom, S.M.; Demorest, P.B.; Arzoumanian, Z.; Blumer, H.; Brook, P.R.; DeCesar, M.E.; Dolch, T.; Ellis, J.A.; et al. Relativistic Shapiro delay measurements of an extremely massive millisecond pulsar. *Nat. Astron.* **2020**, *4*, 72–76. [CrossRef]
17. Tews, I.; Margueron, J.; Reddy, S. Critical examination of constraints on the equation of state of dense matter obtained from GW170817. *Phys. Rev. C* **2018**, *98*, 045804. [CrossRef]
18. Shibata, M.; Zhou, E.; Kiuchi, K.; Fujibayashi, S. Constraint on the maximum mass of neutron stars using GW170817 event. *Phys. Rev. D* **2019**, *100*, 023015. [CrossRef]
19. Farrow, N.; Zhu, X.J.; Thrane, E. The Mass Distribution of Galactic Double Neutron Stars. *Astrophys. J.* **2019**, *876*, 18. [CrossRef]
20. Gompertz, B.P.; Cutter, R.; Steeghs, D.; Galloway, D.K.; Lyman, J.; Ulaczyk, K.; Dyer, M.J.; Ackley, K.; Dhillon, V.S.; O'Brien, P.T.; et al. Searching for electromagnetic counterparts to gravitational-wave merger events with the prototype Gravitational-Wave Optical Transient Observer (GOTO-4). *Mon. Not. R. Astron. Soc.* **2020**, *497*, 726–738. [CrossRef]
21. Riley, T.E.; Watts, A.L.; Bogdanov, S.; Ray, P.S.; Ludlam, R.M.; Guillot, S.; Arzoumanian, Z.; Baker, C.L.; Bilous, A.V.; Chakrabarty, D.; et al. A NICER View of PSR J0030+0451: Millisecond Pulsar Parameter Estimation. *Astrophys. J. Lett.* **2019**, *887*, L21. [CrossRef]
22. Miller, M.C.; Lamb, F.K.; Dittmann, A.J.; Bogdanov, S.; Arzoumanian, Z.; Gendreau, K.C.; Guillot, S.; Harding, A.K.; Ho, W.C.G.; Lattimer, J.M.; et al. PSR J0030+0451 Mass and Radius from NICER Data and Implications for the Properties of Neutron Star Matter. *Astrophys. J. Lett.* **2019**, *887*, L24. [CrossRef]
23. Rajagopal, K.; Frank Wilczek, F. The condensed matter physics of QCD. In *At the Frontier of Particle Physics*; World Scientific: Singapore, 2001; pp. 2061–2151.
24. Alford, M.G. Color superconducting quark matter. *Ann. Rev. Nucl. Part. Sci.* **2001**, *51*, 131–160. [CrossRef]
25. Alford, M.G.; Schmitt, A.; Rajagopal, K.; Schäfer, T. Color superconductivity in dense quark matter. *Rev. Mod. Phys.* **2008**, *80*, 1455–1515. [CrossRef]
26. Bardeen, J.; Cooper, L.N.; Schrieffer, J.R. Microscopic Theory of Superconductivity. *Phys. Rev.* **1957**, *106*, 162–164. [CrossRef]
27. Ranea-Sandoval, I.F.; Orsaria, M.G.; Han, S.; Weber, F.; Spinella, W.M. Color superconductivity in compact stellar hybrid configurations. *Phys. Rev. C* **2017**, *96*, 065807. [CrossRef]
28. Lugones, G.; Horvath, J.E. High-density QCD pairing in compact star structure. *Astron. Astrophys.* **2003**, *403*, 173–178. [CrossRef]

29. Orsaria, M.; Rodrigues, H.; Weber, F.; Contrera, G.A. Quark deconfinement in high-mass neutron stars. *Phys. Rev. C* **2014**, *89*, 015806. [CrossRef]
30. Klähn, T.; Fischer, T. Vector interaction enhanced bag model for astrophysical applications. *Astrophys. J.* **2015**, *810*, 134. [CrossRef]
31. Ferreira, M.; Pereira, R.C.; Providência, C. Quark matter in light neutron stars. *Phys. Rev. D* **2020**, *102*, 083030. [CrossRef]
32. Simonov, Y.A.; Trusov, M.A. Deconfinement transition for nonzero baryon density in the field correlator method. *JETP Lett.* **2007**, *85*, 598–601. [CrossRef]
33. Nefediev, A.V.; Simonov, Y.A.; Trusov, M.A. Deconfinement and Quark—Gluon plasma. *Int. J. Mod. Phys. E* **2009**, *18*, 549–599. [CrossRef]
34. Mariani, M.; Orsaria, M.; Vucetich, H. Constant entropy hybrid stars: A first approximation of cooling evolution. *Astron. Astrophys.* **2017**, *601*, A21. [CrossRef]
35. Malfatti, G.; Orsaria, M.G.; Contrera, G.A.; Weber, F.; Ranea-Sandoval, I.F. Hot quark matter and (proto-) neutron stars. *Phys. Rev. C* **2019**, *100*, 015803. [CrossRef]
36. Pereira, J.P.; Flores, C.V.; Lugones, G. Phase Transition Effects on the Dynamical Stability of Hybrid Neutron Stars. *Astrophys. J.* **2018**, *860*, 12. [CrossRef]
37. Voskresensky, D.; Yasuhira, M.; Tatsumi, T. Charge screening at first order phase transitions and hadron quark mixed phase. *Nucl. Phys. A* **2003**, *723*, 291–339. [CrossRef]
38. Endo, T. Region of hadron-quark mixed phase in hybrid stars. *Phys. Rev. C* **2011**, *83*, 068801. [CrossRef]
39. Wu, X.; Shen, H. Nuclear symmetry energy and hadron-quark mixed phase in neutron stars. *Phys. Rev. C* **2019**, *99*, 065802. [CrossRef]
40. Maslov, K.; Yasutake, N.; Blaschke, D.; Ayriyan, A.; Grigorian, H.; Maruyama, T.; Tatsumi, T.; Voskresensky, D.N. Hybrid equation of state with pasta phases, and third family of compact stars. *Phys. Rev. C* **2019**, *100*, 025802. [CrossRef]
41. Weber, F.; Farrell, D.; Spinella, W.M.; Malfatti, G.; Orsaria, M.G.; Contrera, G.A.; Maloney, I. Phases of Hadron-Quark Matter in (Proto) Neutron Stars. *Universe* **2019**, *5*, 169. [CrossRef]
42. Annala, E.; Gorda, T.; Kurkela, A.; Nättilä, J.; Vuorinen, A. Evidence for quark-matter cores in massive neutron stars. *Nat. Phys.* **2020**, *16*, 907–910. [CrossRef]
43. Mariani, M.; Orsaria, M.G.; Ranea-Sandoval, I.F.; Lugones, G. Magnetized hybrid stars: Effects of slow and rapid phase transitions at the quark-hadron interface. *Mon. Not. R. Astron. Soc.* **2019**, *489*, 4261–4277. [CrossRef]
44. Bombaci, I.; Lugones, G.; Vidana, I. Effects of color superconductivity on the nucleation of quark matter in neutron stars. *Astron. Astrophys.* **2007**, *462*, 1017–1022. [CrossRef]
45. Haensel, P.; Zdunik, J.L.; Schaeffer, R. Phase transitions in dense matter and radial pulsations of neutron stars. *A&A* **1989**, *217*, 137–144.
46. Bombaci, I.; Parenti, I.; Vidaña, I. Quark Deconfinement and Implications for the Radius and the Limiting Mass of Compact Stars. *Astrophys. J.* **2004**, *614*, 314–325. [CrossRef]
47. Bombaci, I.; Logoteta, D.; Panda, P.K.; Providência, C.; Vidaña, I. Quark matter nucleation in hot hadronic matter. *Phys. Lett. B* **2009**, *680*, 448–452. [CrossRef]
48. Lugones, G.; Grunfeld, A.G. Critical spectrum of fluctuations for deconfinement at protoneutron star cores. *Phys. Rev. D* **2011**, *84*, 085003. [CrossRef]
49. Bombaci, I.; Logoteta, D.; Vidaña, I.; Providência, C. Quark matter nucleation in neutron stars and astrophysical implications. *Eur. Phys. J. A* **2016**, *52*, 58. [CrossRef]
50. Glendenning, N.K. Neutron stars are giant hypernuclei? *Astrophys. J.* **1985**, *293*, 470–493. [CrossRef]
51. Alford, M.; Rajagopal, K. Absence of two-flavor color-superconductivity in compact stars. *J. High Energy Phys.* **2002**, *2002*, 31. [CrossRef]
52. Typel, S.; Wolter, H.H. Relativistic mean field calculations with density dependent meson nucleon coupling. *Nucl. Phys. A* **1999**, *656*, 331–364. [CrossRef]
53. Spinella, W.M. A Systematic Investigation of Exotic Matter in Neutron Stars. Ph.D. Thesis, Claremont Graduate University & San Diego State University, Claremont, CA, USA, 2017.
54. Malfatti, G.; Orsaria, M.G.; Ranea-Sandoval, I.F.; Contrera, G.A.; Weber, F. Delta baryons and diquark formation in the cores of neutron stars. *Phys. Rev. D* **2020**, *102*, 063008. [CrossRef]
55. Lattimer, J.M.; Lim, Y. Constraining the Symmetry Parameters of the Nuclear Interaction. *Astrophys. J.* **2013**, *771*, 51. [CrossRef]
56. Lattimer, J.M. Neutron Star Mass and Radius Measurements. *Universe* **2019**, *5*, 159. [CrossRef]
57. Horowitz, C.J.; Brown, E.F.; Kim, Y.; Lynch, W.G.; Michaels, R.; Ono, A.; Piekarewicz, J.; Tsang, M.B.; Wolter, H.H. A way forward in the study of the symmetry energy: Experiment, theory, and observation. *J. Phys. G Nucl. Part. Phys.* **2014**, *41*, 093001. [CrossRef]
58. Hofmann, F.; Keil, C.M.; Lenske, H. Application of the density dependent hadron field theory to neutron star matter. *Phys. Rev. C* **2001**, *64*, 025804. [CrossRef]
59. Simonov, Y.; Trusov, M. Vacuum phase transition at nonzero baryon density. *Phys. Lett. B* **2007**, *650*, 36–40. [CrossRef]
60. Shovkovy, I.A. Two Lectures on Color Superconductivity*. *Found. Phys.* **2005**, *35*, 1309–1358. [CrossRef]
61. Baym, G.; Pethick, C.; Sutherland, P. The Ground State of Matter at High Densities: Equation of State and Stellar Models. *Astrophys. J.* **1971**, *170*, 299. [CrossRef]
62. Baym, G.; Bethe, H.A.; Pethick, C.J. Neutron star matter. *Nucl. Phys. A* **1971**, *175*, 225–271. [CrossRef]

63. Plumari, S.; Burgio, G.; Greco, V.; Zappala, D. Quark matter in neutron stars within the field correlator method. *Phys. Rev. D* **2013**, *88*, 083005. [CrossRef]
64. Logoteta, D.; Bombaci, I. Quark deconfinement transition in neutron stars with the field correlator method. *Phys. Rev. D* **2013**, *88*, 063001. [CrossRef]
65. Burgio, G.; Zappalà, D. Hybrid star structure with the Field Correlator Method. *Eur. Phys. J. A* **2016**, *52*, 1–14. [CrossRef]
66. Khanmohamadi, S.; Moshfegh, H.; Tehrani, S.A. Structure and tidal deformability of a hybrid star within the framework of the field correlator method. *Phys. Rev. D* **2020**, *101*, 123001. [CrossRef]
67. Char, P.; Traversi, S.; Pagliara, G. A Bayesian Analysis on Neutron Stars within Relativistic Mean Field Models. *Particles* **2020**, *3*, 621–629. [CrossRef]
68. Xie, W.J.; Li, B.A. Bayesian Inference of the Symmetry Energy of Superdense Neutron-rich Matter from Future Radius Measurements of Massive Neutron Stars. *Astrophys. J.* **2020**, *899*, 4. [CrossRef]
69. Tolman, R.C. Static solutions of Einstein's field equations for spheres of fluid. *Phys. Rev.* **1939**, *55*, 364–373. [CrossRef]
70. Oppenheimer, J.R.; Volkoff, G.M. On Massive Neutron Cores. *Phys. Rev.* **1939**, *55*, 374–381. [CrossRef]
71. Ranea-Sandoval, I.F.; Han, S.; Orsaria, M.G.; Contrera, G.A.; Weber, F.; Alford, M.G. Constant-sound-speed parametrization for Nambu–Jona-Lasinio models of quark matter in hybrid stars. *Phys. Rev. C* **2016**, *93*, 045812. [CrossRef]
72. Alford, M.; Sedrakian, A. Compact Stars with Sequential QCD Phase Transitions. *Phys. Rev. Lett.* **2017**, *119*, 161104. [CrossRef]
73. Rodríguez, M.; Ranea-Sandoval, I.F.; Mariani, M.; Orsaria, M.G.; Malfatti, G.; Guilera, O. Hybrid stars with sequential phase transitions: The emergence of the g2 mode. *J. Cosmol. Astropart. Phys.* **2021**, *2021*, 9. [CrossRef]
74. Pagliara, G.; Schaffner-Bielich, J. Stability of color-flavor-locking cores in hybrid stars. *Phys. Rev. D* **2008**, *77*, 063004. [CrossRef]
75. Bonanno, L.; Sedrakian, A. Composition and stability of hybrid stars with hyperons and quark color-superconductivity. *Astron. Astrophys.* **2012**, *539*, A16. [CrossRef]

Review

Magnetic Dual Chiral Density Wave: A Candidate Quark Matter Phase for the Interior of Neutron Stars

Efrain J. Ferrer [1,*,†] and Vivian de la Incera [2,†]

Department of Physics and Astronomy, University of Texas Rio Grande Valley, 1201 West University Dr., Edinburg, TX 78539, USA; vivian.incera@utrgv.edu
* Correspondence: efrain.ferrer@utrgv.edu
† These authors contributed equally to this work.

Abstract: In this review, we discuss the physical characteristics of the magnetic dual chiral density wave (MDCDW) phase of dense quark matter and argue why it is a promising candidate for the interior matter phase of neutron stars. The MDCDW condensate occurs in the presence of a magnetic field. It is a single-modulated chiral density wave characterized by two dynamically generated parameters: the fermion quasiparticle mass m and the condensate spatial modulation q. The lowest-Landau-level quasiparticle modes in the MDCDW system are asymmetric about the zero energy, a fact that leads to the topological properties and anomalous electric transport exhibited by this phase. The topology makes the MDCDW phase robust against thermal phonon fluctuations, and as such, it does not display the Landau–Peierls instability, a staple feature of single-modulated inhomogeneous chiral condensates in three dimensions. The topology is also reflected in the presence of the electromagnetic chiral anomaly in the effective action and in the formation of hybridized propagating modes known as axion-polaritons. Taking into account that one of the axion-polaritons of this quark phase is gapped, we argue how incident γ-ray photons can be converted into gapped axion-polaritons in the interior of a magnetar star in the MDCDW phase leading the star to collapse, a phenomenon that can serve to explain the so-called missing pulsar problem in the galactic center.

Keywords: chiral symmetry; axion QED; quark–hole pairing; cold-dense QCD; magnetic DCDW

1. Introduction

A fundamental question in nuclear physics/astrophysics currently is what is the state of matter that is realized in the interior of neutron stars (NS). Neutron stars are among the densest objects in the universe. They are produced by the gravitational collapse of very massive stars that can have up to 30 solar masses or by binary NS merger events such as GW170817 [1]. Their inner densities can reach values several times larger than the nuclear density $\rho_n = 4 \times 10^{17}$ kg/m^3. One possibility is that at those densities, baryons are so close that they can be smashed together, producing quark deconfinement. Once the quarks are liberated, there exists the possibility to have NSs exclusively formed by strange matter, the so-called strange stars [2]. The idea of a strange star was prompted by the Bodmer–Terazawa–Witten hypothesis [3–5] based on the idea that strange matter has a lower energy per baryon than ordinary nuclei, even including $_{56}Fe$. Thus, the true ground state of the hadrons may be strange matter. Later on, the equilibrium composition and the equation of state (EoS) for strange matter were studied by other authors [2,6–10]. Thus, a strange star will be formed by an absolutely stable phase consisting of roughly equal numbers of up, down, and strange quarks plus a smaller number of electrons (to guarantee charge neutrality). More recently, by using a phenomenological quark–meson model that includes the flavor-dependent feedback of the quark gas on the QCD vacuum, it was demonstrated in [11] that u-d quark matter is in general more stable than strange quark matter, and it can be more stable than the ordinary nuclear matter when the baryon number is sufficiently large.

Considering effective models of the Nambu–Jona–Lasinio (NJL)-type with parameters matched to nuclear data, we can simulate the one-gluon exchange interaction of QCD, which contains a dominant attractive diquark channel. This attractive interaction gives rise to color superconductivity (CS) [12–15]. NJL models have predicted that the most favored phase of CS at asymptotically high densities is the three-flavor color-flavor-locked (CFL) phase with a significantly large gap. The existence of a large superconducting gap together with a repulsive vector interaction, which is always present in a dense medium [16], can help to make the EoS stiff enough to reach the high stellar masses measured for two compact objects, PSR J1614-2230 and PSR J0348+0432 with $M = 1.97 \pm 0.04 M_\odot$ [17] and $M = 2.01 \pm 0.04 M_\odot$ [18], respectively, where $M_\odot$ is the solar mass. In a recent paper [19], it was found that in addition to the previously cited agreement with respect to the stellar maximum mass, there is also a strong correlation between the predictions of the CFL model in a plausible range of parameters, even including the radiative effects of gluons [20], and the mass/radius fits to NICER data for PSR J003+0451, as well as the tidal deformabilities of the GW170817 event. Despite these encouraging results, the CFL phase fails to pass another important astrophysical test: the heat capacity lower limit obtained from temperature observations of accreting NSs in quiescence. As found in [21], the heat capacity of the NS core has a lower limit $\tilde{C}_V \geq 10^{36}(T/10^8)$ erg/K. Thus, NS matter-phase candidates that do not satisfy this constraint should be ruled out. Superfluid/superconducting phases where all the fermions are paired do not obey the constraint since they have a very small heat capacity proportional to $e^{-a/T}$ at small T, with a a model-dependent function of the gap. Only superfluid/superconducting phases where not all the fermions are paired have the possibility to produce sufficient heat capacity to satisfy the lower limit thanks to the contribution of nonpaired fermions. These arguments were explicitly corroborated in [21,22] for a pure CFL phase, showing that its heat capacity is strongly depleted, not only because all the quarks form Cooper pairs, but also because the system does not have many electrons as its electrical neutrality is ensured by the almost equal numbers of u, d, and s quarks alone. These results indicate that a pure CFL phase is not a suitable choice for the inner composition of compact stars.

NSs are not only the natural objects with the highest density in the universe, but they also exhibit the strongest magnetic fields, which become extremely large in the case of magnetars, with inner values that have been estimated to range from 10^{18} G for nuclear matter [23] to 10^{20} G for quark matter [24]. The facts that strong magnetic fields populate the vast majority of the astrophysical compact objects and that they can significantly affect several properties of the star have served as the motivation for many works focused on the study of the EoS of magnetized NSs [24–32]. An important characteristic is that the EoS in a uniform magnetic field becomes anisotropic, with different pressures along the field and transverse to it [24–31]. The magnetic field has been shown to play an important role in CS [27,33–42], as well as in inhomogeneous chiral phases [43–47].

The presence of a magnetic field is relevant due to the activation of new channels of interaction and, occasionally, also due to the generation of additional condensates. For instance, in the quarkyonic phase of dense quark matter, a magnetic field is responsible for the appearance of a new chiral spiral between the pion and magnetic moment condensates, $\langle \bar{\psi}\gamma^5\psi \rangle$ and $\langle \bar{\psi}\gamma^1\gamma^2\psi \rangle$, respectively [48]. Similarly, additional condensates emerge in the homogeneous chiral phase [49], as well as in color superconductivity [38].

On the other hand, various QCD effective model studies, as well as QCD calculations in the large-Nc limit indicate that spatially inhomogeneous chiral phases, characterized by particle–hole pairs that carry total momentum, can be formed at relatively low temperatures and intermediate densities [50–63]. Such inhomogeneous chiral phases emerge when the baryon density increases from low values, where the hadronic phase is favored, to densities a few times the nuclear saturation density.

Interestingly enough, approaching the low-temperature/intermediate-density region from the other side, i.e., from the very-high-density region, also favors the formation of spatially inhomogeneous phases, only that in this case, they are CS phases since their ground state contains quark–quark pairs [12,64]. This phenomenon can be understood as follows. The CFL phase, favored at asymptotically large densities, is based on BCS quark pairing. In this phase, the quarks pair at the Fermi surface with equal and opposite momenta, so the phase is homogenous. However, with decreasing density, the combined effect of the strange quark mass, neutrality constraint, and beta equilibrium create a mismatch in the Fermi momenta of different flavors. The mismatch in turn imposes an extra energy cost on Cooper pair formation. BCS pairing can then dominate as long as the energy cost of forcing all species to have the same Fermi momentum is compensated by the win in pairing energy due to Cooper pair formation. The consequence of these competing effects is that eventually, as the density decreases, the CFL phase becomes the gapless CFL (gCFL) [65], on which not all the Cooper pairs remain stable energetically anymore and, as a consequence, some of the quarks become gapless. More importantly, the onset of gCFL produces chromomagnetic instabilities (CMIs) [66,67], meaning some of the gluons acquire imaginary Meissner masses, a sign that one is working in the wrong ground state. A viable solution, free of CMIs, involves a momentum-dependent quark–quark condensate that spontaneously breaks translational invariance [68–71] and hence forms a spatially inhomogeneous CS phase. Most inhomogeneous CS phases are based on the idea of Larkin and Ovchinnikov (LO) [72] and Fulde and Ferrell (FF) [73], originally applied to condensed matter. In the CS LOFF phases [74–76], quarks of different flavors pair even though they have different Fermi momenta, because they form Cooper pairs with nonzero momentum. CS inhomogeneous phases with gluon vortices that break rotational symmetry [77] have also been considered to remove the instability.

Even though the above-mentioned studies suggest that the inhomogeneous phases must be unavoidable at intermediate densities and low temperatures, the question of which phase is the most energetically favorable on each segment of the intermediate region still remains unanswered. Exploring it will require involved calculations due to the fact that the pairing energies between particle–particle, particle–antiparticle, and particle–hole are comparable at these densities.

In the present review, we focus our attention on one particular spatially inhomogeneous phase, a chiral phase known as the magnetic dual chiral density wave (MDCDW) phase [43–46]. The MDCDW ground state is characterized by a chiral density wave made of scalar and pseudo-scalar condensate components, hence the term "dual" in its name. This phase occurs in the presence of a magnetic field and exhibits a wealth of interesting topological properties. The MDCDW phase has profound differences from the so-called dual chiral density wave (DCDW) phase [63] where no external field is present, even though both are characterized by the same type of inhomogeneous chiral condensate. The magnetic field explicitly reduces the rotational and isospin symmetries that are present in the DCDW case, significantly enhances the window for inhomogeneity [43], and leads to topologically nontrivial transport properties [45,46].

An additional effect that makes the MDCDW phase a particularly viable candidate for the NS's inner state of matter is that it is not washed out by thermal fluctuations at low temperatures. This property is significant because even though single-modulated chiral condensates are energetically favored over their homogeneous counterpart at increasing densities and favored even over higher-dimensional modulations in three dimensions, the long-order range in single-modulated condensates is always washed out by the thermal fluctuations of the Goldstone bosons at arbitrarily small temperatures. This occurs due to the existence of soft modes of the fluctuation spectrum in the direction normal to the modulation, a phenomenon known in the literature as the Landau–Peierls instability [78,79]. In dense QCD models, the Landau–Peierls instability occurs in the periodic real kink crystal phase [80]; in the DCDW phase [81]; and in the quarkyonic phase [82]. The Landau–Peierls instability signals the lack of long-range correlations at any finite temperature, hence the lack of a true order parameter. Only a quasi-long-range order remains in all these cases, a situation that resembles what happens in smectic liquid crystals [83].

Thanks to the external magnetic field, the Landau–Peierls instability is absent in the MDCDW phase [84]. The field produces two main effects. First, it acts as an external vector that explicitly breaks the rotational and isospin symmetries, allowing the formation of additional structures in the Ginzburg–Landau (GL) expansion of the MDCDW thermodynamic potential and reducing to one the number of Goldstone bosons in the spontaneously broken symmetry theory. Second, it induces a nontrivial topology in the system that manifests itself in the asymmetry of the lowest Landau level (LLL) modes and in the appearance of odd-in-q terms in the GL expansion. These two features in turn affect the low-energy theory of the thermal fluctuations, stiffening the dispersion relation in the direction normal to the modulation vector, thereby preventing the washout of the long-range order, hence removing the Landau–Peierls instability.

In this review, we discuss the main properties of the MDCDW phase, including how the interaction of the MDCDW medium with an electromagnetic field modifies the propagation of electromagnetic waves, thereby leading to interesting implications for astrophysics.

The review is organized as follows. In Section 2, we introduce the two-flavor NJL model that serves as the basis for the MDCDW phase of dense quark matter in a magnetic field, outlining the derivations that lead to the emergence of a chiral anomaly term in the effective action of the system. In Section 3, we discuss the realization of axion electrodynamics in the MDCDW phase and the implications for electric transport. In Section 4, we demonstrate the lack of the Landau–Peierls instability in the MDCDW system and discuss the role played by the background magnetic field on this property. In Section 5, we go beyond the mean-field approximation to study the anomalous matter–light interaction that takes place in this inhomogeneous phase. We show how photons couple to the fluctuation of the axion field (proportional to the phonon fluctuation) to produce hybrid modes of propagation called axion polaritons. A possible consequence of the formation of these hybridized modes inside a quark star bombarded by γ-rays is then proposed in Section 6 to explain the so-called missing pulsar problem in the galactic center. Section 7 summarizes the main results and our concluding remarks.

2. The Magnetic Dual Chiral Density Wave Phase

To study the MDCDW phase, we start from a two-flavor NJL model of strongly interacting quarks at finite baryon density that includes the electromagnetic interaction and a background magnetic field:

$$\mathcal{L} = -\frac{1}{4}F_{\mu\nu}F^{\mu\nu} + \bar{\psi}[i\gamma^\mu(\partial_\mu + iQA_\mu) + \gamma_0\mu]\psi + G[(\bar{\psi}\psi)^2 + (\bar{\psi}i\tau\gamma_5\psi)^2], \quad (1)$$

Here, $Q = \mathrm{diag}(e_u, e_d) = \mathrm{diag}(\frac{2}{3}e, -\frac{1}{3}e)$, $\psi^T = (u, d)$; μ is the quark chemical potential; G is the four-fermion coupling. The electromagnetic potential A^μ is formed by the background $\bar{A}^\mu = (0, 0, Bx, 0)$, which corresponds to a constant and uniform magnetic field **B** pointing in the z-direction, with $x^\mu = (t, x, y, z)$, and a fluctuation field $\tilde{A}$. Because of the electromagnetic coupling, the flavor symmetry in this model is $U(1)_L \times U(1)_R$. In addition, the background magnetic field explicitly breaks the rotational symmetry that exists in its absence, so that the spatial symmetry of (1) is $SO(2) \times R^3$.

It has been shown that at finite baryon density, the two condensates:

$$\langle\bar{\psi}\psi\rangle = \Delta \cos q_\mu x^\mu, \quad \langle\bar{\psi}i\tau_3\gamma_5\psi\rangle = \Delta \sin q_\mu x^\mu, \quad (2)$$

obtain expectation values different from zero, forming a dual chiral density wave condensate, with its modulation vector favored along the field direction $q^\mu = (0, 0, 0, q)$ [43,44]. Notice that this means that the modulation is q for the u-quarks and $-q$ for the d-quarks.

Expanding the Lagrangian (1) about this inhomogenous condensate, bozonizing the four-fermion interaction via the Hubbard–Stratonovich approach, and taking the local chiral transformations:

$$\psi \to e^{i\tau_3\gamma_5\theta}\psi, \quad \bar{\psi} \to \bar{\psi}e^{i\tau_3\gamma_5\theta} \qquad (3)$$

with $\theta = qz/2$, we arrive at the mean-field Lagrangian:

$$\mathcal{L}_{MF} = \bar{\psi}[i\gamma^\mu(\partial_\mu + iQA_\mu + i\tau_3\gamma_5\partial_\mu\theta) + \gamma_0\mu - m]\psi - \frac{m^2}{4G} - \frac{1}{4}F_{\mu\nu}F^{\mu\nu} \qquad (4)$$

where $m = -2G\Delta$; thus, the quasiparticle mass is proportional to the condensate magnitude.

The energy spectrum of the theory (4) separates into two sets:
(1) Lowest Landau level (LLL) ($l = 0$):

$$E^0 = \epsilon\sqrt{m^2 + k_3^2} + q/2, \quad \epsilon = \pm; \qquad (5)$$

(2) Higher Landau levels (HLLs) ($l \neq 0$):

$$E^l = \epsilon\sqrt{(\xi\sqrt{m^2 + k_3^2} + q/2)^2 + 2|e_f B|l}, \quad \epsilon = \pm, \xi = \pm, l = 1,2,3,... \qquad (6)$$

The HLL spectrum has four branches, with $\xi = \pm$ indicating spin projections and $\epsilon = \pm$ the energy sign. In contrast, the LLL has only two branches because only one spin projection contributes to the LLL modes. Here, ϵ loses the energy sign interpretation as long as $q \neq 0$ [43]. An important feature of this spectrum is that the LLL energies are not symmetric about the zero-energy level. This asymmetry in the LLL spectrum gives rise to nontrivial topological effects, which are pointed out below.

It is important to note that the fermion measure in the path integral is not invariant under the local chiral transformation (3), and hence, it produces a contribution to the action through the transformation's Jacobian $J(\theta(x)) = (\text{Det}\,\mathcal{U}_A)^{-2}$:

$$\mathcal{D}\bar{\psi}(x)\mathcal{D}\psi(x) \to (\text{Det}\,\mathcal{U}_A)^{-2}\mathcal{D}\bar{\psi}(x)\mathcal{D}\psi(x), \qquad (7)$$

with $\mathcal{U}_A = e^{i\tau_3\gamma_5\theta}$. However, $J(\theta(x))$ is ill-defined and needs to be regularized. This can be done using the Fujikawa method [85], so that the measure contribution to the mean-field action turns out to be an axion term given by the electromagnetic chiral anomaly $\frac{\kappa}{4}\theta(x)F_{\mu\nu}\tilde{F}^{\mu\nu}$ [45,46]. Then,

$$S_{eff} = \int d^4x \{\bar{\psi}[i\gamma^\mu(\partial_\mu + iQA_\mu + i\tau_3\gamma_5\partial_\mu\theta) + \gamma_0\mu - m]\psi - \frac{m^2}{4G}$$
$$+ \frac{\kappa}{4}\theta(x)F_{\mu\nu}\tilde{F}^{\mu\nu} - \frac{1}{4}F_{\mu\nu}F^{\mu\nu}\}, \qquad (8)$$

The coupling between the background axion field $\theta(x)$ and the electromagnetic tensor is given by $\frac{\kappa}{4} = \frac{3(e_u^2 - e_d^2)}{8\pi^2} = \frac{e^2}{8\pi^2} = \frac{\alpha}{2\pi}$. It contains the contribution of all the quark flavors and colors.

The one-loop thermodynamic potential of the mean-field theory was found in Refs. [43,46] to be:

$$\Omega = \Omega_{vac}(B) + \Omega_{anom}(B,\mu) + \Omega_\mu(B,\mu) + \Omega_T(B,\mu,T) + \frac{m^2}{4G}, \qquad (9)$$

where Ω_{vac} is the vacuum contribution; Ω_{anom} is the anomalous contribution, extracted from the LLL part of the medium term after proper regularization [43]; Ω_μ is the zero-temperature medium contribution and Ω_T the thermal contribution. For a single quark flavor f, they are [46]:

$$\Omega_{vac}^f = \frac{1}{4\sqrt{\pi}} \frac{N_c |e_f B|}{(2\pi)^2} \int_{-\infty}^{\infty} dk \sum_{l\xi\epsilon} \int_{1/\Lambda^2}^{\infty} \frac{ds}{s^{3/2}} e^{-s(E)^2} \tag{10}$$

$$\Omega_{anom}^f = -\frac{N_c |e_f B|}{(2\pi)^2} q\mu \tag{11}$$

$$\Omega_\mu^f = -\frac{1}{2} \frac{N_c |e_f B|}{(2\pi)^2} \int_{-\infty}^{\infty} dk \sum_{\xi,l>0} 2[(\mu - E)\Theta(\mu - E)]|_{\epsilon=+}$$
$$+ \Omega_\mu^{fLLL} \tag{12}$$

$$\Omega_T^f = -\frac{N_c |e_f B|}{(2\pi)^2 \beta} \int_{-\infty}^{\infty} dk \sum_{l\xi\epsilon} \ln\left(1 + e^{-\beta(|E - \mu|)}\right) \tag{13}$$

with E the energy modes (5) and (6) and the LLL zero-temperature medium contribution given by:

$$\Omega_\mu^{fLLL} = -\frac{1}{2} \frac{N_c |e_f B|}{(2\pi)^2} \int_{-\infty}^{\infty} dk \sum_\epsilon (|E^0 - \mu| - |E^0|)_{reg}$$
$$= -\frac{N_c |e_f B|}{(2\pi)^2} \left\{ \left[Q(\mu) + m^2 \ln\left(m/R(\mu)\right) \right] \Theta(q/2 - \mu - m)\Theta(q/2 - m) \right.$$
$$- \left[Q(0) + m^2 \ln\left(m/R(0)\right) \right] \Theta(q/2 - m) \tag{14}$$
$$+ \left[Q(\mu) + m^2 \ln\left(m/R(\mu)\right) \right] \Theta(\mu - q/2 - m)$$
$$\left. - \left[Q(0) + m^2 \ln\left(m/R(0)\right) \right] \Theta(\mu - q/2 - m)\Theta(-q/2 - m) \right\},$$

Here, we introduced the notation:

$$Q(\mu) = |q/2 - \mu|\sqrt{(q/2 - \mu)^2 - m^2}, \quad Q(0) = |q/2|\sqrt{(q/2)^2 - m^2}$$
$$R(\mu) = |q/2 - \mu| + \sqrt{(q/2 - \mu)^2 - m^2}, \quad R(0) = |q/2| + \sqrt{(q/2)^2 - m^2}$$

Notice that the anomalous term Ω_{anom}^f favors a nonzero modulation q since it decreases the free-energy of the system. Such a term is a direct consequence of the asymmetry of the LLL spectrum and, hence, has a topological origin.

The minimum solutions for m and q in terms of the chemical potential and the external magnetic field can be found by numerically solving the gap equations [43,47]:

$$\frac{\partial \Omega}{\partial m} = 0, \quad \frac{\partial \Omega}{\partial q} = 0. \tag{15}$$

Figure 1 shows the resulting m and $b = q/2$ vs. μ at undercritical coupling $G = 2.5$ for two strong magnetic strengths. Thanks to the magnetic field, the MDCDW solution exists even in the undercritical regime. Notice that the condensate magnitude is quite sensitive to the change in the field strength, while its modulation is not. For $\sqrt{eB} = 0.4$, m is at least one order of magnitude smaller than for $\sqrt{eB} = 0.6$ for the entire range of μ considered. Figure 2 shows the solutions in the supercritical case. In this case, the effect of increasing the magnetic field is also noticeable in m, but still not significant in b, except that increasing the field tends to smooth out the behavior of the dynamical parameters in the region before and after they cross each other. Comparing the two set of curves, it becomes apparent that at a given magnetic field, larger coupling leads to a larger condensate magnitude, but not a larger modulation. All the quantities in the figures are normalized with respect to the proper-time regularization parameter $\Lambda = 636.790$ MeV, thus dimensionless.

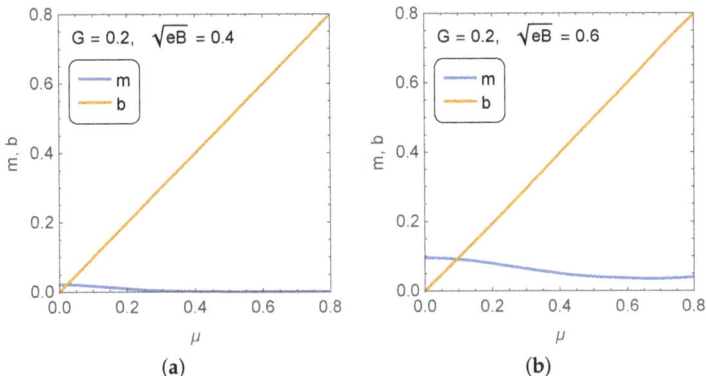

Figure 1. Solutions of the MDCDW gap equations versus the quark chemical potential at subcritical coupling ($G = 2.5$) and magnetic fields (**a**) $\sqrt{eB} = 0.4$ and (**b**) $\sqrt{eB} = 0.6$.

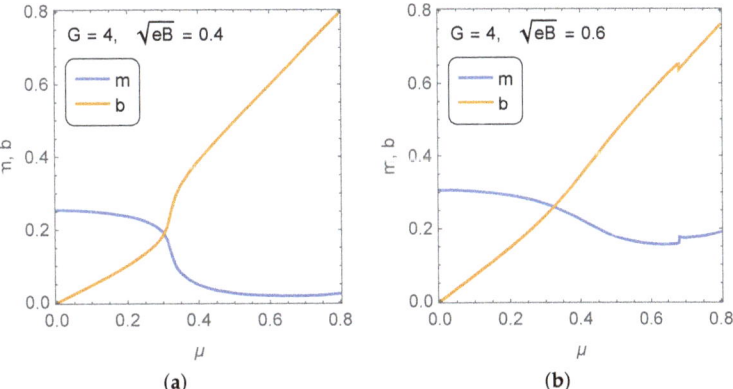

Figure 2. Solutions of the MDCDW gap equations versus the quark chemical potential at supercritical coupling ($G = 4$) and magnetic fields (**a**) $\sqrt{eB} = 0.4$ and (**b**) $\sqrt{eB} = 0.6$.

3. Electromagnetism in the MDCDW Phase

To obtain the electromagnetic effective action $\Gamma(A)$ in the MDCDW phase, we start from the formula:

$$\Gamma = -i \log Z, \qquad (16)$$

where the partition function Z is:

$$Z = e^{i\Gamma} = \int \mathcal{D}\bar{\psi}(x)\mathcal{D}\psi(x)e^{iS_{eff}} \qquad (17)$$

with S_{eff} given in (8).

Integrating in the fermion fields, performing the Matsubara sum, taking the zero-temperature limit, and expanding Γ in powers of the fluctuation field $\tilde{A}$, we obtain:

$$\Gamma(A) = -V\Omega + \int d^4x \left[-\frac{1}{4} F_{\mu\nu} F^{\mu\nu} + \frac{\kappa}{4} \theta(x) F_{\mu\nu} \tilde{F}^{\mu\nu} \right] \tag{18}$$

$$+ \sum_{i=1}^{\infty} \int dx_1 ... dx_i \Pi^{\mu_1,\mu_2,...\mu_i}(x_1, x_2, ... x_i) \tilde{A}_{\mu_1}(x_1)...\tilde{A}_{\mu_i}(x_i),$$

with V the four-volume, Ω the mean-field thermodynamic potential in the one-loop approximation (9), and $\Pi^{\mu_1,\mu_2,...\mu_i}$ the i-vertex tensors corresponding to the one-loop polarization operators with internal lines of fermion Green functions in the MDCDW phase and i external lines of photons.

We are interested in the linear response of the MCDCW phase to a small electromagnetic probe $\tilde{A}$. For the consistency of the approximation, we can neglect all the radiative corrections of order higher than α, as α is the order of the axion term in (18). These conditions imply that we shall cut the series at $i = 1$, which can be shown to provide the medium corrections to the Maxwell equations that are linear in the electromagnetic field and in α.

Hence, the electromagnetic effective action becomes:

$$\Gamma(A) = -V\Omega + \int d^4x \left[-\frac{1}{4} F_{\mu\nu} F^{\mu\nu} - \kappa \int d^4x \epsilon^{\mu\alpha\nu\beta} A_\alpha \partial_\nu A_\beta \partial_\mu \theta \right]$$

$$- \int d^4x \tilde{A}_\mu(x) J^\mu(x), \tag{19}$$

where we integrated by parts the third term in the r.h.s. of (18). The four-current $J^\mu(x) = (J^0, \mathbf{J})$ represents the contribution of the ordinary (nonanomalous) electric four-current, obtained from the one-loop tadpole diagrams.

The Euler–Lagrange equations derived from this effective action turn out to be the equations of axion electrodynamics:

$$\nabla \cdot \mathbf{E} = J^0 + \frac{e^2}{4\pi^2} q B, \tag{20}$$

$$\nabla \times \mathbf{B} - \partial \mathbf{E}/\partial t = \mathbf{J} - \frac{e^2}{4\pi^2} \mathbf{q} \times \mathbf{E}, \tag{21}$$

$$\nabla \cdot \mathbf{B} = 0, \quad \nabla \times \mathbf{E} + \partial \mathbf{B}/\partial t = 0, \tag{22}$$

where we already used $\theta = \frac{qz}{2}$ [46]. Hence, electromagnetism in the MDCDW phase is described by a particular case of the axion electrodynamic equations proposed many years ago for a general axion field θ [86].

The q-dependent terms in (20) and (21) are directly connected to the chiral anomaly and, thus, give rise to an anomalous electric charge density,

$$J^0_{anom} = \frac{e^2}{4\pi^2} q B, \tag{23}$$

and to an anomalous Hall current density,

$$\mathbf{J}_{anom} = -\frac{e^2}{4\pi^2} \mathbf{q} \times \mathbf{E}. \tag{24}$$

The anomalous electric charge density (23) can be also found by multiplying the flavor electric charge e_f by the anomalous quark number density of that flavor, obtained as the derivative of $\Omega^f_{anom} = -\frac{N_c |e_f B|}{(2\pi)^2} q\mu$ with respect to μ, and then summing in flavor [46]. As it should be, the anomalous Hall current $\mathbf{J}_{anom}$ is perpendicular to the background magnetic field and the probe electric field, since $\mathbf{q}$ is aligned with $\mathbf{B}$.

In (20), J^0 and **J** denote ordinary charge and current densities, respectively, which are calculated through radiative corrections. The contribution of the LLL to the ordinary charge density can be found from the tadpole diagram [45,46] and is:

$$J^0_{LLL} = \sum_f J^0_{LLL}(\text{sgn}(e_f)) \tag{25}$$

$$= \frac{e^2 B}{2\pi^2}\sqrt{(\mu - q/2)^2 - m^2}[\Theta(\mu - q/2 - m) - \Theta(q/2 - \mu - m)],$$

Since the LLL ordinary charge density is linear in the magnetic field, one can use the Středa formula [45,46,87]:

$$\sigma_{xy} = \frac{\partial J^0}{\partial B} \tag{26}$$

to show that the LLL contribution to the ordinary Hall conductivity is given by:

$$\sigma^{ord}_{xy} = \frac{\partial J^0_{LLL}}{\partial B} = \frac{e^2}{2\pi^2}\sqrt{(\mu - q/2)^2 - m^2}[\Theta(\mu - q/2 - m) - \Theta(q/2 - \mu - m)], \tag{27}$$

which in turn leads to the LLL ordinary Hall current:

$$\mathbf{J}^{ord}_{LLL} = (\sigma^{ord}_{xy} E_y, -\sigma^{ord}_{xy} E_x, 0). \tag{28}$$

Likewise, the anomalous Hall conductivity can be found either from the anomalous charge (23),

$$\sigma^{anom}_{xy} = \frac{\partial J^0_{anom}}{\partial B} = \frac{e^2}{4\pi^2} q, \tag{29}$$

or directly from the anomalous Hall current (24). As J^0_{anom} is due to the LLL, so is σ^{anom}_{xy}, thereby underlining once again the LLL origin of $\mathbf{J}_{anom}$.

The anomalous Hall conductivity has a topological origin since it is a direct consequence of the chiral anomaly. That means that it has a universal character, and as such, it is robust against dissipative effects. This is quite analogous to what occurs in Weyl semimetals [88], where an anomalous Hall conductivity very similar to (29) is also connected to the chiral anomaly. The only difference is that there, the modulation q is replaced by the separation in momentum between the two Weyl nodes. A more important difference is that in Weyl semimetals, a gap term that explicitly breaks chiral symmetry may exist, in contrast to the MDCDW, where the theory is initially massless and the mass m is dynamically generated by the spontaneous breaking of chiral symmetry induced by the inhomogeneous condensate. Even when there is an initial gap, there are still gapless Weyl points, as long as the separation between them is larger than the gap. Hence, even in this case, the anomalous Hall current of the Weyl semimetal is given by the same expression and remains robust against impurity scattering potentials, electron–electron interactions, or other similar dissipative effects [88].

Something worth noticing is that the LLL contribution to the ordinary charge J^0_{LLL} and Hall current $\mathbf{J}^{ord}_{LLL}$ do not cancel out their corresponding anomalous counterparts (23) and (24) [45,46], in sharp contrast to what occurs in the chiral magnetic effect in equilibrium where the anomalous and ordinary currents completely cancel out [89]. Nevertheless, in the limit when the order parameter m becomes very small, $m \ll \frac{q}{2} < \mu$, one can expand the square root in the LLL ordinary part of the electric charge (25) to see that the anomalous contribution is effectively canceled out by one of the terms from the expansion of the ordinary part, leaving only terms that explicitly depend on μ, hence nontopological. The same type of cancellation happens between the anomalous Hall conductivity and a term coming from expanding the LLL ordinary Hall conductivity at very small m. This occurs near the phase transition line that separates the MDCDW phase from the chirally restored phase, where it is physically expected that the topology (or the lack of it) at the two sides of the transition line should match. Therefore, the topological properties of the MDCDW phase become practically inoperative near the phase transition.

We point out that in [44,90], a different method was employed to obtain the anomalous contributions to the fermion number, electric charge, and Hall current of the MDCDW phase. That method was based on the regularized Atiyah–Patodi–Singer index $\eta_H = \lim_{s\to 0} \sum_l \mathrm{sgn}(\lambda_l) \lambda_l^{-s}$ using an approach discussed in [91]. As found in [44], the index gives different results for the anomalous fermion number depending on whether $m > q/2$ or vice versa. Since $m > q/2$ occurs at low chemical potentials, where no Fermi surface is generated, while $m < q/2$ occurs at chemical potentials large enough for a Fermi surface to exist, these results seem to indicate that there is an additional contribution to the anomalous fermion number in the region of high chemical potentials. Specifically, when $m > q/2$, Reference [44] found that $\eta_H = -\frac{|eB|q}{2\pi^2}$, while when $m < q/2$, it was $\eta_H = \frac{|eB|}{2\pi}[-\frac{q}{\pi} + \frac{\sqrt{q^2-4m^2}}{\pi}]$. Based on these results, Reference [90] claimed that a similar additional contribution entered in the anomalous Hall conductivity. Since such a term does not appear when one extracts the anomalous fermion number contribution using an energy cutoff regularization, as done in [43,45,46], the authors of [90] concluded that the energy cutoff method is not good to extract the complete anomalous parts of physical parameters as the fermion number, Hall conductivity, electric charge, etc. What the authors of [90] failed to realize is that the additional term they found using the index approach and that they interpreted as the "anomalous" Hall conductivity for the region of $m < q/2$ (Equation (18) in [90]) not only is not anomalous, but it is actually eliminated by an equal and opposite contribution coming from the ordinary part of the Hall conductivity (Equation (20) in [90]). Therefore, the actual anomalous Hall conductivity is $\sigma_{xy}^{anom} = \frac{e^2}{4\pi^2}q$. Not only is it the same in all the regions, but it can be correctly extracted from the anomalous charge derived using the energy cutoff regularization approach employed in [43] or from the chiral anomaly obtained using the Fujikawa approach, as done in [45,46].

As the above discussion illustrates, in the region of large chemical potentials, the regularized Atiyah–Patodi–Singer index may contain, besides the genuinely anomalous part, some spurious nonanomalous contributions that cancel out with others coming from the ordinary part of the fermion number. To extract the correct anomalous contribution using the regularized index, one has to be particularly careful when using Niemi's approach for theories with finite chemical potential [92]. Indeed, one first has to add the index and the ordinary (Fermi surface) contributions to the fermion number, since only after that is it possible to cancel any spurious terms and then correctly separate the anomalous from the nonanomalous contributions in the fermion number and similarly in other quantities such as the Hall conductivity. On the other hand, the advantage of finding the anomalous fermion number and electric charge with the energy cutoff approach or the anomalous charge and current from the chiral anomaly is that these approaches manage to extract the actual anomalous contribution without producing spurious terms.

Another interesting property of the MDCDW medium becomes apparent by rewriting Equations (20) and (21) in terms of the D and H fields:

$$\nabla \cdot \mathbf{D} = J^0, \quad \nabla \times \mathbf{H} - \frac{\partial \mathbf{D}}{\partial t} = \mathbf{J} \tag{30}$$

which shows that in this model, the fields $\mathbf{D}$ and $\mathbf{H}$ are:

$$\mathbf{D} = \mathbf{E} - \kappa\theta\mathbf{B}, \quad \mathbf{H} = \mathbf{B} + \kappa\theta\mathbf{E} \tag{31}$$

with κ and θ defined in Section 2. Equation (31) shows that a magnetic field induces an electric polarization $\mathbf{P} = -\kappa\theta\mathbf{B}$ and an electric field induces a magnetization $\mathbf{M} = -\kappa\theta\mathbf{E}$, a phenomenon known as magnetoelectricity. The linear magnetoelectricity of the MDCDW medium is a direct consequence of the chiral anomaly. It reflects the fact that the ground state of the MDCDW medium breaks the parity and time-inversion symmetries. The magnetoelectricity in the MDCDW phase is different from the one found in the magnetic

CFL phase of CS, where parity was not broken and the effect was a consequence of an anisotropic electric susceptibility [39], thus not linear. It also follows from (30) that the anomalous Hall current is given by a medium-induced, magnetic current density $\nabla \times \mathbf{M}$, due to the space-dependent anomalous magnetization coming from the axion term.

The above results might have some connotations for astrophysics. If the MDCDW phase is realized in the interior of NSs, any electric field in the medium, whether due to local separation of charges or any other possible reason, could trigger dissipationless Hall currents in the plane perpendicular to the magnetic field. This current in turn could have a back effect on the magnetic field. Currents of this type could serve to resolve the issue about the stability of the magnetic field strength in magnetars [93,94].

4. Condensate Stability at Finite Temperature

Let us discuss now how the finite temperature can affect the inhomogeneous condensate. As mentioned in the Introduction, single-modulated phases in three spatial dimensions exhibit the Landau–Peierls instability [78,79]. The Landau–Peierls instability is characterized by the fact that at nonzero temperatures, thermal fluctuations of the Nambu–Goldstone bosons, whose dispersions are anisotropic and soft in the direction normal to the modulation vector, wash out the long-range order at any finite temperature, signaling the lack of a true order parameter. Some inhomogeneity may remains, however, due to the algebraically decaying long-range correlations of the order parameter, forming a phase with a quasi-long-range order similar to smectic liquid crystals [83]. Depending on the size of the system, this much smoother inhomogeneity may or may not be relevant for the observables.

Nevertheless, the presence of a magnetic field changes the properties of the low-energy theory in such a way that it completely removes the Landau–Peierls instability [84]. To show that, we start from the low-energy theory of the MDCDW phase, described by a generalized GL expansion of the thermodynamic potential in powers of the order parameter and its derivatives. In the context of NS astrophysics, the region of interest is that of intermediate chemical potentials and low temperatures. Henceforth, we focus our investigation on that region and work near the phase transition to the chirally restored phase.

The validity of the GL expansion in this region is justified by the fact that the order parameters satisfy $m/\mu \ll 1$ and $q/2\mu < 1$ [43]. One can readily show [95], following an approach similar to the one used in [96] for the DCDW case, that the power series in q effectively becomes an expansion in powers of $q/2\mu$, hence corroborating the consistency of the expansion and the truncation used. The GL expansion of the MDCDW phase near the critical point (CP), that is in the region of large temperatures and low chemical potentials, was explored in [44].

The GL expansion in our case should reflect the invariance with respect to the symmetries of the theory in the presence of the external magnetic field. In the MDCDW system, the order parameter is characterized by the scalar and pseudoscalar fields $\sigma = -2G\bar{\psi}\psi$ and $\pi = -2G\bar{\psi}i\gamma^5\tau_3\psi$, respectively. Under a global chiral transformation $e^{i\gamma_5\tau_3\theta/2}$ of the fermion fields, they transform as $\sigma \to \sigma \cos\theta + \pi \sin\theta$ and $\pi \to \pi \cos\theta - \sigma \sin\theta$, reflecting the isomorphism between the chiral group $U_A(1)$ and the $SO(2)$ of internal rotations acting on the two-dimensional vector $\phi^T = (\sigma, \pi)$. In a similar way, one can see that the $U_V(1)$ transformation of the fermions reduces to the trivial group acting on the vector ϕ.

Therefore, the GL expansion, in the $SO(2)$ representation, can be written as:

$$\begin{aligned}
\mathcal{F} &= a_{2,0}\phi^T\phi + \frac{b_{3,1}}{2}\left[\phi^T\hat{B}\cdot\tilde{\nabla}\phi + \hat{B}\cdot(\tilde{\nabla}\phi)^T\phi\right] + a_{4,0}(\phi^T\phi)^2 \\
&+ a_{4,2}^{(0)}(\tilde{\nabla}\phi)^T\cdot\tilde{\nabla}\phi + a_{4,2}^{(1)}\hat{B}\cdot(\tilde{\nabla}\phi)^T\hat{B}\cdot\tilde{\nabla}\phi \\
&+ \frac{b_{5,1}}{2}(\phi^T\phi)\left[\phi^T\hat{B}\cdot\tilde{\nabla}\phi + \hat{B}\cdot(\tilde{\nabla}\phi)^T\phi\right] \\
&+ \frac{b_{5,3}}{2}\left[(\tilde{\nabla}^2\phi)^T\hat{B}\cdot\tilde{\nabla}\phi + \hat{B}\cdot(\tilde{\nabla}\phi)^T\tilde{\nabla}^2\phi\right] + a_{6,0}(\phi^T\phi)^3 \\
&+ a_{6,2}^{(0)}(\phi^T\phi)(\tilde{\nabla}\phi)^T\cdot\tilde{\nabla}\phi + a_{6,2}^{(1)}(\phi^T\phi)[\hat{B}\cdot(\tilde{\nabla}\phi)^T\hat{B}\cdot\tilde{\nabla}\phi] \\
&+ a_{6,4}(\tilde{\nabla}^2\phi)^T(\tilde{\nabla}^2\phi) + ...,
\end{aligned}$$
(32)

where we introduced the additional structural terms that are consistent with the symmetry of the theory in a magnetic field. The notation $\hat{B} = \mathbf{B}/|\mathbf{B}|$ for the normalized vector in the direction of the magnetic field was used, and the gradient operator $-i\nabla$ in the $SO(2)$ representation was introduced as:

$$\tilde{\nabla} = \begin{pmatrix} 0 & 1 \\ -1 & 0 \end{pmatrix}\nabla \quad .$$
(33)

The coefficients a and b are functions of T, μ, and B. They can be derived from the MDCDW thermodynamic potential (9) found in [43,46], although their explicit expressions are not relevant for the present study. The first subindex in the coefficients a and b indicates the power of the order parameter plus its derivatives in that term, and the second index denotes the power of the derivatives alone.

We can now take advantage of the isomorphism between $SO(2)$ and $U_A(1)$ to represent the order parameter as a complex function $M(x) = \sigma(x) + i\pi(x)$. In terms of $M(x)$, the GL expansion of the free-energy (32) takes the form:

$$\begin{aligned}
\mathcal{F} &= a_{2,0}|M|^2 - i\frac{b_{3,1}}{2}\left[M^*(\hat{B}\cdot\nabla M) - (\hat{B}\cdot\nabla M^*)M\right] + a_{4,0}|M|^4 + a_{4,2}^{(0)}|\nabla M|^2 \\
&+ a_{4,2}^{(1)}(\hat{B}\cdot\nabla M^*)(\hat{B}\cdot\nabla M) - i\frac{b_{5,1}}{2}|M|^2\left[M^*(\hat{B}\cdot\nabla M) - (\hat{B}\cdot\nabla M^*)M\right] \\
&+ \frac{ib_{5,3}}{2}\left[(\nabla^2 M^*)\hat{B}\cdot\nabla M - \hat{B}\cdot\nabla M^*(\nabla^2 M)\right] + a_{6,0}|M|^6 + a_{6,2}^{(0)}|M|^2|\nabla M|^2 \\
&+ a_{6,2}^{(1)}|M|^2(\hat{B}\cdot\nabla M^*)(\hat{B}\cdot\nabla M) + a_{6,4}|\nabla^2 M|^2 + ...
\end{aligned}$$
(34)

The magnetic field produces two distinguishable effects on the GL expansion. First, it allows terms even in $\hat{B}$ that are responsible for the explicit separation of transverse and parallel derivatives, as it is expected to occur in any theory where the rotational symmetry is broken by an external vector. These are the terms with coefficients $a_{i,j}^{(1)}$, which have similar structures to those with coefficients $a_{i,j}^{(0)}$, except that the gradient operator is replaced by the projection of the gradient along the field. Second, the symmetries of the theory also allow constructing B-dependent terms that are linear in $\hat{B}$. These are the structures with coefficients $b_{i,j}$. As B is odd under the T symmetry, the rest of the structure has to be also odd under T, hence odd in the pseudoscalar order parameter. Even though these terms are permitted from general symmetry arguments, they are not a common feature of theories with an external vector, but they exist instead when the system exhibits a nontrivial topology. We shall see below that, as was shown in [84], in the MDCDW case, the existence of nonzero $b_{i,j}$ can be indeed traced back to the nontrivial topology manifested through the spectral asymmetry of the LLL fermions.

We call the readers attention to the fact that the anisotropy between transverse and parallel (to the magnetic field direction) vectors created by the explicit breaking of the rotational symmetry by the magnetic field in the MDCDW system is fundamentally different from the one created by the direction of the modulation in the DCDW case, where it is a result of the spontaneous breaking of the rotational symmetry. This difference leads to quite different low-energy theories of the fluctuations in these two models.

Considering that the preferred density wave in the MDCDW case is a single-modulated density wave with its modulation vector parallel to the magnetic field, $M(z) = me^{iqz}$, $m \equiv -2G\Delta$, the free-energy (34) can be written as:

$$\begin{aligned}\mathcal{F} &= a_{2,0}m^2 + b_{3,1}qm^2 + a_{4,0}m^4 + a_{4,2}q^2m^2 + b_{5,1}qm^4 \\ &+ b_{5,3}q^3m^2 + a_{6,0}m^6 + a_{6,2}q^2m^4 + a_{6,4}q^4m^2,\end{aligned} \quad (35)$$

where $a_{4,2} = a_{4,2}^{(0)} + a_{4,2}^{(1)}$, $a_{6,2} = a_{6,2}^{(0)} + a_{6,2}^{(1)}$. In (35), we keep up to sixth-order terms to ensure the stability of the MDCDW phase in the mean-field approximation.

It is important to point out that straight derivations [95] show that the a coefficients receive contributions from all Landau levels l, while the b-coefficients do not receive contributions from the higher Landau levels (HLLs) $l > 1$. This follows from the fact that the b-terms in (35) are odd in q, which leaves the LLL modes as the only possible source of the b-terms. Indeed, the LLL contribution is not invariant under $q \to -q$, due to the asymmetry of the LLL modes (5). In principle, the LLL part of the thermodynamic potential can have q-odd and q-even terms. Obviously, the b-terms come from the odd part. Such an odd part is topological in nature, a fact that manifests in the existence of several anomalous quantities, such as the anomalous part of the quark number, which is proportional to a topological invariant [44], or the anomalous electric charge and the anomalous Hall current [45,46], all of which are odd in q.

In summary, the additional a and b terms have quite different origins. $a^{(1)}$-type terms will always appear in the presence of an external magnetic field, because they reflect the explicit breaking of the rotational symmetry produced by the field direction. On the other hand, the b terms are associated with the topology of the modified fermion spectrum in the presence of the field. As the LLL part of the thermodynamic potential is linear in the magnetic field B, so will be the b-coefficients.

The stationary equations from which the ground state solutions for m and q can be found are:

$$\begin{aligned}\partial \mathcal{F}/\partial m &= 2m\{a_{2,0} + 2a_{4,0}m^2 + 3a_{6,0}m^4 + q^2[a_{4,2} + 2a_{6,2}m^2 + a_{6,4}q^2] \\ &+ [b_{3,1} + 2b_{5,1}m^2 + b_{5,3}q^2]\} = 0,\end{aligned} \quad (36)$$

$$\partial \mathcal{F}/\partial q = m^2\{2q[a_{4,2} + a_{6,2}m^2 + 2a_{6,4}q^2] + b_{3,1} + b_{5,1}m^2 + 3b_{5,3}q^2\} = 0 \quad (37)$$

The minimum equations of the DCDW phase can be readily found from the zero-magnetic-field limit of (36) and (37), where the $a_{i,j}^{(1)}$ and $b_{i,j}$ coefficients vanish.

Following [84], we now explore the theory beyond the mean-field approximation to check if the Landau–Peierls instability found in the absence of a magnetic field (the DCDW phase) [81] is present here as well. With this goal in mind, we investigated the low-energy thermal fluctuations that may affect the long-range order of the inhomogeneous ground state. Notice that in principle, there can be fluctuations of the condensate magnitude and of the condensate phase, but we only need to care about fluctuations associated with the spontaneous breaking of global symmetries, as those are the ones that could in principle have soft modes that lead to the instability. In other words, to probe the instability of the ground state at arbitrarily low temperatures, the relevant fluctuations are those that can be excited at very low energies, i.e., those generated by the Goldstone bosons of the system. Hence, in our analysis, we did not consider the magnitude fluctuations because they are not associated with a Goldstone mode.

The symmetry group of the MDCDW phase is $U_V(1) \times SO(2) \times R^2$, since the ground state of this phase spontaneously breaks the chiral symmetry $U_A(1)$ and the translation along z. Hence, there are two Goldstone bosons: the neutral pion, τ, associated with the breaking of the chiral symmetry, and the phonon, ξ, associated with the breaking of the translation symmetry. Now, the effect of the global transformations of these broken groups on the order parameter is:

$$M(x) \to e^{i\tau} M(z+\xi) = e^{i(\tau+q\xi)} M(z), \tag{38}$$

from which one clearly sees that there is a locking between the chiral rotation and the z-translation. Therefore, we can always express them as two orthogonal combinations, one that leaves the order parameter invariant and one that changes it. As a consequence, there is only one legitimate Goldstone field in the MDCDW theory. One can arbitrarily choose it as either the pion, the phonon, or a linear combination of them. Henceforth, without loss of generality, we consider it to be the phonon.

Let us consider now a small phonon fluctuation $u(x)$ on the order parameter and expand it about the condensate solution up to quadratic order in the fluctuation,

$$M(x) = M(z+u(x)) \simeq M_0(z) + M_0'(z) u(x) + \frac{1}{2} M_0''(z) u^2(x), \tag{39}$$

where $M_0(z) = \bar{m} e^{i\bar{q}z}$ is the ground state solution with $\bar{m}$ and $\bar{q}$ given as the solutions of (36) and (37).

Substituting (39) into (34) and keeping terms up to quadratic order in $u(x)$, we arrive at the phonon free-energy:

$$\mathcal{F}[M(x)] = \mathcal{F}_0 + v_z^2 (\partial_z \theta)^2 + v_\perp^2 (\partial_\perp \theta)^2 + \zeta^2 (\partial_z^2 \theta + \partial_\perp^2 \theta)^2, \tag{40}$$

For convenience, we write (40) in terms of the pseudo scalar $\theta = \bar{q} m u(x)$, which is proportional to the phonon, but with the dimension of a spin-zero field. Here, $\mathcal{F}_0 = \mathcal{F}(M_0)$, $(\partial_\perp \theta)^2 = (\partial_x \theta)^2 + (\partial_y \theta)^2$ and $\zeta^2 = a_{6,4}$. Notice that in deriving (40), the term linear in $\partial_z \theta$ cancels out after using (37).

The coefficients v_z^2, $v_\perp^2$ in (40) are given by:

$$v_z^2 = a_{4,2} + \bar{m}^2 a_{6,2} + 6\bar{q}^2 a_{6,4} + 3\bar{q} b_{5,3} \tag{41}$$

$$v_\perp^2 = a_{4,2} + \bar{m}^2 a_{6,2} + 2\bar{q}^2 a_{6,4} + \bar{q} b_{5,3} - a_{4,2}^{(1)} - \bar{m}^2 a_{6,2}^{(1)} \tag{42}$$

They represent the squares of the parallel and transverse group velocities, respectively. The fluctuation low-energy Lagrangian density is then:

$$\mathcal{L}_\theta = \frac{1}{2}[(\partial_0 \theta)^2 - v_z^2 (\partial_z \theta)^2 - v_\perp^2 (\partial_\perp \theta)^2 - \zeta^2 (\partial_z^2 \theta + \partial_\perp^2 \theta)^2], \tag{43}$$

from which we find the spectrum:

$$E \simeq \sqrt{v_z^2 k_z^2 + v_\perp^2 k_\perp^2}, \tag{44}$$

with $k_\perp^2 = k_x^2 + k_y^2$.

The spectrum of the fluctuations is anisotropic and linear in both the longitudinal and transverse directions. It is easy to see that $v_z \neq 0$ because $a_{6,4}$ cannot be zero for the minimum solution to exist [58]. As for $v_\perp^2$, one can gather from (37) and (42) that the $a_{i,j}^{(1)}$ and $b_{i,j}$ coefficients entering in the transverse group velocity serve to avoid the softness in the transverse direction normally seen in single-modulated phases such as the DCDW. Let us recall that in the DCDW phase, there is no magnetic field, and thus, these coefficients are zero. In such a case, the remaining combination in (42) vanishes due to the stationary condition (37), thereby leading to $v_\perp = 0$. On the other hand, the lack of soft modes ensured by the additional coefficients in the MDCDW phase has remarkable consequences for the stability of the condensate, as shown below.

In order to investigate the stability of the condensate against the fluctuations, we need to calculate its average:

$$\langle M \rangle = \bar{m} e^{i\bar{q}z} \langle \cos \bar{q}u \rangle, \tag{45}$$

with the average defined as:

$$\langle ... \rangle = \frac{\int \mathcal{D}u(x)... e^{-S(u^2)}}{\int \mathcal{D}u(x) e^{-S(u^2)}} \tag{46}$$

where:

$$S(u^2) = T \sum_n \int_{-\infty}^{\infty} \frac{d^3k}{(2\pi)^3} [\omega_n^2 + (v_z^2 k_z^2 + v_\perp^2 k_\perp^2 + \zeta^2 k^4)] \bar{q}^2 \bar{m}^2 u^2 \tag{47}$$

denotes the finite-temperature effective action of the phonon and $\omega_n = 2n\pi T$ the Matsubara frequency.

Considering the relation:

$$\langle \cos \bar{q}u \rangle = e^{-\langle (\bar{q}u)^2 \rangle / 2} \tag{48}$$

and using (46), we find the mean square of the fluctuation as:

$$\begin{aligned}\langle \bar{q}^2 u^2 \rangle &= \frac{1}{(2\pi)^2} \int_0^\infty dk_\perp k_\perp \int_{-\infty}^\infty dk_z \frac{T}{\bar{m}^2 (v_z^2 k_z^2 + v_\perp^2 k_\perp^2 + \zeta^2 k^4)} \\ &\simeq \frac{\pi T}{\bar{m} \sqrt{v_z^2 v_\perp^2}}.\end{aligned} \tag{49}$$

where we took into account that the lowest Matsubara mode is dominant in the infrared.

From (45), (48), and (49), we can see that $\langle M \rangle \neq 0$ since $\langle \bar{q}^2 u^2 \rangle$ is finite. This implies that the MDCDW system does not exhibit the Landau–Peierls instability, meaning that at $B \neq 0$, the fluctuations do not wipe out the condensate at arbitrarily low T. As can be gathered from our derivations, the lack of Landau–Peierls instabilities in the presence of a magnetic field is a direct consequence of the stiffening of the spectrum in the transverse direction, which in turn is due to the explicit breaking of the rotational symmetry by the external field.

We should point out that the lack of Landau–Peierls instabilities in the presence of a magnetic field will not be changed by a nonzero current quark mass, since this property comes from the effect of the magnetic field on the low-energy behavior of the phonon, which remains a Goldstone boson even at nonzero quark masses.

5. Hybrid Propagation Modes in the MDCDW Medium

In this section, we investigate the propagation of electromagnetic waves in the MDCDW phase by going beyond the mean-field approximation to study the effects of the phonon fluctuations when the MDCD medium interacts with photons. This question is not only of fundamental interest to understand the properties of matter–light interaction in the MDCDW medium, but it may also be relevant to explain the stability of NSs in very active γ-ray regions, as will be discussed in Section 6.

In the previous section, we saw that the low-energy theory of the fluctuations in the MDCDW phase is given by (43). This result considered a background magnetic field interacting with the quark medium, but assumed no other electromagnetic field was present. However, there are situations where the MDCDW medium may be penetrated by photons, and we need to understand if their interaction with the medium can produce new physical effects.

When photons are present in the MDCDW medium, the low-energy theory of the fluctuations acquires the following additional contributions:

$$\mathcal{L}_{A-\theta} = -\frac{1}{4}F_{\mu\nu}F^{\mu\nu} + J^\mu A_\mu + \frac{\kappa}{8}\theta_0(x)F_{\mu\nu}\tilde{F}^{\mu\nu} + \frac{\kappa}{8}\theta(x)F_{\mu\nu}\tilde{F}^{\mu\nu}, \quad (50)$$

The first two terms are the conventional Maxwell and ordinary four-current contributions, respectively, the latter obtained after integrating out the fermions in the original MDCDW effective action [45,46]. The last two terms are the axial anomaly with the background axion field $\theta_0(x) = mqz$ and its (phonon-induced) fluctuation $\theta(x)$. Here, $\kappa = 2\alpha/\pi m$.

The combined Lagrangian $\mathcal{L} = \mathcal{L}_\theta + \mathcal{L}_{A-\theta}$ effectively describes the low-energy theory of an axion field $\theta(x)$ interacting nonlinearly with the photon via the chiral anomaly. Let us now assume that a linearly polarized electromagnetic wave, with its electric field **E** parallel to the background magnetic field **B**$_0$, propagates in the MDCDW medium [97]. The field equations of this theory are:

$$\nabla \cdot \mathbf{E} = J^0 + \tfrac{\kappa}{2}\nabla\theta_0 \cdot \mathbf{B} + \tfrac{\kappa}{2}\nabla\theta \cdot \mathbf{B}, \quad (51)$$

$$\nabla \times \mathbf{B} - \partial\mathbf{E}/\partial t = \mathbf{J} - \tfrac{\kappa}{2}(\tfrac{\partial\theta}{\partial t}\mathbf{B} + \nabla\theta \times \mathbf{E}), \quad (52)$$

$$\nabla \cdot \mathbf{B} = 0, \quad \nabla \times \mathbf{E} + \partial\mathbf{B}/\partial t = 0 \quad (53)$$

$$\partial_0^2\theta - v_z^2\partial_z^2\theta - v_\perp^2\partial_\perp^2\theta + \tfrac{\kappa}{2}\mathbf{B}\cdot\mathbf{E} = 0, \quad (54)$$

which contains terms coupling the axion with the photon. In (51), **B** is the total magnetic field, meaning the background field plus the wave magnetic field.

Since we are interested in applications to NSs, we should consider a neutral medium; hence, we assumed that J^0 contains an electron background charge that ensures overall neutrality.

$$J^0 + \frac{\kappa}{2}\nabla\theta_0 \cdot \mathbf{B} + \frac{\kappa}{2}\nabla\theta \cdot \mathbf{B} = 0. \quad (55)$$

The linearized field equations can then be written as:

$$\partial^2\mathbf{E}/\partial t^2 = \nabla^2\mathbf{E} + \tfrac{\kappa}{2}(\partial^2\theta/\partial t^2)\mathbf{B}_0 \quad (56)$$

$$\partial^2\theta/\partial t^2 - v_z^2(\partial^2\theta/\partial z^2) - v_\perp^2(\partial^2\theta/\partial x^2 + \partial^2\theta/\partial y^2) + \tfrac{\kappa}{2}\mathbf{B}_0 \cdot \mathbf{E} = 0. \quad (57)$$

Their solutions describe two hybridized propagating modes of coupled axion and photon fields that we call axion polaritons (APs), borrowing the term from condensed matter. In general, polaritons are hybridized propagating modes that emerge when a collective mode such as phonons, magnons, etc., couples linearly to light.

The energy spectrum of the hybrid modes is:

$$\omega_0^2 = A - B, \quad (58)$$

$$\omega_m^2 = A + B \quad (59)$$

with:

$$A = \frac{1}{2}[p^2 + q^2 + (\frac{\kappa}{2}B_0)^2], \quad (60)$$

$$B = \frac{1}{2}\sqrt{[p^2 + q^2 + (\frac{\kappa}{2}B_0)^2]^2 - 4p^2q^2}, \quad (61)$$

and $q^2 = v_z^2 p_z^2 + v_\perp^2 p_\perp^2$.

From (58)–(61), we identify ω_0 as the gapless mode and ω_m as the gapped mode with field-dependent gap:

$$\omega_m(\vec{p} \to 0) = m_{AP} = \alpha B_0/\pi m \quad (62)$$

Similarly coupled modes of axion and photon have been found in topological magnetic insulators [98], underlining once again the striking similarities between MDCDW quark matter and topological materials in condensed matter.

6. Axion Polariton and the Missing Pulsar Problem

The fact that the MDCDW medium can create massive APs when it is bombarded with electromagnetic radiation may have important implications for the physics of NSs in the galactic center (GC) [97]. A long-standing puzzle in astrophysics, known as the missing pulsar problem, refers to the failed expectation to observe a large number of pulsars within 10 pc of the galactic center. Theoretical predictions have indicated that there should be more than 10^3 active radio pulsars in that region [99], but these numbers have not been observed. This paradox has been magnified by pulse observations of the magnetar SGR J1745-2900 detected by the NuSTAR and Swift satellites [100–102]. These observations revealed that the failures to detect ordinary pulsars at low frequencies cannot be simply due to strong interstellar scattering, but instead should be connected to an intrinsic deficit produced by other causes.

Furthermore, as pointed out in [103], the detection of the young ($T \sim 10^4$ year) magnetar SGR J1745-2900 indicates high efficiency for magnetars' formation from massive stars in the GC, because it would be unlikely to see a magnetar unless magnetar formation is efficient there. In fact, it has been argued that the detection of SGR 1745-2900, with a projected offset of only 0.12 pc from the GC, should not have been expected unless magnetar formation is efficient in the GC with an order unity efficiency [103] and that the missing pulsar problem could be explained as a consequence of a tendency to create short-lived magnetars rather than long-lived ordinary pulsars. On the other hand, there is evidence that several magnetars are associated with massive stellar progenitors ($M > 40 M_\odot$) [104], a fact that supports the idea that magnetars formed in the GC could be very massive compact objects made of quark matter. These massive magnetars can be $2M_\odot$ quark stars with inner magnetic field $B = 10^{17}$ G. Although the original argument for the existence of quark stars was based on the stability of strange quark matter, in recent years, it has been demonstrated [11], using a phenomenological quark–meson model that includes the flavor-dependent feedback of the quark gas on the QCD vacuum, that u-d quark mater is in general more stable than strange quark matter, and it can be more stable than the ordinary nuclear matter when the baryon number is sufficiently large. Based on this result, for the analysis below, we will consider the hypothesis that the massive magnetars in the GC are two-flavor quark stars in the MDCDW phase.

The Milky Way GC is a very active astrophysical environment with numerous γ-ray-emitting point sources [105]. Extragalactic sources of GRBs show an isotropic distribution over the whole sky, flashing with a rate of 1000/year. The energy output of these events is $\sim 10^{56}$ MeV, with photon energies of order 0.1–1 MeV [106], meaning that each one of these events can produce 10^{56} or more photons. If we assume that only 10% of these photons reach the star, which is a conservative estimate if the star is in the narrow cone of a GRB beam, about 10^{55} of those photons can reach the NS.

For fields $B = 10^{17}$ G, the mass gap m_{AP} of the gapped AP is in the range $[0.06, 0.3]$ MeV for the corresponding parameter intervals $\mu \in [340.1, 342.5]$ MeV and $m \in [23.5, 4.7]$ MeV [95]. Hence, one can gather that many of the photons reaching the interior of a quark star in the MDCDW phase can have enough energy to propagate inside as gapped APs. The conversion of a large number of γ-photons into APs once they hit the NS interior can take place through the so-called Primakoff effect [107]. The Primakoff effect is a mechanism that can occur in theories that contain a vertex between a scalar or a pseudoscalar and two photons, so that via this vertex and in the presence of background electric or magnetic fields, the photon can be transformed into these bosons. In the context of the MDCDW dense quark matter, the Primakoff effect allows the incident photons to be transformed into APs thanks to the anomalous axion–two-photon vertex and the existence of a background magnetic field. This effect can produce a large number of gapped APs, which being bosons, will be gravitationally attracted to the center of the star where they will accumulate with high density.

If the number of APs that accumulate in the star's center is higher than the Chandrasekhar limit for these bosons, the AP's will create a mini black hole in the star center that will destroy the host NS, leaving a remnant black hole. We explored this possibility in [97], where we considered the Chandrasekhar limit that determines the number of AP's required to induce the collapse, ignoring the gravitational energy associated with the quarks. For boson particles, this limit is given by [108,109]:

$$N_{AP}^{Ch} = \left(\frac{M_{pl}}{m_{AP}}\right)^2 = 1.5 \times 10^{44} \left(\frac{MeV}{m_{AP}}\right)^2 \quad (63)$$

where $M_{pl} = 1.22 \times 10^{19}$ GeV is the Planck scale. Using the largest AP mass $m_{AP} = 0.3$ MeV for the $B = 10^{17}$ G field, we find $N_{AP}^{Ch} = 1.7 \times 10^{45}$. This implies that if just 10^{-8}% of the 10^{55} photons reach the star with energies ~ 0.3 MeV or larger, they can in principle generate a large enough number of APs to produce a mini black hole in the star's center and induce its collapse. Similarly, for an AP mass $m_{AP} = 0.06$ MeV, we find $N_{AP}^{Ch} = 4.2 \times 10^{46}$, so in this case, 10^{-7}% of the total number of photons will have to reach the star to create the conditions for the collapse. Notice that this mechanism is purely a bosonic effect, since it is related to the Chandrasekhar limit of the bosons.

We should point out that the likelihood of reaching the Chandrasekhar limit in the star interior is not just determined by the number and energies of the γ-rays hitting the star, but also by the capacity of these photons to penetrate the quark medium and then generate a large enough number of APs that become trapped by the star's gravity. Hence, for the above AP mechanism to be operative, one has to estimate the γ-rays' attenuation in the MCDCW quark medium and use it to determine whether the star can trap or not the APs that form in its interior [110].

In a medium, γ-rays are mainly attenuated by their interaction with electrons. The main process driving the attenuation in an NS is Compton scattering. The attenuation at a given depth can be found from the formula:

$$I = I_0 e^{-\sigma n_e L}, \quad (64)$$

where I_0 is the incident radiation intensity, I the intensity at a thickness L inside the medium, σ the cross-section of Compton scattering, and n_e the electron number density. In a quark star, to reach the quark medium, the γ-rays have to cross an electron cloud of thickness a few hundred fm, since quark stars exhibit a macroscopic quark matter surface shrouded with this very thin electron cloud [8]. The quark-star surface acts as a membrane that allows only ultrarelativistic matter to escape: photons, neutrinos, electron–positron pairs, and magnetic fields. For the incoming γ-rays to reach the quark matter medium and activate the Primakoff effect, they first need to go through the electron cloud without big attenuation losses.

The formula that gives the Compton scattering cross-section is known as the Klein–Nishina formula [111,112] and is given by:

$$\begin{aligned}\sigma &= \frac{3e^4}{48\pi\epsilon_0^2 m_e^2 c^4}\left[\frac{1}{x}\left(1 - \frac{2(x+1)}{x^2}\right)ln(2x+1) + \frac{x+8}{2x^2} - \frac{1}{2x(2x+2)^2}\right] \\ &= 2.49 \times 10^{-25}\left[\left(\frac{x^2 - 2(x+1)}{x^3}\right)ln(2x+1) + \frac{x+8}{2x^2} - \frac{1}{2x(2x+2)^2}\right]\text{cm}^2\end{aligned} \quad (65)$$

where $x = \omega/m_e c^2$ is the ratio between the photon energy and the rest energy of the electron. For the maximum incident photon energy $\omega \approx 1$ MeV, $x \approx 2$, and the cross-section is:

$$\sigma \approx 2.58 \times 10^{-25}\text{cm}^2 \quad (66)$$

The electron number density of the cloud can be found from [8]:

$$n_e = \frac{9.49 \times 10^{35} \text{cm}^{-3}}{[1.2(z/10^{-11}\text{cm}) + 4]^3} \qquad (67)$$

Here, z is the height above the quark surface.

From Equations (64), (66), and (67), we obtain that the ratio of intensities for $L \approx z \approx 300\,fm$ is $I/I_0 \approx 0.983$, which shows that for 1MeV γ-rays the attenuation is negligible. A similar calculation for the least-energetic incident γ-ray, with 0.1 MeV, still shows small attenuation $I/I_0 \approx 0.64$. In the case of hybrid stars, the situation is different since the γ-rays have to cross several kilometers of hadronic matter with a relatively large electron density before reaching the quarks in the core. It can be proven that in this case, the γ radiation will be absorbed in a distance of less than a hundred fm into the mantle [110].

Back to the quark star case, once the γ rays reach the quark medium, they are converted to APs via the Primakoff effect, and a natural question immediately follows: Are these AP trapped inside the star? To answer this question, we need to compare the velocity of the AP with the star's escape velocity $v_e/c = \sqrt{2GM_{star}/c^2 R_{star}}$. For a star with $M_{star} = 2M_\odot$ and $R_{star} = 10$ km, we have $v_e = 0.8c$. The velocity v_{AP} that an AP of mass m_{AP} can reach depends on the energy E it acquires from the incident γ-rays:

$$v_{AP}/c = \sqrt{1 - \left(\frac{m_{AP} c^2}{E}\right)^2}. \qquad (68)$$

For instance, for $m_{AP} c^2 = 0.3$ MeV, all the APs with energy $E < 0.5$ MeV cannot escape. Similarly, if $m_{AP} c^2 = 0.06$ MeV, the APs with energies $E < 0.1$ MeV will be gravitationally trapped. This implies that for incident γ-photons in the energy interval $(0.1, 0.5)$ MeV, there will always be APs that will be trapped. The use of $2M_\odot$ stars in the escape velocity is motivated by recent indications [113] that the heaviest neutron stars, with masses $\sim 2M_\odot$, should have deconfined quark matter inside.

The constraint in the interval of photon energies needed to generate APs that will be trapped in turn affects the estimate of the percentages of incident photons needed to reach the Chandrasekhar limit. If we conservatively assume that the number of photons per energy is the same throughout the entire interval of γ-ray energies, then we can estimate that photons in the energy interval $(0.3, 0.5)$ MeV roughly represent 22% of the total number of incident photons that reach the quark medium, i.e., about $\approx 10^{54}$ photons. Of these photons, only 10^{-7}% are needed to generate enough APs to reach the Chandrasekhar limit. We then conclude that the AP mechanism to collapse the star by creating a mini black hole from the creation and subsequent accumulation of AP particles in the star's center is viable for quark stars and can serve to explain the missing pulsar problem.

There are several reasons why the presence of a magnetic field is crucial for the AP mechanism to work: first, because a background magnetic field is needed for the density wave phase of quarks to be stable against low-energy fluctuations [84], second, because a background magnetic field is needed to create APs through the Primakoff effect [97], and third, because the AP gap is proportional to the magnetic field [97]. It is worth mentioning that the AP mechanism does not require unrealistically large magnetic fields to be viable. Fields of magnitude 10^{16}–10^{17} G are enough to make the MDCDW phase energetically favored over the chirally restored one at intermediate densities. These are plausible fields for the interior of magnetars, whose surface magnetic fields can be as high as 10^{15}G. All these facts, together with the intense γ-ray activity in the galaxy center, create the conditions needed for the collapse of those short-lived magnetars via the AP scenario.

7. MDCDW Condensate versus Magnetically Catalyzed Chiral Condensate

It is well known that in a system of massless charged fermions in a magnetic field, the dimensional reduction in the infrared dynamics of the particles in the LLL favors the formation of an homogeneous particle–antiparticle chiral condensate even at the weakest attractive interaction between fermions. This phenomenon is due to the fact that there is no energy gap between the infrared fermions in the LLL and their antiparticles in the Dirac sea. This phenomenon is known as the magnetic catalysis of chiral symmetry breaking (MCχSB) [114–119]. The MCχSB is a universal phenomenon that has been tested in many different contexts [120–126].

In the original studies of the MCχSB [114–126], the catalyzed chiral condensate was assumed to generate only a fermion dynamical mass. However, it was later shown that in QED [127,128], the MCχSB inevitably leads also to the emergence of a dynamical anomalous magnetic moment (AMM). The reason is that the AMM does not break any symmetry that has not already been broken by the chiral condensate. The dynamical AMM in massless QED leads, in turn, to a nonperturbative Lande g-factor and a Bohr magneton proportional to the inverse of the dynamical mass. The induction of the AMM also yields a nonperturbative Zeeman effect [127,128].

Just as in QED, the magnetically catalyzed ground state of an NJL model of massless quarks at subcritical coupling turns out to be actually richer than previously thought with the emergence of two homogeneous condensates, the usual $\langle\overline{\psi}\psi\rangle$ and a magnetic moment condensate $\langle\overline{\psi}\Sigma^3\psi\rangle$ aligned with the magnetic field direction [49]. An effect of the magnetic moment is to significantly enhance the critical temperature for chiral symmetry restoration.

The above examples assumed zero chemical potential. A chemical potential can affect the picture significantly because once the density becomes different from zero and a Fermi surface is formed, the energy cost to pair particles with antiparticles grows, so that eventually, the pairing is no longer energetically favored. At nonzero chemical potential, the MCχSB then occurs until μ reaches a critical value at which a first-order phase transition takes place and the chiral symmetry is restored [129].

In Section 2, we saw that the MDCDW condensate can be formed even in the subcritical coupling regime, as long as the chemical potential is nonzero. That means that there is a region of chemical potentials where the MDCDW chiral condensate and the homogeneous MCχSB condensate compete with each other. Which of them is more energetically favored can be gathered from Figure 3, where the plots of the free-energy vs. the chemical potential are displayed for the MCχSB phase (yellow lines) and the MDCDW phase (blue lines), at different magnetic fields and/or couplings. Clearly, the spatially inhomogeneous condensate wins over the homogeneous one in the entire region of chemical potentials in all the situations.

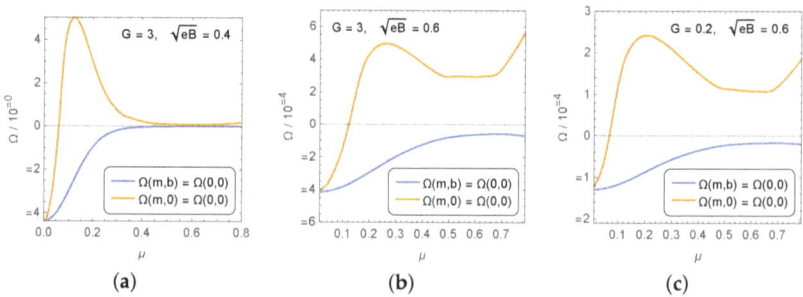

Figure 3. Comparison of free-energies for two phases at subcritical couplings: a homogeneous phase with a magnetically catalyzed condensate (yellow line) and a spatially inhomogeneous phase (blue line) with an MDCDW condensate.

Comparing the plots in Figure 3a,b, one can see that a larger magnetic field decreases the free-energy of the inhomogeneous phase and increases that of the homogeneous one. A similar behavior occurs at fixed field B, but different couplings, as can be seen from (b) and (c). Here, the separation between the two free-energies increases with the coupling, clearly favoring the MDCDW phase. These results underline how robust the MDCDW is even at subcritical coupling, an effect that can be connected to the topological contribution to the free-energy from the LLL quarks.

It is worth stressing another difference between these two phases. While a driven factor in the MCχSB case is the LLL infrared dynamics, as already pointed out, in the MDCDW phase, there is a connection between ultraviolet (UV) and infrared (IR) phenomena. The appearance of Ω_{anom} (11) in the thermodynamic potential is a consequence of the regularization of the high-energy modes in the difference of two ill-defined sums from which the anomalous and the finite medium contributions are extracted [43]. Since the anomalous term contributes to the gap equation for q, whose origin is IR because it comes from the quark–hole pairing, we have that the UV physics and the IR properties of the system are interrelated.

Finally, we should comment on the fact that while in the original MCχSB phenomenon, the condensate increases with the magnetic field, more recently, it was found that if the effect of the magnetic field on the coupling constant is taken into consideration, the chiral condensate actually decreases with the magnetic field, a phenomenon known as inverse magnetic catalysis [130–134]. It remains as an open and interesting question what will be the consequence of including the effect of the magnetic field on the strong coupling constant for the inhomogeneous condensate of the MDCDW phase.

8. Conclusions

In this paper, we reviewed the main physical characteristics of the MDCDW phase of dense quark matter and its possible connection with the astrophysics of NSs. One main attribute of this phase is its nontrivial topology, which is due to the combined effect of the density wave ground state and the dimensional reduction produced by the magnetic field on the LLL, which together give rise to an asymmetric spectrum for the LLL modes. As a consequence, the MDCDW phase displays anomalous properties such as an anomalous electric charge that depends on the applied magnetic field and the modulation q, a nondissipative anomalous Hall current, and magnetoelectricity.

The topological nature of the the MDCDW phase is also reflected in the matter–light interactions and how they affect the propagation of photons in this medium, which occurs via axion polaritons, a transport behavior that could help to explain the so-called missing pulsar problem in the GC.

A very important feature of the MDCDW phase is its stability against thermal phonon fluctuations at arbitrarily small temperatures. In other words, this system is protected against the Landau–Peierls instability [78,79] that usually erodes single-modulated phases in three spatial dimensions, leading to the lack of a long-range order. The lack of the instability is due to magnetic-field-induced terms in the low-energy GL expansion, some of which have a topological origin, since they are connected to the spectral asymmetry, and some of which are just the effect of the explicit breaking of the rotational symmetry by the magnetic field. The lack of Landau–Peierls instabilities in the MDCDW phase makes this phase particularly robust and, hence, a good candidate for the inner matter phase of neutron stars.

Although the emphasis of this paper was on NSs, the results of this review can also be of interest for heavy-ion collision (HIC) physics. Future HIC experiments plan to explore the region of lower temperatures and higher densities, and in doing that, they will certainly generate strong magnetic and electric fields in their off-central collisions, so opening a much more sensitive window to look into a very challenging region of QCD [135]. For example, the second phase of the RHIC energy scan (BES-II) [136], the planned experiments at the Facility for Antiproton and Ion Research (FAIR) [137] at the GSI site in Germany, and the Nuclotron-based Ion Collider Facility (NICA) [138,139] at JINR laboratory in Dubna,

Russia, are all designed to run at unprecedented collision rates to provide high-precision measures of observables in the high-baryon-density and lower-temperature region.

Searching for signals of inhomogeneous quark phases in these planned experiments is a necessary step to probe their realization in this yet unexplored region of the QCD phase map. Recently, a proposal to detect those signatures was discussed in [140]. The idea is that in regimes with periodic spatial modulation, particles can have a "moat" spectrum, where the minimum of the energy is not at zero momentum, but lies over a sphere at nonzero spatial momentum. On the basis that the particle distribution with a moat spectrum should peak at nonzero momentum [141], the authors of [140] argued that this feature can leave distinctive signatures in the production of particles and their correlations, which are measurable in heavy-ion collisions. The properties of the MDCDW phase discussed in this review, together with the upcoming findings of the range of critical temperatures at which the condensate evaporates [95], can serve to guide the experiments to better pinpoint the region of parameters where the signatures of a moat spectrum are most likely to be detected.

Finally, we should call the reader's attention to the fact that the anomalous effects of the MDCDW phase share many similarities with topological condensed matter systems as topological insulators [142], where θ depends on the band structure of the insulator; Dirac semimetals [143–146], a 3D bulk analogue of graphene with nontrivial topological structures; and WSM [88], where the derivative of the angle θ is related to the momentum separation between the Weyl nodes. Therefore, the discovery of new physical properties of these materials can shed light on the physics governing the challenging region of strongly coupled QCD, thereby inspiring new strategies to probe the presence of the MDCDW and other suitable phases in NSs and HICs.

Funding: NSF Grant PHY-2013222.

Acknowledgments: This work was supported in part by NSF Grant PHY-2013222. We are grateful to W. Gyory for helpful discussions and for his help with several graphs.

Conflicts of Interest: The authors declare no conflict of interest.

References

1. Abbott, B.P. (LIGO Scientific Collaboration and Virgo Collaboration). GW170817: Observation of gravitational waves from a binary neutron star inspiral. *Phys. Rev. Lett.* **2017**, *119*, 161101. [CrossRef] [PubMed]
2. Weber, F. Strange quark matter and compact stars. *Prog. Part Nucl. Phys.* **2005**, *54*, 193. [CrossRef]
3. Bodmer, A.R. Collapsed nuclei. *Phys. Rev. D* **1971**, *4*, 1601. [CrossRef]
4. Terazawa, H.; Akama, K.; Chikashige, Y. How to liberate quarks from chromodynamical confinement. *Prog. Theor. Phys.* **1978**, *60*, 1521–1525. [CrossRef]
5. Witten, E. Cosmic separation of phases. *Phys. Rev. D* **1984**, *30*, 272. [CrossRef]
6. Farhi, E.; Jaffe, R.L. Strange matter. *Phys. Rev. D* **1984**, *30*, 2379. [CrossRef]
7. Paczynski, B.; Haensel, P. Gamma-ray bursts from quark stars. *Mon. Not. Astron. Soc.* **2005**, *362*, L4. [CrossRef]
8. Alcock, C.; Farhi, E.; Olinto, A. Strange stars. *Astrophys. J.* **1986**, *310*, 261. [CrossRef]
9. Xu, R.X.; Zhang, B.; Qiao, G.J. Electric character of strange stars. *Chin. Phys. Lett.* **1999**, *16*, 778. [CrossRef]
10. Xu, R.X.; Zhang, B.; Qiao, G.J. What if pulsars are born as strange stars? *Astropart. Phys.* **2001**, *15*, 101. [CrossRef]
11. Holdom, B.; Ren, J.; Zhang, C. Quark matter may not be strange. *Phys. Rev. Lett.* **2018**, *120*, 222001. [CrossRef]
12. Alford, M.G.; Schmitt, A.; Rajagopal, K.; Schäfer, T. Color superconductivity in dense quark matter. *Rev. Mod. Phys.* **2008**, *80*, 1455. [CrossRef]
13. Schmitt, A. *Dense Matter in Compact Stars, Lecture Notes in Physics v. 811*; Springer: Berlin/Heidelberg, Germany, 2010.
14. Fukushima, K.; Hatsuda, T. The phase diagram of dense QCD. *Rep. Prog. Phys.* **2011**, *74*, 014001. [CrossRef]
15. Alford, M.; Rajagopal, K.; Wilczek, F. Color-flavor locking and chiral symmetry breaking in high density QCD. *Nucl. Phys. B* **1999**, *537*, 443. [CrossRef]
16. Kitazawa, M.; Koide, T.; Kunihiro, T.; Nemoto, Y. Chiral and color superconducting phase transitions with vector interaction in a simple model. *Prog. Theor. Phys.* **2002**, *108*, 929. [CrossRef]
17. Demorest, P.B.; Pennucci, T.; Ransom, S.M.; Roberts, M.S.E.; Hessels, J.W.T. A two-solar-mass neutron star measured using Shapiro delay. *Nature* **2010**, *467*, 1081. [CrossRef]
18. Antoniadis, J.; Freire, P.C.C.; Wex, N.; Tauris, T.M.; Lynch, R.S.; van Kerkwijk, M.H. A Massive pulsar in a compact relativistic binary. *Science* **2013**, *340*, 6131. [CrossRef]

19. Lourenço, O.; Lenzi, C.H.; Dutra, M.; Ferrer, E.J.; de la Incera, V.; Paulucci, L.; Horvath, J.E. Tidal deformability of strange stars and the GW170817 event. *Phys. Rev. D* **2021**, *103*, 103010. [CrossRef]
20. Ferrer, E.J.; de la Incera, V.; Paulucci, L. Gluon effects on the equation of state of color superconducting strange stars. *Phys. Rev. D* **2015**, *92*, 043010. [CrossRef]
21. Cumming, A.; Brown, E.F.; Fattoyev, F.J.; Horowitz, C.J.; Page, D.; Reddy, S. A lower limit on the heat capacity of the neutron star core. *Phys. Rev. C* **2017**, *95*, 025806. [CrossRef]
22. Ferrer, E.J.; de la Incera, V.; Sanson, P. Quark matter contribution to the heat capacity of magnetized neutron stars. *Phys. Rev. D* **2021**, *103*, 123013. [CrossRef]
23. Dong, L.; Shapiro, S.L. Cold equation of state in a strong magnetic field: Effects of inverse β-decay. *Astrophys. J.* **1991**, *383*, 745.
24. Ferrer, E.J.; de la Incera, V.; Keith, J.P.; Portillo, I.; Springsteen, P.L. Equation of state of a dense and magnetized fermion system. *Phys. Rev. C* **2010**, *82*, 065802. [CrossRef]
25. Canuto, V.; Chiu, H.Y. Quantum theory of an electron gas in intense magnetic fields. *Phys. Rev.* **1968**, *173*, 1210. [CrossRef]
26. Chaichian, M.; Masood, S.S.; Montonen, C.; Perez Martinez, A.; Perez Rojas, H. Quantum magnetic and gravitational collapse. *Phys. Rev. Lett.* **2000**, *84*, 5261. [CrossRef] [PubMed]
27. Paulucci, L.; Ferrer, E.J.; de la Incera, V.; Horvath, J.E. Equation of state for the MCFL phase and its implications for compact star models. *Phys. Rev. D* **2011**, *83*, 043009. [CrossRef]
28. Dexheimer, V.; Menezes, D.P.; Strickland, M. The influence of strong magnetic fields on proto-quark stars. *J. Phys. G* **2014**, *41*, 015203. [CrossRef]
29. Ferrer, E.J.; de la Incera, V.; Manreza Paret, D.; Perez Martinez, A.; Sanchez, A. Insignificance of the anomalous magnetic moment of charged fermions for the equation of state of a magnetized and dense medium. *Phys. Rev. D* **2015**, *91*, 085041. [CrossRef]
30. Carignano, S.; Ferrer, E.J.; de la Incera, V.; Paulucci, L. Crystalline chiral condensates as a component of compact stars. *Phys. Rev. D* **2015**, *92*, 105018. [CrossRef]
31. Ferrer, E.J.; Hackebill, A. Thermodynamics of neutrons in a magnetic field and its implications for neutron stars. *Phys. Rev. C* **2019**, *99*, 065803. [CrossRef]
32. Broderick, A.; Prakash, M.; Lattimer, J.M. The Equation of state of neutron star matter in strong magnetic fields. *Astrophys. J.* **2000**, *537*, 351. [CrossRef]
33. Ferrer, E.J.; de la Incera, V.; Manuel, C. Magnetic color flavor locking phase in high density QCD. *Phys. Rev. Lett.* **2005**, *95*, 152002. [CrossRef] [PubMed]
34. Ferrer, E.J.; de la Incera, V.; Manuel, C. Color-superconducting gap in the presence of a magnetic field. *Nucl. Phys. B* **2006**, *747*, 88. [CrossRef]
35. Ferrer, E.J.; de la Incera, V. Paramagnetism in color superconductivity and compact stars. *J. Phys. A* **2007**, *40*, 6913. [CrossRef]
36. Noronha, J.L.; Shovkovy, I.A. Color-flavor locked superconductor in a magnetic field. *Phys. Rev. D* **2007**, *76*, 105030. [CrossRef]
37. Fukushima, K.; Warringa, H.J. Color superconducting matter in a magnetic field. *Phys. Rev. Lett.* **2008**, *100*, 03200. [CrossRef]
38. Feng, B.; Ferrer, E.J.; de la Incera, V. Cooper pair's magnetic moment in MCFL color superconductivity. *Nucl. Phys. B* **2011**, *853*, 213. [CrossRef]
39. Feng, B.; Ferrer, E.J.; de la Incera, V. Magnetoelectric effect in strongly magnetized color superconductivity. *Phys. Lett. B* **2011**, *706*, 232. [CrossRef]
40. Ferrer, E.J.; de la Incera, V. Magnetism in dense quark matter. In *Strongly Interacting Matter in Magnetic Fields*; Lecture Notes in Physics; Springer: Berlin/Heidelberg, Germany, 2013; Volume 871, p. 399.
41. Mandal, T.; Jaikumar, P. Neutrality of a magnetized two-flavor quark superconductor. *Phys. Rev. C* **2013**, *87*, 045208. [CrossRef]
42. Mandal, T.; Jaikumar, P. Effect of temperature and magnetic field on two-flavor superconducting quark matter. *Phys. Rev. D* **2016**, *94*, 074016. [CrossRef]
43. Frolov, I.E.; Zhukovsky, V.C.; Klimenko, K.G. Chiral density waves in quark matter within the Nambu–Jona–Lasinio model in an external magnetic field. *Phys. Rev. D* **2010**, *82*, 076002. [CrossRef]
44. Tatsumi, T.; Nishiyama, K.; Karasawa, S. Novel Lifshitz point for chiral transition in the magnetic field. *Phys. Lett. B* **2015**, *743*, 66. [CrossRef]
45. Ferrer, E.J.; de la Incera, V. Dissipationless Hall current in dense quark matter in a magnetic field. *Phys. Lett. B* **2017**, *69*, 208. [CrossRef]
46. Ferrer, E.J.; de la Incera, V. Novel topological effects in dense QCD in a magnetic field. *Nucl. Phys. B* **2018**, *931*, 192. [CrossRef]
47. Feng, B.; Ferrer, E.J.; Portillo, I. Lack of Debye and Meissner screening in strongly magnetized quark matter at intermediate densities. *Phys. Rev. D* **2020**, *101*, 056012. [CrossRef]
48. Ferrer, E.J.; de la Incera, V.; Sanchez, A. Quarkyonic Chiral spirals in a magnetic field. *Acta Phys. Pol. B* **2012**, *5*, 679.
49. Ferrer, E.J.; de la Incera, V.; Portillo, I.; Quiroz, M. New look at the QCD ground state in a magnetic field. *Phys. Rev. D* **2014**, *89*, 085034. [CrossRef]
50. Deryagin, D.V.; Grigoriev, D.Y.; Rubakov, V.A. Standing wave ground state in high density, zero temperature QCD at large N(c). *Int. J. Mod. Phys. A* **1992**, *7*, 659. [CrossRef]
51. Shuster, E.; Son, D.T. On finite density QCD at large N(c). *Nucl. Phys. B* **2000**, *573*, 434. [CrossRef]
52. Park, B.-Y.; Rho, M.; Wirzba, A.; Zahed, I. Dense QCD: Overhauser or BCS pairing? *Phys. Rev. D* **2000**, *62*, 034015. [CrossRef]
53. Kojo, T.; Hidaka, Y.; McLerran, L.; Pisarski, R.D. Quarkyonic chiral spirals. *Nucl. Phys. A* **2010**, *843*, 37. [CrossRef]

54. Kojo, T.; Hidaka, Y.; Fukushima, K.; McLerran, L.D.; Pisarski, R.D. Interweaving chiral spirals. *Nucl. Phys. A* **2010**, *875*, 94. [CrossRef]
55. Kojo, T.; Pisarski, R.D.; Tsvelik, A.M. Covering the Fermi surface with patches of quarkyonic chiral spirals. *Phys. Rev. D* **2010**, *82*, 074015. [CrossRef]
56. Kojo, T. A (1+1) dimensional example of quarkyonic matter. *Nucl. Phys. A* **2012**, *877*, 70. [CrossRef]
57. Nickel, D. How many phases meet at the chiral critical point? *Phys. Rev. Lett.* **2009**, *103*, 072301. [CrossRef] [PubMed]
58. Nickel, D. Inhomogeneous phases in the Nambu-Jona-Lasino and quark–meson model. *Phys. Rev. D* **2009**, *80*, 074025. [CrossRef]
59. Rapp, R.; Shuryak, E.; Zahed, I. A Chiral crystal in cold QCD matter at intermediate densities? *Phys. Rev. D* **2001**, *63*, 034008. [CrossRef]
60. Gubina, N.V.; Klimenko, K.G.; Kurbanov, S.G.; Zhukovsky, V.C. Inhomogeneous charged pion condensation phenomenon in the NJL2 model with quark number and isospin chemical potentials. *Phys. Rev. D* **2012**, *86*, 085011. [CrossRef]
61. Carignano, S.; Nickel, D.; Buballa, M. Influence of vector interaction and Polyakov loop dynamics on inhomogeneous chiral symmetry breaking phases. *Phys. Rev. D* **2010**, *82*, 054009. [CrossRef]
62. Abuki, H.; Ishibashi, D.; Suzuki, K. Crystalline chiral condensates off the tricritical point in a generalized Ginzburg–Landau approach. *Phys. Rev. D* **2012**, *85*, 074002. [CrossRef]
63. Nakano, E.; Tatsumi, T. Chiral symmetry and density waves in quark matter. *Phys. Rev. D* **2005**, *71*, 114006. [CrossRef]
64. Anglani, R.; Casalbuoni, R.; Ciminale, M.; Ippolito, N.; Gatto, R.; Mannarelli, M.; Ruggieri, M. Crystalline color superconductors. *Rev. Mod. Phys.* **2014**, *86*, 509. [CrossRef]
65. Alford, M.; Kouvaris, C.; Rajagopal, K. Gapless Color-Flavor-Locked Quark Matter. *Phys. Rev. Lett.* **2004**, *92*, 222001. [CrossRef] [PubMed]
66. Casalbuoni, R.; Gatto, R.; Mannarelli, M.; Nardulli, G.; Ruggieri, M. Meissner masses in the gCFL phase of QCD. *Phys. Lett. B* **2005**, *605*, 362. [CrossRef]
67. Fukushima, K. Analytical and numerical evaluation of the Debye and Meissner masses in dense neutral three-flavor quark matter. *Phys. Rev. D* **2005**, *72*, 074002. [CrossRef]
68. Reddy, S.; Rupak, G. Phase structure of two-flavor quark matter: Heterogeneous superconductors. *Phys. Rev. C* **2005**, *71*, 025201. [CrossRef]
69. Fukushima, K. Characterizing the Larkin-Ovchinnikov-Fulde-Ferrel phase induced by the chromomagnetic instability. *Phys. Rev. D* **2006**, *73*, 094016. [CrossRef]
70. Hashimoto, M. Manifestation of instabilities in Nambu–Jona-Lasinio type models. *Phys. Lett. B* **2006**, *642*, 93. [CrossRef]
71. Huang, M. Spontaneous current generation in the 2SC phase. *Phys. Rev. D* **2006**, *73*, 045007. [CrossRef]
72. Larkin, A.I.; Ovchinnikov, Y.N. Nonuniform state of superconductors. *Sov. Phys. JETP* **1965**, *20*, 762.
73. Fulde, P.; Ferrell, R.A. Superconductivity in a strong spin-exchange field. *Phys. Rev. A* **1964**, *135*, 550. [CrossRef]
74. Alford, M.G.; Bowers, J.A.; Rajagopal, K. Crystalline color superconductivity. *Phys. Rev. D* **2001**, *63*, 074016. [CrossRef]
75. Bowers, J.A.; Rajagopal, K. Crystallography of color superconductivity. *Phys. Rev. D* **2001**, *66*, 065002. [CrossRef]
76. Casalbuoni, R.; Nardulli, G. Inhomogeneous superconductivity in condensed matter and QCD. *Rev. Mod. Phys.* **2004**, *76*, 263. [CrossRef]
77. Ferrer, E.J.; de la Incera, V. Chromomagnetic Instability and induced magnetic field in neutral two-flavor color superconductivity. *Phys. Rev. D* **2007**, *76*, 114012. [CrossRef]
78. Peierls, R. Remarks on transition temperatures. *Helv. Phys. Acta* **1934**, *7*, 81.
79. Landau, L.D. On the theory of phase transitions. *Phys. Z Sowjet. Union* **1937**, *11*, 26. [CrossRef]
80. Hidaka, Y.; Kamikado, K.; Kanazawa, T.; Noumi, T. Phonons, pions, and quasi-long-range order in spatially modulated chiral condensates. *Phys. Rev. D* **2015**, *92*, 034003. [CrossRef]
81. Lee, T.-G.; Nakano, E.; Tsue, Y.; Tatsumi, T.; Friman, B. Landau–Peierls instability in a Fulde-Ferrell type inhomogeneous chiral condensed phase. *Phys. Rev. D* **2015**, *92*, 034024. [CrossRef]
82. Pisarski, R.D.; Skokov, V.V.; Tsvelik, A.M. Fluctuations in cool quark matter and the phase diagram of quantum chromodynamics. *Phys. Rev. D* **2019**, *99*, 074025. [CrossRef]
83. De Gennes, P.G.; Prost, J. *The Physics of Liquid Crystals*; Oxford University Press: New York, NY, USA, 1993.
84. Ferrer, E.J.; de la Incera, V. Absence of Landau–Peierls instability in the magnetic dual chiral Density wave phase of dense QCD. *Phys. Rev. D* **2020**, *102*, 014010. [CrossRef]
85. Fujikawa, K. Path Integral for Gauge Theories with fermions. *Phys. Rev. D* **1980**, *21*, 2848. [CrossRef]
86. Wilczek, F. Two applications of axion electrodynamics. *Phys. Rev. Lett.* **1987**, *58*, 1799. [CrossRef] [PubMed]
87. Středa, P. Theory of quantised Hall conductivity in two dimensions. *J. Phys. C Solid State Phys.* **1982**, *15*, L717. [CrossRef]
88. Burkov, A.A. Weyl Metals. *Annu. Rev. Condens. Matter Phys.* **2018**, *9*, 359. [CrossRef]
89. Ferrer, E.J.; de la Incera, V. No net charge separation in hot QCD in a magnetic field. *Phys. Rev. D* **2018**, *98*, 074009. [CrossRef]
90. Tatsumi, T.; Yoshiike, R.; Kashiwa, K. Anomalous Hall effect in dense QCS matter. *Phys. Lett. B* **2018**, *785*, 46. [CrossRef]
91. Niemi, A.J.; Semenoff, G.W. Fermion Number Fractionization in Quantum Field Theories. *Phys. Rep.* **1986**, *135*, 99. [CrossRef]
92. Niemi, A.J. Topological solitons in a hot and dense Fermi gas. *Nucl. Phys. B* **1985**, *251*, 155. [CrossRef]
93. Harding, A.K.; Lai, D. Physics of strongly magnetized neutron stars. *Rep. Prog. Phys.* **2006**, *69*, 2631. [CrossRef]
94. Spruit, H.C. Origin of neutron star magnetic fields. *AIP Conf. Proc.* **2008**, *983*, 391.

95. Gyory, W.; de la Incera, V. Phase transitions and resilience of the MDCDW phase at finite temperature and density. in preparation.
96. Carignano, S.; Mannarelli, M.; Anzuini, F.; Benhar, O. Crystalline phases by an improved gradient expansion technique. *Phys. Rev. D* **2018**, *97*, 036009. [CrossRef]
97. Ferrer, E.J.; de la Incera, V. Axion-Polariton in dense quark matter: A solution to the missing pulsar problem. *arXiv* **2020**, arXiv:2010.02314.
98. Li, R.; Wang, J.; Qi, X.-L.; Zhang, S.-C. Dynamical axion field in topological magnetic insulators. *Nature* **2010**, *6*, 284. [CrossRef]
99. Macquart, J.-P.; Kanekar, N.; Frail, D.; Ransom, S. A high-frequency search for pulsars within the central parsec of Sgr A. *Astrophys. J.* **2010**, *715*, 939. [CrossRef]
100. Mori, K.; Gotthelf, E.V.; Zhang, S.; An, H.; Baganoff, F.K.; Barriere, N.M.; Beloborodov, A.M.; Boggs, S.E.; Christensen, F.E.; Craig, W.W.; et al. NuSTAR discovery of A 3.76 s transient magnetar near Sagittarius A*. *ApJL* **2013**, *770*, L23. [CrossRef]
101. Kennea, J.A.; Burrows, D.N.; Kouveliotou, C. Swift Discovery of a new soft gamma repeater, SGR J1745–29, near Sagittarius A. *ApJL* **2013**, *770*, L24. [CrossRef]
102. Spitler, L.G.; Lee, K.J.; Eatough, R.P.; Kramer, M.; Karuppusamy, R.; Bassa, C.G.; Cognard, I.; Desvignes, G.; Lyne, A.G.; Stappers, B.W.; et al. Pulse broadening measurements from the galactic center pulsar J1745-2900. *ApJL* **2014**, *780*, L3. [CrossRef]
103. Dexter, J.; O'Leary, R.M. The peculiar pulsar population of the central parsec. *ApJL* **2014**, *783*, L7. [CrossRef]
104. Figer, D.F.; Najarro, F.; Geballe, T.R.; Blum, R.D.; Kudritzki, R.P. Massive stars in the SGR 1806-20 cluster. *ApJL* **2005**, *622*, L49. [CrossRef]
105. Nolan, P.L.; Abdo, A.A.; Ackermann, M.; Ajello, M.; Allafort, A.; Antolini, E.; Atwood, W.B.; Axelsson, M.; Baldini, L.; Ballet, J.; et al. (Fermi-LAT Collaboration), Fermi large area the telescope second source catalog. *Astrophys. J. Suppl. Ser.* **2012**, *199*, 31. [CrossRef]
106. Meszaros, P. Gamma-ray bursts. *Rept. Prog. Phys.* **2006**, *69*, 2259. [CrossRef]
107. Primakoff, H. Photo-Production of neutral mesons in nuclear electric fields and the mean life of the neutral meson. *Phys. Rev.* **1951**, *81*, 899. [CrossRef]
108. Ruffini, R.; Bonazzola, S. Systems of self-gravitating particles in general relativity and the concept of an equation of state. *Phys. Rev.* **1969**, *187*, 1767. [CrossRef]
109. Goldman, I.; Nussinov, S. Weakly interacting massive particles and neutron stars. *Phys. Rev. D* **1989**, *40*, 3221. [CrossRef]
110. Ferrer, E.J.; de la Incera, V. Axion-Polariton in the Magnetic Dual Chiral Density Wave Phase of Dense QCD. in preparation.
111. Klein, O.; Nishina, Y. The scattering of light by free electrons according to Dirac's new relativistic dynamics. *Nature* **1928**, *122*, 398. [CrossRef]
112. Longair, M.S. *High Energy Astrophysics*; Cambridge University Press: Cambridge, UK, 2011; pp. 235–237.
113. Annala, E.; Gorda, T.; Kurkela, A.; Nattila, J.; Vuorinen, A. Evidence for quark-matter cores in massive neutron stars. *Nat. Phys.* **2020**, *16*, 907. [CrossRef]
114. Suganuma, H.; Tatsumi, T. On the Behavior of Symmetry and Phase Transitions in a Strong Electromagnetic Field. *Ann. Phys.* **1991**, *208*, 470. [CrossRef]
115. Klimenko, K.G. Three-dimensional Gross-Neveu model at nonzero temperature and in an external magnetic field. *Theor. Math. Phys.* **1992**, *90*, 1. [CrossRef]
116. Gusynin, V.P.; Miransky, V.A.; Shovkovy, I.A. Catalysis of Dynamical Flavor Symmetry Breaking by a Magnetic Field in 2 + 1 Dimensions. *Phys. Rev. Lett.* **1994**, *73*, 3499. [CrossRef]
117. Lee, D.-S.; Leung, C.N.; Ng, Y.J. Chiral symmetry breaking in a uniform external magnetic field. *Phys. Rev. D* **1997**, *55*, 6504. [CrossRef]
118. Ferrer, E.J.; de la Incera, V. Ward-Takahashi identity with an external field in ladder QED. *Phys. Rev. D* **1998**, *58*, 065008. [CrossRef]
119. Gusynin, V.P.; Miransky, V.A.; Shovkovy, I.A. Theory of the magnetic catalysis of chiral symmetry breaking in QED. *Nucl. Phys. B* **1999**, *563*, 361. [CrossRef]
120. Ferrer, E.J.; de la Incera, V. Magnetic catalysis in the presence of scalar fields. *Phys. Lett. B* **2000**, *481*, 287. [CrossRef]
121. Yu, I.; Shilnov, Y.I.; Chitov, V.V. Phase structure of the Nambu–Jona–Lasinio model in a constant electromagnetic field in d-dimensional curved spacetime. *Phys. Atom. Nucl.* **2001**, *64*, 2051.
122. Elizalde, E.; Ferrer, E.J.; de la Incera, V. Beyond-constant-mass-approximation magnetic catalysis in the gauge Higgs-Yukawa model. *Phys. Rev. D* **2003**, *68*, 096004 [CrossRef]
123. Rojas, E.; Ayala, A.; Bashir, A.; Raya, A. Dynamical mass generation in QED with magnetic fields: Arbitrary field strength and coupling constant. *Phys. Rev. D* **2008**, *77*, 093004. [CrossRef]
124. Leung, C.N.; Wang, S.-Y. Gauge independent approach to chiral symmetry breaking in a strong magnetic field. *Nucl. Phys. B* **2006**, *747*, 266. [CrossRef]
125. Ferrer, E.J.; de la Incera, V.; Sanchez, A. Paraelectricity in Magnetized Massless QED. *Phys. Rev. Lett.* **2011**, *107*, 041602. [CrossRef]
126. Ferrer, E.J.; de la Incera, V.; Sanchez, A. Non-perturbative Euler-Heisenberg Lagrangian and paraelectricity in magnetized massless QED. *Nucl. Phys.* **2012**, *864*, 469. [CrossRef]
127. Ferrer, E.J.; de la Incera, V. Dynamically Induced Zeeman Effect in Massless QED. *Phys. Rev. Lett.* **2009**, *102*, 050402. [CrossRef]
128. Ferrer, E.J.; de la Incera, V. Dynamically Generated Anomalous Magnetic Moment in Massless QED. *Nucl. Phys. B* **2010**, *824*, 217. [CrossRef]

129. Lee, D.S.; Leung, C.N.; Ng, Y.J. Chiral symmetry breaking in a uniform external magnetic field. II. Symmetry restoration at high temperatures and chemical potentials. *Phys. Rev. D* **1998**, *57*, 5224. [CrossRef]
130. Bali, G.S.; Bruckmann, F.; Endrodi, G.; Fodor, Z.; Katz, S.D.; Krieg, S.; Schaefer, A.; Szabo, K.K. The QCD phase diagram for external magnetic fields. *JHEP* **2012**, *2*, 44. [CrossRef]
131. D'Elia, M. Lattice QCD simulations in external background fields Lect. *Notes Phys.* **2013**, *871*, 181.
132. Farias, R.L.S.; Gomes, K.P.; Krein, G.I.; Pinto, M.B. Importance of asymptotic freedom for the pseudocritical temperature in magnetized quark matter. *Phys. Rev. C* **2014**, *90*, 025203. [CrossRef]
133. Ayala, A.; Loewe, M.; Zamora, R. Inverse magnetic catalysis in the linear sigma model with quarks. *Phys. Rev. D* **2015**, *91*, 016002. [CrossRef]
134. Ferrer, E.J.; de la Incera, V.; Wen, X.J. Quark antiscreening at strong magnetic field and inverse magnetic catalysis. *Phys. Rev. D* **2015**, *91*, 054006. [CrossRef]
135. Ferrer, E.J.; de la Incera, V. Exploring dense and cold QCD in magnetic fields. *Eur. Phys. J. A* **2016**, *52*, 266. [CrossRef]
136. Odyniec, G. The RHIC Beam Energy Scan program in STAR and what's next. *J. Phys. Conf. Ser.* **2013**, *455*, 012037. [CrossRef]
137. Ablyazimov, T.; Abuhoza, A.; Adak, R.P. Challenges in QCD matter physics—The scientific program of the Compressed Baryonic Matter experiment at FAIR. *Eur. Phys. J. A* **2017**, *53*, 60. [CrossRef]
138. Deng, W.-T.; Huang, X.-G. Event-by-event generation of electromagnetic fields in heavy-ion collisions. *Phys. Rev. C* **2012**, *85*, 044907. [CrossRef]
139. Toneev, V.; Rogachevsky, V.O.; Voronyuk, V. Evidence for creation of strong electromagnetic fields in relativistic heavy-ion collisions. *Eur. Phys. J. A* **2016**, *52*, 264. [CrossRef]
140. Pisarski, R.D.; Rennecke, F. Signatures of Moat Regimes in Heavy-Ion Collisions. *Phys. Rev. Lett.* **2021**, *127*, 152302.
141. Pisarski, R.D.; Rennecke, F.; Tsvelik, A.; Valgushev, S. The Lifshitz Regime and its Experimental Signals. *Nucl. Phys. A* **2021**, *1005*, 121910. [CrossRef]
142. Qi, X.-L.; Hughes, T.L.; Zhang, S.-C. Topological field theory of time-reversal invariant insulators. *Phys. Rev. B* **2008**, *78*, 195424. [CrossRef]
143. Young, S.M.; Zaheer, S.; Teo, J.C.Y.; Kane, C.L.; Mele, E.J.; Rappe, A.M. Dirac semimetal in three dimensions. *Phys. Rev. Lett.* **2012**, *108*, 140405. [CrossRef]
144. Borisenko, S.; Gibson, Q.; Evtushinsky, D.; Zabolotnyy, V.; Buchner, B.; Cava, R.J. Experimental realization of a three-dimensional Dirac semimetal. *Phys. Rev. Lett.* **2014**, *113*, 027603. [CrossRef]
145. Neupane, M.; Xu, S.-Y.; Sankar, R.; Alidoust, N.; Bian, G.; Liu, C.; Belopolski, I. Observation of a three-dimensional topological Dirac semimetal phase in high-mobility Cd3As2. *Nat. Commun.* **2014**, *5*, 3786. [CrossRef]
146. Liu, Z.K.; Jiang, J.; Zhou, B.; Wang, Z.J.; Zhang, Y.; Weng, H.M.; Prabhakaran, D.; Mo, S.-K.; Peng, H.; Dudin, P.; et al. A stable three-dimensional topological Dirac semimetal Cd 3 As 2. *Nat. Mater.* **2014**, *13*, 677. [CrossRef]

Article

Radial Oscillations of Quark Stars Admixed with Dark Matter

José C. Jiménez [1] and Eduardo S. Fraga [2,*]

[1] Instituto de Física, Universidade de São Paulo, São Paulo 05508-090, Brazil; jimenez@if.usp.br
[2] Instituto de Física, Universidade Federal do Rio de Janeiro, Rio de Janeiro 21941-972, Brazil
* Correspondence: fraga@if.ufrj.br

Abstract: We investigated compact stars consisting of cold quark matter and fermionic dark matter treated as two admixed fluids. We computed the stellar structures and fundamental radial oscillation frequencies of different masses of the dark fermion in the cases of weak and strong self-interacting dark matter. We found that the fundamental frequency can be dramatically modified and, in some cases, stable dark strange planets and dark strangelets with very low masses and radii can be formed.

Keywords: quark stars; dark matter; radial oscillations

1. Introduction

Compact stars offer a variety of possibilities for probing the inner structure of matter through astronomical observations. In particular, matter at extremely high densities can only be probed, so far, by investigating unique objects that represent one of the possible final stages of stellar evolution. The structure of compact stars can be determined by solving the Tolman–Oppenheimer–Volkov (TOV) equations, given the equation of state (EoS) for the matter under consideration [1,2].

For high enough central energy densities, one expects to find either hybrid stars, i.e., neutron stars with a quark matter (QM) core, or even more exotic objects, such as quark stars. Quark stars [3] and their structure [4] have been considered for more than half a century, even before the elaboration of quantum chromodynamics (QCD) in the 1970s. Later, after a seminal work by Witten [5], a rich phenomenology of self-bound strange stars [6,7] and quark (hybrid) stars emerged using the MIT bag model [8] as a framework for the EoS at high densities. For a review on quark matter in neutron stars, see Ref. [9].

On the other hand, dark matter (DM) represents about a quarter of the total mass–energy density content of the universe or, equivalently, ∼85% of its matter content. Apart from this, it is needed to explain structure formations without modifying general relativity in the current cosmological standard model [10–12]. Nevertheless, there is still no experimental evidence of DM-constituent particles, and its nature remains one of the greatest mysteries of particle physics. Over the years, many candidates have been proposed as being DM-constituent particles, with masses ranging from 10^{-33} GeV to 10^{15} GeV, including weakly interacting massive particles (WIMPs), axions and axion-like particles (ALPs), sterile neutrinos, neutralinos, and so on [13]. In spite of their nature, if DM-constituent particles do not self annihilate and are non-relativistic at freeze-out (cold dark matter (CDM)), the probability of their interaction with ordinary baryonic matter will increase within the extreme densities found in compact stars. In this case, DM can accumulate and thermalize in a small radius. So, if quark stars are to be found in the universe, they have most likely accumulated some amount of dark matter over the course of their lives.

In this paper, we investigate strange quark stars consisting of cold QM and non self-annihilating fermionic cold DM treated as two admixed fluids, attracted only gravitationally. As our main goal, we aim to compute the fundamental radial oscillation frequency of admixed QM and DM *two-fluid* stars for a relevant range of masses of the dark fermion. We consider the cases of weak and strong self-interacting DM and also study how the total

mass and radius of quark and dark stars are modified by their mutual presence in the admixed star.

We describe the QM component on the framework of the MIT bag model, which represents a choice for simplicity, which was mainly motivated by the possibility of direct comparison to previous work. Moreover, for analyses that depend on a range of values for the dark fermion mass and the intensity of DM self-interaction, it is convenient to avoid other bands in parameters that would come about naturally in more realistic descriptions of the EoS, such as those relying on perturbative QCD [14–24].

Neutron stars and quark stars admixed with DM have previously been considered. The effects of fermionic and bosonic DM on the equilibrium features and radial oscillations of neutron stars (NS) have been discussed, e.g., in Refs. [25–31] (see Ref. [32] for a more complete list of references). Reference [33] considers hybrid NSs with an EoS for neutron star matter that uses perturbative QCD and effective field theory as high and low-density descriptions, respectively, and polytropes as interpolating functions, as discussed in Ref. [18][1], in addition to taking into account inner and outer crusts. The authors also consider white dwarfs admixed with asymmetric DM and find dark, compact (Jupiter-like) planets and limits on the DM content of the stars in order to satisfy the two-solar mass observational constraint [34,35]. A stability analysis is also performed by solving the usual Sturm–Liouville problem for one-fluid stars [36,37]. Reference [13] extends these results to a wider range of dark fermion masses, from 1 GeV to 500 GeV, assuming different amounts of DM at the stellar center. From this analysis, the authors inferred that the total mass decreases with m_D, putting constraints on m_D and on DM capture.

Quark stars admixed with dark matter have been discussed in Ref. [38], where the authors use the MIT bag model to describe the EoS for QM admixed with DM made of dark fermions of mass $m_D = 100$ GeV (on the typical WIMP mass scale). They considered two cases: free and strongly self-interacting DM. Solving the TOV equations with two fluids that interact only gravitationally, they found minor modifications to the maximum mass and radius, of the order of a few percent, though with higher values of the central energy density due to a greater gravitational pull.

So far, the stability against radial oscillations of quark stars admixed with dark matter has been studied using one-fluid formalism, usually with simplified interaction terms and unphysical dark-fermion masses [39,40]. A complete treatment of the stability of two-fluid stars requires a non-trivial extension of the Chandrasekhar second-order differential equation, where a coupled system of equations should be solved for the corresponding Lagrangian displacements associated with each fluid, but which also depend on the displacement of the other fluid [26,27,41,42], as will be discussed in the sequel.

The paper is organized as follows. In Section 2, we briefly describe the two-fluid hydrostatic equilibrium equations together with the general-relativistic formalism used to study radial pulsations of the admixed stars. Section 3 contains our main results and discussion. Section 4 presents our summary and perspectives. We adopt natural units, i.e., $\hbar = c = 1$.

2. Framework

In this section we summarize the main features of the TOV equations for the admixture of two fluids that interact only gravitationally. The one-fluid radial oscillation equations are conveniently partitioned to analyze either the stability of the quark mater core or dark matter core of the whole compact star. For the bag constant we use $B^{1/4} = 145$ MeV, which implements the Bodmer–Witten–Terazawa hypothesis for strange quark matter [2]. This choice yields a maximum mass of 2.01 $M_\odot$ and a radius of $R = 11$ km. As mentioned previously, fermionic dark matter is considered as being either weakly ($y = 0.1$) or strongly ($y = 10^3$) self interacting [43]. Here, $y \equiv m_D/m_{int}$, where m_D is the dark fermion mass, and m_{int} is the scale of interaction. One can consider that $m_{int} \sim 100$ MeV for strong interactions and $m_{int} \sim 300$ GeV for weak interactions. The values $y = 0.1$ and $y = 10^3$ are commonly adopted as typical illustrations.

2.1. Two-Fluid Hydrostatic Equilibrium Equations

Since the structure of spherically symmetric, static one-fluid compact stars is determined from the usual TOV equations, they can be separated in order to deal with two fluids that only interact gravitationally. This can be performed as follows. The (perfect) one-fluid energy-momentum tensor is divided into two parts, i.e., $T^{\mu\nu} = T_1^{\mu\nu} + T_2^{\mu\nu}$. This, in turn, induces a separation of the total pressure and energy density in fluid components, as $p = p_1 + p_2$ and $\epsilon = \epsilon_1 + \epsilon_2$, respectively. Given that this separation does not affect the temporal $e^{\nu(r)}$ or radial $e^{\lambda(r)}$ metric functions, the corresponding equations keep their original forms, depending on the total pressure and energy densities. On the other hand, one has a set of coupled TOV equations for each of the fluids.

In our case, i.e., quark and dark matter fluids, we have these two-fluid TOV equations in its dimensionless form given by [33] (see Ref. [29] for a detailed variational derivation):

$$\begin{aligned}
\frac{dp'_{QM}}{dr'} &= -\frac{(p'_{QM} + \epsilon'_{QM})}{2}\frac{d\nu}{dr'}, \\
\frac{dm'_{QM}}{dr'} &= 4\pi r'^2 \epsilon'_{QM}, \\
\frac{dp'_{DM}}{dr'} &= -\frac{(p'_{DM} + \epsilon'_{DM})}{2}\frac{d\nu}{dr'}, \\
\frac{dm'_{DM}}{dr'} &= 4\pi r'^2 \epsilon'_{DM}, \\
\frac{d\nu}{dr'} &= 2\frac{(m'_{QM} + m'_{DM}) + 4\pi r'^3 (p'_{QM} + p'_{DM})}{r'(r' - 2(m'_{QM} + m'_{DM}))},
\end{aligned} \quad (1)$$

where p' and ϵ' are the dimensionless pressure and energy density, respectively, and $m'_{QM,DM}$ are the dimensionless gravitational masses enclosed inside the dimensionless radial coordinate r'.

The set of equations above is solved simultaneously by specifying the (dimensionless) EoSs for QM, i.e., $p'_{QM} = p'_{QM}(\epsilon'_{QM})$, and DM, i.e., $p'_{DM} = p'_{DM}(\epsilon'_{DM})$. As usual, the conditions at the center should be given for QM and DM in the admixed star. The numerical integration stops when one of the pressures reaches zero, i.e., $p'_{QM/DM}(R'_{QM/DM}) = 0$, characterizing the QM or DM core surface, allowing us to obtain the corresponding gravitational mass $m'_{QM/DM}(R'_{QM/DM}) = M'_{QM/DM}$, where, in general, $R'_{QM} \neq R'_{DM}$. If $R'_{QM} > R'_{DM}$, the admixed star has a DM core and, if $R'_{QM} < R'_{DM}$, it has a DM halo surrounding a QM core.[2]

The boundary conditions for the metric function $\nu(r)$ come from ensuring that it matches the Schwarzschild metric outside the QM or DM core in the admixed star, i.e.,:

$$\nu(R'_{QM}) = \ln\left(1 - \frac{2(M'_{QM} + m'_{DM}(R'_{QM}))}{R'_{QM}}\right) \quad (2)$$

or

$$\nu(R'_{DM}) = \ln\left(1 - \frac{2(m'_{QM}(R'_{DM}) + M'_{DM})}{R'_{DM}}\right), \quad (3)$$

respectively.

2.2. Pulsations of Quark and Dark Matter Cores

The equations that describe the radial pulsations of one-fluid compact stars were obtained for the first time by S. Chandrasekhar [36]. He found that these equations could be arranged as a Sturm–Liouville problem where the eigenvalues are the oscillation frequencies squared, ω^2 (the eigenfunctions being the radial Lagrangian displacements). For numerical purposes, these equations can be conveniently modified to a pair of first-order differential equations for each of the Lagrangian variables with more intuitive boundary conditions [44–48].

Strictly speaking, the dynamic stability of admixed stars must be studied using the full two-fluid formalism[3] of Refs. [27,41], which would produce unified oscillation frequencies for the entire admixed star. However, since this calculation is computationally very expensive and time consuming, we decided to solve the equivalent of the two-fluid TOV equations, realized instead in the form of oscillation equations. In order to perform that function, we used the formalism of Ref. [47], which deals with the relative radial displacement $\Delta r'/r' \equiv \xi' = \xi$ and the Lagrangian perturbation pressure $\Delta p'$, both dimensionless.

Inspired by the previous separation for the total pressure and energy density, we separated the total Lagrangian variables as $\xi = \xi_{QM} + \xi_{DM}$ and $\Delta p' = \Delta p'_{QM} + \Delta p'_{DM}$ (omitting the term $e^{i\omega t}$ in both variables), obtaining the following system of equations:

$$\frac{d\xi_{QM/DM}}{dr'} \equiv -\frac{1}{r'}\left(3\xi_{QM/DM} + \frac{\Delta p'_{QM}}{\Gamma p'}\right) - \frac{dp'}{dr'}\frac{\xi_{QM/DM}}{(p'+\epsilon')}, \quad (4)$$

$$\frac{d\Delta p'_{QM/DM}}{dr'} \equiv \xi_{QM/DM}\left\{\omega'^2 e^{\lambda-\nu}(p'+\epsilon')r' - 4\frac{dp'}{dr'}\right\} +$$
$$\xi_{QM/DM}\left\{\left(\frac{dp'}{dr'}\right)^2 \frac{r'}{(p'+\epsilon')} - 8\pi e^{\lambda}(p'+\epsilon')p'r'\right\} +$$
$$\Delta p'_{QM/DM}\left\{\frac{dp'}{dr'}\frac{1}{p'+\epsilon'} - 4\pi(p'+\epsilon')r'e^{\lambda}\right\}, \quad (5)$$

where ω' is the dimensionless oscillation frequency and Γ is the adiabatic index[4] $\Gamma = (1 + \epsilon'/p')(\partial p'/\partial \epsilon')$. The metric function $\lambda(r')$ is obtained from $\lambda(r') = -\ln(1 - 2(m'_{QM}(r') + m'_{DM}(r'))/r')$ with boundary conditions given by Equations (2) and (3), i.e., $\lambda(R'_{QM}) = -\nu(R'_{QM})$ and $\lambda(R'_{DM}) = -\nu(R'_{DM})$.

So far we have not mentioned whether ω' corresponds to the pulsation of a QM core or a DM core. Recall that these equations represent a Sturm–Liouville problem, which defines its eigenvalues in terms of the associated boundary conditions. In this case, they are

$$(\Delta p'_{QM/DM})_{center} \equiv -3(\xi_{QM/DM}\Gamma p'_{QM/DM})_{center}, \quad (6)$$

demanding smoothness at the QM or DM stellar center, and

$$(\Delta p'_{QM/DM})_{surface} \equiv 0, \quad (7)$$

since $p'_{QM/DM}(R'_{QM/DM}) = 0$, with eigenfunctions normalized to $\xi_{QM/DM}(0) = 1$ as usual. Thus, Equations (6) and (7) lead us to define $\omega'^2 \to \omega'^2_{QM/DM}$ if we are dealing with a QM/DM oscillating core in the admixed star. In other words, only one of the cores oscillates depending on the boundary conditions. The other fluid only affects its oscillation indirectly, by the coupling of the total pressure and energy density.

A word of caution should be added at this point. Usually, two ways of dealing with the radial oscillations of two-fluid compact stars have been explored. In the simplest one, only the radial oscillation of the whole admixed star, i.e., treated as one fluid, is studied without explicitly considering the gravitational coupling between the QM and DM cores (see e.g., Refs. [33,39,40]). In the second, a consistent general-relativistic formalism to deal with the couplings between oscillation amplitudes and Lagrangian perturbations for each fluid is developed [41,42]. Unfortunately, dealing with a system of highly coupled and non-linear differential equations requires very time-consuming numerical calculations which we consider unnecessary when independently solving the oscillation equations for each DM or QM core while keeping the other fluid at rest but still coupled through the coefficients entering in the equations. In this sense, the formalism built in this work occurs more in the line of Ref. [27], which considers the independent oscillations of each fluid, thus forming an Sturm–Liouville-like problem. Notice that our reasoning agrees with the fact that each of the two-fluid TOV equations can be considered an independent 'one-fluid' star only, coupled through $\nu(r')$ to the other 'one-fluid' star. Thus, radial oscillations of each 'one-fluid' star can be associated with a set of one-fluid[5] oscillation equations coupled now by the total pressures, energy densities, and polytropic indices and metric functions, $\nu(r')$ and $\lambda(r')$. For consistency, we have verified that our formalism agrees with the results of Ref. [38] when a delay of the maximal central density is reached at higher densities for increasing amounts of DM when the zero frequencies are reached. We stress that, in this case, $f_{n=0} \to 0$ coincides with $\partial M/\partial \epsilon_c \to 0$, since few amounts of DM were considered, whereas in this work we explore all the available DM densities which notoriously modifies the stability of the admixed stars, so that $\partial M/\partial \epsilon_c$ must be used with caution.

In following sections, we focus on the fundamental mode frequency, $\omega_{n=0}$. It vanishes at the maximal stable QM or DM mass configuration, marking the onset of the instability of the corresponding oscillating core which, in turn, induces the gravitational collapse of the whole admixed star.

3. Results and Discussion

The parameter space for quark stars admixed with weakly or strongly self-interacting DM is large. In this section we show only results where the effects on observables are relevant. As mentioned before, we considered dark fermion masses $m_D =1, 10, 50, 100, 200, 500$ GeV in order to include all possible dark fermion candidates.

Regarding the numerical values we chose for $\epsilon_c^{\rm QM/DM}$ in our calculations and showed in our plots: (i) for QM, the three values of $\epsilon_c^{\rm QM}$ correspond to somewhat above, twice, and nearly twice the value of the maximal central energy density of pure quark stars with $B = (145 \,{\rm MeV})^4$, i.e., $\sim 1\,{\rm GeV/fm}^3$. The reason for this is that higher values of $\epsilon_c^{\rm QM}$ are required when DM is present in the admixed star; (ii) the three values of $\epsilon_c^{\rm DM}$ (for strongly or weakly interacting DM) correspond to near the minimum, intermediate, and near the maximal-mass central densities for corresponding pure DM stars. In Tables 1 and 2 the maximal-mass values of central energy density for each m_D are listed. This choice was made to quantify the full dependence of the stellar structure on the amounts of DM. We will show that, in some cases with a huge amount of DM, only very small objects with strangelet-like and planet-like masses are allowed. This was expected from the results of Ref. [38].

Although the usual criterion for static stability, $\partial M/\partial \epsilon_c \geq 0$, consistently works for one-fluid stars, it should not be taken for granted in two-fluid stars; only the frequency analysis can decide on their stability. Our results for the oscillation frequency of the fundamental mode for QM and DM cores in the admixed stars are written in terms of the linear frequency $f_{n=0}^{\rm QM/DM} = \omega_{n=0}^{\rm QM/DM}/(2\pi)$.

Table 1. Maximum masses $M^{\rm max}$ ($M_\odot$) and their corresponding minimum radii $R^{\rm min}$ (km) and maximum central energy densities $\epsilon_c^{\rm max}$ (GeV/fm^3) obtained for weakly interacting (wDM) pure dark matter stars.

EoSs	$\epsilon_c^{\rm max}$(wDM)	$M^{\rm max}$(wDM)	$R^{\rm min}$(wDM)
DM (m_D/GeV = 1)	~ 3	~ 0.63	~ 8.1
10	$\sim 3 \times 10^4$	$\sim 6.27 \times 10^{-3}$	$\sim 7.8 \times 10^{-2}$
50	$\sim 1.97 \times 10^7$	$\sim 2.50 \times 10^{-4}$	$\sim 3.2 \times 10^{-3}$
100	$\sim 3 \times 10^8$	$\sim 6.27 \times 10^{-5}$	$\sim 8.1 \times 10^{-4}$
200	$\sim 4.99 \times 10^9$	$\sim 1.56 \times 10^{-5}$	$\sim 2 \times 10^{-4}$
500	$\sim 1.97 \times 10^{11}$	$\sim 2.50 \times 10^{-6}$	$\sim 3 \times 10^{-5}$

Table 2. Same notation as in Table 1 but now for strongly interacting (sDM) pure dark matter stars.

EoSs	ϵ_c^{max}(sDM)	M^{max}(sDM)	R^{min}(sDM)
DM (m_D/GeV = 1)	$\sim 4.9 \times 10^{-5}$	$\sim 2.67 \times 10^2$	$\sim 1.87 \times 10^3$
10	~ 0.6	~ 2.67	~ 18.5
50	$\sim 4 \times 10^2$	$\sim 1.07 \times 10^{-1}$	$\sim 7.4 \times 10^{-1}$
100	$\sim 4.9 \times 10^3$	$\sim 2.67 \times 10^{-2}$	$\sim 18.7 \times 10^{-2}$
200	$\sim 8 \times 10^4$	$\sim 6.68 \times 10^{-3}$	$\sim 4.7 \times 10^{-2}$
500	$\sim 4 \times 10^6$	$\sim 1.07 \times 10^{-3}$	$\sim 7.5 \times 10^{-3}$

3.1. Admixtures of Quark Matter and Weakly ($y = 0.1$) Interacting Dark Matter

3.1.1. Solving the Two-Fluid TOV Equations

In Figure 1, we display the results obtained from solving the two-fluid TOV Equation (2) with the condition $p_{QM}(R_{QM}) = 0$ for different central energy densities of weakly interacting DM. One can easily see that only the solutions for $m_D = 1500$ GeV display sizable modifications on the QM stellar masses and radii. In particular, the case of $m_D = 500$ GeV suffers a marked reduction of 1.2 $M_\odot$ due to the very high DM central energy densities ($\sim 10^{11}$ GeV/fm^3). Additionally, the central QM densities increased considerably, by a factor ~ 7. Normally such QM densities would generate unstable pure quark stars with central energy densities at most ~ 1 GeV/fm^3 without the DM component.

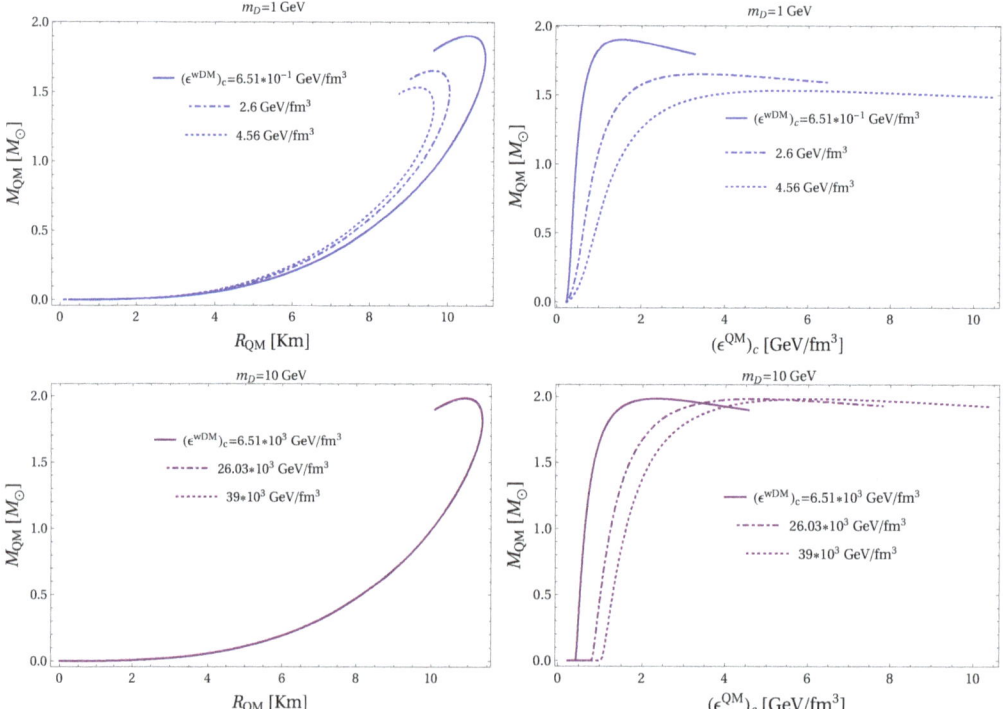

Figure 1. Cont.

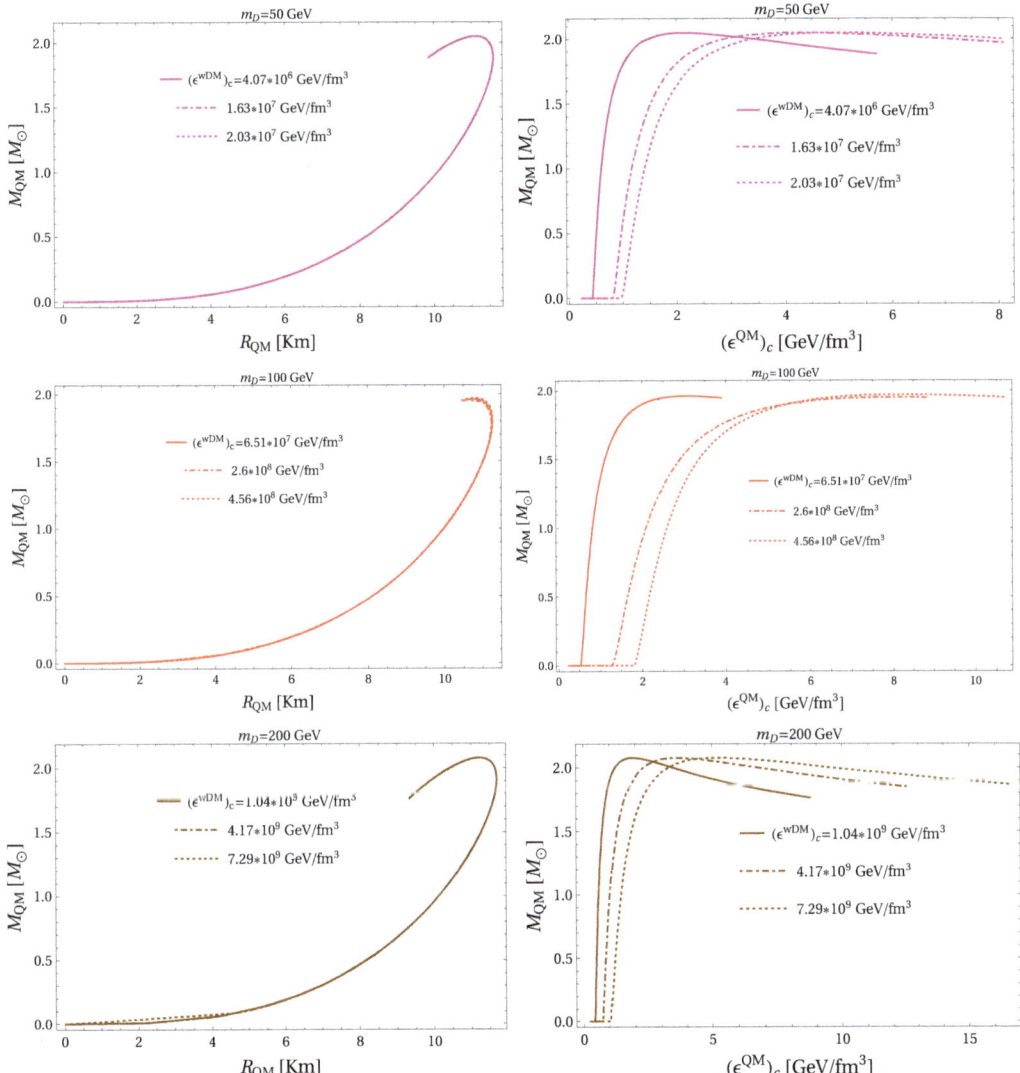

Figure 1. Cont.

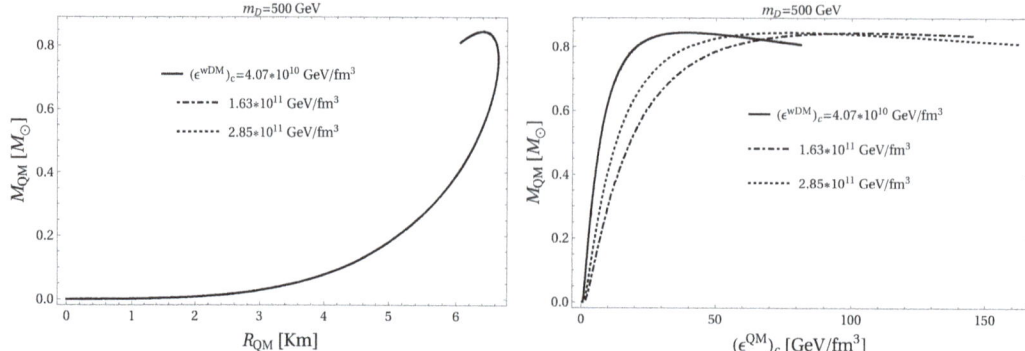

Figure 1. Each pair of panels with the same color for the plots displays the mass–radius relation and the mass as a function of the energy density for quark matter cores, i.e., $p_{QM}(R_{QM}) = 0$, with different amounts of weakly ($y = 0.1$) interacting dark matter (wDM) for dark fermion masses of $m_D = 1, 10, 50, 100, 200, 500$ GeV.

On the other hand, solutions for other values of the dark fermion mass show negligible effects. Again, these QM stars require higher central energy densities in order to compensate for the extra gravitational pull from the DM. Furthermore, solutions for all the dark fermion masses, except $m_D = 1$ and 500 GeV, develop a plateau at low QM stellar masses in the mass vs. central energy density plots, which became wider for higher DM central energy densities. Our calculations show that these QM cores have masses between 10^{-18} to 10^{-4} $M_\odot$ with radii between 10^{-4} and 10^{-2} km, depending on the value of the dark fermion mass. For example, $m_D \sim 10$ GeV mostly commonly produces stellar masses around 10^{-5} $M_\odot$ with radii of 10^{-3} km. As we increase the mass of the dark fermion, the values of M_{QM} and R_{QM} are reduced by many orders of magnitude. We note that all these stars satisfy the criterion $\partial M_{QM}/\partial \epsilon_c^{QM} > 0$ and can be tentatively considered stable objects, "dark strange planets" in analogy to the results of Ref. [33], and "dark strangelets".

Figure 2 shows our results from the two-fluid TOV Equation (2) with the condition $p_{DM}(R_{DM}) = 0$ for different values of QM central energy densities. The DM stars that are most affected by the presence of QM are the ones with $m_D = 1$ and 10 GeV. For stars with $m_D = 1$ GeV, the central QM energy densities are high enough to convert the usual behavior of pure DM stars in the mass–radius diagram into a self-bound-like behavior, making them more compact. To see this more quantitatively, Table 1 shows values of masses and radii for pure $y = 0.1$ DM stars for the whole range of dark fermion masses considered. One can see that the stellar masses and radii are slightly affected by the presence of QM near the maximum mass, but the radii of less massive DM stars are significantly modified. The same is true in the case of $m_D = 10$ GeV. For $m_D = 50, 100, 200, 500$ GeV, the DM high central energy densities completely dominate the QM contribution.

3.1.2. Solving the Coupled Radial Oscillation Equations

The solutions to the coupled radial pulsation Equations (4) and (5), assuming an oscillating QM core with fixed DM central energy density with boundary conditions (6) and (7), are shown in Figure 3. We show the zero-mode frequency as a function of central energy density and stellar mass.

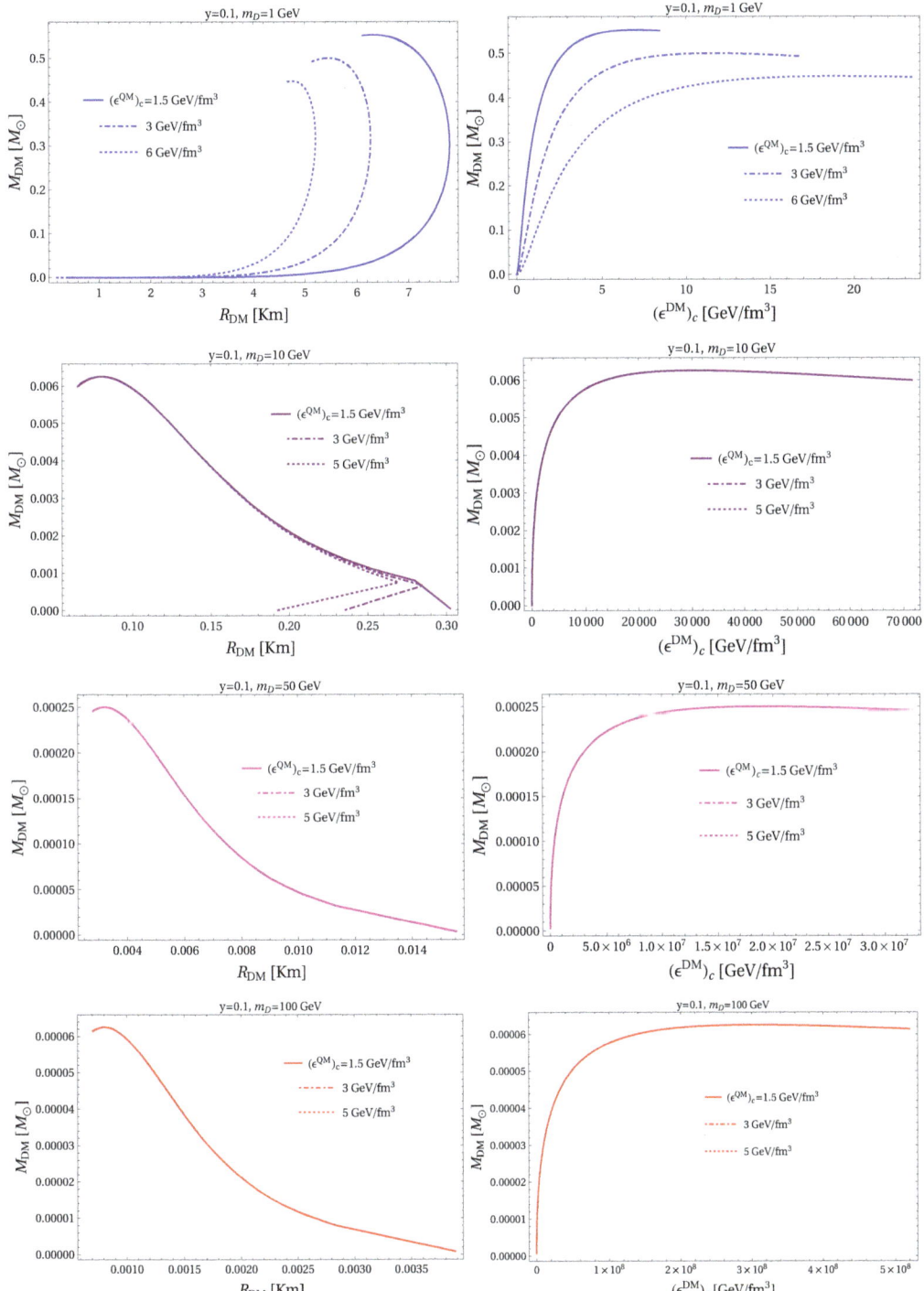

Figure 2. Cont.

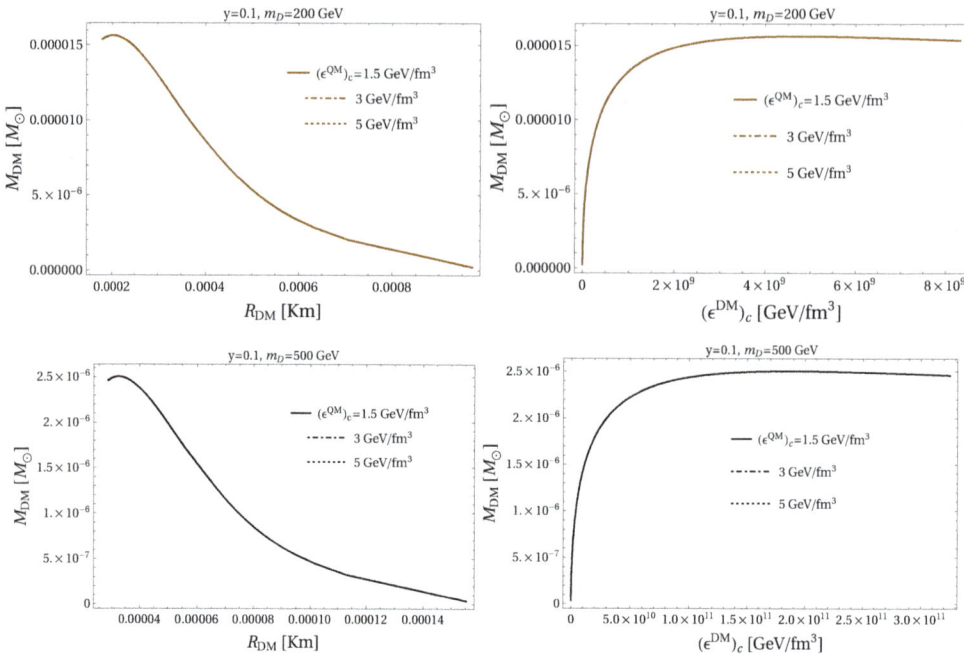

Figure 2. Same notation as in Figure 1 but now for dark matter cores satisfying $p_{DM}(R_{DM}) = 0$.

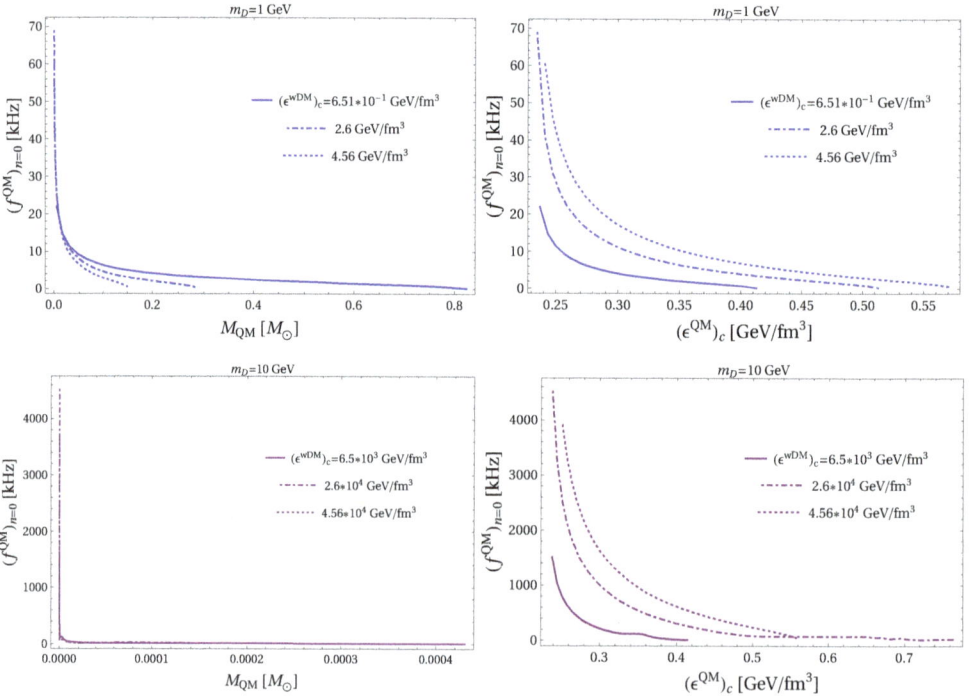

Figure 3. *Cont.*

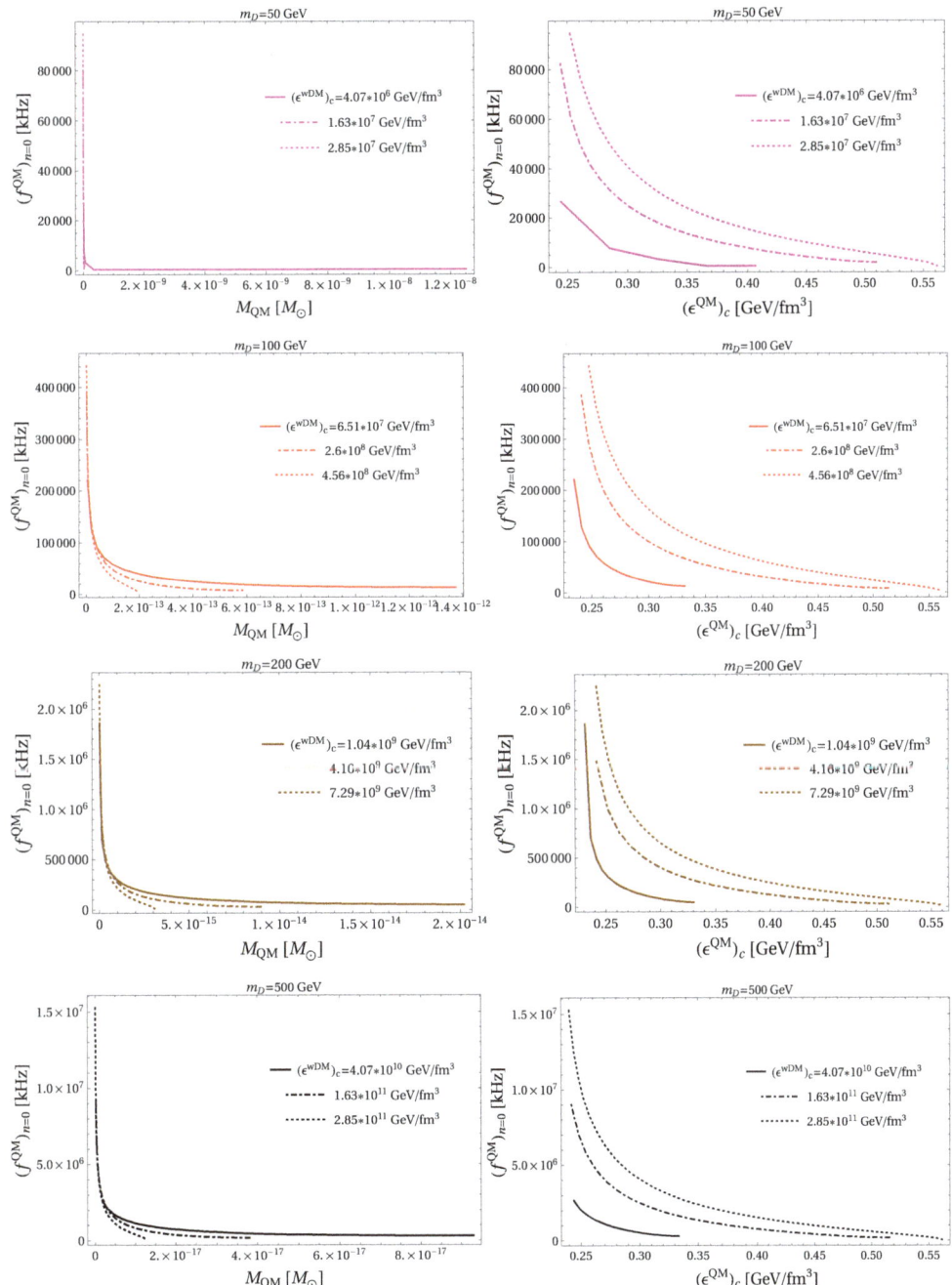

Figure 3. Fundamental-mode frequencies, $f_{n=0}$, versus gravitational masses, M, and central energy densities, ϵ_c, all for the oscillating QM cores with different values of central wDM and dark fermion masses m_D. Panels with the same color belong to the same class of admixed stars. Notice that the behavior in the planes $f_{n=0}(M)$ is highly dependent on the value of ϵ_c^{wDM}, especially for the low-mass QM cores. In a marked contrast, the changes are more modest in the $f_{n=0}(\epsilon_c)$ planes.

One can see in Figure 3 that the increments in the DM central energy density tend to delay the onset of radial instability (except in the case of $m_D = 10$ GeV), which happens when $f_{n=0}^{QM} = 0$. At the same time, this results in the maximum QM stellar masses in the admixed star becoming smaller (in some cases by a factor of 10). This opens a new stability window of ultra-low QM masses (when surrounded by DM) in the range between 10^{-18} and 10^{-4} $M_\odot$, depending on m_D, which correspond to the dark strange planets and strangelets discussed above.

In the same way, Figure 4 shows the results for the coupled radial pulsation Equations (4) and (5) assuming an oscillating DM core with boundary conditions (6) and (7) for different fixed central energy densities of QM. Clearly, the general behavior is qualitatively different, resembling the behavior of nucleonic stars. However, frequencies are very large, reaching $\sim 3 \times 10^5$ kHz, in contrast with the few and tens of kHz for hadronic and quark stars, respectively [50]. In almost all cases, the DM core is essentially unaffected by QM due to its very large central density, the exception being the case with $m_D = 1$ GeV. On the other hand, non-trivial effects show up in the $f_{n=0}^{DM}$ vs. M diagrams: the maximum stable masses do not correspond to the the ones in the mass–radius diagram of Figure 2; they are smaller.

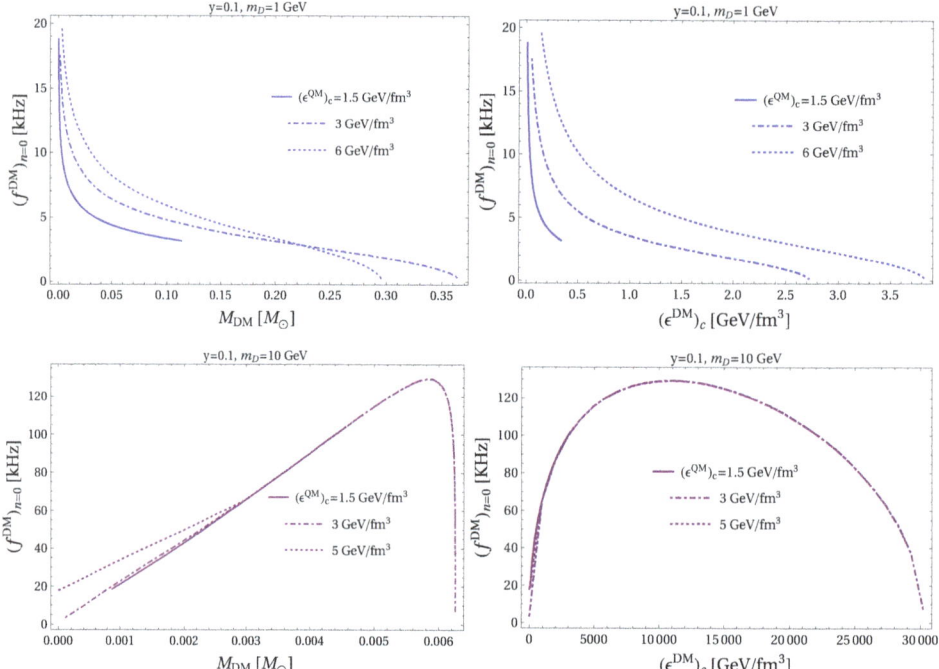

Figure 4. Cont.

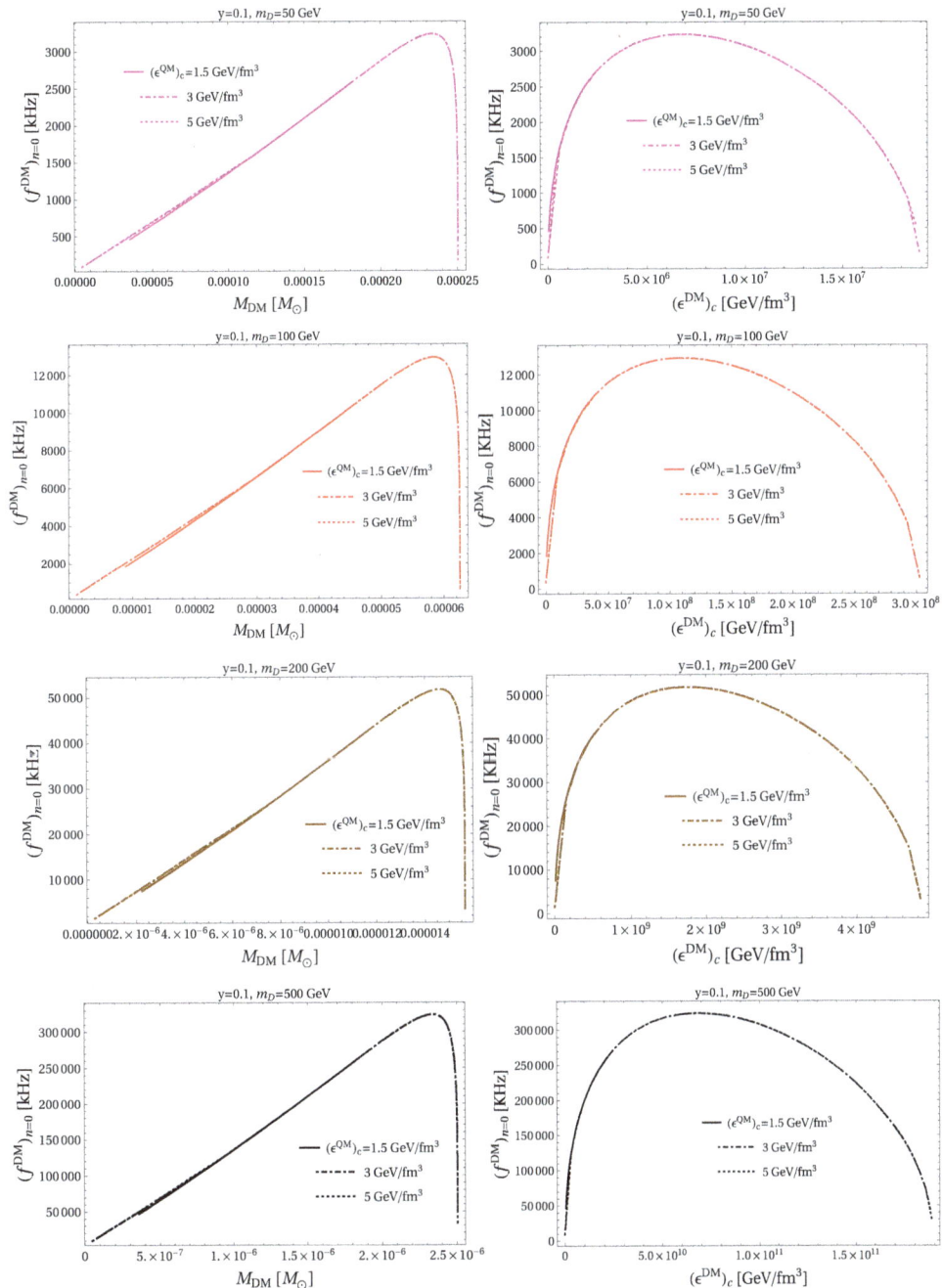

Figure 4. Same notation as in Figure 3 but now for oscillating wDM cores and different central QM energy densities. Notice that, although the frequencies still reach high values, e.g., $\sim 3 \times 10^5$ KHz for $m_D = 1$ GeV, the qualitative behavior in the $f_{n=0}(M)$ and $f_{n=0}(\epsilon_c)$ planes is markedly different and characteristic of dominating wDM in the admixed star for any amount of central QM.

Furthermore, in Figure 4 one sees that, for the case of $\epsilon_c^{QM} = 1.5$ GeV/fm^3 with $m_D = 1$ GeV, zero frequencies are not reached in the corresponding DM stars. After some point, the solutions become mechanically unstable in the sense of having negative QM pressure profiles inside the DM star. A similar phenomenon occurs for larger m_D, though it is much less visible. Systems exhibiting negative pressures, e.g., dark energy inducing an accelerated expansion of the universe, are not strictly prohibited but should be carefully interpreted. For instance, fluids develop negative-pressure states when stresses are applied for long periods. In the case of hybrid neutron stars with a first-order hadron–quark transition, oscillations to negative-pressure states may accelerate the nucleation of bubbles around the transition region, which, in the limit of large amplitudes, induce mechanical instabilities [51]. In our case of oscillating QM and DM cores with small amplitudes having negative-pressure profiles, the two-fluid TOV equations allows for their existence as hydrostatically-equilibrated configurations that are potentially unstable when disturbed by radial perturbations leading to the automatic collapse of the whole admixed star. In other words, negative-pressure interiors lead immediately to complex oscillation frequencies. Only by increasing $\epsilon_c^{QM/DM}$ do the instabilities disappear and one is able to find only real frequencies.

3.2. Admixtures of Quark Matter and Strongly ($y = 10^3$) Interacting Dark Matter

3.2.1. Solving the Two-Fluid TOV Equations

Similar to the case of weakly self-interacting DM, we solved the two-fluid TOV Equation (2) with the condition $p_{QM}(R_{QM}) = 0$ for different central energy densities of strongly self-interacting DM. We present our results in Figure 5. As in the weak limit for DM, in most of the cases stellar masses, radii and central energy densities of the QM core are not appreciably affected. However, for increasing DM central energy densities, some relevant variations occur. In particular, when $m_D = 1, 100, 200$ GeV, the maximum QM central energy densities are increased by a factor of $\sim$20. The cases with $m_D = 10, 50$ GeV show sizable variations of the masses and radii, especially near the maximum mass, where the presence of DM reduces the QM core masses down to $\sim$0.4 $M_\odot$. Interestingly, in the case of $m_D = 10$ GeV, the central QM energy density is almost unaffected by DM, whereas, for $m_D = 50$ GeV, it is dramatically increased. In the case with $m_D = 500$ GeV, the QM masses and radii increase by any amount of DM, and the QM central energy density is augmented by a factor of 10. Analogously to what we have seen before, in the cases with $m_D = 50$ to 500 GeV, there are plateaus whose widths increase with m_D.

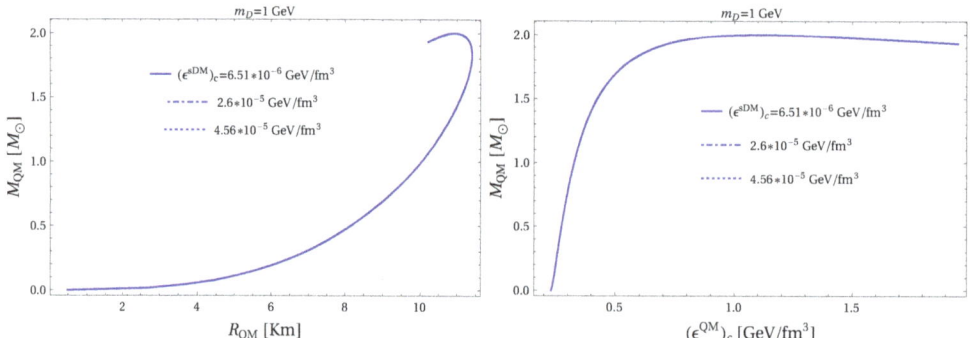

Figure 5. Cont.

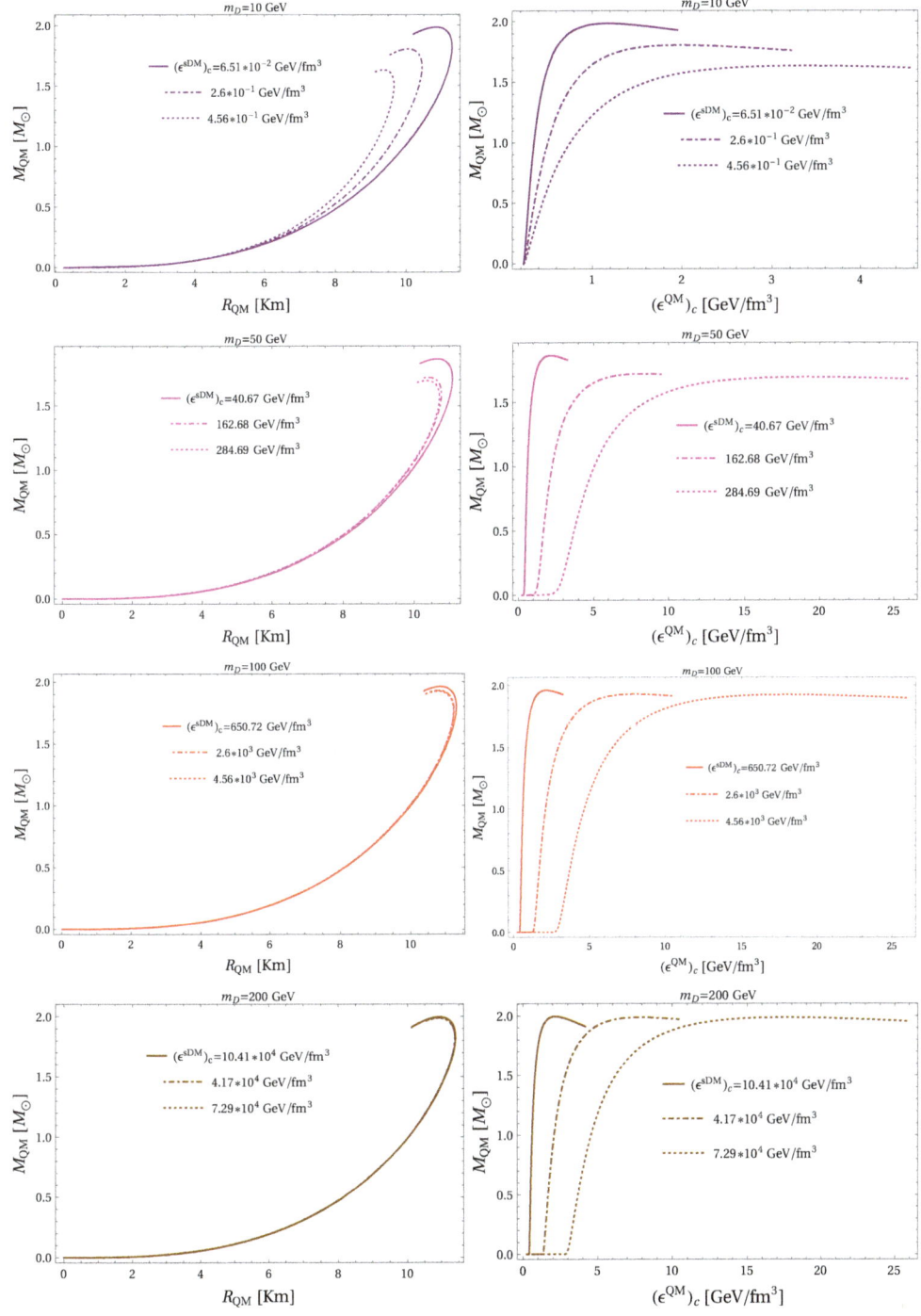

Figure 5. Cont.

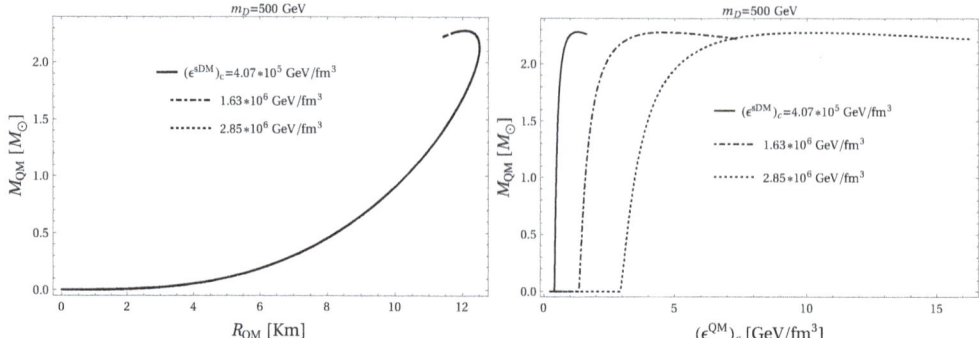

Figure 5. Mass–radius and mass–energy density relationships for QM cores with different amounts of strongly ($y = 10^3$) interacting dark matter (sDM) at the center of the admixed stars. Different values for the dark fermion masses m_D are considered and results characterized by the same color. Notice that the effects of sDM are mainly for high-mass stars and especially marked for $m_D = 10$ GeV.

In order to study the structure of the opposite case, we solved the two-fluid TOV Equations (2) with the condition $p_{DM}(R_{DM}) = 0$ for different central energy densities of QM, as displayed in Figure 6. Pure $y = 10^3$ DM stars display the same qualitative behavior as in the case of $m_D = 500$ GeV, since, in this case, their masses and radii are almost unaffected by any amount of QM due to very large DM central energy densities. The same is true for $m_D = 200$ GeV. See also Table 1.

Although not noticeable in Figure 6, when $m_D = 1$ GeV, our calculations show that the QM in the DM core yields higher masses (not shown in the figure) that are in contradiction with the negative gradient of pressure required by the TOV equations. This happens, because we are considering unstable QM central energy densities for the DM star, as can be seen in Figure 5, which are manifested by producing increasing profiles of pressure then leading to mechanical instabilities associated with complex frequencies, thus destabilizing the whole admixed star. When $m_D = 10$ GeV, we find a self-bound-like behavior for the DM star. This occurs since the DM and QM central energy densities are almost equal in the admixed star, and, in this case, the QM component dominates, modifying the behavior in the mass–radius diagram. As before, the central DM densities are increased by a factor of 10. The cases with $m_D = 50, 100$ GeV display a behavior that is a mixture of dark and quark matter, where QM mainly affects the sector of lower DM stellar masses, and the structure remains almost the same near the maximum mass. There, the central DM energy densities are almost the same since the DM energy densities are enormous compared the QM ones.

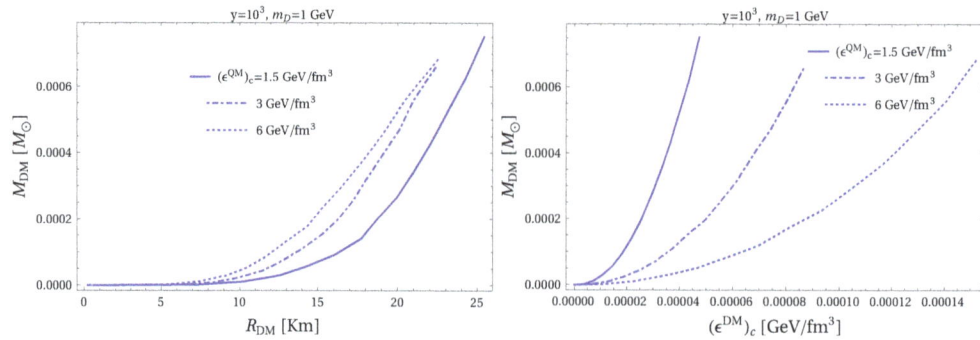

Figure 6. *Cont.*

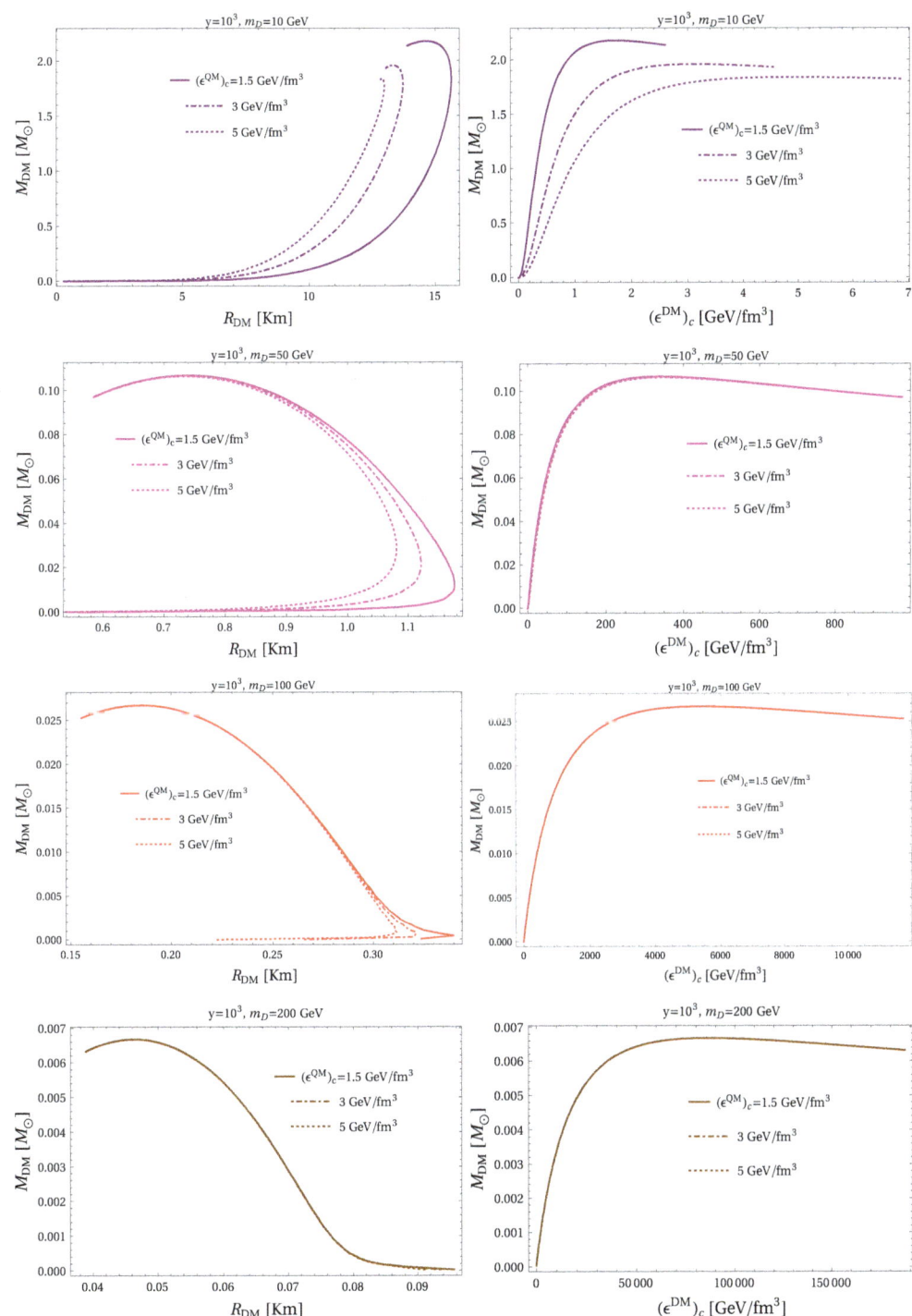

Figure 6. Cont.

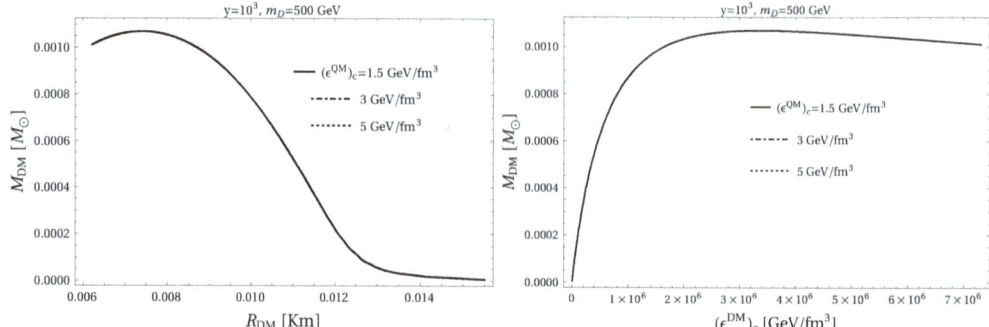

Figure 6. Mass–radius and mass–energy density relations obtained for sDM cores for different fermion masses m_D (indicated by different colors) with increasing amounts of QM at the centers of the admixed stars. Notice that the competition between sDM and QM densities in some cases allows for the presence of very small stars, which are not present in the one-fluid case, producing qualitatively different behavior in the mass–radius relations of sDM stars, especially for low m_D.

3.2.2. Solving the Coupled Radial Oscillation Equations

Finally, we solved the coupled radial pulsation Equations (4) and (5) assuming an oscillating QM core in the admixed star with the boundary conditions (6) and (7) for different fixed central energy densities of strongly interacting DM. The results are displayed in Figure 7. We found that only the case of $m_D = 1$ GeV was unaffected by strongly self-interacting DM. As we increased m_D, the fundamental frequency was strongly affected. In fact, as occurred in the QM cases with weakly self-interacting DM, only low-mass QM stars survived radial oscillations and behaved as strange quark planets and strangelets. The oscillation frequencies of these objects can reach $\sim 10^5$ kHz for $m_D = 500$ GeV.

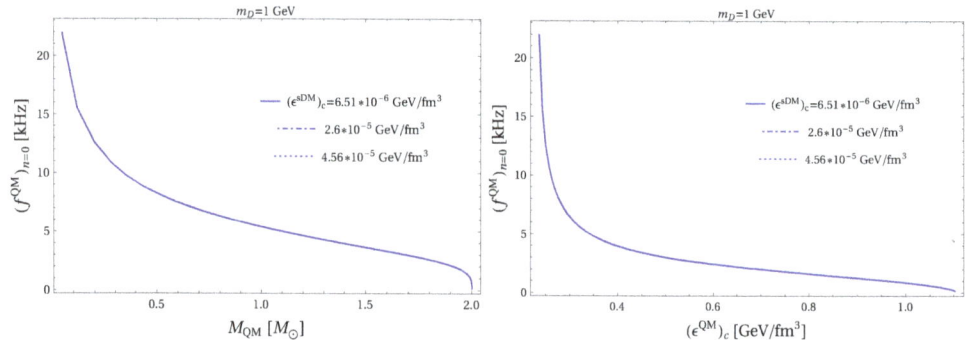

Figure 7. Cont.

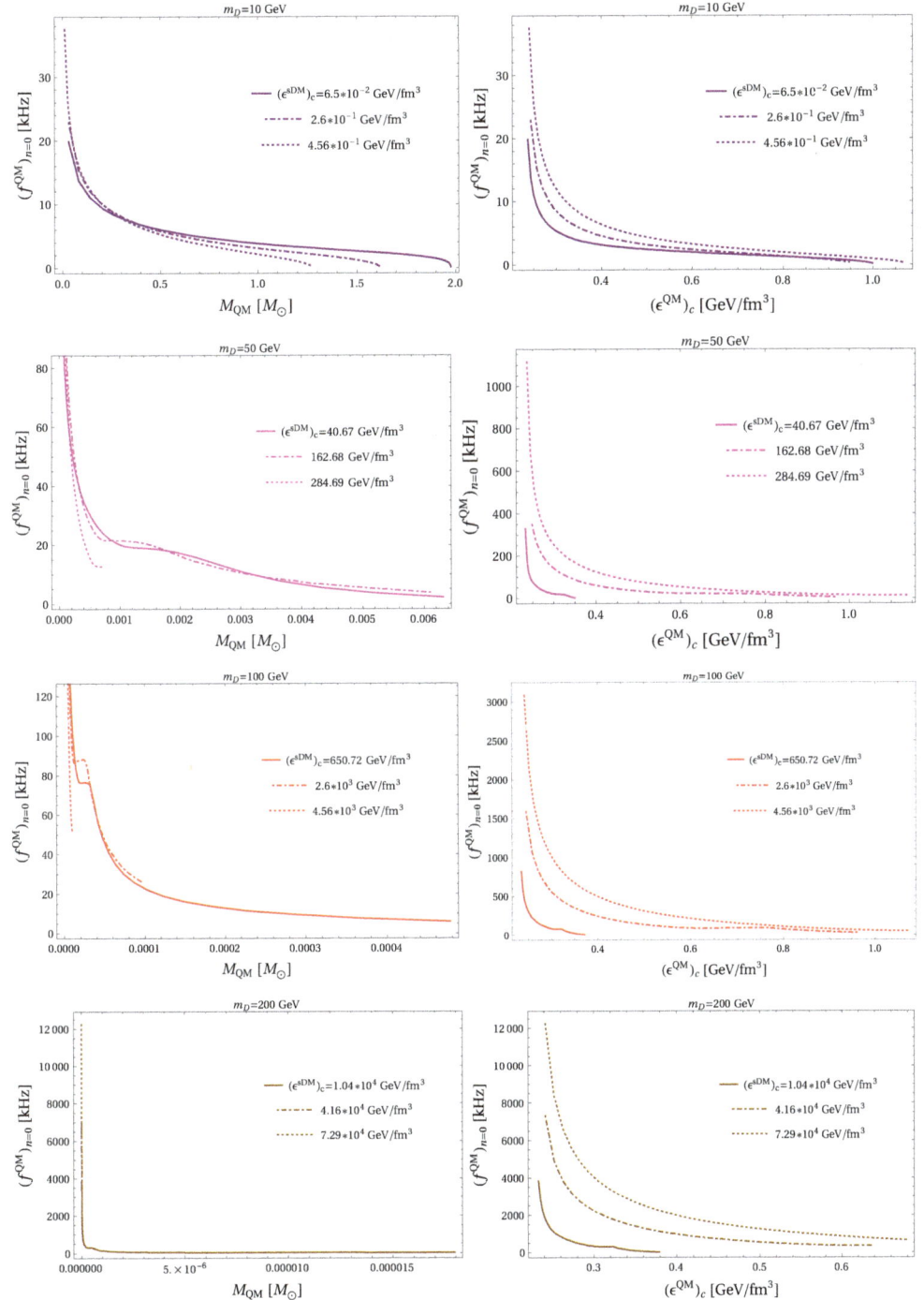

Figure 7. Cont.

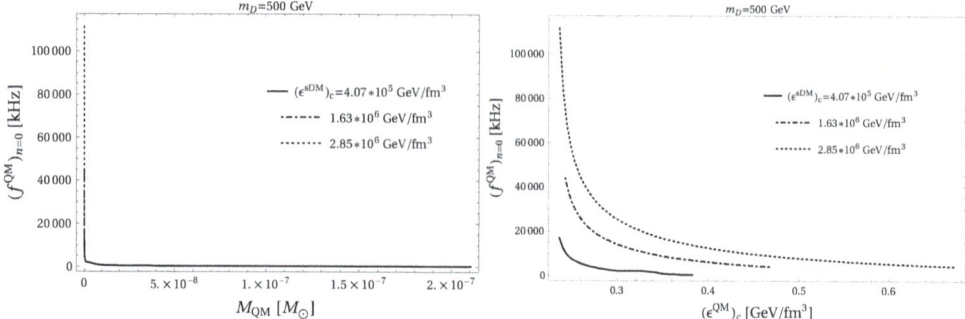

Figure 7. Fundamental-mode frequency, $f_{n=0}$, versus QM core masses and central energy densities with different amounts of sDM for increasing values of the dark fermion masses, m_D, denoted by different colors. It can be seen that the densities of sDM for $m_D = 1$ GeV have almost no effect on the stability of the corresponding QM cores. Nevertheless, as one increases m_D, the stable QM core masses are reduced to lower and lower values and require higher QM central densities.

In Figure 8, we show our results[6] after solving the coupled radial pulsation Equations (4) and (5), assuming an oscillating DM core with boundary conditions (6) and (7) for different central energy densities of QM. In correspondence with the results of Figure 6 for the cases $m_D = 1, 10$ GeV, only a small family of DM stars survived the radial oscillation analysis for low mass stars. These DM stars increase their stability as long as one increases the QM component. The qualitative behavior resembles that of a strange star. This occurs due to the high QM central energy densities compared to the DM ones, with the QM component dominating the stability of the admixed star. On the other hand, the cases with $m_D = 50, 100, 200, 500$ GeV display the standard behavior of pure $y = 10^3$ DM stars due to the very high DM central energy densities. Interestingly, the same phenomenon of increasing stability for higher central QM energy densities occurs in all these cases. The physical picture indicates that low QM central energy densities support a small subset of DM stars against gravitational collapse. As we increase the central energy densities, the admixed star supports higher and higher central DM energy densities.

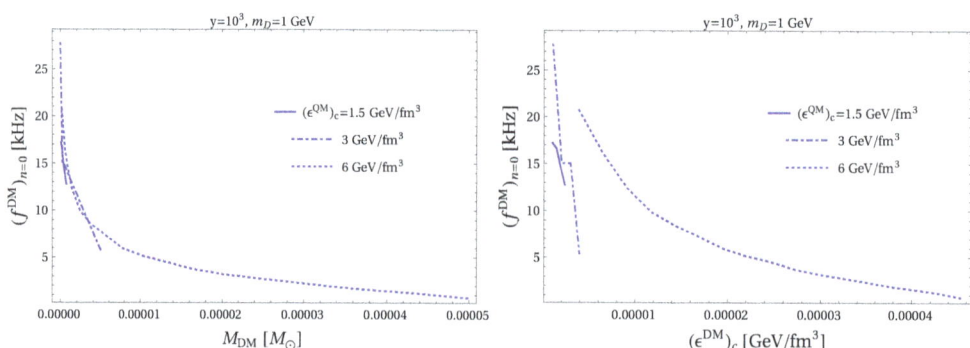

Figure 8. Cont.

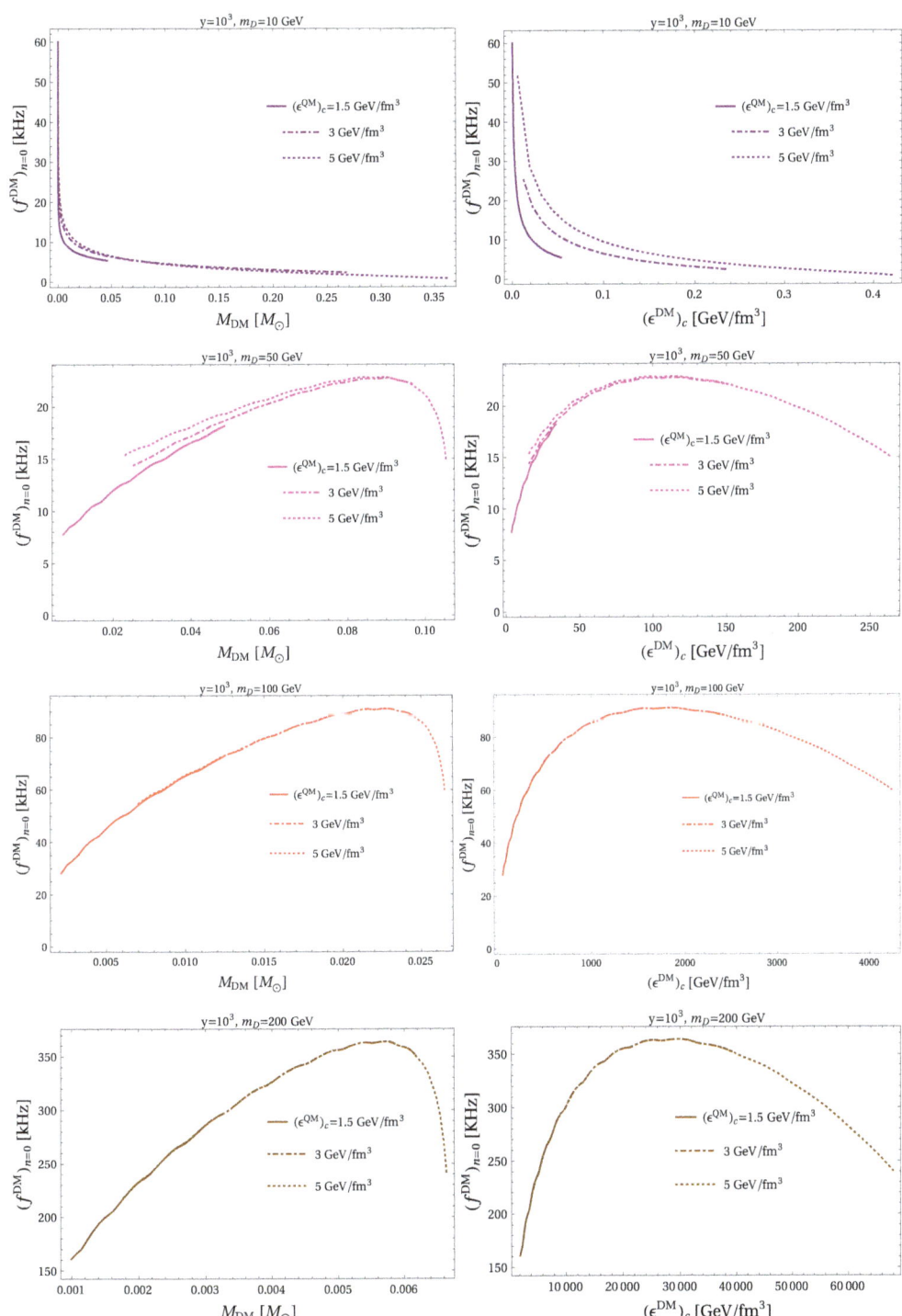

Figure 8. Cont.

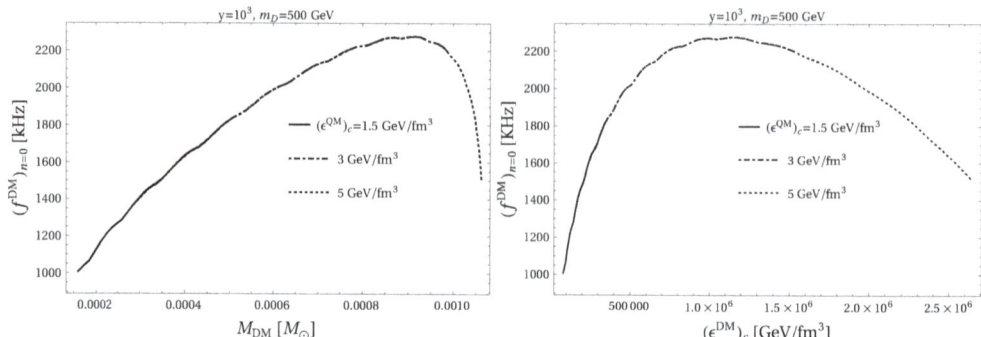

Figure 8. Same notation as in Figure 7, but now for the oscillating core composed of sDM corresponding to increasing m_D (with different colors) and increasing values of central QM densities. Notice the changing qualitative behavior when QM densities dominate over sDM for low $m_D = 1, 10$ GeV but the opposite happening for larger m_D, where QM only allows for more stable sDM cores.

4. Summary and Outlook

We have studied the stability and main global features of strange quark stars admixed with fermionic dark matter in a large parameter space, allowing dark fermion masses from 1 to 500 GeV and considering weakly and strongly self-interacting dark matter. For simplicity, cold quark matter was described within the MIT bag model with $B^{1/4} = 145$ MeV which, in the one-fluid case, produces strange quark stars.

After solving the two-fluid TOV equations, we computed the associated stellar structure. We found that, depending on m_D and the interaction parameter y, some of the obtained QM and DM stars display significant modifications of their stellar masses and radii, whereas others show no change at all. Furthermore, some of the DM stars display a self-bound-like behavior in the mass–radius diagram. In most situations, the central QM and DM densities are increased by the presence of the other component in the admixed star.

For the radial pulsation analysis, a full general-relativistic two-fluid Sturm–Liouville-like problem should, in principle, be solved. Instead, inspired by the way one usually solves the two-fluid TOV equations by separating the total pressure and energy density into QM and DM components, we developed a framework where we separate the total Lagrangian variables entering the oscillation equations into QM and DM contributions. This method allowed us to solve the problem, assuming that we disturb only one component and the other is affected only indirectly.

Our calculations indicate that the static stability criterion $\partial M_{QM/DM}/\partial \epsilon_c^{QM/DM} \geq 0$ alone might produce misleading and incomplete results when applied to two-fluid stars. We found that, in the case of QM stars admixed with DM, predominantly in the case of $y = 0.1$, only very small QM stellar masses are dynamically stable leading to *dark strange planets* and *dark strangelets*. On the other hand, DM stars are mainly affected when small values of m_D are considered, since larger dark fermion masses induce ultra-dense cores for which the QM contribution is almost negligible.

Although our results are still very sensitive, both to the dark fermion mass m_D and the kind of self-interaction involved in the dark sector, whose scale is encoded in the dimensionless variable y, there is hope that the parameter space can be dramatically constrained by gravitational wave events, as discussed recently in Ref. [52].

In a future publications, we plan to refine our description using an equation of state obtained from perturbative QCD [17]. It would also be interesting to explore the effects of adding a nuclear mantle to our dark strange planets.

Author Contributions: J.C.J. and E.S.F. contributed significantly to this work. All authors have read and agreed to the published version of the manuscript.

Funding: This work is a part of the project INCT-FNA Proc. No. 464898/2014-5. J.C.J. acknowledges the support of Fundação de Amparo à Pesquisa do Estado de São Paulo (FAPESP), Grants No. 2020/07791-7 and 2018/24720-6. E.S.F. is partially supported by Coordenação de Aperfeicoamento de Pessoal de Nível Superior (CAPES), Finance Code 001; Conselho Nacional de Desenvolvimento Científico e Tecnológico (CNPq); Fundação de Amparo à Pesquisa do Estado do Rio de Janeiro (FAPERJ).

Conflicts of Interest: The authors declare no conflict of interest.

Notes

1. In fact, the EoS considered corresponds to the most compact of three cases presented in tabulated format in Ref. [18].
2. Equivalently, the total radius R and total mass M of the whole admixed star can be determined by the condition of the total pressure $p(R) = 0$ and $M = m(R)$, where $m(r) = m_{QM}(r) + m_{DM}(r)$. In any case, our code for the two-fluid TOV equations matches the results of Ref. [38] very well.
3. This general-relativistic formalism was studied many years ago in different papers (see e.g. Ref. [49] and references therein) when investigating matter with different properties in compact-star interiors, e.g. one fluid being a proton (neutron) superconductor (superfluid) and the other being normal nuclear matter.
4. The physical and dimensionless definitions have the same mathematical form after being rescaled by an arbitrary factor.
5. In the limit of one-fluid stars, our code for radial oscillations agrees very well with previous works, see e.g., Ref. [48].
6. Some results in this figure display a non-smooth behavior associated only with numerical limitations when using standard root-finding routines to obtain the frequencies for dimensionless central sDM ($\sim 10^{-8}$) and QM (reaching $\sim 10^{-14}$ for $m_D = 500$ GeV) values, i.e., being different by many orders of magnitude, very small, and sensitive to different numerical methods. For these reasons, systematic differences are introduced and manifest as non-smooth curves due to variations in numerical precision when obtaining the dimensionless frequencies with values around 10^{-4} for large m_D, which otherwise would require very time-consuming computations. It should be noted that the same root-finding routines work very well when obtaining the other results shown in this work. In future studies, we propose to use improved theoretical and numerical approaches.

References

1. Glendenning, N.K. *Compact Stars–Nuclear Physics, Particle Physics and General Relativity*; Springer: New York, NY, USA, 2000.
2. Schaffner-Bielich, J. *Compact Star Physics*; Cambridge University Press: Cambridge, MA, USA, 2020.
3. Ivanenko, D.D.; Kurdgelaidze, D.F. Hypothesis concerning quark stars. *Astrophysics* **1965**, *1*, 251–252. [CrossRef]
4. Itoh, N. Hydrostatic Equilibrium of Hypothetical Quark Stars. *Prog. Theor. Phys.* **1970**, *44*, 291. [CrossRef]
5. Witten, E. Cosmic Separation of Phases. *Phys. Rev. D* **1984**, *30*, 272–285. [CrossRef]
6. Alcock, C.; Farhi, E.; Olinto, A. Strange stars. *Astrophys. J.* **1986**, *310*, 261–272. [CrossRef]
7. Haensel, P.; Zdunik, J.L.; Schaeffer, R. Strange quark stars. *Astron. Astrophys.* **1986**, *160*, 121–128.
8. Farhi, E.; Jaffe, R.L. Strange Matter. *Phys. Rev. D* **1984**, *30*, 2379. [CrossRef]
9. Buballa, M.; Dexheimer, V.; Drago, A.; Fraga, E.; Haensel, P.; Mishustin, I.; Pagliara, G.; Schaffner-Bielich, J.; Schramm, S.; Sedrakian, A.; et al. EMMI rapid reaction task force meeting on quark matter in compact stars. *J. Phys. G* **2014**, *41*, 123001. [CrossRef]
10. Bertone, G.; Hooper, D.; Silk, J. Particle dark matter: Evidence, candidates and constraints. *Phys. Rept.* **2005**, *405*, 279–390. [CrossRef]
11. Betoule, M.E.A.; Kessler, R.; Guy, J.; Mosher, J.; Hardin, D.; Biswas, R.; Astier, P.; El-Hage, P.; Konig, M.; Kuhlmann, S.; et al. Improved cosmological constraints from a joint analysis of the SDSS-II and SNLS supernova samples. *Astron. Astrophys.* **2014**, *568*, A22. [CrossRef]
12. Ade, P.A.; Aghanim, N.; Armitage-Caplan, C.; Arnaud, M.; Ashdown, M.; Atrio-Barandela, F.; Aumont, J.; Baccigalupi, C.; Banday, A.J.; Barreiro, R.B.; et al. Planck 2013 results. XVI. Cosmological parameters. *Astron. Astrophys.* **2014**, *571*, A16.
13. Deliyergiyev, M.; Popolo, A.D.; Tolos, L.; Delliou, M.L.; Lee, X.; Burgio, F. Dark compact objects: An extensive overview. *Phys. Rev. D* **2019**, *99*, 063015. [CrossRef]
14. Fraga, E.S.; Pisarski, R.D.; Schaffner-Bielich, J. Small, dense quark stars from perturbative QCD. *Phys. Rev. D* **2001**, *63*, 121702. [CrossRef]
15. Fraga, E.S.; Romatschke, P. The Role of quark mass in cold and dense perturbative QCD. *Phys. Rev. D* **2005**, *71*, 105014. [CrossRef]
16. Kurkela, A.; Romatschke, P.; Vuorinen, A. Cold Quark Matter. *Phys. Rev. D* **2010**, *81*, 105021. [CrossRef]
17. Fraga, E.S.; Kurkela, A.; Vuorinen, A. Interacting quark matter equation of state for compact stars. *Astrophys. J. Lett.* **2014**, *781*, L25. [CrossRef]
18. Kurkela, A.; Fraga, E.S.; Schaffner-Bielich, J.; Vuorinen, A. Constraining neutron star matter with Quantum Chromodynamics. *Astrophys. J.* **2014**, *789*, 127. [CrossRef]

19. Fraga, E.S.; Kurkela, A.; Vuorinen, A. Neutron star structure from QCD. *Eur. Phys. J. A* **2016**, *52*, 49. [CrossRef]
20. Ghisoiu, I.; Gorda, T.; Kurkela, A.; Romatschke, P.; Säppi, M.; Vuorinen, A. On high-order perturbative calculations at finite density. *Nucl. Phys. B* **2017**, *915*, 102–118. [CrossRef]
21. Annala, E.; Gorda, T.; Kurkela, A.; Vuorinen, A. Gravitational-wave constraints on the neutron-star-matter Equation of State. *Phys. Rev. Lett.* **2018**, *120*, 172703. [CrossRef] [PubMed]
22. Gorda, T.; Kurkela, A.; Romatschke, P.; Säppi, M.; Vuorinen, A. Next-to-Next-to-Next-to-Leading Order Pressure of Cold Quark Matter: Leading Logarithm. *Phys. Rev. Lett.* **2018**, *121*, 202701. [CrossRef] [PubMed]
23. Annala, E.; Gorda, T.; Kurkela, A.; Nättilä, J.; Vuorinen, A. Evidence for quark-matter cores in massive neutron stars. *Nat. Phys.* **2020**, *16*, 907–910. [CrossRef]
24. Gorda, T.; Kurkela, A.; Paatelainen, R.; Säppi, S.; Vuorinen, A. Cold quark matter at NNNLO: Soft contributions. *arXiv* **2021**, arXiv:2103.07427.
25. Ciarcelluti, P.; Sandin, F. Have neutron stars a dark matter core? *Phys. Lett. B* **2011**, *695*, 19–21. [CrossRef]
26. Leung, S.C.; Chu, M.C.; Lin, L.M. Dark-matter admixed neutron stars. *Phys. Rev. D* **2011**, *84*, 107301. [CrossRef]
27. Leung, S.C.; Chu, M.C.; Lin, L.M. Equilibrium Structure and Radial Oscillations of Dark Matter Admixed Neutron Stars. *Phys. Rev. D* **2012**, *85*, 103528. [CrossRef]
28. Li, A.; Huang, F.; Xu, R.X. Too massive neutron stars: The role of dark matter? *Astropart. Phys.* **2012**, *37*, 70–74. [CrossRef]
29. Xiang, Q.F.; Jiang, W.Z.; Zhang, D.R.; Yang, R.Y. Effects of fermionic dark matter on properties of neutron stars. *Phys. Rev. C* **2014**, *89*, 025803. [CrossRef]
30. Ellis, J.; Hütsi, G.; Kannike, K.; Marzola, L.; Raidal, M.; Vaskonen, V. Dark Matter Effects On Neutron Star Properties. *Phys. Rev. D* **2018**, *97*, 123007. [CrossRef]
31. Karkevandi, D.R.; Shakeri, S.; Sagun, V.; Ivanytskyi, O. Bosonic Dark Matter in Neutron Stars and its Effect on Gravitational Wave Signal. *arXiv* **2021**, arXiv:2109.03801.
32. Popolo, A.D.; Delliou, M.L.; Deliyergiyev, M. Neutron Stars and Dark Matter. *Universe* **2020**, *6*, 222. [CrossRef]
33. Tolos, L.; Schaffner-Bielich, J. Dark Compact Planets. *Phys. Rev. D* **2015**, *92*, 123002; Erratum in *Phys. Rev. D* **2021**, *103*, 109901. [CrossRef]
34. Demorest, P.; Pennucci, T.; Ransom, S.; Roberts, M.; Hessels, J. Shapiro Delay Measurement of A Two Solar Mass Neutron Star. *Nature* **2010**, *467*, 1081–1083. [CrossRef] [PubMed]
35. Antoniadis, J.; Freire, P.C.C.; Wex, N.; Tauris, T.M.; Lynch, R.S.; van Kerkwijk, M.H.; Kramer, M.; Bassa, C.; Dhillon, V.S.; Driebe, T.; et al. A Massive Pulsar in a Compact Relativistic Binary. *Science* **2013**, *340*, 6131. [CrossRef] [PubMed]
36. Chandrasekhar, S. Dynamical Instability of Gaseous Masses Approaching the Schwarzschild Limit in General Relativity. *Phys. Rev. Lett.* **1964**, *12*, 114. [CrossRef]
37. Shapiro, S.L.; Teukolsky, S.A. *Black Holes, White Dwarfs, and Neutron Stars: The Physics of Compact Objects*; Wiley: New York, NY, USA, 1983.
38. Mukhopadhyay, P.; Schaffner-Bielich, J. Quark stars admixed with dark matter. *Phys. Rev. D* **2016**, *93*, 083009. [CrossRef]
39. Panotopoulos, G.; Lopes, I. Radial oscillations of strange quark stars admixed with condensed dark matter. *Phys. Rev. D* **2017**, *96*, 083013. [CrossRef]
40. Panotopoulos, G.; Lopes, I. Radial oscillations of strange quark stars admixed with fermionic dark matter. *Phys. Rev. D* **2018**, *98*, 083001. [CrossRef]
41. Kain, B. Radial oscillations and stability of multiple-fluid compact stars. *Phys. Rev. D* **2020**, *102*, 023001. [CrossRef]
42. Kain, B. Dark matter admixed neutron stars. *Phys. Rev. D* **2021**, *103*, 043009. [CrossRef]
43. Narain, G.; Schaffner-Bielich, J.; Mishustin, I.N. Compact stars made of fermionic dark matter. *Phys. Rev. D* **2006**, *74*, 063003. [CrossRef]
44. Misner, C.W.; Thorne, K.S.; Wheeler, J.A. *Gravitation*; W. H. Freeman: San Francisco, CA, USA, 1973.
45. Chanmugam, G. Radial oscillations of zero-temperature white dwarfs and neutron stars below nuclear densities. *Astrophys. J.* **1977**, *217*, 799. [CrossRef]
46. Glass, E.N.; Lindblom, L. The radial oscillations of neutron stars. *Astrophys. J. Suppl. Ser.* **1983**, *53*, 93. [CrossRef]
47. Gondek, D.; Haensel, P.; Zdunik, J.L. Radial pulsations and stability of protoneutron stars. *Astron. Astrophys.* **1997**, *325*, 217–227.
48. Kokkotas, K.D.; Ruoff, J. Radial oscillations of relativistic stars. *Astron. Astrophys.* **2001**, *366*, 565. [CrossRef]
49. Comer, G.L.; Langlois, D.; Lin, L.M. Quasinormal modes of general relativistic superfluid neutron stars. *Phys. Rev. D* **1999**, *60*, 104025. [CrossRef]
50. Jiménez, J.C.; Fraga, E.S. Radial oscillations of quark stars from perturbative QCD. *Phys. Rev. D* **2019**, *100*, 114041. [CrossRef]
51. Kapusta, J.I.; Gale, C. *Finite-Temperature Field Theory: Principles and Applications*; Cambridge University Press: New York, NY, USA, 2006.
52. Wystub, S.; Schaffner-Bielich, J.; Christian, J.; Dengler, Y. Constraining exotic compact stars composed of bosonic and fermionic dark matter with gravitational wave events. *arXiv* **2021**, arXiv:2110.12972.

Article

The Macro-Physics of the Quark-Nova: Astrophysical Implications

Rachid Ouyed

Department of Physics and Astronomy, The University of Calgary, Calgary, AB T2N 1N4, Canada; rouyed@ucalgary.ca

Abstract: A quark-nova is a hypothetical stellar evolution branch where a neutron star converts explosively into a quark star. Here, we discuss the intimate coupling between the micro-physics and macro-physics of the quark-nova and provide a prescription for how to couple the Burn-UD code to the stellar evolution code in order to simulate neutron-star-to-quark-star burning at stellar scales and estimate the resulting energy release and ejecta. Once formed, the thermal evolution of the proto-quark star follows. We found much higher peak neutrino luminosities (>10^{55} erg/s) and a higher energy neutrino (i.e., harder) spectrum than previous stellar evolution studies of proto-neutron stars. We derived the neutrino counts that observatories such as Super-Kamiokande-III and Halo-II should expect and suggest how these can differentiate between a supernova and a quark-nova. Due to the high peak neutrino luminosities, neutrino pair annihilation can deposit as much as 10^{52} ergs in kinetic energy in the matter overlaying the neutrinosphere, yielding relativistic quark-nova ejecta. We show how the quark-nova could help us understand many still enigmatic high-energy astrophysical transients, such as super-luminous supernovae, gamma-ray bursts and fast radio bursts.

Keywords: neutron stars; nuclear matter aspects; quark deconfinement; quark-gluon plasma production; phase-transition

Citation: Ouyed, R. The Macro-Physics of the Quark-Nova: Astrophysical Implications. *Universe* **2022**, *8*, 322. https://doi.org/10.3390/universe8060322

Academic Editors: Veronica Dexheimer and Rodrigo Negreiros

Received: 21 March 2022
Accepted: 30 May 2022
Published: 9 June 2022

Publisher's Note: MDPI stays neutral with regard to jurisdictional claims in published maps and institutional affiliations.

Copyright: © 2022 by the author. Licensee MDPI, Basel, Switzerland. This article is an open access article distributed under the terms and conditions of the Creative Commons Attribution (CC BY) license (https://creativecommons.org/licenses/by/4.0/).

1. Introduction

1.1. The Energetic Problem in Astrophysics

High-energy astrophysics suffers from an energy problem. The total integrated luminosity observed in the universe cannot be completely accounted for by existing theoretical models. In almost all astrophysical explosive events that generate 10^{53} ergs or more in kinetic energy and radiation, the engine remains elusive. For example, the energies observed in core-collapse supernovae [1] or gamma-ray bursts cannot be reproduced consistently with computer simulations [2]. Specifically, in the case of core-collapse supernovae, computer simulations cannot form robust explosions from first principles for all the relevant progenitor masses [1]. In the case of even more energetic phenomena, such as superluminous supernova, that have kinetic energies of around 10^{52} ergs, the engine remains even more elusive. Similar issues appear with gamma-ray bursts, which suffer from related energy budget problems. Recently, the associated gamma-ray burst observation of the gravitational wave [3] of a neutron star merger showed the same energy budget problems, where the observed luminosity was much milder than for other known GRBs. These anomalies suggest the need for a novel source that can "balance" this budget problem and can be accounted for by the physics required to fix it.

There are various observational phenomena that indicate the explosion of a neutron star. For example, most models that seek to explain the large luminosities and kinetic energy of super-luminous supernovae do so by using a "point source" that injects energy into an envelope of (1–20) $M_\odot$, whether this point source is a core-collapse supernova, or a magnetar [4]. However, in the case of transforming a core-collapse supernova's energy into luminosity by shocking it with a 1 $M_\odot$ envelope or "wall", it is necessary to explain the source of the envelope itself, which is a non-trivial problem. In the case of a magnetar, it is necessary to assume almost 100 percent efficiency of conversion between the rotational energy and the luminosity/kinetic energy of the envelope [4]. Furthermore, it is necessary to explain the source of the large magnetic field.

1.2. Exploding Neutron Stars?

We argue that this points to the explosive transition (i.e., combustion) of a neutron star to a quark star. In the canonical case, a neutron-star is the final evolutionary path of massive (>8 $M_\odot$) stars which are the remnants of a core-collapse supernova explosion. However, we propose a further evolutionary stage for some of these neutron stars, that is, their explosive collapse into a more compact configuration—the quark star. We refer to this "explosion pathway" as a quark-nova [5]. The energy released in the explosion is a combination of the gravitational binding energy during the neutron star's core-collapse and the nuclear binding energy released from the neutron matter decaying to more stable quark matter made of up, down and strange quarks (hereafter *(u,d,s)*). The model makes use of the Bodmer–Witten–Terazawa hypothesis (BWTH; [6–8]), which argues that *(u,d,s)*, not baryonic matter, is the most stable form of matter in the universe. The Quark-Nova group have developed this model theoretically and primarily numerically (by developing the Burn-UD code) over many years, starting with their pioneering paper of 2002 [5].

If *(u,d,s)* quark-matter is the most stable form of matter in the universe, then it follows that neutron stars may decay into more stable quark stars through an exothermic process. According to the BWT hypothesis, the reason why hadronic matter does not spontaneously decay into *(u,d,s)* matter is that there is an intermediate higher energy state of *(u,d)* matter. To diminish this energy barrier, there need to be sufficient s-quarks available to trigger the combustion process. Another way of stating this, is that s-quarks act as catalysts that lower the free energy barrier, allowing hadronic matter to decay into a lower state of *(u,d,s)* matter. This energy barrier could explain why *(u,d,s)* matter is much scarcer than hadronic matter to the extent that we have not detected the former. In other words, although empirically we do not find two-flavour-quark matter at zero pressure, the addition of an extra degree of freedom, such as strange quarks, could decrease the Fermi energy for the same baryon number density, lowering the quark matter's free energy below the free energies of both hadronic and two-flavoured quark matter.

Since this hypothesis was proposed, many interesting scenarios have been postulated in both astrophysics and particle physics. For example, the existence of pure strange quark stars, and fragments of *(u,d,s)* matter, called strangelets, have been suggested. Beyond the existence of macroscopic objects, such as strange quark stars, another interesting consequence of the BWTH is the release of large amounts of energy when hadronic matter converts to *(u,d,s)* matter. Assuming a bag constant of $B = 145$ MeV, using the above model, the energy per baryon becomes $\sim$840 MeV which is roughly 100 MeV less than for ordinary hadronic matter ($\sim$930 MeV) [9]. This implies that a conversion from hadronic to *(u,d,s)* matter should release about 100 MeV per converted baryon. Assuming a neutron star has about 10^{57} baryons, conversion of every baryon into *(u,d,s)* matter would generate $\sim 10^{53}$ ergs in total energy. While this is of the same order of magnitude for typical explosive events in astrophysics, such as core-collapse supernovae, the energy is hardly harnessed since it is emitted as neutrinos. The advent of the quark-nova allowed novel channels which would convert this energy to photon fireballs and to the kinetic energy of the quark-nova ejecta which can be easily harnessed with revolutionary consequences for high-energy astrophysics. We discuss how it can be harnessed in a newly born neutron star (i.e., embedded deep within its supernova ejecta) or in an old one (in isolation). This contribution focuses on the macro-physics of the neutron-star-to-quark star conversion in order to understand the unique features of quark-nova dynamics and energetics at stellar scales. We refer the reader to a complementary paper [10] where we discuss in detail the micro-physics of the *hadron*-to-*(u,d,s)* conversion which is briefly reviewed here in Section 1.4. Firstly, however, we remind the reader of strategies described in the literature when exploring the transition. In particular, we explain why the correct choice for the thermodynamic potential in a transition which is not in mechanical equilibrium (as in the quark-nova scenario) is the Helmholtz potential, rather than the Gibbs potential which is usually cited in the literature.

1.3. The Hadron-Quark Transition: The Thermodynamics

Glendenning [11] pointed out that, in complex systems of more than one conserved charge, the system does not need to be locally electrically neutral, only globally so. This allows for a complex mixed phase to exist during the transition of nuclear to quark matter where various charges, including baryon number, electric charge, and quark flavors, are conserved. This led to a rich literature exploring the hadron-to-quark matter transition which can be divided into three main streams including smooth (i.e., cross-over), Gibbs (i.e., soft) and Maxwell (i.e., sharp first-order) transitions. The nature of the transition depends strongly on the EoS of the hadronic and quark matter. In the Maxwell construction, the nuclear-quark phase transition is first-order (e.g., [12–15] and references therein) and the imposition of local charge neutrality would lead to a sharp interface (because of the high surface tension) with a width in the order of femtometers (for details see [11,16–18]). This is in contrast to a Gibbs construction where there is a mixed region where hadron matter and quark matter coexist [19–24]. In the case of a smooth cross-over, interpolation procedures are used to connect the two phases (e.g., [25,26] and references therein). The Gibbs construction also appeals to a smooth transition into the mixed phase but the fraction of each phase is determined self-consistently and is independent of the interpolation method adopted. For completeness, we mention other examples of a smooth cross-over transition, such as the chiral model [27] and the quarkyonic model [28]. A quark phase with additional hadronic admixtures, such as hyperons and meson condensates, has also been explored in early work [29].

The Gibbs potential is typically chosen to model most phase transitions since the timescales are usually large enough that the sound waves flatten any pressure spatial gradient across the interface. The Gibbs potential is generally deployed in many studies of phases of matter inside compact stars, since the objects of study are in a steady state, sufficient time has passed so that the phases are in mechanical equilibrium, and the variables that are being studied, such as the radius and mass, are steady-state, time-independent values. Yet, not all phase transitions are in mechanical equilibrium. If the timescales are short enough so that sound waves have not flattened the pressure gradients, then the Gibbs potential becomes inaccurate. The correct choice for the thermodynamic potential to represent the free energy depends on which thermodynamic quantities are approximated as constant when a system changes its thermodynamic state. If it is assumed that the pressure P and the temperature T remain constant through the change (i.e., $dP = dT = 0$), then the decrease in free energy $dG \leq 0$ is equivalent to the second law; that is, the increase in entropy $dS \geq 0$. In the case of the Helmholtz energy, $dF \leq 0$ is equivalent to $dS \geq 0$ if $dV = 0$ (where V is the volume) and $dT = 0$. This difference between the Gibbs and Helmholtz potential is crucial in the context of hadron-quark phase transitions (see discussion in [10]).

In our case, the first-order phase transition of nuclear to quark matter conserves various charges, including baryon number, electric charge, and quark flavors. The fact that the system does not have to be locally neutral gives rise to a complex mixed phase made of differently shaped bubbles of quark matter embedded in hadronic matter. We find that the correct choice for the thermodynamic potential is the Helmholtz potential, which contrasts with the usual Gibbs potential found in the literature. To justify the use of the Helmholtz instead of the Gibbs potential, we note that the most relevant (i.e., the largest) timescale in our approach to the hadron-quark matter phase transition is the weak interaction timescale which is of the order of 10^{-8} s; the timescale of energy release due to quark beta equilibration is also relevant. Our study must also resolve the sonic timescales which are of the order of 10^{-11} s, as the pressure gradients are dynamically important. Since the sonic time is twelve orders of magnitude larger than the strong interaction ($\sim 10^{-23}$ s), a study that resolves the sonic time cannot assume the interface is in mechanical equilibrium—in other words, that $dP = 0$. In the case of the hadron-quark phase transition, the strong interaction acts at a timescale of $\sim 10^{-23}$ s, which is much faster than the hydrodynamics that may flatten the pressure gradient. Therefore, we must choose the Helmholtz thermodynamic potential over the Gibbs one. In other words, hadronic matter will convert to quark matter if the Helmholtz free energy is lower for quark matter than for hadronic matter, a point discussed in detail in Section 2.2 in [10] (and references therein).

1.4. Quark-Nova: A Brief Review of the Microphysics

The mechanism of the quark-nova is intimately linked to the strong force which governs the interaction between quarks and also gives rise to the nuclear force. In astrophysics, quantum chromodynamics (QCD) becomes relevant in the context of compact objects. This is because the cores of compact objects are so dense that they become thermodynamically ideal sites for the phase-transition of hadronic to quark matter.

Quark deconfinement appears at extremely high temperatures or densities. This is due to the property of asymptotic freedom where the high momentum exchange between quarks weakens the attractive interaction between them. So, for the "quarks" to be released/deconfined, they need to collide with extreme momenta. Since temperature is a measure of kinetic energies, high temperatures are a way to trigger this deconfinement. In the case of high densities, fermions, such as quarks, are compressed into having high Fermi energies, triggering high momentum exchange.

In Earth-based experiments, particle accelerators tap into the high temperature regime by triggering very high energy collisions. However quark deconfinement in compact stars cannot be probed through experiments, since deconfinement appears at low temperatures but high ($\sim 10^{15}$ g cm^{-3}) densities. This give rise to the need to use compact star observations to probe the QCD phase diagram. The existence of exotic particles in the core of compact stars is, therefore, an ideal laboratory for the study of exotic particles. Given the high Fermi energies, and, therefore, high momentum exchanges in the cores of compact stars, nucleation of quark matter inside them can be expected.

The BWTH hypothesis referred to previously states that matter with the lowest binding energy could be (u,d,s) quark matter. The main reason for this is that the existence of a third degree of freedom in the form of s-quarks in general lowers the Fermi energy of the matter. In the MIT bag model, a simple approximation is that quark matter is in the form of a Fermi gas with a constant B that acts as the confinement pressure. A range of bag constants can be found where (u,d,s) quark matter is lower than the hadronic binding energy of $\sim$930 MeV, but, at the same time, where (u,d) matter has a higher binding energy than hadronic matter. This hypothesis therefore implies that macroscopic objects made of (u,d,s) matter are thermodynamically plausible.

The conversion of hadronic to quark matter could occur in the following way: Once two-flavoured quark matter is nucleated in the core of neutron stars, the weak interaction can turn some of the d quarks into s-quarks, lowering the Fermi energy of the quark matter. Because, at this point, the free energy of (u,d,s) matter is lower than the free energy of hadrons, the hadrons accreted by the quark core would find it energetically favourable to deconfine into lower energy quark matter. Eventually, the quark core would grow, engulfing the whole compact star, turning it into a pure (u,d,s) star. There are alternate scenarios for conversion of a whole compact star to a (u,d,s) star including, for example, through "seeding" of cosmic strangelets (e.g., [30]), or dark-matter annihilation in neutron stars heating up parcels of neutron star matter making conditions favorable for the creation of quark bubbles [31].

Although the 10^{53} ergs of energy release predicted by energetics compares favorably to explosive events such as supernovae, whether this energy is released explosively or in a slow simmer is not defined. Since the 1980s, different groups have sought to elucidate the phenomenology of this energy release. Olinto [30] pioneered a hydrodynamic formalism for exploring the conversion of hadronic to (u,d,s) quark matter as a hydrodynamic combustion process. The conversion was modeled as a "combustion front" that "burns" hadronic fuel into (u,d,s) ash. However, the exact equations that govern this reaction zone, the reaction-diffusion-advection equations, cannot be solved in analytic form since they are non-linear. Olinto therefore needed to linearize the equations and impose mechanical equilibrium and derive semi-analytic, steady-state solutions. The study yielded timescales of conversion of minutes to days for the whole compact star, which would imply a slow simmer, since the timescale of a supernova explosion is about one second.

Another pioneering paper was published by Benvenuto et al. [32] in the late 1980s. In contrast to Olinto, the authors assumed an initial shock and solved the relativistic jump conditions. The model proposed leads to a steady-state solution but without the mechanical equilibrium assumed by Olinto. The approach yields a supersonic detonation, which Benvenuto et al. argue can provide enough kinetic energy to make a core-collapse supernova explode. Although this explosive solution contrasts with Olinto's much slower timescales, the reason is that a shock is assumed on an a priori basis, with arguments presented that the initial deconfined bubble of quark matter creates a sharp pressure discontinuity. Drago et al. [33] also solved the jump conditions without assuming mechanical equilibrium, but in their case they found that the combustion takes the form of subsonic deflagration.

All the literature on hadron-quark combustion before the 2010s can be roughly categorized as following either a mechanical equilibrium approach [30] or a jump condition approach [33], and has always assumed a steady state. Because of the variety of the assumptions made, such as whether a pressure equilibrium is assumed or not, or whether a shock is hypothesized as an initial condition or not, the timescales of conversion predicted for the compact star have varied by various orders of magnitude, from milliseconds to days.

1.5. The Burn-UD Code and Non-Premixed Combustion

Previous literature on this topic has reported very different results on the transition speed and energy as a consequence of incorrectly assuming premixed combustion (see discussion on this in [34]). However, the (u,d)-to-(u,d,s) combustion is of the non-premixed type, a distinction that is critically important. In a hadron-quark combustion flame, the thermal conductivity plays a negligible role, since the activation occurs through the s-quark fraction, because it is ultimately the quantity of s-quarks in the quark phase that determines whether the quark matter has a lower free energy than the hadronic matter. A minimal amount of s-quarks in the NS core is sufficient to create "oxidation" (to represent it in chemical activation terminology). In traditional pre-mixed combustion, the oxidant must be mixed with the fuel so that, once the activation temperature is achieved, the fuel is burned. Some fuels come premixed with the oxidant, and, therefore, the combustion is fundamentally mediated by thermal conductivity. In our case, as the fuel and oxidant are not mixed, the transport of oxidants into the fuel becomes an important process, alongside the thermal conductivity. Since the s-quarks can be thought of as related to the activation temperature and as an oxidant, a proper treatment of the hadron-quark combustion process should be studied as a diffusion flame. Equally important, and unlike previous work, we include neutrinos which carry a non-negligible energy (in the hadron-quark combustion system, mass and energy are interchangeable) and momentum. We found a much more complex interplay between fluid dynamics and radiation which makes it impossible to compare our work to past investigations. Ultimately, it is the transport of s-quarks, in concert with neutrino transport and leptonic dynamics, that decides the behavior of the flame, which is very different from the way thermal conductivity acts in Arrhenius-type reactions. Thus, fundamentally, the non-premised scenario in the quark-nova model is different from that of past work (see in-depth analysis and discussion in [35,36]).

A hydrodynamic combustion code (the Burn-UD code; [35,36]) was developed by the Quark-Nova group to model in detail the non-premixed phase transition of hadronic to quark matter. The Burn-UD code allows the adoption of the Helmholtz, instead of the

Gibbs, potential (see Section 1.3) and self-consistently couples the thermodynamics to the hydrodynamics, which is of crucial importance. It can be shown that this coupling allows for a more rigorous capture of the propagation of the burning front with implications for the energetics in the case of a burning neutron star. For example, if the propagation of the burning front is too slow, the energy released is not efficiently transformed into kinetic energy, with the energy simply leaking out slowly as transparent neutrinos. The Burn-UD code consistently calculates how the weak interaction gives rise to particle and temperature spatial gradients that, in turn, trigger pressure gradients. A pressure gradient acts as a source of momentum density in the fluid, transforming some of the energy released into mechanical energy. The inclusion of the Helmholtz thermodynamic potential was found to lead to much larger neutrino luminosities (about two orders of magnitude larger than for the Gibbs potential) and larger burning speeds. Furthermore, the Helmholtz approach offers advantages numerically since it can borrow from the Gibbs construction, which avoids sharp density gradients in numerical experiments by employing a mixed phase (see Section 2.2 in [10]).

The Burn-UD code models the flame micro-physics for different equations of state (EOS) on both sides of the interface, i.e., for both the ash (up-down-strange quark phase) and the fuel (up-down quark phase). It also allows the user to explore strange-quark seeding produced by different processes. It is an *advection-reaction-diffusion* code which is essential for a proper treatment of the micro-physics of a burning front. Furthermore, having a precise understanding of the phase transition dynamics for different EOSs further aids in constraining the nature of the non-perturbative regimes of QCD in general (see Section 4.1). The Burn-UD code has evolved into a platform/software which can be used and shared by the QCD community exploring the phases of quark matter and by astrophysicists working on compact stars. The code provides a unique physical window to diagnose whether the combustion process will simmer quietly and slowly, lead to a transition from deflagration to detonation, or entail a (quark) core-collapse explosion.

Niebergal et al. [37], for the first time, in 2010 published a study that numerically solved the reaction-diffusion-advection equations for hadron-quark combustion. This study combined transport, chemical, and entropic processes into a numerical simulation. Not only was the burning velocity much faster than many of the previous estimates, but Niebergal et al. suggested that leptons may trigger feedback that can accelerate the burning front into supersonic detonation or quench it. Their argument was based on solving the jump conditions and parameterizing the cooling behind the front.

Later, Ouyed et al. [38] solved the reaction-diffusion-advection equations and coupled them to neutrino transport using a flux-limited diffusion scheme, and added an electron EOS and a hadronic matter (HM) EOS. Ouyed et al. confirmed numerically that leptons can trigger extreme feedbacks, with the burning halting completely for certain choices of the initial conditions. Ouyed et al.'s study was important in that it showed that, due to non-linear couplings between lepton physics and hydrodynamics, the simulation was extremely sensitive to the details of neutrino transport. This indicated that the system is genuinely a non-linear, dynamic process, and that simplifying it by imposing mechanical equilibrium or steady-state conditions was extremely inaccurate.

There are multiple ways that a quark-nova could be triggered. There are two "mechanisms" for initiating the combustion of a neutron star into a quark star. One mechanism relates to the core of a neutron star in some way reaching sufficiently high densities that favour the deconfinement of quark matter. These nucleated (u,d) quark bubbles, in turn, would beta equilibrate into (u,d,s) matter, and then, in accordance with the BWTH, grow, engulfing the whole neutron star [39]. However, the density at which quark matter deconfines is very uncertain. It could be that most neutron stars achieve the deconfinement density and, therefore, turn into quark stars. However if the deconfinement density is higher than that of the average core of a neutron star, then sufficiently high density could be achieved through other processes, such as accretion, fall-back from supernovae, or spin-down evolution, leading to a two-family compact star scenario, where quark stars and neutron stars coexist [40].

The other mechanism for triggering a quark-nova could be through "seeding". According to the BWTH, a strangelet that interacts with hadronic matter can convert the latter, provided that there is not an electrostatic barrier preventing the interaction. Since neutrons do not have a charge, neutron stars are an ideal site for strangelet contamination. The source of strangelets can be arbitrary; for example, cosmic strangelets can be released by a (u,d,s) star merger, or stranglets may be formed through the annihilation of dark matter in the core of neutron stars.

In summary, the quark-nova hypothesis (and the underlying microphysics) implies that the traditional picture of stellar evolution is not the whole story. There is the possibility that the neutron star would experience further collapse into a (u,d,s) star. Such a phenomenon would have similar dynamics and energetics as a core-collapse supernova, with approximately $\sim 10^{53}$ ergs released of both chemical and gravitational binding energy. Such an addition to the stellar evolution picture has immense phenomenological consequences. This hypothesis essentially argues that the neutron star "explodes" (i.e., the neutron-star-to-quark-star combustion is explosive). The neutron-rich ejecta released from the outer layers of the exploding neutron star also constitute a very suitable site for nucleosynthesis and r-process elements, since there is a very low proton fraction (Y_e; see Section 3.4).

In the quark-nova investigations, it was found that a very natural way of triggering the detonation of a neutron star is via a "quark core-collapse" where the neutron star core simply collapses into a more compact, (u,d,s) configuration, releasing massive amounts of energy. This relies on the crucial coupling between the conversion front (the micro-physics; see [10]) and the dynamics it induces at the scale of the star ($\sim 10^6$ cm; the macro-physics), as discussed in the next section.

2. Quark-Nova: The Macrophysics

The initial setup consist of a cold NS. The conversion from hadronic matter (HM) to (u,d,s) is triggered by s-quark seeding in the core [38]. If sufficient s-quarks are seeded into a parcel of quark matter, then the conversion of HM to (u,d,s) can proceed unimpeded because s-quarks can behave as catalysts. In the results presented in this review, we chose the Hempel & Schaffner-Bielich (2010; [41]) tabulated EOS to describe the HM layers (overlaying the quark core) because it is well-cited, and, more importantly, its tabular structure is fairly simple and well-documented. The EOS also satisfies the two-solar-mass neutron star constraint. For the (u,d,s) EOS, we chose the MIT bag model which consists simply of a Fermi gas with a negative pressure B that confines the gas—the Fermi gas pushes outward but the confinement pressure B pushes inward. In the language of free energy, (u,d) acts as an energy barrier between two energy minima, which are the hadronic state (i.e., HM) and the (u,d,s) state. Since (u,d) exists as a barrier, the hadronic matter will not decay by itself. For some values of B, (u,d,s)'s binding energy is lower than for the hadronic matter, while at the same time the binding energy of (u,d) is higher than for the hadronic matter. Therefore the absolute stability of (u,d,s) can exist while respecting the empirical reality of unstable (u,d). For this work, we have extended the MIT bag EOS to include first-order corrections for the strong coupling constant and included temperature dependencies. Nevertheless, inherent uncertainties to the quark matter EOS we use exist as we assume zero entropy and massless quarks. Moreover, only for certain choices of B does the MIT bag model predict absolutely stable (u,d,s) matter. In Figure 1, we compare the free energy per baryon versus temperature for the hadronic EOS of [41], and the (u,d,s) matter represented by the MIT bag EOS with strong coupling constant corrections. As can be seen from the figure, the free energy of (u,d,s) becomes higher around $T \sim 40$ MeV, which blocks the conversion from hadronic to quark matter. In our simulations, we set an initial temperature of $T = 20$ MeV yielding thermodynamic conditions of a neutron star that will be converted into a proto-quark star (PQS). We tested other hadronic EOSs, but, as stated in our work (see [10] and references therein), the effects of the leptonic weak interaction, including the corresponding weak decay rates and the EOS of electrons and neutrinos, are at least as important as the uncertainties related to the EOS of HM, (u,d) and (u,d,s) (see discussion in Section 4.1).

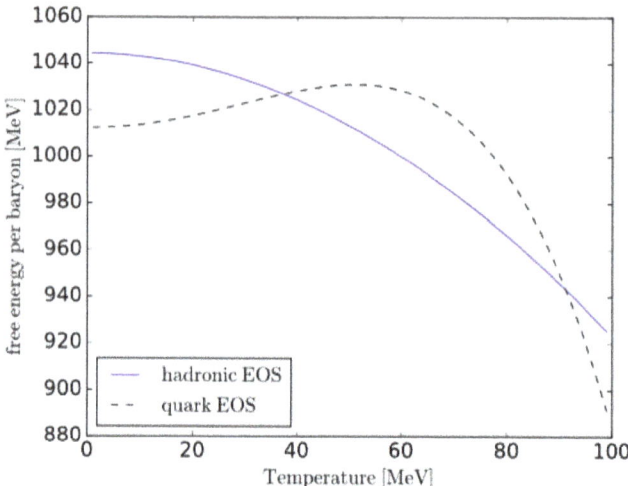

Figure 1. Free energy per baryon versus temperature for the hadronic EOS [41] and that of (u,d,s) (the MIT bag EOS with strong coupling constant corrections) used in this work. The free energy of (u,d,s) becomes higher around $T \sim 40$ MeV, which blocks the conversion from hadronic to quark matter. Reprinted from Ref. [36].

2.1. The Code

The micro-physics of the quark-nova focuses merely on length-scales of ~0.1 cm to cm (width of the reaction zone) and timescales of about 10^{-8} s (the timescale of the weak interaction that converts d quarks to s quarks). However, in order to study the final fate of a neutron star combusting to a quark star, it is necessary to take into account larger scales.

To truly study this combustion process at a large scale it would be necessary to build a three-dimensional code that combusts the neutron star into a quark star. This code would need to solve the reaction-diffusion-advection equations for the whole star. Such a simulation, although feasible, would be quite difficult to build, since the scales that dominate in the reaction zone (cm) are various orders of magnitude smaller than the scales of the whole compact star (10^6 cm). It would be necessary to use an adaptive computational mesh that uses smaller computational zones for the reaction zone while using larger zones for the rest of the star.

Such a computational code does not exist yet. However, if it is assumed that the burning front remains somewhat well-defined, and therefore instabilities do not distort it significantly, some macroscopic properties of the combustion process can still be derived.

The original attempts to derive the "macroscopic" phenomenology of microphysical studies of the hadron-quark interface hark back to the 1980s, when Olinto et al. wrote their pioneering paper on hadron-quark combustion [30]. In their case, and other similar studies (e.g., [42]), the burning speed was calculated for different densities and then this speed was assumed to be the same for the whole compact star. This approach, even under the assumption that instabilities will not distort the interface too much, or that the boundary conditions of the microphysical problem reflect the macroscopic physics, does not say a great deal about the phenomenology of the conversion, i.e., what the conversion would "look like" through detectors and telescopes. This approach can only be used to calculate a rough timescale for the conversion of the whole neutron star into a quark star, but without calculating the signal detected on Earth.

An interesting imprint that the combustion process leaves behind that should be detectable is a large neutrino signal. Electron neutrinos are produced copiously in quark matter by leptonic processes:

$$u + e^- \to d + \nu_e \tag{1}$$

$$u + e^- \to s + \nu_e \tag{2}$$

$$d \to e^- + \bar{\nu}_e + u \tag{3}$$

$$s \to e^- + \bar{\nu}_e + u \tag{4}$$

Furthermore, copious τ_ν and μ_ν neutrinos are created through quark breemstralung processes. Neutrinos provide an excellent probe into the combustion process because of their high luminosity and high energies. The reason for the large luminosity is the immense release of energy by the beta equilibration of quark matter. Since the quarks are degenerate, their relaxation into a more stable energy state implies changes of 100 MeV in binding energy. Much of this binding energy is released as neutrinos. Furthermore, the binding energy release is what heats the quark matter, which in turn traps neutrinos and thermalizes them into high temperatures of MeV. Given their energies and luminosities (e.g., peak neutrino luminosities of $>10^{55}$ erg/s), neutrinos may serve as a means of confirming the combustion process.

Furthermore, since the expected luminosities and neutrino temperatures are higher than for other phenomena, such as core-collapse supernovae, the spectrum and photometry of neutrinos for the quark-nova should provide an unambiguous probe to discriminate this phenomenon macroscopically from other explosive astrophysical events.

Finally, neutrinos are also important because they are the most dynamic aspect of the quark star's energy budget. Once combustion burns the star, which would happen over timescales shorter than a second (e.g., [37]), assuming that instabilities do not really distort the interface significantly or quench it, the change in the energy density of the profile becomes a function of neutrino transport, much like the case for proto-neutron stars. At this point, hydrodynamic processes, such as convection, become secondary to the process of neutrino transport. In other words, the evolution of the proto-quark star is defined by the evolution of the neutrino profile, and the hydrodynamics are higher-order effects. Therefore, to detect a "signal" that discriminates this combustion process, it would be essential to examine the evolution of the neutrino profile.

2.2. The Hot Proto-Quark Star

Fortunately, there are approaches to studying the neutrino-driven evolution of a compact star without building a complicated three-dimensional code for the hydrodynamics of the combustion process. There is a class of codes called "stellar evolution" codes originally designed to probe the evolution and luminosities of ordinary stars. They solve, through implicit numerical techniques, the transport equations for heat, and couple these transport processes to the equations for the hydrostatic equilibrium of the star (e.g., [43]). This technique was applied to neutron stars. In the neutron star case, the transport equations deal with the general relativistic transport of neutrinos, and the hydrostatic equations are replaced by the general relativistic version of these equations (the Tolman–Openheimer–Volkoff (TOV) equations).

The reason why these equations must be solved in the general relativistic case, as opposed to the Newtonian case, is the extreme compactness of neutron stars and quark stars which distort space and time because their radius is close to their Schwarzschild radius: $r_s = 2GM/c^2$ where G is the gravitational constant, M is the mass of the object, and c is the speed of light.

For example, neutrinos look "cooler" and "less energetic" to an observer far away from the compact star because of a gravitational red-shifting of the neutrinos, which decrease their frequency from a frame of reference at infinity.

So, under the following assumptions, we can simulate the evolution of the proto-quark star (PQS):

- *Short combustion timescale*: We must assume that the combustion process is much faster than the neutrino evolution process. The reason we should make such an assumption is that, if the neutrino cooling is much longer, it can be assumed that the temperature profile produced by the combustion process "freezes" and is only affected by neutrino transport. Since, outside the combustion process, all other cooling processes that affect the partitioning of the energy budget are much slower than neutrino transport, the microphysical combustion problem can reasonably be decoupled from the large-scale evolution problem, if we assume that combustion is much faster than neutrino transport.

  This assumption of combustion may be supported by microphysical simulations (e.g., [37]). Numerical simulations show that laminar burning speeds can reach 0.001c–0.1c. Assuming these speeds are sustained in the microscopic case, and that instabilities do not slow down the burning front too much, using these numbers would mean that the neutron star would combust into a quark star in a fraction of a second. This timescale must be smaller than the timescale for cooling/deleptonization. We can make a rough order-of-magnitude estimate of the timescale of deleptonization/cooling through dimensional analysis. For the high temperatures > 20 MeV and high densities of a quark star (a few times nuclear saturation density), the neutrino mean free path is about $\lambda_\nu \sim 1$ cm, much smaller than the radius of the PQS of $R_{PQS} = 10^6$ cm. Through dimensional analysis, we find the timescale of cooling: $\tau_{cool.} \sim R_{PQS}^2/(\lambda_\nu c) \sim 33$ s. Since this cooling timescale is much larger than the estimated combustion timescale, this particular assumption is valid.

- *Hydrostatic equilibrium*: This assumption is justified if the timescales studied in the stellar evolution simulation are longer than the hydrodynamic timescales. This can be tested by looking at the sonic time, which is the time a sound wave takes to cross the whole length that is studied. The reason neutrino cooling needs to be slower than the hydrodynamic processes is that the time-steps of the simulation need to be large enough so that pressure gradients along the star are smoothed out by sound waves. In our case, the length-scale is the radius of the PQS. Because the sound speed of degenerate matter is of the order of the speed of light c, the sonic time will be $\tau_s \sim R_{PQS}/c \sim 3 \times 10^{-5}$ s. Since the cooling timescale, as calculated above, is of the order of 10 s, we can argue that the neutrino cooling is much slower than the hydrodynamic processes, which justifies the hydrostatic assumption.

- *Neutrino trapping*: Most stellar evolution codes for compact stars assume neutrino trapping to be able to simulate neutrino transport with a simple application of Fick's law. Since we know that the mean free path of neutrinos is about 1 cm, while the radius of the quark star is $R \sim 10$ km, the neutrino trapping assumption is reasonable.

- *β-equilibrium*: We must assume that the quarks in the PQS are in chemical equilibrium at each time-step. This assumption makes it possible not to have to keep track of the time-dependent reaction rates that regulate the chemical composition of quark matter. Since the weak interaction in the context of the conversion of two-flavoured to three-flavoured matter has a timescale of $\sim 10^{-8}$ s, we can effectively assume chemical equilibrium, since the cooling/deleptonization timescale, as calculated above, is ~ 10 s.

- *Thermal equilibrium*: In order to assume thermodynamic variables such as pressure, temperature, and chemical potential, we must assume that the neutrinos are thermalized. By thermalized, we imply that the neutrinos have collided and scattered sufficiently so that they can be considered to be at thermal equilibrium. In much of the Universe, neutrinos are seldom thermalized, since their interaction cross-section is tiny; so, once emitted, they pass through matter mostly unperturbed. However, compact stars, such as quark stars, are the only existing systems in the Universe that emit a spectrum of thermal neutrinos. This is due to the extreme densities and temperatures of these objects; such thermodynamic conditions enlarge the cross-section of neutrinos to the point that they scatter and collide easily with other particles.

2.3. Thermalized Neutrinos and Heat Transport

The fact that neutrinos are thermalized ($\lambda_\nu \ll R_{PQS}$) makes the simulation much easier than if the neutrinos were not thermal, since the neutrino's temperature is the same as the quark matter's temperature. In this case, the transport equation for the energy density of neutrinos simply corresponds to one diffusion-like equation per flavour. In contrast, if the neutrinos were not thermalized, one would have to solve the Boltzmann transport equations, which requires a very complicated six-dimensional integral, and therefore requires more computational and programming sophistication/resources.

Following the assumptions above, we can outline the equations that our simulation will solve. First, we must write down the relevant space-time metric of the problem:

$$ds^2 = -e^{2\phi}dt^2 + e^{2\lambda}dr^2 + r^2 d\Omega \tag{5}$$

Here, dt is an infinitesimal element of the coordinate time at infinity. $d\Omega$ is an infinitesimal element of the solid angle, and ϕ and λ are metric functions.

The TOV equations that compute the structure of the compact star, that is, the pressure, radius, and density, will be outlined using the above metric and the assumption of hydrostatic equilibrium. The TOV equations in Lagrangian coordinates are:

$$\frac{dr}{da} = \frac{1}{4\pi r^2 n_B e^\lambda} \tag{6}$$

$$\frac{dm}{da} = \frac{\epsilon}{n_B e^\lambda} \tag{7}$$

$$\frac{d\phi}{da} = \frac{e^\lambda}{4\pi r^4 n_B}(m + 4\pi r^2 P) \tag{8}$$

$$\frac{dP}{da} = -(\epsilon + P)\frac{e^\lambda}{4\pi r^4 n_B}(m + 4\pi r^3 P) \tag{9}$$

$$e^{-\lambda} = \sqrt{1 - \frac{2m}{r}} \tag{10}$$

where r stands for the radial coordinates, n_B for number density, P for pressure, a for the number of baryons enclosed by a sphere of radius r, and m is the gravitational mass enclosed by radius r. The reason why we choose Lagrangian coordinates over the more common derivation that uses Eulerian coordinates, and therefore r as the integrated quantity, is that the radius of the compact star is time-dependent. Since the radius is not a conserved quantity, the numerical treatment becomes complicated as a computational grid made of radial coordinates would keep changing spatially. In contrast, the total baryon number of the star is conserved, so a computational grid that discretizes along a baryonic coordinate can be constructed.

The transport equations (for lepton fraction Y_L and energy density ϵ) are the following:

$$\frac{\partial Y_L}{\partial t} + \frac{\partial(e^\phi 4\pi r^2 (F_{\nu,e}))}{\partial a} = 0 \tag{11}$$

$$\frac{\partial \epsilon}{\partial t} + \frac{\partial(e^{2\phi} 4\pi r^2 (H_{\nu,e} + H_{\nu,\mu}))}{\partial a} = 0 \tag{12}$$

$$F_{\nu,e} = \frac{\lambda_{\nu,e}}{3}\frac{n_\nu}{dr} \tag{13}$$

$$H_{\nu,i} = \frac{\lambda_{\nu,i}}{3} \frac{\epsilon_{\nu_i}}{dr} \quad (14)$$

where $F_{\nu,e}$ is the neutrino number density flux and $H_{\nu,i}$ is the neutrino energy density flux. These equations are simply Fick's law as applied to neutrino number densities (n_ν) and neutrino energy density (ϵ_{ν_i}).

The stellar evolution code requires some initial conditions to be set in order to solve the problem. Three important radial parameters that need to be imposed as initial conditions are the baryonic mass, the lepton fraction and the temperature. The initial values of these parameters must be imposed a priori. A useful observation that enables the derivation of these initial distributions is the fact that neutrino transport is probably much slower than the combustion speed; as calculated above, the timescale of neutrino transport is about ~ 10 s while the timescale of combustion is at most a fraction of a second. We can therefore make the following assumptions that simplify our calculations considerably:

- *Frozen initial temperature profile*: Since the dominant process of cooling is neutrino emission/transport, we assume that the initial temperature profile can be interpolated from local microscopic simulations that calculate the temperature for a given initial fuel density. This implies that we can decouple the problem into two sets of microphysical and macrophysical simulations: the former calculates the temperature profile through interpolation of temperature calculations for various initial densities, and the latter solves the global, macroscopic equations of neutrino transport. This decoupling simplifies the calculations considerably.
- *Frozen lepton fraction*: Since the combustion process happens at a much faster timescale than the neutrino transport, we can assume that the initial lepton fraction of the unburned neutron star is equivalent to the initial lepton fraction distribution of the hot quark star that is evolved in the code. Through this assumption, we can directly extract the initial lepton fraction from the EOS of a neutron star.
- *Convergence of combustion temperature at low initial hadronic densities*: Our simulations can only calculate the temperature for initial hadronic densities that are not lower than 0.05 fm^{-3}, since, otherwise, the density gradient would be too large, generating numerical instabilities. However, for lower initial densities, such as those found on the edge of the hadronic star, the temperatures of the ash will converge to a similar temperature of ~ 20 MeV, as the ash will also converge to the same density, since the large confinement pressure of B forces the ash to have a non-zero density in the order of nuclear saturation. Therefore, even if we do not pursue a simulation, we can calculate the neutrinospheric temperature from the binding energy released through two-flavour to three-flavour quark matter equilibration using an analytical argument. Using a zero entropy MIT bag model, in previous sections, we found that the temperature of a baryon can increase to about ~ 30 MeV. In the numerical scheme for 0.05 fm^{-3} initial hadronic density, this quantity ends up lower, but of the same magnitude, around ~ 20 MeV, mostly because of the effect of the s-quark mass, where a finite mass leads to less binding energy release.

The temperature of a neutrinospheric baryon that is about ~ 20 MeV will mostly cool through neutrino emission. To ensure that the neutrinospheric temperature will remain high for sufficiently long after the combustion process, in order to assume the same high initial neutrinospheric temperature, it is necessary to calculate the cooling timescale. Assuming neutrinos are not trapped in the neutrinosphere, then the neutrinos of neutrinospheric quark matter will automatically escape the moment they are emitted. We can calculate the timescale of cooling analytically with the following prescription obtained from Iwamoto et al. [44].

$$\tau_{cool} \sim 3153 \text{ s} \times \left(\frac{Y_e}{0.01}\right)^{-1/3} \times (T_{f_9}^{-4} - T_{i_9}^{-4}). \quad (15)$$

In the above, T_{f_9} and T_{i_9} are the neutrinosphere's final and initial temperatures in units of 10^9 K. For an initial temperature of around 20 MeV, how long it will take for the temperature to cool off by 50 percent can be determined, assuming that there is no combustion to "reheat" the interface. Using the above equation, the time necessary for the neutrinosphere to lose 50 percent of its temperature is about $\tau_{cool} \sim 10^{-5}$ s. This timescale is actually a lower bound, as the emissivity is proportional to $Y_e^{1/3}$, and, therefore, the emissivity becomes less intense as the lepton fraction lowers due to deleptonization. In order to assume this neutrinosphere temperature, this timescale must be much longer than the time required for the combustion interface to cross its own width. We can calculate the minimum combustion speed where this approximation is valid through the estimate $v = l/\tau_{cool}$. Assuming the reaction zone width is $l = 0.1$ cm and $\tau \sim 10^{-5}$ s, as calculated from Equation (15), we obtain $v = 10^4$ cm/s. As even the slowest burning speeds calculated in the literature (e.g., Olinto et al. [30] indicate a lower limit of 1 km/s, we can assume that the neutrinosphere remains "hot" throughout the combustion process.

The first assumption, that of a "frozen initial temperature distribution", simplifies the problem and calculations. Using these assumptions, we can run the Burn-UD code for different initial hadronic densities to calculate the "frozen" temperatures that will be plugged into a stellar evolution code. We ran the Burn-UD microphysical code for five different initial densities (0.05 fm^{-3}, 0.1 fm^{-3}, 0.2 fm^{-3}, 0.3 fm^{-3}, 0.4 fm^{-3}). Due to the "frozen lepton fraction" assumption, we can impose a lepton profile extracted from a cold neutron star in beta equilibrium [45], which is generally of the order of $Y_e = 0.1$ or less. We ran the simulations with a timescale of the weak interaction $\sim 10^{-8}$ s, which amounts to about 10^5 time-steps. These simulations lead to a two-column table of temperature vs. initial density (Table 1). These temperatures and densities can be easily interpolated into a function of temperature that is a function of initial hadronic density.

Table 1. Final temperatures of (u,d,s) ash for different initial hadronic number densities, as calculated by solving the reaction-diffusion-advection equations. Burning speed is also included for each initial hadronic number density. Reprinted from Ref. [36].

n_B [fm^{-3}]	T [MeV]	v/c
0.05	22.9	0.00083
0.1	23.1	0.0016
0.2	23.4	0.0025
0.3	26.4	0.0058
0.4	30.4	0.010

In order to impose this temperature distribution into a stellar evolution macroscopic simulation, we perform the following. We solve the TOV equations for a cold neutron star at temperature $T = 0.1$ MeV. This gives a density profile of the hadronic star. Since we have an interpolated function of temperature vs. hadronic density, we can compute the temperature at each computational zone as a function of the density in the zone. This creates a temperature profile. We maintain the temperature fixed at each baryonic coordinate a (see Equation (6)), and then simply switch the EOS from hadronic to quark matter. We solve the TOV equations again to obtain a new quark star density profile, radius, and gravitational mass, while still maintaining the same temperature profile and the same baryonic mass.

2.4. The Neutrino Spectrum

Now that we have constructed our hot PQS, a simulation based on the above assumptions and equations produces the following behavior behind a nascent, hot quark star: the production of entropy by the combustion process creates a nascent quark star with central temperatures of $T \sim 30$ MeV and outer temperatures of about $T \sim 20$ MeV. The initial lepton fraction is of the order of $Y_L \sim 0.1$ since it corresponds to the same lepton fraction as that of a cold neutron star in beta equilibrium. This nascent quark star also has a neutrino density profile with a very high neutrino chemical potential profile of ~100 MeV, since the quark star's densities are always of the order of nuclear saturation density, with the density decreasing sharply to zero in a height scale of a femtometer (the length scale of the strong interaction). This very hot object of $T > 20$ MeV will cool off in a period of tens of seconds since the heat will utimately be carried away by neutrinos. There is also a Joule heating effect in the neutrino transport, since the initial chemical potential of neutrinos is high, and some of the chemical potential energy is transformed into heat as the neutrinos escape from the quark star (see [10] for the micro-physics of the combustion).

The main ways in which this stellar evolution differs from proto-neutron stars are the following: First, the initial neutrinosphere will be much hotter for the quark star case. As mentioned previously in this section, the neutrinosphere temperature is ~20 MeV if calculated numerically. This has tremendous consequences for the spectrum and luminosity, as the neutrino energy will be roughly ~60 MeV and the luminosity is proportional to T_ν^4, where T_ν is the neutrinospheric temperature.

Since the neutrino spectrum is both harder and more luminous for the PQS than the PNS, the neutrino signal, as detected from Earth, will be different for the PQS and the PNS (Figures 2 and 3). First, the PQS will have a very hard spectrum composed of high temperature $T > 20$ MeV neutrinos, which will produce a very different Fermi–Dirac distribution, and, therefore, detected signal, than the PNS, where neutrinos have a temperature of only T~5 MeV. This harder spectrum also leads to a higher peak luminosity for the PQS, which is $>10^{55}$ erg/s, a luminosity that cannot be produced by PNSs.

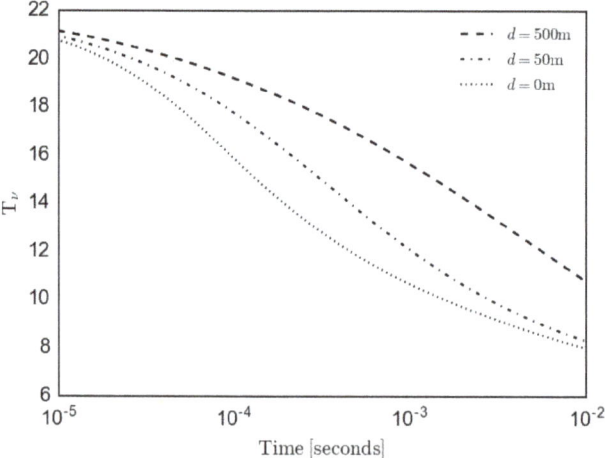

Figure 2. Evolution of the neutrinospheric temperature for the PQS. Each curve represents a different length of the mixed-phase d (in meters). Reprinted from Ref. [36].

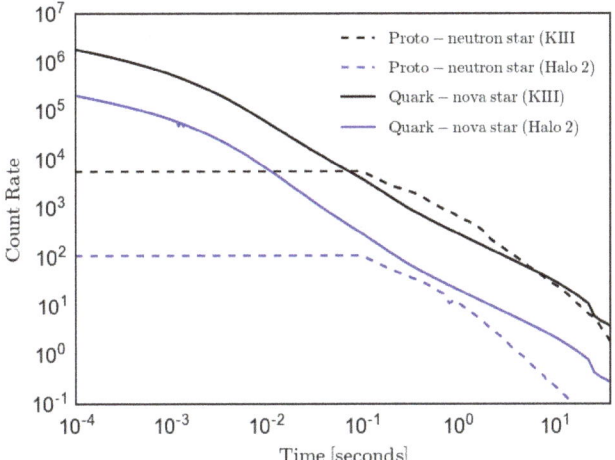

Figure 3. Detector count rates for a quark-nova vs. proto-neutron star for Super-Kamiokande III and Halo 2. Reprinted from Ref. [36].

An interesting question is how would this neutrino signal look in a detector? We will focus in water-based detectors (KIII) and lead-based detectors (Halo 2). In the case of water-based detectors, neutrinos are detected through the emission of secondary positrons by proton absorption of electron anti-neutrinos:

$$\bar{\nu}_e + p \rightarrow e^+ + n. \tag{16}$$

where p, is a proton, n is a neutron, and e^+ is a positron. This cross-section is proportional to E_ν^2, where E_ν is the energy of neutrinos. In the context of Halo II, neutrinos are detected by the emission of neutrons through neutrino capture by lead nuclei:

$$\nu_e + (N, Z) = (N - 1, Z + 1) + e^- + n, \tag{17}$$

where (N, Z) is an arbitrary nucleus of N neutrons and Z protons.

Detector counts for the two types of detectors are found in Figure 3. For the first 10^{-2} s, PQS count rates are about two orders of magnitude higher than for the PNS case. Furthermore, the PQS spectrum will be very different, as the neutrinospheric temperatures are much higher for the PQS case, as can be seen from Figure 2. Therefore, we can deduce that the PQS will release a fairly clean signal that should be very different from the case of PNS.

2.5. The Ejecta

Another important aspect is that the large neutrino luminosity of the PQS can potentially transform into kinetic energy through neutrino-antineutrino pair annihilation. This effect arises from the fact that there will be a high density of both neutrinos and antineutrinos, and therefore a high probability of head-on collisions which would annihilate them. The formula for neutrino pair-annihilation is:

$$L_{e^-e^+} = 1.09 \times 10^{-5} \times (D_1 L_{\nu_e,51}^{9/4} + D_2 L_{\nu_\mu,51}^{9/4} + D_2 L_{\nu_\tau,51}^{9/4}) R_{PQS,6}^{-3/2} \tag{18}$$

where $L_{e^-e^+}$ is the energy per second deposited as e^-e^+ pairs and $L_{\nu_i,51}$ is neutrino luminosity in units of 10^{51} erg/s, $D_1 = 1.23$ and $D_2 = 0.814$ [46]; the proto-quark star radius R_{PQS} is in units 10^6 cm.

This implies that annihilation is proportional to T_ν^9, which means this effect is extremely sensitive to temperature. The pair annihilation mechanism has already been explored in the context of core-collapse supernovae and neutron star mergers (e.g., [47]). In the case of supernovae, it was originally conceived as a mechanism that could inject sufficient energy to revive the stalled shock, with Goodman et al. [47] arguing that the pair annihilation mechanism could inject as much as 10^{51} ergs in mechanical energy, which is the same kinetic energy observed in ordinary core-collapse explosions. However Cooperstein et al. [48] found that the original value of 10^{51} ergs was a gross overestimation, since Goodman et al. had overestimated the energy of neutrinos, and had not taken into account the fact that the reverse pair annihilation reaction could annihilate the electron-positron pairs to produce cooling, which sapped the shock from the energy necessary to eject the supernova shell. Therefore, in the case of supernovae, the pair annihilation mechanism contributes negligibly to the explosion.

However, in the case of the PQS, there are differences in the physics of the neutrinosphere from the PNS case that makes the pair annihilation mechanism a powerful explosive engine. First, there is the fact that the neutrinosphere of the PQS is extremely hot, with a temperature of about $T \sim 20$ MeV. This high temperature is due to combustion, which heats up the whole star, including the neutrinosphere. This large temperature makes an immense difference in the energy deposited by the pair annihilation mechanism for the PQS in contrast to the PNS. We can calculate the ratio between the two by noting that the pair annihilation mechanism is proportional to T_ν^9. Assuming the neutrinospheric temperature of PNS is $T_{\nu PNS} \sim 5$ MeV, and that for the PQS is $T_{\nu PQS} \sim 20$ MeV, the ratio between the two is:

$$\frac{T_{\nu PQS}^4}{T_{\nu PNS}^4} = 4^9 \sim 3 \times 10^5 . \tag{19}$$

In other words, the energy deposited through pair annihilation in PQS is more than five orders of magnitude larger than for PNS! Furthermore, the PQS does not suffer the same sort of electron-positron annihilation cooling as for the case of the PNS, since in the PQS case, along the interface, there is an extreme temperature drop of 20 MeV with a scale height of less than one centimeter. Since the cross-section for electron-positron annihilation is proportional to temperature, then the cooling rates are of lesser magnitude than the neutrino annihilation heating rates, since the latter have a much larger temperature than the former.

We can estimate how much energy is injected through pair annihilation by using the time-dependent output of the stellar evolution code, since the pair annihilation mechanism ultimately depends on temperature.

Preliminary calculations have found that the kinetic energy deposited by pair annihilation can be as much as $\sim 10^{52}$ ergs, depending on the existence of a strangelet-electron mixed phase at the edge of the star [49]. The larger the mixed phase, the more energy is deposited through pair annihilation, as the luminosity is larger. The neutrino luminosity is larger with larger mixed phases because the mean free path becomes enlarged, since a PQS without a mixed phase is extremely dense, of the order of the nuclear saturation density throughout the whole profile, since the density falls very sharply to zero in a scale height of Fermis.

We can estimate how much matter is ejected by the pair annihilation mechanism. A more precise calculation would require solving the hydrodynamic equations behind the PQS wind. However, we can find an analytic approximation of the hydrodynamic equations that can be used to estimate the mass ejection with the use of the time-dependent output of the stellar evolution code. The equations of mass continuity imply that:

$$\frac{dM}{dt} = 4\pi \rho R^2 v_s , \tag{20}$$

where $\frac{dM}{dt}$ is the mass ejected per second, ρ is the mass density, R is the radius, and v_s is the velocity of the wind. We assume the mass ejected is the leftover hadronic mass that hovers above the quark-star. We can assume that pair-annihilation "happens" before the whole quark star is burnt; therefore, there will be a small amount of hadronic matter overlaying the quark star that can be ejected. The same can be said for a mixed phase, where the quark-nuggets that are gravitationally bound to an electron lattice can also be ejected by the pair annihilation.

Furthermore, we must have an energy conservation equation where mass is ejected, only if: (i) the energy injected by pair annihilation is more than the gravitational potential energy of the parcel ejected, and (ii) the energy does not transport away as fast as it is injected. Under these two assumptions, we can write the equation of energy conservation:

$$L - GM\frac{dM}{dt}/R = 4\pi\rho v_s^3 R^2 , \qquad (21)$$

where v_s is the sound speed, M is the mass of the quark star, and G is the gravitational constant.

As the speed of sound, M and R, and L are given, we can solve the two equations above to obtain a solution for the $\frac{dM}{dt}$. The existence of mass ejection through pair-annihilation implies an explosive mechanism that does not require supersonic detonation or core-collapse—it merely requires that the neutrinosphere is hot enough and that the combustion front is faster than the neutrino transport timescale. These conditions are weaker and easier to achieve than core-collapse of the quark core or detonation to a deflagration transition.

We conclude this section by briefly enumerating the mechanisms that can trigger the ejection of the relativistic ejecta. An important set of mechanisms is what we will refer to as "shock-induced ejection". This implies that, in a compact star, the ongoing conversion of hadronic to quark matter shrinks the core too quickly for the overlaying layers to respond, creating a separation or a gap. Given that this requires supersonic falling speeds, this will create a shock. This scenario is similar to core-collapse supernova, where the core shrinks supersonically, separating the outer layers. In this scenario, a couple of things could happen:

- *Mechanical core bounce*: In the case of supersonic core-collapse, the increasing density in the core would make it stiffer, eventually making the infalling matter bounce back. This mechanism has been used in supernova simulations with quark cores (e.g., [50]).
- *Thermal photon fireball*: The surface of a quark star can achieve very high temperatures of $T \sim 20$ MeV. This would generate an intense photon flux that could push the crust towards relativistic speeds. This picture is sustained by the fact that the crust "floats" on top of the quark star, leaving a gap between the quark surface and the crust. The photon flux would then act as a piston that pushes the crust outwards. The other issue that occurs in the case of a transition to CFL, is that neutrino emissivities are shut off, making photons the explosive mechanism [51].
- *Detonation*: it could be that instabilities accelerate the laminar flame into supersonic speeds. This would generate an effect referred to as a deflagration to detonation transition (DDT). This would generate a shock that could eject the outer layers of the compact star.
- *Neutrino-induced ejection*: Originally Keränen et al. [52] calculated the mass ejection that is induced by neutrino deposition. From this perspective, the core shrinks supersonically and at the same time emits neutrinos that are absorbed by the overlaying layers, unbounding them gravitationally. In this case, 10^{51} ergs are deposited into the outer hadronic layers.

Here, we argue that, since the neutrinospheric temperature in a PQS will reach ~ 20 MeV, there will be copious neutrino-antineutrino pairs. These pairs will annihilate above the neutrinosphere into electron-positron pairs that will become tightly coupled with the overlying hadronic matter. Due to momentum conservation, these neutrinos will deposit their momentum. Our preliminary calculations show that about $\sim 10^{52}$ ergs can be deposited using this mechanism.

Given that, in the case of an isolated quark-nova, the only remaining hadronic matter will be the overlaying crust, then the ejecta will only contain about $\sim 10^{-5} M_\odot$ matter. If we assume that about $\sim 10^{52}$ ergs are injected into that crust, we will obtain a Lorenz factor of about a few hundred. Thus the quark-nova has the potential to convert an important percentage of the NS-to-QS conversion energy to relativistic ejecta with interesting implications for astrophysics, as discussed below.

3. Some Applications to High-Energy Astrophysics

The findings presented above did not take into account the presence of a color superconductive quark matter phase. This would allow the channelling of some of the neutrino energy to a photon fireball (see [51] and references therein) making relativistic quark-nova ejecta an even more likely outcome. The relativistic quark-nova ejecta (see Section 2.5) enable an efficient harnessing of the HM-to-(u,d,s) conversion energy, converting it to extreme radiation via shock following collision with the environment. An interesting aspect of the mass ejection mechanism is the possibility that it produces strong electromagnetic signatures with a total energy of 10^{52} ergs. There are two avenues for the production of these signatures. The first avenue is when the quark-nova explodes in isolation; in other words, the quark-deconfinement that produces the mass ejection appears in a fairly old neutron star, where the supernova ejecta of the progenitor explosion has dispersed, giving rise to a neutron star in isolation. The other case is when a neutron star explodes while still embedded within the ejected envelope of its supernova progenitor. Under these two scenarios, the quark-nova model was found to account for the main high-energy astrophysical phenomena and, in particular, those facing the energy budget discussed in the introduction.

3.1. Superluminous SuperNovae (SLSNe)

A dual-shock quark-nova (dsQN) happens when the quark-nova occurs days to weeks after the supernova (SN) explosion of the progenitor star. The time delay means that the quark-nova ejecta catch up and collide with the SN ejecta after it has expanded to large radii [53]. Effectively, the quark-nova re-energizes the extended SN ejecta causing a re-brightening of the SN; most of the ejecta's energy (i.e., $\sim 10^{52}$ ergs) can thus be converted to radiation! For time delays not exceeding a few days, and because of PdV losses, the size of the SN ejecta is small enough that only a modest re-brightening results when the quark-nova ejecta collides with the preceding SN ejecta; this yields a moderately energetic, high-velocity, SN. However, in this case, the quark-nova model predicts that the interaction of the quark-nova neutrons with the SN ejecta leads to unique nuclear spallation products [54]. For longer time delays, extreme re-brightening occurs when the two ejecta collide yielding light curves very similar to those of SLSNe [55]. For time-delays exceeding many weeks, the SN ejecta is too large and too diffuse to experience any substantial re-brightening.

A quark-nova could also occur in tight binaries where the NS can accrete/gain enough mass to increase its core density and experience a quark-nova event. The NS can accrete either from the companion overflowing its Roche lobe [56] or while inside a binary's common envelope. Quark-novae in binaries have proven successful in fitting properties of unusual SNe (see [57] for details). The quark-nova model (applied to buried and isolated NS) has been used to fit a large number of superluminous and double-humped supernovae (see http://www.quarknova.ca/LCGallery.html (accessed on 20 March 2022) for a picture gallery of the fits).

3.2. Gamma-Ray Bursts (GRBs)

For longer delays of years to decades following the core-collapse of a massive star (e.g., a Type Ic SN), Ref. [58] built a model capable of explaining many of the key characteristics of gamma-ray bursts (GRBs). Here, one appeals to the turbulent (i.e., filamentary and magnetically saturated) SN ejecta, shaped by its interaction with an underlying pulsar wind nebula (PWN), and sprayed by the relativistic quark-nova ejecta. Synchrotron radiation is emitted as the quark-nova ejecta passes through successive filaments explaining the light-curves of many observed GRBs including the flares and the afterglow. We successfully fitted the light-curves in the XRT-band (including the afterglow and the flares when present) simultaneously with the spectrum for each of the many GRBs we selected; see Section 5.3.1 and Figure 6 in [58].

3.3. Fast Radio Bursts (FRBs)

Old, slowly rotating and isolated NSs in the outskirts of galaxies experiencing a quark-nova event can yield fast radio bursts [59]. The quark-nova ejecta expanding in a low-density medium develops plasma instabilities (Buneman and Weibel successively) yielding electron bunching and coherent synchrotron emission with properties of repeating and non-repeating FRBs, such as the GHz frequency, the milli-second duration and a fluence in the Jy ms range. (The reader is encouraged to run the quark-nova FRB simulator at http://www.quarknova.ca/FRBSimulator/ (accessed on 20 March 2022)).

3.4. R-Process Nucleo-Synthesis

The presence of neutron-rich, large Z nuclei in the QN ejecta (i.e., the neutron star's outermost layers with $(40, 95) < (Z, A) < (70, 177)$), the large neutron-to-seed ratio, and the low electron fraction $Y_e \sim 0.03$ in the decompressing ejecta present favorable conditions for rapid neutron capture (r-process) nucleosynthesis. The quark-nova provides a rich supply of exotic nuclei and generates an r-process environment that is similar, though not identical, to neutron star mergers (NSMs). The QN and NSM scenarios both utilize decompression of neutron matter for the r-process, but the underproduction of elements at $A < 130$, known as a feature of NSM yields, is less pronounced in the QN [60,61]. The quark-nova ejecta is a natural rapid neutron-capture (r-process) site [61]. With an estimated quark-nova rate of 0.1 that of core-collapse supernovae and an ejecta of $\sim 10^{-5} M_\odot$ per quark-nova, these could be an important source of r-process elements ejecting $\sim 10^{-8} M_\odot$ per year per galaxy of r-process products. This is of the same order as the contribution from binary mergers which occur at a much lower rate of $\sim 10^{-6} M_\odot$ per year per galaxy but with a much higher ejecta mass of $\sim 10^{-2} M_\odot$ per merger.

There are implications of the quark-nova r-process nucleosynthesis for astrophysics. These include: (i) A neutron star experiencing a quark-nova event while still embedded within the supernova remnant can deposit NSM-like r-process material into the expanding shell; (ii) quark-novae occur naturally within Pop. III stars, thus contributing to the r-enrichment of the interstellar medium much before NSMs which would instead lead to a sudden and late r-enrichment [62]; (iii) The neutron-rich relativistic quark-nova ejecta was shown to be an efficient spallation process converting ^{56}Ni to ^{44}Ti when interacting with the preceding SN ejecta [54]. This novel process of destroying ^{56}Ni would have the unexpected effect of dimming some supernovae (e.g., [63]).

4. Discussion

The work of the Quark-Nova group in simulating the non-premixed hadron-to-quark combustion starting with Niebergal [35] was seminal, since the time-dependent solutions were solved for the first time. These early investigations used neither neutrino transport, nor a hadronic EOS, and the halting solution (of the burning front) was based on hybrid arguments which appeal to semi-analytic and numerical analyses. In subsequent work [36], the Burn-UD code was extended by adding neutrino transport, electron EOS, neutrino EOS, and a hadronic EOS. From these additions, we found, for the first time, that neutrinos do indeed induce mechanical instabilities, since they can quench the burning. Furthermore, the addition of hadronic EOS (i.e., HM-to-(u,d,s) combustion compared to the (u,d)-to-(u,d,s) version) leads to thermodynamic effects that may quench or accelerate burning. A major result is that the neutrino heating experienced by hadronic matter due to absorption of neutrinos produced by the beta equilibrating of (u,d,s) ash, will lead to a free-energy barrier between the *(u,d,s)* ash and the hadronic fuel (see [10] for a recent review). This energy barrier can quench the burning. Specifically, in comparing *(u,d)*-to-*(u,d,s)* versus HM-to-*(u,d,s)* burning, the latter (i.e., the inclusion of a hadronic EOS) can generate non-linear thermodynamic effects where the coupling of neutrino transport and the free energy of the hadronic EOS can lead to quenching. This quenching appears since the hadronic fuel can absorb neutrinos emitted by the hot *(u,d,s)*, which can lead to the erection of a free-energy barrier that makes combustion thermodynamically unfavourable. These results suggest that a multidimensional code is necessary, since instability would lead to a wrinkling of the interface, and, therefore, only through a multidimensional study can we unearth the final fate of the burning neutron star.

4.1. Quark-Novae and the EOS of Dense Matter

We note that the formation and properties (e.g., temperature) of the hot proto-quark star, driven by the pressure gradients that drive the burning interface, are controlled primarily by leptonic weak decays rather than by the EOS of the hadronic matter. Specifically, the effects of the leptonic weak interaction, including the corresponding weak decay rates and the EOS of electrons and neutrinos, are at least as important as the uncertainties related to the EOS of high density matter (see [10,36] for details). In the work presented here, we explored hadronic EOSs with a proton fraction less than 0.1, but, in general, the proton fraction, while important, is not as crucial as the strong pressure gradients induced by leptonic weak decays which drastically slow down the burning speed (by orders of magnitude), which is thereafter controlled by the much slower burning process driven by back-flowing downstream matter. The relativistic mean-field approach used in [41] is not unique and other approaches taking into account nuclear many-body interactions rather than reducing the interactions to mean fields exist [64,65]. We plan to explore other hadronic EOSs, both stiff and soft ones including hyperons.

The MIT bag EOS only includes confinement but does not emulate chiral symmetry breaking (the process that gives hadrons their large masses compared to the quark masses that constitute them). Some chiral models, such as the Nambu–Jona–Lasinio (NJL) model tend to reduce the stability of *(u,d,s)*, since the quarks become massive [66]. It is evident that at least some quark matter EOS would not release as much energy through beta equilibration, and therefore lead to lower temperatures for the *(u,d,s)* ash. We are currently exploring a wider parameterization across different quark matter EOSs.

The observation of an energetic quark-nova (e.g., in re-energized core-collapse SNe or in double-humped SNe; see Section 3.1) would support the suggestion that: (i) The transition was first-order (i.e., release of latent heat during the HM-to-*(u,d,s)* transition); (ii) Interface instabilities (e.g., deleptonization; [34]) would have taken place which would favor HM EOS poor in proton fraction in concert with neutrino trapping; (iii) From the total energy released, one could, in principle, differentiate a deflagration-to-detonation from a (quark) core-collapse scenario; (iv) The time delay between the supernova and the quark-nova (weeks in the case of double-humped SNe; see Section 3.1) could be used to investigate: (iv-a) The density at which quark matter deconfines (which is very uncertain). The time delay is the time it takes the core of the neutron star to reach quark deconfinement density due to either spin-down or accretion; (iv-b) s-quark seeding timescales as the most likely mechanisms.

While constraints on the HM and *(u,d,s)* EOSs could be gleaned from the observation of a quark-nova as described above, better interpretation of the observations depends on exploring more EOSs to understand their exact role in the conversion front compared to pressure gradients (from leptonic weak decays and for different electron EOSs) that drive the burning interface.

4.2. Quark-Novae and Binary Neutron Star Mergers

Section 2.5 discusses the quark-nova ejecta which consists mainly of the NS's outermost layers (i.e., the crust) with $M_{\rm QN} \sim 10^{-5} M_\odot$. With up to 10^{52} ergs of conversion energy converted to kinetic energy, this means an ejecta with a Lorentz factor of hundreds. In other words, compared to binary mergers and SNe, the quark-nova ejecta, besides being neutron-rich and efficient at r-process nucleo-synthesis (see Section 3.4), is highly relativistic. Numerical simulations of NSMs suggest that the type of merger depends strongly on the total mass of the binaries, the mass ratio and on the HM EOS. Prompt black hole formation would naturally be expected if the EOS is soft, while a stiff EOS would yield a hyper-massive NS (HMNS; e.g., [67–69]). Of relevance to the quark-nova model, is the long-lived (>100 ms) HMNS scenario where the massive NS may undergo a quark-nova transition before a black hole forms. An HMNS is more likely to harbour a quark core; once two-lavoured quark matter is nucleated in the core of the HMNS, the weak interaction can turn some of the d quarks into s-quarks, lowering the Fermi energy of the quark matter. The conversion of the HMNS to a quark star is not unrealistic if it occurs on timescales shorter than the black hole formation. An interesting outcome is a short gamma-ray burst from the interaction of the relativistic quark-nova ejecta with the binary's ejecta (see Section 3.2).

Adding the quark-nova into the NSM picture would help relax the need for a short-duration gamma-ray burst driven by accretion onto the black-hole and would provide a new channel for gravitational wave (GW) signals (see Section 4.3). The GWs would be emitted in the time frame between the formation of the HMNS and the collapse to a black hole. Our model would thus predict a short-duration gamma-ray burst prior to black hole formation but following the quark-nova GW signal. The NSM ejecta ($\sim 10^{-2} M_\odot$) dwarfs the QN ejecta ($\sim 10^{-5} M_\odot$). Nevertheless, the relativistic nature of the QN ejecta plausibly implies the presence of unique exotic nuclei at $A < 130$ not expected from NSMs (see Section 3.4).

4.3. Quark-Novae and Gravitational Waves

Preliminary investigation of gravitational waves from a quark-nova used Newtonian gravity (see Appendix in [70]). The ultimate goal is to compute the GW signal during the HM-to-(u,d,s) burning (i.e., during the outward expansion of the hadronic-to-quark matter conversion front) using a full general relativistic treatment which is currently being pursued by the Quark-Nova group. The extreme densities in the burning NS core and instabilities unique to the HM-to-(u,d,s) burning (e.g., the deleptonization) should favour specific modes. Ultimately, we hope to isolate unique features of quark-nova GWs to differentiate them from supernovae and binary mergers.

5. Conclusions

By coupling a stellar evolution code to the Burn-UD code, we studied the formation and evolution of a hot proto-quark star (the macro-physics of the quark-nova). We found much higher peak neutrino luminosities (>10^{55} erg/s) and a harder neutrino spectrum than previous stellar evolution studies on proto-quark stars (e.g., Pagliara et al. (2013)). The neutrino counts derived were those that observatories such as Super-Kamiokande-III and Halo-II should expect and could be used to differentiate between a supernova and a quark-nova. Due to the high peak neutrino luminosities in a quark-nova, neutrino pair annihilation can deposit as much as 10^{52} ergs in kinetic energy in the matter overlaying the neutrinosphere, yielding a relativistic ejecta. The energetics of the quark-nova and the dynamics of its ejecta have interesting implications for high-energy astrophysics and could aid in our understanding of many still enigmatic astrophysical transients, such as super-luminous supernovae, gamma-ray bursts and fast radio bursts.

Funding: This research is funded by the Natural Sciences and Engineering Research Council of Canada.

Conflicts of Interest: The authors declare no conflict of interest.

References

1. Janka, H.-T.; Melson, T.; Summa, A. Physics of core-collapse supernovae in three dimensions: A sneak preview. *Annu. Rev. Nucl. Part. Sci.* **2016**, *66*, 341–375. [CrossRef]
2. Kumar, P.; Zhang, B. The physics of gamma-ray bursts and relativistic jets. *Phys. Rep.* **2015**, *561*, 1–109. [CrossRef]
3. Abbott, B.; Abbott, R.; Abbott, T.; Acernese, F.; Ackley, K.; Adams, C.; Adams, T.; Addesso, P.; Adhikari, R.; Adya, V.; et al. Gravitational waves and gamma-rays from a binary neutron star merger: GW170817 and GRB 170817A. *Astrophys. J. Lett.* **2017**, *848*, L13. [CrossRef]
4. Sukhbold, T.; Woosley, S. The most luminous supernovae. *Astrophys. J. Lett.* **2016**, *820*, L38. [CrossRef]
5. Ouyed, R.; Dey, J.; Dey, M. Quark-Nova. *Astron. Astrophys.* **2002**, *390*, L39–L42. [CrossRef]
6. Bodmer, A. Collapsed nuclei. *Phys. Rev. D* **1971**, *4*, 1601. [CrossRef]
7. Terazawa, H. *Tokyo University Report INS336*; Tokyo University: Tokyo, Japan, 1979.
8. Witten, E. Cosmic separation of phases. *Phys. Rev. D* **1984**, *30*, 272. [CrossRef]
9. Weber, F. Strange quark matter and compact stars. *Prog. Part. Nucl. Phys.* **2005**, *54*, 193–288. [CrossRef]
10. Ouyed, R. The micro-physics of the Quark-Nova: Recent developments. In *Exploring the Astrophysics of the XXI Century with Compact Stars*; World Scientific Publishing: Singapore, 2022; ISBN 978-981-122-093-7.
11. Glendenning, N.K. First-order phase transitions with more than one conserved charge: Consequences for neutron stars. *Phys. Rev. D* **1992**, *46*, 1274. [CrossRef]
12. Alford, M.G.; Rajagopal, K.; Reddy, S.; Wilczek, F. Minimal color-flavor-locked–nuclear interface. *Phys. Rev. D* **2001**, *64*, 074017. [CrossRef]
13. Lugones, G.; Grunfeld, A.G.; Ajmi, M.A. Surface tension and curvature energy of quark matter in the Nambu–Jona-Lasinio model. *Phys. Rev. C* **2013**, *88*, 045803. [CrossRef]
14. Paschalidis, V.; Yagi, K.; Alvarez-Castillo, D.; Blaschke, D.B.; Sedrakian, A. Implications from GW170817 and I-Love-Q relations for relativistic hybrid stars. *Phys. Rev. D* **2018**, *97*, 084038. [CrossRef]
15. Alvarez-Castillo, D.E.; Blaschke, D.B.; Grunfeld, A.G.; Pagura, V.P. Third family of compact stars within a nonlocal chiral quark model equation of state. *Phys. Rev. D* **2019**, *99*, 063010. [CrossRef]
16. Bhattacharyya, A.; Mishustin, I.N.; Greiner, W. Deconfinement phase transition in compact stars: Maxwell versus Gibbs construction of the mixed phase. *J. Phys. G Nucl. Phys.* **2010**, *37*, 025201. [CrossRef]
17. Yasutake, N.; Lastowiecki, R.; Benic, S.; Blaschke, D.; Maruyama, T.; Tatsumi, T. Finite-size effects at the hadron-quark transition and heavy hybrid stars. *Phys. Rev. C* **2014**, *89*, 065803. [CrossRef]
18. Alford, M.G.; Han, S. Characteristics of hybrid compact stars with a sharp hadron-quark interface. *Eur. Phys. J. A* **2016**, *52*, 62. [CrossRef]
19. Glendenning, N.K. Phase transitions and crystalline structures in neutron star cores. *Phys. Rept.* **2001**, *342*, 393. [CrossRef]
20. Carroll, J.D.; Leinweber, D.B.; Williams, A.G.; Thomas, A.W. Phase transition from quark-meson coupling hyperonic matter to deconfined quark matter. *Phys. Rev. C* **2009**, *79*, 045810. [CrossRef]
21. Weissenborn, S.; Sagert, I.; Pagliara, G.; Hempel, M.; Schaffner-Bielich, J. Quark matter in massive compact stars. *Astrophys. J.* **2011**, *740*, L14. [CrossRef]
22. Fischer, T.; Sagert, I.; Pagliara, G.; Hempel, M.; Schaffner-Bielich, J.; Rauscher, T.; Liebendörfer, M. Core-collapse supernova explosions triggered by a quark–hadron phase transition during the early post-bounce phase. *Astrophys. J. Suppl.* **2011**, *194*, 39. [CrossRef]
23. Schulze, H.-J.; Rijken, T. Maximum mass of hyperon stars with the Nijmegen ESC08 model. *Phys. Rev. C* **2011**, *84*, 035801. [CrossRef]
24. Maruyama, T.; Chiba, S.; Schulze, H.-J.; Tatsumi, T. Hadron-quark mixed phase in hyperon stars. *Phys. Rev. D* **2007**, *76*, 123015. [CrossRef]
25. Masuda, K.; Hatsuda, T.; Takatsuka, T. Hadron–quark cross-over and massive hybrid stars. *Prog. Theor. Exp. Phys.* **2013**, *7*, 073.
26. Alvarez-Castillo, D.; Blaschke, D.; Typel, S. Mixed phase within the multi-polytrope approach to high-mass twins. *Astron. Nachr.* **2017**, *338*, 1048. [CrossRef]
27. Dexheimer, V.; Negreiros, R.; Schramm, S. Role of strangeness in hybrid stars and possible observables. *Phys. Rev. C* **2015**, *91*, 055808. [CrossRef]
28. McLerran, L.; Reddy, S. Quarkyonic Matter and Neutron Stars. *Phys. Rev. Lett.* **2019**, *122*, 122701. [CrossRef]
29. Prakash, M.; Bombaci, I.; Prakash, M.; Ellis, P.J.; Lattimer, J.M.; Knorren, R. Composition and structure of proto-neutron stars. *Phys. Rept.* **1997**, *280*, 1. [CrossRef]
30. Olinto, A.V. On the conversion of neutron stars into strange stars. *Phys. Lett. B* **1987**, *192*, 71–75. [CrossRef]
31. Perez-Garcia, M.A.; Silk, J.; Stone, J.R. Dark matter, neutron stars, and strange quark matter. *Phys. Rev. Lett.* **2010**, *105*, 141101. [CrossRef]
32. Benvenuto, O.; Horvath, J. Evidence for strange matter in super-novae? *Phys. Rev. Lett.* **1989**, *63*, 716. [CrossRef]
33. Drago, A.; Lavagno, A.; Parenti, I. Burning of a hadronic star into a quark or a hybrid star. *Astrophys. J.* **2007**, *659*, 1519. [CrossRef]
34. Ouyed, R.; Niebergal, B.; Jaikumar, P. Explosive Combustion of a Neutron Star into a Quark Star: The non-premixed scenario. In Proceedings of the Compact Stars in the QCD Phase Diagram III (CSQCD III), Guarujá, Brazil, 12–15 December 2012.

35. Niebergal, B. Hadronic-to-Quark-Matter Phase Transition: Astrophysical Implications. Ph.D. Thesis, University of Calgary, Calgary, AB, Canada, 2011; Publication Number: AAT NR81856.
36. Ouyed, A. The Neutrino Sector in Hadron-Quark Combustion: Physical and Astrophysical Implications. Ph.D. Thesis, University of Calgary, Calgary, AB, Canada, 2018.
37. Niebergal, B.; Ouyed, R.; Jaikumar, P. Numerical simulation of the hydrodynamical combustion to strange quark matter. *Phys. Rev. C* **2010**, *82*, 062801. [CrossRef]
38. Ouyed, A.; Ouyed, R.; Jaikumar, P. Numerical simulation of the hydrodynamical combustion to strange quark matter in the trapped neutrino regime. *Phys. Lett. B* **2018**, *777*, 184–190. [CrossRef]
39. Lugones, G. From quark drops to quark stars. *Eur. Phys. J. A* **2016**, *52*, 53. [CrossRef]
40. Drago, A.; Pagliara, G. The scenario of two families of compact stars. *Eur. Phys. J. A* **2016**, *52*, 41. [CrossRef]
41. Hempel, M.; Schaffner-Bielich, J. A statistical model for a complete supernova equation of state. *Nucl. Phys. A* **2010**, *837*, 210–254. [CrossRef]
42. Furusawa, S.; Sanada, T.; Yamada, S. Hydrodynamical study on the conversion of hadronic matter to quark matter: I. shock-induced conversion. *Phys. Rev. D* **2016**, *93*, 043018. [CrossRef]
43. Pons, J.A.; Steiner, A.W.; Prakash, M.; Lattimer, J.M. Evolution of proto-neutron stars with quarks. *Phys. Rev. Lett.* **2001**, *86*, 5223. [CrossRef]
44. Iwamoto, N. Neutrino emissivities and mean free paths of degenerate quark matter. *Ann. Phys.* **1982**, *141*, 1–49. [CrossRef]
45. Gao, Z.-F.; Shan, H.; Wang, W.; Wang, N. Reinvestigation of the electron fraction and electron fermi energy of neutron star. *Astron. Nachrichten* **2017**, *338*, 1066–1072. [CrossRef]
46. Salmonson, J.D.; Wilson, J.R. Neutrino annihilation between binary neutron stars. *Astrophys. J.* **2001**, *561*, 950. [CrossRef]
47. Goodman, J.; Dar, A.; Nussinov, S. Neutrino annihilation in type ii supernovae. *Astrophys. J.* **1987**, *314*, L7–L10. [CrossRef]
48. Cooperstein, J.; Horn, L.V.D.; Baron, E. Neutrino pair energy deposition in supernovae. *Astrophys. J.* **1987**, *321*, L129–L132. [CrossRef]
49. Jaikumar, P.; Reddy, S.; Steiner, A.W. Strange star surface: A crust with nuggets. *Phys. Rev. Lett.* **2006**, *96*, 041101. [CrossRef]
50. Gentile, N.; Aufderheide, M.; Mathews, G.; Swesty, F.; Fuller, G. The QCD phase transition and supernova core collapse. *Astrophys. J.* **1993**, *414*, 701–711. [CrossRef]
51. Ouyed, R.; Rapp, R.; Vogt, C. Fireballs from quark stars in the color-flavor locked phase: Application to gamma-ray bursts. *Astrophys. J.* **2005**, *632*, 1001. [CrossRef]
52. Keränen, P.; Ouyed, R.; Jaikumar, P. Neutrino emission and mass ejection in Quark-Novae. *Astrophys. J.* **2005**, *618*, 485. [CrossRef]
53. Ouyed, R.; Leahy, D. Dynamical and thermal evolution of the Quark-Nova ejecta. *Astrophys. J.* **2009**, *696*, 562. [CrossRef]
54. Ouyed, R.; Leahy, D.; Ouyed, A.; Jaikumar, P. Spallation Model for the Titanium-Rich Supernova Remnant Cassiopeia A. *Phys. Rev. Lett.* **2011**, *107*, 151103. [CrossRef]
55. Ouyed, R.; Kostka, M.; Koning, N.; Leahy, D.A.; Steffen, W. Quark nova imprint in the extreme supernova explosion SN 2006gy. *MNRAS* **2012**, *423*, 1652. [CrossRef]
56. Ouyed, R.; Staff, J.E. Quark-novae in neutron star—White dwarf binaries: A model for luminous (spin-down powered) sub-Chandrasekhar-mass Type Ia supernovae? *Res. Astron. Astrophys.* **2013**, *13*, 435. [CrossRef]
57. Ouyed, R.; Leahy, D.; Koning, N. Quark-Novae in massive binaries: A model for double-humped, hydrogen-poor, superluminous Supernovae. *Mon. Not. R. Astron. Soc.* **2015**, *454*, 2353–2359. [CrossRef]
58. Ouyed, R.; Leahy, D.; Koning, N. A Quark-Nova in the wake of a core-collapse supernova: A unifying model for long duration gamma-ray bursts and fast radio bursts. *Res. Astron. Astrophys.* **2020**, *20*, 27. [CrossRef]
59. Ouyed, R.; Leahy, D.; Koning, N. Quark-Novae in the outskirts of galaxies: An explanation of the fast radio burst phenomenon. *Mon. Not. R. Astron. Soc.* **2021**, *500*, 4414–4421. [CrossRef]
60. Jaikumar, P.; Meyer, B.S.; Otsuki, K.; Ouyed, R. Nucleosynthesis in neutron-rich ejecta from quark-novae. *A&A* **2007**, *471*, 227–236.
61. Kostka, M. Investigating astrophysical r-process sites: Code (r-Java 2.0) and model (dual-shock Quark-Nova) development. Ph.D. Thesis, University of Calgary, Calgary, AB, Canada, 2014.
62. Ouyed, R.; Pudritz, R.E.; Jaikumar, P. Quark-Novae, cosmic reionization, and early r-process element production. *Astrophys. J.* **2009**, *702*, 1575–1583. [CrossRef]
63. Ouyed, R.; Leahy, D.; Koning, N. Hints of a second explosion (a quark nova) in Cassiopeia A Supernova. *Res. Astron. Astrophys.* **2015**, *15*, 483. [CrossRef]
64. Weber, F.; Weigel, M. Neutron star properties and the relativistic nuclear equation of state of many-baryon matter. *Nucl. Phys. A* **1989**, *493*, 549–582. [CrossRef]
65. Camelio, G.; Lovato, A.; Gualtieri, L.; Benhar, O.; Pons, J.A.; Ferrari, V. Evolution of a proto-neutron star with a nuclear many-body equation of state: Neutrino luminosity and gravitational wave frequencies. *Phys. Rev. D* **2017**, *96*, 043015. [CrossRef]
66. Buballa, M. NJL-model analysis of dense quark matter. *Phys. Rep.* **2005**, *407*, 205–376. [CrossRef]
67. Shibata, M.; Taniguchi, K.; Uryu, K.K. Merger of binary neutron stars with realistic equations of state in full general relativity. *Phys. Rev. D* **2005**, *71*, 084021. [CrossRef]
68. Hotokezaka, K.; Kyutoku, K.; Okawa, H.; Shibata, M.; Kiuc, K. Binary Neutron Star Mergers: Dependence on the Nuclear Equation of State. *Phys. Rev. D* **2011**, *83*, 124008. [CrossRef]

69. Drago, A.; Pagliara, G.; Popov, S.B. The Merger of Two Compact Stars: A Tool for Dense Matter Nuclear Physics. *Universe* **2018**, *4*, 50. [CrossRef]
70. Staff, J.E.; Jaikumar, P.; Chan, V.; Ouyed, R. Spindown of Isolated Neutron Stars: Gravitational Waves or Magnetic Braking? *Astrophys. J.* **2012**, *751*, 24. [CrossRef]

Article

Beta Equilibrium under Neutron Star Merger Conditions

Mark G. Alford [1], Alexander Haber [1,*], Steven P. Harris [2] and Ziyuan Zhang [1,3]

[1] Physics Department, Washington University in Saint Louis, Saint Louis, MO 63130, USA; alford@wustl.edu (M.G.A.); ziyuan.z@wustl.edu (Z.Z.)
[2] Institute for Nuclear Theory, University of Washington, Seattle, WA 98195, USA; harrissp@uw.edu
[3] McDonnell Center for the Space Sciences, Washington University in St. Louis, St. Louis, MO 63130, USA
* Correspondence: ahaber@physics.wustl.edu

Abstract: We calculate the nonzero-temperature correction to the beta equilibrium condition in nuclear matter under neutron star merger conditions, in the temperature range $1\,\text{MeV} < T \lesssim 5\,\text{MeV}$. We improve on previous work using a consistent description of nuclear matter based on the IUF and SFHo relativistic mean field models. This includes using relativistic dispersion relations for the nucleons, which we show is essential in these models. We find that the nonzero-temperature correction can be of order 10 to 20 MeV, and plays an important role in the correct calculation of Urca rates, which can be wrong by factors of 10 or more if it is neglected.

Keywords: nuclear matter; neutron star merger; beta equilibration; weak interaction

1. Introduction

Nuclear matter in neutron stars settles into beta equilibrium, meaning that the proton fraction is in equilibrium with respect to the weak interactions. In this paper, we will study the conditions for beta equilibrium in ordinary nuclear matter (where all the baryon number is contributed by neutrons (n) and protons (p)) in the temperature range $1\,\text{MeV} \lesssim T \lesssim 5\,\text{MeV}$. This regime, which arises in neutron star mergers [1–4], is cool enough so that neutrinos are not trapped, but warm enough so that there are corrections to the low-temperature equilibrium condition. It has previously been shown [5] that in this regime the full beta equilibrium condition is

$$\mu_n = \mu_p + \mu_e + \Delta\mu, \tag{1}$$

where $\Delta\mu$ is a correction that arises from the violation of detailed balance (neutrino transparency) and the breakdown of the Fermi surface approximation (see Section 2). In nuclear matter in the temperature regime discussed here, the proton fraction will equilibrate towards the value given by Equation (1). Even if equilibrium is not reached on the timescale of a merger, one needs to know the correct equilibration condition in order to analyze phenomena associated with this relaxation process, such as bulk viscosity and neutrino emission. At low temperatures ($T \ll 1\,\text{MeV}$) $\Delta\mu$ is negligible, but in the temperature regime under consideration here it has been estimated to be up to tens of MeV [5]. The calculation in Ref. [5] went beyond the Fermi surface approximation by performing the phase space integral for the equilibration rate over the entire momentum space. However, it used a very crude model of the in-medium nucleons, assigning them their vacuum mass and assuming that their kinematics remained nonrelativistic at all densities.

In this paper, we improve on the analysis of Ref. [5]. We treat nuclear matter consistently using relativistic mean field models [6,7] with fully relativistic dispersion relations for the nucleons. We show that this makes a considerable difference to the beta equilibration rates because in these models the nucleons at the Fermi surface become relativistic at densities of a few times nuclear saturation density n_0. We calculate the direct Urca rate using the entire weak-interaction matrix element rather than its nonrelativistic limit, and evaluate the full phase space integral.

Other authors have evaluated direct Urca phase space integrals in calculations of the direct Urca rate, the neutrino emissivity, or the neutrino mean free path. Fully relativistic computations of direct Urca phase space integrals are uncommon in the literature, but they do appear. Refs. [8–11] calculate the neutrino mean free path using a fully relativistic formalism, while integrating over the full phase space. Ref. [10] calculates the direct Urca electron capture rate using a fully relativistic formalism and performs the full phase space integration. Although these calculations perform the full integration over phase space, they focus on high temperatures ($T \gtrsim 5$ MeV) where neutrinos are trapped and where the direct Urca threshold is blurred over a wide density range. In this temperature regime, which can be reached in mergers as well [1,12–14], beta equilibrium is given by

$$\mu_n + \mu_\nu = \mu_p + \mu_e, \qquad (2)$$

with μ_ν being the neutrino chemical potential. As discussed in more detail in Section 2, the neutrino-trapped beta equilibration condition does not require an additional finite-temperature correction. This paper will examine the phase space integral at lower temperatures where the direct Urca threshold is apparent and a key feature in the physics of beta equilibration or neutrino emission.

Other works use the relativistic formalism, but assume the nuclear matter is strongly degenerate (using the Fermi surface approximation, described below), and thus their results have a sharp direct Urca threshold density [15–17]. Ref. [18] uses the Fermi surface approximation, but develops a way to incorporate the finite 3-momentum of the neutrino, slightly blurring the threshold at finite temperature. Some works do the full phase space integration, but use nonrelativistic approximations for the matrix element and nucleon dispersion relations [5,19–21]. The vast majority of calculations use nonrelativistic approximations of the matrix element and the nucleon dispersion relations, together with the Fermi surface approximation [22–34]. All of these calculations are approximations of the full phase space integration using the fully relativistic formalism. Under certain conditions, the approximations match well with the full calculation, and have the advantage of being simple.

In Section 3 we introduce the two relativistic mean field models, IUF and SFHo, that we use. Section 4 describes our calculation of the rate of direct Urca processes, where we integrate over the entire phase space in order to include contributions from the region that would be kinematically forbidden in the low-temperature limit. Section 5 describes our calculation of the modified Urca contribution to the rate, where we use the Fermi surface approximation since there is no kinematically forbidden region for those processes in the density range that we consider. Section 6 presents our results, and Section 7 provides our conclusions.

We work in natural units, where $\hbar = c = k_B = 1$.

2. Beta Equilibration

Beta equilibration in npe^- matter is established by the Urca processes [35]. The modified Urca processes

$$N + n \to N + p + e^- + \bar{\nu} \qquad (3)$$
$$N + p + e^- \to N + n + \nu,$$

(here, N represents a "spectator" neutron or proton) operate at all densities in the core of the neutron star. In uniform npe^- matter, the proton-spectator modified Urca process only operates at densities where $x_p > 1/65$ [25,31], though this condition is only violated (if ever) in the inner crust of neutron stars [36] where the matter is not uniform and thus the calculations in this paper would not apply. The direct Urca processes

$$n \to p + e^- + \bar{\nu} \tag{4}$$
$$p + e^- \to n + \nu,$$

are exponentially suppressed when the temperature is much less than the Fermi energies and the density is in the range where $k_{Fn} > k_{Fp} + k_{Fe}$. In nuclear matter, the proton fraction rises as the density rises above n_0 and eventually may reach a "direct Urca threshold" where $k_{Fn} = k_{Fp} + k_{Fe}$. Above this threshold density beta equilibration is dominated by direct Urca, since (when kinematically allowed) it is faster than modified Urca.

In nuclear matter at temperatures greater than, say, 10 MeV, the neutrino mean free path is short and the nuclear matter system (for example, a protoneutron star) is neutrino-trapped and has conserved lepton number $Y_L = (n_e + n_\nu)/n_B$. In this case, the Urca processes (3) and (4) can proceed forward and backward, as the nuclear matter contains a population of neutrinos (or antineutrinos). In beta equilibrum, the forward and reverse processes have equal rates (detailed balance), and the beta equilibrium condition is given by balancing the chemical potentials of the participants in the equilibration reactions [6,37]

$$\mu_n + \mu_\nu = \mu_p + \mu_e \quad (\nu\text{-trapped}). \tag{5}$$

In cooler nuclear matter, at the temperatures considered in this work, the neutrino mean free path is comparable to or longer than the system size and therefore neutrinos are not in thermodynamic equilibrium: they escape from the star. Neutrinos can then occur in the final state but not the initial state of the Urca processes. Beta equilibrium is still achieved, but now by a balance of the neutron decay and the electron capture processes. However, the principle of detailed balance is not applicable because electron capture is not the time-reverse of neutron decay.

There is then no obvious equilibrium condition that can be written down a priori. In the limit of low temperature ($T \ll 1$ MeV) the Fermi surface approximation becomes valid: the particles participating in the Urca processes are close to their Fermi surfaces, and the neutrino carries negligible energy $\sim T$. The beta equilibrium condition can then be obtained by neglecting the neutrino, so that neutron decay and electron capture are just different time orderings of the same process $n \leftrightarrow p \, e^-$, and detailed balance gives

$$\mu_n = \mu_p + \mu_e \quad (\text{low temperature, } \nu\text{-transparent}). \tag{6}$$

The same condition on the chemical potentials can be reached by examining the phase space integrals for the direct Urca neutron decay and electron capture rates, taking the limit where the neutrino energy and momentum go to zero [38]. At temperatures $T \gtrsim 1$ MeV corrections to the Fermi surface approximation start to become significant, particularly for the protons whose Fermi energy is in the 10 MeV range. Then one cannot neglect the finite-temperature correction to (6)

$$\mu_n = \mu_p + \mu_e + \Delta\mu \quad (\text{general, } \nu\text{-transparent}). \tag{7}$$

The correction $\Delta\mu$ is a function of density and temperature, and its value in beta equilibrium is found by explicitly calculating the neutron decay and electron capture rates and adjusting $\Delta\mu$ so that they balance [5] (see also [39], where a similar calculation was done in the context of a hot plasma). In this paper, we perform that calculation.

For weak interactions we use the Fermi effective theory, which is an excellent approximation at nuclear energy scales. The main approximations arise in our treatment of the strong interaction. To describe nuclear matter and the nucleon excitations we use two different relativistic mean field models, both consistent with known phenomenology and chosen to illustrate a plausible range of behaviors. We describe these models in Section 3.

For the modified Urca process we model the nucleon-nucleon interaction with one-pion exchange [31,40].

3. Nuclear Matter Models

We will use two different equations of state, IUF [41] and SFHo [42], to calculate the Urca rates and the nonzero-temperature correction $\Delta\mu$. These are both consistent at the 2σ level with observational constraints on the maximum mass and the radius of neutron stars.

IUF predicts a maximum mass of neutron star to be $1.95 M_\odot$, and SFHo predicts $2.06 M_\odot$. Both are consistent with the observed limits, which are:

- $M_{\max} > 2.072^{+0.067}_{-0.066} M_\odot$ from NICER and XMM analysis of PSR J0740+6620 [43];
- $M_{\max} = 1.928^{+0.017}_{-0.017} M_\odot$ from NANOGrav analysis of PSR J1614-2230 [44];
- $M_{\max} = 2.01^{+0.14}_{-0.14} M_\odot$ from pulsar timing analysis of PSR J0348+0432 [45].

For the radius of a star of mass $2.06 M_\odot$, SFHo predicts $R = 10.3$ km, consistent with $R = 12.39^{+1.30}_{-0.98}$ km from NICER and XMM analysis of PSR J0740+6620 [43]. For the radius of a $1.4 M_\odot$ neutron star, IUF predicts $R = 12.7$ km and SFHo predicts $R = 11.9$ km, consistent with $R = 11.94^{+0.76}_{-0.87}$ km obtained by a combined analysis of X-ray and gravitational wave measurements of PSR J0740+6620 in Ref. [46].

It is still not determined whether there is a direct Urca threshold or not in nuclear matter at neutron star densities [47–51], so we choose one equation of state (IUF) with a threshold at $4.1 n_0$ and one (SFHo) with no threshold, as shown in Figure 1. Our approach could be applied to any equation of state where the beta process rates can be calculated. As we will see in Section 6.3, the density dependence of the momentum surplus $k_{Fp} + k_{Fe} - k_{Fn}$ is an important factor in the behavior of the direct Urca rates at low temperature, but the density dependence of the nucleon effective masses and Fermi momenta has a noticeable impact as well.

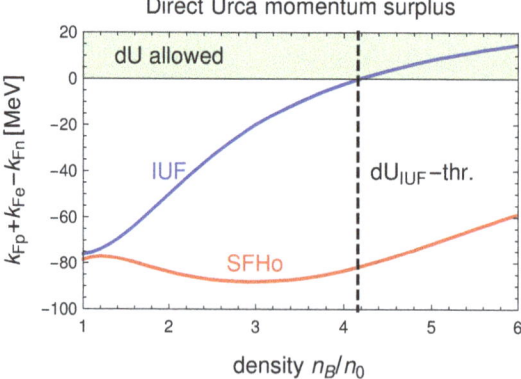

Figure 1. Direct Urca momentum surplus $k_{Fp} + k_{Fe} - k_{Fn}$ for IUF and SFHo equations of state at $T = 0$. When the surplus is negative, direct Urca is forbidden. IUF has an upper density threshold above which direct Urca is allowed; SFHo does not.

The coupling constants for SFHo are shown in Appendix A. Notice that the constants are taken from the online CompOSE database (https://compose.obspm.fr/, accessed on 27 April 2021), and are different from the values provided in Ref. [42].

A key feature of our calculation is that we use the full relativistic dispersion relations for the nucleons. In Figures 2 and 3 we illustrate the importance of this in relativistic mean field theories, where the nucleon effective mass drops rapidly with density. Although the precipitous drop in the nucleon Dirac effective mass with increasing density is a common feature in relativistic mean field theories [52,53], we note that in two recent treatments that go beyond the mean field approximation, the drop in the effective mass was not as dramatic [54,55]. We plot the Dirac effective mass [56] and the Fermi momentum of the neutrons and protons in these two EoSs. Although around nuclear saturation density n_0, the nucleons are nonrelativistic, as the density rises to several times n_0, the nucleon effective mass has dropped significantly below its vacuum value. Neutrons on their Fermi surface become relativistic at $2 - 3n_0$, while protons on their Fermi surface remain nonrelativistic until the density rises to $3 - 6n_0$. In Figures 4 and 5, we show that using a nonrelativistic approximation would lead to Urca rates that are incorrect by about an order of magnitude, although for direct Urca neutron decay the discrepancy can be many orders of magnitude.

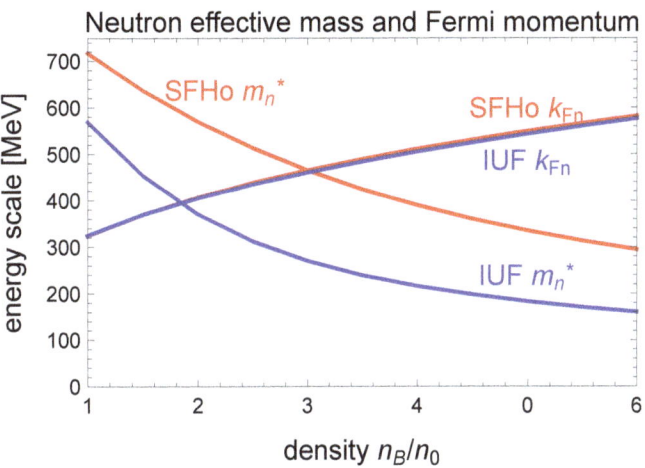

Figure 2. Density dependence of the neutron's (Dirac) effective mass and Fermi momentum for the IUF and SFHo EoSs, showing that neutrons at the Fermi surface become relativistic at densities above 2 to $3 n_0$.

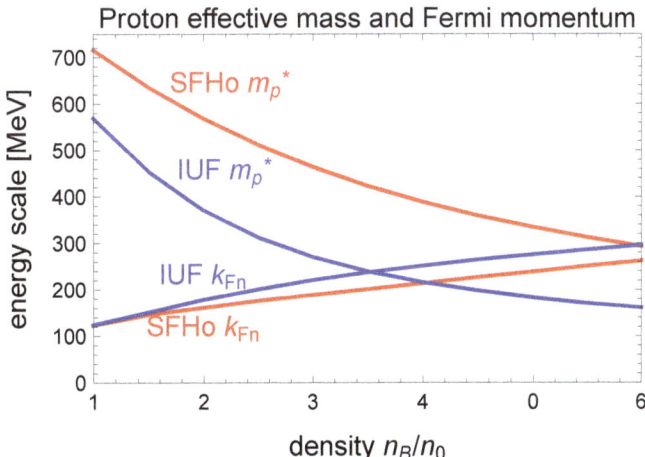

Figure 3. Density dependence of the proton's (Dirac) effective mass and Fermi momentum for the IUF and SFHo EoSs, showing that protons at the Fermi surface become relativistic starting at densities between $3 - 6n_0$.

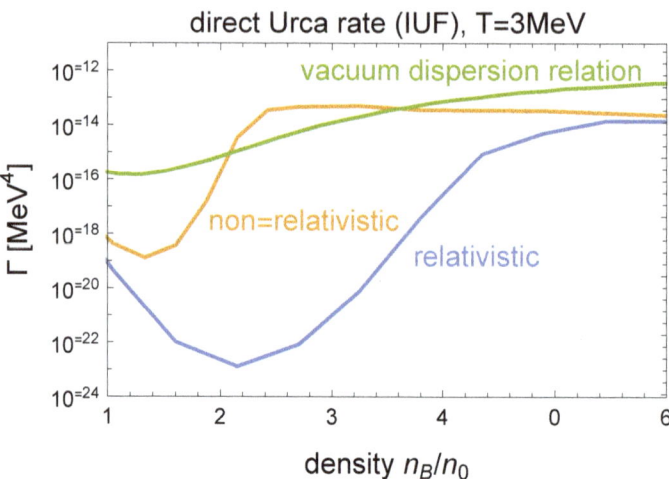

Figure 4. Direct Urca neutron decay rate calculated using relativistic, nonrelativistic and the vacuum dispersion relations at $T = 3$ MeV for IUF.

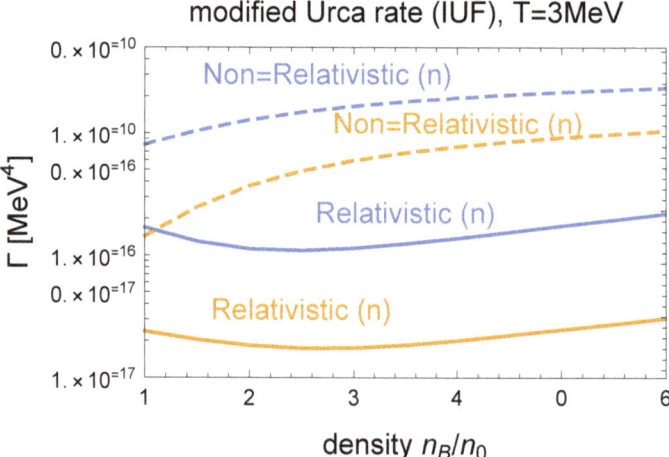

Figure 5. Modified Urca rate calculated using relativistic and nonrelativistic dispersion relations at $T = 3$ MeV for IUF. (n) stands for neutron-spectator modified Urca and (p) stands for proton-spectator modified Urca.

4. Beta Equilibration via Direct Urca

We calculate the in-medium direct Urca rates for neutron decay and electron capture using the relativistic weak-interaction matrix element and the relativistic dispersion relations for the nucleons and electrons. We also integrate over the full momentum phase space, not relying on the Fermi surface approximation. This is important because in the "dUrca-forbidden" density range the Fermi surface approximation would say the direct Urca rate is zero, so nonzero-temperature corrections are the leading contribution. These become significant (comparable to modified Urca) at the temperatures of interest here, $T \gtrsim 1$ MeV [5].

In relativistic mean field models the dispersion relations for the neutrons, protons, and electrons are

$$E_n = \underbrace{\sqrt{m_n^{*2} + k_n^2}}_{E_n^*} + U_n$$

$$E_p = \underbrace{\sqrt{m_p^{*2} + k_p^2}}_{E_p^*} + U_p \qquad (8)$$

$$E_e = \sqrt{m_e^2 + k_e^2}$$

$$E_\nu = k_\nu,$$

where the nucleons' effective mass m_i^* and energy shift U_i depend on density and temperature [10]. The unshifted energies E_i^* arise in the phase space normalization and the Dirac traces [9].

4.1. Neutron Decay

The direct Urca neutron decay rate is [31,57]

$$\Gamma_{nd} = \int \frac{d^3k_n}{(2\pi)^3} \frac{d^3k_p}{(2\pi)^3} \frac{d^3k_e}{(2\pi)^3} \frac{d^3k_\nu}{(2\pi)^3} f_n (1-f_p)(1-f_e) \frac{\sum |M|^2}{(2E_n^*)(2E_p^*)(2E_e)(2E_\nu)}$$
$$(2\pi)^4 \delta^{(4)}(k_n - k_p - k_e - k_\nu). \qquad (9)$$

For a more detailed explanation of this expression and its evaluation, see Appendix B. As described there, it can be reduced to 5-dimensional momentum integral (43)

$$\Gamma_{nd} = \frac{G^2}{16\pi^6} \int_0^\infty dk_n \int_0^{k_p^{max}} dk_p \int_0^{k_e^{max}} dk_e k_n^2 k_p^2 k_e^2 f_n (1-f_p)(1-f_e) \Theta(E_\nu)$$
$$\int_{z_p^{min}}^{z_p^{max}} dz_p \int_{z_e^-}^{z_e^+} dz_e \frac{4 E_\nu \mathcal{M}_{\phi_0}}{\sqrt{S^2 - (E_\nu^2 - R)^2}}, \qquad (10)$$

where R, S, and $\mathcal{M}_{\phi_0}$ are defined in Equations (24)–(26). The antineutrino energy E_ν is given by

$$E_\nu = E_n - E_p - E_e, \qquad (11)$$

which becomes a function of the remaining integration variables, k_n, k_p, and k_e. Please note that there are Fermi-Dirac distributions for the neutrons, proton vacancies, and electron vacancies, but none for the neutrinos because we work in the neutrino-transparent regime where neutrinos escape from the star and do not form a Fermi gas. We evaluate this integral numerically using a Monte-Carlo algorithm.

4.2. Electron Capture

The expression for the electron capture rate can be obtained from that for neutron decay (A10) by making the following changes: (1) the energy-momentum delta function now corresponds to the process $p\, e^- \to n\, \nu$, and (2) there are Fermi-Dirac distributions for proton and electron particles, and neutron vacancies,

$$\Gamma_{ec} = \int \frac{d^3k_n}{(2\pi)^3} \frac{d^3k_p}{(2\pi)^3} \frac{d^3k_e}{(2\pi)^3} \frac{d^3k_\nu}{(2\pi)^3} (1 - f_n) f_p f_e \frac{\sum |M|^2}{(2E_n^*)(2E_p^*)(2E_e)(2E_\nu)}$$
$$(2\pi)^4 \delta^{(4)}(k_p + k_e - k_n - k_\nu). \qquad (12)$$

Evaluating this expression takes us through the same steps as for neutron decay, except that the neutrino energy is now

$$E_\nu = E_p + E_e - E_n,\tag{13}$$

and the requirement that this be positive leads to different limits on the momentum integrals,

$$\Gamma_{ec} = \frac{G^2}{16\pi^6} \int_0^\infty dk_n \int_0^\infty dk_p \int_0^\infty dk_e k_n^2 k_p^2 k_e^2 f_n (1-f_p)(1-f_e) \Theta(E_\nu)$$
$$\int_{z_p^{\min}}^{z_p^{\max}} dz_p \int_{z_e^-}^{z_e^+} dz_e \frac{4 E_\nu \mathcal{M}_{\phi_0}}{\sqrt{S^2 - (E_\nu^2 - R)^2}}.\tag{14}$$

5. Beta Equilibration via Modified Urca

We calculate the rate of the modified Urca processes (3) using the relativistic dispersion relations of the nucleons in the phase space integration, but unlike the direct Urca rate we do not perform the phase space integration exactly, which would be difficult because the involvement of the spectator particles would lead to an 11-dimensional numerical integral over momentum. Instead we use the Fermi surface approximation. This is reasonable for modified Urca as long as the Fermi surfaces are not too thermally blurred, i.e. when the temperature is below the lowest Fermi kinetic energy, which is that of the proton. The modified Urca processes do not have a density threshold in the range of densities we consider here (see Section 2), so the Fermi surface approximation never predicts a vanishing rate. In this work we explore the temperature range $1\,\text{MeV} < T < 5\,\text{MeV}$, and the proton's Fermi kinetic energy is at least $10\,\text{MeV}$ in the density range $n > n_0$, so the Fermi surface approximation is justified for modified Urca rates. The first paragraph of Section 4 contains a discussion of why we need to go beyond the Fermi surface approximation in our direct Urca rate calculations. For the matrix elements that arise in modified Urca (44) and (59), we use the standard results (see, e.g., [31]), which were calculated assuming nonrelativistic nucleons. It has been pointed out [58] that the standard calculation of the modified Urca matrix element [40], which we use here, is based on a very crude approximation for the propagator of the internal off-shell nucleon. A more accurate treatment would lead to different modified Urca rates and shift our predicted values of $\Delta\mu$; we defer such a calculation to future work.

5.1. Neutron Decay

Modified Urca can proceed with either a neutron spectator or a proton spectator. From Fermi's Golden rule, we have the rate for the neutron decay process

$$\Gamma_{mU,nd} = \int \frac{d^3 k_n}{(2\pi)^3} \frac{d^3 k_p}{(2\pi)^3} \frac{d^3 k_e}{(2\pi)^3} \frac{d^3 k_\nu}{(2\pi)^3} \frac{d^3 k_{N_1}}{(2\pi)^3} \frac{d^3 k_{N_2}}{(2\pi)^3} \left(s \frac{\sum |M|^2}{2^6 E_n^* E_p^* E_e E_\nu E_{N_1}^* E_{N_2}^*} \right)$$
$$(2\pi)^4 \delta^{(4)}(k_n + k_{N_1} - k_p - k_e - k_\nu - k_{N_2}) f_n f_{N_1}(1-f_p)(1-f_e)(1-f_{N_2}).\tag{15}$$

Here, $s = 1/2$ because of the identical particles appearing in the process. N_1 and N_2 are neutrons in the n-spectator process and for the p-spectator neutron decay process, N_1 and N_2 are protons. The matrix element is different for each process see Equations (44) and (59). The detailed derivation of the modified Urca rates is in Appendix C. For n-spectator neutron decay, allowing the system to deviate from the low-temperature beta equilibrium condition (6) by amount

$$\xi = \frac{\mu_n - \mu_p - \mu_e}{T},\tag{16}$$

we obtain

$$\Gamma_{mU,nd(n)}(\xi) = \frac{7}{64\pi^9}G^2 g_A^2 f^4 \frac{(E_{Fn}^*)^3 E_{Fp}^*}{m_\pi^4} \frac{k_{Fn}^4 k_{Fp}}{(k_{Fn}^2 + m_\pi^2)^2} F(\xi) T^7 \theta_n, \qquad (17)$$

where $f \approx 1$ is the N-π coupling [31],

$$F(\xi) \equiv -(\xi^4 + 10\pi^2 \xi^2 + 9\pi^4)\text{Li}_3(-e^\xi) + 12(\xi^3 + 5\pi^2 \xi)\text{Li}_4(-e^\xi) \\ - 24(3\xi^2 + 5\pi^2)\text{Li}_5(-e^\xi) + 240\xi\text{Li}_6(-e^\xi) - 360\text{Li}_7(-e^\xi), \qquad (18)$$

and

$$\theta_n \equiv \begin{cases} 1 & k_{Fn} > k_{Fp} + k_{Fe} \\ 1 - \dfrac{3}{8}\dfrac{(k_{Fp} + k_{Fe} - k_{Fn})^2}{k_{Fp} k_{Fe}} & k_{Fn} < k_{Fp} + k_{Fe}. \end{cases} \qquad (19)$$

The functions $\text{Li}_n(x)$ are polylogarithms of order n [59]. For p-spectator neutron decay, we obtain

$$\Gamma_{mU,nd(p)}(\xi) = \frac{1}{64\pi^9}G^2 g_A^2 f^4 \frac{(E_{Fp}^*)^3 E_{Fn}^*}{m_\pi^4} \frac{(k_{Fn} - k_{Fp})^4 k_{Fn}}{((k_{Fn} - k_{Fp})^2 + m_\pi^2)^2} F(\xi) T^7 \theta_p, \qquad (20)$$

where

$$\theta_p \equiv \begin{cases} 0 & \text{if } k_{Fn} > 3k_{Fp} + k_{Fe} \\ \dfrac{(3k_{Fp} + k_{Fe} - k_{Fn})^2}{k_{Fn} k_{Fe}} & \text{if } \begin{array}{l} k_{Fn} > 3k_{Fp} - k_{Fe} \\ k_{Fn} < 3k_{Fp} + k_{Fe} \end{array} \\ 4\dfrac{3k_{Fp} - k_{Fn}}{k_{Fn}} & \text{if } \begin{array}{l} 3k_{Fp} - k_{Fe} > k_{Fn} \\ k_{Fn} > k_{Fp} + k_{Fe} \end{array} \\ \left(2 + 3\dfrac{2k_{Fp} - k_{Fn}}{k_{Fe}} - 3\dfrac{(k_{Fp} - k_{Fe})^2}{k_{Fn} k_{Fe}}\right) & \text{if } k_{Fn} < k_{Fp} + k_{Fe}. \end{cases} \qquad (21)$$

5.2. Electron Capture

The electron capture modified Urca rate can be obtained in a similar way to neutron decay, by changing the sign of the neutrino 4-momentum in the energy-momentum delta function and interchanging the particle and hole Fermi-Dirac factors,

$$\Gamma_{mU,ec} = \int \frac{d^3 k_n}{(2\pi)^3}\frac{d^3 k_p}{(2\pi)^3}\frac{d^3 k_e}{(2\pi)^3}\frac{d^3 k_\nu}{(2\pi)^3}\frac{d^3 k_{N_1}}{(2\pi)^3}\frac{d^3 k_{N_2}}{(2\pi)^3}\left(s\frac{\sum |M|^2}{2^6 E_n^* E_p^* E_e E_\nu E_{N_1}^* E_{N_2}^*}\right) \\ (2\pi)^4 \delta^{(4)}(k_p + k_e + k_{N_1} - k_n - k_\nu - k_{N_2})f_p f_e f_{N_1}(1 - f_n)(1 - f_{N_2}). \qquad (22)$$

Through a similar calculation, we find that the modified Urca neutron decay and electron capture rates in the Fermi surface approximation are related by

$$\Gamma_{mU,ec(n)}(\xi) = \Gamma_{mU,nd(n)}(-\xi), \qquad (23)$$

and

$$\Gamma_{mU,ec(p)}(\xi) = \Gamma_{mU,nd(p)}(-\xi). \qquad (24)$$

6. Results

6.1. Beta Equilibrium at Nonzero Temperature

Figures 6 and 7 show our final results for the nonzero-temperature correction $\Delta\mu$ required to achieve beta equilibrium, for the IUF and SFHo equations of state, respectively. The key features are

- At low temperatures $T \lesssim 1\,\text{MeV}$, the Fermi surface approximation is valid and beta equilibrium is achieved with a negligible correction $\Delta\mu$ (see Section 2).
- At the temperature rises through the neutrino-transparent regime, the value of $\Delta\mu$ rises.
- We only provide results for temperatures up to 5 MeV because at temperatures of around 5 to 10 MeV the neutrino mean free path will become smaller than the star, invalidating our assumption of neutrino transparency.
- The figures indicate that the nonzero-temperature correction reaches values of 10 to 20 MeV before neutrino trapping sets in.
- The density dependence of $\Delta\mu$ appears very different for different EoSs. For IUF the largest values are reached at moderate densities, near the direct Urca threshold. For SFHo, $\Delta\mu$ has a minimum at those densities.

In the rest of this section we will explain these features of our results.

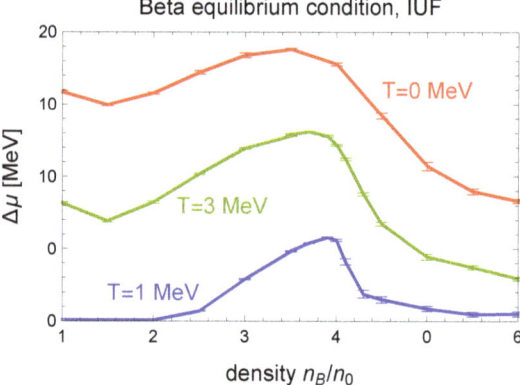

Figure 6. Nonzero-temperature correction $\Delta\mu$ required for beta equilibrium Equation (7) with the IUF EoS.

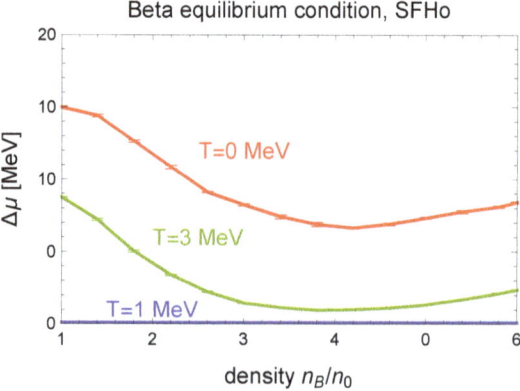

Figure 7. Nonzero-temperature correction $\Delta\mu$ required for beta equilibrium Equation (7) with the SFHo EoS.

The temperature dependence follows from the breakdown of the Fermi surface approximation. At $T \lesssim 1$ MeV the Urca processes are dominated by modes close to the Fermi surfaces of the neutron, protons, and electrons. The energy of the emitted neutrino is of order T which is negligible, so the direct Urca process is effectively $n \leftrightarrow p\,e^-$, for which the equilibrium condition is $\mu_n = \mu_p + \mu_e$, i.e., $\Delta\mu = 0$. As the temperature approaches the Fermi energy of the protons, the Fermi surface approximation breaks down. Modes far from the proton and electron Fermi surfaces begin to play a role, and the energy of the emitted neutrino becomes important. The processes that establish beta equilibrium, $n \to p\,e^-\,\bar{\nu}_e$ and $p\,e^- \to n\,\nu_e$, are not related by time reversal, so the principle of detailed balance does not apply. This means that even below the direct Urca threshold density, direct Urca processes can be fast enough and sufficiently different in their rates to require a correction $\Delta\mu$ to bring them into balance. As we will explain below, at $\Delta\mu = 0$ electron capture is much less suppressed than neutron decay, requiring a positive value of $\Delta\mu$ to decrease the proton fraction and equalize the rates.

The density dependence of the correction $\Delta\mu$ is more complicated, depending on specific features of the equations of state. We will discuss this in more detail below.

6.2. Urca Rates

Figure 8 illustrates how, without a nonzero-temperature correction $\Delta\mu$ (dashed lines), the neutron decay (nd) and electron capture (ec) rates become very different when the temperature rises to 3 MeV. For both EoSs, electron capture is significantly faster than neutron decay, so a positive $\Delta\mu$ will be required to balance the rates and establish beta equilibrium (solid lines). This is because a positive $\Delta\mu$ reduces the proton fraction. The resultant change in the phase space near the neutron and proton Fermi surfaces enhances the neutron decay rate and suppresses electron capture, bringing the two processes into balance with each other.

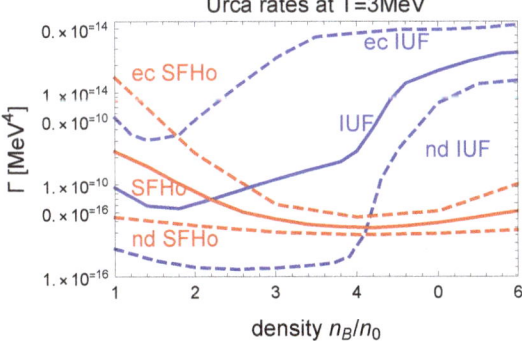

Figure 8. Urca (direct plus modified) rates for IUF and SFHo EoSs at $T = 3$ MeV. When $\Delta\mu = 0$ (dashed lines) the rates for neutron decay (nd) and electron capture (ec) do not balance. With the correct choice of $\Delta\mu$ (Figures 6 and 7) the neutron decay and electron capture rates (solid lines) become equal, and the system is in beta equilibrium.

For IUF, the mismatch between electron capture and neutron decay is greatest just below the IUF direct Urca threshold density of $4\,n_0$, which explains why for IUF $\Delta\mu$ reaches its highest value there (Figure 6). For SFHo, the mismatch is smallest at that density, which explains why for SFHo $\Delta\mu$ reaches a local minimum there (Figure 7).

Figures 9 and 10 give further insight into the density dependence of the rates by showing the separate contributions from direct and modified Urca.

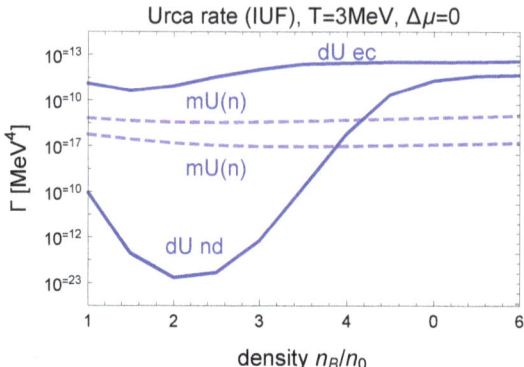

Figure 9. Urca rates calculated using the IUF EoS at $T = 3\,\text{MeV}$. Because $\Delta\mu = 0$ there is a large mismatch between the direct Urca rates for neutron decay and electron capture. Modified Urca (with neutron spectator (n) and proton spectator (p)) rates are calculated in the Fermi surface approximation and therefore match automatically.

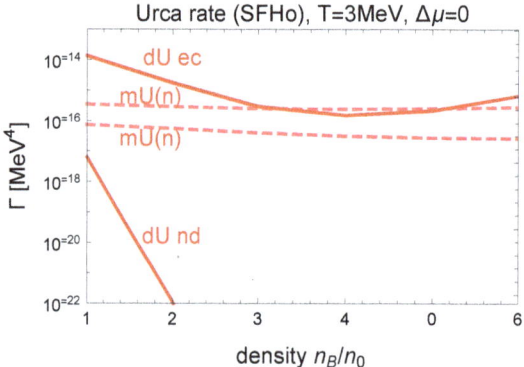

Figure 10. Urca rates calculated using the SFHo EoS at $T = 3\,\text{MeV}$. Because $\Delta\mu = 0$ there is a large mismatch between the direct Urca rates for neutron decay and electron capture. Modified Urca (with neutron spectator (n) and proton spectator (p)) rates are calculated in the Fermi surface approximation and therefore match automatically.

For IUF (Figure 9), in the dUrca-forbidden density range one would expect that the direct Urca rates should be exponentially suppressed at low temperature, leaving the modified Urca rates which automatically balance when $\Delta\mu = 0$ because they are calculated in the Fermi surface approximation. We see that the direct Urca neutron capture rate is indeed strongly suppressed, but the direct Urca electron capture rate only shows a slight reduction below the threshold, and remains well above the modified Urca rates. This mismatch is what leads to a positive correction $\Delta\mu$ in beta equilibrium. We will explain below why this is the case.

For SFHo (Figure 10), the analysis is similar: neutron decay is heavily suppressed as expected in the dUrca-forbidden region (up to infinite density), but electron capture is much less suppressed. In the middle density range (3 to 5 n_0) where mUrca is dominant there is no need for a correction, since the mUrca rates balance at $\Delta\mu = 0$. However, at lower or higher densities the direct Urca electron capture rate becomes large enough to dominate, so a positive $\Delta\mu$ will be required to pull it down and establish equilibrium between neutron decay and electron capture.

In the next subsection we analyze the imbalance between electron capture and neutron decay rates in the dUrca-forbidden density range. This imbalance is the reason a nonzero

$\Delta\mu$ is required in beta equilibrium. We can understand the difference in the rates, and their density dependence, by looking at which parts of the phase space dominate the rate integrals. This is largely determined by the Fermi-Dirac factors in the rate integrals, since the matrix element depends only weakly on the magnitudes of the momenta.

6.3. Direct Urca Suppression Factors

The density and temperature dependence of the direct Urca rates is dominated by the Fermi-Dirac factors. Below the dUrca threshold density, at zero temperature all direct Urca processes would be forbidden, but at nonzero temperature the Fermi surfaces are blurred, so there is some nonzero occupation of particle and hole states in regions of momentum space where the direct Urca process is kinematically allowed. The rate is governed by the Fermi-Dirac suppression factors for those momentum states.

At each density and temperature we search for the combination of momenta that is least suppressed, i.e., that maximizes the product of Fermi-Dirac factors in the rate integral while maintaining energy-momentum conservation. The magnitude of that product of Fermi-Dirac factors tells us how suppressed the whole process will be, at that density and temperature.

Below the direct Urca threshold density, considering particles near their Fermi surfaces, the neutron has a momentum larger than the sum of proton and electron momenta, even if the proton and electron are coaligned (see Figure 1). In this regime, the direct Urca kinematics will become essentially one-dimensional, as this is how the electron and proton momenta can come closest to adding up to the large neutron momentum. We take the neutron momentum to be positive, so a negative momentum indicates motion in the direction opposite of the neutron. For momentum conservation to hold, the electron and proton will have to be away from their Fermi surfaces. In the assumption of one-dimensional kinematics, we determine the optimal momenta $\{k_n^{opt}, k_p^{opt}, k_e^{opt}, k_\nu^{opt}\}$ as follows. For neutron decay, we maximize $f_n(1-f_p)(1-f_e)$ and for electron capture we maximize $(1-f_n)f_pf_e$. Energy and (one-dimensional) momentum conservation impose two constraints on the momentum, leaving two independent momenta over which to maximize.

The results of this maximization exercise are shown for the IUF EoS in Figures 11 and 12, and for SFHo in Figures 13 and 14.

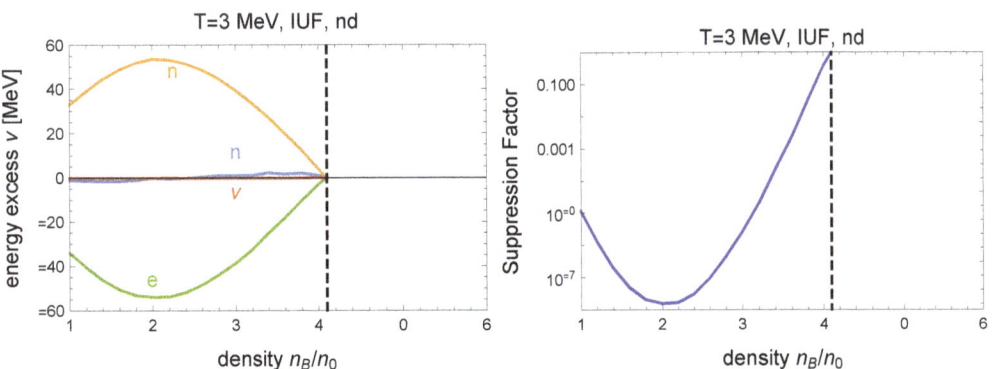

Figure 11. The optimal kinematics for neutron decay for the IUF EoS. **Left panel**: the least suppressed kinematic arrangement, showing the energy distance γ of each particle from its Fermi surface. **Right panel**: the Fermi-Dirac suppression factor, $e^{-|\gamma_e|/T}e^{-|\gamma_n|\Theta(\gamma_n)/T}$ which is dominated by the difficulty of finding an electron hole at energy γ_e below its Fermi surface.

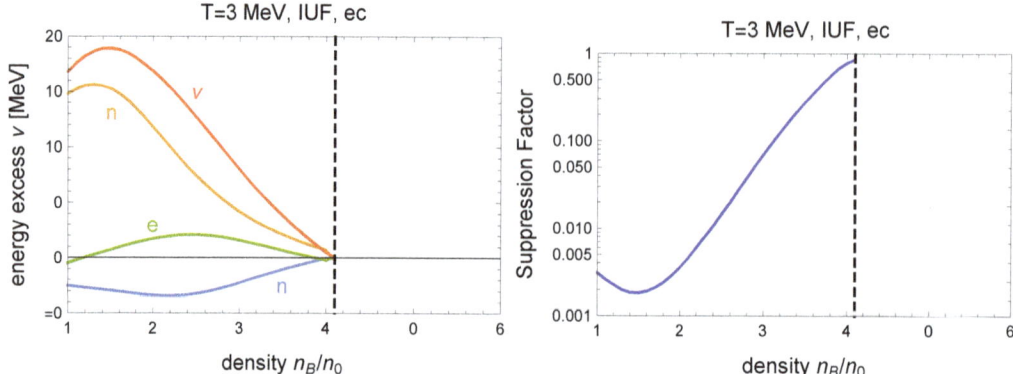

Figure 12. The optimal kinematics for electron capture for the IUF EoS. **Left panel**: the least suppressed kinematic arrangement, showing the energy distance γ of each particle from its Fermi surface. **Right panel**: the overall Fermi-Dirac suppression factor, $e^{-|\gamma_p|/T} e^{-|\gamma_e|\Theta(\gamma_e)/T} e^{-|\gamma_n|\Theta(-\gamma_n)/T}$, which is dominated by the difficulty of finding a proton at energy γ_p above its Fermi surface.

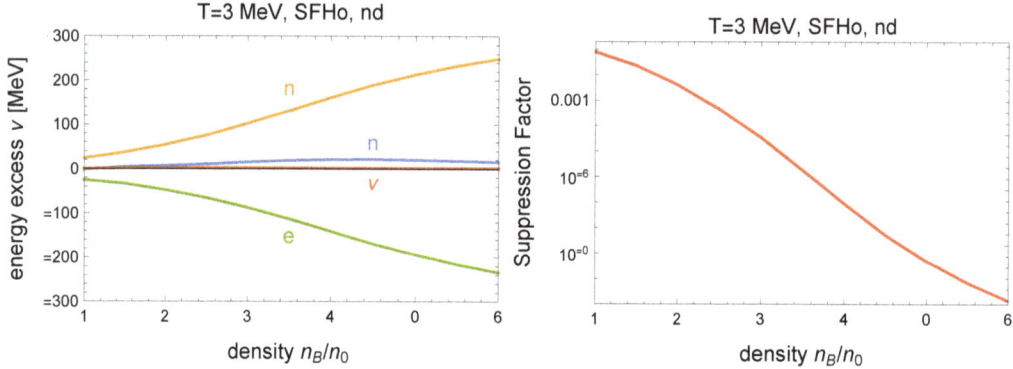

Figure 13. The optimal kinematics for neutron decay at $T = 3$ MeV for SFHo, obtained by maximizing the Fermi-Dirac products. The suppression factor, $e^{-|\gamma_e|/T} e^{-|\gamma_n|\Theta(\gamma_n)/T}$ is dominated by the difficulty of finding an electron hole below its Fermi surface.

The left panels show how far from their Fermi surfaces the particles are in the least Fermi-Dirac-suppressed kinematic configuration. For each particle i we show $\gamma_i \equiv E_i^{\rm opt} - E_{Fi}$, which is the extra energy the particle with its optimal momentum has relative to its Fermi energy. The curves only exist in the dUrca-forbidden region, which for IUF ends at 4.1 n_0. (In the dUrca-allowed region all particles can be on their Fermi surfaces, so the curves would be trivially zero and are not shown). The right panels show the maximum value of the Fermi-Dirac factor, which gives the overall suppression of the process.

6.3.1. Neutron Decay

Direct Urca neutron decay is suppressed because the neutrons at their Fermi surface have just enough energy to make a proton and electron near their Fermi surfaces (this is a consequence of the beta equilibrium condition (6)), but too much momentum (Figure 1). The process can still proceed (with an exponential suppression factor) by exploiting the thermal blurring of the Fermi surfaces. Figure 11 (IUF) and Figure 13 (SFHo) show that the best option is to create a proton at energy γ_p above its Fermi surface and an electron at energy $\gamma_e = -\gamma_p$ which is below its Fermi surface. The co-linear proton and electron now have more momentum then when they were both on their Fermi surfaces because the proton's momentum rises rapidly with γ_p because the proton is less relativistic, whereas the electron's momentum drops more slowly as γ_e becomes more negative, because the electron is ultrarelativistic. The creation of the proton incurs no Fermi-Dirac suppression because states above the Fermi surface are mostly empty, but the creation of the electron is suppressed by a Fermi-Dirac factor of $e^{-|\gamma_e|/T}$ reflecting the scarcity of electron holes available to take such an electron. The net suppression of the rate, $e^{-|\gamma_e|/T}e^{-|\gamma_n|\Theta(\gamma_n)/T}$, is shown in the right panels of Figure 11 (IUF) and Figure 13 (SFHo). For IUF we see the strongest suppression at around $2\,n_0$, which explains the density dependence of the IUF neutron decay rate shown in Figure 9. For SFHo, since the dUrca-forbidden region extends up to infinite density, and the momentum deficit remains large across the density range surveyed, we see stronger suppression that does not relent at the upper end of the density range, explaining the almost total suppression seen in Figure 10.

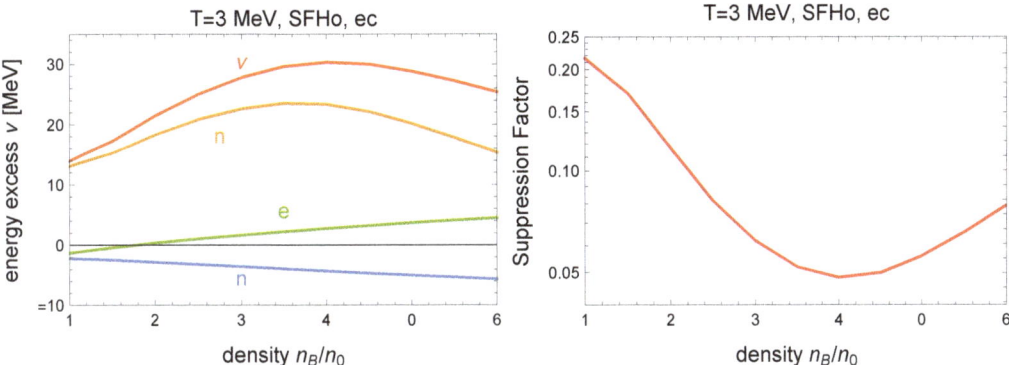

Figure 14. The optimal kinematics for electron capture at $T = 3$ MeV for SFHo, obtained by maximizing the Fermi-Dirac products. The suppression factor, $e^{-|\gamma_p|/T}e^{-|\gamma_e|\Theta(\gamma_e)/T}e^{-|\gamma_n|\Theta(-\gamma_n)/T}$, is dominated by the difficulty of finding a proton above its Fermi surface.

We can understand the density dependence of γ_p in terms of the one-dimensional model within which the maximization was performed.

We assume that as seen in Figure 11 (IUF) and Figure 13 (SFHo), the neutron remains on its Fermi surface, and the neutrino takes negligible energy/momentum, since lack of momentum to build the final state is the main obstacle. Conservation of energy and momentum then tells us that

$$k_{Fn} = k_p^{opt} + k_e^{opt}, \qquad (25)$$

$$E_{Fn} = E_p(k_p^{opt}) + k_e^{opt}. \qquad (26)$$

Using the dispersion relations (8) we can solve for k_p^{opt} and k_e^{opt} and, after using that $E_{Fn} = E_{Fp} + E_{Fe}$ (since we have assumed $\Delta\mu = 0$), we find

$$k_p^{opt} - k_{Fp} = \frac{\Delta k(2E_{Fp}^* - \Delta k)}{2(E_{Fp}^* + k_{Fp} - k_{Fn})}, \qquad (27)$$

where $\Delta k \equiv k_{Fn} - k_{Fp} - k_{Fe}$ is the momentum deficit (we plotted the surplus $-\Delta k$ in Figure 1). From this analysis, we learn that the density dependence of γ_p, and therefore the rate, not only depends on the momentum deficit Δk, but on the relative behavior of the neutron and proton Fermi momenta and their effective masses.

Although the momentum deficit Δk in IUF monotonically shrinks with density, γ_p shows a slight increase at low densities due to the fast drop of the effective proton mass m_p^* (see Figure 3). This fast decrease counter-intuitively leads E_{Fp}^* to drop with density, while the real Fermi energy, which includes the nuclear mean field, U_p, rises with density as expected. Closer to the threshold density, the momentum deficit dominates the behavior of γ_p and the rate, so that γ_p goes to zero at the threshold as Δk approaches zero, leading to $k_p^{\text{opt}} = k_{Fp}$ as expected.

For the SFHo EoS, the direct Urca momentum deficit is only varying weakly with density (see again Figure 1). Although the momentum deficit is slowly falling, γ_p continues to rise with density as shown in Figure 13. This is due to the neutron Fermi momentum which rises fast enough that the denominator in Equation (27) decreases by more than a factor of five in the studied density range while the momentum surplus stays nearly constant in comparison.

6.3.2. Electron Capture

In the dUrca-forbidden density range, using the one-dimensional kinematics described above, we find that the optimal kinematics for electron capture has a proton above its Fermi surface and an electron close to its Fermi surface combining to make a neutron slightly below its Fermi surface and a neutrino. The Fermi-Dirac suppression factor is $e^{-\gamma_p/T} e^{-|\gamma_e|\Theta(\gamma_e)/T} e^{-|\gamma_n|\Theta(-\gamma_n)/T}$, reflecting the scarcity of protons and electrons above their Fermi surfaces, and of neutron holes below the neutron Fermi surface.

Figures 12 and 14 show the corresponding energy excesses γ_i and Fermi-Dirac suppression factors. In the right panels we see that in the dUrca-forbidden region, electron capture is somewhat suppressed but not nearly as suppressed as neutron decay. This is because, as we explain below, it is able to proceed using a proton that is much closer to its Fermi surface than is possible for neutron decay, and there is correspondingly less Fermi-Dirac suppression (compare the left panels of Figure 11 vs. Figure 12, and Figure 13 vs. Figure 14).

The special feature of electron capture is that there is a very efficient way to exploit the thermal blurring of the Fermi surfaces. Given a momentum shortfall $\Delta k \equiv k_{Fn} - k_{Fp} - k_{Fe}$, we can start with a proton whose momentum is less than Δk above the Fermi surface. The rarity of finding such a proton leads to a Fermi-Dirac suppression factor of $e^{-|\gamma_p|/T}$. This proton captures an electron near its Fermi surface with momentum parallel to the proton's. At this point their combined momentum is not enough to make a neutron on its Fermi surface, and there is excess energy. However, we can use that excess energy to create, along with a neutron on its Fermi surface, a neutrino whose momentum partly cancels the neutron momentum, so the combined momentum of the proton and electron is enough to create that final state.

Because of the "help" from the neutrino, the proton does not need to be as far above its Fermi surface as the proton in neutron decay, so the electron capture rate is suppressed by a smaller Fermi-Dirac factor,

The density dependence of the suppression factors (right panels of Figure 12 for IUF and Figure 14 for SFHo) explain the density dependence of the direct Urca electron capture rates shown in Figures 9 and 10.

To understand the density dependence of γ_p, we can perform a similar analysis as for neutron decay. We now assume neutron and electron to be on their Fermi surfaces, as shown in Figure 12 (IUF) and Figure 14 (SFHo), which is not as good as an assumption compared to the neutron decay analysis, but still helps us to gain insight into the behavior of the rates. Energy-momentum conservation again allows us to deduce that

$$k_{Fn} = k_p^{\text{opt}} + k_{Fe} + k_\nu^{\text{opt}}, \tag{28}$$

$$E_{Fn} + k_\nu^{\text{opt}} = E_p(k_p^{\text{opt}}) + k_{Fe}^{\text{opt}}, \tag{29}$$

which leads, following the same procedure as in the neutron decay case, to

$$k_p^{\text{opt}} - k_{Fp} = \frac{\Delta k (\Delta k + 2 E_{Fp}^*)}{2(E_{Fp}^* + k_{Fn} - k_{Fp})}. \tag{30}$$

For IUF at low densities, we can neglect the proton Fermi momentum compared to the effective mass. The behavior of γ_p is then again dominated by the effective proton mass, whose rapid decrease overcomes the rising neutron Fermi momentum at low densities. This pushes the proton further away from its Fermi surface at low densities, before the momentum surplus dominates the behavior of γ_p as the threshold is approached. As for neutron decay, $\Delta k = 0$ at the threshold, therefore the rate is again dominated by particles on their respective Fermi surfaces.

For SFHo, the momentum surplus is becoming smaller from n_0 to $3\,n_0$ while the combination of the effective masses and Fermi momenta in (30) varies slowly with density. This allows the behavior of the momentum surplus Δk to dominate the behavior of γ_p at low densities, so both are increasing and therefore pushing the proton further away from its Fermi surface initially. At higher densities, SFHo is seemingly approaching asymptotically a direct Urca threshold. Both the momentum surplus and the Fermi momenta and effective masses in Equation (30) are pushing the ideal proton momentum back closer to the Fermi surface. Overall, the behavior of the electron capture rate in SFHo can therefore largely be explained by the density dependence of the momentum surplus.

6.4. Nonrelativistic Rate vs. Relativistic Rate

In Section 3 we emphasized that as the density rises above about $2n_0$ relativistic corrections become important in the nucleon dispersion relations. In this section, we illustrate the importance of relativistic corrections in the neutron decay rate.

6.4.1. Direct Urca Neutron Decay

Figure 4 shows various approximations to the direct Urca neutron decay rate at $T = 3\,\text{MeV}$ (with $\Delta\mu = 0$). We show the rate calculated with fully relativistic dispersion relations, with the nonrelativistic dispersion relation

$$E_N = m_N^* + \frac{p_N^2}{2m_N^*} + U_N, \tag{31}$$

and with the "vacuum dispersion relation" used in [5],

$$E_N = m_{\text{eff},N} + \frac{p_N^2}{2m_N}, \tag{32}$$

where $m_N = 940\,\text{MeV}$, and $m_{\text{eff},N}$ is chosen such that $E_N(p_F) = \mu_N$.

For the nonrelativistic curves, we use a corresponding nonrelativistic approximation of the rescaled matrix element (12),

$$M = 1 + 3g_A^2 + (1 - g_A^2)\frac{\vec{p}_e \cdot \vec{p}_\nu}{E_e E_\nu}, \tag{33}$$

see Refs. [5,31], and the derivation in Appendix C of [60]. We see that relativistic corrections make an enormous difference to the rate. The nonrelativistic approximation is reasonably accurate at low density (where the nucleons are indeed nonrelativistic) but overestimates the rate by up to eight orders of magnitude (at $T = 3\,\text{MeV}$) between $2\,n_0$ and the direct Urca threshold at $4.1\,n_0$. Due to the breakdown of the nonrelativistic approximation, the direct Urca threshold condition is incorrectly already fulfilled below two times saturation density, which explains the steep increase of the nonrelativistic rate around this density. For a detailed discussion of the density dependence of the relativistic rate, see Section 6.3.

The thermal blurring of the Fermi energy, which is proportional to the temperature T, translates to a blurring in momentum space of order T/v_F, where v_F is the Fermi velocity. In the correct relativistic treatment, v_F has an upper bound of 1, whereas for the nonrelativistic dispersion relation, the Fermi velocity grows without a limit. This leads to a suppression of the nonrelativistic rate at higher densities which partially cancels the effects of the earlier threshold.

The "vacuum dispersion relation" gives a rate that is one to eight orders of magnitude too large (at $T = 3$ MeV), and is less suppressed at higher densities since the corresponding Fermi velocity stays comparatively small in the plotted density range.

6.4.2. Modified Urca Neutron Decay

Figure 5 shows the importance of using relativistic dispersion relations in calculating modified Urca. The rates are calculated for the IUF equation of state in the Fermi surface approximation at $T = 3$ MeV. The relativistic rate is about 1 to 2 orders of magnitude smaller than the nonrelativistic rate. The modified Urca rates are not sensitive to the direct Urca threshold because of the spectator providing extra momenta. Much of the difference between the nonrelativistic calculation and the relativistic calculation comes from the prefactors, as shown in Section 5 and Equations (57), (58), (60) and (61). The relativistic rates are suppressed by $\prod_i m_i^*/E_i^*$, where i is the index for each of the nucleons participating the interaction. Notice that the proton-spectator modified Urca rate is always less than the neutron-spectator rate because the proton Fermi surface, and its accompanying phase space, is smaller.

7. Conclusions

We have investigated the conditions for beta equilibrium in nuclear matter in neutron stars, focusing on the temperature range where the material is cool enough so that neutrinos escape ($T \lesssim 5$ MeV) but warm enough so that nonzero-temperature corrections to the Fermi surface approximation play an important role ($T \gtrsim 1$ MeV).

Previous work [5] found that a nonzero-temperature correction $\Delta\mu$ to the traditional beta equilibrium condition (Equation (7)) was required to balance the rate of neutron decay against the rate of electron capture. We have improved on that calculation using a consistent description of nuclear matter, based on two relativistic mean field models, IUF and SFHo.

We find that when using relativistic mean field models it is important to use the full relativistic dispersion relations of the nucleons. In these theories the effective masses drop quickly with density, so the neutrons become relativistic at densities of 2 to 3 n_0. Using nonrelativistic nucleon dispersion relations can make the modified Urca rates wrong by an order of magnitude and the direct Urca rates wrong by many orders of magnitude.

Our results for the nonzero-temperature correction $\Delta\mu$ are shown in Figures 6 and 7. We find that it rises with the temperature, and can be of order 10 to 20 MeV for temperatures in the 3 to 5 MeV range. The density dependence is quite different for the two EoSs that we studied, and we showed in detail how it depends on specific properties of the EoS.

We find that the nonzero-temperature correction plays an important role in the correct calculation of Urca rates. Using the naive (low-temperature) beta equilibrium condition $\mu_n = \mu_p + \mu_e$ at $T = 3$ MeV would yield electron capture rates that are too large by an order of magnitude, and neutron decay rates that are too small by an order of magnitude (Figure 8). This would significantly affect calculations of neutrino emissivity in the cooler regions of a neutron star merger, and therefore the estimated energy loss due to neutrinos. Currently used neutrino leakage schemes (e.g., Ref. [61] and references therein), which often treat the temperature range $T \lesssim 5$ MeV as neutrino free streaming, need to be adapted to the corrected beta equilibrium. Additionally, the bulk viscosity of nuclear matter [62] depends on the rate of the Urca process which restores the system to beta equilibrium. The improved calculation of the Urca rates presented here will modify the temperatures and densities at which bulk viscosity reaches its maximum strength. Using the correct beta equilibrium condition also affects the equation of state: a recent study estimated its impact to be at the 5% level [63], and it would be interesting to evaluate the impact by performing a merger simulation using an EoS that incorporates the finite-temperature correction described in this paper.

Author Contributions: Conceptualization, M.G.A., A.H., S.P.H.; methodology, all authors; formal analysis, all authors; writing, all authors; visualization, Z.Z. All authors have read and agreed to the published version of the manuscript.

Funding: M.G.A., A.H. and Z.Z. are partly supported by the U.S. Department of Energy, Office of Science, Office of Nuclear Physics, under Award No. #DE-FG02-05ER41375. Z.Z. received additional support from the McDonnell Center for the Space Sciences at Washington University. S.P.H. is supported by the U. S. Department of Energy grant DE-FG02-00ER41132 as well as the National Science Foundation grant No. PHY-1430152 (JINA Center for the Evolution of the Elements).

Institutional Review Board Statement: No application.

Informed Consent Statement: No application.

Data Availability Statement: No application.

Acknowledgments: We thank A. Steiner for useful discussions.

Conflicts of Interest: The authors declare no conflict of interest.

Appendix A. The SFHo Relativistic Mean Field Theory

The Lagrangian for the SFHo relativistic mean field model is given in Refs. [42,64] and reads

$$\mathcal{L} = \mathcal{L}_N + \mathcal{L}_M + \mathcal{L}_l, \tag{A1}$$

$$\mathcal{L}_N = \bar{\psi}(i\gamma^\mu \partial_\mu - m_N + g_\sigma \sigma - g_\omega \gamma^\mu \omega_\mu - \frac{g_\rho}{2}\boldsymbol{\tau}\cdot\boldsymbol{\rho}_\mu \gamma^\mu)\psi, \tag{A2}$$

with bold symbols being vectors in iso-space, $\boldsymbol{\tau}$ being the iso-spin generators, and

$$\begin{aligned}\mathcal{L}_M =& \frac{1}{2}\partial_\mu \sigma \partial^\mu \sigma - \frac{1}{2}m_\sigma^2 \sigma^2 - \frac{bM}{3}(g_\sigma\sigma)^3 - \frac{c}{4}(g_\sigma\sigma)^4 - \frac{1}{4}\omega_{\mu\nu}\omega^{\mu\nu} + \frac{1}{2}m_\omega^2 \omega_\mu \omega^\mu \\ &+ \frac{\zeta}{24}g_\omega^4 (\omega_\mu \omega^\mu)^2 - \frac{1}{4}\boldsymbol{B}_{\mu\nu}\cdot\boldsymbol{B}^{\mu\nu} + \frac{1}{2}m_\rho^2 \boldsymbol{\rho}_\mu \cdot \boldsymbol{\rho}^\mu + \frac{\xi}{24}g_\rho^4 (\boldsymbol{\rho}_\mu \cdot \boldsymbol{\rho}^\mu)^2 \\ &+ g_\rho^2 \left[\sum_{i=1}^{6}a_i \sigma^i + \sum_{j=1}^{3}b_j (\omega_\mu \omega^\mu)^j \right]\boldsymbol{\rho}_\mu \cdot \boldsymbol{\rho}^\mu,\end{aligned} \tag{A3}$$

where

$$\omega_{\mu\nu} = \partial_\mu \omega_\nu - \partial_\nu \omega_\mu, \tag{A4}$$
$$\boldsymbol{B}_{\mu\nu} = \partial_\mu \boldsymbol{\rho}_\nu - \partial_\nu \boldsymbol{\rho}_\mu. \tag{A5}$$

The lepton contribution

$$\mathcal{L}_l = \bar{\psi}_e (i\gamma^\mu \partial_\mu - m_e)\psi_e, \tag{A6}$$

consists of free electrons with a mass of $m_e = 0.511$ MeV. In our calculations we use the values of the masses and couplings given in the online CompOSE database. These are listed in Table A1. In the table,

$$C_\sigma = g_\sigma/m_\sigma, \tag{A7}$$
$$C_\omega = g_\omega/m_\omega, \tag{A8}$$
$$C_\rho = g_\rho/m_\rho. \tag{A9}$$

Table A1. SFHo parameter values taken from CompOSE (https://compose.obspm.fr/eos/34/, accessed on 27 April 2021). The last three masses are taken from [42].

Quantity	Unit	Value
c_σ	fm	3.1791606374
c_ω	fm	2.2752188529
c_ρ	fm	2.4062374629
b		$7.3536466626 \times 10^{-3}$
c		$-3.8202821956 \times 10^{-3}$
ζ		$-1.6155896062 \times 10^{-3}$
ξ		$4.1286242877 \times 10^{-3}$
a_1	fm^{-1}	$-1.9308602647 \times 10^{-1}$
a_2		$5.6150318121 \times 10^{-1}$
a_3	fm	$2.8617603774 \times 10^{-1}$
a_4	fm^2	2.7717729776
a_5	fm^3	1.2307286924
a_6	fm^4	$6.1480060734 \times 10^{-1}$
b_1		5.5118461115
b_2	fm^2	-1.8007283681
b_3	fm^4	4.2610479708×10^2
m_σ	fm^{-1}	2.3689528914
m_ω	fm^{-1}	3.9655047020
m_ρ	fm^{-1}	3.8666788766
m_n	MeV	939.565346
m_p	MeV	938.272013
M	MeV	939

Appendix B. Direct Urca Neutron Decay Rate

From Fermi's Golden rule, we have the rate Equation (9) [31,57]

$$\Gamma_{nd} = \int \frac{d^3k_n}{(2\pi)^3} \frac{d^3k_p}{(2\pi)^3} \frac{d^3k_e}{(2\pi)^3} \frac{d^3k_\nu}{(2\pi)^3} \frac{\sum |M|^2}{(2E_n^*)(2E_p^*)(2E_e)(2E_\nu)} (2\pi)^4 \delta^{(4)}(k_n - k_p - k_e - k_\nu)$$
$$f_n (1 - f_p)(1 - f_e). \tag{A10}$$

There is no neutrino Fermi-Dirac factor because we assume the medium is neutrino-transparent, i.e., neutrinos escape the star. The spin-summed matrix element is [11]

$$\sum |M|^2 = 32 G^2 [(g_A^2 - 1) m_n^* m_p^* (k_e \cdot k_\nu) + (g_A - 1)^2 (k_e \cdot k_n)(k_p \cdot k_\nu)$$
$$+ (1 + g_A)^2 (k_p \cdot k_e)(k_n \cdot k_\nu)], \tag{A11}$$

where $G = G_F \cos\theta_c$, $G_F = 1.166 \times 10^{-11}$ MeV^{-2} is the Fermi constant and $\theta_c = 13.04°$ is the Cabbibo angle. As they originate from spin summations (see Appendix B of [9]), the 4-vector dot products in the matrix element (A11) are $k^\mu = (E^*, \mathbf{k})$.

It is convenient to define the rescaled dimensionless matrix element

$$\mathcal{M} \equiv \frac{\sum |M|^2}{32 G^2 E_n^* E_p^* E_e E_\nu} \tag{12}$$
$$= \frac{(g_A^2 - 1) m_n^* m_p^* (k_e \cdot k_\nu) + (g_A - 1)^2 (k_e \cdot k_n)(k_p \cdot k_\nu) + (1 + g_A)^2 (k_p \cdot k_e)(k_n \cdot k_\nu)}{E_n^* E_p^* E_e E_\nu}.$$

In the nonrelativistic limit, since $g_A \approx 1$, $\mathcal{M} \approx (1 + 3g_A^2) \sim 4$ [11,20,31,34,65,66].

The neutron decay rate can now be written

$$\Gamma_{nd} = \frac{2G^2}{(2\pi)^8} \int d^3k_n d^3k_p d^3k_e d^3k_\nu \, \mathcal{M} \, \delta^{(4)}(k_n - k_p - k_e - k_\nu) f_n (1 - f_p)(1 - f_e). \quad (13)$$

The 12-dimensional integral can be reduced to a 5-dimensional integral as follows. Integrating over the 3-momentum conservation delta functions reduces the integral to 9 dimensions (compare (E.1) in Ref. [60])

$$\Gamma_{nd} = \frac{2G^2}{(2\pi)^8} \int d^3k_n d^3k_p d^3k_e \, \mathcal{M} \delta(E_n - E_p - E_e - |\vec{k}_n - \vec{k}_p - \vec{k}_e|) f_n (1 - f_p)(1 - f_e). \quad (14)$$

The remaining delta function imposes energy conservation in the creation of the neutrino: $E_\nu = |\vec{k}_\nu|$, so the argument of the delta function is

$$g(\phi) \equiv E_\nu - |\vec{k}_n - \vec{k}_p - \vec{k}_e|, \quad (15)$$
$$E_\nu \equiv E_n - E_p - E_e.$$

Each momentum integral can be written in polar co-ordinates as $d^3k = k^2 dk dz d\phi$ where $z = \cos\theta$. Setting up the following coordinate system (see Appendix E in [60])

$$\vec{k}_n = k_n(0, 0, 1), \quad (16)$$
$$\vec{k}_p = k_p(\sqrt{1 - z_p^2}, 0, z_p), \quad (17)$$
$$\vec{k}_e = k_e(\sqrt{1 - z_e^2}\cos\phi, \sqrt{1 - z_e^2}\sin\phi, z_e), \quad (18)$$

allows us to integrate over z_n and ϕ_n yielding a factor of 4π and over ϕ_p yielding a factor of 2π, which eliminates three angular integrals, so that (compare (E.5) in [60])

$$\Gamma_{nd} = \frac{G^2}{16\pi^6} \int_0^\infty dk_n \int_0^{k_p^{max}} dk_p \int_0^{k_e^{max}} dk_e k_n^2 k_p^2 k_e^2 f_n (1 - f_p)(1 - f_e) I(k_n, k_p, k_e), \quad (19)$$

where

$$I(k_n, k_p, k_e) \equiv \Theta(E_\nu) \int_{-1}^1 dz_p \int_{-1}^1 dz_e \int_0^{2\pi} d\phi \, \mathcal{M} \, \delta(g(\phi)). \quad (20)$$

Please note that for simplicity we label the electron azimuthal angle as ϕ (rather than ϕ_e). The factor of $\Theta(E_\nu)$ restricts the integral to the region of momentum space where the neutrino energy $E_\nu(k_n, k_p, k_e)$ is positive, which is a requirement for the emission of a neutrino. This condition leads to the upper limits on the proton and electron momenta. If we perform the integrals in the order shown in (19) then the electron momentum integral is the inner integral, so it is performed for known values of k_n and k_p, so the constraint $E_\nu > 0$ corresponds to $E_e < E_n - E_p$. Similarly, the k_p integral is performed for a known value of k_n, so its range is constrained by requiring that there be enough energy to create an electron (of unknown momentum) and a neutrino, $E_p < E_n - m_e$. This leads to upper limits on the proton and electron integral,

$$k_p^{max} = \Theta(E_n - U_p - m_p - m_e)\sqrt{(E_n - U_p - m_e)^2 - m_p^2}, \quad (21)$$

$$k_e^{max} = \Theta(E_n - E_p - m_e)\sqrt{(E_n - E_p)^2 - m_e^2}. \quad (22)$$

In the delta function in Equation (20),

$$g(\phi) = E_v - \sqrt{R + S\cos\phi}, \tag{23}$$

$$\text{where} \quad R \equiv k_n^2 + k_p^2 + k_e^2 - 2k_n k_e z_e - 2k_n k_p z_p + 2k_p k_e z_p z_e, \tag{24}$$

$$S \equiv 2k_p k_e \sqrt{1 - z_p^2}\sqrt{1 - z_e^2}. \tag{25}$$

Since $g(\phi)$ depends on ϕ only via $\cos\phi$ there will be either zero or two solutions to $g(\phi) = 0$, so

$$I(k_n, k_p, k_e) = 2\Theta(E_v) \int_{-1}^{1} dz_p \int_{-1}^{1} dz_e \, \Theta(S - |E_v^2 - R|) \frac{\mathcal{M}_{\phi_0}}{|g'(\phi_0)|}, \tag{26}$$

where $\mathcal{M}_{\phi_0}$ is the dimensionless rescaled matrix element (12) evaluated at ϕ_0, which can be either of the two solutions of $g(\phi) = 0$,

$$\cos\phi_0 = \frac{E_v^2 - R}{S}. \tag{27}$$

It does not matter which solution we use for ϕ_0 because g is a function of $\cos\phi$ and $\mathcal{M}$ depends only on $\cos\phi$ and $\sin^2\phi$, so the integrand has the same value for both the solutions. The theta function $\Theta(S - |E_v^2 - R|)$ imposes the condition that there are two solutions (rather than none), by limiting the integral to the domain where $-1 < \cos\phi_0 < 1$.

We now use (23) and (27) to evaluate the integrand in (26).

First, the Jacobian of the delta function is

$$|g'(\phi_0)| = \frac{\sqrt{S^2 - (E_v^2 - R)^2}}{2E_v}. \tag{28}$$

Using (28) in (26),

$$I = 4E_v \Theta(E_v) \int_{-1}^{1} dz_p \int_{-1}^{1} dz_e \, \frac{\Theta(S - |E_v^2 - R|)}{\sqrt{S^2 - (E_v^2 - R)^2}} \mathcal{M}_{\phi_0}. \tag{29}$$

Secondly, substituting (27) in to (A11) gives the matrix element

$$\mathcal{M}_{\phi_0} = \frac{1}{2} \frac{(g_A - 1)^2 F_1 + (g_A + 1)^2 F_2 + (g_A^2 - 1) F_3}{E_n^* E_p^* E_e E_v}, \tag{30}$$

where

$$F_1 = \left(k_n^2 + k_e^2 - k_p^2 - 2E_p^* E_v - E_v^2 - 2k_n k_e z_e\right)\left(k_n k_e z_e - E_e E_n^*\right), \tag{31}$$

$$F_2 = \left(k_n^2 + k_p^2 + k_e^2 + 2E_p^* E_e - E_v^2 - 2k_n(k_p z_p + k_e z_e)\right)\left(E_n^* E_v + k_n(k_p z_p + k_e z_e - k_n)\right), \tag{32}$$

$$F_3 = m_n^{*2}\left(k_e^2 - k_n^2 - k_p^2 + 2E_e E_v + E_v^2 + 2k_n k_p z_p\right). \tag{33}$$

Limits of Angular Integration

To speed up the numerical evaluation of (29) we implement the theta function as limits on the range of integration over z_p and z_e. The condition $S > |E_\nu^2 - R|$ can be written (using (24), (25)) as

$$|a + bz_e| < c\sqrt{1 - z_e^2}, \tag{34}$$

$$\text{where} \quad a \equiv q^2 - k_n^2 - k_p^2 - k_e^2 + 2k_n k_p z_p, \tag{35}$$

$$b \equiv 2k_e(k_n - k_p z_p), \tag{36}$$

$$c \equiv 2k_e k_p \sqrt{1 - z_p^2}. \tag{37}$$

The inequality (34) is obeyed for $z_e^- < z_e < z_e^+$ where

$$z_e^\pm = \frac{-ab \pm c\sqrt{c^2 + b^2 - a^2}}{b^2 + c^2}. \tag{38}$$

Please note that if the roots are real then they are always within the physical range $z_e \in [-1, 1]$. We can therefore put bounds on z_p by requiring that (38) has real roots,

$$c^2 + b^2 > a^2$$
$$\Rightarrow 2k_p E_\nu > |E_\nu^2 + k_e^2 - k_n^2 - k_p^2 + 2k_n k_p z_p|. \tag{39}$$

This means that $z_p^- < z_p < z_p^+$, where

$$z_p^\pm = \frac{k_n^2 + k_p^2 - k_e^2 - E_\nu^2 \pm 2k_e E_\nu}{2k_n k_p}. \tag{40}$$

In this case, however, these bounds are not necessarily within the physical range $z_p \in [-1, 1]$, so the true bounds on the z_p integral are

$$[z_p^{\min}, z_p^{\max}] = [z_p^+, z_p^-] \cap [-1, 1]. \tag{41}$$

We can now write the angular integral as

$$I = 4E_\nu \Theta(E_\nu) \int_{z_p^{\min}}^{z_p^{\max}} dz_p \int_{z_e^-}^{z_e^+} dz_e \frac{\mathcal{M}_{\phi_0}}{\sqrt{S^2 - (E_\nu^2 - R)^2}}. \tag{42}$$

Using this in (19) we obtain

$$\Gamma_{\rm nd} = \frac{G^2}{16\pi^6} \int_0^\infty dk_n \int_0^{k_p^{\max}} dk_p \int_0^{k_e^{\max}} dk_e\, k_n^2 k_p^2 k_e^2 f_n (1 - f_p)(1 - f_e)$$
$$\Theta(E_\nu) \int_{z_p^{\min}}^{z_p^{\max}} dz_p \int_{z_e^-}^{z_e^+} dz_e \frac{4 E_\nu \mathcal{M}_{\phi_0}}{\sqrt{S^2 - (E_\nu^2 - R)^2}}. \tag{43}$$

The second line corresponds to the I integral (20), (42). It is natural to group a factor of E_ν with $\mathcal{M}_{\phi_0}$ to cancel the factor of E_ν in the denominator (30) which can cause numerical problems at the edge of the kinematically allowed momentum range where $E_\nu \to 0$.

The neutron decay rate can therefore be computed as a 5-dimensional momentum integral (43), obtaining the integration ranges from (21), (22), (38) and (41), the matrix element from (30), and the Jacobian (square root denominator) from (24), (25).

C. Modified Urca Neutron Decay Rate

The matrix element is (4.16) in [31,60]

$$\left(s\frac{\sum|M_n|^2}{2^6 E_n^* E_p^* E_e E_\nu E_{N_1}^* E_{N_2}^*}\right) = 42 G^2 \frac{f^4}{m_\pi^4} \frac{g_A^2}{E_e^2} \frac{k_{Fn}^4}{(k_{Fn}^2+m_\pi^2)^2}, \quad (44)$$

where $f \approx 1$ is the N-π coupling and $s = 1/2$ for the identical particles. The conventional way of doing the integral is to divide the integral into an energy integral and an angular integral (termed "phase space decomposition" [35])

$$\int dk_n^3 dk_p^3 dk_e^3 dk_\nu^3 dk_{N_1}^3 dk_{N_2}^3 = \int dk_n dk_p dk_e dk_\nu dk_{N_1} dk_{N_2} k_n^2 k_p^2 k_e^2 k_\nu^2 k_{N_1}^2 k_{N_2}^2$$
$$\times \int d\Omega_n d\Omega_p d\Omega_e d\Omega_\nu d\Omega_{N_1} d\Omega_{N_2}. \quad (45)$$

We use relativistic dispersion relations for nucleons

$$E_N = \sqrt{k^2 + m_N^{*2}} + U_N, \quad (46)$$

where U is the mean field contribution to the energy. We define $E^* \equiv \sqrt{k^2 + m^{*2}}$, then $dE^* = kdk/E^*$. We use ultrarelativistic dispersion relations for electron and neutrino,

$$E = k, \quad (47)$$

then $dE = dk$ (the electron mass $m_e = 0.511$ MeV is negligible compared to its momentum). Therefore, we can convert the momentum integral to an energy integral, and the rate integral becomes

$$\Gamma_{mU,nd(n)} = \frac{42 G^2 g_A^2 f^4}{(2\pi)^{14} m_\pi^4} \int d\Omega_n d\Omega_p d\Omega_e d\Omega_\nu d\Omega_{N_1} d\Omega_{N_2}$$
$$\times \delta^{(3)}(\vec{k}_n + \vec{k}_{N_1} - \vec{k}_p - \vec{k}_e - \vec{k}_{N_2}) k_n^2 k_p^2 k_e^2 k_\nu^2 k_{N_1}^2 k_{N_2}^2 \frac{1}{E_e^2} \frac{k_{Fn}^4}{(k_{Fn}^2+m_\pi^2)^2}$$
$$\times \int dE_n^* dE_p^* dE_e dE_\nu dE_{N_1}^* dE_{N_2}^* \frac{E_n^*}{k_n} \frac{E_p^*}{k_p} \frac{E_{N_1}^*}{k_{N_1}} \frac{E_{N_2}^*}{k_{N_2}}$$
$$\times \delta(E_n + E_{N_1} - E_p - E_e - E_\nu - E_{N_2}) f_n f_{N_1}(1-f_p)(1-f_e)(1-f_{N_2}). \quad (48)$$

Notice that it is most common to set $\vec{k}_\nu = 0$ in the momentum conserving delta function but keep E_ν in the energy delta function.

In the Fermi surface approximation, we set all momenta to Fermi momenta and we will have $E_e = k_e = k_{Fe}$, $k_\nu = E_\nu$.

Now, the rate integral becomes

$$\Gamma_{mU,nd(n)} = \frac{42 G^2 g_A^2 f^4}{(2\pi)^{14} m_\pi^4} k_{Fn}^2 k_{Fp}^2 k_{Fe}^2 k_{FN_1}^2 k_{FN_2}^2 \frac{1}{k_{Fe}^2} \frac{k_{Fn}^4}{(k_{Fn}^2+m_\pi^2)^2} \frac{E_n^*}{k_{Fn}} \frac{E_p^*}{k_{Fp}} \frac{E_{N_1}^*}{k_{FN_1}} \frac{E_{N_2}^*}{k_{N_2}}$$
$$\times \int d\Omega_n d\Omega_p d\Omega_e d\Omega_\nu d\Omega_{N_1} d\Omega_{N_2} \delta^{(3)}(\vec{k}_n + \vec{k}_{N_1} - \vec{k}_p - \vec{k}_e - \vec{k}_{N_2})$$
$$\times \int dE_n^* dE_p^* dE_e dE_\nu dE_{N_1}^* dE_{N_2}^* E_\nu^2 f_n f_{N_1}(1-f_p)(1-f_e)(1-f_{N_2})$$
$$\times \delta(E_n^* + E_{N_1}^* - E_p^* - E_e - E_\nu - E_{N_2}^* + (U_n - U_p)). \quad (49)$$

For the energy integral, we do a change of variable,

$$x = \frac{E^* - \mu^*}{T}, \tag{50}$$

then, $dx = (1/T)dE^*$ and $\mu = 0$ for the neutrino. For the integral bounds, we have

$$\int_{m^*}^{+\infty} dE^* = T\int_{(m^*-\mu^*)/T}^{+\infty} dx = T\int_{-(\mu^*-m^*)/T}^{+\infty} dx \approx T\int_{-\infty}^{+\infty} dx, \tag{51}$$

where the approximation is valid because $\mu^* \gg T$. For neutrino, $\mu^* = 0$ and $m = 0$, so the lower bound is 0. Then, the energy integral, which we denote as I, becomes

$$\begin{aligned}
I \equiv &\int dE_n^* dE_p^* dE_e dE_v dE_{N_1}^* dE_{N_2}^* E_v^2 f_n f_{N_1}(1-f_p)(1-f_e)(1-f_{N_2}) \\
&\times \delta(E_n^* + E_{N_1}^* - E_p^* - E_e - E_v - E_{N_2}^* + (U_n - U_p)) \\
=& T^7 \int dx_n dx_p dx_e dx_v dx_{N_1} dx_{N_2}\, x_v^2 f(x_n) f(x_{N_1})(1-f(x_p))(1-f(x_e)) \\
&\times (1-f(x_{N_2}))\delta(x_n + x_{N_1} - x_p - x_e - x_v - x_{N_2} + \frac{\mu_n - \mu_p - \mu_e}{T}) \\
=& T^7 \int_0^{+\infty} dx_v x_v^2 \int_{-\infty}^{+\infty} dx_n dx_p dx_e dx_{N_1} dx_{N_2}\, f(x_n)f(x_{N_1})f(-x_p)f(-x_e) \\
&\times f(-x_{N_2})\delta(x_n + x_{N_1} - x_p - x_e - x_v - x_{N_2} + \frac{\mu_n - \mu_p - \mu_e}{T}) \\
=& T^7 \int_0^{+\infty} dx_v x_v^2 \int_{-\infty}^{+\infty} dx_n dx_p dx_e dx_{N_1} dx_{N_2}\, f(x_n)f(x_{N_1})f(x_p)f(x_e)f(x_{N_2}) \\
&\times \delta(x_n + x_{N_1} + x_p + x_e - x_v + x_{N_2} + \frac{\mu_n - \mu_p - \mu_e}{T}).
\end{aligned} \tag{52}$$

One can use Mathematica to obtain an analytical expression,

$$I = \frac{1}{12}F(\xi), \tag{53}$$

where $\xi \equiv (\mu_n - \mu_p - \mu_e)/T$, and

$$F(\xi) \equiv -(\xi^4 + 10\pi^2\xi^2 + 9\pi^4)\text{Li}_3(-e^\xi) + 12(\xi^3 + 5\pi^2\xi)\text{Li}_4(-e^\xi) \\
- 24(3\xi^2 + 5\pi^2)\text{Li}_5(-e^\xi) + 240\xi\text{Li}_6(-e^\xi) - 360\text{Li}_7(-e^\xi). \tag{54}$$

For the angular integral, we can look up [25], which calculated the n-dimensional angular integral for n=3,4,5, and obtain

$$A = \frac{32\pi(2\pi)^4}{k_n^3}\theta_n, \tag{55}$$

where

$$\theta_n = \begin{cases} 1 & k_{Fn} > k_{Fp} + k_{Fe} \\ 1 - \dfrac{3}{8}\dfrac{(k_{Fp} + k_{Fe} - k_{Fn})^2}{k_{Fp}k_{Fe}} & k_{Fn} < k_{Fp} + k_{Fe}. \end{cases} \tag{56}$$

Therefore, the neutron decay modified Urca rate with n-spectator under Fermi surface approximation is

$$\Gamma_{mU,nd(n)}(\xi) = \frac{7}{64\pi^9}G^2 g_A^2 f^4 \frac{(E_{Fn}^*)^3 E_{Fp}^*}{m_\pi^4} \frac{k_{Fn}^4 k_{Fp}}{(k_{Fn}^2 + m_\pi^2)^2} F(\xi) T^7 \theta_n. \tag{57}$$

Similarly, we can calculate the electron capture mU rate with n-spectator

$$\Gamma_{mU,ec(n)}(\xi) = \Gamma_{mU,nd(n)}(-\xi).\tag{58}$$

For p-spectator processes, the matrix element is

$$\left(s \frac{\sum |M_p|^2}{2^6 E_n^* E_p^* E_e E_\nu E_{N_1}^* E_{N_2}^*}\right) = 48 G^2 \frac{f^4}{m_\pi^4} \frac{g_A^2}{E_e^2} \frac{(k_{Fn} - k_{Fp})^4}{((k_{Fn} - k_{Fp})^2 + m_\pi^2)^2},\tag{59}$$

where we still have $s = 1/2$. Then we have the mU rates with p-spectator

$$\Gamma_{mU,nd(p)}(\xi) = \frac{1}{64\pi^9} G^2 g_A^2 f^4 \frac{(E_{Fp}^*)^3 E_{Fn}^*}{m_\pi^4} \frac{(k_{Fn} - k_{Fp})^4 k_{Fn}}{((k_{Fn} - k_{Fp})^2 + m_\pi^2)^2} F(\xi) T^7 \theta_p,\tag{60}$$

$$\Gamma_{mU,ec(p)}(\xi) = \Gamma_{mU,nd(p)}(-\xi),\tag{61}$$

where

$$\theta_p = \begin{cases} 0 & k_{Fn} > 3k_{Fp} + k_{Fe} \\ \dfrac{(3k_{Fp} + k_{Fe} - k_{Fn})^2}{k_{Fn} k_{Fe}} & 3k_{Fp} + k_{Fe} > k_{Fn} > 3k_{Fp} - k_{Fe} \\ \dfrac{4(3k_{Fp} - k_{Fn})}{k_{Fn}} & 3k_{Fp} - k_{Fe} > k_{Fn} > k_{Fp} + k_{Fe} \\ 2 + \dfrac{3(2k_{Fp} - k_{Fn})}{k_{Fe}} - \dfrac{3(k_{Fn} - k_{Fe})^2}{k_{Fn} k_{Fe}} & k_{Fn} < k_{Fp} + k_{Fe}. \end{cases}\tag{62}$$

References

1. Perego, A.; Bernuzzi, S.; Radice, D. Thermodynamics conditions of matter in neutron star mergers. *Eur. Phys. J. A* **2019**, *55*, 124. [CrossRef]
2. Endrizzi, A.; Perego, A.; Fabbri, F.M.; Branca, L.; Radice, D.; Bernuzzi, S.; Giacomazzo, B.; Pederiva, F.; Lovato, A. Thermodynamics conditions of matter in the neutrino decoupling region during neutron star mergers. *Eur. Phys. J. A* **2020**, *56*, 15. [CrossRef]
3. Hanauske, M.; Steinheimer, J.; Motornenko, A.; Vovchenko, V.; Bovard, L.; Most, E.R.; Papenfort, L.; Schramm, S.; Stöcker, H. Neutron Star Mergers: Probing the EoS of Hot, Dense Matter by Gravitational Waves. *Particles* **2019**, *2*, 44–56. [CrossRef]
4. Most, E.R.; Harris, S.P.; Plumberg, C.; Alford, M.G.; Noronha, J.; Noronha-Hostler, J.; Pretorius, F.; Witek, H.; Yunes, N. Projecting the likely importance of weak-interaction-driven bulk viscosity in neutron star mergers. *Mon. Not. R. Astron. Soc.* **2021**, stab2793. [CrossRef]
5. Alford, M.G.; Harris, S.P. Beta equilibrium in neutron star mergers. *Phys. Rev.* **2018**, *C98*, 065806. [CrossRef]
6. Glendenning, N.K. *Compact Stars: Nuclear Physics, Particle Physics, and General Relativity*; Springer: New York, NY, USA, 1997.
7. Dutra, M.; Lourenco, O.; Avancini, S.S.; Carlson, B.V.; Delfino, A.; Menezes, D.P.; Providencia, C.; Typel, S.; Stone, J.R. Relativistic Mean-Field Hadronic Models under Nuclear Matter Constraints. *Phys. Rev. C* **2014**, *90*, 055203. [CrossRef]
8. Fischer, T.; Guo, G.; Dzhioev, A.A.; Martinez-Pinedo, G.; Wu, M.R.; Lohs, A.; Qian, Y.Z. Neutrino signal from proto-neutron star evolution: Effects of opacities from charged-current–neutrino interactions and inverse neutron decay. *Phys. Rev. C* **2020**, *101*, 025804. [CrossRef]
9. Roberts, L.F.; Reddy, S. Charged current neutrino interactions in hot and dense matter. *Phys. Rev.* **2017**, *C95*, 045807. [CrossRef]
10. Fu, W.J.; Wang, G.H.; Liu, Y.X. Electron Capture and Its Reverse Process in Hot and Dense Astronuclear Matter. *Astrophys. J.* **2008**, *678*, 1517–1529. [CrossRef]
11. Reddy, S.; Prakash, M.; Lattimer, J.M. Neutrino interactions in hot and dense matter. *Phys. Rev. D* **1998**, *58*, 013009. [CrossRef]
12. Oechslin, R.; Janka, H.T.; Marek, A. Relativistic neutron star merger simulations with non-zero temperature equations of state. 1 Variation of binary parameters and equation of state. *Astron. Astrophys.* **2007**, *467*, 395. [CrossRef]
13. Baiotti, L.; Rezzolla, L. Binary neutron star mergers: A review of Einstein's richest laboratory. *Rept. Prog. Phys.* **2017**, *80*, 096901. [CrossRef] [PubMed]
14. Raithel, C.; Paschalidis, V.; Özel, F. Realistic finite-temperature effects in neutron star merger simulations. *Phys. Rev. D* **2021**, *104*, 063016. [CrossRef]
15. Leinson, L.B.; Perez, A. Relativistic direct Urca processes in cooling neutron stars. *Phys. Lett. B* **2001**, *518*, 15, [Erratum: *Phys. Lett. B* **2001**, *522*, 358]. [CrossRef]

16. Ding, W.B.; Qi, Z.Q.; Hou, J.W.; Mi, G.; Bao, T.; Yu, Z.; Liu, G.Z.; Zhao, E.G. Relativistic Correction on Neutrino Emission from Neutron Stars in Various Parameter Sets. *Commun. Theor. Phys.* **2016**, *66*, 474–478. [CrossRef]
17. Qi, Z.; Ding, W.; Zhang, C.; Hou, J. Relativistic Correction of Neutrino Emission in Neutron Stars. *Chin. Astron. Astrophys.* **2018**, *42*, 69–80. [CrossRef]
18. Wadhwa, A.; Gupta, V.K.; Singh, S.; Anand, J.D. On the cooling of neutron stars. *J. Phys. Nucl. Part. Phys.* **1995**, *21*, 1137–1147. [CrossRef]
19. Alford, M.; Harutyunyan, A.; Sedrakian, A. Bulk Viscous Damping of Density Oscillations in Neutron Star Mergers. *Particles* **2020**, *3*, 500–517. [CrossRef]
20. Alford, M.; Harutyunyan, A.; Sedrakian, A. Bulk viscosity of baryonic matter with trapped neutrinos. *Phys. Rev.* **2019**, *D100*, 103021. [CrossRef]
21. Alford, M.G.; Harris, S.P. Damping of density oscillations in neutrino-transparent nuclear matter. *Phys. Rev.* **2019**, *C100*, 035803. [CrossRef]
22. Yakovlev, D.G.; Gusakov, M.E.; Haensel, P. Bulk viscosity in a neutron star mantle. *Mon. Not. Roy. Astron. Soc.* **2018**, *481*, 4924–4930. [CrossRef]
23. Arras, P.; Weinberg, N.N. Urca reactions during neutron star inspiral. *Mon. Not. Roy. Astron. Soc.* **2019**, *486*, 1424–1436. [CrossRef]
24. Schmitt, A.; Shternin, P. Reaction rates and transport in neutron stars. *Astrophys. Space Sci. Libr.* **2018**, *457*, 455–574. [CrossRef]
25. Kaminker, A.D.; Yakovlev, D.G.; Haensel, P. Theory of neutrino emission from nucleon-hyperon matter in neutron stars: Angular integrals. *Astrophys. Space Sci.* **2016**, *361*, 267. [CrossRef]
26. Kolomeitsev, E.E.; Voskresensky, D.N. Viscosity of neutron star matter and r-modes in rotating pulsars. *Phys. Rev. C* **2015**, *91*, 025805. [CrossRef]
27. Yin, P.; Zuo, W. Three-body force effect on neutrino emissivities of neutron stars within the framework of the Brueckner-Hartree-Fock approach. *Phys. Rev. C* **2013**, *88*, 015804. [CrossRef]
28. Alford, M.G.; Mahmoodifar, S.; Schwenzer, K. Large amplitude behavior of the bulk viscosity of dense matter. *J. Phys. G* **2010**, *37*, 125202. [CrossRef]
29. Yang, S.H.; Zheng, X.P.; Pi, C.M. Radiative viscosity of neutron stars. *Phys. Lett. B* **2010**, *683*, 255–258. [CrossRef]
30. Gusakov, M.E.; Yakovlev, D.G.; Haensel, P.; Gnedin, O.Y. Direct Urca process in a neutron star mantle. *Astron. Astrophys.* **2004**, *421*, 1143–1148. [CrossRef]
31. Yakovlev, D.G.; Kaminker, A.D.; Gnedin, O.Y.; Haensel, P. Neutrino emission from neutron stars. *Phys. Rept.* **2001**, *354*, 1. [CrossRef]
32. Haensel, P.; Schaeffer, R. Bulk viscosity of hot-neutron-star matter from direct URCA processes. *Phys. Rev. D* **1992**, *45*, 4708–4712. [CrossRef]
33. Haensel, P. Non-equilibrium neutrino emissivities and opacities of neutron star matter. *Astron. Astrophys.* **1992**, *262*, 131–137.
34. Lattimer, J.M.; Prakash, M.; Pethick, C.J.; Haensel, P. Direct URCA process in neutron stars. *Phys. Rev. Lett.* **1991**, *66*, 2701–2704. [CrossRef]
35. Shapiro, S.L.; Teukolsky, S.A. *Black Holes, White Dwarfs, and Neutron Stars: The Physics of Compact Objects*; Wiley: Hoboken, NJ, USA, 1983.
36. Piekarewicz, J.; Toledo Sanchez, G. Proton fraction in the inner neutron-star crust. *Phys. Rev. C* **2012**, *85*, 015807. [CrossRef]
37. Greiner, W.; Neise, L.; Stocker, H.; Stöcker, H.; Rischke, D. *Thermodynamics and Statistical Mechanics*; Classical theoretical physics; Springer: Berlin/Heidelberg, Germany, 1995.
38. Yuan, Y.F. Electron positron capture rates and the steady state equilibrium condition for electron-positron plasma with nucleons. *Phys. Rev. D* **2005**, *72*, 013007. [CrossRef]
39. Liu, M.Q. Steady state equilibrium condition of npe±gas and its application to astrophysics. *Res. Astron. Astrophys.* **2010**, *11*, 91–102. [CrossRef]
40. Friman, B.L.; Maxwell, O.V. Neutron Star Neutrino Emissivities. *Astrophys. J.* **1979**, *232*, 541–557. [CrossRef]
41. Fattoyev, F.J.; Horowitz, C.J.; Piekarewicz, J.; Shen, G. Relativistic effective interaction for nuclei, giant resonances, and neutron stars. *Phys. Rev. C* **2010**, *82*, 055803. [CrossRef]
42. Steiner, A.W.; Hempel, M.; Fischer, T. Core-collapse supernova equations of state based on neutron star observations. *Astrophys. J.* **2013**, *774*, 17. [CrossRef]
43. Riley, T.E.; Watts, A.L.; Ray, P.S.; Bogdanov, S.; Guillot, S.; Morsink, S.M.; Bilous, A.V.; Arzoumanian, Z.; Choudhury, D.; Deneva, J.S.; et al. A NICER View of the Massive Pulsar PSR J0740+6620 Informed by Radio Timing and XMM-Newton Spectroscopy. *Astrophys. J. Lett.* **2021**, *918*, L27. [CrossRef]
44. Fonseca, E.; Pennucci, T.T.; Ellis, J.A.; Stairs, I.H.; Nice, D.J.; Ransom, S.M.; Demorest, P.B.; Arzoumanian, Z.; Crowter, K.; Dolch, T.; et al The NANOGrav Nine-year Data Set: Mass and Geometric Measurements of Binary Millisecond Pulsars. *Astrophys. J.* **2016**, *832*, 167. [CrossRef]
45. Antoniadis, J.; Freire, P.C.; Wex, N.; Tauris, T.M.; Lynch, R.S.; Van Kerkwijk, M.H.; Kramer, M.; Bassa, C.; Dhillon, V.S.; Driebe, T.; et al. A Massive Pulsar in a Compact Relativistic Binary. *Science* **2013**, *340*, 6131. [CrossRef]
46. Pang, P.T.H.; Tews, I.; Coughlin, M.W.; Bulla, M.; Van Den Broeck, C.; Dietrich, T. Nuclear-Physics Multi-Messenger Astrophysics Constraints on the Neutron-Star Equation of State: Adding NICER's PSR J0740+6620 Measurement. *arXiv* **2021**, arXiv:2105.08688.

47. Brown, E.F.; Cumming, A.; Fattoyev, F.J.; Horowitz, C.J.; Page, D.; Reddy, S. Rapid neutrino cooling in the neutron star MXB 1659-29. *Phys. Rev. Lett.* **2018**, *120*, 182701. [CrossRef] [PubMed]
48. Beloin, S.; Han, S.; Steiner, A.W.; Odbadrakh, K. Simultaneous Fitting of Neutron Star Structure and Cooling Data. *Phys. Rev. C* **2019**, *100*, 055801. [CrossRef]
49. Wei, J.B.; Burgio, G.F.; Schulze, H.J. Neutron star cooling with microscopic equations of state. *Mon. Not. Roy. Astron. Soc.* **2019**, *484*, 5162. [CrossRef]
50. Reed, B.T.; Fattoyev, F.J.; Horowitz, C.J.; Piekarewicz, J. Implications of PREX-2 on the Equation of State of Neutron-Rich Matter. *Phys. Rev. Lett.* **2021**, *126*, 172503. [CrossRef]
51. Page, D.; Lattimer, J.M.; Prakash, M.; Steiner, A.W. Minimal cooling of neutron stars: A New paradigm. *Astrophys. J. Suppl.* **2004**, *155*, 623–650. [CrossRef]
52. Serot, B.D.; Walecka, J.D. Recent progress in quantum hadrodynamics. *Int. J. Mod. Phys. E* **1997**, *6*, 515–631. [CrossRef]
53. Char, P.; Traversi, S.; Pagliara, G. A Bayesian Analysis on Neutron Stars within Relativistic Mean Field Models. *Particles* **2020**, *3*, 621–629. [CrossRef]
54. Zhang, X.; Prakash, M. Hot and dense matter beyond relativistic mean field theory. *Phys. Rev. C* **2016**, *93*, 055805. [CrossRef]
55. Friman, B.; Weise, W. Neutron Star Matter as a Relativistic Fermi Liquid. *Phys. Rev. C* **2019**, *100*, 065807, doi:10.1103/PhysRevC.100.065807. [CrossRef]
56. Li, B.A.; Cai, B.J.; Chen, L.W.; Xu, J. Nucleon Effective Masses in Neutron-Rich Matter. *Prog. Part. Nucl. Phys.* **2018**, *99*, 29–119. [CrossRef]
57. Villain, L.; Haensel, P. Non-equilibrium beta processes in superfluid neutron star cores. *Astron. Astrophys.* **2005**, *444*, 539. [CrossRef]
58. Shternin, P.S.; Baldo, M.; Haensel, P. In-medium enhancement of the modified Urca neutrino reaction rates. *Phys. Lett. B* **2018**, *786*, 28–34. [CrossRef]
59. Olver, F.W.; Lozier, D.W.; Boisvert, R.F.; Clark, C.W. *NIST Handbook of Mathematical Functions Hardback and CD-ROM*; Cambridge University Press: Cambridge, UK, 2010.
60. Harris, S.P. Transport in Neutron Star Mergers. Ph.D. Thesis, Washington University in Saint Louis: St. Louis, MO, USA, 2020.
61. Radice, D.; Perego, A.; Hotokezaka, K.; Fromm, S.A.; Bernuzzi, S.; Roberts, L.F. Binary Neutron Star Mergers: Mass Ejection, Electromagnetic Counterparts and Nucleosynthesis. *Astrophys. J.* **2018**, *869*, 130. [CrossRef]
62. Alford, M.G.; Bovard, L.; Hanauske, M.; Rezzolla, L.; Schwenzer, K. Viscous Dissipation and Heat Conduction in Binary Neutron-Star Mergers. *Phys. Rev. Lett.* **2018**, *120*, 041101. [CrossRef] [PubMed]
63. Hammond, P.; Hawke, I.; Andersson, N. Thermal aspects of neutron star mergers. *arXiv preprint* **2021**, arXiv:2108.08649. [PubMed]
64. Steiner, A.W.; Prakash, M.; Lattimer, J.M.; Ellis, P.J. Isospin asymmetry in nuclei and neutron stars. *Phys. Rept.* **2005**, *411*, 325–375. [CrossRef]
65. Haensel, P.; Levenfish, K.P.; Yakovlev, D.G. Bulk viscosity in superfluid neutron star cores. I. direct urca processes in npe mu matter. *Astron. Astrophys.* **2000**, *357*, 1157–1169.
66. Sawyer, R.F.; Soni, A. Transport of neutrinos in hot neutron-star matter. *Astrophys. J.* **1979**, *230*, 859–869. [CrossRef]

Article

High-Order Multipole and Binary Love Number Universal Relations

Daniel A. Godzieba [1,*] and David Radice [1,2,3]

1. Department of Physics, The Pennsylvania State University, University Park, PA 16802, USA; dur566@psu.edu
2. Institute for Gravitation & The Cosmos, The Pennsylvania State University, University Park, PA 16802, USA
3. Department of Astronomy & Astrophysics, The Pennsylvania State University, University Park, PA 16802, USA
* Correspondence: dag5611@psu.edu

Abstract: Using a data set of approximately 2 million phenomenological equations of state consistent with observational constraints, we construct new equation-of-state-insensitive universal relations that exist between the multipolar tidal deformability parameters of neutron stars, Λ_l, for several high-order multipoles ($l = 5, 6, 7, 8$), and we consider finite-size effects of these high-order multipoles in waveform modeling. We also confirm the existence of a universal relation between the radius of the $1.4 M_\odot$ NS, $R_{1.4}$ and the reduced tidal parameter of the binary, $\tilde{\Lambda}$, and the chirp mass. We extend this relation to a large number of chirp masses and to the radii of isolated NSs of different mass M, R_M. We find that there is an optimal value of M for every $\mathcal{M}$ such that the uncertainty in the estimate of R_M is minimized when using the relation. We discuss the utility and implications of these relations for the upcoming LIGO O4 run and third-generation detectors.

Keywords: neutron star; equation of state; universal relation

1. Introduction

Due to the constraints imposed by general relativity and causality, there exist quasi-universal relations between various bulk physical properties of neutron stars (NSs) that are mostly insensitive to the actual equation of state (EOS) of nuclear matter [1–14]. Since the nuclear EOS in the high-density regime of NSs is still unknown, these universal relations are a great utility for gravitational wave (GW) astronomy. Universal relations reduce a group of several seemingly independent physical properties to a family characterized by only a few parameters. Ideally, this allows one to break the degeneracies between parameters in the analysis of GW data as well as in waveform modelling.

A robust set of universal relations (called multipole Love relations) holds between the l-th order dimensionless gravitoelectric tidal deformability coefficients of NSs [12], Λ_l, which are defined by

$$\Lambda_l \equiv \frac{2}{(2l-1)!!} \frac{k_l}{C^{2l+1}}, \tag{1}$$

where $C = M/R$ is the compactness of the NS (here we take $G = c = 1$) and k_l is its l-th order gravitoelectric tidal Love number [15]. The GW waveform of a binary NS (BNS) merger is, quite understandably, highly sensitive to these tidal parameters. How deformable a NS is in a tidal potential affects how its mass ultimately gets distributed during the inspiral of a merger, which, in turn, shapes the GW waveform, especially during the late stages of the inspiral [15–19]. The tidal parameters enter into the waveform at different post-Newtonian orders; however, they are degenerate in the signal [12]. The multipole relations allow this degeneracy to be broken by reducing all of the tidal deformabilities to a family determined by a single parameter. This parameter is always chosen to be the quadrupolar tidal deformability Λ_2, which is the source of the leading-order finite-size effect in the GW signal and, consequently, is the easiest to measure [12]. Thus, higher-order ($l > 2$) tidal deformabilities can be expressed through the multipole Love relations as functions of Λ_2. The authors and others have demonstrated that the improvements to the accuracy of tidal deformability measurements, to parameter estimation, and to GW modelling offered by the multipole Love relations are significant [12,14,15,20,21] and will become particularly important with the increased sensitivity of upcoming third-generation GW detectors like LIGO III, the Einstein Telescope, and Cosmic Explorer [12,15,22–25].

Motivated by these potential improvements, we present entirely new fits to several previously un-fitted high-order multipole Love relations, specifically for $l = 5, 6, 7$, and 8. Though the finite-size effects of these orders of tidal parameters are currently smaller than measurement error, they will become more measurable with increased sensitivity; hence, faithful GW waveform modelling will need to incorporate them. Previosu studies, such as Flanagan and Hinderer [26] and Damour et al. [27], have discussed the finite-size effects of the $l \leq 4$ multipoles.

Zhao and Lattimer [19], De et al. [28] have demonstrated the existence of an intriguing EOS-insensitive relation for BNSs between the radius of the $1.4 M_\odot$ NS, $R_{1.4}$ and the reduced tidal deformability (also called the binary tidal deformability), $\tilde{\Lambda}$. The quadrupolar deformabilities of the individual NSs enter into the GW signal of the merger via $\tilde{\Lambda}$, which is defined as

$$\tilde{\Lambda} \equiv \frac{16}{13} \frac{(12q+1)\Lambda_{2,1} + (12+q)\Lambda_{2,2}}{(1+q)^5}, \quad (2)$$

where $\Lambda_{2,1}$ and $\Lambda_{2,2}$ are the deformabilities of the primary and the secondary stars, respectively. The quadrupolar tidal Love number k_2 is known to scale roughly as C^{-1} independently of the EOS [15,29]. According to Equation (1), this means Λ_2 scales approximately as C^{-6}. In an apparently analogous fashion, $\tilde{\Lambda}$ seems to go as $(\mathcal{M}/R_{1.4})^{-6}$, where $\mathcal{M}$ is the chirp mass of the BNS given by

$$\mathcal{M} \equiv \frac{(m_1 m_2)^{3/5}}{(m_1 + m_2)^{1/5}}. \quad (3)$$

Combining this observation with the definition of $\tilde{\Lambda}$ in the manner done by Zhao and Lattimer [19] yields a mostly EOS-insensitive estimate of $R_{1.4}$ in terms of $\tilde{\Lambda}$ and $\mathcal{M}$ that is also mostly insensitive to the binary mass ratio q:

$$R_{1.4} \simeq (11.5 \pm 0.3 \text{ km}) \frac{\mathcal{M}}{M_\odot} \left(\frac{\tilde{\Lambda}}{800}\right)^{1/6}. \quad (4)$$

The immediate utility of this relation is the ability to produce an EOS-agnostic estimate of $R_{1.4}$ from just tidal parameter measurements. This is an alternative to the more involved method of using the universal relation for binaries between the symmetric and antisymmetric combinations of $\Lambda_{2,1}$ and $\Lambda_{2,2}$ [14,30] combined with the relation for individual NSs between Λ_2 and the compactness C [14,31] (a relation which intuitively follows from the definition of Λ_l in Equation (1)). One would first use the symmetric-antisymmetric relation to break the degeneracy between $\Lambda_{2,1}$ and $\Lambda_{2,2}$ and estimate them individually from $\tilde{\Lambda}$, and then use the Λ_2-C relation and the masses of the binary to extract the radii of both stars. The LIGO/VIRGO analysis of GW170817 is an example of this latter approach [28,32,33]. One need not appeal to universal relations to estimate stellar radii, however. Instead, one could perform an inference of the EOS directly using a parametric representation of the EOS as was also done in the LIGO/VIRGO analysis [32], or using a much more sophisticated nonparametric representation, as described in Essick et al. [34].

It is an appealing question, then, whether this relation can be extended using the radius of a NS with a generic mass M, $R(M) = R_M$. A R_M-$\tilde{\Lambda}$ relation would allow one to use measurements of tidal parameters and $\mathcal{M}$ to place robust constrains on R_M directly without the need for a more complicated procedure. Hence, our motivation in this work is to provide a phenomenological study of the R_M-$\tilde{\Lambda}$ relation. We look at the relation for several values of M. For a given M, we compute fits to the relation for twelve fixed values of $\mathcal{M}$ between $0.9M_\odot$ and $1.4M_\odot$. We then generalize the fit for all $\mathcal{M} \in [0.9M_\odot, 1.4M_\odot]$ by interpolating the fitting parameters as functions of $\mathcal{M}$. Fitting to the relation from across a vast set of phenomenological EOSs incorporates the effects of higher-order terms that are dropped when one analytically derives the expression in Equation (4) as was done in [19]. Equation (4) assumes that the $R_{1.4}$-$\tilde{\Lambda}$ relation (and, by extension, the R_M-$\tilde{\Lambda}$ relation) is only linearly dependent on $\mathcal{M}$, i.e., that $\mathcal{M}$ simply scales the relation but does not change its dependence on $\tilde{\Lambda}$. A phenomenological study permits us to observe directly the effect changing $\mathcal{M}$ has on the relation.

The outline of this paper is as follows. In Section 2, we describe the parameterization scheme and algorithm by which we generate our phenomenological EOS data and the statistics for our analyses. In Section 3, we present the fitting parameters of the high-order multipole Love relations, followed in Section 4 by an phenomenological analysis of and fits to the $R_{1.4}$-$\tilde{\Lambda}$ relation as well as to the general R_M-$\tilde{\Lambda}$ relation. We also discuss the implications of these new fits to GW waveform analysis for the LIGO O4 run. A concluding summary is given in Section 5.

2. Methods

We parameterize the space of all possible EOSs consistent with theoretical calculations and astronomical observations using the piecewise polytropic interpolation developed in Read et al. [35], with the only modification being that we allow the transition densities ρ_1 and ρ_2 to vary. We then generate random piecewise EOSs using a Markov chain Monte Carlo (MCMC) algorithm, with the basic summary as follows. For a given candidate EOS, the algorithm first computes a series of solutions to the Tolman-Oppenheimer-Volkoff (TOV) equation using the publically available TOVL code described in Bernuzzi and Nagar [36] and Damour and Nagar [17], and then accepts the EOS if and only if it satisfies three weak physical constraints:

1. Causality of the maximum mass NS is preserved (i.e., the maximum sound speed c_s is less than the speed of light c below the maximum stable central density);
2. The maximum stable mass of a non-rotating NS, M_{max}, is greater than $1.97M_\odot$, and
3. $\Lambda_2 < 800$ for the $1.4M_\odot$ NS.

The full details of parameterization and the MCMC algorithm can be found in Godzieba et al. [14]. With this scheme, we generate a set of 1,966,225 phenomenological EOSs.

To study the multipole Love relations, for each EOS in our data set, we solve the TOV equation for sixteen evenly spaced central densities between $\rho_c = 3.09 \times 10^{14}$ g/cm^3 and the maximum stable central density of that EOS, and then extract Λ_l for $l = 2$ through $l = 8$ from each solution.

To study the R_M-$\tilde{\Lambda}$ relation, we follow a similar procedure. First, we choose a fixed value of $\mathcal{M}$. Next, for each EOS in a random sample of a quarter of all EOS in the data set, we generate twenty random binary NSs (BNSs). We uniformly sample the binary mass ratio $q = m_2/m_1$ (where $m_2 \leq m_1$) on the interval $1/2 \leq q \leq 1$. This range is not intended to represent the complete range of values that q could take in Nature, but rather simply to capture the general behavior of q based on observational and theoretical considerations. Observations of the most massive known pulsars indicate that $M_{max} \gtrsim 2M_\odot$ [37–42], and the analysis of GW170817 suggests that $M_{max} \lesssim 2.3M_\odot$ [43–47]; though, as we await upcoming precision measurements of millisecond pulsar radii by NICER, we cannot as of yet categorically rule out the possibility of extreme EOSs with $M_{max} < 2.5M_\odot$ [48]. Meanwhile, the least massive known pulsar has a mass of $1.17M_\odot$ [49], and, depending on the true nuclear EOS, the minimum stable gravitational mass, M_{min}, could be as low as $1.15M_\odot$ [50]. Hence, $q \geq M_{min}/M_{max} \approx 1/2$, and the vast majority of BNSs, being far from either mass extreme, will fall well within this range.

Each q is then converted into the actual binary masses m_1 and m_2 using the value of $\mathcal{M}$ and Equation (3):

$$m_1 = \mathcal{M} q^{-3/5}(1+q)^{1/5}, \quad m_2 = \mathcal{M} q^{2/5}(1+q)^{1/5}. \quad (5)$$

The TOV equation is then solved with the corresponding EOS for NSs with these two masses, and Λ_2 is extracted from both solutions to compute $\tilde{\Lambda}$. We apply this procedure for twelve different values of $\mathcal{M}$ between $0.9 M_\odot$ and $1.4 M_\odot$. The $\tilde{\Lambda}$ values are then plotted versus R_M for eight different values of M. These R_M values are pulled from our EOS data set.

3. High-Order Multipole Relations

From our phenomenological EOS data set, we compute 21,994,104 valid individual NS solutions to the TOV equation as our statistics for analyzing the multipole Love relations. Λ_3, Λ_4, Λ_5, Λ_6, Λ_7, and Λ_8 are plotted against Λ_2 in Figure 1, and one can appreciate the universality of each relation across a vast range of scales. (We observe that all the intersections between the six curves lie around $\Lambda_2 \sim 100$, but we are not sure why this is the case.) As in the authors' previous work [14], we employ a fitting function of the form

$$\ln \Lambda_l = \sum_{k=0}^{6} a_k (\ln \Lambda_2)^k, \quad (6)$$

which is an extended version of the fitting function originally used by Yagi and Yunes [11]. The fitting parameters $\vec{a} = \{a_k\}$ for each relation are given in Table 1.

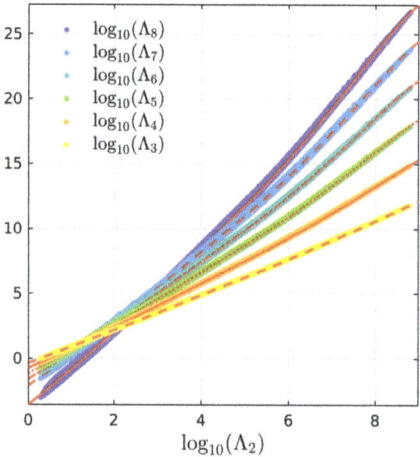

Figure 1. Universal multipole Love relations for $l = 3$ through $l = 8$ from the collection of phenomenological EOSs. We use the fitting function function in Equation (6), and the fit to each relation is plotted in red.

Table 1. Fitting parameters $\vec{a} = \{a_k\}$ of the multipole Love relations given in Equation (6).

Relation	a_0	a_1	a_2	a_3	a_4	a_5	a_6
Λ_3–Λ_2	−0.82195	1.2110	1.0494×10^{-2}	1.6581×10^{-3}	-3.1933×10^{-4}	1.8607×10^{-5}	-3.5027×10^{-7}
Λ_4–Λ_2	−1.6887	1.4719	7.1803×10^{-3}	5.4042×10^{-3}	-8.3262×10^{-4}	4.6940×10^{-5}	-8.9092×10^{-7}
Λ_5–Λ_2	−2.6473	1.7485	-5.1199×10^{-4}	9.7085×10^{-3}	-1.3990×10^{-3}	7.8465×10^{-5}	-1.5055×10^{-6}
Λ_6–Λ_2	−3.7032	2.0313	-1.0038×10^{-2}	1.4083×10^{-2}	-1.9640×10^{-3}	1.1029×10^{-4}	-2.1380×10^{-6}
Λ_7–Λ_2	−4.8568	2.3209	-2.2063×10^{-2}	1.8533×10^{-2}	-2.5050×10^{-3}	1.4020×10^{-4}	-2.7305×10^{-6}
Λ_8–Λ_2	−8.2442	2.6203	-1.8152×10^{-2}	2.5720×10^{-2}	-3.6087×10^{-3}	2.0231×10^{-4}	-3.9399×10^{-6}

In Figure 2, we show the 68%, 95%, and 99.7% relative error of each fit. For each line in the error plot, the corresponding percentage of data points lie below it. We restrict our attention to the domain $1 < \Lambda_2 < 10^4$, as this is the range of Λ_2 most relevant to current LIGO measurements. The estimate error of each Λ_l over this range stays mostly flat with a slight downward trend. (The small ripples that can be seen in the error plots over this range are simply artifacts of how the distribution of NS solutions was computed.) The universality of the multipole relations weaken gradually as l increases, as can be seen in the increasing thickness of the distributions in Figure 1. This then increases the maximum estimate error of Λ_l for larger l despite the faithfulness of each fit to the shape of the corresponding relation (see Figure 1). While 95% of estimate errors are smaller than $\sim$7% for the Λ_3–Λ_2 relation, 95% are only smaller than $\sim$50% for Λ_8–Λ_2.

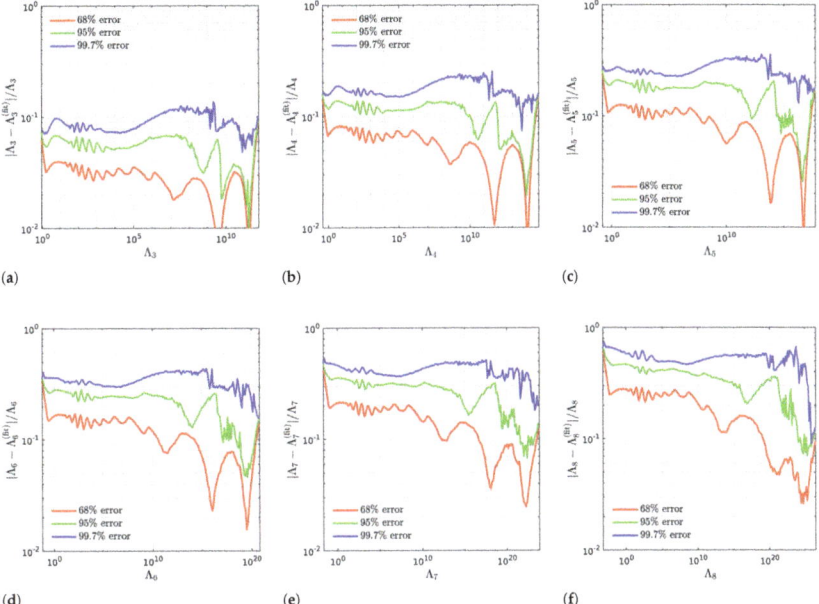

Figure 2. 68%, 95%, and 99.7% relative errors of the fits to (**a**) Λ_3–Λ_2, (**b**) Λ_4–Λ_2, (**c**) Λ_5–Λ_2, (**d**) Λ_6–Λ_2, (**e**) Λ_7–Λ_2, and (**f**) Λ_8–Λ_2 relations. The small ripple in the error seen at small values of each Λ_l is simply an artifact of how the distribution of NS solutions were generated. The fits are faithful to the shape of the curves of the relations; however, universality weakens and the distributions of points spread out as l increases, resulting in the maximum error of the estimate increasing with l.

The phase of a GW in waveform modelling is affected by the highest order out to which one carries finite-size corrections (The leading-terms of the finite-size correction from Λ_l is given in [12]). We demonstrate this with a baseline model of a binary with $m_1 = m_2 = 2.7 M_\odot$ and $\Lambda_1 = \Lambda_2 = 1000$ using the spin-aligned effective-one-body waveform model TEOBResumS [18]. Often when universal relations are not employed, all finite-size effects are dropped except for the leading-order ($l = 2$) effect. In the baseline model, just the $l = 2$ correction alone contributes a phase difference of 36.7 radians compared to a waveform model with no tidal corrections. Further corrections from the $l = 3$ and $l = 4$ effects using the Λ_3–Λ_2 and Λ_4–Λ_2 relations, respectively, incur an additional 2.89 radians. Finally, including the $l = 5, 6, 7$, and 8 corrections using the relations given in this work adds 0.02 radians of dephasing on top of that. (The dephasing between the $l \leq 8$ waveform model and models with fewer corrections is plotted in Figure 3 as a function of time. For all models, most of the dephasing is accumulated in the last 5 milliseconds before the merger.) Combined, the $l > 2$ corrections contribute 2.91

radians of dephasing. This demonstrates the importance of the multipole Love relations for faithful waveform modelling.

The dephasing of the $l > 4$ corrections are currently smaller than GW detector uncertainties, but this could only have been known after fitting to the $l > 4$ multipole relations. Additionally, with the greater sensitivity of future detectors, the $l > 4$ finite-size effects will start to come into view. The order out to which one should carry finite-size corrections in the waveform analysis of actual GW data is dependent on several factors (the EOS model, the signal-to-noise ratio of the merger, etc.); however, in general it is recommended that corrections up to $l = 4$ be included in the analysis of data from current detectors [12,14,27].

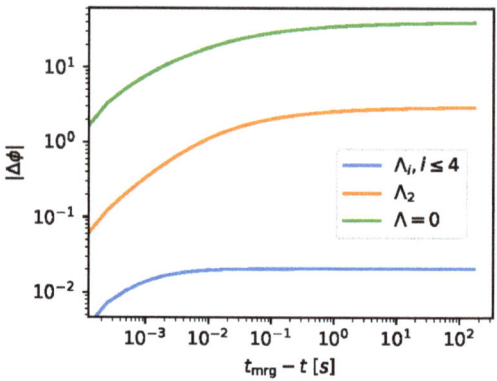

Figure 3. An example of dephasing between different waveform models (one with no tides, one with only the $l = 2$ correction, and one with all corrections up to $l = 4$) and the full model (all corrections up to $l = 8$). The overall dephasing is very small between the $l \leq 4$ model and the full model. Most of the dephasing is accumulated in the last 5 milliseconds, just a few orbits prior to the merger.

4. R_M-$\tilde{\Lambda}$ Relation

We analyze the $R_{1.4}$-$\tilde{\Lambda}$ relation at twelve different fixed values of the chirp mass $\mathcal{M}$, which are given in Table 2. We compute between 750,000 and 1,000,000 valid individual binaries for each value of $\mathcal{M}$. Several example plots of the relation are shown in Figure 4. The relation's dependence on the binary mass ratio q is illustrated by the coloring of the points in these plots. Each point in the plot represents a BNS. Points with smaller values of q are plotted on top. An important conclusion to draw from these plots is that the relation does not depend upon both stars having the same radius [19]. For $\mathcal{M} \lesssim 1.25 M_\odot$, the relation remains fairly tight for all values of q. Further, for $\mathcal{M} \gtrsim 1.1 M_\odot$ (The smallest physical value $\mathcal{M}$ can take is when $m_1 = m_2 = M_{\min} \approx 1.15 M_\odot$ (see Section 2). Using Equation (3), this gives us $\mathcal{M} \gtrsim 1.001 M_\odot$. Since we permit m_1 and m_2 to be less than $1.15 M_\odot$, we are able to reach as low as $\mathcal{M} = 0.9 M_\odot$.), the relation actually becomes *tighter* as q decreases (i.e., as the radii of the two stars differ more and more), which can be understood by considering the definition of $\tilde{\Lambda}$ in Equation (2). For fixed $R_{1.4}$, the range of possible values $\tilde{\Lambda}$ can take is constrained by q. When $q = 1$, the masses of the binary can span the range from the minimum to the maximum mass, $M_{\min} \leq m_1 = m_2 \leq M_{\max}$. Hence, $\min(\Lambda_2) \leq \Lambda_{2,1} = \Lambda_{2,2} \leq \max(\Lambda_2)$, and $\min(\Lambda_2) \leq \tilde{\Lambda} \leq \max(\Lambda_2)$. As q decreases, the bounds for both m_1 and m_2 shrink and no longer overlap, causing the same to happen for $\Lambda_{2,1}$ and $\Lambda_{2,2}$. This, as we see, also shrinks the bounds on $\tilde{\Lambda}$. Thus, we expect the relation to tighten as q decreases.

Table 2. Fitting parameters of the general $R_{1.4}$-$\tilde{\Lambda}$ relation given in Equation (7) for different values of $\mathcal{M}$.

$\mathcal{M}/M_\odot$	α (km)	β
0.900	11.832	6.7621
0.950	11.668	6.5775
1.000	11.548	6.4189
1.045	11.473	6.3020
1.100	11.412	6.1972
1.150	11.377	6.1515
1.180	11.359	6.1513
1.219	11.330	6.1906
1.250	11.302	6.2441
1.300	11.228	6.4147
1.350	11.102	6.7139
1.400	10.921	7.1305

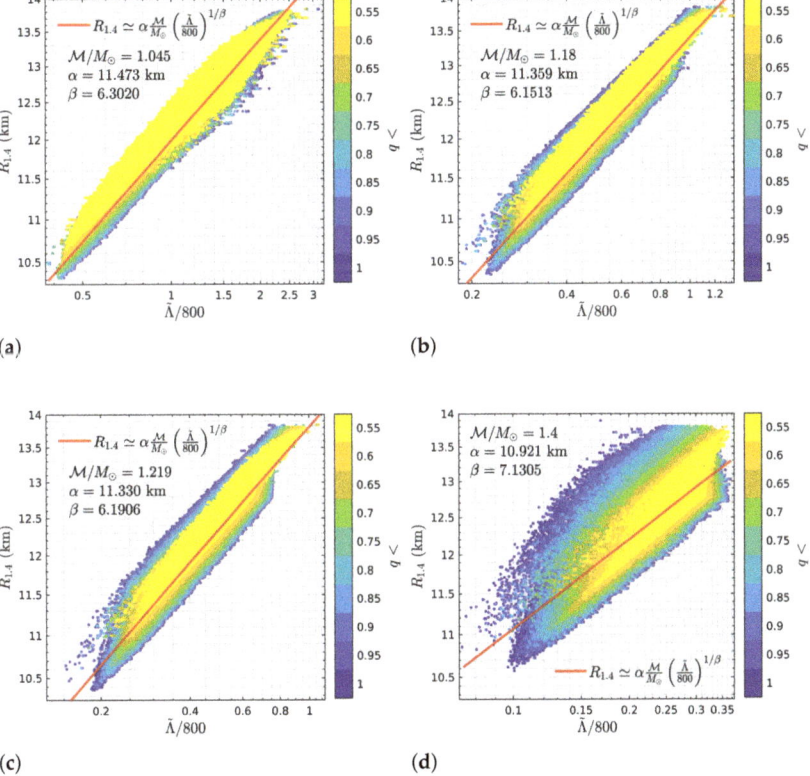

Figure 4. Example fits to the $R_{1.4}$-$\tilde{\Lambda}$ relation for (**a**) $\mathcal{M} = 1.045 M_\odot$, (**b**) $\mathcal{M} = 1.18 M_\odot$, (**c**) $\mathcal{M} = 1.219 M_\odot$, and (**d**) $\mathcal{M} = 1.4 M_\odot$. Each point represents a BNS and is colored according to the value of the binary mass ratio $q = m_2/m_1$. Points with smaller values of q are drawn on top. The upper limit on the value of $\tilde{\Lambda}$ for each $\mathcal{M}$ derives from the $\Lambda_2 < 800$ cutoff for the $1.4 M_\odot$ NS imposed on the EOSs generated by our algorithm (see Section 2). The relation does not depend on both NSs having the same radius, and indeed for $\mathcal{M}/M_\odot \gtrsim 1.1$ it becomes tighter as q decreases.

We construct a fitting function for the $R_{1.4}$-$\tilde{\Lambda}$ relation by considering a slightly generalized form of Equation (4):

$$R_M \simeq \alpha \frac{M}{M_\odot} \left(\frac{\tilde{\Lambda}}{800}\right)^{1/\beta}, \qquad (7)$$

where, in this case, $M = 1.4 M_\odot$. Here the proportionality constant α and the inverse exponent β are the fitting parameters and, consequently, will be dependent on M. These fits are also shown in Figure 4. The fitting parameters for all values of M are given in Table 2. A sense of the accuracy of the estimated value of $R_{1.4}$ from the fit can be gathered from Figure 5, where we plot the 68%, 95%, and 99.7% relative error of the example fits. Overall, the estimates are accurate to within $\mathcal{O}(10\%)$ error for all values of M, and are, in fact, accurate to within $\sim$5% for most values of $R_{1.4}$.

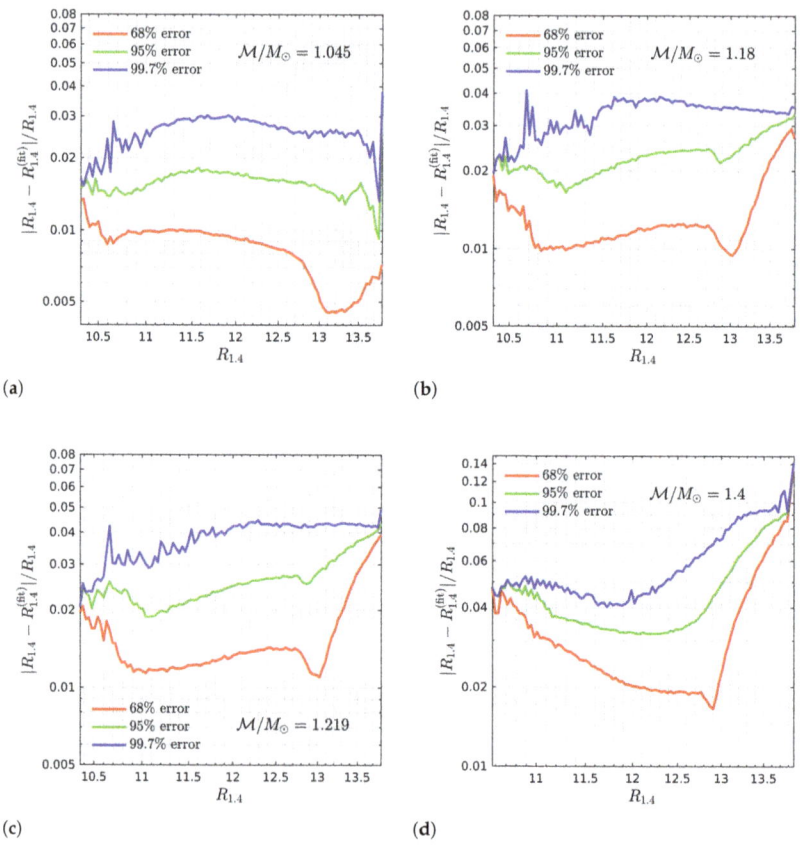

Figure 5. 68%, 95%, and 99.7% relative errors of the fits to the $R_{1.4}$-$\tilde{\Lambda}$ relation for (**a**) $M = 1.045 M_\odot$, (**b**) $M = 1.18 M_\odot$, (**c**) $M = 1.219 M_\odot$, and (**d**) $M = 1.4 M_\odot$. The error overall stays below $\mathcal{O}(10\%)$ with 95% of the estimates generally below 4–5% error, for all values of M.

We can extend our fitting results to all $M \in [0.9 M_\odot, 1.4 M_\odot]$ by fitting the dependence of α and β on M. We construct the rational fitting functions

$$\alpha(x) = \frac{\sum_{k=0}^{3} p_k x^k}{\sum_{k=0}^{2} q_k x^k} \text{ km} \quad \text{and} \quad \beta(x) = \frac{\sum_{k=0}^{2} p_k x^k}{\sum_{k=0}^{2} q_k x^k}, \qquad (8)$$

where $x = (\mathcal{M}/M_\odot - \mu_\mathcal{M})/\sigma_\mathcal{M}$, $\mu_\mathcal{M} = 1.1537$, and $\sigma_\mathcal{M} = 0.15927$. These fits, which are in excellent agreement the values in Table 2, are shown in Figure 6. The fitting parameters $\vec{p} = \{p_k\}$ and $\vec{q} = \{q_k\}$ for $\alpha(x)$ and $\beta(x)$ are given in Table 3. What is interesting is that the inverse exponent β is not monotonic. Rather, it has a minimum at $\mathcal{M} = 1.1661 M_\odot$. A possible contributor to this effect is the decrease in the variety of possible binaries as $\mathcal{M}$ increases. The maximum value M could take for a given EOS is found by letting $m_1 = m_2 = M_{max}$ in Equation (3), which yields $\mathcal{M}_{max} = 2^{-1/5} M_{max}$. For $1/2 \leq q \leq 1$, m_1 and m_2 are bounded by

$$2^{1/5}\mathcal{M} \leq m_1 \leq \min\left(12^{1/5}\mathcal{M}, M_{max}\right), \qquad (9)$$

$$(3/8)^{1/5}\mathcal{M} \leq m_2 \leq 2^{1/5}\mathcal{M}. \qquad (10)$$

Table 3. Fitting parameters $\vec{p} = \{p_k\}$ and $\vec{q} = \{q_k\}$ for α and β as functions of $x = (\mathcal{M}/M_\odot - \mu_\mathcal{M})/\sigma_\mathcal{M}$, where $\mu_\mathcal{M} = 1.1537$ and $\sigma_\mathcal{M} = 0.15927$ for several values of $\mathcal{M}$. The fitting functions are given in Equation (3).

$\mathcal{M}/M_\odot$		p_0	p_1	p_2	p_3	q_0	q_1	q_2
1.4	$\beta(x)$	404.40	−96.991	26.475	-	65.755	−15.259	1
	$\alpha(x)$	224.75	−24.553	11.832	−1.8434	19.758	−1.9914	1
1.5	$\beta(x)$	502.01	−119.44	32.193	-	79.153	−16.598	1
	$\alpha(x)$	282.86	−29.568	12.893	−2.2628	24.833	−2.3357	1
1.6	$\beta(x)$	642.10	−152.88	40.447	-	98.054	−18.391	1
	$\alpha(x)$	386.63	−42.102	14.780	−3.0054	33.942	−3.2743	1
1.7	$\beta(x)$	877.56	−210.98	54.468	-	129.67	−21.419	1
	$\alpha(x)$	598.97	−73.554	18.854	−4.5818	52.655	−5.7193	1
1.8	$\beta(x)$	1442.2	−356.28	88.775	-	206.20	−29.608	1
	$\alpha(x)$	1291.3	−192.50	32.831	−10.064	113.87	−15.207	1
1.9	$\beta(x)$	2734.1	−709.62	174.36	-	380.72	−46.815	1
	$\alpha(x)$	3282.2	−592.78	80.705	−27.980	291.00	−48.054	1
2	$\beta(x)$	63,061	−19,071	3663.7	-	8959.4	−1478.5	1
	$\alpha(x)$	9986.9	−2011.9	232.61	−82.091	887.58	−167.09	1
2.14	$\beta(x)$	93,209	−34,415	6102.8	-	12,686	−2286.4	1
	$\alpha(x)$	58,353	−18,272	1904.6	−609.58	5234.8	−1543.2	1

Hence, as $\mathcal{M}$ increases, the relation becomes gradually dominated by (1) EOSs with $M_{max} \geq 2^{1/5}\mathcal{M}$ and (2) only those BNSs from each EOS that lie in the increasingly narrow range in Equation (9). This decrease of BNS variety could play a role in the non-monotonic behavior of $\beta(x)$.

One could, of course, consider more generally the relation between $\tilde{\Lambda}$ and the radius of a NS with some mass M, R_M. We pursue this thought by looking at R_M-$\tilde{\Lambda}$ for $M/M_\odot = 1.4$, 1.5, 1.6, 1.7, 1.8, 1.9, 2, and 2.14. Just as for the $R_{1.4}$-$\tilde{\Lambda}$ relation, we utilize the fitting function in Equation (4), and then find α and β as functions of x using Equation (8). In Table 3, we show the fitting parameters $\vec{p} = \{p_k\}$ and $\vec{q} = \{q_k\}$ of $\alpha(x)$ and $\beta(x)$ for each M. The tightness of the R_M-$\tilde{\Lambda}$ relation (and thus the general quality of the estimate from the fit) is dependent on both M and $\mathcal{M}$. We illustrate this in Figure 7 by plotting the approximate uncertainty of the estimated value of R_M as a function of $\mathcal{M}$ for several values of M. Since our EOSs and BNSs do not come from prior probability distributions, we non-stringently define the uncertainty here as the half-width of the symmetric interval centered at $\Delta R_M = R_M - R_M^{(fit)} = 0$ that encloses 95% of the data points in the histogram of ΔR_M for fixed $\mathcal{M}$. Interestingly, the uncertainty for each M reaches a minimum at some particular value of $\mathcal{M}$, with the minimum uncertainty for each M being around 0.2 km in the range of $\mathcal{M}$ we considered. The minima for $M = 1.4 M_\odot$ through $1.8 M_\odot$ are visible in Figure 7. This reveals that there is an optimal $\mathcal{M}$ for each M such that R_M is maximally constrained by the R_M–$\tilde{\Lambda}$ relation at that $\mathcal{M}$. Thus, for example, a chirp mass of $\mathcal{M} \approx 1.05 M_\odot$ would yield the best estimate of $R_{1.4}$, while a chirp mass of $\mathcal{M} \approx 1.4 M_\odot$ would yield the best estimate of $R_{1.8}$. Further, there appears to be a linear dependence of the optimal $\mathcal{M}$ on M; however, a wider range of $\mathcal{M}$ would need to be considered to confirm this. The change in the variety of BNSs as $\mathcal{M}$ increases, as previously described, may contribute to this. At larger $\mathcal{M}$, the relation becomes dominated by larger mass NSs; thus, the relation may become more sensitive to the radii of larger mass NSs as $\mathcal{M}$ increases.

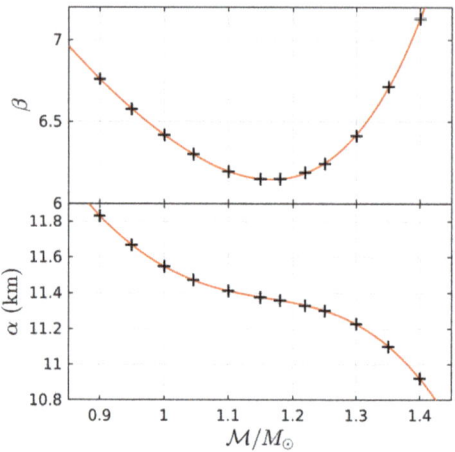

Figure 6. Fitting parameters α and β of the $R_{1.4}$–$\tilde{\Lambda}$ relation as functions of $\mathcal{M}/M_\odot$. $\beta(x)$ does not vary monotonically with x, but has a minimum.

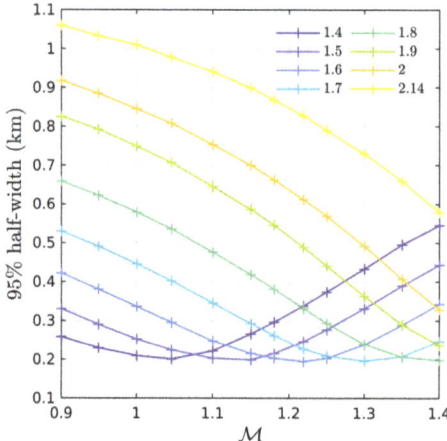

Figure 7. The approximate uncertainty of the estimated value of R_M computed using the R_M–$\tilde{\Lambda}$ relation as a function of $\mathcal{M}$. Each curve is colored according to the value of M (given in units of $M_\odot$). The uncertainty is defined as the half-width of the symmetric interval centered at $\Delta R_M = R_M - R_M^{(\text{fit})} = 0$ that encloses 95% of the data points in the histogram of ΔR_M. For every M, there is an optimal value of $\mathcal{M}$ such that this uncertainty is minimized.

The R_M-$\tilde{\Lambda}$ relation, then, allows one to use any binary to place a robust, EOS-agnostic constraint on R_M using just $\tilde{\Lambda}$ and $\mathcal{M}$. This offers great prospects for the upcoming LIGO O4 run and for third-generation detectors. The O4 run expects to see 10^{+52}_{-10} detections within a search volume of 1.6×10^7 Mpc^3 year [51]. Every BNS detection can be transformed into a maximum constrain on some R_M. However, even the weaker constraints afforded by R_M-$\tilde{\Lambda}$ are of still great utility. Just 10 weak constraints on $R_{1.4}$ using the $R_{1.4}$-$\tilde{\Lambda}$ relation will yield a reliable value for $R_{1.4}$. Further, a reduction in statistical uncertainty thanks to increased sensitivity improves the effectiveness of universal relations, as, for example, the systematic errors of fits to multipole relations are generally smaller than statistical uncertainty [12].

5. Conclusions

We supplement the tool set of GW analysis and waveform modelling by presenting entirely new fits to several universal relations between high-multipole-order dimensionless gravitoelectric tidal deformabilities Λ_l and to the universal relation for BNS between the radius of the $1.4 M_\odot$ NS, $R_{1.4}$, and the reduced tidal deformability $\tilde{\Lambda}$. We compute these utilizing a data set of nearly two-million phenomenological EOS sampled from across a broad parameter space using an MCMC algorithm.

First, we present fits to the multipole relations. Previous fits [12,14] had been made to just the Λ_3-Λ_2 and Λ_4-Λ_2 relations. We extend the library of fits by looking at the Λ_5-Λ_2, Λ_6-Λ_2, Λ_7-Λ_2, and Λ_8-Λ_2 relations. The tightness of the relations weakens as l increases. Consequently, though the fits are faithful to the shapes of the relations, the maximum estimate error of the fits increases to the order of 50% for Λ_8. The inclusion of the finite-size effects of the $l < 4$ multipoles in waveform analysis can incur as much as 0.02 radians of dephasing compared to including only the $l \leq 4$ effects. Collectively, the $l > 2$ effects contribute as much as 2.91 radians of dephasing, and it is recommended that finite-size corrections for $l > 2$ multipoles be included in the analysis of GW data wherever they are at least comparable to detector uncertainties. The full usefulness of these $l > 4$ relations in GW data analysis will be realized with the increased sensitivity of the upcoming third-generation GW detectors like LIGO III [22], the Einstein Telescope [23,24], and Cosmic Explorer [25], as the finite-size effects of these multipole orders are currently smaller than measurement error.

Next, we analyze the $R_{1.4}$-$\tilde{\Lambda}$ relation. The original derivation of the relation [19] yields an expression, given in Equation (4), that is linearly dependent on the chirp mass $\mathcal{M}$ of the BNS. Fitting the relation for different fixed values of $\mathcal{M}$ reveals any nonlinear dependence the relation may have on $\mathcal{M}$ and allows us to compute an expression that more accurately estimates $R_{1.4}$. We do this for twelve different values of $\mathcal{M}$ between $0.9 M_\odot$ and $1.4 M_\odot$, using the fitting function in Equation (7). We then interpolate the fitting parameters to all $\mathcal{M} \in [0.9 M_\odot, 1.4 M_\odot]$ by fitting them as functions of $\mathcal{M}$. The accuracy of the estimate of $R_{1.4}$ for any value of $\mathcal{M}$ is found to be quite good. 95% of the estimates are within $\sim$5% of $R_{1.4}$.

We then consider a generalized form of the relation R_M-$\tilde{\Lambda}$ for a generic NS mass M. We perform the same analysis as for the $R_{1.4}$-$\tilde{\Lambda}$ relation for seven other values of M. We find that the level of uncertainty in the estimate of R_M depends on both M and $\mathcal{M}$. There is, in fact, an optimal value of M for each $\mathcal{M}$ such that R_M is maximally constrained by the relation at that value of $\mathcal{M}$. Therefore, this relation will be an excellent tool for combining the results from multiple GW detections of BNSs into constraints on NS radii.

The parameter space of possible EOS explored by our MCMC algorithm to compute our EOS data set can be further restricted with the inclusion of possible future LIGO/Virgo/KAGRA O4 constraints, laboratory constraints, such as those from heavy-ion collisions [52] and PREX [53], X-ray burst observations from NICER [54–56], and by combining the phenomenological EOSs with results from pQCD calculations [57].

Author Contributions: D.A.G. generated and analyzed the TOV data, D.A.G. and D.R. interpreted the results and wrote the manuscript. Both authors have read and agreed to the published version of the manuscript.

Funding: This research was funded by U.S. Department of Energy, Office of Science, Division of Nuclear Physics under Award Number(s) DE-SC0021177 and from the National Science Foundation under Grants No. PHY-2011725 and PHY-2116686. Computations for this research were performed on the Pennsylvania State University's Institute for Computational and Data Sciences Advanced CyberInfrastructure (ICDS-ACI).

Data Availability Statement: EOS parameters and bulk properties of reference NSs generated for this work are publicly available on Zenodo [58].

Acknowledgments: The authors gratefully wish to acknowledge R. Gamba for waveform dephasing calculations and S. Bernuzzi for discussions that motivated us to start this work.

Conflicts of Interest: The authors declare no conflict of interest. The funders had no role in the design of the study; in the collection, analyses, or interpretation of data; in the writing of the manuscript, or in the decision to publish the results.

Abbreviations

The following abbreviations are used in this manuscript:

EOS	Equation of state
NS	Neutron star
BNS	Binary neutron star
GW	Gravitational wave
MCMC	Markov chain Monte Carlo
TOV	Tolman-Oppenheimer-Volkoff

References

1. Andersson, N.; Kokkotas, K.D. Gravitational Waves and Pulsating Stars: What Can We Learn from Future Observations? *Phys. Rev. Lett.* **1996**, *77*, 4134–4137. [CrossRef] [PubMed]
2. Andersson, N.; Kokkotas, K.D. Towards gravitational wave asteroseismology. *Mon. Not. R. Astron. Soc.* **1998**, *299*, 1059–1068. [CrossRef]
3. Benhar, O.; Berti, E.; Ferrari, V. The imprint of the equation of state on the axial w-modes of oscillating neutron stars. *Mon. Not. R. Astron. Soc.* **1999**, *310*, 797–803. [CrossRef]
4. Benhar, O.; Ferrari, V.; Gualtieri, L. Gravitational wave asteroseismology reexamined. *Phys. Rev. D* **2004**, *70*, 124015. [CrossRef]
5. Tsui, L.K.; Leung, P.T. Universality in quasi-normal modes of neutron stars. *Mon. Not. R. Astron. Soc.* **2005**, *357*, 1029–1037. [CrossRef]
6. Lau, H.K.; Leung, P.T.; Lin, L.M. Inferring Physical Parameters of Compact Stars from their f-mode Gravitational Wave Signals. *Astrophys. J.* **2010**, *714*, 1234–1238. [CrossRef]
7. Bejger, M.; Haensel, P. Moments of inertia for neutron and strange stars: Limits derived for the Crab pulsar. *Astron. Astrophys.* **2002**, *396*, 917–921. [CrossRef]
8. Lattimer, J.M.; Schutz, B.F. Constraining the Equation of State with Moment of Inertia Measurements. *Astophys. J.* **2005** *629*, 979–984. [CrossRef]
9. Urbanec, M.; Miller, J.C.; Stuchlík, Z. Quadrupole moments of rotating neutron stars and strange stars. *Mon. Not. R. Astron. Soc.* **2013**, *433*, 1903–1909. [CrossRef]
10. Yagi, K.; Yunes, N. I-Love-Q: Unexpected Universal Relations for Neutron Stars and Quark Stars. *Science* **2013**, *341*, 365–368. [CrossRef]
11. Yagi, K.; Yunes, N. I-Love-Q relations in neutron stars and their applications to astrophysics, gravitational waves, and fundamental physics. *Phys. Rev. D* **2013**, *88*, 023009. [CrossRef]
12. Yagi, K. Multipole Love relations. *Phys. Rev. D* **2014**, *89*, 043011. [CrossRef]
13. Yagi, K.; Stein, L.C.; Pappas, G.; Yunes, N.; Apostolatos, T.A. Why I-Love-Q: Explaining why universality emerges in compact objects. *Phys. Rev. D* **2014**, *90*, 063010. [CrossRef]
14. Godzieba, D.A.; Gamba, R.; Radice, D.; Bernuzzi, S. Updated universal relations for tidal deformabilities of neutron stars from phenomenological equations of state. *Phys. Rev. D* **2021**, *103*, 063036. [CrossRef]
15. Hinderer, T.; Lackey, B.D.; Lang, R.N.; Read, J.S. Tidal deformability of neutron stars with realistic equations of state and their gravitational wave signatures in binary inspiral. *Phys. Rev. D* **2010**, *81*, 123016. [CrossRef]
16. Hinderer, T. Tidal Love Numbers of Neutron Stars. *Astrophys. J.* **2008**, *677*, 1216–1220. [CrossRef]

17. Damour, T.; Nagar, A. Relativistic tidal properties of neutron stars. *Phys. Rev. D* **2009**, *80*, 084035. [CrossRef]
18. Nagar, A.; Messina, F.; Rettegno, P.; Bini, D.; Damour, T.; Geralico, A.; Akcay, S.; Bernuzzi, S. Nonlinear-in-spin effects in effective-one-body waveform models of spin-aligned, inspiralling, neutron star binaries. *Phys. Rev. D* **2019**, *99*, 044007. [CrossRef]
19. Zhao, T.; Lattimer, J.M. Tidal deformabilities and neutron star mergers. *Phys. Rev. D* **2018**, *98*, 063020. [CrossRef]
20. Yagi, K.; Yunes, N. Approximate universal relations for neutron stars and quark stars. *Phys. Rep.* **2017**, *681*, 1–72. [CrossRef]
21. Gamba, R.; Breschi, M.; Bernuzzi, S.; Agathos, M.; Nagar, A. Waveform systematics in the gravitational-wave inference of tidal parameters and equation of state from binary neutron star signals. *arXiv* **2020**, arXiv:2009.08467.
22. Adhikari, R.X. Gravitational radiation detection with laser interferometry. *Rev. Mod. Phys.* **2014**, *86*, 121–151. [CrossRef]
23. Einstein Telescope. Available online: http://www.et-gw.eu/ (accessed on 29 September 2021).
24. Hild, S.; Chelkowski, S.; Freise, A. Pushing towards the ET sensitivity using 'conventional' technology. *arXiv* **2008**, arXiv:0810.0604.
25. Reitze, D.; Adhikari, R.X.; Ballmer, S.; Barish, B.; Barsotti, L.; Billingsley, G.; Brown, D.A.; Chen, Y.; Coyne, D.; Eisenstein, R.; et al. Cosmic Explorer: The U.S. Contribution to Gravitational-Wave Astronomy beyond LIGO. *Bull. Am. Astron. Soc.* **2019**, *51*, 35.
26. Flanagan, É.É.; Hinderer, T. Constraining neutron-star tidal Love numbers with gravitational-wave detectors. *Phys. Rev. D* **2008**, *77*, 021502. [CrossRef]
27. Damour, T.; Nagar, A.; Villain, L. Measurability of the tidal polarizability of neutron stars in late-inspiral gravitational-wave signals. *Phys. Rev. D* **2012**, *85*, 123007. [CrossRef]
28. De, S.; Finstad, D.; Lattimer, J.M.; Brown, D.A.; Berger, E.; Biwer, C.M. Tidal Deformabilities and Radii of Neutron Stars from the Observation of GW170817. *Phys. Rev. Lett.* **2018**, *121*, 091102. [CrossRef]
29. Postnikov, S.; Prakash, M.; Lattimer, J.M. Tidal Love numbers of neutron and self-bound quark stars. *Phys. Rev. D* **2010**, *82*, 024016. [CrossRef]
30. Yagi, K.; Yunes, N. Binary Love relations. *Class. Quantum Gravity* **2016**, *33*, 13LT01. [CrossRef]
31. Maselli, A.; Cardoso, V.; Ferrari, V.; Gualtieri, L.; Pani, P. Equation-of-state-independent relations in neutron stars. *Phys. Rev. D* **2013**, *88*, 023007. [CrossRef]
32. Abbott, B. GW170817: Observation of Gravitational Waves from a Binary Neutron Star Inspiral. *Phys. Rev. Lett.* **2017**, *119*, 161101. [CrossRef]
33. Abbott, B. GW170817: Measurements of Neutron Star Radii and Equation of State. *Phys. Rev. Lett.* **2018**, *121*, 161101. [CrossRef]
34. Essick, R.; Landry, P.; Holz, D.E. Nonparametric inference of neutron star composition, equation of state, and maximum mass with GW170817. *Phys. Rev. D* **2020**, *101*, 063007. [CrossRef]
35. Read, J.S.; Lackey, B.D.; Owen, B.J.; Friedman, J.L. Constraints on a phenomenologically parametrized neutron-star equation of state. *Phys. Rev. D* **2009**, *79*, 124032. [CrossRef]
36. Bernuzzi, S.; Nagar, A. Gravitational waves from pulsations of neutron stars described by realistic Equations of State. *Phys. Rev.* **2008**, *D78*, 024024. [CrossRef]
37. Demorest, P.; Pennucci, T.; Ransom, S.; Roberts, M.; Hessels, J. Shapiro Delay Measurement of A Two Solar Mass Neutron Star. *Nature* **2010**, *467*, 1081–1083. [CrossRef]
38. Fonseca, E. The NANOGrav Nine-year Data Set: Mass and Geometric Measurements of Binary Millisecond Pulsars. *Astrophys. J.* **2016**, *832*, 167. [CrossRef]
39. Arzoumanian, Z. The NANOGrav 11-year Data Set: High-precision timing of 45 Millisecond Pulsars. *Astrophys. J. Suppl.* **2018**, *235*, 37. [CrossRef]
40. Antoniadis, J. A Massive Pulsar in a Compact Relativistic Binary. *Science* **2013**, *340*, 6131. [CrossRef] [PubMed]
41. Cromartie, H.T. Relativistic Shapiro delay measurements of an extremely massive millisecond pulsar. *Nat. Astron.* **2019**, *4*, 72–76. [CrossRef]
42. Linares, M.; Shahbaz, T.; Casares, J. Peering into the dark side: Magnesium lines establish a massive neutron star in PSR J2215+5135. *Astrophys. J.* **2018**, *859*, 54. [CrossRef]
43. Margalit, B.; Metzger, B.D. Constraining the Maximum Mass of Neutron Stars From Multi-Messenger Observations of GW170817. *Astrophys. J. Lett.* **2017**, *850*, L19. [CrossRef]
44. Shibata, M.; Fujibayashi, S.; Hotokezaka, K.; Kiuchi, K.; Kyutoku, K.; Sekiguchi, Y.; Tanaka, M. Modeling GW170817 based on numerical relativity and its implications. *Phys. Rev.* **2017**, *D96*, 123012. [CrossRef]
45. Rezzolla, L.; Most, E.R.; Weih, L.R. Using gravitational-wave observations and quasi-universal relations to constrain the maximum mass of neutron stars. *Astrophys. J. Lett.* **2018**, *852*, L25. [CrossRef]
46. Ruiz, M.; Shapiro, S.L.; Tsokaros, A. GW170817, General Relativistic Magnetohydrodynamic Simulations, and the Neutron Star Maximum Mass. *Phys. Rev.* **2018**, *D97*, 021501. [CrossRef]
47. Shibata, M.; Zhou, E.; Kiuchi, K.; Fujibayashi, S. Constraint on the maximum mass of neutron stars using GW170817 event. *Phys. Rev.* **2019**, *D100*, 023015. [CrossRef]
48. Godzieba, D.A.; Radice, D.; Bernuzzi, S. On the Maximum Mass of Neutron Stars and GW190814. *Astrophys. J.* **2021**, *908*, 122. [CrossRef]
49. Martinez, J.G.; Stovall, K.; Freire, P.C.C.; Deneva, J.S.; Jenet, F.A.; McLaughlin, M.A.; Bagchi, M.; Bates, S.D.; Ridolfi, A. Pulsar J0453+1559: A Double Neutron Star System with a Large Mass Asymmetry. *Astrophys. J.* **2015**, *812*, 143. [CrossRef]
50. Suwa, Y.; Yoshida, T.; Shibata, M.; Umeda, H.; Takahashi, K. On the minimum mass of neutron stars. *Mon. Not. R. Astron. Soc.* **2018**, *481*, 3305–3312. [CrossRef]

51. Abbott, B.P. Prospects for observing and localizing gravitational-wave transients with Advanced LIGO, Advanced Virgo and KAGRA. *Living Rev. Relativ.* **2020**, *23*, 3. [CrossRef]
52. Danielewicz, P.; Lacey, R.; Lynch, W.G. Determination of the Equation of State of Dense Matter. *Science* **2002**, *298*, 1592–1596. [CrossRef]
53. Reed, B.T.; Fattoyev, F.J.; Horowitz, C.J.; Piekarewicz, J. Implications of PREX-2 on the Equation of State of Neutron-Rich Matter. *Phys. Rev. Lett.* **2021**, *126*, 172503. [CrossRef]
54. Steiner, A.W.; Lattimer, J.M.; Brown, E.F. The Equation of State from Observed Masses and Radii of Neutron Stars. *Astrophys. J.* **2010**, *722*, 33–54. [CrossRef]
55. Lattimer, J.M. The Nuclear Equation of State and Neutron Star Masses. *Annu. Rev. Nucl. Part. Sci.* **2012**, *62*, 485–515. [CrossRef]
56. Özel, F.; Freire, P. Masses, Radii, and the Equation of State of Neutron Stars. *Ann. Rev. Astro. Astrophys.* **2016**, *54*, 401–440. [CrossRef]
57. Annala, E.; Gorda, T.; Kurkela, A.; Nättilä, J.; Vuorinen, A. Evidence for quark-matter cores in massive neutron stars. *Nat. Phys.* **2020**, *16*, 907–910. [CrossRef]
58. Godzieba, D.A.; Radice, D.; Bernuzzi, S. Phenomenological EOS Data Set. *Zenodo* **2020**. [CrossRef]

Correction

Correction: Godzieba, D.A.; Radice, D. High-Order Multipole and Binary Love Number Universal Relations. *Universe* 2021, 7, 368

Daniel A. Godzieba [1,*] and David Radice [1,2,3]

1 Department of Physics, The Pennsylvania State University, University Park, PA 16802, USA; dur566@psu.edu
2 Institute for Gravitation & The Cosmos, The Pennsylvania State University, University Park, PA 16802, USA
3 Department of Astronomy & Astrophysics, The Pennsylvania State University, University Park, PA 16802, USA
* Correspondence: dag5611@psu.edu

The authors wish to make the following corrections to their paper [1]:

In Section 4, we accidentally swapped the numerators in the definitions of the fitting functions $\alpha(x)$ and $\beta(x)$ in Equation (8). The definitions are corrected as

$$\alpha(x) = \frac{\sum_{k=0}^{3} p_k x^k}{\sum_{k=0}^{2} q_k x^k} \text{ km} \quad \text{and} \quad \beta(x) = \frac{\sum_{k=0}^{2} p_k x^k}{\sum_{k=0}^{2} q_k x^k}, \qquad (8)$$

where $x = (M/M_\odot - \mu_M)/\sigma_M$, $\mu_M = 1.1537$, and $\sigma_M = 0.15927$.

As a consequence of this error, Table 3 in Section 4 has the fitting parameters for $\alpha(x)$ and $\beta(x)$ incorrectly labelled. Additionally, it was not originally made clear in the table that we fix $q_2 = 1$ for all fits. The table is corrected to Table 3. All other results are unaffected by these corrections. The authors would like to apologize for any inconvenience caused to the readers by these changes.

Table 3. Fitting parameters $\vec{p} = \{p_k\}$ and $\vec{q} = \{q_k\}$ for α and β as functions of $x = (M/M_\odot - \mu_M)/\sigma_M$, where $\mu_M = 1.1537$ and $\sigma_M = 0.15927$ for several values of M. The fitting functions are given in Equation (3).

$M/M_\odot$		p_0	p_1	p_2	p_3	q_0	q_1	q_2
1.4	$\beta(x)$	404.40	−96.991	26.475	-	65.755	−15.259	1
	$\alpha(x)$	224.75	−24.553	11.832	−1.8434	19.758	−1.9914	1
1.5	$\beta(x)$	502.01	−119.44	32.193	-	79.153	−16.598	1
	$\alpha(x)$	282.86	−29.568	12.893	−2.2628	24.833	−2.3357	1
1.6	$\beta(x)$	642.10	−152.88	40.447	-	98.054	−18.391	1
	$\alpha(x)$	386.63	−42.102	14.780	−3.0054	33.942	−3.2743	1
1.7	$\beta(x)$	877.56	−210.98	54.468	-	129.67	−21.419	1
	$\alpha(x)$	598.97	−73.554	18.854	−4.5818	52.655	−5.7193	1
1.8	$\beta(x)$	1442.2	−356.28	88.775	-	206.20	−29.608	1
	$\alpha(x)$	1291.3	−192.50	32.831	−10.064	113.87	−15.207	1
1.9	$\beta(x)$	2734.1	−709.62	174.36	-	380.72	−46.815	1
	$\alpha(x)$	3282.2	−592.78	80.705	−27.980	291.00	−48.054	1
2	$\beta(x)$	63,061	−19,071	3663.7	-	8959.4	−1478.5	1
	$\alpha(x)$	9986.9	−2011.9	232.61	−82.091	887.58	−167.09	1
2.14	$\beta(x)$	93,209	−34,415	6102.8	-	12,686	−2286.4	1
	$\alpha(x)$	58,353	−18,272	1904.6	−609.58	5234.8	−1543.2	1

Reference

1. Godzieba, D.A.; Radice, D. High-Order Multipole and Binary Love Number Universal Relations. *Universe* **2021**, *7*, 368. [CrossRef]

MDPI
St. Alban-Anlage 66
4052 Basel
Switzerland
Tel. +41 61 683 77 34
Fax +41 61 302 89 18
www.mdpi.com

Universe Editorial Office
E-mail: universe@mdpi.com
www.mdpi.com/journal/universe

www.ingramcontent.com/pod-product-compliance
Lightning Source LLC
LaVergne TN
LVHW070048120526
838202LV00101B/1652